1000
FREEZER
RECIPES

1000 FREEZER RECIPES

Edited by
Carole Handslip
&
Jeni Wright

INTRODUCTION

When cooking for the freezer it is important to use only good quality fresh food. Freezing will not improve food and food to be frozen must be of the best quality, hygienically prepared, and correctly packed and stored. Keep all utensils, materials, work surfaces and hands scrupulously clean and work quickly, handling the food as little as possible.

For best results, cool food as rapidly as possible before freezing, in order to preserve it in prime condition and to avoid contamination by harmful bacteria.

All materials or containers used for packaging must be moisture- and vapour-proof. Packaging must also protect food from damage during storage and be durable at low temperatures. All glass containers and serving dishes should be tested for toughness at low temperatures. To do this, fill them with water, leaving a 2.5 cm/1 inch headspace, place in a freezer bag and freeze. (Always pack glass in a freezer bag, in any case; should the container shatter, the pieces will be held safely in the bag.)

Correct and careful packaging of food is essential. One of the results of bad packaging is dehydration, which takes place if air is not completely excluded from the package before freezing. Moisture and juices are lost from the food and in extreme cases freezer burn appears on the surface of the food in the form of greyish or brown patches. These are not harmful and can be removed when the food is thawed. Oxidation is another result of bad packaging and occurs in products with a high fat content. Oxygen penetrates animal tissues, causing fats to go rancid. Correct wrapping and the removal of air from packages prevents oxidation occurring.

Always overwrap highly spiced or strong-smelling foods in freezer bags or heavy-duty foil. Insufficiently wrapped foods containing garlic and onions, for example, will transfer their flavours to foods nearby.

When liquid freezes it expands, so it is necessary to leave room for this expansion in the package. A headspace of 2–2.5 cm/¾–1 inch per 600 ml/1 pint/2½ cups of liquid is usually sufficient, but a little more is required for tall narrow containers.

Pack food in usable quantities and label all packages clearly, giving the date of freezing. It is important to keep a record of the contents of the freezer to ensure that food is not kept beyond its recommended storage time.

Many frozen cooked foods can be reheated without thawing, either in the oven or on top of the stove. Cooked foods in foil containers may be transferred directly from the freezer to a preheated oven. When reheating soups, stews and casseroles on top of the stove, reheat very gently and slowly. Make sure that cooked food is heated right through before serving.

CONTENTS

First published 1979 by Octopus Books Limited
59 Grosvenor Street, London W1
Reprinted 1981, 1982, 1983, 1984

ISBN 0 7064 0765 2
Printed in Czechoslovakia
50383/8

HUNTER'S PÂTÉ

METRIC/IMPERIAL

450 g/1 lb boneless belly pork, skinned
225 g/½ lb pig's liver
225 g/½ lb pork sausagemeat
225 g/½ lb garlic sausage
1 medium onion, peeled and roughly chopped
450 g/1 lb boneless rabbit or hare meat, cut into small pieces
3 × 15 ml spoons/3 tablespoons dry sherry
2 × 15 ml spoons/2 tablespoons freshly chopped parsley
1 × 5 ml spoon/1 teaspoon dried thyme
salt
freshly ground black pepper
450 g/1 lb streaky bacon rashers, rinds removed

AMERICAN

1 lb salt pork, skinned
½ lb pork liver
1 cup pork sausagemeat
½ lb garlic sausage
1 medium onion, peeled and roughly chopped
1 lb boneless rabbit or hare meat, cut into small pieces
3 tablespoons dry sherry
2 tablespoons freshly chopped parsley
1 teaspoon dried thyme
salt
freshly ground black pepper
1 lb fatty bacon slices

Mince (grind) the pork, liver, sausagemeat, garlic sausage and onion, then put in a bowl with the remaining ingredients except the bacon. Stir well to mix.

Flatten the bacon with the blade of a knife and use to line the bottom and sides of a greased 1 litre/2 pint/5 cup loaf tin. Spoon in the pâté mixture and press down lightly. Fold the bacon ends over the mixture and cover with foil. Put the loaf tin in a roasting tin half filled with water and bake in a preheated moderate oven (160°C/325°F or Gas Mark 3) for 2 to 2½ hours or until set.

To freeze: cool quickly. Put heavy weights on top of the pâté, then chill in the refrigerator until firm. Turn out, wrap in foil, then overwrap in a freezer bag. Seal, label and freeze.

To thaw and serve: remove wrappings and arrange the pâté on a serving platter. Thaw in the refrigerator overnight. Serve cut into thick slices.

SERVES 8 to 10

SMOKED MACKEREL PÂTÉ

METRIC/IMPERIAL

2 large smoked mackerel, skinned and boned
275 g/10 oz butter, softened
100 g/4 oz cream cheese
juice of ½ lemon
freshly ground black pepper
parsley sprigs, to garnish

AMERICAN

2 large smoked mackerel, skinned and boned
1¼ cups butter, softened
½ cup cream cheese
juice of ½ lemon
freshly ground black pepper
parsley sprigs, to garnish

Line a 450 g/1 lb loaf tin with foil.
Work the mackerel to a purée in an electric blender or mash well with a fork. Add the remaining ingredients gradually, blending or mashing until smooth and evenly mixed. Spoon into the prepared tin and smooth over the top.
To freeze: open (flash) freeze until firm, then turn out and wrap in foil. Seal, label and return to the freezer.
To thaw and serve: remove wrappings and arrange the pâté on a serving platter. Thaw in the refrigerator overnight. Garnish with parsley sprigs just before serving.
SERVES 6

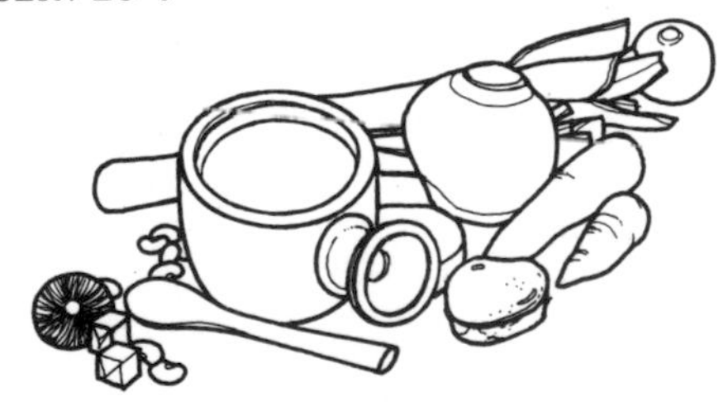

SMOKED TROUT PÂTÉ

METRIC/IMPERIAL

2 large smoked trout, skinned and boned
225 g/½ lb butter, softened
4 × 15 ml spoons/4 tablespoons double cream
2 × 15 ml spoons/2 tablespoons lemon juice
freshly ground black pepper
watercress, to garnish

AMERICAN

2 large smoked trout, skinned and boned
1 cup butter, softened
¼ cup heavy cream
2 tablespoons lemon juice
freshly ground black pepper
watercress, to garnish

Mash the trout and butter together with a fork, then gradually beat in the cream, lemon juice and pepper to taste.
To freeze: chill in the refrigerator, then spoon into a rigid container. Seal, label and freeze.
To thaw and serve: thaw in the container at room temperature for 4 hours, then spoon into a serving dish and garnish with watercress.
SERVES 6

TERRINE MAISON

METRIC/IMPERIAL

225 g/½ lb pig's liver
225 g/½ lb boneless belly pork, skinned
225 g/½ lb pork sausagemeat
1 onion, peeled and finely chopped
2 garlic cloves, peeled and crushed
2 × 5 ml spoons/2 teaspoons freshly chopped parsley
salt
freshly ground black pepper
6 streaky bacon rashers, rinds removed
1 bay leaf

AMERICAN

½ lb pork liver
½ lb salt pork, skinned
1 cup pork sausagemeat
1 onion, peeled and finely chopped
2 garlic cloves, peeled and crushed
2 teaspoons freshly chopped parsley
salt
freshly ground black pepper
6 fatty bacon slices
1 bay leaf

Mince (grind) the liver and pork, then put in a bowl with the remaining ingredients except the bacon and bay leaf. Stir well to mix.
Flatten the bacon with the blade of a knife and use to line the bottom and sides of a greased 675 g/1½ lb loaf tin. Spoon in the pâté mixture and press down lightly. Put the bay leaf on top and cover with foil.
Put in a roasting tin half filled with water and bake in a preheated moderate oven (160°/325°F or Gas Mark 3) for 2 hours or until set. Remove the bay leaf.
To freeze: cool quickly. Put heavy weights on top of the pâté, then chill in the refrigerator until firm. Turn out, wrap in foil, then overwrap in a freezer bag. Seal, label and freeze.
To thaw and serve: remove wrappings and arrange the pâté on a serving platter. Thaw in the refrigerator overnight. Serve cut into thick slices.
SERVES 6

DANISH LIVER PÂTÉ

METRIC/IMPERIAL

25 g/1 oz butter
25 g/1 oz flour
150 ml/¼ pint milk
salt
freshly ground black pepper
350 g/¾ lb pig's liver
100 g/4 oz streaky bacon
1 egg, beaten
2 × 5 ml spoons/2 teaspoons grated onion
2 × 5 ml spoons/2 teaspoons dry sherry (optional)

AMERICAN

2 tablespoons butter
¼ cup flour
⅔ cup milk
salt
freshly ground black pepper
¾ lb pork liver
¼ lb fatty bacon
1 egg, beaten
2 teaspoons grated onion
2 teaspoons dry sherry (optional)

Melt the butter in a pan, stir in the flour and cook for 2 minutes, stirring constantly. Remove from the heat and gradually stir in the milk. Return to the heat and bring to the boil, stirring constantly. Simmer until thick, then add salt and pepper to taste and remove from the heat.

Mince (grind) the liver and bacon together and put into a bowl with the sauce and the remaining ingredients. Stir well to mix. Spoon into a greased 900 ml/1½ pint/3¾ cup ovenproof dish and press down lightly. Cover with foil.

Put the dish in a roasting tin half filled with water and bake in a preheated moderate oven (180°C/350°F or Gas Mark 4) for 1 hour or until set.

To freeze: cool quickly, then wrap in foil, seal, label and freeze.

To thaw and serve: thaw in the refrigerator overnight. Remove wrappings and serve from the dish.

SERVES 4 to 6

PORK PÂTÉ

METRIC/IMPERIAL

225 g/½ lb pig's liver
100 g/4 oz pork sausagemeat
1 onion, peeled and chopped
1 garlic clove, peeled and crushed
1 × 5 ml spoon/1 teaspoon anchovy essence
1 × 2.5 ml spoon/½ teaspoon ground mace
1 × 2.5 ml spoon/½ teaspoon dried mixed herbs
freshly ground black pepper
75 g/3 oz fresh white breadcrumbs
25 g/1 oz butter, softened
2 × 15 ml spoons/2 tablespoons milk
1 egg
6 streaky bacon rashers, rinds removed

AMERICAN

½ lb pork liver
½ cup pork sausagemeat
1 onion, peeled and chopped
1 garlic clove, peeled and crushed
1 teaspoon anchovy extract
½ teaspoon ground mace
½ teaspoon dried mixed herbs
freshly ground black pepper
1½ cups fresh white breadcrumbs
2 tablespoons butter, softened
2 tablespoons milk
1 egg
6 fatty bacon slices

Put the liver, sausagemeat, onion, garlic, anchovy essence (extract), mace, herbs and pepper to taste in an electric blender and work until smooth. Transfer to a bowl.

Put the remaining ingredients, except the bacon, in the blender and work to a smooth paste. Add to the bowl and stir well to mix.

Flatten the bacon with the blade of a knife and use to line the bottom and sides of a greased 450 g/1 lb loaf tin. Spoon in the pâté mixture and press down lightly. Cover with foil.

Put in a roasting tin half filled with water and bake in a preheated moderate oven (160°C/325°F or Gas Mark 3) for 1 to 1½ hours or until set.

To freeze: cool quickly. Put heavy weights on top of the pâté, then chill in the refrigerator until firm. Turn out, wrap in foil, then overwrap in a freezer bag. Seal, label and freeze.

To thaw and serve: remove wrappings and arrange the pâté on a serving platter. Thaw in the refrigerator overnight. Serve cut into thick slices.

SERVES 4 to 6

LIVER PÂTÉ EN CROUTE

METRIC/IMPERIAL

1 × 225 g/½ lb piece of streaky bacon
100 g/4 oz chicken livers
1 onion, peeled and chopped
1 × 15 ml spoon/1 tablespoon flour
2 × 15 ml spoons/2 tablespoons milk
2 × 15 ml spoons/2 tablespoons dry sherry
1 × 2.5 ml spoon/½ teaspoon grated nutmeg
freshly ground black pepper
1 egg, beaten
6 streaky bacon rashers, rinds removed
1 × 225 g/8 oz packet frozen puff pastry, thawed

AMERICAN

1 × ½ lb piece of fatty bacon
¼ lb chicken livers
1 onion, peeled and chopped
1 tablespoon flour
2 tablespoons milk
2 tablespoons dry sherry
½ teaspoon grated nutmeg
freshly ground black pepper
1 egg, beaten
6 fatty bacon slices
1 × ½ lb package frozen puff paste, thawed

Put the bacon in a pan, cover with water and bring to the boil. Drain, then cut off any rind. Mince (grind) the bacon finely, then mince (grind) again with the chicken livers and onion. Transfer to a bowl, add the flour, milk, sherry, nutmeg, pepper and half the egg and stir well. Flatten the bacon with the blade of a knife and use to line the bottom and sides of a greased 450 g/1 lb loaf tin. Spoon in the pâté mixture and press down lightly. Cover with foil.

Bake in a preheated moderate oven (180°C/350°F or Gas Mark 4) for 30 minutes, then remove from the oven and leave to cool for 10 minutes. Turn the pâté out of the tin and brush with some of the remaining egg.

Roll out the dough on a floured surface and use to cover the pâté, sealing the edges well with beaten egg. Use any trimmings to decorate the top of the dough and brush all over with the remaining egg.

Bake in a preheated moderately hot oven (200°C/400°F or Gas Mark 6) for 30 minutes or until the pastry is golden brown.

To freeze: cool quickly. Open (flash) freeze until firm, then wrap in a freezer bag or foil. Seal, label and return to the freezer.

To thaw and serve: remove wrappings and arrange the pâté on a serving platter. Thaw in the refrigerator overnight. Serve cut into thick slices.

SERVES 8

FRENCH PÂTÉ

METRIC/IMPERIAL

4 slices of white bread, crusts removed
3 × 15 ml spoons/3 tablespoons milk
225 g/½ lb chicken livers
175 g/6 oz lean bacon rashers, rinds removed
1 small onion, peeled and chopped
1 garlic clove, peeled
1 × 2.5 ml spoon/½ teaspoon dried mixed herbs
2 × 5 ml spoons/2 teaspoons mustard powder
salt
freshly ground black pepper
1 egg, beaten
3 streaky bacon rashers, rinds removed

AMERICAN

4 slices of white bread, crusts removed
3 tablespoons milk
½ lb chicken livers
6 oz Canadian bacon slices
1 small onion, peeled and chopped
1 garlic clove, peeled
½ teaspoon dried mixed herbs
2 teaspoons mustard powder
salt
freshly ground black pepper
1 egg, beaten
3 fatty bacon slices

Put the bread in a bowl, add the milk and leave to soak.

Meanwhile, mince (grind) the chicken livers, lean (Canadian) bacon rashers, onion and garlic together. Squeeze the bread as dry as possible and add to the liver mixture with the remaining ingredients, except the streaky (fatty) bacon.

Flatten the bacon with the blade of a knife and use to line a small greased ovenproof bowl. Spoon in the pâté mixture and press down lightly. Cover with foil.

Put in a roasting tin half filled with water and bake in a preheated moderate oven (180°C/350°F or Gas Mark 4) for 1 to 1½ hours or until set.

To freeze: cool quickly. Put heavy weights on top of the pâté, then chill in the refrigerator until firm. Turn out, wrap in foil, then overwrap in a freezer bag. Seal, label and freeze.

To thaw and serve: remove wrappings and arrange the pâté on a serving platter. Thaw in the refrigerator overnight. Serve cut into thick slices.

SERVES 4 to 6

MIXED FISH PÂTÉ

METRIC/IMPERIAL

175 g/6 oz fresh white breadcrumbs
100 g/4 oz butter, melted
finely grated rind and juice of 1 lemon
1 × 200 g/7 oz can salmon, skinned, boned and flaked
1 × 200 g/7 oz can tuna fish, flaked
100 g/4 oz peeled prawns
3 × 15 ml spoons/3 tablespoons anchovy essence
2 × 15 ml spoons/2 tablespoons Worcestershire sauce
300 ml/½ pint single cream
freshly ground black pepper
1 slice of lemon, to garnish

AMERICAN

3 cups fresh white breadcrumbs
½ cup butter, melted
finely grated rind and juice of 1 lemon
1 × 7 oz can salmon, skinned, boned and flaked
1 × 7 oz can tuna fish, flaked
⅔ cup shelled shrimp
3 tablespoons anchovy extract
2 tablespoons Worcestershire sauce
1¼ cups light cream
freshly ground black pepper
1 slice of lemon, to garnish

Put all the ingredients in a bowl, except the slice of lemon, and beat well to mix.
To freeze: chill in the refrigerator, then spoon into a rigid container. Seal, label and freeze.
To thaw and serve: thaw at room temperature for 4 hours, then spoon into a serving dish and garnish with a twist of lemon.
SERVES 8

CHOPPED CHICKEN LIVER PÂTÉ

METRIC/IMPERIAL

25 g/1 oz butter
225 g/½ lb chicken livers
2 lean bacon rashers, rinds removed and finely chopped
1 small onion, peeled and finely grated
1 × 15 ml spoon/1 tablespoon brandy or sherry (optional)
salt
freshly ground black pepper

AMERICAN

2 tablespoons butter
½ lb chicken livers
2 Canadian bacon slices, finely chopped
1 small onion, peeled and finely grated
1 tablespoon brandy or sherry (optional)
salt
freshly ground black pepper

Melt the butter in a pan, add the chicken livers and bacon and fry for 8 to 10 minutes, turning frequently. Remove from the pan, place on a board and chop finely. Return to the pan, add the remaining ingredients and fry for a further 5 minutes, stirring constantly.
To freeze: cool quickly, then pack into a rigid container. Seal, label and freeze.
To thaw and serve: thaw in the container at room temperature for 4 hours, then spoon into a serving dish.
SERVES 4 to 6

CHICKEN LIVER PÂTÉ

METRIC/IMPERIAL

100 g/4 oz butter
225 g/½ lb chicken livers
1 medium onion, peeled and chopped
1 garlic glove, peeled and crushed
1 × 15 ml spoon/1 tablespoon chopped fresh mixed herbs
salt
freshly ground black pepper
1 × 15 ml spoon/1 tablespoon brandy

AMERICAN

½ cup butter
½ lb chicken livers
1 medium onion, peeled and chopped
1 garlic clove, peeled and crushed
1 tablespoon chopped fresh mixed herbs
salt
freshly ground black pepper
1 tablespoon brandy

Melt half the butter in a pan, add the chicken livers and fry for 4 minutes, turning frequently. Remove from the pan. Add the onion and garlic to the pan and fry gently until soft. Add the remaining butter, the herbs and salt and pepper to taste, and cook for a further 1 minute.
Put the chicken livers, the contents of the pan and the brandy into an electric blender or wire sieve (strainer) and work to a smooth purée. Spoon the mixture into 6 individual ramekins.
To freeze: chill in the refrigerator, then wrap in foil, seal, label and freeze.
To thaw and serve: remove wrappings and thaw at room temperature for 4 hours.
SERVES 6

TERRINE OF CHICKEN

METRIC/IMPERIAL
1 × 1.5 kg/3½ lb chicken, skinned and boned
225 g/½ lb lean pork
350 g/¾ lb streaky bacon rashers, rinds removed
salt
freshly ground black pepper
225 g/½ lb pork sausagemeat
4 × 15 ml spoons/4 tablespoons strong chicken stock, made from the giblets
1 × 15 ml spoon/1 tablespoon freshly chopped parsley

AMERICAN
1 × 3½ lb chicken, skinned and boned
½ lb lean pork
¾ lb fatty bacon slices
salt
freshly ground black pepper
1 cup pork sausagemeat
¼ cup strong chicken stock, made from the giblets
1 tablespoon freshly chopped parsley

Cut the chicken breast meat into neat slices, then mince (grind) the remaining meat with the pork and 2 bacon rashers (slices). Put the minced (ground) mixture in a bowl, add the sausagemeat, half the stock and salt and pepper to taste, then stir well to mix.
Flatten the remaining bacon with the blade of a knife, then use half to line the bottom of an oval ovenproof dish. Put a layer of the minced (ground) mixture in the dish, then arrange some of the sliced chicken breast on top and sprinkle lightly with stock and chopped parsley. Continue with these layers until all the ingredients are used up, finishing with a layer of the minced (ground) mixture.
Cover with the remaining bacon rashers (slices), then cover with foil and put the dish in a roasting tin half filled with water. Bake in a preheated moderate oven (160°C/325°F or Gas Mark 3) for 1½ hours or until set.
To freeze: cool quickly. Put heavy weights on top of the pâté, then chill in the refrigerator until firm. Turn out, wrap the pâté in foil, then overwrap in a freezer bag. Seal, label and freeze.
To thaw and serve: remove wrappings and thaw in the refrigerator overnight. Serve cut into thick slices.
SERVES 6 to 8

WHITING PÂTÉ

METRIC/IMPERIAL
100 g/4 oz buttered shrimps
40 g/1½ oz butter
100 g/4 oz soft cream cheese
275 g/10 oz whiting fillets, poached, skinned and flaked
2 × 15 ml spoons/2 tablespoons single cream
2 × 5 ml spoons/2 teaspoons lemon juice
salt
freshly ground black pepper
To garnish:
4–6 slices of lemon
4–6 sprigs of parsley

AMERICAN
½ cup buttered shrimp
3 tablespoons butter
½ cup soft cream cheese
10 oz whiting fillets, poached, skinned and flaked
2 tablespoons light cream
2 teaspoons lemon juice
salt
freshly ground black pepper
To garnish:
4–6 slices of lemon
4–6 sprigs of parsley

Put the buttered shrimps in a warm dish, then drain off the butter into a bowl. Cream the two butters together, then add the cheese and the fish and beat until smooth and evenly blended. Stir in the cream, lemon juice and salt and pepper to taste, then fold in the shrimps.
Spoon the mixture into individual freezerproof ramekins or serving dishes and smooth the tops.
To freeze: wrap in foil, seal, label and freeze.
To thaw and serve: remove wrappings and thaw in the refrigerator overnight. Garnish each ramekin or dish with 1 lemon slice and 1 parsley sprig.
SERVES 4 to 6

SMOKED HADDOCK PÂTÉ

METRIC/IMPERIAL
450 g/1 lb smoked haddock fillets
75 g/3 oz butter
150 ml/¼ pint double cream
150 ml/¼ pint single cream
freshly ground black pepper

AMERICAN
1 lb smoked haddock fillets
⅜ cup butter
⅔ cup heavy cream
⅔ cup light cream
freshly ground black pepper

Brush the haddock fillets with butter and grill (broil) for about 5 minutes on each side or until the fish flakes easily with a fork. Discard the skin and any bones, put the flesh in an electric blender with any cooking juices and the remaining butter and work to a smooth purée. Transfer to a bowl.
Put the two creams in a separate bowl, beat together until thick, then fold into the haddock purée. Add pepper to taste, then spoon into a 600 ml/1 pint/2½ cup loaf tin and smooth the top.
To freeze: wrap in a freezer bag or foil, seal, label and freeze.
To thaw and serve: thaw in the refrigerator overnight, then turn the pâté out onto a serving platter.
SERVES 6

TUNA FISH PÂTÉ

METRIC/IMPERIAL
2 × 200 g/7 oz cans tuna fish, drained and flaked
50 g/2 oz butter
1 × 15 ml spoon/1 tablespoon olive oil
finely grated rind and juice of ½ lemon
25 g/1 oz fresh white breadcrumbs
salt
freshly ground black pepper
To garnish:
lemon wedges
1 parsley sprig

AMERICAN
2 × 7 oz cans tuna fish, drained and flaked
¼ cup butter
1 tablespoon olive oil
finely grated rind and juice of ½ lemon
½ cup fresh white breadcrumbs
salt
freshly ground black pepper
To garnish:
lemon wedges
1 parsley sprig

Put the tuna, butter and oil in an electric blender and work to a smooth purée. Transfer to a bowl, add the remaining ingredients and beat well to mix.
To freeze: spoon into a rigid container, seal, label and freeze.
To thaw and serve: thaw in the container at room temperature for 4 hours, then spoon into a serving dish and garnish with lemon wedges and parsley.
SERVES 4

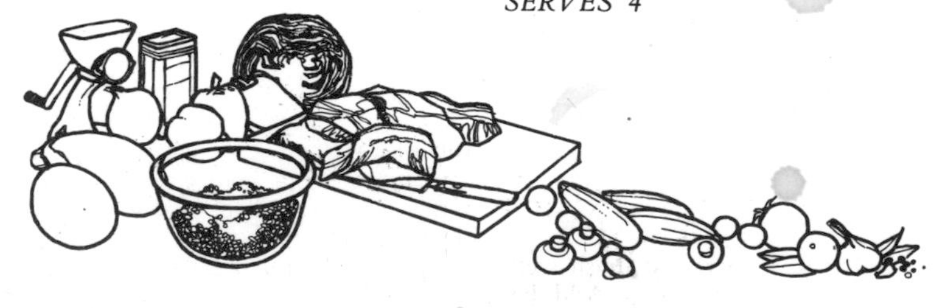

KIPPER PÂTÉ

METRIC/IMPERIAL

1 × 350 g/12 oz packet boil-in-the-bag kipper fillets
2 × 5 ml spoons/2 teaspoons lemon juice
2 × 5 ml spoons/2 teaspoons horseradish sauce
freshly ground black pepper
225 g/½ lb cream cheese
a little milk, to mix

AMERICAN

1 × 12 oz package boil-in-the-bag kipper fillets
2 teaspoons lemon juice
2 teaspoons horseradish sauce
freshly ground black pepper
1 cup cream cheese
a little milk, to mix

Boil the kipper fillets according to packet directions, drain and reserve 4 × 15 ml spoons/4 tablespoons/¼ cup of the cooking juices. Remove any skin and bones from the kippers and flake the flesh. Put the flesh in an electric blender with the reserved juice, the lemon juice, horseradish sauce and pepper to taste and work to a smooth purée.

Beat the cream cheese with enough milk to give a soft consistency, then stir in the kipper mixture. Beat until smooth and evenly blended.

To freeze: chill in the refrigerator, then spoon into a rigid container, seal, label and freeze.

To thaw and serve: thaw in the container in the refrigerator overnight, then spoon into a serving dish.

SERVES 6

BUCKLING PÂTÉ

METRIC/IMPERIAL

6 buckling, skinned and boned
4 × 15 ml spoons/4 tablespoons horseradish sauce
150 ml/¼ pint double cream
2 × 5 ml spoons/2 teaspoons lemon juice
freshly ground black pepper
1 parsley sprig, to garnish

AMERICAN

6 buckling, skinned and boned
¼ cup horseradish sauce
⅔ cup heavy cream
2 teaspoons lemon juice
freshly ground black pepper
1 parsley sprig, to garnish

Put the buckling flesh in a bowl and mash well with a fork, removing any large bones. Add the remaining ingredients and beat well to mix.

To freeze: chill in the refrigerator, then spoon into a rigid container. Seal, label and freeze.

To thaw and serve: thaw at room temperature for 4 hours, then spoon into a serving dish and garnish with a sprig of parsley.

SERVES 12

PÂTÉ DE CAMPAGNE

METRIC/IMPERIAL

450 g/1 lb pig's liver
225 g/½ lb pork fat
1 egg, beaten
25 g/1 oz fine semolina
2 garlic cloves, peeled and crushed
pinch of dried mixed herbs
1 × 2.5 ml spoon/½ teaspoon ground mace
1–2 × 5 ml spoons/1–2 teaspoons salt
freshly ground black pepper
2 × 15 ml spoons/2 tablespoons brandy
3 bay leaves
4 streaky bacon rashers, rinds removed

AMERICAN

1 lb pork liver
½ lb pork fat
1 egg, beaten
2 tablespoons semolina flour
2 garlic cloves, peeled and crushed
pinch of dried mixed herbs
½ teaspoon ground mace
1–2 teaspoons salt
freshly ground black pepper
2 tablespoons brandy
3 bay leaves
4 fatty bacon slices

Mince (grind) the liver and pork fat, then put in a bowl with the remaining ingredients except the bay leaves and bacon. Stir well to mix.

Arrange the bay leaves in a flower pattern on the bottom of a greased 600 ml/1 pint/2½ cup ovenproof dish. Flatten the bacon with the blade of a knife and use to line the bottom of the dish. Spoon in the pâté mixture and press down lightly. Put the dish in a roasting tin half filled with water. Cover with foil and bake in a preheated moderate oven (160°C/325°F or Gas Mark 3) for 2 to 2½ hours or until set.

To freeze: cool quickly. Put heavy weights on top of the pâté, then chill in the refrigerator until firm. Turn out, wrap in foil, then overwrap in a freezer bag. Seal, label and freeze.

To thaw and serve: remove wrappings and thaw the pâté in the refrigerator overnight. Serve cut into thick slices.

SERVES 6 to 8

STUFFED PORK PÂTÉ

METRIC/IMPERIAL

For the pâté:

1 kg/2 lb boneless pork
1 onion, peeled and roughly chopped
2 garlic cloves, peeled
2–3 × 15 ml spoons/2–3 tablespoons freshly chopped parsley
salt
freshly ground black pepper
4 small eggs, beaten

For the stuffing:

100 g/4 oz stoned prunes, chopped
100 g/4 oz cooked ham, chopped
100 g/4 oz Gouda cheese, diced

AMERICAN

For the pâté:

2 lb boneless pork
1 onion, peeled and roughly chopped
2 garlic cloves, peeled
2–3 tablespoons freshly chopped parsley
salt
freshly ground black pepper
4 small eggs, beaten

For the stuffing:

⅔ cup pitted prunes, chopped
½ cup chopped cooked ham
¼ lb Gouda cheese, diced

Mince (grind) the pork, onion and garlic, then put in a bowl with the remaining pâté ingredients. Stir well to mix.

Line a greased 1 kg/2 lb loaf tin with three-quarters of the pâté mixture. Mix together the ingredients for the stuffing and spoon into the centre of the tin. Cover with the remaining pâté mixture and press down lightly.

Put in a roasting tin half filled with water. Cover with foil and bake in a preheated moderate oven (160°C/325°F or Gas Mark 3) for 2 hours or until set.

To freeze: cool quickly. Put heavy weights on top of the pâté, then chill in the refrigerator until firm. Turn out, wrap in foil, then overwrap in a freezer bag. Seal, label and freeze.

To thaw and serve: remove wrappings and thaw the pâté in the refrigerator overnight. Serve cut into thick slices.

SERVES 10

FARMHOUSE PÂTÉ

METRIC/IMPERIAL

225 g/½ lb belly pork
225 g/½ lb lean veal
100 g/4 oz pig's liver
100 g/4 oz fat bacon, rind removed
1 × 5 ml spoon/1 teaspoon salt
freshly ground black pepper
pinch of ground mace
2 × 15 ml spoons/2 tablespoons dry white wine
1 × 15 ml spoon/1 tablespoon brandy
1 small garlic clove, peeled and crushed

AMERICAN

½ lb salt pork
½ lb lean veal
¼ lb pork liver
¼ lb fat bacon
1 teaspoon salt
freshly ground black pepper
pinch of ground mace
2 tablespoons dry white wine
1 tablespoon brandy
1 garlic clove, peeled and crushed

Mince (grind) the pork, veal and liver two or three times until very fine. Dice half the bacon and put in a bowl with the minced (ground) mixture and the remaining ingredients. Stir well to mix, then leave in a cool place for 2 hours.

Spoon the mixture into a 600 ml/1 pint/2½ cup ovenproof dish, press down lightly and cover with strips of the remaining fat bacon. Put the dish in a roasting tin half filled with water, cover with foil and bake in a preheated moderate oven (160°C/325°F or Gas Mark 3) for 1¼ to 1½ hours or until set.

To freeze: cool quickly. Put heavy weights on top of the pâté, then chill in the refrigerator until firm. Turn out, wrap in foil, then overwrap in a freezer bag. Seal, label and freeze.

To thaw and serve: remove wrappings and thaw the pâté in the refrigerator overnight. Serve cut into thick slices.

SERVES 4 to 6

SARDINE PÂTÉ

METRIC/IMPERIAL

225 g/½ lb cream cheese
finely grated rind and juice of 1 lemon
2 × 5 ml spoons/2 teaspoons freshly chopped parsley
1 × 200 g/7 oz can sardines in oil, mashed
salt
freshly ground black pepper
4–6 lemon slices, to garnish

AMERICAN
1 cup cream cheese
finely grated rind and juice of 1 lemon
2 teaspoons freshly chopped parsley
1 × 7 oz can sardines in oil, mashed
salt
freshly ground black pepper
4–6 lemon slices, to garnish

Put the cream cheese and lemon juice in a bowl and beat until soft. Add the remaining ingredients and beat well to mix. Spoon into 6 individual dishes.
To freeze: wrap in foil, seal, label and freeze.
To thaw and serve: thaw at room temperature for 2 hours, then chill in the refrigerator and garnish with lemon slices before serving. Serve with hot toast.
SERVES 6

COUNTRY PÂTÉ

METRIC/IMPERIAL
100 g/4 oz pig's liver
100 g/4 oz garlic sausage
1 onion, peeled and chopped
100 g/4 oz pork sausagemeat
225 g/½ lb cooked chicken, finely chopped
1 × 15 ml spoon/1 tablespoon freshly chopped parsley
2 × 5 ml spoons/2 teaspoons dried sage
salt
freshly ground black pepper
6 streaky bacon rashers, rinds removed

AMERICAN
¼ lb pork liver
¼ lb garlic sausage
1 onion, peeled and chopped
½ cup pork sausagemeat
1 cup finely chopped cooked chicken
1 tablespoon freshly chopped parsley
2 teaspoons dried sage
salt
freshly ground black pepper
6 fatty bacon slices

Mince (grind) the liver, garlic sausage and onion and put into a bowl with the remaining ingredients, except the bacon. Stir well to mix. Flatten the bacon with the blade of a knife and use to line the bottom and sides of a 450 g/1 lb loaf tin. Spoon in the pâté mixture and press down lightly. Cover with foil.
Put in a roasting tin half filled with water and bake in a preheated moderate oven (160°C/325°F or Gas Mark 3) for 2 to 2¼ hours or until set.
To freeze: cool quickly. Put heavy weights on top of the pâté, then chill in the refrigerator until firm. Turn out, wrap in foil, then overwrap in a freezer bag. Seal, label and freeze.
To thaw and serve: remove wrappings and arrange the pâté on a serving platter. Thaw in the refrigerator overnight. Serve cut into thick slices.
SERVES 4 to 6

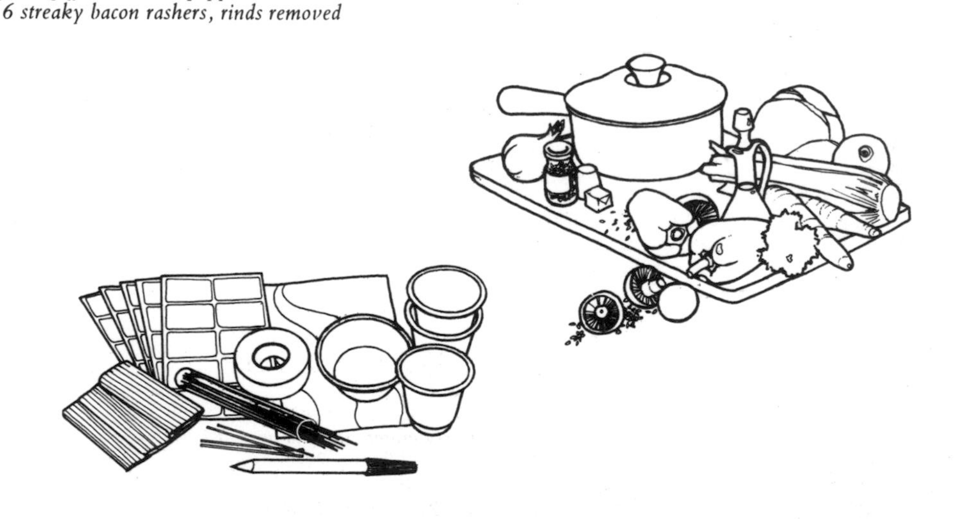

TOMATO JELLY RING

METRIC/IMPERIAL

1 × 400 g/4 oz can tomatoes
1 × 15 ml spoon/1 tablespoon tomato purée
4 × 15 ml spoons/4 tablespoons dry white wine
juice of ½ lemon
1 garlic clove, peeled and crushed
6 peppercorns
1 bay leaf
salt
1 × 5 ml spoon/1 teaspoon sugar
15 g/½ oz gelatine
4 × 15 ml spoons/4 tablespoons water
To serve:
a few sprigs of watercress
French dressing

AMERICAN

1 × 14 oz can tomatoes
1 tablespoon tomato paste
¼ cup dry white wine
juice of ½ lemon
1 garlic clove, peeled and crushed
6 peppercorns
1 bay leaf
salt
1 teaspoon sugar
2 envelopes unflavored gelatin
¼ cup water
To serve:
a few sprigs of watercress
French dressing

Put the tomatoes in a pan with the remaining ingredients except the gelatine and water. Bring to the boil and simmer for 5 minutes. Remove the peppercorns and bay leaf and rub the mixture through a sieve (strainer).

Sprinkle the gelatine over the water, leave for 5 minutes until spongy, then heat gently until dissolved. Strain into the tomato pulp and stir well to mix. Taste for seasoning, then pour into a lightly oiled 600 ml/1 pint/2½ cup ring mould. Chill in the refrigerator until set.

To freeze: wrap in a freezer bag or foil, seal, label and freeze.

To thaw and serve: turn the frozen jelly ring out onto a serving platter and thaw in the refrigerator for 6 hours. Fill the centre with watercress and serve with French dressing handed separately.

SERVES 4 to 6

PRAWNS (SHRIMP) EN COQUILLES

METRIC/IMPERIAL

25 g/1 oz butter
100 g/4 oz peeled prawns
100 g/4 oz white fish fillets, poached and flaked
300 ml/½ pint white coating sauce
100 g/4 oz Cheddar cheese, grated
dash of Worcestershire sauce
salt
freshly ground black pepper

AMERICAN

2 tablespoons butter
⅔ cup shelled shrimp
¼ lb white fish fillets, poached and flaked
1½ cups white coating sauce
1 cup grated Cheddar cheese
dash of Worcestershire sauce
salt
freshly ground black pepper

Melt the butter in a pan, add the prawns (shrimp) and white fish and cook gently for 2 minutes. Stir in the white sauce and heat through, then stir in half the grated cheese, the Worcestershire sauce and salt and pepper to taste.
Divide the mixture equally between 4 buttered scallop shells or individual ovenproof dishes and scatter over the remaining cheese.
To freeze: cool quickly. Open (flash) freeze until firm, wrap individually in foil, then pack in a freezer bag. Seal, label and return to the freezer.
To thaw and serve: remove wrappings and thaw at room temperature for 2 hours. Place on a baking sheet and cook in a preheated moderately hot oven (200°C/400°F or Gas Mark 6) for 15 to 20 minutes until crisp and golden brown.
SERVES 4

GARLIC LOAF

METRIC/IMPERIAL
1 French loaf
100 g/4 oz butter, softened
2 garlic cloves, peeled and crushed
salt
freshly ground black pepper

AMERICAN
1 French loaf
½ cup butter, softened
2 garlic cloves, peeled and crushed
salt
freshly ground black pepper

Cut the loaf into 2.5cm/1 inch thick slices without cutting right through the base. Put the remaining ingredients in a bowl, beat well to mix, then spread between the slices. Spread any remaining butter on the top and sides of the loaf.
To freeze: wrap in foil, then pack in a freezer bag. Seal, label and freeze.
To thaw and serve: put the foil-wrapped loaf on a baking sheet and bake from frozen in a preheated moderate oven (180°C/350°F or Gas Mark 4) for 20 minutes. Fold back the foil to uncover the loaf, increase the heat to hot (220°C/425°F or Gas Mark 7) and bake for a further 10 minutes until crisp.
SERVES 4

ANCHOVY LOAF

Make as for Garlic Loaf (see above), substituting 6 anchovy fillets and 1 × 5 ml spoon/1 teaspoon anchovy essence (extract) for the garlic.
Soak the anchovies in a little milk for 30 minutes before using, then drain and chop.
Freeze, thaw and serve as for Garlic Loaf.
SERVES 4

HERB LOAF

Make as for Garlic Loaf (see above), substituting 1 × 15 ml spoon/1 tablespoon chopped fresh herbs for the garlic.
Freeze, thaw and serve as for Garlic Loaf.
SERVES 4

SALMON MOUSSE

METRIC/IMPERIAL
1 × 225 g/8 oz can red salmon, skin and bones removed
300 ml/½ pint aspic jelly
2 × 15 ml spoons/2 tablespoons lemon juice
1 × 15 ml spoon/1 tablespoon freshly chopped parsley
salt
freshly ground black pepper
150 ml/¼ pint double cream, whipped
To garnish:
a few sprigs of watercress
a few slices of cucumber

AMERICAN
1 × ½ lb can red salmon, skin and bones removed
1¼ cups aspic jelly
2 tablespoons lemon juice
1 tablespoon freshly chopped parsley
salt
freshly ground black pepper
⅔ cup heavy cream, whipped
To garnish:
a few sprigs of watercress
a few slices of cucumber

Put the salmon in an electric blender with the aspic jelly, lemon juice, parsley and salt and pepper to taste. Work until smooth, transfer to a bowl, then fold in the cream.
Spoon the mixture into a wetted 750 ml/1¼ pint/3 cup ring mould and chill in the refrigerator until set.
To freeze: cover with foil, then pack in a freezer bag. Seal, label and freeze.
To thaw and serve: remove wrappings and turn the frozen mousse out onto a serving platter. Thaw at room temperature for 3 hours, then garnish with watercress sprigs and cucumber slices just before serving.
SERVES 6

TUNA AND TOMATO RING

METRIC/IMPERIAL
40 g/1½ oz butter
40 g/1½ oz flour
450 ml/¾ pint milk
salt
freshly ground black pepper
150 ml/¼ pint thick homemade mayonnaise
1 × 200 g/7 oz can tuna fish, drained and flaked
1 × 15 ml spoon/1 tablespoon Worcestershire sauce
2 × 15 ml spoons/2 tablespoons tomato purée
1 × 15 ml spoon/1 tablespoon lemon juice
3 spring onions, trimmed and finely chopped
15 g/½ oz gelatine
2 × 15 ml spoons/2 tablespoons water
To serve:
a few sprigs of watercress

AMERICAN
3 tablespoons butter
⅜ cup flour
2 cups milk
salt
freshly ground black pepper
⅔ cup thick homemade mayonnaise
1 × 7 oz can tuna fish, drained and flaked
1 tablespoon Worcestershire sauce
2 tablespoons tomato paste
1 tablespoon lemon juice
3 scallions, trimmed and finely chopped
2 envelopes unflavored gelatin
2 tablespoons water
To serve:
a few sprigs of watercress

Melt the butter in a pan, stir in the flour and cook for 2 minutes, stirring constantly. Remove from heat and gradually stir in the milk. Return to the heat and bring to the boil, stirring constantly. Simmer until thick, add salt and pepper to taste, then pour into a bowl, cover with foil and leave to cool.
Put all the remaining ingredients, except the gelatine and the water, in a bowl and stir well to mix. Beat the cooled sauce and fold into the mixture. Taste for seasoning.
Sprinkle the gelatine over the water, leave for 5 minutes until spongy, then heat gently until dissolved. Stir into the tuna mixture. Pour into a dampened 900 ml/1½ pint/3¾ cup ring mould and chill in the refrigerator until set.
To freeze: wrap in a freezer bag or foil, seal, label and freeze.
To thaw and serve: turn the frozen ring out onto a serving platter and thaw at room temperature for 4 hours. Fill the centre of the ring with watercress to serve.
SERVES 6 to 8

TARAMASALATA

METRIC/IMPERIAL
2 thick slices of white bread, crusts removed
4 × 15 ml spoons/4 tablespoons milk
1 × 175 g/6 oz jar smoked cods' roe
1 garlic clove, peeled and crushed
150 ml/¼ pint corn oil
2 × 15 ml spoons/2 tablespoons lemon juice
freshly ground black pepper
To garnish:
1 lemon, cut into wedges
4–6 black olives

AMERICAN
2 thick slices of white bread, crusts removed
¼ cup milk
1 × 6 oz jar smoked cods' roe
1 garlic clove, peeled and crushed
⅔ cup corn oil
2 tablespoons lemon juice
freshly ground black pepper
To garnish:
1 lemon, cut into wedges
4–6 black olives

Put the bread in a bowl, cover with the milk and leave to soak for 10 minutes.
Squeeze the bread dry, then put in an electric blender with the remaining ingredients and work to a smooth purée. Taste for seasoning and add more lemon juice, if liked.
To freeze: chill in the refrigerator, then spoon into a rigid container. Seal, label and freeze.
To thaw and serve: thaw in the container in the refrigerator overnight, then spoon into a serving dish. Garnish with lemon and olives just before serving.
SERVES 4 to 6

WHITING MORNAY

METRIC/IMPERIAL
225 g/½ lb whiting fillets, skinned
300 ml/½ pint milk
salt
freshly ground black pepper
25 g/1 oz cornflour
1 × 15 ml spoon/1 tablespoon water
75 g/3 oz Cheddar cheese, grated
450 g/1 lb potatoes, peeled, boiled and mashed with butter and milk

AMERICAN

½ lb whiting fillets, skinned
1¼ cups milk
salt
freshly ground black pepper
¼ cup cornstarch
1 tablespoon water
¾ cup grated Cheddar cheese
1 lb potatoes, peeled, boiled and mashed with butter and milk

Put the fish in a pan with the milk and salt and pepper to taste and cook gently for 15 minutes or until the fish is tender. Drain and reserve the cooking liquid in the pan.
Flake the fish and divide equally between 4 buttered scallop shells or individual ovenproof dishes. Mix the cornflour (cornstarch) to a paste with the water, then stir into the reserved cooking liquid. Bring to the boil, stirring constantly, then remove from the heat and stir in 50 g/2 oz/½ cup cheese.
Pour the sauce over the fish in the shells or dishes, dividing it equally between them. Pipe the mashed potatoes in a border around the shells or dishes, then sprinkle with the remaining cheese.
To freeze: cool quickly. Open (flash) freeze until firm, then wrap individually in freezer bags or foil. Seal, label and return to the freezer.
To thaw and serve: remove wrappings and thaw at room temperature for 1 hour. Reheat in a preheated moderately hot oven (200°C/400°F or Gas Mark 6) for 20 minutes or until heated through and golden brown on top.
SERVES 4

POTTED SHRIMPS

METRIC/IMPERIAL

100 g/4 oz butter
225 g/½ lb peeled shrimps
juice of ½ lemon
1 × 2.5 ml spoon/½ teaspoon freshly ground black pepper
pinch of cayenne pepper
1 × 2.5 ml spoon/½ teaspoon ground mace
lemon wedges, to garnish

AMERICAN

½ cup butter
1 cup shelled shrimp
juice of ½ lemon
½ teaspoon freshly ground black pepper
pinch of cayenne pepper
½ teaspoon ground mace
lemon wedges, to garnish

Melt 25 g/1 oz/2 tablespoons butter in a pan, add the remaining ingredients and fry briskly for 1 minute, stirring constantly. Taste and add more lemon juice, if liked.
Divide the mixture equally between 4 individual ramekins or serving dishes and smooth the tops. Melt the remaining butter until frothy, skim and pour over the shrimps. Leave to set.
To freeze: wrap in foil, seal, label and freeze.
To thaw and serve: remove wrappings and thaw at room temperature for 4 hours. Garnish with lemon wedges just before serving.
SERVES 4

POTTED HAM

METRIC/IMPERIAL

75 g/3 oz butter, softened
225 g/½ lb cooked ham, minced or finely chopped
salt
1 × 2.5 ml spoon/½ teaspoon mustard powder
pinch of cayenne pepper

AMERICAN

⅜ cup butter, softened
1 cup ground or finely chopped cooked ham
salt
½ teaspoon mustard powder
pinch of cayenne pepper

Put all the ingredients in a bowl and beat until smooth and evenly blended. Taste for seasoning, then press into a rigid container.
To freeze: wrap in foil, seal, label and freeze.
To thaw and serve: thaw in the container at room temperature for 4 hours.
SERVES 4

POTTED SALMON

METRIC/IMPERIAL

225g/½ lb fresh salmon, poached, skinned and boned
75 g/3 oz butter
salt
freshly ground black pepper
1 × 5 ml spoon/1 teaspoon lemon juice

AMERICAN

½ lb fresh salmon, poached, skinned and boned
⅜ cup butter
salt
freshly ground black pepper
1 teaspoon lemon juice

Prepare, freeze, thaw and serve as for Potted Ham (see above).

MARINATED KIPPERS

METRIC/IMPERIAL

8 kipper fillets
freshly chopped parsley, to garnish
For the marinade:
1 onion, peeled and sliced into rings
2 bay leaves
300 ml/½ pint dry white wine
150 ml/¼ pint wine vinegar
2 × 15 ml spoons/2 tablespoons vegetable oil
1 × 15 ml spoon/1 tablespoon soft brown sugar
1 × 2.5 ml spoon/½ teaspoon salt
6 black peppercorns, crushed

AMERICAN

8 kipper fillets
freshly chopped parsley, to garnish
For the marinade:
1 onion, peeled and sliced into rings
2 bay leaves
1¼ cups dry white wine
⅔ cup wine vinegar
2 tablespoons vegetable oil
1 tablespoon light brown sugar
1 teaspoon salt
6 black peppercorns, crushed

Put the kipper fillets in a shallow dish. Mix all the ingredients for the marinade together and pour over the fish. Leave to marinate in the refrigerator for 24 hours.
To freeze: transfer to a rigid container, seal, label and freeze.
To thaw and serve: thaw in the container at room temperature for 4 hours. Serve chilled, garnished with parsley.
SERVES 4

MUSHROOM-STUFFED PANCAKES (CRÊPES)

METRIC/IMPERIAL

8 pancakes made from 300 ml/½ pint batter
75 g/3 oz Cheddar cheese, grated
300 ml/½ pint white coating sauce
For the filling:
25 g/1 oz butter
½ onion, peeled and finely chopped
1 garlic clove, peeled and crushed
225 g/½ lb mushrooms, chopped
1 × 5 ml spoon/1 teaspoon dried mixed herbs
25 g/1 oz fresh white breadcrumbs
salt
freshly ground black pepper

AMERICAN

8 crêpes made from 1¼ cups batter
¾ cup grated Cheddar cheese
1¼ cups white coating sauce
For the filling:
2 tablespoons butter
½ onion, peeled and finely chopped
1 garlic clove, peeled and crushed
2 cups chopped mushrooms
1 teaspoon dried mixed herbs
½ cup fresh white breadcrumbs
salt
freshly ground black pepper

To make the filling: melt the butter in a pan, add the onion, garlic and mushrooms and fry gently until reduced to a pulp. Stir in the herbs, breadcrumbs and salt and pepper to taste. Remove from the heat, divide equally between the pancakes (crêpes) and fold or roll up.
Put the pancakes (crêpes) in an ovenproof dish or foil container. Stir 50 g/2 oz/½ cup cheese into the white sauce, add salt and pepper to taste, then pour over the pancakes (crêpes). Sprinkle the remaining cheese on the top.
To freeze: cool quickly, then cover with foil. Seal, label and freeze.
To thaw and serve: remove wrappings and thaw at room temperature for 4 hours. Bake in a preheated moderately hot oven (190°C/375°F, or Gas Mark 5) for 30 to 35 minutes or until heated through.
SERVES 4

SMOKED TROUT AND APPLE MOUSSE

METRIC/IMPERIAL

1 medium cooking apple, peeled, cored and sliced
2 × 15 ml spoons/2 tablespoons water
3 smoked trout, skinned and boned
300 ml/½ pint soured cream
2 × 5 ml spoons/2 teaspoons horseradish sauce
freshly ground black pepper
2 × 5 ml spoons/2 teaspoons gelatine
juice of 1 lemon
2 egg whites
To garnish:
a few lettuce leaves, shredded
a few sprigs of watercress
a few slices of cucumber

AMERICAN

1 medium baking apple, peeled, cored and sliced
2 tablespoons water
3 smoked trout, skinned and boned
1¼ cups sour cream
2 teaspoons horseradish sauce
freshly ground black pepper

2 teaspoons unflavored gelatin
juice of 1 lemon
2 egg whites
To garnish:
a few lettuce leaves, shredded
a few sprigs of watercress
a few slices of cucumber

Put the apple and water in a pan, cover and cook gently for 10 minutes. Remove from the heat and leave to cool.
Mash the trout flesh and mix with the sour(ed) cream. Add the apple, then work to a smooth purée in an electric blender. Stir in the horseradish sauce and pepper to taste.
Sprinkle the gelatine over the lemon juice, leave for 5 minutes until spongy, then heat gently until dissolved. Fold into the fish mixture.
Beat the egg whites until stiff, fold into the fish mixture, then spoon into a dampened 900 ml/1½ pints/3¾ cup ring mould. Chill in the refrigerator until set.
To freeze: wrap in a freezer bag or foil, seal, label and freeze.
To thaw and serve: turn out onto a serving platter and thaw in the refrigerator overnight. Garnish with lettuce, watercress and cucumber.
SERVES 6 to 8

SPINACH AND HAM PANCAKES (CRÊPES)

METRIC/IMPERIAL
For the batter:
75 g/3 oz flour
salt
1 egg, beaten
1 egg yolk
175 ml/6 fl oz milk
1 × 15 ml spoon/1 tablespoon vegetable oil or melted butter
vegetable oil for frying
For the filling:
25 g/1 oz butter
675 g/1½ lb spinach, boiled, drained and sieved
1 × 15 ml spoon/1 tablespoon grated Gruyère cheese
freshly ground black pepper
8 thin slices of cooked ham
For the sauce:
25 g/1 oz butter
25 g/1 oz flour
450 ml/¾ pint milk
50 g/2 oz Cheddar cheese, grated
1 × 2.5 ml spoon/½ teaspoon prepared French mustard
25 g/1 oz grated Parmesan cheese, to finish

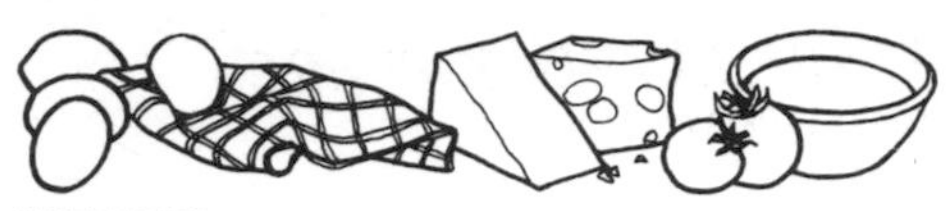

AMERICAN
For the batter:
¾ cup flour
salt
1 egg, beaten
1 egg yolk
¾ cup milk
1 tablespoon vegetable oil or melted butter
vegetable oil for frying
For the filling:
2 tablespoons butter
1½ lb spinach, boiled, drained and strained
1 tablespoon grated Gruyère cheese
freshly ground black pepper
8 thin slices of cooked ham
For the sauce:
2 tablespoons butter
¼ cup flour
2 cups milk
½ cup grated Cheddar cheese
½ teaspoon prepared French mustard
¼ cup grated Parmesan cheese, to finish

To make the pancakes (crêpes): sift the flour and salt into a bowl. Add the beaten egg and egg yolk and half the milk and beat until smooth. Stir in the remaining milk and the oil or melted butter. Leave the batter to stand for 1 hour, then make 8 paper thin pancakes (crêpes), frying the batter in hot oil.
To make the filling: melt the butter in a pan, add the spinach and cook until dry. Remove from the heat and stir in the cheese and salt and pepper to taste. Put 1 pancake (crêpe) in a buttered ovenproof dish or foil container, spoon over a little of the spinach mixture and top with a slice of ham. Repeat these layers until all the ingredients are used up, finishing with a pancake (crêpe).
To make the sauce: melt the butter in a pan, stir in the flour and cook for 2 minutes, stirring constantly. Remove from the heat and gradually stir in the milk. Return to the heat and bring to the boil, stirring constantly. Simmer until thick, then add the cheese and mustard. Pour over the pancakes (crêpes) and sprinkle with the Parmesan cheese.
To freeze: cool quickly. Open (flash) freeze until firm, then wrap in foil. Seal, label and return to the freezer.
To thaw and serve: remove wrappings and reheat from frozen in a preheated moderately hot oven (200°C/400°F or Gas Mark 6) for 30 to 40 minutes or until heated through.
SERVES 8

SMOKED HADDOCK MOUSSE

METRIC/IMPERIAL
450 g/1 lb smoked haddock fillets
600 ml/1 pint milk
50 g/2 oz butter
50 g/2 oz flour
15 g/½ oz gelatine
5 × 15 ml spoons/5 tablespoons water
300 ml/½ pint double cream, lightly whipped
freshly ground black pepper
To garnish:
1 hard-boiled egg, sliced
a few parsley sprigs

AMERICAN
1 lb smoked haddock fillets
2½ cups milk
¼ cup butter
½ cup flour
2 envelopes unflavored gelatin
⅓ cup water
1¼ cups heavy cream, lightly whipped
freshly ground black pepper
To garnish:
1 hard-cooked egg, sliced
a few parsley sprigs

Put the haddock in a pan, add the milk and poach gently until tender. Remove the skin and bones and flake the flesh. Strain the cooking liquid and reserve.

Melt the butter in a clean pan, stir in the flour and cook for 2 minutes, stirring constantly. Stir in the reserved cooking liquid and bring to the boil. Simmer until thick, then remove from the heat and stir in the flaked fish. Leave to cool.

Sprinkle the gelatine over the water, leave for 5 minutes until spongy, then heat gently until dissolved. Stir into the haddock mixture. Fold in the cream and add pepper to taste. Pour into a buttered 1 litre/1¾ pint/4¼ cup soufflé dish and chill in the refrigerator until set.

To freeze: wrap in a freezer bag or foil, seal, label and freeze.

To thaw and serve: remove wrappings and thaw in the refrigerator overnight. Decorate the top of the mousse with slices of egg and parsley sprigs.

SERVES 6

COQUILLES ST JACQUES

METRIC/IMPERIAL
6 large scallops, with shells
150 ml/¼ pint dry white wine
150 ml/¼ pint water
1 × 5 ml spoon/1 teaspoon lemon juice
15 g/½ oz butter
15 g/½ oz flour
150 ml/¼ pint double cream
pinch of cayenne pepper
salt
freshly ground black pepper
25 g/1 oz grated Parmesan cheese

AMERICAN
6 large scallops, with shells
⅔ cup dry white wine
⅔ cup water
1 teaspoon lemon juice
1 tablespoon butter
2 tablespoons flour
⅔ cup heavy cream
pinch of cayenne pepper
salt
freshly ground black pepper
¼ cup grated Parmesan cheese

Put the scallops in a pan with the wine, water and lemon juice and poach gently for 10 minutes. Remove from the heat and leave to cool.

Strain the scallops and slice finely. Reserve the cooking liquid in the pan and boil to reduce to 150 ml/¼ pint/⅔ cup.

Melt the butter in a separate pan, stir in the flour and cook for 2 minutes, stirring constantly. Stir in the reduced cooking liquid and bring to the boil, stirring. Simmer for 4 minutes, then add the cream and boil until thick. Add the cayenne and salt and pepper to taste, then remove from the heat and stir in the sliced scallops.

Divide the mixture equally between 4 buttered scallop shells and sprinkle the cheese on the top.

To freeze: cool quickly. Open (flash) freeze until firm, then wrap individually in freezer bags or foil. Seal, label and return to the freezer.

To thaw and serve: remove wrappings and thaw in the refrigerator overnight. Bake in a preheated moderately hot oven (190°C/375°F or Gas Mark 5) for 20 minutes or until heated through and golden brown on top.

MAKES 4

COTTAGE CHEESE AND CRAB MOUSSE

METRIC/IMPERIAL

15 g/½ oz gelatine
150 ml/¼ pint water
450 g/1 lb cottage cheese
½ bunch of watercress, stalks removed and leaves finely chopped
1 × 225 g/8 oz can crab meat, drained and flaked
3 × 15 ml spoons/3 tablespoons single cream
2 × 5 ml spoons/2 teaspoons lemon juice
salt
freshly ground black pepper
a few sprigs of watercress, to garnish

AMERICAN

2 envelopes unflavored gelatin
⅔ cup water
2 cups cottage cheese
½ bunch of watercress, stalks removed and leaves finely chopped
1 × ½ lb can crab meat, drained and flaked
3 tablespoons light cream
2 teaspoons lemon juice
salt
freshly ground black pepper
a few sprigs of watercress, to garnish

Prepare, freeze, thaw and serve as for Sour(ed) Cream and Tuna Mousse (see page 24).

DANISH BLUE MOUSSE

METRIC/IMPERIAL

1 × 300 ml/½ pint packet aspic jelly crystals
150 ml/¼ pint boiling water
100 g/4 oz Danish blue cheese, sieved
150 ml/¼ pint soured cream
2 egg whites

AMERICAN

1 × 1¼ cup package aspic jelly crystals
⅔ cup boiling water
¼ lb Danish blue cheese, strained
⅔ cup sour cream
2 egg whites

Put the aspic crystals in a bowl, pour over the boiling water and stir to dissolve.
Put the cheese and sour(ed) cream in a separate bowl and beat well to mix. Stir in the aspic jelly and leave in a cool place until on the point of setting.
Beat the egg whites until stiff, then fold into the mixture and pour into a dampened 450 g/1 lb loaf tin. Chill in the refrigerator until the mousse has set.
To freeze: open (flash) freeze until firm, then turn the mousse out of the tin and wrap in foil. Seal, label and return to the freezer.
To thaw and serve: remove wrappings and arrange the mousse on a serving platter. Thaw in the refrigerator overnight.
SERVES 6 to 8

SMOKED MACKEREL MOUSSE

METRIC/IMPERIAL

15 g/½ oz gelatine
250 ml/8 fl oz chicken stock
225 g/½ lb smoked mackerel, skinned, boned and flaked
75 g/3 oz Gouda cheese, grated
75 g/3 oz butter, melted
1.5 × 15 ml spoons/1½ tablespoons lemon juice
freshly ground black pepper
1 × 15 ml spoon/1 tablespoon freshly chopped parsley
To garnish:
1 lemon, sliced
a few slices of cucumber

AMERICAN

2 envelopes unflavored gelatin
1 cup chicken stock
½ lb smoked mackerel, skinned, boned and flaked
¾ cup grated Gouda cheese
⅜ cup butter, melted
1½ tablespoons lemon juice
freshly ground black pepper
1 tablespoon freshly chopped parsley
To garnish:
1 lemon, sliced
a few slices of cucumber

Sprinkle the gelatine over the stock, leave for 5 minutes until spongy, then heat gently until dissolved. Leave to cool slightly, then pour into an electric blender. Add the remaining ingredients, except the parsley, and work to a smooth purée. Stir in the parsley, then pour the mixture into a lightly buttered mould or serving dish. Chill in the refrigerator until set.
Dip the mould or dish in hot water, invert over a plate and turn out the mousse.
To freeze: open (flash) freeze until firm, then wrap in a freezer bag or foil. Seal, label and return to the freezer.
To thaw and serve: remove wrappings and place the mousse on a serving platter. Thaw at room temperature for 4 hours, then garnish with lemon and cucumber slices just before serving.
SERVES 6

SOURED CREAM AND TUNA MOUSSE

METRIC/IMPERIAL

15 g/½ oz gelatine
150 ml/¼ pint water
300 ml/½ pint soured cream
½ bunch of watercress, stalks removed and leaves finely chopped
1 × 200 g/7 oz can tuna fish, drained and flaked
2 × 5 ml spoons/2 teaspoons lemon juice
salt
freshly ground black pepper
a few sprigs of watercress, to garnish

AMERICAN

2 envelopes unflavored gelatin
⅔ cup water
1¼ cups sour cream
½ bunch of watercress, stalks removed and leaves finely chopped
1 × 7 oz can tuna fish, drained and flaked
2 teaspoons lemon juice
salt
freshly ground black pepper
a few sprigs of watercress, to garnish

Sprinkle the gelatine over the water, leave for 5 minutes until spongy, then heat gently until dissolved.

Put the remaining ingredients in a bowl and stir well to mix. Stir in the dissolved gelatine, then pour into a 900 ml/1½ pint/3¾ cup soufflé dish and chill in the refrigerator until set.

To freeze: wrap in a freezer bag or foil, seal, label and freeze.

To thaw and serve: remove wrappings and thaw in the refrigerator overnight. Garnish the top of the mousse with watercress just before serving.

SERVES 4 to 6

SUMMER CHICKEN MOUSSE

METRIC/IMPERIAL

3 eggs, separated
15 g/½ oz gelatine
2 × 15 ml spoons/2 tablespoons water
300 ml/½ pint chicken stock
1 × 15 ml spoon/1 tablespoon horseradish sauce
salt
freshly ground black pepper
275 g/10 oz cooked chicken meat, minced
2 celery stalks, minced
few tomato slices, to garnish

AMERICAN

3 eggs, separated
2 envelopes unflavored gelatin
2 tablespoons water
1¼ cups chicken stock
1 tablespoon horseradish sauce
salt
freshly ground black pepper
1¼ cups ground cooked chicken meat
2 celery stalks, ground
few tomato slices, to garnish

Put the egg yolks in a heatproof bowl, stand over a pan of hot water and beat until thick. Sprinkle the gelatine over the water, leave for 5 minutes until spongy, then heat gently until dissolved. Stir into the stock with the horseradish sauce and salt and pepper to taste, then pour onto the egg yolks and stir well to mix. Fold in the chicken and celery and leave to cool. Beat the egg whites until stiff, then fold into the chicken mixture. Pour into a buttered 900 ml/1½ pint/3¾ cup soufflé dish and chill in the refrigerator until set.

To freeze: wrap in a freezer bag or foil, seal, label and freeze.

To thaw and serve: remove wrappings and thaw in the refrigerator overnight. Garnish the top of the mousse with thin tomato slices just before serving.

SERVES 6

SMOKED HADDOCK EN COQUILLES

METRIC/IMPERIAL

40 g/1½ oz butter
100 g/4 oz mushrooms, sliced
300 ml/½ pint white coating sauce
1 × 2.5 ml spoon/½ teaspoon prepared English mustard
275 g/10 oz smoked haddock fillets, poached, skinned and flaked
freshly ground black pepper
25 g/1 oz Cheddar cheese, grated
15 g/½ oz fresh white breadcrumbs

AMERICAN

3 tablespoons butter
1 cup sliced mushrooms
1¼ cups white coating sauce
½ teaspoon prepared English mustard
10 oz smoked haddock fillets, poached, skinned and flaked
freshly ground black pepper
¼ cup grated Cheddar cheese
¼ cup fresh white breadcrumbs

Melt 25 g/1 oz/2 tablespoons butter in a pan, add the mushrooms and fry for 3 minutes. Stir in the white sauce, mustard, fish and pepper to taste. Divide the mixture equally between 4 buttered scallop shells or individual ovenproof dishes and sprinkle with the grated cheese and breadcrumbs.

To freeze: cool quickly. Open (flash) freeze until firm, then wrap individually in freezer bags or foil. Seal, label and return to the freezer.

To thaw and serve: remove wrappings and thaw at room temperature for 1 hour. Dot with the remaining butter and reheat in a preheated moderately hot oven (200°C/400°F or Gas Mark 6) for 20 minutes or until heated through and golden brown on top.

MAKES 4

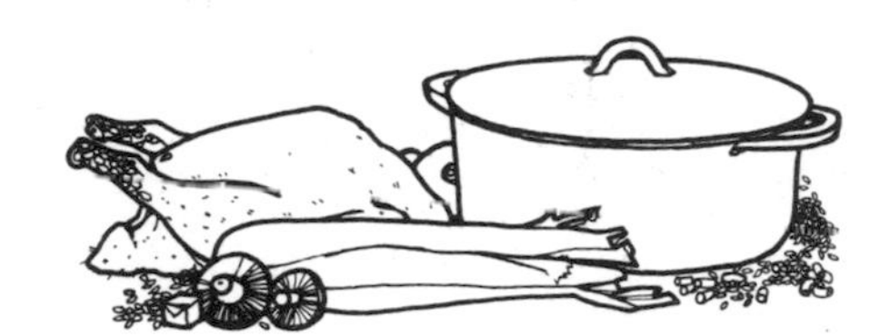

CHICKEN BALLS AND MUSTARD DIP

METRIC/IMPERIAL

125 g/4½ oz fine semolina
450 ml/¾ pint chicken stock
225 g/½ lb cooked chicken meat, minced or finely chopped
225 g/½ lb cooked ham, minced or finely chopped
1 × 5 ml spoon/1 teaspoon freshly chopped parsley
salt
freshly ground black pepper
1 egg, beaten
vegetable oil for deep-frying
To serve:
1 × 15 ml spoon/1 tablespoon prepared French mustard
150 ml/¼ pint double cream, lightly whipped

AMERICAN

¾ cup fine semolina flour
2 cups chicken stock
1 cup ground or finely chopped cooked chicken meat
1 cup ground or finely chopped cooked ham
1 teaspoon freshly chopped parsley
salt
freshly ground black pepper
1 egg, beaten
vegetable oil for deep-frying
To serve:
1 tablespoon prepared French mustard
⅔ cup heavy cream, lightly whipped

Put 75 g/3 oz/½ cup semolina and the stock in a pan and blend together. Bring to the boil and simmer for 2 minutes, stirring constantly. Remove from the heat, stir in the chicken, ham, parsley and salt and pepper to taste, then leave to cool.

Shape the mixture into very small balls, dip into the beaten egg one at a time, then coat in the remaining semolina. Deep-fry in hot oil until golden brown on all sides, then drain on paper towels.

To freeze: cool quickly. Open (flash) freeze until firm, then pack in a rigid container, separating each layer with foil. Seal, label and return to the freezer.

To thaw and serve: thaw at room temperature for 4 hours, then reheat on a baking sheet in a preheated moderately hot oven (200°C/400°F or Gas Mark 6) for 20 to 30 minutes or until heated through. Beat the mustard into the cream, spoon into a serving dish and hand separately.

SERVES 6

CAMEMBERT MOUSSE

METRIC/IMPERIAL

3 individual portions of Camembert cheese, rinds removed
1 × 15 ml spoon/1 tablespoon melted butter
1 individual portion of Petit Suisse cheese
3 × 15 ml spoons/3 tablespoons double cream, whipped
1 × 5 ml spoon/1 teaspoon prepared mustard
1 × 5 ml spoon/1 teaspoon freshly chopped parsley

AMERICAN

3 individual portions of Camembert cheese, rinds removed
1 tablespoon melted butter
1 individual portion of Petit Suisse cheese
3 tablespoons heavy cream, whipped
1 teaspoon prepared mustard
1 teaspoon freshly chopped parsley

Put the Camembert and butter in a bowl and beat together until smooth. Add the Petit Suisse and beat well to mix. Fold in the cream, then stir in the mustard and parsley. Press into a lightly oiled mould.

To freeze: chill in the refrigerator, then open (flash) freeze until firm. Remove from the mould and wrap in foil. Seal, label and return to the freezer.

To thaw and serve: remove wrappings and arrange the mousse on a serving platter. Thaw in the refrigerator overnight.

SERVES 4

PRAWN (SHRIMP) AND TOMATO RAMEKINS

METRIC/IMPERIAL

25 g/1 oz butter
1 onion, peeled and chopped
1 garlic clove, peeled and crushed
25 g/1 oz flour
1 × 225 g/8 oz can tomatoes
1 × 5 ml spoon/1 teaspoon tomato purée
salt
freshly ground black pepper
225 g/½ lb peeled prawns
25 g/1 oz grated Parmesan cheese

AMERICAN

2 tablespoons butter
1 onion, peeled and chopped
1 garlic clove, peeled and crushed
¼ cup flour
1 × ½ lb can tomatoes
1 teaspoon tomato paste
salt
freshly ground black pepper
1⅓ cups shelled shrimp
¼ cup grated Parmesan cheese

Melt the butter in a pan, add the onion and garlic and fry gently until soft. Stir in the flour, then the tomatoes, tomato purée (paste) and salt and pepper to taste. Simmer for 20 minutes, then work through a sieve (strainer) and mix with the prawns (shrimp).

Spoon the mixture into 6 individual freezer-proof ramekins or ovenproof dishes, smooth the tops and sprinkle with the Parmesan cheese.

To freeze: cool quickly, then wrap in foil, seal, label and freeze.

To thaw and serve: remove wrappings and thaw at room temperature for 2 hours. Reheat in a preheated moderate oven (180°C/350°F or Gas Mark 4) for 20 minutes or until heated through and golden brown on top.

MAKES 6

CURRIED HADDOCK SCALLOPS

METRIC/IMPERIAL

50 g/2 oz butter
1 onion, peeled and chopped
1 × 5 ml spoon/1 teaspoon curry powder
300 ml/½ pint white coating sauce
225 g/½ lb haddock fillets, poached, skinned and flaked
salt
freshly ground black pepper
15 g/½ oz fresh white breadcrumbs
450 g/1 lb potatoes, peeled, boiled and mashed with butter and milk

AMERICAN

¼ cup butter
1 onion, peeled and chopped
1 × 5 ml spoon/1 teaspoon curry powder
1¼ cups white coating sauce
½ lb haddock fillets, poached, skinned and flaked
salt
freshly ground black pepper
¼ cup fresh white breadcrumbs
1 lb potatoes, peeled, boiled and mashed with butter and milk

Melt half the butter in a pan, add the onion and fry gently for 3 minutes. Stir in the curry powder and cook for 1 minute. Add the white sauce, fish and salt and pepper to taste, then stir well to mix.

Divide the mixture equally between 4 buttered scallop shells or individual ovenproof dishes. Sprinkle with the breadcrumbs. Pipe the mashed potatoes in a border around the shells or dishes.

To freeze: cool quickly. Open (flash) freeze until firm, then wrap individually in freezer bags or foil. Seal, label and return to the freezer.

To thaw and serve: remove wrappings and thaw at room temperature for 1 hour. Dot with the remaining butter and reheat in a preheated moderately hot oven (200°C/400°F or Gas Mark 6) for 20 minutes or until heated through and golden brown on top.

MAKES 4

SEAFOOD TIMBALE

METRIC/IMPERIAL
450 g/1 lb whiting fillets, skinned
300 ml/½ pint milk
pinch of dried mixed herbs
salt
freshly ground black pepper
25 g/1 oz butter
25 g/1 oz flour
50 g/2 oz cooked ham, finely chopped
2 × 5 ml spoons/2 teaspoons freshly chopped parsley
450 g/1 lb mashed potatoes

AMERICAN
1 lb whiting fillets, skinned
1¼ cups milk
pinch of dried mixed herbs
salt
freshly ground black pepper
2 tablespoons butter
¼ cup flour
¼ cup finely chopped cooked ham
2 teaspoons freshly chopped parsley
2 cups mashed potato

Put the fish in a pan with the milk, herbs and salt and pepper to taste and cook gently for 15 minutes or until the fish is tender. Drain, reserve the cooking liquid and flake the fish. Melt the butter in a clean pan, stir in the flour and cook for 2 minutes, stirring constantly. Remove from the heat and gradually stir in the reserved cooking liquid. Return to the heat and bring to the boil, stirring constantly. Simmer until thick, then stir in the flaked fish, ham and parsley.
Put a layer of mashed potatoes into the bottom of a buttered ovenproof dish or foil container and pipe or press the remaining potatoes around the sides. Pour the sauce into the centre.
To freeze: cool quickly. Open (flash) freeze until firm, then wrap in a freezer bag or foil. Seal, label and return to the freezer.
To thaw and serve: remove wrappings and thaw at room temperature for 4 hours. Bake in a preheated moderately hot oven (190°C/375°F or Gas Mark 5) for 30 to 40 minutes or until heated through.
SERVES 4

DEVILLED SAUSAGES ON TOAST

METRIC/IMPERIAL
25 g/1 oz butter
225 g/½ lb skinless pork sausages, sliced
2 streaky bacon rashers, rinds removed
1 medium onion, peeled and finely chopped
2 tomatoes, peeled and quartered
2 × 5 ml spoons/2 teaspoons curry powder
1 × 5 ml spoon/1 teaspoon prepared English mustard
2 × 5 ml spoons/2 teaspoons tomato ketchup
1 × 15 ml spoon/1 tablespoon chutney
pinch of cayenne pepper
salt
freshly ground black pepper
To serve:
4 slices of hot buttered toast
freshly chopped parsley

AMERICAN
2 tablespoons butter
½ lb skinless pork sausages, sliced
2 fatty bacon slices
1 medium onion, peeled and finely chopped
2 tomatoes, peeled and quartered
2 teaspoons curry powder
1 teaspoon prepared English mustard
2 teaspoons tomato ketchup
1 tablespoon chutney
pinch of cayenne pepper
salt
freshly ground black pepper
To serve:
4 slices of hot buttered toast
freshly chopped parsley

Melt the butter in a pan, add the sausages, bacon and onion and fry gently for 5 minutes until lightly coloured. Add the remaining ingredients and cook for a further 5 minutes, stirring constantly.
To freeze: cool quickly, then transfer to a rigid container, seal, label and freeze.
To thaw and serve: thaw in the container at room temperature for 2 hours, then reheat gently on top of the stove, stirring occasionally. Pile onto hot toast and sprinkle with parsley just before serving.
SERVES 4

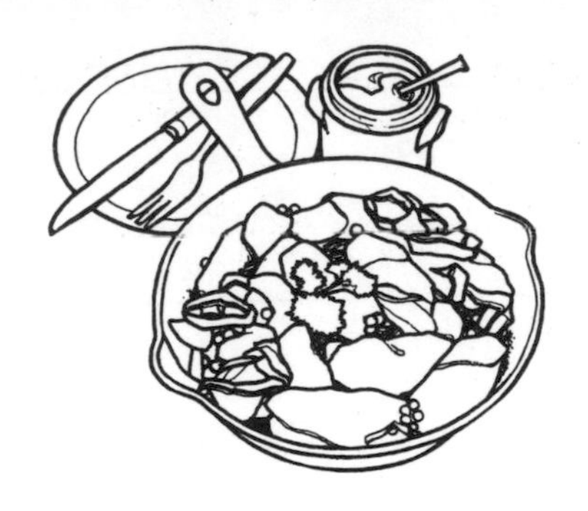

MUSHROOM-STUFFED PEPPERS

METRIC/IMPERIAL

40 g/1½ oz butter
100 g/4 oz mushrooms, finely chopped
100 g/4 oz cooked ham, finely chopped
1 onion, peeled and finely chopped
100 g/4 oz long-grain rice, boiled and drained
2 × 15 ml spoons/2 tablespoons tomato purée
1 × 5 ml spoon/1 teaspoon dried sage
salt
freshly ground black pepper
4 green peppers, cored, seeded and blanched

AMERICAN

3 tablespoons butter
1 cup finely chopped mushrooms
½ cup finely chopped cooked ham
1 onion, peeled and finely chopped
⅔ cup long-grain rice, boiled and drained
2 tablespoons tomato paste
1 teaspoon dried sage
salt
freshly ground black pepper
4 green peppers, cored, seeded and blanched

Melt the butter in a pan, add the remaining ingredients, except the green peppers, and fry gently for 10 minutes.

Put the peppers in a buttered ovenproof dish or foil container and divide the filling equally between them. Cover and bake in a preheated moderate oven (180°C/350°F or Gas Mark 4) for 40 minutes.

To freeze: cool quickly, then wrap individually in foil, seal, label and freeze.

To thaw and serve: remove wrappings and thaw at room temperature for 4 hours, then reheat in a covered dish or container in a preheated moderate oven for 30 to 35 minutes or until heated through.

SERVES 4

SQUID IN GARLIC SAUCE

METRIC/IMPERIAL

675 g/1½ lb fresh squid
2 × 15 ml spoons/2 tablespoons olive oil
1 large onion, peeled and cut into thin rings
2 garlic cloves, peeled and finely chopped
150 ml/¼ pint dry white wine
150 ml/¼ pint water
1 parsley sprig
1 bay leaf
salt
freshly ground black pepper
1 × 15 ml spoon/1 tablespoon cornflour
To finish:
3 × 15 ml spoons/3 tablespoons double cream
freshly chopped parsley

AMERICAN

1½ lb fresh squid
2 tablespoons olive oil
1 large onion, peeled and cut into thin rings
2 garlic cloves, peeled and finely chopped
⅔ cup dry white wine
⅔ cup water
1 parsley sprig
1 bay leaf
salt
freshly ground black pepper
1 tablespoon cornstarch
To finish:
3 tablespoons heavy cream
freshly chopped parsley

Wash and skin the squid. Remove the long transparent backbone and clean the inside. Remove the head and ink bag and pull out the hard core at the centre of the tentacles. Cut the body into rings about 1 cm/½ inch wide. Leave the tentacles whole or, if too large, cut into 2.5 cm/1 inch lengths.

Heat the oil in a pan, add the onion and garlic and fry gently for 1 minute. Add the squid and the remaining ingredients except the cornflour (cornstarch). Cover and simmer for 1 hour or until tender, then remove the squid from the pan and discard the parsley sprig and bay leaf. Mix the cornflour (cornstarch) to a paste with a little water. Stir into the pan to thicken the cooking liquid.

To freeze: cool quickly. Put the squid in a rigid container and cover with the sauce. Seal, label and freeze.

To thaw and serve: thaw in the container at room temperature for 4 hours, then stir in the cream. Transfer to a serving dish, sprinkle with parsley and chill in the refrigerator for at least 30 minutes before serving.

SERVES 6

MELON AND GINGER COCKTAIL

METRIC/IMPERIAL

1 honeydew melon
50 g/2 oz caster sugar
pinch of ground ginger
finely grated rind and juice of 1 lemon
a little chopped stem ginger, to finish

AMERICAN

1 honeydew melon
¼ cup sugar
pinch of ground ginger
finely grated rind and juice of 1 lemon
a little chopped preserved ginger, to finish

Cut the melon in half, discard the seeds and, using a melon baller, scoop out as many melon balls as possible. Place in a rigid container.
Make the melon juice up to 150 ml/¼ pint/⅔ cup with water and put in a pan with the remaining ingredients except the stem (preserved) ginger. Bring slowly to the boil, stirring constantly, then strain.
To freeze: cool quickly. Pour the sauce over the melon balls in the container, seal, label and freeze.
To thaw and serve: thaw in the container in the refrigerator for 6 hours, then stir thoroughly, transfer to a serving dish and sprinkle with chopped stem (preserved) ginger.
SERVES 4 to 6

SALMON CRISP CRUMBLE

METRIC/IMPERIAL

1 × 212 g/7½ oz can salmon, drained, skinned and flaked
1 × 298 g/10½ oz can condensed tomato soup
4 × 15 ml spoons/4 tablespoons cooked peas
salt
freshly ground black pepper
25 g/1 oz flour
15 g/½ oz butter
65 g/2½ oz plain potato crisps, crushed

AMERICAN

1 × 7½ oz can salmon, drained, skinned and flaked
1 × 10½ oz can condensed tomato soup
¼ cup cooked peas
salt
freshly ground black pepper
¼ cup flour
1 tablespoon butter
1¼ cups crushed plain potato chips

Blend the salmon, soup and peas together, add salt and pepper to taste, then spoon into an ovenproof dish or foil container.
Sift the flour into a bowl, rub in the butter with the fingertips, then stir in the crisps (chips). Sprinkle over the salmon mixture.
To freeze: wrap in foil, seal, label and freeze.
To thaw and serve: thaw at room temperature for 4 hours, then bake, uncovered, in a preheated moderate oven (180°C/350°F or Gas Mark 4) for 20 to 30 minutes or until heated through.
SERVES 4

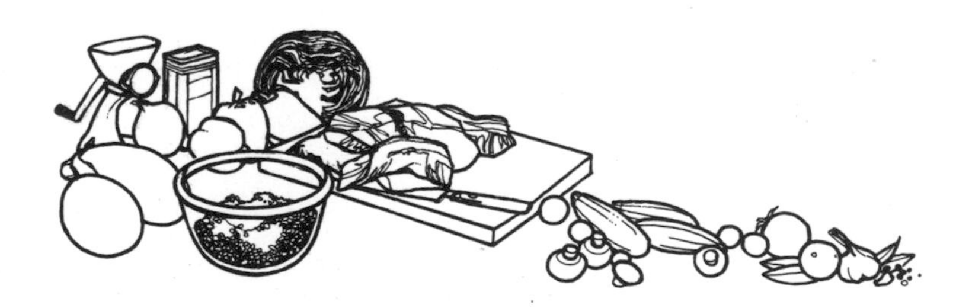

CHILLED PUMPKIN SOUP

METRIC/IMPERIAL

900 ml/1½ pints beef stock
1 × 200 g/7 oz can tomatoes, drained
1 onion, peeled and chopped
1 bay leaf
225 g/½ lb cooked pumpkin, puréed
salt
freshly ground black pepper
To finish:
300 ml/½ pint single cream
a few snipped chives

AMERICAN

3¾ cups beef stock
1 × 7 oz can tomatoes, drained
1 onion, peeled and chopped
1 bay leaf
1 cup puréed cooked pumpkin
salt
freshly ground black pepper
To finish:
1¼ cups light cream
a few snipped chives

Put the stock, tomatoes, onion and bay leaf in a pan, cover and simmer for 15 minutes. Remove the bay leaf, leave the soup to cool slightly, then work to a smooth purée in an electric blender or Mouli-légumes (food mill), or rub through a sieve (strainer). Return to the heat, add the pumpkin and salt and pepper to taste, then simmer for 2 minutes.
To freeze: cool quickly, then pour into a rigid container. Seal, label and freeze.
To thaw and serve: thaw in the refrigerator for 8 hours, then add the cream, stir thoroughly and sprinkle with chives.
SERVES 6

SUMMER FISH SOUP

METRIC/IMPERIAL

1 × 400 g/14 oz can lobster bisque
1 × 450 g/1 lb can tomato juice
150 ml/¼ pint single cream
pinch of cayenne pepper
juice of ½ lemon
100 g/4 oz peeled shrimps, roughly chopped
salt
freshly ground black pepper
To finish:
4–6 × 15 ml spoons/4–6 tablespoons single cream
2 × 15 ml spoons/2 tablespoons finely chopped parsley

AMERICAN

1 × 14 oz can lobster bisque
1 × 1 lb can tomato juice
⅔ cup light cream
pinch of cayenne pepper
juice of ½ lemon
½ cup shelled shrimp, roughly chopped
salt
freshly ground black pepper
To finish:
4–6 tablespoons light cream
2 tablespoons finely chopped parsley

Put the lobster bisque, tomato juice, cream, cayenne and lemon juice in a bowl and beat well to mix. Stir in the shrimps and salt and pepper to taste.
To freeze: pour into a rigid container, seal, label and freeze.
To thaw and serve: thaw in the refrigerator overnight, then stir thoroughly. Serve with a swirl of cream and a sprinkling of chopped parsley in each individual serving bowl.
SERVES 4 to 6

CHILLED AVOCADO SOUP

METRIC/IMPERIAL

2 ripe avocados, peeled, stoned and roughly chopped
600 ml/1 pint chicken stock
1 × 15 ml spoon/1 tablespoon finely chopped onion
2 × 5 ml spoons/2 teaspoons lemon juice
1 × 5 ml spoon/1 teaspoon Worcestershire sauce
salt
freshly ground white pepper
To finish:
150 ml/¼ pint single cream
a few snipped chives

AMERICAN

2 ripe avocados, peeled, seeded and roughly chopped
2½ cups chicken stock
1 tablespoon finely chopped onion
2 teaspoons lemon juice
1 teaspoon Worcestershire sauce
salt
freshly ground white pepper
To finish:
⅔ cup light cream
a few snipped chives

Work the avocados, stock, onion, lemon juice and Worcestershire sauce to a smooth purée in an electric blender or Mouli-légumes (food mill). Add salt and pepper to taste.
To freeze: pour into a rigid container, seal, label and freeze.
To thaw and serve: thaw in the refrigerator for 8 hours, then add the cream, stir thoroughly and sprinkle with chives.
SERVES 4

GAZPACHO

METRIC/IMPERIAL

¼ cucumber, peeled, seeded and finely chopped
450 g/1 lb tomatoes, peeled, seeded and chopped
1 × 187 g/6½ oz can pimentos, drained and finely chopped
1 small onion, peeled and finely chopped
1 garlic clove, peeled and crushed
a few snipped chives
15 g/½ oz parsley, finely chopped
300 ml/½ pint cold chicken stock
5 × 15 ml spoons/5 tablespoons vegetable oil
3 × 15 ml spoons/3 tablespoons lemon juice
salt
freshly ground black pepper
To serve:
toasted croûtons
diced cucumber
diced green pepper

AMERICAN

¼ cucumber, peeled, seeded and finely chopped
2 cups peeled, seeded and chopped tomatoes
1 × 6½ oz can pimientos, drained and finely chopped
1 small onion, peeled and finely chopped
1 garlic clove, peeled and crushed
a few snipped chives
⅓ cup finely chopped parsley
1¼ cups cold chicken stock
⅓ cup vegetable oil
3 tablespoons lemon juice
salt
freshly ground black pepper
To serve:
toasted croûtons
diced cucumber
diced green pepper

Work the vegetables and herbs to a purée in an electric blender or Mouli-légumes (food mill). Add the stock, oil, lemon juice and salt and pepper to taste and stir well to mix.
To freeze: pour into a rigid container, seal, label and freeze.
To thaw and serve: thaw in the refrigerator overnight, then stir thoroughly. Serve with croûtons, cucumber and green pepper passed separately.
SERVES 4

CHILLED APPLE AND APRICOT SOUP

METRIC/IMPERIAL

1 kg/2 lb apples, peeled, cored and chopped
225 g/½ lb dried apricots
1.2 litres/2 pints chicken stock
150 ml/¼ pint dry white wine
150 ml/¼ pint soured cream

AMERICAN

2 lb apples, peeled, cored and chopped
1¼ cups dried apricots
5 cups chicken stock
⅔ cup dry white wine
⅔ cup sour cream

Put the apples, apricots and stock in a pan and cook gently until soft. Leave to cool slightly, then work to a smooth purée in an electric blender or Mouli-légumes (food mill). Stir in the remaining ingredients.
To freeze: cool quickly, then pour into a rigid container. Seal, label and freeze.
To thaw and serve: thaw in the refrigerator overnight, then stir thoroughly before serving.
SERVES 8

CHILLED ASPARAGUS SOUP

METRIC/IMPERIAL

1 × 450 g/1 lb can asparagus spears, drained
1.2 litres/2 pints chicken stock
1 × 5 ml spoon/1 teaspoon lemon juice
salt
freshly ground black pepper
To finish:
150 ml/¼ pint single cream
a few snipped chives

AMERICAN

1 × 1 lb can asparagus spears, drained
5 cups chicken stock
1 teaspoon lemon juice
salt
freshly ground black pepper
To finish:
⅔ cup light cream
a few snipped chives

Work the asparagus and half the stock to a smooth purée in an electric blender of Mouli-légumes (food mill). Put the purée in a pan with the remaining stock, lemon juice and salt and pepper to taste. Cover, bring to the boil and boil for 1 minute, then strain.
To freeze: cool quickly, then pour into a rigid container. Seal, label and freeze.
To thaw and serve: thaw in the refrigerator for 8 hours, then add the cream, stir thoroughly and sprinkle with chives.
SERVES 6

FRUIT SOUP

METRIC/IMPERIAL

450 g/1 lb fruit (morello cherries, apples, elderberries, pears, blueberries or gooseberries), peeled, stoned or cored and diced
1.2 litres/2 pints water
1 strip of lemon peel
25 g/1 oz cornflour
50–150 g/2–5 oz sugar (according to taste)
a little fresh lemon juice
toasted croûtons, to serve

AMERICAN

1 lb fruit (bing cherries, apples, elderberries, pears, bilberries or gooseberries), peeled, pitted or cored and diced
5 cups water
1 strip of lemon peel
¼ cup cornstarch
¼–⅔ cup sugar (according to taste)
a little lemon juice
toasted croûtons, to serve

Put the fruit in a pan with the water and lemon peel and bring to the boil in an enamel pan. Cover and simmer until the fruit is tender. Rub through a sieve (strainer), return the fruit purée to the rinsed-out pan and bring to the boil.
Mix the cornflour (cornstarch) to a paste with a little water, then stir into the pan and bring to the boil. Simmer until the soup thickens, stirring constantly. Add sugar and lemon juice to taste.
To freeze: cool quickly, then pour into a rigid container. Seal, label and freeze.
To thaw and serve: reheat gently from frozen on top of the stove, stirring occasionally. Serve with croûtons. To serve cold, thaw in the refrigerator overnight and stir thoroughly.
SERVES 6 to 8

ICED LEBANESE SOUP

METRIC/IMPERIAL

450 ml/¾ pint chicken stock
150 ml/¼ pint tomato juice
300 ml/½ pint natural yogurt
150 ml/¼ pint single cream
1 garlic clove, peeled
salt
freshly ground black pepper
To finish:
1 small cucumber, peeled, seeded and diced
1 hard-boiled egg, finely chopped
1 × 15 ml spoon/1 tablespoon freshly chopped mint

AMERICAN

2 cups chicken stock
⅔ cup tomato juice
1¼ cups unflavored yogurt
⅔ cup light cream
1 garlic clove, peeled
salt
freshly ground black pepper
To finish:
1 small cucumber, peeled, seeded and diced
1 hard-cooked egg, finely chopped
1 tablespoon freshly chopped mint

Put all the ingredients in an electric blender and work to a smooth purée.
To freeze: pour into a rigid container, seal, label and freeze.
To thaw and serve: thaw in the refrigerator for 8 hours, then stir thoroughly or work again in the electric blender if the soup has separated. Stir in the cucumber, egg and mint just before serving.
SERVES 4 to 6

VICHYSSOISE

METRIC/IMPERIAL
25 g/1 oz butter
3 medium leeks, sliced
3 medium potatoes, peeled and sliced
1 celery stalk, chopped
900 ml/1½ pints jellied stock
salt
freshly ground white pepper
To finish:
150 ml/¼ pint double cream
a few snipped chives

AMERICAN
2 tablespoons butter
3 medium leeks, sliced
3 medium potatoes, peeled and sliced
1 celery stalk, chopped
3¾ cups jellied stock
salt
freshly ground white pepper
To finish:
⅔ cup heavy cream
a few snipped chives

Melt the butter in a pan, add the leeks and fry gently for 5 minutes. Add the potatoes, celery, stock and salt and pepper to taste and bring to the boil. Cover and simmer for 30 minutes or until the vegetables are cooked. Leave to cool slightly, then work to a smooth purée in an electric blender or Mouli-légumes (food mill), or rub through a sieve (strainer).
To freeze: cool quickly, then pour into a rigid container. Seal, label and freeze.
To thaw and serve: reheat gently from frozen on top of the stove, stirring occasionally. Stir in the cream, adjust seasoning and sprinkle with chives just before serving. To serve cold, thaw overnight in the refrigerator, then add the cream and stir thoroughly.
SERVES 6

CUCUMBER SOUP

METRIC/IMPERIAL
1 large cucumber, peeled, seeded and chopped
600 ml/1 pint chicken stock
1 small onion, peeled and chopped
To finish:
150 ml/¼ pint soured cream
salt
freshly ground white pepper
freshly chopped mint

AMERICAN
1 large cucumber, peeled, seeded and chopped
2½ cups chicken stock
1 small onion, peeled and chopped
To finish:
⅔ cup sour cream
salt
freshly ground white pepper
freshly chopped mint

Put the cucumber, stock and onion in a pan and bring to the boil. Cover and simmer for 10 minutes or until the cucumber is tender. Leave to cool slightly, then work to a smooth purée in an electric blender or Mouli-légumes (food mill), or rub through a sieve (strainer).
To freeze: cool quickly, then pour into a rigid container. Seal, label and freeze.
To thaw and serve: thaw in the refrigerator overnight, then add the sour(ed) cream and salt and pepper to taste. Stir thoroughly and sprinkle with mint just before serving.
SERVES 4

CHILLED RASPBERRY SOUP

METRIC/IMPERIAL
450 g/1 lb fresh raspberries
2 × 15 ml spoons/2 tablespoons honey
5 × 15 ml spoons/5 tablespoons red wine
150 ml/¼ pint soured cream
200 ml/⅓ pint water

AMERICAN
1 lb fresh raspberries
2 tablespoons honey
⅓ cup red wine
⅔ cup sour cream
⅞ cup water

Rub the raspberries through a sieve (strainer) to make 300 ml/½ pint/1¼ cups raspberry purée. Put the honey, 2 × 15 ml spoons/2 tablespoons red wine and 2 × 15 ml spoons/2 tablespoons water in a pan and heat gently until the honey has dissolved, stirring occasionally. Leave to cool slightly, then stir into the raspberry purée with half the sour(ed) cream, the remaining wine and the water. Chill in the refrigerator for several hours.
To freeze: pour into a rigid container, seal, label and freeze.
To thaw and serve: thaw in the refrigerator overnight, then stir thoroughly and serve with a little sour(ed) cream in each individual serving bowl.
SERVES 4

CHILLED PROVENÇALE SOUP

METRIC/IMPERIAL

1 × 575 g/1 lb 3 oz can tomato juice
300 ml/½ pint single cream
50 g/2 oz cooked ham, finely chopped
2 spring onions, trimmed and chopped
1 small green pepper, cored, seeded and chopped
salt
freshly ground black pepper

AMERICAN

1 × 1 lb 3 oz can tomato juice
1¼ cups light cream
¼ cup chopped cooked ham
2 scallions, trimmed and chopped
1 small green pepper, cored, seeded and chopped
salt
freshly ground black pepper

Blend together the tomato juice and cream, then stir in the remaining ingredients.
To freeze: pour into a rigid container, seal, label and freeze.
To thaw and serve: thaw in the refrigerator overnight, then stir thoroughly before serving.
SERVES 4

TOMATO ORANGE SOUP

METRIC/IMPERIAL

1 onion, peeled and sliced
1 carrot, peeled and sliced
1 bay leaf
a few black peppercorns
1.2 litres/2 pints chicken stock
1 × 400 g/14 oz can tomatoes
salt
40 g/1½ oz butter
40 g/1½ oz flour
200 ml/⅓ pint orange juice
finely grated rind of 1 orange
To garnish:
4–6 × 15 ml spoons/4–6 tablespoons single cream
a few slices of orange, rinds removed

AMERICAN

1 onion, peeled and sliced
1 carrot, peeled and sliced
1 bay leaf
a few black peppercorns
5 cups chicken stock
1 × 14 oz can tomatoes
salt
3 tablespoons butter
6 tablespoons flour
⅞ cup orange juice
finely grated rind of 1 orange
To garnish:
4–6 tablespoons light cream
a few slices of orange, rinds removed

Put the onion, carrot, bay leaf, peppercorns, stock, tomatoes and salt in a pan. Bring to the boil, then cover and simmer for 30 minutes. Remove the bay leaf, leave to cool slightly, then work to a smooth purée in an electric blender or Mouli-légumes (food mill).
Melt the butter in a separate pan, stir in the flour and cook for 2 minutes, stirring constantly. Stir in the puréed liquid and bring to the boil. Simmer for 5 minutes, then add the orange juice and rind.
To freeze: cool quickly, then pour into a rigid container. Seal, label and freeze.
To thaw and serve: thaw in the refrigerator overnight, then stir thoroughly. Serve with a swirl of cream and a slice of orange in each individual serving bowl.
SERVES 4 to 6

COCK-A-LEEKIE

METRIC/IMPERIAL

1 × 1.5 kg/3 lb chicken
2.25 litres/4 pints water
1 kg/2 lb leeks, sliced
50 g/2 oz pearl barley, rinsed
salt
freshly ground black pepper

AMERICAN

1 × 3 lb chicken
5 pints (10 cups) water
2 lb leeks, sliced
¼ cup pearl barley, rinsed
salt
freshly ground black pepper

Put the chicken, water and a quarter of the leeks in a pan, bring to the boil, then cover and simmer for 1 hour or until the chicken is tender. Remove the chicken from the pan and leave to cool.
Skim off the scum from the top of the liquid. Add the remaining leeks, the pearl barley and salt and pepper to taste, then simmer for 30 minutes. Remove the meat from the chicken and chop into small pieces.
To freeze: cool the soup quickly. Put the chicken in the bottom of a rigid container, then pour in the soup. Seal, label and freeze.
To thaw and serve: thaw at room temperature for 4 hours, then reheat gently on top of the stove, stirring occasionally.
SERVES 8

NUTTY VEGETABLE SOUP

METRIC/IMPERIAL

450 g/1 lb mixed vegetables (potatoes, carrots, leeks, celery, turnips, peas), prepared and sliced
900 ml/1½ pints stock
1 × 15 ml spoon/1 tablespoon cornflour
65 g/2½ oz peanut butter
150 ml/¼ pint milk
salt
freshly ground black pepper
freshly chopped parsley, to garnish

AMERICAN

1 lb mixed vegetables (potatoes, carrots, leeks, celery, turnips, peas), prepared and sliced
3¾ cups stock
1 tablespoon cornstarch
¼ cup peanut butter
⅔ pint milk
salt
freshly ground black pepper
freshly chopped parsley, to garnish

Put the vegetables and stock in a pan, bring to the boil, then cover and simmer for 20 minutes or until the vegetables are tender.
Mix the cornflour (cornstarch) with the peanut butter, then gradually add the milk. Stir into the vegetable mixture, add salt and pepper to taste, then bring to boil, stirring constantly. Simmer until the soup thickens.
To freeze: cool quickly, then pour into a rigid container. Seal, label and freeze.
To thaw and serve: reheat gently from frozen on top of the stove, stirring occasionally. Sprinkle with parsley just before serving.
SERVES 4

CURRY AND APPLE SOUP

METRIC/IMPERIAL

25 g/1 oz butter
1 onion, peeled and finely chopped
40 g/1½ oz flour
1 × 15 ml spoon/1 tablespoon curry powder
900 ml/1½ pints chicken stock
675 g/1½ lb cooking apples, peeled, cored and sliced
juice of ½ lemon
salt
freshly ground black pepper
150 ml/¼ pint single cream, to finish

AMERICAN

2 tablespoons butter
1 onion, peeled and finely chopped
⅜ cup flour
1 tablespoon curry powder
3¾ cups chicken stock
1½ lb baking apples, peeled, cored and sliced
juice of ½ lemon
salt
freshly ground black pepper
⅔ cup light cream, to finish

Melt the butter in a pan, add the onion and fry gently until soft. Stir in the flour and curry powder and cook for 1 minute, stirring constantly. Add the stock, apples, lemon juice and salt and pepper to taste. Bring to the boil and simmer for 15 minutes. Leave to cool slightly, then work to a smooth purée in an electric blender or Mouli-légumes (food mill).
To freeze: cool quickly, then pour into a rigid container. Seal, label and freeze.
To thaw and serve: reheat gently from frozen on top of the stove with 2 × 15 ml spoons/2 tablespoons water, stirring occasionally. Serve with a swirl of cream in each individual serving bowl.
SERVES 6

CHICKEN AND CELERY SOUP

METRIC/IMPERIAL

3 celery stalks, finely chopped
600 ml/1 pint chicken stock
100 g/4 oz cooked chicken, chopped
25 g/1 oz butter
25 g/1 oz flour
salt
freshly ground black pepper
1 × 1.25 ml spoon/¼ teaspoon celery salt

AMERICAN

3 celery stalks, finely chopped
2½ cups chicken stock
½ cup chopped cooked chicken
2 tablespoons butter
¼ cup flour
salt
freshly ground black pepper
¼ teaspoon celery salt

Put the celery and stock in a pan and bring to the boil. Cover and simmer for 10 to 15 minutes or until the celery is tender.
Leave to cool slightly, then add the remaining ingredients and bring to the boil, beating constantly. Simmer until the soup thickens.
To freeze: cool quickly, then pour into a rigid container. Seal, label and freeze.
To thaw and serve: thaw at room temperature for 4 hours, then reheat gently on top of the stove, stirring occasionally.
SERVES 4

QUICK PEA SOUP

METRIC/IMPERIAL

25 g/1 oz butter
1 onion, peeled and chopped
outer leaves of 1 lettuce, roughly shredded
450 g/1 lb frozen peas
1 litre/1¾ pints chicken stock
salt
freshly ground black pepper
To finish:
4 × 15 ml spoons/4 tablespoons single cream
freshly chopped parsley

AMERICAN

2 tablespoons butter
1 onion, peeled and chopped
outer leaves of 1 lettuce, roughly shredded
1 lb frozen peas
4¼ cups chicken stock
salt
freshly ground black pepper
To finish:
¼ cup light cream
freshly chopped parsley

Melt the butter in a pan, add the onions and lettuce leaves and cook for 2 minutes. Add the peas, stock and salt and pepper to taste, then bring to the boil and simmer for 5 minutes.

Leave to cool slightly, then work to a smooth purée in an electric blender or Mouli-légumes (food mill), or rub through a sieve (strainer).

To freeze: cool quickly, then pour into a rigid container. Seal, label and freeze.

To thaw and serve: thaw for 3 to 4 hours at room temperature, then reheat gently on top of the stove, stirring occasionally. Stir in the cream and sprinkle with parsley just before serving.

SERVES 4

LENTIL SOUP WITH FRANKFURTERS

METRIC/IMPERIAL

350 g/¾ lb lentils
175 g/6 oz streaky bacon rashers, rinds removed and chopped
2 carrots, peeled and finely chopped
1 leek, finely sliced
4 celery stalks, chopped
40 g/1½ oz butter
1 large onion, peeled and finely chopped
1 × 15 ml spoon/1 tablespoon flour
2 × 5 ml spoons/2 teaspoons wine vinegar
salt
freshly ground black pepper
6 frankfurters

AMERICAN

1½ cups lentils
9 fatty bacon slices, chopped
2 carrots, peeled and finely chopped
1 leek, finely sliced
4 celery stalks, chopped
3 tablespoons butter
1 large onion, peeled and finely chopped
1 tablespoon flour
2 teaspoons wine vinegar
salt
freshly ground black pepper
6 frankfurters

Put the lentils in a bowl, add 900 ml/1½ pints/3¾ cups water and leave to soak for 3 to 4 hours. Transfer the lentils and water to a heavy pan, add a further 1 litre/1¾ pints/4¼ cups water, the bacon, carrots, leek and celery. Bring to the boil, then cover and simmer for 45 minutes.

Melt the butter in a separate pan, add the onion and fry gently until soft. Stir in the flour and cook for 2 minutes, then gradually stir in 300 ml/½ pint/1¼ cups water. Bring to the boil, stirring constantly. Beat the onion mixture into the soup, then add the vinegar and salt and pepper to taste. Cover and simmer for a further 30 to 40 minutes or until the lentils are tender.

To freeze: cool quickly. Put the frankfurters in a rigid container, then pour over the soup. Seal, label and freeze.

To thaw and serve: reheat gently from frozen on top of the stove, stirring occasionally.

SERVES 6

FRENCH ONION SOUP

METRIC/IMPERIAL

3 × 15 ml spoons/3 tablespoons vegetable oil
2 large onions, peeled and sliced into rings
900 ml/1½ pints beef stock
salt
freshly ground black pepper
2 × 15 ml spoons/2 tablespoons dry sherry
To finish:
4 slices of French bread
100 g/4 oz Cheddar cheese, grated
freshly chopped parsley

AMERICAN

3 tablespoons vegetable oil
2 large onions, peeled and sliced into rings
3¾ cups beef stock
salt
freshly ground black pepper
2 tablespoons dry sherry
To finish:
4 slices of French bread
1 cup grated Cheddar cheese
freshly chopped parsley

Heat the oil in a pan, add the onions and fry until a deep golden brown. Add the stock and salt and pepper to taste, bring to the boil, then cover and simmer for 45 minutes. Stir in the sherry and simmer for 1 minute.
To freeze: cool quickly, then pour into a rigid container. Seal, label and freeze.
To thaw and serve: thaw at room temperature for 4 hours, then reheat gently on top of the stove, stirring occasionally. Pour into 4 individual heatproof serving bowls, put 1 slice of bread in each bowl, then sprinkle with the cheese. Put under a preheated grill (broiler) for 2 to 3 minutes to melt the cheese. Sprinkle with parsley just before serving.
SERVES 4

LETTUCE AND POTATO SOUP

METRIC/IMPERIAL

50 g/2 oz butter
1 onion, peeled and sliced
350 g/¾ lb potatoes, peeled and sliced
600 ml/1 pint chicken stock
salt
freshly ground white pepper
2 heads of lettuce, roughly shredded
To finish:
450 ml/¾ pint milk
150 ml/¼ pint single cream
a few sprigs of watercress

AMERICAN

¼ cup butter
1 onion, peeled and sliced
¾ lb potatoes, peeled and sliced
2½ cups chicken stock
salt
freshly ground white pepper
2 heads of lettuce, roughly shredded
To finish:
2 cups milk
⅔ cup light cream
a few sprigs of watercress

Melt the butter in a pan, add the onion and potatoes and fry gently for 5 minutes. Add the stock and salt and pepper to taste, then bring to the boil. Cover and simmer for 15 minutes. Leave to cool slightly, then work to a smooth purée in an electric blender or Mouli-légumes (food mill), or rub through a sieve (strainer).
To freeze: cool quickly, then pour into a rigid container. Seal, label and freeze.
To thaw and serve: thaw in the refrigerator overnight, then reheat gently on top of the stove with the milk and cream. Float the watercress on top of the soup just before serving.
SERVES 6 to 8

KIDNEY SOUP

METRIC/IMPERIAL

50 g/2 oz butter
1 onion, peeled and finely chopped
4 lambs' kidneys, chopped
600 ml/1 pint beef stock
1 × 15 ml spoon/1 tablespoon tomato purée
25 g/1 oz flour
150 ml/¼ pint milk
salt
freshly ground black pepper
2 × 15 ml spoons/2 tablespoons sherry
freshly chopped parsley, to garnish

AMERICAN

¼ cup butter
1 onion, peeled and finely chopped
4 lambs' kidneys, chopped
2½ cups beef stock
1 tablespoon tomato paste
¼ cup flour
⅔ cup milk
salt
freshly ground black pepper
2 tablespoons sherry
freshly chopped parsley, to garnish

Melt the butter in a pan, add the onion and kidneys and fry gently until the kidneys are evenly browned. Stir in the stock and tomato purée (paste), cover and simmer for 15 minutes. Blend the flour with the milk, then stir into the kidney mixture with salt and pepper to taste. Simmer for 2 to 3 minutes until the soup thickens, stirring constantly. Stir in the sherry.
To freeze: cool quickly, then pour into a rigid container. Seal, label and freeze.
To thaw and serve: thaw at room temperature for 4 hours, then reheat gently on top of the stove, stirring. Sprinkle with parsley to serve.
SERVES 4

TURNIP SOUP

METRIC/IMPERIAL

50 g/2 oz butter
3 turnips, peeled and diced
1 large onion, peeled and chopped
1 small potato, peeled and diced
1 litre/1¾ pints chicken stock
1 bay leaf
1 × 2.5 ml spoon/½ teaspoon grated nutmeg
salt
freshly ground black pepper
To finish:
150 ml/¼ pint single cream
freshly chopped parsley

AMERICAN

¼ cup butter
3 turnips, peeled and diced
1 large onion, peeled and chopped
1 small potato, peeled and diced
4¼ cups chicken stock
1 bay leaf
½ teaspoon nutmeg
salt
freshly ground black pepper
To finish:
⅔ cup light cream
freshly chopped parsley

Melt the butter in a pan, add the turnips, onion and potato and fry gently for 5 minutes. Stir in the stock, bay leaf, nutmeg and salt and pepper to taste and bring to the boil. Cover and simmer for 20 minutes or until the vegetables are tender, then remove the bay leaf.

Leave to cool slightly, then work to a smooth purée in an electric blender or Mouli-légumes (food mill), or rub through a sieve (strainer).

To freeze: cool quickly, then pour into a rigid container. Seal, label and freeze.

To thaw and serve: reheat gently from frozen on top of the stove, stirring occasionally, then stir in the cream and heat through gently without boiling. Sprinkle with parsley just before serving.

SERVES 4 to 6

CAULIFLOWER SOUP

METRIC/IMPERIAL

50 g/2 oz butter
1 large onion, peeled and sliced
1 garlic clove, peeled and crushed
1 small cauliflower, divided into florets
900 ml/1½ pints chicken stock
salt
freshly ground black pepper
To finish:
4 × 15 ml spoons/4 tablespoons single cream
freshly chopped parsley

AMERICAN

¼ cup butter
1 large onion, peeled and sliced
1 garlic clove, peeled and crushed
1 small cauliflower, divided into florets
3¾ cups chicken stock
salt
freshly ground black pepper
To finish:
¼ cup light cream
freshly chopped parsley

Melt the butter in a pan, add the onion and garlic and fry gently for 5 minutes until soft. Add the cauliflower, stock and salt and pepper to taste. Bring to the boil, then cover and simmer for 25 minutes.

Leave to cool slightly, then work to a smooth purée in an electric blender or Mouli-légumes (food mill), or rub through a sieve (strainer).

To freeze: cool quickly, then pour into a rigid container. Seal, label and freeze.

To thaw and serve: reheat gently from frozen on top of the stove, stirring occasionally. Stir in the cream and sprinkle with parsley just before serving.

SERVES 4

COUNTRY LENTIL SOUP

METRIC/IMPERIAL

450–675 g/1–1½ lb knuckle of bacon, soaked overnight in cold water
175 g/6 oz red lentils
1 medium carrot, peeled and sliced
1 celery stalk, chopped
1 medium onion, peeled and sliced
1.5 litres/2½ pints water
1 × 15 ml spoon/1 tablespoon Worcestershire sauce
freshly ground black pepper
100 g/4 oz frozen peas
toasted croûtons, to serve

AMERICAN

1–1½ lb smoked ham hock, soaked overnight in cold water
¾ cup red lentils
1 medium carrot, peeled and sliced
1 celery stalk, chopped
1 medium onion, peeled and sliced
6¼ cups water
1 tablespoon Worcestershire sauce
freshly ground black pepper
¾ cup frozen peas
toasted croûtons, to serve

Drain the bacon (ham hock) and rinse under cold running water. Put in a pan with the remaining ingredients except the peas and croûtons. Bring slowly to the boil, then skim with a slotted spoon. Half cover with a lid and simmer for 2 hours or until the meat is tender.

Remove the bacon (ham hock) from the pan, take the meat from the bone and cut into dice or thin slices. Work the soup to a smooth purée in an electric blender or Mouli-légumes (food mill).

To freeze: cool quickly. Put meat, peas and liquid in a rigid container, seal, label and freeze.

To thaw and serve: reheat gently from frozen on top of the stove, stirring occasionally. Float croûtons on top of the soup just before serving.

SERVES 6 to 8

LEEK AND ARTICHOKE SOUP

METRIC/IMPERIAL

25 g/1 oz butter
225 g/½ lb leeks, sliced
2 celery stalks, chopped
675 g/1½ lb Jerusalem artichokes, peeled and sliced
900 ml/1½ pints chicken stock
1 bay leaf
salt
freshly ground black pepper
300 ml/½ pint milk, to finish

AMERICAN

2 tablespoons butter
½ lb leeks, sliced
2 celery stalks, chopped
1½ lb Jerusalem artichokes, peeled and sliced
3¾ cups chicken stock
1 bay leaf
salt
freshly ground black pepper
1¼ cups milk, to finish

Melt the butter in a pan, add the leeks and celery and fry gently for 2 to 3 minutes. Add the artichokes, stock, bay leaf and salt and pepper to taste, cover and simmer for 30 to 40 minutes or until the artichokes are tender. Remove the bay leaf.

Leave to cool slightly, then work to a smooth purée in an electric blender or Mouli-légumes (food mill), or rub through a sieve (strainer).

To freeze: cool quickly, then pour into a rigid container. Seal, label and freeze.

To thaw and serve: thaw at room temperature for 3 to 4 hours, then reheat gently on top of the stove, stirring occasionally. Stir in the milk and heat through before serving.

SERVES 4 to 6

ONION AND PEPPER SOUP

METRIC/IMPERIAL

40 g/1½ oz butter
2 large onions, thinly sliced
1 garlic clove, peeled and crushed
1 green pepper, cored, seeded and cut into strips
1 red pepper, cored, seeded and cut into strips
25 g/1 oz flour
1 × 200 g/7 oz can tomatoes, chopped
900 ml/1½ pints beef stock
salt
freshly ground black pepper
freshly chopped parsley, to garnish

AMERICAN

3 tablespoons butter
2 large onions, thinly sliced
1 garlic clove, peeled and crushed
1 green pepper, cored, seeded and cut into strips
1 red pepper, cored, seeded and cut into strips
¼ cup flour
1 × 7 oz can tomatoes, chopped
3¾ cups beef stock
salt
freshly ground black pepper
freshly chopped parsley, to garnish

Melt the butter in a pan, add the onions, garlic and peppers and fry gently for about 10 minutes until soft. Stir in the flour and cook for 2 minutes, stirring constantly, then stir in the tomatoes and stock. Add salt and pepper to taste, then simmer for 20 minutes.

To freeze: cool quickly, then pour into a rigid container. Seal, label and freeze.

To thaw and serve: reheat gently from frozen on top of the stove, stirring occasionally. Sprinkle with parsley just before serving.

SERVES 4

GOULASH SOUP

METRIC/IMPERIAL

225 g/½ lb shin of beef, cut into small cubes
1 × 15 ml spoon/1 tablespoon flour
2 × 5 ml spoons/2 teaspoons paprika pepper
salt
freshly ground black pepper
25 g/1 oz dripping
2 onions, peeled and thinly sliced
2 garlic cloves, peeled and chopped
1 × 15 ml spoon/1 tablespoon tomato purée
1 litre/2 pints beef stock
To finish:
2 large potatoes, peeled and sliced
150 ml/¼ pint soured cream

AMERICAN

½ lb foreshank of beef, cut into small cubes
1 tablespoon flour
2 teaspoons paprika pepper
salt
freshly ground black pepper
2 tablespoons dripping
2 onions, peeled and thinly sliced
2 garlic cloves, peeled and chopped
1 tablespoon tomato paste
5 cups beef stock
To finish:
2 large potatoes, peeled and sliced
⅔ cup sour cream

Coat the beef in the flour seasoned with the paprika and salt and pepper. Melt the dripping in a pan, add the beef and fry briskly until browned on all sides. Add the onions and garlic, cover and cook gently until the onions are soft. Stir in the tomato purée (paste) and stock, then cover and simmer for 2 to 3 hours until the meat is tender.

To freeze: cool quickly, then pour into a rigid container. Seal, label and freeze.

To thaw and serve: reheat gently from frozen on top of the stove, stirring occasionally. Add the potatoes and cook for 15 to 20 minutes or until tender. Stir in the sour(ed) cream just before serving.

SERVES 8

COUNTRY SOUP

METRIC/IMPERIAL

1 × 15 ml spoon/1 tablespoon vegetable oil
175 g/6 oz streaky bacon rashers, rinds removed and diced
3 medium onions, peeled and chopped
450 g/1 lb potatoes, peeled and thinly sliced
1 × 400 g/14 oz can tomatoes
600 ml/1 pint chicken stock
pinch of ground mace
freshly ground black pepper
To finish:
150 ml/¼ pint soured cream
2 streaky bacon rashers, crisply fried and crumbled

AMERICAN

1 tablespoon vegetable oil
9 fatty bacon slices, diced
3 medium onions, peeled and chopped
1 lb potatoes, peeled and thinly sliced
1 × 14 oz can tomatoes
2½ cups chicken stock
pinch of ground mace
freshly ground black pepper
To finish:
⅔ cup sour cream
2 fatty bacon slices, crisply fried and crumbled

Heat the oil in a pan, add the bacon and fry until crisp and golden brown. Remove from the pan with a slotted spoon and drain on paper towels. Add the onions to the pan and fry gently for 5 minutes until soft. Add the remaining ingredients, bring to the boil, then cover and simmer for 1 hour.

Leave to cool slightly, then work to a smooth purée in an electric blender or Mouli-légumes (food mill), or rub through a sieve (strainer).

To freeze: cool quickly, then pour into a rigid container. Seal, label and freeze.

To thaw and serve: reheat gently from frozen on top of the stove, stirring occasionally. Stir in the sour(ed) cream and heat through gently, without boiling. Add a little water if the soup is too thick. Sprinkle with the crumbled bacon before serving.

SERVES 4

SPINACH SOUP

METRIC/IMPERIAL

15 g/½ oz butter
1 large onion, peeled and chopped
1 × 15 ml spoon/1 tablespoon flour
450 ml/¾ pint chicken stock
675 g/1½ lb spinach, stalks removed
1 × 1.25 ml spoon/¼ teaspoon grated nutmeg
salt
freshly ground black pepper
To finish:
150 ml/¼ pint single cream
1 hard-boiled egg, sieved

AMERICAN

1 tablespoon butter
1 large onion, peeled and chopped
1 tablespoon flour
2 cups chicken stock
1½ lb spinach, stalks removed
¼ teaspoon grated nutmeg
salt
freshly ground black pepper
To finish:
⅔ cup light cream
1 hard-cooked egg, pressed through a strainer

Melt the butter in a pan, add the onion and fry gently for 5 minutes until soft. Stir in the flour and cook for 2 minutes, stirring constantly, then stir in the stock. Add the spinach, nutmeg and salt and pepper to taste, then bring to the boil. Cover and simmer for 25 minutes.
Cool slightly, then work to a purée in an electric blender or rub through a sieve (strainer).
To freeze: cool quickly, then pour into a rigid container. Seal, label and freeze.
To thaw and serve: reheat gently from frozen on top of the stove, stirring occasionally. Stir in the cream and heat through gently without boiling. Sprinkle with the egg just before serving.
SERVES 4

MUSHROOM AND ONION SOUP

METRIC/IMPERIAL

40 g/1½ oz butter
225 g/½ lb mushrooms, finely chopped
1 large onion, peeled and chopped
1 × 15 ml spoon/1 tablespoon flour
1.2 litres/2 pints chicken stock
1 bouquet garni
salt
freshly ground black pepper
To finish:
150 ml/¼ pint milk
150 ml/¼ pint single cream
freshly chopped parsley

AMERICAN

3 tablespoons butter
2 cups finely chopped mushrooms
1 large onion, peeled and chopped
1 tablespoon flour
5 cups chicken stock
1 bouquet garni
salt
freshly ground black pepper
To finish:
⅔ cup milk
⅔ cup light cream
freshly chopped parsley

Melt the butter in a pan, add the mushrooms and onion, cover and cook gently for 5 minutes. Stir in the flour and cook for 2 minutes, stirring constantly, then stir in the stock. Bring to the boil, add the bouquet garni and salt and pepper to taste, then cover and simmer for 20 minutes. Remove the bouquet garni.
To freeze: cool quickly, then pour into a rigid container. Seal, label and freeze.
To thaw and serve: reheat gently from frozen on top of the stove, stirring occasionally. Stir in the milk and cream and heat through without boiling. Sprinkle with parsley just before serving.
SERVES 6

LEEK AND CELERY SOUP

METRIC/IMPERIAL

50 g/2 oz butter
3 medium onions, peeled and chopped
3 celery stalks, chopped
1 medium potato, peeled and diced
1 kg/2 lb leeks, sliced
1 litre/1¾ pints chicken stock
salt
freshly ground black pepper
600 ml/1 pint creamy milk, to finish

AMERICAN

¼ cup butter
3 medium onions, peeled and chopped
3 celery stalks, chopped
1 medium potato, peeled and diced
2 lb leeks, sliced
4¼ cups chicken stock
salt
freshly ground black pepper
2½ cups creamy milk, to finish

Melt the butter in a pan, add the onions, celery, potato and leeks and fry gently for 5 minutes. Stir in the stock and bring to the boil, then cover and simmer for 40 minutes or until the vegetables are tender.
Add salt and pepper to taste, then work to a smooth purée in an electric blender or Mouli-légumes (food mill), or rub through a sieve (strainer).
To freeze: cool quickly, then pour into a rigid container. Seal, label and freeze.
To thaw and serve: add the milk and reheat gently from frozen on top of the stove, stirring occasionally.
SERVES 10

BROAD (LIMA) BEAN SOUP

METRIC/IMPERIAL

1 × 15 ml spoon/1 tablespoon vegetable oil
2 bacon rashers, rinds removed and chopped
1 onion, peeled and chopped
900 ml/1½ pints chicken stock
450 g/1 lb broad beans, shelled
salt
freshly ground black pepper
To finish:
1 × 5 ml spoon/1 teaspoon cornflour
150 ml/¼ pint single cream
1 × 2.5 ml spoon/½ teaspoon lemon juice

AMERICAN

1 tablespoon vegetable oil
2 bacon slices, chopped
1 onion, peeled and chopped
3¾ cups chicken stock
1 lb lima beans, shelled
salt
freshly ground black pepper
To finish:
1 teaspoon cornstarch
⅔ cup light cream
½ teaspoon lemon juice

Heat the oil in a pan, add the bacon and onion and fry gently for 5 minutes. Stir in the stock and bring to the boil, then add the beans and simmer for 20 to 30 minutes or until tender.
Leave to cool slightly, then work to a smooth purée in an electric blender or Mouli-légumes (food mill), or rub through a sieve (strainer). Return the purée to the rinsed-out pan, add salt and pepper to taste and simmer for 10 minutes.
To freeze: cool quickly, then pour into a rigid container. Seal, label and freeze.
To thaw and serve: thaw at room temperature for 4 hours, then reheat gently on top of the stove, stirring occasionally. Mix the cornflour (cornstarch) and cream together, stir into the soup and bring to boiling point. Simmer for 2 to 3 minutes until the soup has thickened, stirring constantly, then stir in the lemon juice.
SERVES 6

MINTED CHICKEN SOUP

METRIC/IMPERIAL

1.2 litres/2 pints chicken stock
75 g/3 oz cooked chicken, diced
75 g/3 oz long-grain rice, boiled and drained
salt
freshly ground black pepper
To finish:
juice of 1 lemon
2 × 15 ml spoons/2 tablespoons freshly chopped mint
6 thin lemon slices, to garnish

AMERICAN

5 cups chicken stock
⅓ cup diced cooked chicken
½ cup long-grain rice, boiled and drained
salt
freshly ground black pepper
To finish:
juice of 1 lemon
2 tablespoons freshly chopped mint
6 thin lemon slices, to garnish

Put all the ingredients in a pan and simmer for 5 minutes.
To freeze: cool quickly, then pour into a rigid container. Seal, label and freeze.
To thaw and serve: reheat gently from frozen on top of the stove, stirring occasionally. Stir in the lemon juice and mint and garnish with lemon slices before serving.
SERVES 6

SPLIT PEA AND HAM SOUP

METRIC/IMPERIAL

25 g/1 oz butter
1 large onion, peeled and sliced
1 large carrot, peeled and sliced
1 celery stalk, chopped
100 g/4 oz dried split peas, soaked in cold water overnight
1 × 100 g/4 oz piece of ham or bacon
1.2 litres/2 pints stock
salt
freshly ground black pepper
150 ml/¼ pint double cream, to finish

AMERICAN

2 tablespoons butter
1 large onion, peeled and sliced
1 large carrot, peeled and sliced
1 celery stalk, chopped
½ cup dried split peas, soaked in cold water overnight
1 × ¼ lb piece of ham or bacon
5 cups stock
salt
freshly ground black pepper
⅔ cup heavy cream, to finish

Melt the butter in a pan, add the onion, carrot and celery and cook gently for 5 minutes. Drain the split peas and refresh under cold running water. Add to the pan with the ham or bacon, the stock and salt and pepper to taste. Bring

slowly to the boil, then cover and simmer gently for 2½ hours.
Remove the ham or bacon and cut into cubes. Work the vegetables and liquid to a smooth purée in an electric blender or Mouli-légumes (food mill), or rub through a sieve (strainer).
To freeze: cool quickly. Put both the ham or bacon and the puréed liquid in a rigid container, seal, label and freeze.
To thaw and serve: reheat gently from frozen on top of the stove, stirring occasionally. Stir in the cream just before serving.
SERVES 4 to 6

MIXED FISH CHOWDER

METRIC/IMPERIAL
450 g/1 lb coley fillets
225 g/½ lb smoked haddock fillets
3 bacon rashers, rinds removed and chopped
1 onion, peeled and finely sliced
450 g/1 lb potatoes, peeled and diced
100 g/4 oz mushrooms, sliced
1 × 200 g/7 oz can sweetcorn, drained
450 ml/¾ pint milk
1.5 × 5 ml spoons/1½ teaspoons mustard powder
freshly ground black pepper
freshly chopped parsley, to garnish

AMERICAN
1 lb cod fillets
½ lb smoked haddock fillets
3 bacon slices, chopped
1 onion, peeled and finely sliced
1 lb potatoes, peeled and diced
1 cup sliced mushrooms
1 × 7 oz can corn kernels, drained
2 cups milk
1½ teaspoons mustard powder
freshly ground black pepper
freshly chopped parsley, to garnish

Put the fish in a pan, cover with water and poach gently for 8 to 10 minutes. Strain and reserve 300 ml/½ pint/1¼ cups poaching liquid, then skin and flake the fish.
Put the bacon and onion in a separate pan and fry for a few minutes until lightly coloured. Add the fish, the reserved liquid and the remaining ingredients except the parsley. Cover and simmer gently until the potatoes are cooked.
To freeze: cool quickly, then pour into a rigid container. Seal, label and freeze.
To thaw and serve: reheat gently from frozen on top of the stove, stirring occasionally. Sprinkle with parsley just before serving.
SERVES 4

COD CHOWDER

METRIC/IMPERIAL
25 g/1 oz butter
1 large onion, peeled and chopped
450 g/1 lb cod steaks or fillets
300 ml/½ pint milk
300 ml/½ pint water
salt
freshly ground black pepper
225 g/½ lb potatoes, peeled and diced
175 g/6 oz cooked ham, diced
75 g/3 oz peeled prawns
2 × 15 ml spoons/2 tablespoons freshly chopped parsley

AMERICAN
2 tablespoons butter
1 large onion, peeled and chopped
1 lb cod steaks or fillets
1¼ cups milk
1¼ cups water
salt
freshly ground black pepper
½ lb potatoes, peeled and diced
¾ cup diced cooked ham
½ cup shelled shrimp
2 tablespoons freshly chopped parsley

Melt the butter in a pan, add the onion and fry gently until soft. Set aside.
Put the fish in a pan with the milk, water and salt and pepper to taste and poach gently for 8 to 10 minutes. Strain and reserve the poaching liquid, then skin and flake the fish.
Put the potatoes in the reserved liquid, cover and simmer until cooked. Add the onion, fish, ham, prawns (shrimp) and half the parsley and simmer for a further 5 minutes.
To freeze: cool quickly, then pour into a rigid container. Seal, label, and freeze.
To thaw and serve: reheat gently from frozen on top of the stove, stirring occasionally. Sprinkle with the remaining parsley just before serving.
SERVES 4

CAULIFLOWER AND CHEESE SOUP

METRIC/IMPERIAL

1 medium cauliflower, divided into florets
2 medium onions, peeled and chopped
1 litre/1¾ pints chicken stock
40 g/1½ oz butter
25 g/1 oz flour
50 g/2 oz Danish blue cheese, grated
freshly ground black pepper
To garnish:
fried croûtons
freshly chopped parsley

AMERICAN

1 medium cauliflower, divided into florets
2 medium onions, peeled and chopped
4¼ cups chicken stock
3 tablespoons butter
¼ cup flour
½ cup grated Danish blue cheese
freshly ground black pepper
To garnish:
fried croûtons
freshly chopped parsley

Put the cauliflower in a pan with the onions and stock. Cover and cook gently for 10 to 15 minutes or until the cauliflower is tender. Leave to cool slightly, then work to a smooth purée in an electric blender or Mouli-légumes (food mill), or rub through a sieve (strainer).
Melt the butter in the rinsed-out pan, stir in the flour and cook for 1 minute, stirring constantly. Stir in the purée, then bring to the boil and simmer for 3 minutes. Add the cheese and pepper to taste, then heat gently until the cheese melts, stirring constantly.
To freeze: cool quickly, then pour into a rigid container. Seal, label and freeze.
To thaw and serve: reheat gently from frozen on top of the stove, stirring occasionally. Sprinkle with croûtons and parsley just before serving.
SERVES 4

MINESTRONE

METRIC/IMPERIAL

4 × 15 ml spoons/4 tablespoons olive or vegetable oil
3 bacon rashers, rinds removed and diced
2 onions, peeled and chopped
2 carrots, peeled and sliced
1 small potato, peeled and diced
3 celery stalks, sliced
½ cabbage heart, shredded
2 leeks, sliced
4 tomatoes, peeled and chopped
100 g/4 oz frozen peas
100 g/4 oz dried haricot beans, soaked overnight in cold water
2 × 15 ml spoons/2 tablespoons tomato purée
1 litre/1¾ pints chicken stock
2 × 5 ml spoons/2 teaspoons dried mixed herbs
salt
freshly ground black pepper
25 g/1 oz raw spaghetti, broken into pieces
grated Parmesan cheese, to serve

AMERICAN

¼ cup olive or vegetable oil
3 bacon slices, diced
2 onions, peeled and chopped
2 carrots, peeled and sliced
1 small potato, peeled and diced
3 celery stalks, sliced
½ cabbage heart, shredded
2 leeks, sliced
4 tomatoes, peeled and chopped
¾ cup frozen peas
⅓ cup dried navy beans, soaked overnight in cold water
2 tablespoons tomato paste
4¼ cups chicken stock
2 teaspoons dried mixed herbs
salt
freshly ground black pepper
¼ cup broken raw spaghetti
grated Parmesan cheese, to serve

Heat the oil in a pan, add the bacon and fry until lightly coloured. Add the vegetables, except the haricot (navy) beans, cover and cook gently for 5 minutes or until just tender, stirring occasionally. Drain the beans and refresh under cold

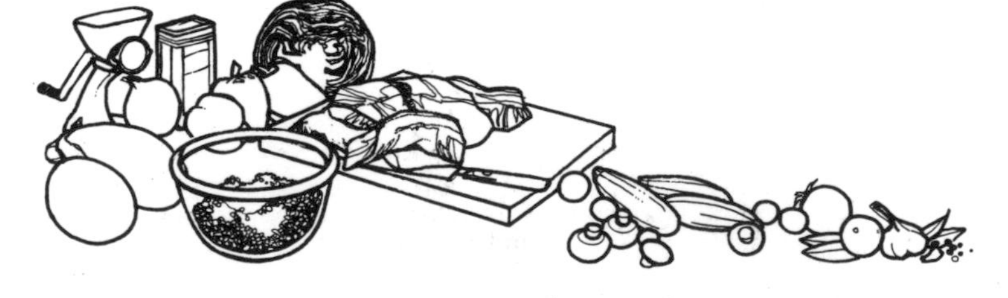

running water. Add to the pan with the tomato purée (paste), mixed herbs and salt and pepper to taste. Stir in the stock and bring to the boil, then cover and simmer for 1 hour. Add the spaghetti 10 minutes before the end of cooking.
To freeze: cool quickly, then pour into a rigid container. Seal, label and freeze.
To thaw and serve: reheat gently from frozen on top of the stove, stirring occasionally. Serve with Parmesan cheese handed separately.
SERVES 6 to 8

TOMATO SOUP

METRIC/IMPERIAL
50 g/2 oz butter
1 large carrot, peeled and diced
2 medium onions, peeled and chopped
1 kg/2 lb tomatoes, peeled and chopped
25 g/1 oz flour
1 × 15 ml spoon/1 tablespoon tomato purée
1 litre/1¾ pints chicken stock
1 bay leaf
pinch of grated nutmeg
1 sugar lump
salt
freshly ground black pepper

AMERICAN
¼ cup butter
1 large carrot, peeled and diced
2 medium onions, peeled and chopped
4 cups peeled and chopped tomatoes
¼ cup flour
1 tablespoon tomato paste
4¼ cups chicken stock
1 bay leaf
pinch of grated nutmeg
1 sugar lump
salt
freshly ground black pepper

Melt the butter in a pan, add the carrot and onions and fry gently until lightly coloured. Add the tomatoes, cover and cook gently for 5 minutes, stirring occasionally. Stir in the flour, add the remaining ingredients and bring to the boil. Cover and simmer for 45 minutes.
Remove the bay leaf, leave the soup to cool slightly, then work to a smooth purée in an electric blender or Mouli-légumes (food mill), or rub through a sieve (strainer).
To freeze: cool quickly, then pour into a rigid container. Seal, label and freeze.
To thaw and serve: reheat gently from frozen on top of the stove, stirring occasionally.
SERVES 6

OXTAIL SOUP

METRIC/IMPERIAL
25 g/1 oz butter
1 oxtail, cut into serving pieces
2 onions, peeled and sliced
2 carrots, peeled and chopped
2 celery stalks, chopped
2 lean bacon rashers, rinds removed and chopped
1 × 2.5 ml spoon/½ teaspoon dried thyme
salt
freshly ground black pepper
1.75 litres/3 pints water
1 × 15 ml spoon/1 tablespoon sherry
2 × 5 ml spoons/2 teaspoons tomato purée
25 g/1 oz flour
To finish:
freshly chopped parsley
toasted croûtons

AMERICAN
2 tablespoons butter
1 oxtail, cut into serving pieces
2 onions, peeled and sliced
2 carrots, peeled and chopped
2 celery stalks, chopped
2 Canadian bacon slices, chopped
½ teaspoon dried thyme
salt
freshly ground black pepper
7½ cups water
1 tablespoon sherry
2 teaspoons tomato paste
¼ cup flour
To finish:
freshly chopped parsley
toasted croûtons

Melt the butter in a pan, add the oxtail and fry until golden brown. Drain off the excess fat, then add the vegetables, bacon, herbs, and salt and pepper to taste. Pour in the water, bring to the boil, then cover and simmer for about 3 hours, or until the meat falls away from the bone.
Remove the oxtail from the pan and discard the bones. Skim off excess fat, return the oxtail meat to the pan and stir in the sherry and tomato purée (paste). Mix the flour to a paste with a little cold water, pour a few spoons of the stock onto the blended flour, then stir into the pan. Bring to the boil, then simmer for a further 5 minutes, stirring constantly.
To freeze: cool quickly, then pour into a rigid container. Seal, label and freeze.
To thaw and serve: thaw at room temperature for 3 hours, then reheat gently on top of the stove, stirring occasionally. Sprinkle with parsley and croûtons just before serving.
SERVES 8 to 10

CREAM OF MUSHROOM SOUP

METRIC/IMPERIAL

25 g/1 oz butter
1 small onion, peeled and sliced
225 g/½ lb flat mushrooms, sliced
25 g/1 oz flour
600 ml/1 pint well-flavoured chicken stock
150 ml/¼ pint milk
salt
freshly ground black pepper
To finish:
150 ml/¼ pint double cream
freshly chopped parsley

AMERICAN

2 tablespoons butter
1 small onion, peeled and sliced
2 cups sliced flat mushrooms
¼ cup flour
2½ cups well-flavored chicken stock
⅔ cup milk
salt
freshly ground black pepper
To finish:
⅔ heavy cream
freshly chopped parsley

Melt the butter in a pan, add the onion and fry gently until soft. Add the mushrooms and fry for 5 minutes. Stir in the flour and cook for 2 minutes, stirring constantly. Remove from the heat, then gradually stir in the stock and milk. Return to the heat and bring to the boil, stirring constantly. Add salt and pepper to taste, cover and simmer for 20 minutes. Leave to cool slightly, then work to a smooth purée in an electric blender or Mouli-légumes (food mill).
To freeze: cool quickly, then pour into a rigid container. Seal, label and freeze.
To thaw and serve: reheat gently from frozen on top of the stove, stirring occasionally. Stir in the cream and sprinkle with parsley to serve.
SERVES 4

CREAM OF CELERY SOUP

METRIC/IMPERIAL

15 g/½ oz butter
1 head of celery, chopped
1 onion, peeled and chopped
1 × 15 ml spoon/1 tablespoon flour
750 ml/1¼ pints well-flavoured chicken stock
salt
freshly ground black pepper
1 bouquet garni
croûtons, to garnish

AMERICAN

1 tablespoon butter
1 head of celery, chopped
1 onion, peeled and chopped
1 tablespoon flour
3 cups well-flavored chicken stock
salt
freshly ground black pepper
1 bouquet garni
croûtons, to garnish

Melt the butter in a pan, add the celery and onion and fry gently for a few minutes. Stir in the flour and cook for 2 minutes, stirring constantly. Add the stock and bring to the boil, stirring constantly. Add salt and pepper to taste and the bouquet garni, cover and simmer for 30 minutes or until the celery is tender. Remove the bouquet garni, leave to cool slightly, then work to a smooth purée in an electric blender or Mouli-légumes (food mill).
To freeze: cool quickly, then pour into a rigid container. Seal, label and freeze.
To thaw and serve: reheat gently from frozen on top of the stove, stirring occasionally. Sprinkle with croûtons just before serving.
SERVES 4

CREAM OF BROCCOLI SOUP

METRIC/IMPERIAL

600 ml/1 pint chicken stock
1 × 250 g/9 oz packet frozen broccoli
25 g/1 oz butter
2 × 5 ml spoons/2 teaspoons grated onion
25 g/1 oz flour
600 ml/1 pint milk
salt
freshly ground black pepper
To finish:
150 ml/¼ pint single cream
fried croûtons

AMERICAN

2½ cups chicken stock
1 × 9 oz package frozen broccoli
2 tablespoons butter
2 teaspoons grated onion
¼ cup flour
2½ cups milk
salt
freshly ground black pepper
To finish:
⅔ cup light cream
fried croûtons

Put the stock in a pan, bring to the boil and add the broccoli. Cook for about 10 minutes or until the broccoli is tender. Leave to cool slightly, then work to a smooth purée in an electric blender or Mouli-légumes (food mill), or rub through a sieve (strainer). Melt the butter in a pan, add the onion and fry gently until soft. Stir in the flour and cook for 2 minutes, stirring constantly. Remove from the heat and gradually stir in the milk, then return to the heat and bring to the boil, stirring constantly. Simmer until thick, then stir in the puréed broccoli and salt and pepper to taste. Simmer for 3 to 4 minutes.
To freeze: cool quickly, then pour into a rigid container. Seal, label and freeze.
To thaw and serve: reheat gently from frozen on top of the stove, stirring occasionally. Stir in the cream and heat through, then float croûtons on top of the soup just before serving.
SERVES 6

BEAN SOUP

METRIC/IMPERIAL
450 g/1 lb dried haricot beans, soaked in cold water overnight
1.75 litres/3 pints water
1 × 15 ml spoon/1 tablespoon olive oil
1 medium onion, peeled and sliced
1 medium potato, peeled and diced
1 garlic clove, peeled and crushed
salt
freshly ground black pepper
freshly chopped parsley, to garnish

AMERICAN
2 cups dried navy beans, soaked in cold water overnight
7½ cups water
1 tablespoon olive oil
1 medium onion, peeled and sliced
1 medium potato, peeled and diced
1 garlic clove, peeled and crushed
salt
freshly ground black pepper
freshly chopped parsley, to garnish

Drain the beans and refresh under cold running water. Put in a pan with the water, cover and simmer for 1½ to 2 hours or until soft.
Heat the oil in a separate pan, add the onion, potato and garlic and fry gently until lightly coloured.
Work half the beans (with their cooking liquid) to a smooth purée in an electric blender or Mouli-légumes (food mill), or rub through a sieve (strainer). Add to the onion and potato mixture with the remaining beans and salt and pepper to taste, then bring to the boil. Cover and simmer for a further 20 minutes.
To freeze: cool quickly, then pour into a rigid container. Seal, label and freeze.
To thaw and serve: reheat gently from frozen on top of the stove, stirring occasionally. Sprinkle with parsley just before serving.
SERVES 8 to 10

PARSLEY SOUP

METRIC/IMPERIAL
100 g/4 oz fresh parsley
50 g/2 oz butter
2 onions, peeled and chopped
2 potatoes, peeled and chopped
1.2 litres/2 pints chicken stock
salt
freshly ground black pepper
To finish:
150 ml/¼ pint single cream
freshly chopped parsley

AMERICAN
¼ lb fresh parsley
¼ cup butter
2 onions, peeled and chopped
2 potatoes, peeled and chopped
5 cups chicken stock
salt
freshly ground black pepper
To finish:
⅔ cup light cream
freshly chopped parsley

Cut the tops off the parsley stalks and set aside. Melt the butter in a pan, add the onions and potatoes and fry gently for 5 minutes. Stir in the stock and the parsley stalks and cook for 10 minutes or until the potatoes are cooked. Remove the parsley stalks. Leave the soup to cool slightly, add the parsley tops, then work to a smooth purée in an electric blender or Mouli-légumes (food mill). Add salt and pepper to taste.
To freeze: cool quickly, then pour into a rigid container. Seal, label and freeze.
To thaw and serve: reheat gently from frozen on top of the stove, stirring occasionally. Stir in the cream and sprinkle with parsley just before serving. To serve cold, thaw at room temperature for 4 hours or in the refrigerator overnight, then add the cream and sprinkle with parsley.
SERVES 6

BORSHCH

METRIC/IMPERIAL
25 g/1 oz butter
1 small onion, peeled and chopped
450 g/1 lb freshly cooked beetroot, peeled and diced
1 × 15 ml spoon/1 tablespoon flour
1.2 litres/2 pints chicken stock
salt
freshly ground black pepper
150 ml/¼ pint soured cream, to finish

AMERICAN
2 tablespoons butter
1 small onion, peeled and chopped
1 lb freshly cooked beets, peeled and diced
1 tablespoon flour
5 cups chicken stock
salt
freshly ground black pepper
⅔ cup sour cream, to finish

Melt the butter in a pan, add the onion and beetroot (beets) and fry gently for 5 minutes, stirring occasionally. Stir in the flour, then the stock. Bring to the boil, stirring constantly, then add salt and pepper to taste. Cover and simmer for 30 minutes. Leave to cool slightly, then work to a purée in an electric blender or Mouli-légumes (food mill), or rub through a sieve (strainer).
To freeze: cool quickly, then pour into a rigid container. Seal, label and freeze.
To thaw and serve: thaw in the refrigerator overnight, then reheat gently on top of the stove, stirring occasionally. Stir in the sour(ed) cream.
SERVES 4

JERUSALEM ARTICHOKE SOUP

METRIC/IMPERIAL
25 g/1 oz butter
1 onion, peeled and chopped
1.5 kg/3 lb Jerusalem artichokes, peeled and sliced
1.2 litres/2 pints chicken stock
salt
freshly ground white pepper
To finish:
300 ml/½ pint milk
freshly chopped parsley

AMERICAN
2 tablespoons butter
1 onion, peeled and chopped
3 lb Jerusalem artichokes, peeled and sliced
5 cups chicken stock
salt
freshly ground white pepper
To finish:
1¼ cups milk
freshly chopped parsley

Melt the butter in a pan, add the onion and fry gently until soft. Add the artichokes and fry gently for 1 to 2 minutes. Stir in the stock, add salt and pepper to taste, then cover and simmer until the artichokes are cooked. Leave to cool slightly, then work to a smooth purée in an electric blender or Mouli-légumes (food mill), or rub through a sieve (strainer).
To freeze: cool quickly, then pour into a rigid container. Seal, label and freeze.
To thaw and serve: reheat gently from frozen on top of the stove with the milk, stirring occasionally. Sprinkle with parsley just before serving.
SERVES 8

CHESTNUT SOUP

METRIC/IMPERIAL
25 g/1 oz butter
1 onion, peeled and chopped
2 celery stalks, chopped
2 × 5 ml spoons/2 teaspoons flour
900 ml/1½ pints beef stock
300 ml/½ pint double cream
150 ml/¼ pint Madeira or sherry
450 g/1 lb unsweetened chestnut purée
freshly chopped parsley, to garnish

AMERICAN
2 tablespoons butter
1 onion, peeled and chopped
2 celery stalks, chopped
2 teaspoons flour
3¾ cups beef stock
1¼ cups heavy cream
⅔ cup Madeira or sherry
1 lb unsweetened chestnut purée
freshly chopped parsley, to garnish

Melt the butter in a saucepan and sauté the onion and celery for 5 minutes. Add the flour and cook for 1 minute, then blend in the stock and bring to the boil. Simmer for 20 minutes. Mix the cream and sherry with the chestnut purée and beat to a smooth paste. Add a little soup to the chestnut mixture then pour into the soup and simmer for a further 5 to 10 minutes.
To freeze: cool quickly, pour into a rigid container, seal, label and freeze.
To thaw and serve: thaw at room temperature for 3 to 4 hours, then reheat gently on top of the stove. Sprinkle with chopped parsley to serve.
SERVES 8

QUICK CORN SOUP

METRIC/IMPERIAL
40 g/1½ oz butter
50 g/2 oz flour
900 ml/1½ pints chicken stock or water
1 × 175 g/6 oz packet frozen sweetcorn
salt
freshly ground black pepper
1 × 5 ml spoon/1 teaspoon Worcestershire sauce
150 ml/¼ pint evaporated milk
2 lean bacon rashers, rinds removed and chopped
To garnish:
freshly chopped parsley
paprika pepper

AMERICAN
3 tablespoons butter
½ cup flour
3¾ cups chicken stock or water
1 × 6 oz package frozen corn kernels
salt
freshly ground black pepper
1 teaspoon Worcestershire sauce
⅔ cup evaporated milk
2 Canadian bacon slices, chopped
To garnish:
freshly chopped parsley
paprika pepper

Melt the butter in a pan, stir in the flour and cook for 2 minutes, stirring constantly. Remove from the heat and gradually stir in the stock, corn, salt and pepper to taste and the Worcestershire sauce. Return to the heat and bring to the boil, stirring constantly. Simmer for 5 minutes, then stir in the evaporated milk.
Grill (broil) the bacon until crisp, add to the soup and simmer for a further few minutes.
To freeze: cool quickly, then pour into a rigid container. Seal, label and freeze.
To thaw and serve: thaw at room temperature for 4 hours, then reheat gently on top of the stove, stirring occasionally. Sprinkle with parsley and paprika just before serving.
SERVES 4

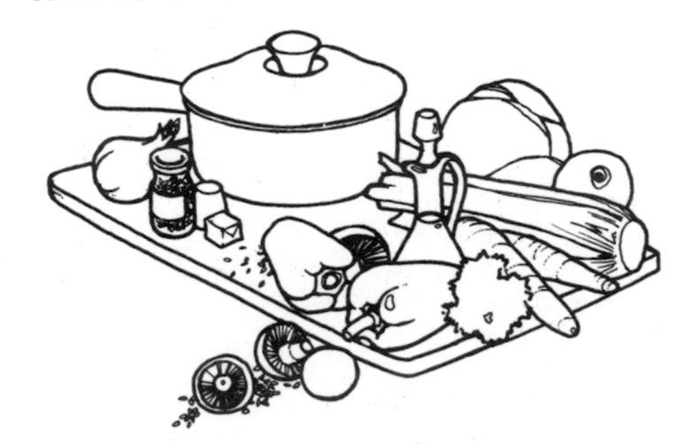

CHEESY VEGETABLE SOUP

METRIC/IMPERIAL
25 g/1 oz butter
1 large onion, peeled and sliced
100 g/4 oz mushrooms, sliced
1 × 225 g/8 oz packet frozen mixed vegetables
25 g/1 oz flour
450 ml/¾ pint chicken stock
300 ml/½ pint milk
2 × 15 ml spoons/2 tablespoons lemon juice
salt
freshly ground black pepper
To finish:
100 g/4 oz Cheddar cheese, grated
4 slices of French bread

AMERICAN
2 tablespoons butter
1 large onion, peeled and sliced
1 cup sliced mushrooms
1 × 8 oz package frozen mixed vegetables
¼ cup flour
2 cups chicken stock
1¼ cups milk
2 tablespoons lemon juice
salt
freshly ground black pepper
To finish:
1 cup grated Cheddar cheese
4 slices of French bread

Melt the butter in a pan, add the onion and mushrooms and fry gently until soft. Add the mixed vegetables and flour and stir well to mix. Stir in the stock and milk gradually, then bring to the boil and simmer until thick, stirring constantly.
Add the lemon juice and salt and pepper to taste. Cover and simmer until the vegetables are tender.
To freeze: cool quickly, then pour into a rigid container. Seal, label and freeze.
To thaw and serve: thaw at room temperature for 4 hours, then reheat gently on top of the stove, stirring occasionally. Stir in 75 g/3 oz/¾ cup cheese, turn off the heat and stir until the cheese has melted. Pour into 4 individual heatproof serving bowls and put 1 slice of bread in each bowl. Sprinkle with the remaining cheese and put under a preheated grill (broiler) for 2 to 3 minutes to melt the cheese.
SERVES 4

BUTTER BEAN AND TOMATO SOUP

METRIC/IMPERIAL

25 g/1 oz butter
1 large onion, peeled and sliced
1 × 400 g/14 oz can tomatoes
100 g/4 oz dried butter beans, soaked in cold water overnight
1 bay leaf
1 litre/1¾ pints stock or water
salt
freshly ground black pepper
freshly chopped parsley, to garnish

AMERICAN

2 tablespoons butter
1 large onion, peeled and sliced
1 × 14 oz can tomatoes
⅔ cup dried white beans, soaked in cold water overnight
1 bay leaf
4¼ cups stock or water
salt
freshly ground black pepper
freshly chopped parsley, to garnish

Melt the butter in a pan, add the onions and fry gently until soft. Add the tomatoes and fry for a further 2 minutes.
Drain the beans and rinse under cold running water. Add to the pan with the bay leaf, stock or water and salt and pepper to taste. Bring to the boil, cover and simmer for 2 to 2½ hours or until the beans are soft.
Remove the bay leaf. Work the soup to a smooth purée in an electric blender or Mouli-légumes (food mill), or rub through a sieve (strainer).
To freeze: cool quickly, then pour into a rigid container. Seal, label and freeze.
To thaw and serve: thaw at room temperature for 4 hours, then reheat gently on top of the stove, stirring occasionally. Sprinkle with parsley.
SERVES 6

CHEESE AND POTATO SOUP

METRIC/IMPERIAL

450 g/1 lb potatoes, peeled and diced
1 onion, peeled and chopped
1 large celery stalk, chopped
300 ml/½ pint water
freshly ground black pepper
25 g/1 oz flour
300 ml/½ pint milk
1 × 200 g/7 oz can sweetcorn, drained
175 g/6 oz Double Gloucester cheese, grated, to finish

AMERICAN

1 lb potatoes, peeled and diced
1 onion, peeled and chopped
1 large celery stalk, chopped
1¼ cups water
freshly ground black pepper
¼ cup flour
1¼ cups milk
1 × 7 oz can corn kernels, drained
1½ cups grated Double Gloucester cheese, to finish

Put the vegetables in a pan with the water and salt and pepper to taste. Bring to the boil, cover and simmer for 30 minutes or until the potatoes are cooked.
Mix the flour to a paste with a little of the milk, then stir into the vegetable mixture. Bring to the boil, then simmer until the soup thickens, stirring constantly. Add the remaining milk and the corn.
To freeze: cool quickly, then pour into a rigid container. Seal, label and freeze.
To thaw and serve: thaw at room temperature for 4 hours, then reheat gently on top of the stove, stirring occasionally. Stir in the grated cheese and heat through until melted.
SERVES 4 to 6

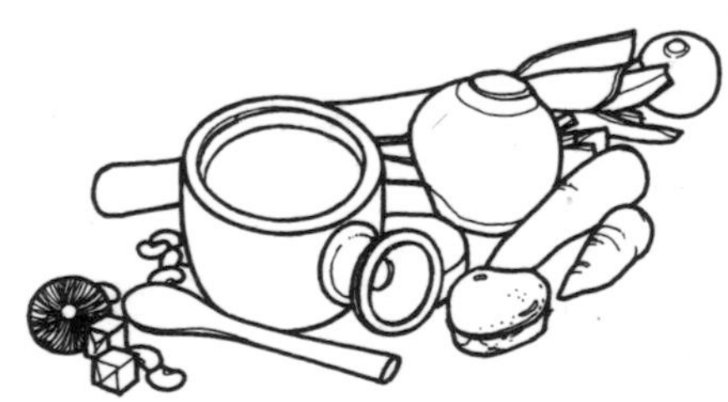

COURGETTE (ZUCCHINI) SOUP

METRIC/IMPERIAL

1 litre/2 pints chicken stock
675 g/1½ lb courgettes, trimmed and finely chopped
2 medium onions, peeled and grated
2 × 15 ml spoons/2 tablespoons lemon juice
salt
freshly ground black pepper
croûtons, to serve

AMERICAN

5 cups chicken stock
1½ lb zucchini, trimmed and finely chopped
2 medium onions, peeled and grated
2 tablespoons lemon juice
salt
freshly ground black pepper
croûtons, to serve

Heat the stock in a pan, add the courgettes (zucchini) and onions, cover and simmer for 15 minutes or until the courgettes (zucchini) are tender. Add the lemon juice and salt and pepper to taste. Leave to cool slightly, then work to a smooth purée in an electric blender or Mouli-légumes (food mill), or rub through a sieve (strainer).
To freeze: cool quickly, then pour into a rigid container. Seal, label and freeze.
To thaw and serve: reheat gently from frozen on top of the stove, stirring occasionally. Serve with croûtons.
SERVES 6

CARROT AND COURGETTE (ZUCCHINI) SOUP

METRIC/IMPERIAL
50 g/2 oz butter
225 g/½ lb carrots, peeled and sliced
225 g/½ lb courgettes, trimmed and sliced
600 ml/1 pint chicken stock
1 bay leaf
1 × 15 ml spoon/1 tablespoon tomato purée
1 × 15 ml spoon/1 tablespoon caster sugar
salt
freshly ground black pepper

AMERICAN
¼ cup butter
½ lb carrots, peeled and sliced
½ lb zucchini, trimmed and sliced
2½ cups chicken stock
1 bay leaf
1 tablespoon tomato paste
1 tablespoon sugar
salt
freshly ground black pepper

Melt the butter in a pan, add the carrots and courgettes (zucchini), cover and cook gently for 10 minutes until soft. Pour in the stock and add the remaining ingredients. Bring the soup to the boil, then simmer for 30 minutes. Remove the bay leaf, leave the soup to cool slightly, then work to a smooth purée in an electric blender or Mouli-légumes (food mill).
To freeze: cool quickly, then pour into a rigid container. Seal, label and freeze.
To thaw and serve: reheat gently from frozen on top of the stove with 2 × 15 ml spoons/2 tablespoons stock or water, stirring occasionally.
SERVES 4

CREAMY TURKEY SOUP

METRIC/IMPERIAL
1 turkey carcass
1 bouquet garni
25 g/1 oz butter
2 × 15 ml spoons/2 tablespoons chopped onion
1 × 5 ml spoon/1 teaspoon curry powder
175 g/6 oz potatoes, peeled and diced
1 medium carrot, peeled and finely diced
2 celery stalks, chopped
salt
freshly ground black pepper
To finish:
150 ml/¼ pint evaporated milk or single cream
freshly chopped parsley

AMERICAN
1 turkey carcass
1 bouquet garni
2 tablespoons butter
2 tablespoons chopped onion
1 teaspoon curry powder
1 cup peeled and diced potatoes
1 medium carrot, peeled and finely diced
2 celery stalks, chopped
salt
freshly ground black pepper
To finish:
⅔ cup evaporated milk or single cream
freshly chopped parsley

Remove any remaining meat from the carcass, cut into small pieces and set aside. Put the carcass in a pan and cover with water. Add the bouquet garni, bring to the boil, then half cover and simmer for about 2 hours.
Strain the stock and leave to cool, then skim off excess fat and measure 900 ml/1½ pints/3¾ cups. Add water to the stock if there is not enough.
Melt the butter in a pan, add the onion and fry gently until soft. Stir in the curry powder, cook for 1 minute, then add the vegetables, measured stock and salt and pepper to taste. Cover and simmer for 30 minutes or until the vegetables are tender. Stir in the reserved turkey meat.
To freeze: cool quickly, then pour into a rigid container. Seal, label and freeze.
To thaw and serve: thaw at room temperature for 4 hours, then reheat gently on the top of the stove, stirring occasionally. Blend together the evaporated milk or cream and the flour, then stir into the soup. Simmer until the soup thickens, stirring constantly. Sprinkle with parsley just before serving.
SERVES 6

POTAGE CRÈCY

METRIC/IMPERIAL

40 g/1½ oz butter
450 g/1 lb carrots, peeled and chopped
100 g/4 oz turnips, peeled and chopped
350 g/¾ lb potatoes, peeled and diced
1.5 litres/2½ pints warm water
salt
freshly ground black pepper
1 large onion, peeled and chopped
croûtons, to serve

AMERICAN

3 tablespoons butter
1 lb carrots, peeled and chopped
⅔ cup peeled and chopped turnips
2 cups peeled and diced potatoes
6¼ cups warm water
salt
freshly ground black pepper
1 large onion, peeled and chopped
croûtons, to serve

Melt 25 g/1 oz/2 tablespoons butter in a pan, add the carrots and turnips, cover and cook gently for 20 minutes or until soft, stirring occasionally. Add the potatoes, water and salt and pepper to taste. Bring to the boil, then simmer, uncovered, for 1 hour.
Melt the remaining butter in a separate pan, add the onion and fry gently until soft. Work the soup to a smooth purée in an electric blender or Mouli-légumes (food mill), then stir in the cooked onion and simmer for a further 10 minutes.
To freeze: cool quickly, then pour into a rigid container. Seal, label and freeze.
To thaw and serve: reheat gently from frozen on top of the stove, stirring occasionally. If the soup seems too thick, add a little milk or water. Serve with croûtons.
SERVES 8

CREAM OF VEGETABLE SOUP

METRIC/IMPERIAL

50 g/2 oz butter
2 large carrots, peeled and diced or grated
175 g/6 oz swede, peeled and diced
2 medium onions, peeled and sliced, or 2 medium leeks, sliced
450 ml/¾ pint stock
freshly ground black pepper
To finish:
150 ml/¼ pint milk
6 × 15 ml spoons/6 tablespoons single cream

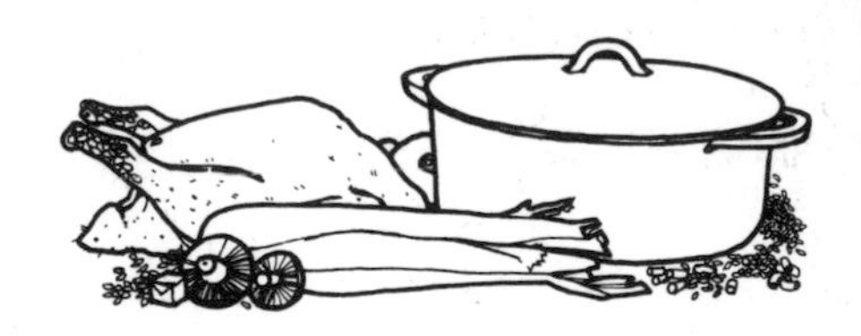

AMERICAN

¼ cup butter
2 large carrots, peeled and diced or grated
1 cup peeled and diced rutabaga
2 medium onions, peeled and sliced, or 2 medium leeks, sliced
2 cups stock
freshly ground black pepper
To finish:
⅔ cup milk
6 tablespoons light cream

Melt the butter in a pan, add the carrots, swede (rutabaga) and onions or leeks and fry gently for 5 to 10 minutes or until lightly coloured. Stir in the stock and salt and pepper to taste and bring to the boil. Cover and simmer for 15 to 20 minutes or until the vegetables are tender. Leave to cool slightly, then work to a smooth purée in an electric blender or Mouli-légumes (food mill), or rub through a sieve (strainer).
To freeze: cool quickly, then pour into a rigid container. Seal, label and freeze.
To thaw and serve: reheat gently from frozen on top of the stove, stirring occasionally. Stir in the milk and cream and heat through. Do not allow to boil.
SERVES 4

WATERCRESS SOUP

METRIC/IMPERIAL

1 bunch of watercress, finely chopped
1 celery stalk, finely chopped
300 ml/½ pint single cream
finely grated rind of 1 lemon
300 ml/½ pint milk
450 ml/¾ pint chicken stock
1 × 15 ml spoon/1 tablespoon butter
2 × 15 ml spoons/2 tablespoons flour
salt
freshly ground black pepper

AMERICAN

1 bunch of watercress, finely chopped
1 celery stalk, finely chopped
1¼ cups light cream

finely grated rind of 1 lemon
1¼ cups of milk
2 cups chicken stock
1 tablespoon butter
2 tablespoons flour
salt
freshly ground black pepper

Put the watercress, celery, çream, lemon rind and milk in a pan, bring to just below boiling point, then remove from the heat and stir in the stock.
Blend the butter and flour together and stir into the soup in small pieces. Return to the heat and cook for 2 to 3 minutes or until the soup is thick and smooth, stirring constantly. Add salt and pepper to taste and cook gently for a further 2 minutes.
To freeze: cool quickly, then pour into a rigid container. Seal, label and freeze.
To thaw and serve: reheat gently from frozen on top of the stove, stirring occasionally.
SERVES 4

PARSNIP SOUP

METRIC/IMPERIAL
50 g/2 oz butter
350 g/¾ lb parsnips, peeled and roughly chopped
1 potato, peeled and chopped
1 onion, peeled and chopped
450 ml/¾ pint chicken stock
salt
freshly ground black pepper
1 × 15 ml spoon/1 tablespoon cornflour
450 ml/¾ pint creamy milk
freshly chopped parsley, to garnish

AMERICAN
¼ cup butter
2 cups peeled and roughly chopped parsnips
1 potato, peeled and chopped
1 onion, peeled and chopped
2 cups chicken stock
salt
freshly ground black pepper
1 tablespoon cornstarch
2 cups creamy milk
freshly chopped parsley, to garnish

Melt the butter in a pan, add the parsnips, potato and onion, cover and cook gently for 3 minutes. Stir in the stock and salt and pepper to taste. Bring to the boil, then cover and simmer for 30 minutes.
Leave to cool slightly, then work to a smooth purée in an electric blender or Mouli-légumes (food mill), or rub through a sieve (strainer). Mix the cornflour (cornstarch) to a paste with a little of the milk, then stir into the soup with the remaining milk. Bring to the boil, then simmer until the soup thickens, stirring constantly.
To freeze: cool quickly, then pour into a rigid container. Seal, label and freeze.
To thaw and serve: thaw at room temperature for 4 hours, then reheat gently on top of the stove, stirring occasionally. Sprinkle with parsley just before serving.
SERVES 4

POTATO SOUP

METRIC/IMPERIAL
15 g/½ oz butter
225 g/½ lb peeled potatoes, diced
1 celery stalk, chopped
1 small carrot, peeled and diced
1 small onion, peeled and chopped
450 ml/¾ pint chicken stock
salt
freshly ground black pepper
1 tablespoon flour
150 ml/¼ pint milk

AMERICAN
1 tablespoon butter
1⅓ cups peeled and diced potatoes
1 celery stalk, chopped
1 small carrot, peeled and diced
1 small onion, peeled and chopped
2 cups chicken stock
salt
freshly ground black pepper
1 tablespoon flour
⅔ cup milk

Put the butter and vegetables in a pan with the stock and salt and pepper to taste. Bring to the boil, then cover and simmer for 40 to 50 minutes or until the vegetables are soft.
Leave to cool slightly, then work to a smooth purée in an electric blender or Mouli-légumes (food mill), or rub through a sieve (strainer). Mix the flour to a paste with a little of the milk, then stir into the purée with the remaining milk. Bring to the boil, then simmer until the soup thickens, stirring constantly.
To freeze: cool quickly, then pour into a rigid container. Seal, label and freeze.
To thaw and serve: thaw at room temperature for 4 hours, then reheat gently on top of the stove, stirring occasionally.
SERVES 4

CHICORY (BELGIAN ENDIVE) WITH CHEESE AND HAM

METRIC/IMPERIAL
4 heads of chicory, trimmed
salt
juice of ½ lemon
40 g/1½ oz butter
40 g/1½ oz flour
300 ml/½ pint milk
50 g/2 oz Cheddar cheese, grated
freshly ground black pepper
pinch of grated nutmeg
4 slices of cooked ham
To finish:
50 g/2 oz Cheddar cheese, grated
25 g/1 oz fresh white breadcrumbs
25 g/1 oz butter

AMERICAN
4 heads of Belgian endive, trimmed
salt
juice of ½ lemon
3 tablespoons butter
⅜ cup flour
1¼ cups milk
½ cup grated Cheddar cheese
freshly ground black pepper
pinch of grated nutmeg
4 slices of cooked ham
To finish:
½ cup grated Cheddar cheese
½ cup fresh white breadcrumbs
2 tablespoons butter

Put the chicory (Belgian endive) in boiling salted water with the lemon juice, then cook gently for 25 minutes. Strain and reserve 300 ml/½ pint/1¼ cups liquid.
Melt the butter in a pan, stir in the flour and cook for 2 minutes, stirring constantly. Remove from the heat and gradually stir in the milk and the reserved cooking liquid. Return to the heat, bring to the boil and simmer until thick, stirring constantly. Add the cheese, salt and pepper to taste and the nutmeg.
To freeze: wrap each head of chicory (Belgian endive) in a slice of ham and put in a rigid container. Pour over the sauce. Cool quickly, then seal, label and freeze.
To thaw and serve: reheat from frozen, uncovered, in a preheated moderately hot oven (200°C/400°F or Gas Mark 6) for 30 minutes. Sprinkle with the grated cheese and breadcrumbs, dot with the butter and cook for a further 15 minutes or until golden brown and heated through.
SERVES 4

BRAISED CELERY

METRIC/IMPERIAL

25 g/1 oz butter
1 onion, peeled and finely chopped
2 medium carrots, peeled and diced
2 heads of celery, trimmed, cut in half and blanched
300 ml/½ pint beef stock
salt
freshly ground black pepper

AMERICAN

2 tablespoons butter
1 onion, peeled and finely chopped
2 medium carrots, peeled and diced
2 heads of celery, trimmed, cut in half and blanched
1¼ cups beef stock
salt
freshly ground black pepper

Melt the butter, add the onion and carrots and fry gently for 2 minutes. Put the celery in an ovenproof dish or foil container, add the fried vegetables, the stock and salt and pepper to taste. Cover and cook in a preheated moderate oven (180°C/350°F or Gas Mark 4) for 1 to 1¼ hours or until the celery is tender.

To freeze: cool quickly, then seal, label and freeze.

To thaw and serve: thaw at room temperature for 4 hours, then reheat in a preheated moderate oven (180°C/350°F or Gas Mark 4) for 35 minutes or until heated through.

SERVES 4 to 6

RICE SALAD

225 g/½ lb long-grain rice
salt
3 spring onions, trimmed and finely chopped
50 g/2 oz currants
1 small red pepper, cored, seeded and finely chopped
1 small green pepper, cored, seeded and finely chopped
freshly ground black pepper
4 × 15 ml spoons/4 tablespoons French dressing, to finish

AMERICAN

1⅓ cups long-grain rice
salt
3 scallions, trimmed and finely chopped
⅓ cup currants
1 small red pepper, cored, seeded and finely chopped
1 small green pepper, cored, seeded and finely chopped
freshly ground black pepper
¼ cup French dressing, to finish

Cook the rice in plenty of boiling salted water for 12 minutes or until 'al dente'. Drain and rinse under cold running water, then drain again thoroughly.

Put the rice in a bowl with the remaining ingredients, except the French dressing, and stir with a fork to mix.

To freeze: transfer to a rigid container, seal, label and freeze.

To thaw and serve: thaw at room temperature for 4 hours, then mix thoroughly with the French dressing.

SERVES 6 to 8

STUFFED GREEN PEPPERS

METRIC/IMPERIAL

25 g/1 oz butter
1 large onion, peeled and chopped
225 g/½ lb lean minced beef
100 g/4 oz mushrooms, sliced
100 g/4 oz long-grain rice, boiled and drained
salt
freshly ground black pepper
1 × 5 ml spoon/1 teaspoon Worcestershire sauce
1 × 5 ml spoon/1 teaspoon tomato purée
pinch of dried mixed herbs
4 medium green peppers, cored, seeded and blanched

AMERICAN

2 tablespoons butter
1 large onion, peeled and chopped
1 cup lean ground beef
1 cup sliced mushrooms
⅔ cup long-grain rice, boiled and drained
salt
freshly ground black pepper
1 teaspoon Worcestershire sauce
1 teaspoon tomato paste
pinch of dried mixed herbs
4 medium green peppers, cored, seeded and blanched

Melt the butter in a pan, add the onion and fry gently until soft. Add the beef and fry for 10 minutes, stirring constantly to break up the meat. Add the remaining ingredients, except the green peppers, stir well to mix. Continue cooking for 5 minutes, then divide the filling equally between the peppers.

To freeze: cool quickly, then place in an ovenproof dish or foil container and cover with foil. Seal, label and freeze.

To thaw and serve: reheat from frozen in the covered dish or container in a preheated moderately hot oven (200°C/400°F or Gas Mark 6) for 1 hour or until heated through.

SERVES 4

BEAN AND PEA SALAD

METRIC/IMPERIAL

100 g/4 oz dried haricot beans, soaked in cold water overnight
100 g/4 oz dried red kidney beans, soaked in cold water overnight
100 g/4 oz dried chick peas, soaked in cold water overnight
salt
2 × 15 ml spoons/2 tablespoons peeled and finely chopped onion
100 g/4 oz shelled peas, cooked
freshly ground black pepper
To finish:
4 × 15 ml spoons/4 tablespoons French dressing
freshly chopped parsley

AMERICAN

½ cup dried navy beans, soaked in cold water overnight
⅓ cup dried red kidney beans, soaked in cold water overnight
½ cup dried chick peas (garbanzos), soaked in cold water overnight
salt
2 tablespoons peeled and finely chopped onion
¾ cup shelled peas, cooked
freshly ground black pepper
To finish:
¼ cup French dressing
freshly chopped parsley

Drain the beans and chick peas, then cook in separate pans of boiling water until tender. Add salt halfway through the cooking.
Drain, leave to cool, then put in a bowl with the onion, peas and salt and pepper to taste. Stir well to mix.
To freeze: transfer to a rigid container, seal, label and freeze.
To thaw and serve: thaw at room temperature for 4 hours, then mix thoroughly with the French dressing and sprinkle with parsley.
SERVES 8

CHINESE VEGETABLES

METRIC/IMPERIAL

2 × 15 ml spoons/2 tablespoons corn oil
3 celery stalks, sliced
2 large carrots, peeled and cut into thin strips
1 green pepper, cored, seeded and cut into thin strips
1 small onion, peeled and sliced
1 small cauliflower, divided into florets
100 g/4 oz mushrooms, sliced
4 × 15 ml spoons/4 tablespoons water
1 × 15 ml spoon/1 tablespoon dry sherry
1 × 2.5 ml spoon/½ teaspoon salt
freshly ground black pepper
2 × 5 ml spoons/2 teaspoons soy sauce
1 × 5 ml spoon/1 teaspoon brown sugar
225 g/½ lb bean sprouts, to finish

AMERICAN

2 tablespoons corn oil
3 celery stalks, sliced
2 large carrots, peeled and cut into thin strips
1 green pepper, cored, seeded and cut into thin strips
1 small onion, peeled and sliced
1 small cauliflower, divided into florets
1 cup sliced mushrooms
¼ cup water
1 tablespoon dry sherry
½ teaspoon salt
freshly ground black pepper
2 teaspoons soy sauce
1 teaspoon brown sugar
4 cups bean sprouts, to finish

Heat the oil in a pan, add the celery and carrots and fry gently for 3 minutes. Stir in the remaining vegetables and cook for 2 minutes. Add the remaining ingredients, except the bean sprouts, and cook briskly for 6 to 8 minutes until the vegetables are cooked but still crisp.
To freeze: cool quickly, then transfer to a rigid container. Seal, label and freeze.
To thaw and serve: thaw in the refrigerator overnight, or at room temperature for 4 hours. Stir in the bean sprouts and reheat gently on top of the stove, stirring constantly.
SERVES 4

VEGETABLE MEDLEY

METRIC/IMPERIAL

1 medium aubergine, sliced
salt
1 medium onion, peeled and sliced
1 medium green pepper, cored, seeded and sliced
1 medium red pepper, cored, seeded and sliced
225 g/½ lb tomatoes, peeled and sliced
225 g/½ lb courgettes, sliced
freshly ground black pepper
300 ml/½ pint chicken stock
To finish:
100 g/4 oz cooked ham, chopped
100 g/4 oz Cheddar cheese, grated

AMERICAN

1 medium eggplant, sliced
salt
1 medium onion, peeled and sliced
1 medium green pepper, cored, seeded and sliced

1 medium red pepper, cored, seeded and sliced
½ lb tomatoes, peeled and sliced
½ lb zucchini, sliced
freshly ground black pepper
1¼ cups chicken stock
To finish:
½ cup chopped cooked ham
1 cup grated Cheddar cheese

Sprinkle the aubergine (eggplant) slices with salt and leave for 30 minutes. Drain off any liquid, rinse under cold running water, then dry on paper towels.
Arrange the vegetables in layers in an ovenproof dish or foil container, sprinkling each layer with plenty of salt and pepper. Pour over the stock, then cover and cook in a preheated moderately hot oven (190°C/375°F or Gas Mark 5) for 45 minutes to 1 hour or until the vegetables are tender.
To freeze: cool quickly, then seal, label and freeze.
To thaw and serve: cover the dish or container loosely with foil. Reheat from frozen in a preheated moderate oven (180°C/350°F or Gas Mark 4) for 1 hour or until heated through. Pour off some of the stock, sprinkle the top of the vegetables with the ham and cheese, then cook for a further 10 minutes or until the cheese has melted.
SERVES 6

CHEESE-STUFFED AUBERGINES (EGGPLANTS)

METRIC/IMPERIAL
2 aubergines, stalks removed and cut in half lengthways
75 g/3 oz fresh white breadcrumbs
1 onion, peeled and grated
175 g/6 oz Cheddar cheese, grated
2 × 5 ml spoons/2 teaspoons honey
2 × 5 ml spoons/2 teaspoons soy sauce
1 × 5 ml spoon/1 teaspoon vinegar
1 egg yolk

AMERICAN
2 eggplants, stalks removed and cut in half lengthwise
1½ cups fresh white breadcrumbs
1 onion, peeled and grated
1½ cups grated Cheddar cheese
2 teaspoons honey
2 teaspoons soy sauce
1 teaspoon vinegar
1 egg yolk

Scoop out the flesh from the centre of the aubergines (eggplants) and chop finely. Put in a bowl with the breadcrumbs, onion and 150 g/5 oz/1¼ cups cheese, add the remaining ingredients and stir well to mix.
Divide the filling equally between the aubergine (eggplant) skins, then place in an ovenproof dish and sprinkle with remaining cheese. Cover and cook in a preheated moderately hot oven (200°C/400°F or Gas Mark 6) for 30 minutes.
To freeze: cool quickly, then wrap individually in foil. Pack in a freezer bag, seal, label and freeze.
To thaw and serve: put the foil-wrapped aubergines (eggplants) in an ovenproof dish and reheat from frozen in a preheated moderate oven (180°C/350°F or Gas Mark 4) for 25 minutes. Remove foil and cook for a further 15 minutes.
SERVES 4

LENTIL STEW

METRIC/IMPERIAL
25 g/1 oz butter
1 carrot, peeled and diced
2 leeks, finely sliced
2 celery stalks, finely sliced
1 onion, peeled and finely chopped
1 × 400 g/14 oz can tomatoes
150 ml/¼ pint stock
salt
freshly ground black pepper
1 × 5 ml spoon/1 teaspoon freshly chopped parsley
225 g/½ lb lentils

AMERICAN
2 tablespoons butter
1 carrot, peeled and diced
2 leeks, finely sliced
2 celery stalks, finely sliced
1 onion, peeled and finely chopped
1 × 14 oz can tomatoes
⅔ cup stock
salt
freshly ground black pepper
1 teaspoon freshly chopped parsley
1 cup lentils

Melt the butter in a pan, add the carrot, leeks, celery and onion and fry gently until soft. Add the remaining ingredients, cover and simmer for 1 to 1½ hours or until the lentils are tender.
To freeze: cool quickly, then transfer to a rigid container. Seal, label and freeze.
To thaw and serve: thaw at room temperature for 2 to 3 hours, then reheat gently on top of the stove, stirring occasionally.
SERVES 4

SWEET AND SOUR BEETROOT (BEETS)

METRIC/IMPERIAL

1 × 15 ml spoon/1 tablespoon soft brown sugar
5 × 15 ml spoons/5 tablespoons orange juice
2 × 15 ml spoons/2 tablespoons white vinegar
1 × 15 ml spoon/1 tablespoon cornflour
15 g/½ oz butter
salt
freshly ground black pepper
450 g/1 lb cooked beetroot, peeled and coarsely diced
finely chopped spring onions, to garnish

AMERICAN

1 tablespoon light brown sugar
⅓ cup orange juice
2 tablespoons white vinegar
1 tablespoon cornstarch
1 tablespoon butter
salt
freshly ground black pepper
1 lb cooked beets, peeled and coarsely diced
1 tablespoon finely chopped scallion, to garnish

Put the sugar, orange juice, vinegar and cornflour (cornstarch) in a pan, stir over a low heat until smooth, then bring to the boil, stirring constantly. Reduce the heat and simmer for 2 minutes, stirring occasionally, then beat in the butter and add salt and pepper to taste. Fold the beetroot (beets) into the sauce and heat through gently to just below boiling point.
To freeze: cool quickly, then transfer to a rigid container. Seal, label and freeze.
To thaw and serve: thaw at room temperature for 2 to 3 hours, then reheat gently on top of the stove, stirring occasionally. Sprinkle with the spring onion (scallion) just before serving.
SERVES 4

RED CABBAGE WITH APPLE

METRIC/IMPERIAL

1 kg/2 lb red cabbage, core removed and finely shredded
450 g/1 lb onions, peeled and finely chopped
450 g/1 lb cooking apples, peeled, cored and finely chopped
2 × 15 ml spoons/2 tablespoons soft brown sugar
salt
freshly ground black pepper
2 × 15 ml spoons/2 tablespoons wine vinegar
25 g/1 oz butter

AMERICAN

2 lb red cabbage, core removed and finely shredded
1 lb onions, peeled and finely chopped
1 lb baking apples, peeled, cored and finely chopped
2 tablespoons light brown sugar
salt
freshly ground black pepper
2 tablespoons wine vinegar
2 tablespoons butter

Put the cabbage, onions and apples in layers in an ovenproof or foil container, sprinkling each layer with sugar and salt and pepper to taste. Pour in the wine vinegar and dot with the butter. Cover and cook in a preheated moderate oven (160°C/325°F or Gas Mark 3) for 2 hours.
To freeze: cool quickly, then seal, label and freeze.
To thaw and serve: thaw at room temperature for 4 hours, then reheat gently on top of the stove, stirring occasionally.
SERVES 6 to 8

SPICED CARROTS

METRIC/IMPERIAL

675 g/1½ lb carrots, peeled and sliced
25 g/1 oz butter, melted
2 × 15 ml spoons/2 tablespoons orange juice
1 × 5 ml spoon/1 teaspoon grated orange rind
pinch of ground ginger
pinch of nutmeg
salt
freshly ground black pepper
freshly chopped parsley, to garnish

AMERICAN

1½ lb carrots, peeled and sliced
2 tablespoons butter, melted
2 tablespoons orange juice
1 teaspoon finely grated orange rind
pinch of ground ginger
pinch of grated nutmeg
salt
freshly ground black pepper
freshly chopped parsley, to garnish

Put the carrots in an ovenproof dish or foil container. Mix together the remaining ingredients, except the parsley, and spoon over the carrots. Cover and cook in a preheated moderately hot oven (190°C/375°F or Gas Mark 5) for 45 minutes.
To freeze: cool quickly, then seal, label and freeze.
To thaw and serve: thaw at room temperature for 4 hours, then reheat in a preheated moderate oven (180°C/350°F or Gas Mark 4) for 20 to 30 minutes or until heated through. Sprinkle with parsley just before serving.
SERVES 4

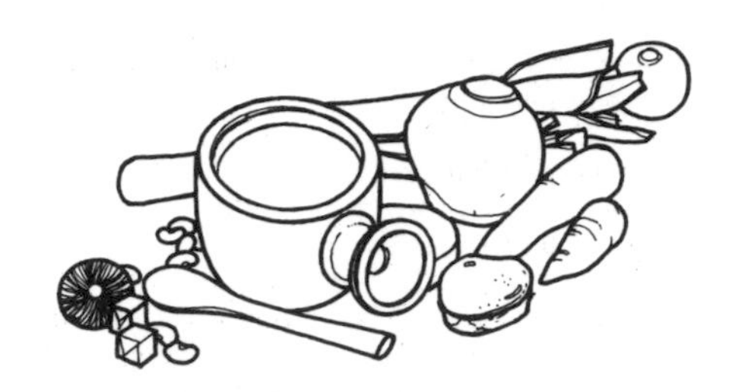

STUFFED COURGETTES (ZUCCHINI)

METRIC/IMPERIAL
450 g/1 lb courgettes, sliced in half lengthways
15 g/½ oz butter
1 medium onion, peeled and finely chopped
450 g/1 lb lean minced beef
pinch of dried thyme
salt
dash of Tabasco sauce
3 tomatoes, peeled and chopped
1 × 15 ml spoon/1 tablespoon tomato purée
50 g/2 oz fresh white breadcrumbs

AMERICAN
1 lb zucchini, sliced in half lengthwise
1 tablespoon butter
1 medium onion, peeled and finely chopped
2 cups lean ground beef
pinch of dried thyme
salt
dash of Tabasco sauce
3 tomatoes, peeled and chopped
1 tablespoon tomato paste
1 cup fresh white breadcrumbs

Scoop out the flesh from the centre of the courgettes (zucchini), put the skins in boiling water for 5 minutes, then drain and arrange in a single layer in a buttered ovenproof dish or foil container.
Melt the butter in a pan, add the onion and fry gently until soft. Add the beef and cook until browned, stirring constantly to break up the meat. Stir in the remaining ingredients, except the breadcrumbs, and cook gently for 5 minutes, stirring occasionally.
Remove from the heat, stir in the breadcrumbs and divide the filling equally between the courgettes (zucchini).
To freeze: cool quickly, then cover with foil. Seal, label and freeze.
To thaw and serve: reheat from frozen in the covered dish or container in a preheated moderate oven (180°C/350°F or Gas Mark 4) for 1 hour or until heated through.
SERVES 4

VEGETABLE CASSEROLE

METRIC/IMPERIAL
1 kg/2 lb mixed vegetables (carrots, parsnips, potatoes, onions, celery, swede), prepared and diced
salt
3 lean bacon rashers, rinds removed and cut into strips
50 g/2 oz butter
50 g/2 oz flour
1 × 15 ml spoon/1 tablespoon prepared German mustard
300 ml/½ pint milk
freshly ground black pepper
75 g/3 oz Cheddar cheese, grated

AMERICAN
2 lb mixed vegetables (carrots, parsnips, potatoes, onions, celery, rutabaga), prepared and diced
salt
3 Canadian bacon slices, cut into strips
¼ cup butter
½ cup flour
1 tablespoon prepared German mustard
1¼ cups milk
freshly ground black pepper
¾ cup grated Cheddar cheese

Cook the vegetables in boiling salted water for 10 to 15 minutes or until tender. Drain and reserve 300 ml/½ pint/1¼ cups cooking liquid.
Fry the bacon in its own fat until crisp, then set aside.
Melt the butter in a separate pan, stir in the flour and mustard and cook for 2 minutes, stirring constantly. Remove from the heat and gradually stir in the milk and the reserved cooking liquid. Return to the heat and bring to the boil, stirring constantly. Simmer until thick, then add salt and pepper to taste.
Pour half of the sauce into an ovenproof dish or foil container. Add the vegetables and bacon and cover with the remaining sauce. Sprinkle with the cheese and cook in a preheated moderate oven (180°C/350°F or Gas Mark 4) for 45 minutes.
To freeze: cool quickly, then cover with foil. Seal, label and freeze.
To thaw and serve: thaw at room temperature for 4 hours, then reheat in the covered dish or container in a preheated moderate oven for 35 to 40 minutes or until heated through.
SERVES 4

DHAL

METRIC/IMPERIAL

175 g/6 oz red lentils
25 g/1 oz butter
1 small onion, peeled and finely chopped
1 × 5 ml spoon/1 teaspoon mustard powder
1 × 2.5 ml spoon/½ teaspoon ground turmeric
1 × 5 ml spoon/1 teaspoon garam masala
600 ml/1 pint stock
salt

AMERICAN

¾ cup red lentils
2 tablespoons butter
1 small onion, peeled and finely chopped
1 teaspoon mustard powder
½ teaspoon ground turmeric
1 teaspoon garam masala
2½ cups stock
salt

Put the lentils in a bowl, cover with hot water and leave to soak for 1 hour. Drain and rinse under cold running water.
Melt the butter in a pan, add the onion and fry gently until soft. Stir in the mustard, turmeric and garam masala and fry for a further 5 minutes, stirring occasionally. Add the lentils and stock, cover and simmer for 50 minutes to 1 hour or until the lentils are soft and the dhal is the consistency of thick pea soup. Add salt to taste.
To freeze: cool quickly, then transfer to a rigid container. Seal, label and freeze.
To thaw and serve: thaw in the refrigerator overnight, then reheat gently on top of the stove, stirring occasionally.
SERVES 6

PURÉE OF SPLIT PEAS

METRIC/IMPERIAL

450 g/1 lb dried split peas, soaked in cold water overnight
40 g/1½ oz butter
1 bay leaf
1 × 5 ml spoon/1 teaspoon mustard powder
salt
1 small onion, peeled and finely chopped

AMERICAN

2 cups dried split peas, soaked in cold water overnight
3 tablespoons butter
1 bay leaf
1 teaspoon mustard powder
salt
1 small onion, peeled and finely chopped

Drain the split peas and rinse under cold running water. Put in a pan, cover with water and add 25 g/1 oz/2 tablespoons butter, the bay leaf and mustard. Cover and simmer for 1 to 1½ hours or until the split peas are soft, adding salt to taste after the first 30 minutes of cooking. Add more water if the mixture becomes too dry. Remove the bay leaf.
Leave to cool slightly, then work to a smooth purée in an electric blender or Mouli-légumes (food mill), or rub through a sieve (strainer).
Melt the remaining butter in a pan, add the onion and fry gently until soft. Stir into the purée.
To freeze: cool quickly, then transfer to a rigid container. Seal, label and freeze.
To thaw and serve: thaw at room temperature for 4 hours, then reheat gently on top of the stove, stirring occasionally. Add a little water if the mixture is too dry.
SERVES 6

SAUTÉED MARROW (SQUASH)

METRIC/IMPERIAL

40 g/1½ oz butter
1 × 15 ml spoon/1 tablespoon vegetable oil
1 medium marrow, peeled, seeded and coarsely chopped
1 medium onion, peeled and sliced
1 garlic clove, peeled and crushed
pinch of dried oregano
salt
freshly ground black pepper

AMERICAN

3 tablespoons butter
1 tablespoon vegetable oil
1 medium summer squash, peeled, seeded and coarsely chopped
1 medium onion, peeled and sliced
1 garlic clove, peeled and crushed
pinch of dried oregano
salt
freshly ground black pepper

Heat the butter and oil in a pan, add the marrow (squash), onion and garlic and fry gently for 3 minutes, stirring occasionally. Stir in the oregano and salt and pepper to taste. Cover and cook very gently for 10 minutes or until the marrow (squash) is tender, shaking the pan occasionally. Add a little water if the mixture becomes too dry.

To freeze: cool quickly, then transfer to a rigid container. Seal, label and freeze.

To thaw and serve: thaw at room temperature for 4 hours, then reheat gently on top of the stove, stirring occasionally.

SERVES 4 to 6

BEAN AND VEGETABLE HOT POT

METRIC/IMPERIAL

1 × 396 g/14 oz can butter beans, drained
225 g/½ lb potatoes, peeled and sliced
2 medium carrots, peeled and sliced
1 green pepper, cored, seeded and finely sliced
2 onions, peeled and sliced
2 celery stalks, chopped
2 tomatoes, peeled and quartered
salt
freshly ground black pepper
450 ml/¾ pint chicken stock

AMERICAN

1 × 14 oz can butter beans, drained
½ lb potatoes, peeled and sliced
2 medium carrots, peeled and sliced
1 green pepper, cored, seeded and finely sliced
2 onions, peeled and sliced
2 celery stalks, chopped
2 tomatoes, peeled and quartered
salt
freshly ground black pepper
2 cups chicken stock

Put the vegetables in a pan, sprinkle with salt and pepper to taste and pour over the stock. Cover and simmer for 30 minutes or until the vegetables are tender.

To freeze: cool quickly, then transfer to a rigid container. Seal, label and freeze.

To thaw and serve: thaw at room temperature for 4 hours, then reheat gently on top of the stove, stirring occasionally.

SERVES 4

BEAN AND TOMATO CASSEROLE

METRIC/IMPERIAL

225 g/½ lb dried haricot beans, soaked in cold water overnight
225 g/½ lb dried red kidney beans, soaked in cold water overnight
salt
50 g/2 oz butter
1 large onion, peeled and finely chopped
2 garlic cloves, peeled and crushed
1 × 400 g/14 oz can tomatoes
2 × 15 ml spoons/2 tablespoons honey
1 × 5 ml spoon/1 teaspoon mustard powder
4 frankfurters, halved
freshly ground black pepper

AMERICAN

1 cup dried navy beans, soaked in cold water overnight
¾ cup dried red kidney beans, soaked in cold water overnight
salt
¼ cup butter
1 large onion, peeled and finely chopped
2 garlic cloves, peeled and crushed
1 × 14 oz can tomatoes
2 tablespoons honey
1 teaspoon mustard powder
4 frankfurters, halved
freshly ground black pepper

Drain the beans and rinse under cold running water. Cook in boiling salted water for 1 to 1½ hours or until soft, then drain and set aside. Melt the butter in a pan, add the onion and garlic and fry gently until soft. Add the remaining ingredients and the beans, cover and simmer for 30 minutes.

To freeze: cool quickly, then transfer to a rigid container. Seal, label and freeze.

To thaw and serve: thaw at room temperature for 4 hours, then reheat in a covered casserole dish in a preheated moderate oven (180°C/350°F or Gas Mark 4) for 30 to 35 minutes or until heated through.

SERVES 4

BRAISED CHICORY (BELGIAN ENDIVE)

METRIC/IMPERIAL

8 heads of chicory, trimmed and blanched
50 g/2 oz butter
pinch of grated nutmeg
juice of ½ lemon
salt
freshly ground black pepper
120 ml/4 fl oz chicken stock

AMERICAN

8 heads of Belgian endive, trimmed and blanched
¼ cup butter
pinch of grated nutmeg
juice of ½ lemon
salt
freshly ground black pepper
½ cup chicken stock

Put the chicory (Belgian endive) in an ovenproof dish or foil container. Dot with the butter, then sprinkle with the nutmeg, lemon juice and salt and pepper to taste. Pour over the stock, cover and cook in a preheated moderate oven (160°C/325°F or Gas Mark 3) for 1 to 1½ hours or until the chicory (Belgian endive) is tender.

To freeze: cool quickly, seal, label and freeze.

To thaw and serve: reheat from frozen in the covered casserole or container in a preheated moderate oven (160°C/325°F or Gas Mark 3)

SERVES 4

CREAMED CABBAGE WITH CHEESE

METRIC/IMPERIAL

675 g/1½ lb white winter cabbage, trimmed and finely shredded
salt
300 ml/½ pint béchamel sauce
1 × 5 ml spoon/1 teaspoon mustard powder
freshly ground black pepper
50 g/2 oz Cheddar cheese, grated
50 g/2 oz fresh white breadcrumbs
25 g/1 oz butter

AMERICAN

1½ lb white winter cabbage, trimmed and finely shredded
salt
1¼ cups béchamel sauce
1 teaspoon mustard powder
freshly ground black pepper
½ cup grated Cheddar cheese
1 cup fresh white breadcrumbs
2 tablespoons butter

Cook the cabbage in boiling salted water for 5 minutes, drain well and keep hot.

Heat the béchamel sauce in a pan, stir in the mustard and salt and pepper to taste, then add the cabbage and stir well to mix. Remove from the heat and stir in 25 g/1 oz/¼ cup cheese. Transfer to an ovenproof dish or foil container, sprinkle with the remaining cheese and the breadcrumbs and dot with the butter.

To freeze: cool quickly, then cover with foil. Seal, label and freeze.

To thaw and serve: reheat from frozen in the covered dish or container in a preheated moderate oven (180°C/350°F or Gas Mark 4) for 50 minutes. Remove the cover and cook for a further 10 minutes or until golden brown and heated through.

SERVES 4 to 6

CAULIFLOWER MORNAY

METRIC/IMPERIAL

1 medium cauliflower, divided into florets
300 ml/½ pint white coating sauce
100 g/4 oz Cheddar cheese, grated
freshly ground black pepper
25 g/1 oz grated Parmesan cheese
2 × 15 ml spoons/2 tablespoons fresh white breadcrumbs

AMERICAN

1 medium cauliflower, divided into florets
1¼ cups white coating sauce
1 cup grated Cheddar cheese
freshly ground black pepper
¼ cup grated Parmesan cheese
2 tablespoons fresh white breadcrumbs

Cook the cauliflower in boiling salted water for 10 minutes until tender but still firm. Drain well, then place in an ovenproof dish or foil container.

Heat the white sauce in a pan, then stir in the Cheddar cheese and salt and pepper to taste. When the cheese has melted, pour over the cauliflower and sprinkle with the Parmesan cheese and breadcrumbs.

To freeze: cool quickly, then cover with foil. Seal, label and freeze.

To thaw and serve: reheat from frozen in the covered dish or container in a preheated moderate oven (160°C/325°F or Gas Mark 3) for 20 minutes. Remove the cover, increase the heat to moderately hot (200°C/400°F or Gas Mark 6) and cook for a further 10 minutes or until golden brown and heated through.

SERVES 4

TURNIP AND POTATO PURÉE

METRIC/IMPERIAL

40 g/1½ oz butter
350 g/¾ lb young turnips, peeled and sliced
350 g/¾ lb potatoes, peeled and sliced
1 small onion, peeled and sliced
300 ml/½ pint milk
1 × 2.5 ml spoon/½ teaspoon grated nutmeg
salt
freshly ground black pepper
50 g/2 oz butter, to finish

AMERICAN

3 tablespoons butter
¾ lb young turnips, peeled and sliced
¾ lb potatoes, peeled and sliced
1 small onion, peeled and sliced
1¼ cups milk
½ teaspoon grated nutmeg
salt
freshly ground black pepper
¼ cup butter, to finish

Melt the butter in a pan, add the turnips, potatoes and onion and fry gently for 3 minutes, stirring occasionally. Stir in the milk and add the nutmeg and salt and pepper to taste. Bring to the boil, then cover and simmer for 10 minutes or until the vegetables are tender. Leave to cool slightly, then work to a smooth purée in an electric blender or Mouli-légumes (food mill), or rub through a sieve (strainer).
To freeze: cool quickly, then transfer to a rigid container. Seal, label and freeze.
To thaw and serve: thaw at room temperature for approximately 4 hours, then reheat gently on top of the stove with the butter, stirring occasionally.
SERVES 4 to 6

MARROW (SQUASH) WITH TOMATO

METRIC/IMPERIAL

4 × 15 ml spoons/4 tablespoons olive oil
2 large onions, peeled and finely chopped
1 garlic clove, peeled and crushed
1 medium marrow, peeled, seeded and diced
6 large tomatoes, peeled and chopped
2 × 15 ml spoons/2 tablespoons tomato purée
2 × 5 ml spoons/2 teaspoons dried basil
salt
freshly ground black pepper

AMERICAN

¼ cup olive oil
2 large onions, peeled and finely chopped
1 garlic clove, peeled and crushed
1 medium summer squash, peeled, seeded and diced
6 large tomatoes, peeled and chopped
2 tablespoons tomato paste
2 teaspoons dried basil
salt
freshly ground black pepper

Heat the oil in a pan, add the onions and garlic and fry gently until soft. Add the marrow (squash) and fry gently for a further 5 minutes. Stir in the remaining ingredients, cover and simmer for 20 minutes or until the vegetables are tender, stirring occasionally.
To freeze: cool quickly, then transfer to a rigid container. Seal, label and freeze.
To thaw and serve: reheat gently from frozen on top of the stove, stirring occasionally.
SERVES 4 to 6

PEPERONATA

METRIC/IMPERIAL

3 × 15 ml spoons/3 tablespoons olive oil
1 × 15 ml spoon/1 tablespoon butter
1 small onion, peeled and finely chopped
1 garlic clove, peeled and crushed
4 red peppers, cored, seeded and cut into thin strips
salt
freshly ground black pepper
4–5 tomatoes, peeled and quartered
freshly chopped parsley, to garnish

AMERICAN

3 tablespoons olive oil
1 tablespoon butter
1 small onion, peeled and finely chopped
1 garlic clove, peeled and crushed
4 red peppers, cored, seeded and cut into thin strips
salt
freshly ground black pepper
4–5 tomatoes, peeled and quartered
freshly chopped parsley, to garnish

Heat the oil and butter in a pan, add the onion and garlic and fry gently until soft. Add the red peppers and salt and pepper to taste, then cover and cook gently for 15 minutes. Stir in the tomatoes, cover and cook for a further 30 minutes.
To freeze: cool quickly, then transfer to a rigid container. Seal, label and freeze.
To thaw and serve: thaw at room temperature for 4 hours and sprinkle with parsley.
SERVES 4

MUSHROOM-STUFFED TOMATOES

METRIC/IMPERIAL

6 large even-sized tomatoes
25 g/1 oz butter
100 g/4 oz mushrooms, finely chopped
1 small onion, peeled and finely chopped
1 × 5 ml spoon/1 teaspoon dried mixed herbs
50 g/2 oz fresh white breadcrumbs
salt
freshly ground black pepper

AMERICAN

6 large even-sized tomatoes
2 tablespoons butter
1 cup finely chopped mushrooms
1 small onion, peeled and finely chopped
1 teaspoon dried mixed herbs
1 cup fresh white breadcrumbs
salt
freshly ground black pepper

Cut the tops off the tomatoes and reserve them. Scoop out the flesh and discard the seeds.

Melt the butter in a pan, add the mushrooms and onion and fry briskly for 2 to 3 minutes. Remove from the heat and stir in the tomato flesh and the remaining ingredients. Divide the filling equally between the tomatoes and replace the tops.

To freeze: cool quickly, then place tomatoes in an ovenproof dish or foil container. Cover with foil, seal, label and freeze.

To thaw and serve: thaw at room temperature for 1 hour, then reheat, uncovered, in a preheated moderately hot oven (190°C/375°F or Gas Mark 5) for 15 to 20 minutes or until heated through.

SERVES 6

GLAZED CARROTS AND PARSNIPS

METRIC/IMPERIAL

50 g/2 oz butter
4 large carrots, peeled and sliced
2 large parsnips, peeled and sliced into rings
1 × 2.5 ml spoon/½ teaspoons ground ginger
1 × 2.5 ml spoon/½ teaspoon grated nutmeg
salt
freshly ground black pepper
2 × 15 ml spoons/2 tablespoons lemon juice
2 × 15 ml spoons/2 tablespoons caster sugar
To finish:
15 g/½ oz butter
freshly chopped parsley

AMERICAN

¼ cup butter
4 large carrots, peeled and sliced
2 large parsnips, peeled and sliced into rings
½ teaspoon ground ginger
½ teaspoon grated nutmeg
salt
freshly ground black pepper
2 tablespoons lemon juice
2 tablespoons sugar
To finish:
1 tablespoon butter
freshly chopped parsley

Melt half the butter in a pan, add the carrots and parsnips and fry gently for 2 minutes, turning frequently. Add the ginger, nutmeg and salt and pepper to taste, then stir well and add the lemon juice and enough water to cover the vegetables.

Cover and simmer for 12 to 15 minutes or until the vegetables are tender and most of the liquid has been absorbed. Add the sugar and the remaining butter, increase the heat and toss the vegetables until they are glossy.

To freeze: cool quickly, then transfer to a rigid container. Seal, label and freeze.

To thaw and serve: thaw at room temperature for 2 to 3 hours, then reheat gently on top of the stove with the butter, stirring occasionally. Sprinkle with parsley just before serving.

SERVES 4

SAVOURY POTATO CAKE

METRIC/IMPERIAL

100 g/4 oz butter
4 celery stalks, chopped
100 g/4 oz mushrooms, sliced
100 g/4 oz flour
1 × 15 ml spoon/1 tablespoon mustard powder
2 × 5 ml spoons/2 teaspoons baking powder
1 kg/2 lb mashed potatoes
100 g/4 oz Cheddar cheese, grated
1 × 15 ml spoon/1 tablespoon single cream

AMERICAN

½ cup butter
4 celery stalks, chopped
1 cup sliced mushrooms
1 cup flour
1 tablespoon mustard powder
2 teaspoons baking powder
4 cups mashed potatoes
1 cup grated Cheddar cheese
1 tablespoon light cream

Melt 25 g/1 oz/2 tablespoons butter in a pan, add the celery, cover and cook gently for 15 minutes. Add the mushrooms and cook for a further 5 minutes. Stir in 1 × 15 ml spoon/1 tablespoon flour and the mustard and cook for 2 minutes, stirring constantly. Remove from the heat and leave to cool.

Beat the remaining butter and flour and the baking powder into the potatoes, then roll out the dough on a floured surface to 2 rounds, one slightly larger than the other.

Put the larger round of dough on a foil dish. Stir the cheese and cream into the cooled vegetable mixture and spread over the dough, leaving a narrow margin. Cover with the remaining round of dough and press firmly to seal. Bake in a preheated moderately hot oven (200°C/400°F or Gas Mark 6) for 30 minutes.

To freeze: cool quickly. Open (flash) freeze until firm, then wrap in foil. Seal, label and return to the freezer.

To thaw and serve: place on a baking sheet and reheat from frozen in a preheated moderate oven (180°C/350°F or Gas Mark 4) for 30 minutes or until heated through.

SERVES 4

STUFFED MARROW (SQUASH)

METRIC/IMPERIAL

1 medium marrow
25 g/1 oz butter
1 onion, peeled and finely chopped
2 bacon rashers, rinds removed and finely chopped
350 g/¾ lb lean minced beef
75 g/3 oz Cheddar cheese, finely grated
100 g/4 oz long-grain rice, boiled and drained
1 × 5 ml spoon/1 teaspoon Worcestershire sauce
salt
freshly ground black pepper
1 small egg, beaten
tomato sauce, to serve

AMERICAN

1 medium summer squash
2 tablespoons butter
1 onion, peeled and finely chopped
2 bacon slices, finely chopped
1½ cups lean ground beef
¾ cup finely grated Cheddar cheese
⅔ cup long-grain rice, boiled and drained
1 teaspoon Worcestershire sauce
salt
freshly ground black pepper
1 small egg, beaten
tomato sauce, to serve

Slice one end off the marrow (squash) and scoop out the seeds.

Melt the butter in a pan, add the onion and bacon and fry gently for a few minutes. Add the beef and fry until browned, stirring constantly to break up the meat. Add the remaining ingredients and stir well to mix.

Spoon the filling into the marrow (squash), wrap in buttered foil and place on a baking sheet. Bake in a preheated moderate oven (180°C/350°F or Gas Mark 4) for 45 minutes to 1 hour or until the marrow (squash) is tender.

To freeze: cool quickly. Open (flash) freeze until firm, then pack in a freezer bag, seal, label and return to the freezer.

To thaw and serve: remove wrappings and place on a baking sheet. Reheat from frozen in a preheated moderate oven for 35 to 40 minutes or until heated through. Serve cut into thick slices with hot tomato sauce.

SERVES 4

BRUSSELS SPROUTS WITH CHESTNUTS

METRIC/IMPERIAL

225 g/½ lb chestnuts
450 g/1 lb Brussels sprouts
salt
25 g/1 oz butter
1 small onion, peeled and finely chopped
freshly ground black pepper
25 g/1 oz butter, to finish

AMERICAN

½ lb chestnuts
1 lb Brussels sprouts
salt
2 tablespoons butter
1 small onion, peeled and finely chopped
freshly ground black pepper
2 tablespoons butter, to finish

Slit the chestnuts and bake in the oven until the skins begin to separate. When cool enough to handle, peel and chop roughly.

Cook the sprouts in boiling salted water for 15 to 20 minutes or until tender, then drain and place in a rigid container.

Melt the butter in a pan, add the onion and chestnuts and fry gently for 5 minutes. Add salt and pepper to taste, then spoon over the sprouts.

To freeze: cool quickly, then seal, label and freeze.

To thaw and serve: thaw at room temperature for 2 to 3 hours, then reheat gently on top of the stove with the butter, stirring occasionally.

SERVES 4 to 6

DOLMAS

METRIC/IMPERIAL

12 medium cabbage leaves
salt
25 g/1 oz lard
1 onion, peeled and finely chopped
1 garlic clove, peeled and crushed
450 g/1 lb lean minced beef
1 × 15 ml spoon/1 tablespoon tomato purée
2 × 5 ml spoons/2 teaspoons Worcestershire sauce
freshly ground black pepper
1 × 5 ml spoon/1 teaspoon dried mixed herbs
120 ml/4 fl oz chicken stock
tomato sauce, to serve

AMERICAN

12 medium cabbage leaves
salt
2 tablespoons lard
1 onion, peeled and finely chopped
1 garlic clove, peeled and crushed
1 lb lean ground beef
1 tablespoon tomato paste
2 teaspoons Worcestershire sauce
freshly ground black pepper
1 teaspoon dried mixed herbs
½ cup chicken stock
tomato sauce, to serve

Blanch the cabbage leaves for 2 minutes in boiling salted water, then plunge into cold water. Drain well and remove any coarse stems. Melt the lard in a pan, add the onion and garlic and fry gently for 5 minutes until soft. Stir in the beef and fry for 5 minutes, stirring constantly to break up the meat. Add the remaining ingredients, except the stock, and stir well to mix.
Put a spoonful of the meat mixture in the middle of each cabbage leaf, then fold up to make a parcel. Place in a buttered foil container and pour over the stock. Cover and bake in a preheated moderate oven (180°C/350°F or Gas Mark 4) for about 30 minutes.
To freeze: cool quickly, then wrap in a freezer bag. Seal, label and freeze.
To thaw and serve: thaw in the refrigerator overnight, then reheat in a preheated moderate oven for 45 minutes or until heated through. Serve with a tomato sauce.
SERVES 6

VEGETABLE CANNELLONI

METRIC/IMPERIAL

12 cannelloni tubes
salt
225 g/½ lb tomatoes, peeled and chopped
100 g/4 oz Cheddar cheese, grated
100 g/4 oz fresh white breadcrumbs
1 × 15 ml spoon/1 tablespoon freshly chopped parsley
freshly ground black pepper
1 egg, beaten
1 × 400 g/14 oz can tomatoes, chopped
1 × 5 ml spoon/1 teaspoon dried oregano

AMERICAN

12 canneloni tubes
salt
½ lb tomatoes, peeled and chopped
1 cup grated Cheddar cheese
2 cups fresh white breadcrumbs
1 tablespoon freshly chopped parsley
freshly ground black pepper
1 egg, beaten
1 × 14 oz can tomatoes, chopped
1 teaspoon dried oregano

Plunge the cannelloni in boiling salted water for 5 minutes or until just soft. Drain, rinse under cold running water, then drain again and dry on paper towels.
Put the remaining ingredients, except the canned tomatoes and oregano, in a bowl and stir well to mix. Fill the cannelloni tubes with the mixture, then place in a single layer in an ovenproof dish or foil container. Pour over the canned tomatoes and sprinkle with the oregano.
To freeze: cover with foil, then pack in a freezer bag. Seal, label and freeze.
To thaw and serve: bake from frozen in the foil-covered dish or container in a preheated moderate oven (180°C/350°F or Gas Mark 4) for 1 to 1½ hours until heated through.
SERVES 4

RATATOUILLE

METRIC/IMPERIAL

2 medium aubergines, sliced
salt
4 × 15 ml spoons/4 tablespoons olive oil
2 medium onions, peeled and sliced
1 garlic clove, peeled and crushed
2 green peppers, cored, seeded and cut into thin strips
225 g/½ lb courgettes, trimmed and sliced
450 g/1 lb tomatoes, peeled, seeded and chopped
freshly ground black pepper

AMERICAN

2 medium eggplants, sliced
salt
¼ cup olive oil
2 medium onions, peeled and sliced
1 garlic clove, peeled and crushed
2 green peppers, cored, seeded and cut into thin strips
½ lb zucchini, trimmed and sliced
1 lb tomatoes, peeled, seeded and chopped
freshly ground black pepper

Sprinkle the aubergines (eggplants) with salt and leave for 30 minutes. Drain off any liquid, rinse under cold running water, then dry on paper towels. Heat half the oil in a pan, add the aubergines (eggplants) and fry until golden brown, then drain on paper towels.

Heat the remaining oil in a pan, add the onions and garlic and fry gently for 5 minutes until the onions are soft. Add the peppers and courgettes (zucchini) and fry for 3 minutes, stirring.

Add the aubergines (eggplants) to the pan with the tomatoes and salt and pepper to taste. Cover and simmer for 45 minutes or until the vegetables are tender.

To freeze: cool quickly, then pour into a rigid container. Seal, label and freeze.

To thaw and serve: reheat from frozen in a covered casserole in a preheated moderate oven (180°C/350°F or Gas Mark 4) for 30 to 40 minutes or until heated through. Ratatouille may also be served chilled: thaw in the container in the refrigerator overnight.

SERVES 4 to 6

VEGETABLE PIE

METRIC/IMPERIAL

For the cheese pastry:
175 g/6 oz flour
100 g/4 oz butter
75 g/3 oz Cheddar cheese, finely grated
a little water, to mix
1 egg, beaten, to finish

For the filling:
50 g/2 oz butter
1 onion, peeled and sliced
3 carrots, peeled and sliced
1 × 200 g/7 oz can sweetcorn, drained
50 g/2 oz mushrooms, sliced
4 celery stalks, chopped
1 leek, sliced
1 × 298 g/10½ oz can condensed tomato soup
150 ml/¼ pint stock
salt
freshly ground black pepper

AMERICAN

For the cheese pastry:
1½ cups flour
½ cup butter
¾ cup finely grated Cheddar cheese
a little water, to mix
1 egg, beaten, to finish

For the filling:
¼ cup butter
1 onion, peeled and sliced
3 carrots, peeled and sliced
1 × 7 oz can corn kernels, drained
½ cup sliced mushrooms
4 celery stalks, chopped
1 leek, sliced
1 × 10½ oz can condensed tomato soup
⅔ cup stock
salt
freshly ground black pepper

To make the pastry: sift the flour into a bowl, add the butter in pieces and rub into the flour until the mixture resembles fine breadcrumbs. Stir in the cheese and bind the mixture together with water. Wrap in foil and leave in a cool place.

To make the filling: melt the butter in a pan, add the vegetables and fry gently for 10 minutes. Transfer to a 900 ml/1½ pint/3¾ cup pie dish, pour in the soup and stock and sprinkle with salt and pepper to taste.

Roll out the dough on a floured surface and use to cover the top of the pie dish. Trim and flute the edges and use the trimmings to decorate the top of the pie.

To freeze: open (flash) freeze until firm, wrap in foil, then pack in a freezer bag. Seal, label and return to the freezer.

To thaw and serve: remove wrappings and brush the dough with the beaten egg. Bake from frozen in a preheated moderately hot oven (200°C/400°F or Gas Mark 6) for 15 minutes, then reduce the heat to moderate (180°C/350°F or Gas Mark 4) and bake for a further 50 minutes to 1 hour until heated through. Cover with foil if pastry becomes too brown during cooking.

SERVES 4

BACON-STUFFED POTATOES

METRIC/IMPERIAL

2 large old potatoes, scrubbed
75 g/3 oz lean bacon rashers, rinds removed, chopped and fried
a little milk
1 × 15 ml spoon/1 tablespoon freshly chopped parsley
salt
freshly ground black pepper

AMERICAN

2 large old potatoes, scrubbed
4–5 lean bacon slices, chopped and fried
a little milk
1 tablespoon freshly chopped parsley
salt
freshly ground black pepper

Prick the potato skins and bake in a preheated moderately hot oven (200°C/400°F or Gas Mark 6) for 1 to 1½ hours until soft. Cut the potatoes in half lengthways and scoop out the flesh. Put the flesh in a bowl with the remaining ingredients, beat well, then spoon into the skins.
To freeze: cool quickly. Open (flash) freeze until firm, then wrap individually in foil and pack in a freezer bag. Seal, label and return to the freezer.
To thaw and serve: remove wrappings and place the frozen potatoes on a baking sheet. Reheat in a preheated moderately hot oven (190°C/375°F or Gas Mark 5) for 10 minutes or until heated through.
SERVES 4

CHEESE-STUFFED POTATOES

Make as for Bacon-Stuffed Potatoes (see above), substituting 75 g/3 oz/¾ cup grated cheese and 1 × 15 ml spoon/1 tablespoon freshly chopped mixed herbs for the bacon and parsley. Freeze, thaw and serve as for Bacon-Stuffed Potatoes.
SERVES 4

RÖSTI

METRIC/IMPERIAL

1 kg/2 lb potatoes, scrubbed
salt
25 g/1 oz butter
100 g/4 oz streaky bacon rashers, rinds removed and chopped
75 g/3 oz Emmenthal or Gruyère cheese, grated
freshly ground black pepper
50 g/2 oz butter, to finish

AMERICAN

2 lb potatoes, scrubbed
salt
2 tablespoons butter
¼ lb fatty bacon slices, chopped
¾ cup grated Emmenthal or Gruyère cheese
freshly ground black pepper
¼ cup butter, to finish

Cook the unpeeled potatoes in boiling salted water for 20 minutes or until just cooked. Leave to cool, then peel and grate the flesh into a bowl. Melt the butter in a pan, add the bacon and fry briskly for 3 to 4 minutes until crisp. Drain, then add to the potatoes with the cheese and salt and pepper to taste. Beat well to mix, then turn the mixture onto a sheet of foil and shape into a circle the size of a frying pan (skillet).
To freeze: cool quickly. Wrap in the foil, then pack in a freezer bag. Seal, label and freeze.
To thaw and serve: melt the remaining butter in the frying pan (skillet), add the frozen potato cake and cook gently for 15 minutes on each side. Turn out onto a warmed serving platter and serve immediately.
SERVES 4

POTATO AND LENTIL GOULASH

METRIC/IMPERIAL

25 g/1 oz butter
1 large onion, peeled and chopped
1 × 225 g/8 oz can tomatoes
2 × 15 ml spoons/2 tablespoons Worcestershire sauce
2 × 15 ml spoons/2 tablespoons tomato purée
150 ml/¼ pint soured cream
salt
freshly ground black pepper
450 g/1 lb potatoes, peeled, boiled and thickly sliced
100 g/4 oz lentils, boiled and drained
50 g/2 oz Cheddar cheese, grated

AMERICAN

2 tablespoons butter
1 large onion, peeled and chopped
1 × ½ lb can tomatoes
2 tablespoons Worcestershire sauce
2 tablespoons tomato paste
⅔ cup sour cream
salt
freshly ground black pepper
1 lb potatoes, peeled, boiled and thickly sliced
½ cup lentils, boiled and drained
½ cup grated Cheddar cheese

Melt the butter in a pan, add the onion and fry gently until soft. Add the tomatoes, Worcestershire sauce and tomato purée (paste), then remove from the heat and stir in the sour(ed) cream with salt and pepper to taste.
Put the potatoes and lentils in layers in a buttered ovenproof dish or foil container, beginning and ending with a layer of potatoes. Pour over the tomato sauce and sprinkle with the cheese.
Cook in a preheated moderately hot oven (190°C/375°F or Gas Mark 5) for about 20 minutes or until the cheese is golden brown.
To freeze: cool quickly, then cover with foil. Seal, label and freeze.
To thaw and serve: thaw at room temperature for 4 hours, then reheat in the covered dish or container in a preheated moderately hot oven for 40 minutes or until heated through.
SERVES 4

SAUSAGE-STUFFED POTATOES

METRIC/IMPERIAL
2 large potatoes, scrubbed and pricked with a skewer
3 streaky bacon rashers, rinds removed and chopped
4 chipolata sausages, sliced
225 g/½ lb cottage cheese
1 × 5 ml spoon/1 teaspoon prepared mustard
salt
freshly ground black pepper
1–2 × 15 ml spoons/1–2 tablespoons single cream
freshly chopped parsley or sprigs of watercress, to garnish

AMERICAN
2 large potatoes, scrubbed and pricked with a skewer
3 fatty bacon slices, chopped
4 link sausages, sliced
1 cup cottage cheese
1 teaspoon prepared mustard
salt
freshly ground black pepper
1–2 tablespoons light cream
freshly chopped parsley or sprigs of watercress, to garnish

Bake the potatoes in a preheated moderately hot oven (200°C/400°F or Gas Mark 6) for about 1 hour or until soft. Leave to cool slightly, then cut in half and scoop out the potato flesh.
Put the bacon in a pan and fry briskly in its own fat for 3 minutes. Add the sausages and fry gently for 8 to 10 minutes until browned on all sides. Remove from the pan with a slotted spoon.
Put the potato flesh, bacon and sausages in a bowl with the remaining ingredients, except the parsley or watercress, and stir well to mix. Divide equally between the potato skins.
To freeze: cool quickly. Open (flash) freeze until firm, wrap individually in foil, then pack in a freezer bag. Seal, label and return to the freezer.
To thaw and serve: remove wrappings and place on a baking sheet. Reheat from frozen in a preheated moderately hot oven (190°C/375°F or Gas Mark 5) for 40 minutes or until heated through. Garnish with parsley or watercress just before serving.
SERVES 4

POTATO HOTCAKES

METRIC/IMPERIAL
1 kg/2 lb potatoes, peeled
2 × 15 ml spoons/2 tablespoons flour
2 × 5 ml spoons/2 teaspoons mustard powder
2 × 15 ml spoons/2 tablespoons finely grated onion
salt
freshly ground black pepper
2 small eggs, beaten
vegetable oil for frying

AMERICAN
2 lb potatoes, peeled
2 tablespoons flour
2 teaspoons mustard powder
2 tablespoons finely grated onion
salt
freshly ground black pepper
2 small eggs, beaten
vegetable oil for frying

Soak the potatoes in cold water for 30 minutes, then drain. Grate into a bowl and drain off any starchy liquid, then add the remaining ingredients, except the oil, and stir well to mix.
Heat the oil in a frying pan (skillet), add the mixture in spoonfuls and fry until browned on both sides.
To freeze: cool quickly. Open (flash) freeze until firm, then pack in a rigid container, separating each layer with foil. Seal, label and return to the freezer.
To thaw and serve: remove wrappings and place on a baking sheet. Reheat from frozen in a preheated moderate oven (180°C/350°F or Gas Mark 4) for 30 minutes or until heated through.
SERVES 6 to 8

POTATO CROQUETTES

METRIC/IMPERIAL

1 kg/2 lb potatoes, peeled and halved
salt
50 g/2 oz butter
1 egg, beaten
1 × 15 ml spoon/1 tablespoon milk
freshly ground black pepper
vegetable oil for deep-frying, to finish
For the coating:
a little flour
2 eggs, beaten
50 g/2 oz fresh white breadcrumbs

AMERICAN

2 lb potatoes, peeled and halved
salt
¼ cup butter
1 egg, beaten
1 × 15 ml spoon/1 tablespoon milk
freshly ground black pepper
vegetable oil for deep-frying, to finish
For the coating:
a little flour
2 eggs, beaten
1 cup fresh white breadcrumbs

Cook the potatoes in boiling salted water for 15 to 20 minutes until tender. Drain well, then mash with the butter and beat in the egg, milk and salt and pepper to taste. Leave to cool.
Shape the mixture into 16 croquettes by rolling with floured hands. Dip the croquettes in the beaten eggs, then roll in the breadcrumbs. Chill in the refrigerator until firm.
To freeze: open (flash) freeze until firm, then pack in a rigid container, separating each layer with foil. Seal, label and return to the freezer.
To thaw and serve: remove from the container and thaw in the refrigerator for 2 hours. Deep-fry in hot oil for 4 to 5 minutes until golden brown, then drain well on paper towels and serve immediately.
MAKES 16

LAMB AND APPLE POTATOES

METRIC/IMPERIAL

6 large potatoes, scrubbed and pricked with a skewer
salt
1 large onion, peeled and finely sliced
2 medium dessert apples, peeled, cored and finely diced
350 g/¾ lb cooked lamb, finely diced
25 g/1 oz butter
freshly ground black pepper
75 g/3 oz Cheddar cheese, grated

AMERICAN

6 large potatoes, scrubbed and pricked with a skewer
salt
1 large onion, peeled and finely sliced
2 medium dessert apples, peeled, cored and finely diced
1½ cups finely diced cooked lamb
2 tablespoons butter
freshly ground black pepper
¾ cup grated Cheddar cheese

Rub the potatoes with salt, wrap in foil and bake in a preheated moderately hot oven (190°C/375°F or Gas Mark 5) for 1 to 1½ hours or until soft.
Leave to cool slightly, then cut in half and scoop out the potato flesh. Put in a bowl with the remaining ingredients, except the cheese, and stir well to mix. Divide the mixture equally between the potato skins, then sprinkle the tops with the cheese.
To freeze: cool quickly. Open (flash) freeze until firm, wrap individually in foil, then pack in a freezer bag. Seal, label and return to the freezer.
To thaw and serve: remove wrappings and thaw at room temperature for 4 hours. Place on a baking sheet and reheat in a preheated moderately hot oven for 30 minutes or until golden brown and heated through.
SERVES 6

POTATOES NORMANDE

METRIC/IMPERIAL

1 kg/2 lb potatoes, peeled and thinly sliced
40 g/1½ oz butter
salt
freshly ground black pepper
300 ml/½ pint milk

AMERICAN

2 lb potatoes, peeled and thinly sliced
3 tablespoons butter
salt
freshly ground black pepper
1¼ cups milk

Put the potato slices in layers in a buttered ovenproof dish or foil container, sprinkling each layer liberally with salt and pepper. Pour in the milk and dot with the butter. Bake in a preheated moderate oven (180°C/350°F or Gas Mark 4) for 1 to 1½ hours until the potatoes are soft.
To freeze: cool quickly, then cover with foil and pack in a freezer bag. Seal, label and freeze.
To thaw and serve: remove wrappings and thaw

at room temperature for 4 hours. Reheat in a preheated moderately hot oven (190°C/375°F or Gas Mark 5) for 30 minutes or until heated through.
SERVES 4 to 6

BUBBLE AND SQUEAK BAKE

METRIC/IMPERIAL
450 g/1 lb green cabbage, shredded
salt
675 g/1½ lb potatoes, peeled, boiled and mashed with milk and butter
1 small onion, peeled and finely chopped
2 tomatoes, peeled and chopped
freshly ground black pepper
75 g/3 oz Cheddar cheese, grated

AMERICAN
1 lb green cabbage, shredded
salt
1½ lb potatoes, peeled, boiled and mashed with milk and butter
1 small onion, peeled and finely chopped
2 tomatoes, peeled and chopped
freshly ground black pepper
¾ cup grated Cheddar cheese

Cook the cabbage in boiling salted water for 5 minutes, then drain and chop finely. Turn into a bowl and add the mashed potatoes, onion, tomatoes and salt and pepper to taste. Stir well to mix.
Spoon into a buttered ovenproof dish or foil container, sprinkle with the cheese and cook in a preheated moderately hot oven (200°C/400°F or Gas Mark 6) for 30 minutes or until evenly browned.
To freeze: cool quickly, then cover with foil. Seal, label and freeze.
To thaw and serve: thaw at room temperature for 3 hours, then reheat in a preheated moderately hot oven (190°C/375°F or Gas Mark 5) for 30 minutes or until heated through.
SERVES 4

GLAZED ONIONS

METRIC/IMPERIAL
50 g/2 oz butter
2 × 15 ml spoons/2 tablespoons vegetable oil
1 kg/2 lb small pickling onions, peeled
150 ml/¼ pint stock or red wine
1 bouquet garni
salt
freshly ground black pepper

AMERICAN
¼ cup butter
2 tablespoons vegetable oil
2 lb baby onions, peeled
⅔ cup stock or red wine
1 bouquet garni
salt
freshly ground black pepper

Heat the butter and oil in a flameproof casserole dish, add the onions and fry until browned, turning frequently. Add the remaining ingredients, cover and cook in a preheated moderate oven (180°C/350°F or Gas Mark 4) for 25 to 30 minutes or until the onions are tender. Remove the bouquet garni.
To freeze: cool quickly. Leave in the casserole or transfer to a rigid container. Cover, then wrap in a freezer bag or foil. Seal, label and freeze.
To thaw and serve: thaw at room temperature for 4 hours, then reheat gently on top of the stove, stirring occasionally.
SERVES 6

SALSIFY WITH PARSLEY AND LEMON

METRIC/IMPERIAL
450 g/1 lb salsify
salt
50 g/2 oz butter
1 × 15 ml spoon/1 tablespoon lemon juice
freshly chopped parsley, to garnish

AMERICAN
1 lb salsify
salt
¼ cup butter
1 tablespoon lemon juice
freshly chopped parsley, to garnish

Cook the salsify in boiling salted water for 30 minutes or until tender. Drain and rinse under cold running water, then peel and cut into 7.5 cm/3 inch pieces.
Melt the butter in a pan, add the salsify and lemon juice and simmer for 10 minutes, stirring occasionally.
To freeze: cool quickly, then transfer to a rigid container. Seal, label and freeze.
To thaw and serve: thaw at room temperature for 2 to 3 hours, then reheat gently on top of the stove, stirring occasionally. Sprinkle with parsley just before serving.
SERVES 4

SPANISH OMELET

METRIC/IMPERIAL
25 g/1 oz butter
1 medium onion, peeled and finely sliced
1 green pepper, cored, seeded and finely sliced
1 red pepper, cored, seeded and finely sliced
225 g/½ lb new potatoes, scrubbed, boiled and finely sliced
6 eggs
3 × 15 ml spoons/3 tablespoons water
salt
freshly ground black pepper

AMERICAN
2 tablespoons butter
1 medium onion, peeled and finely sliced
1 green pepper, cored, seeded and finely sliced
1 red pepper, cored, seeded and finely sliced
½ lb new potatoes, scrubbed, boiled and finely sliced
6 eggs
3 tablespoons water
salt
freshly ground black pepper

Melt the butter in a large frying pan (skillet), add the onion and peppers and fry gently for 7 minutes. Add the potatoes and heat through. Put the eggs in a bowl with the water and salt and pepper to taste, beat well to mix, then pour into the pan. Cook gently until the eggs set, stirring occasionally. Remove from the pan.
To freeze: cool quickly. Open (flash) freeze until firm, then wrap in foil, seal, label and return to the freezer.
To thaw and serve: remove wrappings and place in an ovenproof dish. Cover with foil and reheat from frozen in a preheated moderate oven (180°C/350°F or Gas Mark 4) for 30 minutes or until heated through. Serve cut into wedges. To serve cold, remove wrappings and thaw at room temperature for 4 hours.
SERVES 4

WELSH CASSEROLE

METRIC/IMPERIAL
25 g/1 oz butter
1 large onion, peeled and sliced into rings
1 × 225 g/8 oz can tomatoes
150 ml/¼ pint beef stock
1 × 225 g/8 oz packet frozen Brussels sprouts
1 × 175 g/6 oz packet frozen sweetcorn
salt
freshly ground black pepper
To finish:
50 g/2 oz Cheddar cheese, grated
4 slices of toast, crusts removed and cut into cubes

AMERICAN
2 tablespoons butter
1 large onion, peeled and sliced into rings
1 × ½ lb can tomatoes
⅔ cup beef stock
1 × ½ lb package frozen Brussels sprouts
1 × 6 oz package frozen corn kernels
salt
freshly ground black pepper
To finish:
½ cup grated Cheddar cheese
4 slices of toast, crusts removed and cut into cubes

Melt the butter in a pan, add the onion and fry gently until soft. Add the remaining ingredients, cover and cook gently until the vegetables are tender.
To freeze: cool quickly, then transfer to a rigid container. Seal, label and freeze.
To thaw and serve: thaw at room temperature for 4 hours, then reheat gently on top of the stove, stirring occasionally. Stir in half the cheese and pour into a heatproof serving dish. Top with the cubes of toast, sprinkle with the remaining cheese and put under a preheated grill (broiler) until golden brown.
SERVES 6

AUBERGINE (EGGPLANT) AND TOMATO PIE

METRIC/IMPERIAL
450 g/1 lb aubergines, finely sliced
flour for coating
vegetable oil for frying
225 g/½ lb Bel Paese or Edam cheese, finely sliced
25 g/1 oz grated Parmesan cheese
For the sauce:
1 × 400 g/14 oz can tomatoes
1 small onion, peeled and finely chopped
1 carrot, peeled and finely chopped
1 celery stalk, finely chopped
pinch of dried oregano
pinch of dried basil
1 × 2.5 ml spoon/½ teaspoon sugar
salt
freshly ground black pepper

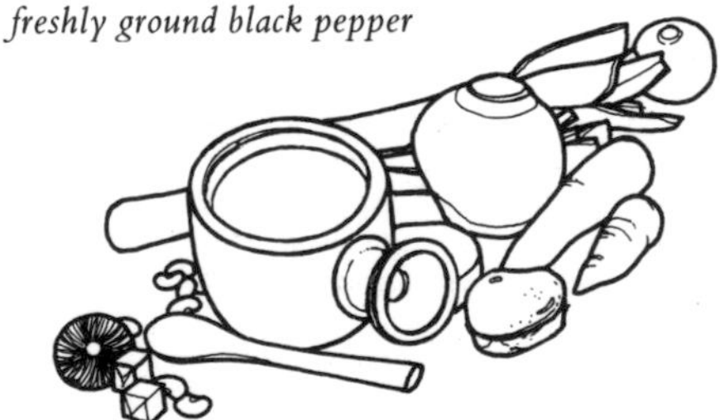

AMERICAN
1 lb eggplants, finely sliced
flour for coating
vegetable oil for frying
½ lb Bel Paese or Edam cheese, finely sliced
¼ cup grated Parmesan cheese
For the sauce:
1 × 14 oz can tomatoes
1 small onion, peeled and finely chopped
1 carrot, peeled and finely chopped
1 celery stalk, finely chopped
pinch of dried oregano
pinch of dried basil
½ teaspoon sugar
salt
freshly ground black pepper

Put all the ingredients for the sauce in a pan, cover and simmer for 30 minutes, then leave to cool slightly.
Meanwhile, sprinkle the aubergine (eggplant) slices with salt and leave for 30 minutes. Drain off any liquid, rinse under cold running water, then dry on paper towels.
Work the sauce to a smooth purée in an electric blender or Mouli-légumes (food mill), or rub through a sieve (strainer).
Fry the aubergines (eggplants) in hot oil until golden brown on both sides, then drain on paper towels.
Arrange the aubergines (eggplants), sauce and Bel Paese or Edam cheese in layers in a buttered ovenproof dish or foil container, finishing with a layer of sauce. Sprinkle with the Parmesan.
Cook in a preheated moderately hot oven (190°C/375°F or Gas Mark 5) for 25 to 30 minutes.
To freeze: cool quickly, then cover with foil. Seal, label and freeze.
To thaw and serve: thaw at room temperature for 4 hours, then reheat in the covered dish or container in a preheated moderately hot oven for 20 to 30 minutes or until heated through.
SERVES 4 to 6

COURGETTES (ZUCCHINI) PROVENÇALE

METRIC/IMPERIAL
2 × 15 ml spoons/2 tablespoons olive oil
450 g/1 lb courgettes, sliced
1 onion, peeled and chopped
1 garlic clove, peeled and crushed
450 g/1 lb tomatoes, peeled and sliced
salt
freshly ground black pepper
100 g/4 oz Cheddar cheese, grated

AMERICAN
2 tablespoons olive oil
1 lb zucchini, sliced
1 onion, peeled and chopped
1 garlic clove, peeled and crushed
1 lb tomatoes, peeled and sliced
salt
freshly ground black pepper
1 cup grated Cheddar cheese

Heat the oil in a pan, add the courgettes (zucchini), onion and garlic and fry gently for 3 minutes. Stir in the tomatoes and salt and pepper to taste and cook for a further 2 to 3 minutes.
Put half the mixture in an ovenproof dish or foil container, sprinkle with half the cheese, then repeat with the remaining vegetable mixture and cheese.
To freeze: cool quickly, then cover with foil. Seal, label and freeze.
To thaw and serve: remove wrappings and reheat from frozen in a preheated moderate oven (180°C/350°F or Gas Mark 4) for 45 minutes or until golden brown and heated through.
SERVES 4

BRAISED CELERIAC

METRIC/IMPERIAL
1 kg/2 lb celeriac, peeled, sliced and blanched
25 g/1 oz butter
approx 450 ml/¾ pint stock
salt
freshly ground black pepper

AMERICAN
2 lb celeriac, peeled, sliced and blanched
2 tablespoons butter
approx 2 cups stock
salt
freshly ground black pepper

Put the celeriac in a pan with the butter and enough stock to cover. Add salt and pepper to taste, cover and simmer for 20 to 30 minutes or until the celeriac is tender but not too soft. Remove the celeriac from the pan with a slotted spoon and place in a rigid container. Boil the cooking liquid to reduce slightly, then pour over the celeriac.
To freeze: cool quickly, then seal, label and freeze.
To thaw and serve: thaw at room temperature for 2 to 3 hours, then reheat gently on top of the stove, stirring occasionally.
SERVES 4

FENNEL AU GRATIN

METRIC/IMPERIAL

50 g/2 oz butter
4 heads of fennel, outer leaves removed, blanched and quartered
25 g/1 oz flour
300 ml/½ pint milk
50 g/2 oz Cheddar cheese, grated
salt
freshly ground black pepper
25 g/1 oz fresh white breadcrumbs

AMERICAN

¼ cup butter
4 heads of fennel, outer leaves removed, blanched and quartered
¼ cup flour
1¼ cups milk
½ cup grated Cheddar cheese
salt
freshly ground black pepper
½ cup fresh white breadcrumbs

Melt the butter in a pan, add the fennel and fry gently for 10 to 20 minutes or until tender, stirring occasionally. Remove from the pan with a slotted spoon and place in an ovenproof dish or foil container.

Stir the flour into the butter remaining in the pan and cook for 2 minutes, stirring constantly. Remove from the heat and gradually stir in the milk. Return to the heat and bring to the boil, stirring constantly. Simmer until thick, then stir in the cheese and salt and pepper to taste. Pour over the fennel and sprinkle with the breadcrumbs.

To freeze: cool quickly, then cover with foil. Seal, label and freeze.

To thaw and serve: remove wrappings and thaw at room temperature for 4 hours. Reheat in a preheated moderately hot oven (190°C/375°F or Gas Mark 5) for 25 to 30 minutes or until golden brown and heated through.

SERVES 4

BROCCOLI AND HAM AU GRATIN

METRIC/IMPERIAL

225 g/½ lb broccoli spears
salt
4 slices of cooked ham
25 g/1 oz butter
25 g/1 oz flour
450 ml/¾ pint milk
75 g/3 oz cheese, grated
freshly ground black pepper

AMERICAN

½ lb broccoli spears
salt
4 slices of cooked ham
2 tablespoons butter
¼ cup flour
2 cups milk
¾ cup grated cheese
freshly ground black pepper

Cook the broccoli in boiling salted water for 10 minutes, then drain and divide into 4 equal portions. Roll a slice of ham around each bundle, then arrange in the bottom of an ovenproof dish or foil container.

Melt the butter in a pan, add the flour and cook for 2 minutes, stirring constantly. Remove from the heat and gradually stir in the milk, then return to the heat and bring to the boil, stirring constantly. Simmer until thick, then stir in 50 g/2 oz/¼ cup cheese and salt and pepper to taste. Pour the sauce over the ham and scatter the remaining cheese over the top.

To freeze: cool quickly, then cover with foil and pack in a freezer bag. Seal, label and freeze.

To thaw and serve: remove wrappings and thaw at room temperature for 4 hours. Bake in a preheated moderately hot oven (200°C/400°F or Gas Mark 6) for 25 to 35 minutes until golden brown and heated through.

SERVES 4

HAM AND LEEK AU GRATIN

METRIC/IMPERIAL

8 large leeks, trimmed
salt
8 thin slices of cooked ham
600 ml/1 pint cheese sauce
For the topping:
2 × 15 ml spoons/2 tablespoons grated Cheddar cheese
2 × 15 ml spoons/2 tablespoons fresh white breadcrumbs

AMERICAN

8 large leeks, trimmed
salt
8 thin slices of cooked ham
2½ cups cheese sauce
For the topping:
2 tablespoons grated Cheddar cheese
2 tablespoons fresh white breadcrumbs

Cook the leeks in boiling salted water for 20 minutes, then drain and pat dry with paper towels.
Wrap each leek in a slice of ham and place in a buttered ovenproof dish or foil container. Pour over the cheese sauce and sprinkle with the cheese and breadcrumbs.
To freeze: cool quickly, then cover with foil. Seal, label and freeze.
To thaw and serve: thaw at room temperature for 4 hours, then reheat, uncovered, in a preheated moderate oven (180°C/350°F or Gas Mark 4) for 20 minutes or until crisp and brown and heated through.
SERVES 4

BRAISED JERUSALEM ARTICHOKES

METRIC/IMPERIAL
25 g/1 oz butter
1 × 15 ml spoon/1 tablespoon sugar
1 kg/2 lb Jerusalem artichokes, peeled and sliced
450 g/1 lb pickling onions, peeled
salt
freshly ground black pepper

AMERICAN
2 tablespoons butter
1 tablespoon sugar
2 lb Jerusalem artichokes, peeled and sliced
1 lb baby onions, peeled
salt
freshly ground black pepper

Melt the butter in a pan, add the sugar and stir. Add the artichokes and onions, cover and braise very gently for about 30 minutes or until tender and golden brown, stirring occasionally. Add salt and pepper to taste.
To freeze: cool quickly, then transfer to a foil container and cover with foil. Seal, label and freeze.
To thaw and serve: thaw at room temperature for 4 hours, then reheat in the covered container in a preheated moderate oven (180°C/350°F or Gas Mark 4) for 30 minutes or until heated through.
SERVES 4

LEEK, CELERY AND CHEESE PIE

METRIC/IMPERIAL
450 g/1 lb leeks, sliced
3 celery stalks, chopped
450 ml/¾ pint milk
salt
freshly ground black pepper
25 g/1 oz butter
25 g/1 oz flour
100 g/4 oz Cheddar cheese, grated
100 g/4 oz cut macaroni
To finish:
25 g/1 oz fresh white breadcrumbs
15 g/½ oz butter

AMERICAN
1 lb leeks, sliced
3 celery stalks, chopped
2 cups milk
salt
freshly ground black pepper
2 tablespoons butter
¼ cup flour
1 cup grated Cheddar cheese
1 cup cut macaroni
To finish:
½ cup fresh white breadcrumbs
1 tablespoon butter

Put the leeks and celery in a pan with the milk and salt and pepper to taste. Cover, simmer until tender, then strain and reserve the cooking liquid.
Melt the butter in the rinsed-out pan, stir in the flour and cook for 2 minutes, stirring constantly. Remove from the heat and gradually stir in the cooking liquid. Simmer until thick, then add the cheese.
Cook the macaroni in boiling salted water until 'al dente', drain and place in a buttered ovenproof dish, or foil container. Add the leeks and celery and pour over the sauce.
To freeze: cool quickly, then cover with foil. Seal, label and freeze.
To thaw and serve: remove wrappings and sprinkle with the breadcrumbs. Dot with the butter and reheat from frozen in a preheated moderately hot oven (200°C/400°F or Gas Mark 6) for 45 minutes or until golden brown and heated through.
SERVES 4

QUICHE LORRAINE

METRIC/IMPERIAL

basic shortcrust pastry dough made with 175 g/6 oz flour
25 g/1 oz butter
1 onion, peeled and chopped
100 g/4 oz streaky bacon rashers, rinds removed and chopped
150 ml/¼ pint milk
300 ml/½ pint single cream
3 eggs, beaten
pinch of grated nutmeg
salt
freshly ground black pepper

AMERICAN

basic pie dough made with 1½ cups flour
2 tablespoons butter
1 onion, peeled and chopped
6 fatty bacon slices, chopped
⅔ cup milk
1¼ cups light cream
3 eggs, beaten
pinch of grated nutmeg
salt
freshly ground black pepper

Roll out the dough on a floured surface and use to line a 20 cm/8 inch flan ring set on a baking sheet.

Melt the butter in a pan, add the onion and bacon and fry gently until lightly coloured. Put in the bottom of the pastry case (pie shell). Put the milk and cream in a pan and heat to just below boiling point. Remove from the heat and beat in the eggs, nutmeg and salt and pepper to taste. Pour over the onion and bacon.

Bake in a preheated moderately hot oven (200°C/400°F or Gas Mark 6) for 10 minutes, then reduce the heat to moderate (160°C/325°F or Gas Mark 3) and bake for a further 35 minutes or until the filling is set. Cool quickly on a wire rack, then remove the flan ring.

To freeze: open (flash) freeze until firm, wrap in foil, then pack in a freezer bag. Seal, label and return to the freezer.

To thaw and serve: remove wrappings and place the quiche on a baking sheet. Thaw at room temperature for 4 hours, then reheat in a preheated moderate oven (180°C/350°F or Gas Mark 4) for 25 minutes or until heated through.

SERVES 4 to 6

INDIVIDUAL SPINACH AND GREEN PEPPER QUICHES

METRIC/IMPERIAL

basic shortcrust pastry dough made with 100 g/4 oz flour
25 g/1 oz butter
1 medium onion, peeled and finely chopped
1 small green pepper, cored, seeded and finely chopped
1 egg, beaten
150 ml/¼ pint single cream
1 × 175 g/6 oz packet frozen chopped spinach, thawed
pinch of grated nutmeg
salt
freshly ground black pepper

AMERICAN

basic pie dough made with 1 cup flour
2 tablespoons butter
1 medium onion, peeled and finely chopped
1 small green pepper, cored, seeded and finely chopped
1 egg, beaten
⅔ cup light cream
1 × 6 oz package frozen chopped spinach, thawed
pinch of grated nutmeg
salt
freshly ground black pepper

Roll out the dough on a floured surface and use to line 4 individual 10 cm/4 inch patty tins. Bake blind in a preheated moderately hot oven (200°C/400°F or Gas Mark 6) for 10 minutes.

Melt the butter in a pan, add the onion and green pepper and fry gently until soft. Transfer to a bowl, add the remaining ingredients and beat well to mix. Pour into the pastry cases

(pie shells), then bake in a preheated moderate oven (180°C/350°F or Gas Mark 4) for 25 minutes or until the filling is set. Cool quickly on a wire rack.
To freeze: open (flash) freeze until firm, remove the tins, then wrap the quiches individually in foil. Pack in a freezer bag. Seal, label and return to the freezer.
To thaw and serve: remove wrappings and return the quiches to the tins. Reheat from frozen in a preheated moderate oven for 25 minutes or until heated through.
MAKES 4

CHEESE AND VEGETABLE QUICHES

METRIC/IMPERIAL
basic shortcrust pastry dough made with 225 g/½ lb flour
25 g/1 oz butter
1 small onion, peeled and finely chopped
1 small red pepper, cored, seeded and finely chopped
2 medium courgettes, thinly sliced
2 eggs
300 ml/½ pint milk
pinch of mustard powder
salt
freshly ground black pepper
25 g/1 oz grated Parmesan cheese, to finish

AMERICAN
basic pie dough made with 2 cups flour
2 tablespoons butter
1 small onion, peeled and finely chopped
1 small red pepper, cored, seeded and finely chopped
2 medium zucchini, thinly sliced
2 eggs
1¼ cups milk
pinch of mustard powder
salt
freshly ground black pepper
¼ cup grated Parmesan cheese, to finish

Roll out the dough on a floured surface and cut out 12 circles using a 10 cm/4 inch plain cutter. Use to line individual foil baking cases.
Melt the butter in a pan, add the onion, red pepper and courgettes (zucchini), cover and cook gently until tender. Leave to cool, then divide equally between the 12 cases.
Put the remaining ingredients, except the Parmesan cheese, in a bowl and beat well to mix. Pour into the pastry cases (pie shells).
To freeze: open (flash) freeze until firm, wrap individually in foil, then pack in a freezer bag. Seal, label and return to the freezer.
To thaw and serve: remove wrappings and place the quiches on a baking sheet. Bake from frozen in a preheated moderately hot oven (200°C/400°F or Gas Mark 6) for 10 minutes, then sprinkle with the Parmesan cheese and bake for a further 15 to 20 minutes or until the filling is set.
MAKES 12

INDIVIDUAL HAM QUICHES

METRIC/IMPERIAL
basic shortcrust pastry dough made with 225 g/½ lb flour
1 shallot, peeled and chopped
15 g/½ oz butter
100 g/4 oz cooked ham, finely chopped
75 g/3 oz Gruyère cheese, grated
2 eggs
6 × 15 ml spoons/6 tablespoons single cream
2 × 5 ml spoons/2 teaspoons snipped chives
salt
freshly ground black pepper

AMERICAN
basic pie dough made with 2 cups flour
1 shallot, peeled and chopped
1 tablespoon butter
½ cup finely chopped cooked ham
¾ cup grated Gruyère cheese
2 eggs
6 tablespoons light cream
2 teaspoons snipped chives
salt
freshly ground black pepper

Roll out the dough on a floured surface and use to line 20 deep patty tins. Bake blind in a preheated moderately hot oven (190°C/375°F or Gas Mark 5) for 15 minutes.
Melt the butter in a pan, add the shallot and fry gently for 5 minutes. Mix with the ham, divide equally between the pastry cases (tart shells), then sprinkle with the cheese. Put the remaining ingredients in a bowl and beat well to mix. Spoon into the cases (shells), then bake in a preheated moderate oven (160°C/325°F or Gas Mark 3) for 20 minutes or until the filling is set.
To freeze: cool quickly. Open (flash) freeze until firm, wrap individually in foil, then pack in foil. Pack in a freezer bag. Seal, label and return to the freezer.
To thaw and serve: remove wrappings and return the quiches to the patty tins. Reheat from frozen in a preheated moderate oven (180°C/350°F or Gas Mark 4) for 15 to 20 minutes or until heated through.
MAKES 20

PISSALADIÈRE

METRIC/IMPERIAL

basic shortcrust pastry dough made with 175 g/6 oz flour
25 g/1 oz butter
2 large onions, peeled and sliced
2 × 5 ml spoons/2 teaspoons cornflour
2 × 5 ml spoons/2 teaspoons tomato purée
1 × 400 g/14 oz can tomatoes
1 × 2.5 ml spoon/½ teaspoon dried mixed herbs
freshly ground black pepper
1 × 50 g/2 oz can anchovy fillets, drained and soaked in milk
few black olives, halved and stoned

AMERICAN

basic pie dough made with 1½ cups flour
2 tablespoons butter
2 large onions, peeled and sliced
2 teaspoons cornstarch
2 teaspoons tomato paste
1 × 14 oz can tomatoes
½ teaspoon dried mixed herbs
freshly ground black pepper
1 × 2 oz can anchovy fillets, drained and soaked in milk
few black olives, halved and pitted

Roll out the dough on a floured surface and use to line a 20 cm/8 inch flan ring set on a baking sheet. Bake blind in a preheated moderately hot oven (200°C/400°F or Gas Mark 6) for 15 minutes.
Melt the butter in a pan, add the onions and fry gently until soft. Mix together the cornflour (cornstarch) and tomato purée (paste), then stir into the onions with the tomatoes, herbs and pepper to taste. Bring to the boil, stirring constantly. Simmer for 10 minutes, then pour into the pastry case (pie shell).
Drain the anchovies and arrange in a lattice pattern on top of the tomato mixture. Put halved olives in each 'window' of the lattice. Return to the moderately hot oven and bake for a further 15 minutes. Cool quickly on a wire rack, then remove the flan ring.
To freeze: open (flash) freeze until firm, wrap in foil, then pack in a freezer bag. Seal, label and return to the freezer.
To thaw and serve: remove wrappings and place the pissaladière on a baking sheet. Reheat from frozen in a preheated moderately hot oven (190°C/375°F or Gas Mark 5) for 30 minutes or until heated through.
SERVES 4 to 6

SWEETCORN AND GARLIC SAUSAGE FLAN

METRIC/IMPERIAL

basic shortcrust pastry dough made with 225 g/½ lb flour
25 g/1 oz butter
1 onion, peeled and chopped
1 × 5 ml spoon/1 teaspoon dried mixed herbs
1 × 200 g/7 oz can sweetcorn, drained
100 g/4 oz garlic sausage, chopped
2 tomatoes, peeled and chopped
300 ml/½ pint creamy milk or single cream
3 eggs
salt
freshly ground black pepper
50 g/2 oz Cheddar cheese, grated

AMERICAN

basic pie dough made with 2 cups flour
2 tablespoons butter
1 onion, peeled and chopped
1 teaspoon dried mixed herbs
1 × 7 oz can corn kernels, drained
¼ lb garlic sausage, chopped
2 tomatoes, peeled and chopped
1¼ cups half and half or light cream
3 eggs
salt
freshly ground black pepper
½ cup grated Cheddar cheese

Roll out the dough on a floured surface and use to line a 25 cm/10 inch flan ring set on a baking sheet.
Melt the butter in a pan, add the onion and fry gently until soft. Transfer the onion to the pastry case (pie shell), then place the corn, garlic sausage and tomatoes on top.
Put the milk or cream, eggs and salt and pepper to taste in a bowl and beat well to mix. Pour over the filling and sprinkle with the cheese. Bake in a preheated moderate oven (180°C/350°F or Gas Mark 4) for 35 minutes or until the filling is set. Cool quickly on a wire rack, then remove the flan ring.
To freeze: pack between 2 cardboard plates, secure with freezer tape, then place in a freezer bag. Seal, label and freeze.
To thaw and serve: remove wrappings and place the flan on a baking sheet. Reheat from frozen in a preheated moderate oven (180°C/350°F or Gas Mark 4) for 35 minutes or until heated through.
SERVES 6 to 8

TOMATO AND COURGETTE (ZUCCHINI) QUICHE

METRIC/IMPERIAL

basic shortcrust pastry dough made with 175 g/6 oz flour
3 tomatoes, sliced
3 small courgettes, sliced
2 eggs
150 ml/¼ pint milk
salt
freshly ground black pepper
75 g/3 oz Cheddar cheese, grated

AMERICAN

basic pie dough made with 1½ cups flour
3 tomatoes, sliced
3 small zucchini, sliced
2 eggs
⅔ cup milk
salt
freshly ground black pepper
¾ cup grated Cheddar cheese

Roll out the dough on a floured surface and use to line a 20 cm/8 inch flan ring set on a baking sheet. Bake blind in a preheated moderately hot oven (200°C/400°F or Gas Mark 6) for 15 minutes.
Arrange the tomatoes and courgettes (zucchini) in the pastry case (pie shell). Put the eggs, milk and salt and pepper to taste in a bowl and beat well to mix. Pour over the filling and sprinkle with the cheese.
Bake in a preheated moderately hot oven (190°C/375°F or Gas Mark 5) for 25 minutes or until the filling is set. Cool quickly on a wire rack, then remove the flan ring.
To freeze: open (flash) freeze until firm, wrap in foil, then pack in a freezer bag. Seal, label and return to the freezer.
To thaw and serve: remove wrappings and place the quiche on a baking sheet. Reheat from frozen in a preheated moderately hot oven (190°C/375°F or Gas Mark 5) for 30 minutes or until heated through.
SERVES 4 to 6

SMOKED HADDOCK AND TOMATO QUICHE

Make as for Tomato and Courgette (Zucchini) Quiche (see above), substituting 175 g/6 oz poached and flaked smoked haddock fillets for the courgettes (zucchini). Freeze, thaw and serve as for Tomato and Courgette (Zucchini) Quiche.
SERVES 4 to 6

PRAWN (SHRIMP) QUICHE

METRIC/IMPERIAL

basic shortcrust pastry dough made with 250 g/9 oz flour
4 celery stalks, chopped
100 g/4 oz mushrooms, chopped
225 g/½ lb peeled prawns
150 ml/¼ pint milk
150 ml/¼ pint single cream
2 eggs
2 egg yolks
1 × 2.5 ml spoon/½ teaspoon dried mixed herbs
salt
freshly ground black pepper
100 g/4 oz Cheddar cheese, grated
few whole prawns, to garnish

AMERICAN

basic pie dough made with 2¼ cups flour
4 celery stalks, chopped
1 cup chopped mushrooms
1¼ cups shelled shrimp
⅔ cup milk
⅔ cup light cream
2 eggs
2 egg yolks
½ teaspoon dried mixed herbs
salt
freshly ground black pepper
1 cup grated Cheddar cheese
few whole shrimp, to garnish

Roll out the dough on a floured surface and use to line a 30 cm/12 inch fluted flan ring set on a baking sheet. Bake blind in a preheated moderately hot oven (200°C/400°F or Gas Mark 6) for 15 minutes.
Arrange the celery, mushrooms and prawns (shrimp) in the pastry case (pie shell). Put the remaining ingredients, except the cheese and the whole prawns (shrimp), in a bowl and beat well to mix. Pour over the filling.
Bake in a preheated moderately hot oven (190°C/375°F or Gas Mark 5) for 40 minutes or until the filling is set. Cool quickly on a wire rack, then remove the flan ring.
To freeze: open (flash) freeze until firm, wrap in foil, then pack in a freezer bag. Seal, label and return to the freezer.
To thaw and serve: remove wrappings and thaw the quiche at room temperature for 4 hours. Reheat on a baking sheet in a preheated moderate oven (180°C/350°F or Gas Mark 4) for 25 minutes or until heated through. Garnish with whole prawns (shrimp).
SERVES 8

COD, SPINACH AND CHEESE FLAN

METRIC/IMPERIAL

basic shortcrust pastry dough made with 175 g/6 oz flour
15 g/½ oz butter
1 onion, peeled and finely chopped
1 × 225 g/8 oz packet frozen cod fillets, poached, skinned and flaked
1 × 225 g/8 oz packet frozen chopped spinach, thawed
75 g/3 oz Gouda cheese, grated
150 ml/¼ pint single cream
1 egg, beaten
pinch of grated nutmeg
salt
freshly ground black pepper
4 slices of Gouda cheese

AMERICAN

basic pie dough made with 1½ cups flour
1 tablespoon butter
1 onion, peeled and finely chopped
1 × ½ lb package frozen cod fillets, poached, skinned and flaked
1 × ½ lb package frozen chopped spinach, thawed
¾ cup grated Gouda cheese
⅔ cup light cream
1 egg, beaten
pinch of grated nutmeg
salt
freshly ground black pepper
4 slices of Gouda cheese

Roll out the dough on a floured surface and use to line a 20 cm/8 inch flan ring set on a baking sheet. Bake blind in a preheated moderately hot oven (200°C/400°F or Gas Mark 6) for 15 minutes.

Melt the butter in a pan, add the onion and fry gently until soft. Transfer to a bowl, add the remaining ingredients, except the slices of cheese, and stir well to mix. Pour into the pastry case (pie shell).

Return to the moderately hot oven and bake for a further 25 minutes or until the filling is set. Arrange the cheese slices on top and put under a preheated grill (broiler) to melt the cheese. Cool on a wire rack, then remove flan ring.

To freeze: open (flash) freeze until firm, wrap in foil, then pack in a freezer bag. Seal, label and return to the freezer.

To thaw and serve: remove wrappings and place the flan on a baking sheet. Reheat from frozen in a preheated moderately hot oven (190°C/375°F or Gas Mark 5) for 30 minutes or until heated through.

SERVES 4 to 6

BLUE CHEESE QUICHE

METRIC/IMPERIAL

basic shortcrust pastry dough made with 225 g/½ lb flour
1 medium onion, peeled and chopped
75 g/3 oz streaky bacon rashers, rinds removed and chopped
175 g/6 oz Stilton cheese, crumbled
150 ml/¼ pint double cream
150 ml/¼ pint milk
2 eggs
1 egg yolk
salt
freshly ground black pepper
snipped chives, freshly chopped parsley or spring onions, to garnish

AMERICAN

basic pie dough made with 2 cups flour
1 medium onion, peeled and chopped
5 fatty bacon slices, chopped
1½ cups crumbled Stilton cheese
⅔ cup heavy cream
⅔ cup milk
2 eggs
1 egg yolk
salt
freshly ground black pepper
snipped chives, freshly chopped parsley or scallions, to garnish

Roll out the dough on a floured board and use to line a 23 cm/9 inch flan dish. Bake blind in a preheated moderately hot oven (200°C/400°F or Gas Mark 6) for 15 minutes.

Put the onion and bacon in a pan and fry until the bacon fat runs and the onion is soft. Arrange in the bottom of the pastry case (pie shell) and cover with the cheese. Put the remaining ingredients in a bowl and beat well to mix. Pour into the case (shell) and bake in a preheated moderately hot oven (190°C/375°F or Gas Mark 5) for 35 minutes or until the filling is set.

To freeze: cool quickly. Open (flash) freeze until firm, remove the flan dish, than wrap the quiche in foil, Pack in a freezer bag. Seal, label and return to the freezer.

To thaw and serve: remove wrappings and return the quiche to the flan dish· Thaw at room temperature for 4 hours, then reheat in a pre-preheated moderate oven (180°C/350°F or Gas Mark 4) for 30 minutes or until heated through. Sprinkle with chives, parsley or spring onions (scallions) just before serving.

SERVES 4 to 6

CHEESE AND VEGETABLE FLAN

METRIC/IMPERIAL

For the cheese pastry:

175 g/6 oz flour

1 × 2.5 ml spoon/½ teaspoon salt

75 g/3 oz butter

75 g/3 oz Cheddar cheese, finely grated

approx 2 × 15 ml spoons/2 tablespoons water

For the filling:

175 g/6 oz cream cheese, softened

2 eggs

300 ml/½ pint milk

salt

freshly ground black pepper

450 g/1 lb mixed seasonal or frozen vegetables (carrots, broad beans, French beans, peas, etc), cooked

AMERICAN

For the cheese pastry:

1½ cups flour

½ teaspoon salt

⅜ cup butter

¾ cup finely grated Cheddar cheese

approx 2 tablespoons water

For the filling:

¾ cup cream cheese, softened

2 eggs

1¼ cups milk

salt

freshly ground black pepper

1 lb mixed seasonal or frozen vegetables (carrots, lima beans, green beans, peas, etc), cooked

To make the pastry: sift the flour and salt into a bowl, add the butter in pieces and rub into the flour until the mixture resembles fine bread-crumbs. Mix in the cheese, then add enough water to give a stiff dough. Form into a ball, wrap in foil, then chill in the refrigerator for 30 minutes.

Roll out the dough on a floured surface and use to line a 30 cm/12 inch flan ring set on a baking sheet. Bake blind in a preheated moderately hot oven (200°C/400°F or Gas Mark 6) for 15 minutes.

To make the filling: put the cream cheese in a bowl and beat until smooth, then beat in the eggs, milk and salt and pepper to taste. Arrange the vegetables in the bottom of the pastry case (pie shell) and pour over the cream cheese mixture. Return to the moderately hot oven and bake for a further 25 minutes or until the filling is set. Cool quickly on a wire rack, then remove the flan ring.

To freeze: open (flash) freeze until firm, wrap in foil, then pack in a freezer bag. Seal, label and return to the freezer.

To thaw and serve: remove wrappings and thaw the flan at room temperature for 4 hours. Reheat on a baking sheet in a preheated moderate oven (180°C/350°F or Gas Mark 4) for 25 minutes or until heated through.

SERVES 6 to 8

SALMON AND ASPARAGUS FLAN

METRIC/IMPERIAL

basic shortcrust pastry dough made with 175 g/6 oz flour

2 eggs

1 × 298 g/10½ oz can condensed asparagus soup

1 × 225 g/8 oz can pink salmon, drained, skinned and flaked

1 onion, peeled and grated

50 g/2 oz cheese, grated

salt

freshly ground black pepper

few canned asparagus spears, to garnish

AMERICAN

basic pie dough made with 1½ cups flour

2 eggs

1 × 10½ oz can condensed asparagus soup

1 × ½ lb can pink salmon, drained, skinned and flaked

1 onion, peeled and grated

½ cup grated cheese

salt

freshly ground black pepper

few canned asparagus spears, to garnish

Roll out the dough on a floured surface and use to line a 20 cm/8 inch flan ring set on a baking sheet. Bake blind in a preheated moderately hot oven (200°C/400°F or Gas Mark 6) for 15 minutes.

Put the eggs and soup in a bowl and beat well to mix. Stir in the salmon, onion, half the cheese, and salt and pepper to taste. Pour into the pastry case (pie shell), then sprinkle with the remaining cheese. Return to the moderately hot oven and bake for a further 25 minutes or until the filling is set. Cool quickly on a wire rack, then remove the flan ring.

To freeze: open (flash) freeze until firm, wrap in foil, then pack in a freezer bag. Seal, label and return to the freezer.

To thaw and serve: remove wrappings and place the flan on a baking sheet. Reheat from frozen in a preheated moderately hot oven (200°C/400°F or Gas Mark 6) for 30 minutes or until heated through. Garnish with asparagus spears.

SERVES 4 to 6

ASPARAGUS QUICHE

METRIC/IMPERIAL

basic shortcrust pastry dough made with 175 g/6 oz flour
225 g/½ lb frozen asparagus spears, thawed
4 × 15 ml spoons/4 tablespoons double cream
150 ml/¼ pint single cream
25 g/1 oz grated Parmesan cheese
salt
freshly ground black pepper
4 eggs, beaten

AMERICAN

basic pie dough made with 1½ cups flour
½ lb frozen asparagus spears, thawed
¼ cup heavy cream
⅔ cup light cream
¼ cup grated Parmesan cheese,
salt
freshly ground black pepper
4 eggs, beaten

Roll out the dough on a floured surface and use to line a 20 cm/8 inch flan ring set on a baking sheet. Trim the asparagus to fit the pastry case/pie shell, cut up the extra pieces and place them in the bottom of the flan. Arrange the trimmed spears as spokes of a wheel on top.

Mix together the remaining ingredients and pour over the asparagus. Bake in a preheated moderately hot oven (200°C/400°F or Gas Mark 6) for 35 minutes or until the filling is set. Cool quickly, then remove the flan ring.

To freeze: open (flash) freeze until firm, wrap in foil, then pack in a freezer bag. Seal, label and return to the freezer.

To thaw and serve: remove wrappings and thaw the quiche at room temperature for 4 hours. Reheat on a baking sheet in a preheated moderate oven (180°C/350°F or Gas Mark 4) for 25 minutes or until heated through.

SERVES 4 to 6

KIPPER AND CHEESE FLAN

METRIC/IMPERIAL

basic shortcrust pastry dough made with 175 g/6 oz flour
3 small kipper fillets, poached and skinned
2 eggs
175 ml/6 fl oz milk
40 g/1½ oz Cheddar cheese, coarsely grated
freshly ground black pepper

AMERICAN

basic pie dough made with 1½ cups flour
3 small kipper fillets, poached and skinned
2 eggs
¾ cup milk
⅓ cup coarsely grated Cheddar cheese
freshly ground black pepper

Roll out the dough on a floured surface and use to line a 20 cm/8 inch flan ring set on a baking sheet. Bake blind in a preheated moderately hot oven (200°C/400°F or Gas Mark 6) for 15 minutes.

Arrange the kippers in the bottom of the pastry case (pie shell). Put the remaining ingredients in a bowl, beat well to mix, then pour over the kippers. Bake in a preheated moderate oven (180°C/350°F or Gas Mark 4) for 30 minutes or until the filling is set. Cool quickly on a wire rack, then remove the flan ring.

To freeze: open (flash) freeze until firm, wrap in foil, then pack in a freezer bag. Seal, label and return to the freezer.

To thaw and serve: remove wrappings and place the flan on a baking sheet. Reheat from frozen in a preheated moderately hot oven (190°C/375°F or Gas Mark 5) for 30 minutes or until heated through.

SERVES 4 to 6

CHEESE AND RATATOUILLE FLAN

METRIC/IMPERIAL

1 small aubergine, sliced
salt
basic shortcrust pastry dough made with 225 g/½ lb flour
50 g/2 oz butter
2 medium courgettes, sliced
2 large tomatoes, peeled and sliced
1 small onion, peeled and chopped
1 small green pepper, cored, seeded and chopped
100 g/4 oz lean bacon rashers, rinds removed and chopped
freshly ground black pepper
225 g/½ lb Cheddar cheese, grated, to finish

AMERICAN

1 small eggplant, sliced
salt
basic pie dough made with 2 cups flour
¼ cup butter
2 medium zucchini, sliced
2 large tomatoes, peeled and sliced
1 small onion, peeled and chopped
1 small green pepper, cored, seeded and chopped
6 Canadian bacon rashers, chopped
freshly ground black pepper
2 cups grated Cheddar cheese, to finish

Sprinkle the aubergine (eggplant) slices with salt and leave for 30 minutes.
Meanwhile, roll out the dough on a floured surface and use to line a 20 cm/8 inch flan ring set on a baking sheet.
Drain the aubergines (eggplants), rinse under cold running water, then dry on paper towels. Melt the butter in a pan, add the vegetables and bacon and fry gently until tender and lightly coloured. Add salt and papper to taste, leave to cool, then spoon into the pastry case (pie shell).
To freeze: open (flash) freeze until firm. Remove the flan ring, wrap the flan in foil, then pack in a freezer bag. Seal, label and return to the freezer.
To thaw and serve: remove wrappings, place the flan on a baking sheet and replace flan ring. Cover with foil and bake from frozen in a preheated moderately hot oven (200°C/400°F or Gas Mark 6) for 45 minutes. Remove the foil, sprinkle with the cheese and bake for a further 15 to 20 minutes or until the cheese has melted.
SERVES 4 to 6

MUSHROOM FLAN

METRIC/IMPERIAL
100 g/4 oz streaky bacon rashers, rinds removed and diced
1 × 600 ml/1 pint packet dried mushroom soup mix
7 × 15 ml spoons/7 tablespoons creamy milk
2 eggs
salt
freshly ground black pepper
1 × 20 cm/8 inch baked pastry case
50 g/2 oz cheese, grated

AMERICAN
6 fatty bacon slices, diced
1 × 2½ cup package dried mushroom soup mix
7 tablespoons half and half
2 eggs
salt
freshly ground black pepper
1 × 8 inch baked pie shell
½ cup grated cheese

Put the bacon in a pan and fry in its own fat for 3 to 5 minutes until lightly coloured. Remove from the pan with a slotted spoon and leave to drain on paper towels.
Put the soup mix in a bowl, add a little of the milk (half and half) and stir well to mix. Beat in the remaining milk (half and half), the eggs and salt and pepper to taste.
Put the bacon in the bottom of the pastry case (pie shell), pour over the milk mixture and sprinkle with the cheese. Bake in a preheated moderately hot oven (200°C/400°F or Gas Mark 6) for 25 minutes or until the filling is set.
To freeze: cool quickly. Open (flash) freeze until firm, wrap in foil, then pack in a freezer bag. Seal, label and return to the freezer.
To thaw and serve: remove wrappings and place the flan on a baking sheet. Thaw at room temperature for 2 hours, then reheat in a preheated moderate oven (180°C/350°F or Gas Mark 4) for 25 minutes or until heated through.
SERVES 4 to 6

CHEESE AND CELERY FLAN

METRIC/IMPERIAL
basic shortcrust pastry dough made with 175 g/6 oz flour
3 celery stalks, finely chopped
100 g/4 oz cheese, grated
2 eggs
150 ml/¼ pint milk
1 × 5 ml spoon/1 teaspoon prepared English mustard
salt
freshly ground black pepper

AMERICAN
basic pie dough made with 1½ cups flour
3 celery stalks, finely chopped
1 cup grated cheese
2 eggs
⅔ cup milk
1 teaspoon prepared English mustard
salt
freshly ground black pepper

Roll out the dough on a floured surface and use to line a 20 cm/8 inch flan ring set on a baking sheet. Prick the bottom of the dough.
Arrange the celery in the bottom of the pastry case (pie shell) and sprinkle with the cheese. Put the remaining ingredients in a bowl, beat well to mix, then pour over the filling.
Bake in a preheated moderately hot oven (190°C/375°F or Gas Mark 5) for 35 minutes or until the filling is set. Cool quickly on a wire rack, then remove the flan ring.
To freeze: open (flash) freeze until firm, wrap in foil, then pack in a freezer bag. Seal, label and return to the freezer.
To thaw and serve: remove wrappings and thaw the flan at room temperature for 4 hours. Place on a baking sheet and reheat in a preheated moderate oven (180°C/350°F or Gas Mark 4) for 25 minutes or until heated through.
SERVES 4 to 6

SMOKED HADDOCK AND COTTAGE CHEESE FLAN

METRIC/IMPERIAL

225 g/½ lb smoked haddock fillets
150 ml/¼ pint water
finely grated rind and juice of 1 lemon
25 g/1 oz butter
1 small onion, peeled and chopped
50 g/2 oz button mushrooms, sliced
1 × 20 cm/8 inch baked pastry case
2 eggs, beaten
3 × 15 ml spoons/3 tablespoons single cream
100 g/4 oz cottage cheese
1 × 15 ml spoon/1 tablespoon freshly chopped parsley
salt
freshly ground black pepper
To garnish:
4–6 lemon wedges
a few sprigs of parsley

AMERICAN

½ lb smoked haddock fillets
⅔ cup water
finely grated rind and juice of 1 lemon
2 tablespoons butter
1 small onion, peeled and chopped
½ cup sliced button mushrooms
1 × 8 inch baked pie shell
2 eggs, beaten
3 tablespoons light cream
½ cup cottage cheese
1 tablespoon freshly chopped parsley
salt
freshly ground black pepper
To garnish:
4–6 lemon wedges
a few sprigs of parsley

Put the fish in a pan with the water and half the lemon juice and poach gently until tender. Drain the fish, remove the skin and flake the flesh. Melt the butter in a pan, add the onion and fry gently until soft. Add the mushrooms, fry for a further 1 minute, then mix with the fish. Put the mixture in the bottom of the pastry case (pie shell) set on a baking sheet.
Put the remaining ingredients in a bowl with the lemon rind and remaining juice and beat well to mix. Pour over the fish mixture and bake in a preheated moderately hot oven (190°C/375°F or Gas Mark 5) for 35 minutes or until the filling is set. Cool quickly on a wire rack.
To freeze: open (flash) freeze until firm, wrap in foil, then pack in a freezer bag. Seal, label and return to the freezer.
To thaw and serve: remove wrappings and place the flan on a baking sheet. Reheat from frozen in a preheated moderate oven (180°C/350°F or Gas Mark 4) for 25 minutes or until heated through. Garnish with lemon wedges and parsley just before serving.
SERVES 4 to 6

INDIVIDUAL SALAMI AND COTTAGE CHEESE FLANS

METRIC/IMPERIAL

basic shortcrust pastry dough made with 100 g/4 oz flour
50 g/2 oz salami, finely sliced
1 small onion, peeled and chopped
225 g/½ lb cottage cheese
2 eggs, beaten
1 × 2.5 ml spoons/½ teaspoon dried mixed herbs
salt
freshly ground black pepper
To garnish:
a few tomato wedges
a few sprigs of parsley

AMERICAN

basic pie dough made with 1 cup flour
2 oz salami, finely sliced
1 small onion, peeled and chopped
1 cup cottage cheese
2 eggs, beaten
½ teaspoon dried mixed herbs
salt
freshly ground black pepper
To garnish:
a few tomato wedges
a few sprigs of parsley

Roll out the dough on a floured surface and use to line 4 individual 10 cm/4 inch patty tins. Bake blind in a preheated moderately hot oven (200°C/400°F or Gas Mark 6) for 15 minutes.
Divide the salami equally between the pastry cases (flan shells). Put the remaining ingredients in a bowl and beat well to mix. Pour over the salami. Bake in a preheated moderate oven (180°C/350°F or Gas Mark 4) for 25 minutes or until the filling is set. Cool quickly on a wire rack.
To freeze: open (flash) freeze until firm, remove the tins, then wrap the flans individually in foil. Pack in a freezer bag. Seal, label and return to the freezer.
To thaw and serve: remove wrappings and return the flans to the tins. Reheat from frozen in a preheated moderate oven for 25 minutes or until heated through. Garnish with tomato and parsley just before serving.
MAKES 4

CHICKEN, HAM AND MUSHROOM QUICHE

METRIC/IMPERIAL
basic shortcrust pastry dough made with 175 g/6 oz flour
25 g/1 oz butter
1 onion, peeled and chopped
100 g/4 oz button mushrooms, chopped
100 g/4 oz cooked ham, chopped
175 g/6 oz cooked chicken, chopped
2 eggs, beaten
150 ml/¼ pint double cream
1 × 2.5 ml/½ teaspoon dried mixed herbs
salt
freshly ground black pepper
watercress, to garnish

AMERICAN
basic pie dough made with 1½ cups flour
2 tablespoons butter
1 onion, peeled and chopped
1 cup sliced button mushrooms
½ cup chopped cooked ham
¾ cup chopped cooked chicken
2 eggs, beaten
⅔ cup heavy cream
½ teaspoon dried mixed herbs
salt
freshly ground black pepper
watercress, to garnish

Roll out the dough on a floured surface and use to line a 20 cm/8 inch flan ring set on a baking sheet. Bake blind in a preheated moderately hot oven (200°C/400°F or Gas Mark 6) for 15 minutes.

Melt the butter in a pan, add the onion and fry gently until soft. Add the mushrooms to the pan and fry for 3 minutes. Stir in the ham and chicken, then transfer to the bottom of the pastry case (pie shell).

Put the remaining ingredients in a bowl and beat well to mix. Pour over the filling and bake in a preheated moderate oven (180°C/350°F or Gas Mark 4) for 25 minutes or until the filling is set. Cool quickly on a wire rack, then remove the flan ring.

To freeze: open (flash) freeze until firm, wrap in foil, then pack in a freezer bag. Seal, label and return to the freezer.

To thaw and serve: remove wrappings and place the quiche on a baking sheet. Reheat from frozen in a preheated moderate oven for 25 minutes or until heated through. Garnish with watercress just before serving.

SERVES 4 to 6

CHEESE AND PRAWN (SHRIMP) FLAN

METRIC/IMPERIAL
basic shortcrust pastry dough made with 175 g/6 oz flour
40 g/1½ oz butter
40 g/1½ oz flour
300 ml/½ pint milk
100 g/4 oz cheese, grated
100 g/4 oz peeled prawns
salt
freshly ground black pepper
1 × 15 ml spoon/1 tablespoon fresh white breadcrumbs
few whole prawns, to garnish

AMERICAN
basic pie dough made with 1½ cups flour
3 tablespoons butter
⅜ cup flour
1¼ cups milk
1 cup grated cheese
¾ cup shelled shrimp
salt
freshly ground black pepper
1 tablespoon fresh white breadcrumbs
few whole shrimp, to garnish

Roll out the dough on a floured surface and use to line a 20 cm/8 inch flan ring set on a baking sheet. Bake blind in a preheated moderately hot oven (200°C/400°F or Gas Mark 6) for 15 minutes. Melt the butter in a pan, stir in the flour and cook for 2 minutes, stirring constantly. Remove from the heat and gradually stir in the milk. Return to the heat and bring to the boil, stirring constantly. Simmer until thick, then stir in the remaining ingredients except the breadcrumbs and whole prawns (shrimp). Pour into the pastry case (pie shell) and sprinkle with the breadcrumbs.

To freeze: cool quickly. Open (flash) freeze until firm, remove the flan ring, then wrap the flan in foil. Pack in a freezer bag. Seal, label and return to the freezer.

To thaw and serve: remove wrappings and place the flan on a baking sheet. Thaw at room temperature for 4 hours, then reheat in a preheated moderate oven (180°C/350°F or Gas Mark 4) for 25 minutes or until heated through. Garnish with whole prawns (shrimp) just before serving.

SERVES 4 to 6

CREAMY SPINACH FLAN

METRIC/IMPERIAL

basic shortcrust pastry dough made with 225 g/½ lb flour
1 × 225 g/8 oz packet frozen chopped spinach, cooked
100 g/4 oz cooked ham, diced
175 g/6 oz cream cheese, softened
salt
freshly ground black pepper
2 eggs, beaten

AMERICAN

basic pie dough made with 2 cups flour
1 × ½ lb package frozen chopped spinach, cooked
½ cup diced cooked ham
¾ cup cream cheese, softened
salt
freshly ground black pepper
2 eggs, beaten

Roll out the dough on a floured surface and use to line a 20 cm/8 inch flan ring set on a baking sheet. Reserve the trimmings.

Put the remaining ingredients in a bowl and beat well to mix. Pour into the pastry case (pie shell). Roll out the dough trimmings and cut out circles using a 5 cm/2 inch plain cutter. Arrange around the edge, overlapping the circles. Bake in a preheated moderately hot oven (200°C/400°F or Gas Mark 6) for 15 minutes, then reduce the heat to moderate (180°C/350°F or Gas Mark 4) and bake for a further 25 minutes or until the filling is set. Cool quickly on a wire rack, then remove the flan ring.

To freeze: open (flash) freeze until firm, wrap in foil, then pack in a freezer bag. Seal, label and return to the freezer.

To thaw and serve: remove wrappings and place the flan on a baking sheet. Thaw at room temperature for 4 hours, then reheat in a preheated moderate oven (180°C/350°F or Gas Mark 4) for 25 minutes or until heated through.

SERVES 6

LIVER AND BACON PASTIES

METRIC/IMPERIAL

basic uncooked shortcrust pastry dough made with 225 g/½ lb flour
1 medium potato, peeled and diced
1 medium onion, peeled and chopped
175 g/6 oz pig's liver, cooked and diced
3 bacon rashers, rinds removed, cooked and diced
salt
freshly ground black pepper
beaten egg, to glaze

AMERICAN

basic pie dough made with 2 cups flour
1 medium potato, peeled and diced
1 medium onion, peeled and chopped
¾ cup cooked and diced pork liver
3 bacon rashers, cooked and diced
salt
freshly ground black pepper
beaten egg, to glaze

Divide the dough in four and roll out each piece on a floured surface to a 15 to 18 cm/6 to 7 inch circle.

Put all the remaining ingredients, except the egg, in a bowl and stir well to mix. Divide equally between the four rounds, leaving a margin around the edges. Moisten the edges with water and draw up the dough to enclose the filling. Press firmly to seal, then flute the edges.

Place the pasties on a baking sheet and brush with the beaten egg. Bake in a preheated hot oven (220°C/425°F or Gas Mark 7) for 40 minutes or until golden brown and cooked through.

To freeze: cool quickly. Open (flash) freeze until firm, wrap in foil, then pack in a freezer bag. Seal, label and return to the freezer.

To thaw and serve: remove wrappings and place the pasties on a baking sheet. Thaw at room temperature for 4 hours, then reheat in a preheated moderate oven (180°C/350°F or Gas Mark 4) for 25 minutes or until heated through.

MAKES 4

WHOLEMEAL (WHOLEWHEAT) PEPPER QUICHE

METRIC/IMPERIAL

For the pastry:
175 g/6 oz wholemeal flour
pinch of salt
75 g/3 oz butter
approx 3 × 15 ml spoons/3 tablespoons water
For the filling:
25 g/1 oz butter
1 onion, peeled and chopped
1 small green pepper, cored, seeded and sliced
1 small red pepper, cored, seeded and sliced
2 eggs
150 ml/¼ pint milk
100 g/4 oz Edam cheese, grated
salt
freshly ground black pepper

AMERICAN

For the pastry:

1½ cups wholewheat flour
pinch of salt
⅜ cup butter
approx 3 tablespoons water

For the filling:

2 tablespoons butter
1 onion, peeled and chopped
1 small green pepper, cored, seeded and sliced
1 small red pepper, cored, seeded and sliced
2 eggs
⅔ cup milk
1 cup grated Edam cheese
salt
freshly ground black pepper

To make the pastry: put the flour and salt into a bowl. Add the butter, in pieces, and rub into the flour until the mixture resembles fine breadcrumbs. Stir in enough water to give a stiff dough. Form into a ball, wrap in foil and chill in the refrigerator for 30 minutes.

Roll out the dough on a floured surface and use to line a 20 cm/8 inch fluted flan ring set on a baking sheet. Prick the bottom of the dough.

To make the filling: melt the butter in a pan, add the onion and peppers and fry gently until soft. Arrange in the bottom of the pastry case (pie shell). Put the remaining ingredients in a bowl, beat well to mix, then pour over the vegetables.

Bake in a preheated moderately hot oven (190°C/375°F or Gas Mark 5) for 35 minutes or until the filling is set. Cool quickly on a wire rack, then remove the flan ring.

To freeze: open (flash) freeze until firm, wrap in foil, then pack in a freezer bag. Seal, label and return to the freezer.

To thaw and serve: remove wrappings and thaw the quiche at room temperature for 4 hours. Place on a baking sheet and reheat in a preheated moderate oven (180°C/350°F or Gas Mark 4) for 25 minutes or until heated through.

SERVES 4 to 6

SARDINE TART

METRIC/IMPERIAL

basic shortcrust pastry dough made with 175 g/6 oz flour
1 × 115 g/4½ oz can sardines in oil
1 small onion, peeled and finely sliced
juice of ½ lemon
5 × 15 ml spoons/5 tablespoons natural yogurt
5 × 15 ml spoons/5 tablespoons single cream
50 g/2 oz cottage cheese
2 eggs
freshly ground black pepper
freshly chopped parsley, to garnish

AMERICAN

basic pie dough made with 1½ cups flour
1 × 4½ oz can sardines in oil
1 small onion, peeled and finely sliced
juice of ½ lemon
⅓ cup unflavored yogurt
⅓ cup light cream
¼ cup cottage cheese
2 eggs
freshly ground black pepper
freshly chopped parsley, to garnish

Roll out the dough on a floured surface and use to line a 20 cm/8 inch flan ring set on a baking sheet.

Drain the oil from the sardines into a pan. Add the onion and fry gently until soft, then put in the bottom of the pastry case (pie shell) and sprinkle with half the lemon juice.

Put the yogurt in a bowl with the cream, cottage cheese, eggs and pepper to taste. Beat well to mix, then pour over the onion. Arrange the sardines as spokes of a wheel on top, then sprinkle with the remaining lemon juice and pepper to taste.

Bake in a preheated hot oven (220°C/425°F or Gas Mark 7) for 15 minutes, then reduce the heat to moderate (180°C/350°F or Gas Mark 4) and bake for a further 25 minutes or until the filling is set. Cool quickly on a wire rack, then remove the flan ring.

To freeze: open (flash) freeze until firm, wrap in foil, then pack in a freezer bag. Seal, label and return to the freezer.

To thaw and serve: remove wrappings and thaw the tart at room temperature for 4 hours. Sprinkle with parsley just before serving.

SERVES 4 to 6

CHEESE AND BACON FLAN

METRIC/IMPERIAL

basic shortcrust pastry dough made with 225 g/½ lb flour
175 g/6 oz lean bacon rashers, rinds removed and diced
3 eggs
450 ml/¾ pint double cream
225 g/½ lb Cheddar cheese, grated
salt
freshly ground black pepper

AMERICAN

basic pie dough made with 2 cups flour
9 Canadian bacon slices, diced
3 eggs
2 cups heavy cream
2 cups grated Cheddar cheese
salt
freshly ground black pepper

Roll out the dough on a floured surface and use to line a 23 cm/9 inch flan tin. Prick the dough.
Put the bacon in a pan and fry in its own fat for 3 to 5 minutes until lightly coloured. Remove from the pan with a slotted spoon, drain on paper towels, then put in the bottom of the pastry case (pie shell).
Put the remaining ingredients in a bowl and beat well to mix. Pour over the bacon. Bake in a preheated moderately hot oven (190°C/375°F or Gas Mark 5) for 35 minutes or until the filling is set.
To freeze: cool quickly. Open (flash) freeze until firm, remove the tin, then wrap the flan in foil. Pack in a freezer bag. Seal, label and return to the freezer.
To thaw and serve: remove wrappings and return the flan to the tin. Thaw at room temperature for 4 hours, then serve cold, or reheat in a preheated moderate oven (180°C/350°F or Gas Mark 4) for 25 minutes or until heated through.
SERVES 4 to 6

BACON LATTICE FLAN

METRIC/IMPERIAL

100 g/4 oz lean bacon rashers, rinds removed and chopped
2 large eggs, beaten
3 × 15 ml spoons/3 tablespoons milk
½ small onion, peeled and grated
freshly ground black pepper
1 × 18 cm/7 inch unbaked pastry case
4 streaky bacon rashers, rinds removed and halved lengthways

AMERICAN

6 Canadian bacon slices, chopped
2 large eggs, beaten
3 tablespoons milk
½ small onion, peeled and grated
freshly ground black pepper
1 × 7 inch unbaked pie shell
4 fatty bacon slices, halved lengthwise

Put the lean (Canadian) bacon, eggs, milk, onion and pepper in a bowl and beat well to mix, then pour into the pastry case (pie shell) set on a baking sheet.
Arrange the streaky (fatty) bacon in a lattice over the top of the filling, trimming them a little wider than the flan to allow for shrinkage during cooking. Bake in a preheated moderately hot oven (200°C/400°F or Gas Mark 6) for 35 minutes or until the filling is set. Cool quickly.
To freeze: open (flash) freeze until firm, wrap in foil, then pack in a freezer bag. Seal, label and return to the freezer.
To thaw and serve: remove wrappings and place the flan on a baking sheet. Reheat from frozen in a preheated moderate oven (180°C/350°F or Gas Mark 4) for 25 minutes or until heated through.
SERVES 4

HOT DOG FLAN

METRIC/IMPERIAL

25 g/1 oz butter
225 g/½ lb skinless pork sausages, sliced
1 small onion, peeled and chopped
2–3 streaky bacon rashers, rinds removed and chopped
1 × 20 cm/8 inch baked pastry case
2 eggs
200 ml/⅓ pint milk
50 g/2 oz Cheddar cheese, grated
salt
freshly ground black pepper
freshly chopped parsley, to garnish

AMERICAN

2 tablespoons butter
½ lb skinless pork sausages, sliced
1 small onion, peeled and chopped
2–3 fatty bacon slices, chopped
1 × 8 inch baked pie shell
2 eggs
⅞ cup milk
½ cup grated Cheddar cheese
salt
freshly ground black pepper
freshly chopped parsley, to garnish

Melt the butter in a pan, add the sausages and fry until golden brown. Remove from the pan with a slotted spoon. Add the onion and bacon to the pan and fry for 3 to 5 minutes until lightly coloured.
Put the sausages, onion and bacon in the bottom of the pastry case (pie shell). Put the remaining ingredients in a bowl, beat well to mix, then pour over the filling.
Bake in a preheated moderately hot oven (190°C/375°F or Gas Mark 5) for 25 minutes or until the filling is set.
To freeze: cool quickly. Open (flash) freeze until firm, wrap in foil, then pack in a freezer bag. Seal, label and return to the freezer.
To thaw and serve: remove wrappings and place the flan on a baking sheet. Thaw at room temperature for 2 hours, then reheat in a preheated moderate oven (180°C/350°F or Gas Mark 4) for 25 minutes or until heated through. Serve sprinkled with parsley.
SERVES 4 to 6

LEEK AND BACON CREAM FLAN

METRIC/IMPERIAL
basic shortcrust pastry dough made with 175 g/6 oz flour
25 g/1 oz butter
225 g/½ lb leeks, finely sliced
100 g/4 oz bacon rashers, rinds removed and chopped
150 ml/¼ pint single cream
2 eggs
1 × 5 ml spoon/1 teaspoon freshly chopped parsley
salt
freshly ground black pepper

AMERICAN
basic pie dough made with 1¼ cups flour
2 tablespoons butter
½ lb leeks, finely sliced
6 bacon slices, chopped
⅔ cup light cream
2 eggs
1 teaspoon freshly chopped parsley
salt
freshly ground black pepper

Roll out the dough on a floured surface and use to line a 20 cm/8 inch flan ring set on a baking sheet.
Melt the butter in a pan, add the leeks and bacon and fry gently until lightly coloured, then put in the bottom of the pastry case (pie shell).
Put the remaining ingredients in a bowl and beat well to mix. Pour over the leeks and bacon. Bake in a preheated moderately hot oven (190°C/375°F or Gas Mark 5) for 35 minutes or until the filling is set. Cool quickly on a wire rack, then remove the flan ring.
To freeze: open (flash) freeze until firm, wrap in foil, then pack in a freezer bag. Seal, label and return to the freezer.
To thaw and serve: remove wrappings and place the flan on a baking sheet. Reheat from frozen in a preheated moderate oven (180°C/350°F or Gas Mark 4) for 25 minutes or until heated through.
SERVES 4 to 6

ONION FLAN

METRIC/IMPERIAL
40 g/1½ oz butter
2 medium onions, peeled and chopped
2 eggs
150 ml/¼ pint single cream or creamy milk
salt
freshly ground black pepper
1 × 20 cm/8 inch baked pastry case
2 × 15 ml spoons/2 tablespoons grated cheese

AMERICAN
3 tablespoons butter
2 medium onions, peeled and chopped
2 eggs
⅔ cup light cream or half and half
salt
freshly ground black pepper
1 × 8 inch baked pie shell
2 tablespoons grated cheese

Melt the butter in a pan, add the onions, cover and cook gently for 5 to 10 minutes or until soft. Transfer to a bowl, add the eggs, cream or milk (half and half) and salt and pepper to taste, then beat well to mix.
Pour into the pastry case (pie shell) set on a baking sheet, sprinkle with the cheese and bake in a preheated moderate oven (180°C/350°F or Gas Mark 4) for 25 minutes or until the filling is set. Cool quickly on a wire rack.
To freeze: open (flash) freeze until firm, wrap in foil, then pack in a freezer bag. Seal, label and return to the freezer.
To thaw and serve: remove wrappings and place the flan on a baking sheet. Thaw at room temperature for 4 hours, then reheat in a preheated moderate oven (180°C/350°F or Gas Mark 4) for 25 minutes or until heated through.
SERVES 4 to 6

SWEETCORN AND PEPPER FLAN

METRIC/IMPERIAL

25 g/1 oz butter
1 medium onion, peeled and chopped
1 large green pepper, cored, seeded and chopped
300 ml/½ pint white coating sauce
75 g/3 oz Cheddar cheese, grated
225 g/½ lb frozen sweetcorn
1 × 5 ml spoon/1 teaspoon prepared mustard
salt
freshly ground black pepper
1 × 20 cm/8 inch baked pastry case

AMERICAN

2 tablespoons butter
1 medium onion, peeled and chopped
1 large green pepper, cored, seeded and chopped
1¼ cups white coating sauce
¾ cup grated Cheddar cheese
1½ cups frozen corn kernels
1 teaspoon prepared mustard
salt
freshly ground black pepper
1 × 8 inch baked pie shell

Melt the butter in a pan, add the onion and green pepper and fry gently for 5 minutes. Stir in the sauce with 50 g/2 oz/½ cup cheese, the corn, mustard and salt and pepper to taste. Bring to the boil, then remove from the heat and pour into the pastry case (pie shell). Sprinkle the remaining cheese over the top.
To freeze: cool quickly. Open (flash) freeze until firm, wrap in foil, then pack in a freezer bag. Seal, label and return to the freezer.
To thaw and serve: remove wrappings and place on a baking sheet. Reheat from frozen in a preheated moderate oven (180°C/350°F or Gas Mark 4) for 25 minutes or until heated through.
SERVES 4 to 6

COTTAGE CHEESE UPSIDE-DOWN SCONE (BISCUIT)

METRIC/IMPERIAL

25 g/1 oz butter
1 medium onion, peeled and sliced into rings
3 tomatoes, peeled and sliced
salt
freshly ground black pepper
For the scone dough:
225 g/½ lb self-raising flour
50 g/2 oz butter
100 g/4 oz cottage cheese
1 egg
2 × 15 ml spoons/2 tablespoons milk

AMERICAN

2 tablespoons butter
1 medium onion, peeled and cut into rings
3 tomatoes, peeled and sliced
salt
freshly ground black pepper
For the biscuit dough:
2 cups self-rising flour
¼ cup butter
½ cup cottage cheese
1 egg
2 tablespoons milk

Grease a 20 cm/8 inch sandwich tin (layer cake pan) and line the bottom with greaseproof paper or non-stick parchment.
Melt the butter in a pan, add the onion and fry gently until soft. Transfer to the tin, cover with the tomato slices and sprinkle with salt and pepper to taste.
To make the dough: sift the flour and a pinch of salt into a bowl. Add the butter in pieces and rub into the flour with the fingertips. Stir in the cottage cheese. Beat the egg and milk together, then pour into the bowl and mix to give a soft dough. Knead lightly on a floured surface until smooth, then roll out and cut a 20 cm/8 inch circle. Put on top of the tomatoes, pressing down lightly.
Bake in a preheated hot oven (220°C/425°F or Gas Mark 7) for 25 minutes or until the dough has risen and is golden brown. Turn out of the tin and remove the greaseproof paper or non-stick parchment.
To freeze: cool quickly. Open (flash) freeze until firm, wrap in foil, then pack in a freezer bag. Seal, label and return to the freezer.
To thaw and serve: remove wrappings and place the scone (biscuit) upside-down in the sandwich tin (layer cake pan) lined with foil. Cover with foil and reheat from frozen in a preheated moderate oven (180°C/350°F or Gas Mark 4) for 25 minutes or until heated through.
SERVES 4 to 6

ITALIAN FLAN

METRIC/IMPERIAL

1 × 20 cm/8 inch baked pastry case
100 g/4 oz salami, finely sliced
225 g/½ lb cottage cheese
2 eggs
1 small onion, peeled and grated
1 × 2.5 ml spoon/½ teaspoon dried mixed herbs
salt
freshly ground black pepper
a few slices of tomato, to garnish

AMERICAN

1 × 8 inch baked pie shell
¼ lb salami, finely sliced
1 cup cottage cheese
2 eggs
1 small onion, peeled and grated
½ teaspoon dried mixed herbs
salt
freshly ground black pepper
a few slices of tomato, to garnish

Cover the bottom of the pastry case (pie shell) with the salami. Put the remaining ingredients, except the tomato slices, in a bowl and beat well to mix. Pour over the salami.

Place on a baking sheet and bake in a preheated moderate oven (180°C/350°F or Gas Mark 4) for 25 minutes or until the filling is set. Cool quickly on a wire rack.

To freeze: open (flash) freeze until firm, wrap in foil, then pack in a freezer bag. Seal, label and return to the freezer.

To thaw and serve: remove wrappings and place the flan on a baking sheet. Reheat from frozen in a preheated moderate oven for 25 minutes or until heated through. Garnish with tomato slices just before serving.

SERVES 4 to 6

HARLEQUIN FLAN

METRIC/IMPERIAL

basic shortcrust pastry dough made with 175 g/6 oz flour
225 g/½ lb cottage cheese
150 ml/¼ pint natural yogurt
100 g/4 oz cooked ham, chopped
100 g/4 oz cucumber, peeled, seeded and chopped
3 × 15 ml spoons/3 tablespoons mayonnaise
50 g/2 oz cheese, grated
salt
freshly ground black pepper

AMERICAN

basic pie dough made with 1½ cups of flour
1 cup cottage cheese
⅔ cup unflavored yogurt
½ cup chopped cooked ham
1 cup peeled, seeded and chopped cucumber
3 tablespoons mayonnaise
½ cup grated cheese
salt
freshly ground black pepper

Roll out the dough on a floured surface and use to line a 20 cm/8 inch flan ring set on a baking sheet. Bake blind in a preheated moderately hot oven (200°C/400°F or Gas Mark 6) for 15 minutes or until the pastry is golden brown and firm.

Put all the remaining ingredients in a bowl and stir well to mix. Spoon into the pastry case (pie shell).

To freeze: open (flash) freeze until firm, wrap in foil, then pack in a freezer bag. Seal, label and return to the freezer.

To thaw and serve: remove wrappings and thaw the flan at room temperature for 4 hours. Serve cold.

SERVES 4 to 6

QUICKIE PIZZAS

METRIC/IMPERIAL

450 g/1 lb self-raising flour
pinch of salt
4 × 15 ml spoons/4 tablespoons vegetable oil
225 g/½ lb salami, sliced
350 g/¾ lb Mozzarella cheese, sliced, or Cheddar cheese, grated
2 × 5 ml spoons/2 teaspoons dried oregano
10 stuffed olives, halved (optional)

AMERICAN

4 cups self-rising flour
pinch of salt
¼ cup vegetable oil
½ lb salami, sliced
¾ lb Mozzarella cheese, sliced, or 3 cups grated Cheddar cheese
2 teaspoons dried oregano
10 stuffed olives, halved (optional)

Sift the flour and salt into a bowl, then stir in the oil and enough water to give a soft dough. Divide the dough in two, roll out on a floured surface and use to line two 23 cm/9 inch flan tins.

Arrange the salami slices overlapping on top of the dough, then top with the cheese and sprinkle with the oregano. Arrange the olives over the top (if using).

Bake in a preheated moderately hot oven (200°C/400°F or Gas Mark 6) for 35 minutes.

To freeze: cool quickly. Open (flash) freeze until firm, then remove from the tins. Wrap the pizzas in foil, then pack in freezer bags. Seal, label and return to the freezer.

To thaw and serve: remove wrappings and return the pizzas to the tins. Reheat from frozen in a preheated moderately hot oven (200°C/400°F or Gas Mark 6) for 45 minutes or until heated through.

EACH PIZZA SERVES 4

ITALIAN PIZZA

METRIC/IMPERIAL

1 × 450 g/1 lb packet white bread mix
1 × 5 ml spoon/1 teaspoon olive oil
1 × 5 ml spoon/1 teaspoon tomato purée
1 × 400 g/14 oz can tomatoes, drained and roughly chopped
pinch of dried oregano
salt
freshly ground black pepper
175 g/6 oz Emmenthal cheese, thinly sliced
1 × 50 g/2 oz can anchovy fillets, drained and soaked in milk for 30 minutes
10 black olives, halved and stoned

AMERICAN

1 × 1 lb package white bread mix
1 teaspoon olive oil
1 teaspoon tomato paste
1 × 14 oz can tomatoes, drained and roughly chopped
pinch of dried oregano
salt
freshly ground black pepper
6 oz Emmenthal cheese, thinly sliced
1 × 2 oz can anchovy fillets, drained and soaked in milk for 30 minutes
10 black olives, halved and pitted

Make up the bread mix as directed on the packet, knead lightly until smooth, then divide into two equal portions. Roll each piece out to a circle 20 cm/8 inches in diameter and place on baking sheets. Brush each circle with the oil and spread with the tomato purée (paste).
Mix the tomatoes with the oregano and salt and pepper to taste, then spread over the dough. Cover with the cheese slices. Arrange a lattice of drained anchovy fillets on top, then place an olive half in each 'window' of the lattice. Leave to rise in a warm place for 30 minutes, then bake in a preheated hot oven (220°C/425°F or Gas Mark 7) for 30 minutes.
To freeze: cool quickly. Open (flash) freeze until firm, wrap in foil, then pack in a freezer bag. Seal, label and return to the freezer.
To thaw and serve: remove wrappings and place the frozen pizzas on baking sheets. Reheat in a preheated hot oven (220°C/425°F or Gas Mark 7) for 15 to 20 minutes until heated through.
EACH PIZZA SERVES 4

BACON AND MUSHROOM PIZZA

METRIC/IMPERIAL

1 × 450 g/1 lb packet white bread mix
25 g/1 oz butter
6 streaky bacon rashers, rinds removed and chopped
225 g/½ lb button mushrooms, sliced
175 g/6 oz Cheddar cheese, grated

AMERICAN

1 × 1 lb package white bread mix
2 tablespoons butter
6 fatty bacon slices, chopped
2 cups sliced button mushrooms
1½ cups grated Cheddar cheese

Make up two circles of dough as for Italian Pizza.
Melt the butter in a pan, add the bacon and mushrooms and fry gently for 5 minutes, stirring occasionally. Spread the mixture over the dough, then cover with the grated cheese. Leave to rise and bake as for Italian Pizza.
Freeze, thaw and serve as for Italian Pizza.
EACH PIZZA SERVES 4

SALAMI PIZZA

METRIC/IMPERIAL

1 × 450 g/1 lb packet white bread mix
8 slices of salami
6 × 15 ml spoons/6 tablespoons tomato chutney
pinch of mixed herbs
6 large tomatoes, peeled and sliced

AMERICAN

1 × 1 lb package white bread mix
8 slices of salami
6 tablespoons tomato chutney
pinch of dried mixed herbs
6 large tomatoes, peeled and sliced

Make up two circles of dough as for Italian Pizza.
Arrange 4 slices of salami on each circle, mix the chutney and herbs together and spread over the salami. Cover with the slices of tomato, then leave to rise and bake as for Italian Pizza.
Freeze, thaw and serve as for Italian Pizza.
EACH PIZZA SERVES 4

SCONE (BISCUIT) PIZZA

METRIC/IMPERIAL

For the dough:

225 g/½ lb self-raising flour
pinch of salt
50 g/2 oz butter
5 × 15 ml spoons/5 tablespoons milk
1 egg, beaten

For the topping:

3 large tomatoes, peeled and sliced
freshly ground black pepper
225 g/½ lb cheese, grated
1 × 50 g/2 oz can anchovies, drained and soaked in milk
few black olives, halved and stoned

AMERICAN

For the dough:

2 cups self-rising flour
pinch of salt
¼ cup butter
⅓ cup milk
1 egg, beaten

For the topping:

3 large tomatoes, peeled and sliced
freshly ground black pepper
2 cups grated cheese
1 × 2 oz can anchovies, drained and soaked in milk
few black olives, halved and pitted

To make the dough: sift the flour and salt into a bowl. Add the butter in pieces and rub into the flour until the mixture resembles fine breadcrumbs. Mix in the milk and egg to give a soft dough.

Roll out the dough on a floured surface to 1 cm/½ inch thickness. Cut out 5 circles using a 7.5 cm/3 inch plain cutter and place on a greased baking sheet.

Put the tomatoes on top of the dough, sprinkle with a little pepper, then cover with the cheese. Drain the anchovies and arrange in a lattice pattern on top, then put halved olives in each 'window' of the lattice. Bake in a preheated hot oven (220°C/425°F or Gas Mark 7) for 20 minutes or until cooked through. Cool quickly on a wire rack.

To freeze: open (flash) freeze until firm, wrap the pizzas individually in foil, then pack in a freezer bag. Seal, label and return to the freezer.

To thaw and serve: remove wrappings and place the pizzas on a baking sheet. Reheat from frozen in a preheated moderately hot oven (200°C/400°F or Gas Mark 6) for 20 minutes or until heated through.

MAKES 5

BEEFBURGER PIZZA

METRIC/IMPERIAL

2 × 15 ml spoons/2 tablespoons vegetable or corn oil
1 medium onion, peeled and chopped
1 × 400 g/14 oz can tomatoes
salt
freshly ground black pepper
450 g/1 lb frozen bread dough, thawed
2 × 5 ml spoons/2 teaspoons dried oregano
6 beefburgers, cooked and cut into thin strips
50 g/2 oz Cheddar cheese, grated
few black olives, halved and stoned (optional)
1–2 × 15 ml spoons/1–2 tablespoons grated Parmesan cheese

AMERICAN

2 tablespoons vegetable or corn oil
1 medium onion, peeled and chopped
1 × 14 oz can tomatoes
salt
freshly ground black pepper
1 lb frozen bread dough, thawed
2 teaspoons dried oregano
6 beefburgers, cooked and cut into thin strips
½ cup grated Cheddar cheese
few black olives, halved and pitted (optional)
1–2 tablespoons grated Parmesan cheese

Heat the oil in a pan, add the onion and fry gently until soft. Add the tomatoes and salt and pepper to taste, then simmer for 10 minutes or until thick.

Divide the dough in two and roll out each piece on a floured surface to a 25 cm/10 inch circle. Place on an oiled baking sheet or ovenproof dinner plates. Divide the tomato mixture equally between the two, leaving a narrow margin around the edge. Sprinkle with the oregano, then arrange the beefburger strips on top as spokes of a wheel.

Sprinkle with the Cheddar cheese and garnish with the olives (if liked). Bake in a preheated moderately hot oven (200°C/400°F or Gas Mark 6) for 30 minutes. Sprinkle with the Parmesan cheese and bake for a further 10 minutes or until the cheese has melted and the bread is golden brown. Cool quickly on a wire rack.

To freeze: open (flash) freeze until firm, wrap each pizza in foil, then pack in freezer bags. Seal, label and return to the freezer.

To thaw and serve: remove wrappings and place the pizzas on a baking sheet. Reheat from frozen in a preheated moderate oven (180°C/350°F or Gas Mark 4) for 30 minutes or until heated through.

EACH PIZZA SERVES 4

COD IN PARSLEY SAUCE

METRIC/IMPERIAL

1 kg/2 lb cod fillets, skinned
finely grated rind and juice of 1 lemon
1 bay leaf
6 peppercorns
50 g/2 oz butter
2 × 15 ml spoons/2 tablespoons cornflour
salt
freshly ground black pepper
2 × 15 ml spoons/2 tablespoons freshly chopped parsley
150 ml/¼ pint single cream
lemon wedges, to garnish

AMERICAN

2 lb cod fillets, skinned
finely grated rind and juice of 1 lemon
1 bay leaf
6 peppercorns
¼ cup butter
2 tablespoons cornstarch
salt
freshly ground black pepper
2 tablespoons freshly chopped parsley
⅔ cup light cream
lemon wedges, to garnish

Roll up the cod fillets and arrange in a buttered ovenproof dish or foil container. Add enough water to cover, then add the lemon rind and juice, the bay leaf and peppercorns. Cover and bake in a preheated moderate oven (160°C/325°F or Gas Mark 3) for 30 minutes. Strain off the stock and reserve 600 ml/1 pint/2½ cups.

Melt the butter in a pan, stir in the cornflour (cornstarch) and cook for 1 minute. Stir in the reserved fish stock and salt and pepper to taste. Bring to the boil, stirring constantly, then simmer until thick. Remove from the heat and stir in the parsley and cream. Pour over the fish.

To freeze: cool quickly, then cover with foil. Seal, label and freeze.

To thaw and serve: reheat from frozen in the covered dish or container in a preheated moderate oven (180°C/350°F or Gas Mark 4) for 30 minutes or until heated through. Arrange in a hot serving dish and garnish with lemon wedges.

SERVES 4 to 6

COD MADRAS

METRIC/IMPERIAL

25 g/1 oz butter
1 small onion, peeled and chopped
15 g/½ oz flour
2 × 5 ml spoons/2 teaspoons curry powder
300 ml/½ pint fish stock
1 × 5 ml spoon/1 teaspoon tomato purée
1 small cooking apple, peeled, cored and diced
25 g/1 oz sultanas
salt
freshly ground black pepper
450 g/1 lb cod fillets, skinned and cut into cubes

AMERICAN

2 tablespoons butter
1 small onion, peeled and chopped
2 tablespoons flour
2 teaspoons curry powder
1¼ cups fish stock
1 teaspoon tomato paste
1 small baking apple, peeled, cored and diced
3 tablespoons seedless white raisins
salt
freshly ground black pepper
1 lb cod fillets, skinned and cut into cubes

Melt the butter in a pan, add the onion and fry gently until soft. Stir in the flour and curry powder and cook for 2 minutes, stirring constantly. Stir in the remaining ingredients, except the fish, bring to the boil and simmer for 8 minutes. Add the fish cubes. Return to the boil, then lower the heat and simmer for a further 7 minutes.
To freeze: cook quickly, then pour into a rigid container. Seal, label and freeze.
To thaw and serve: thaw at room temperature for 4 hours, then reheat gently on top of the stove, stirring occasionally.
SERVES 4

SWEET FISH

METRIC/IMPERIAL

675 g/1½ lb cod fillets, skinned and cut into large pieces, or 6 cod steaks
flour for coating
salt
freshly ground black pepper
2 × 15 ml spoons/2 tablespoons vegetable oil
1 × 5 ml spoon/1 teaspoon dried rosemary
2 × 15 ml spoons/2 tablespoons honey
juice of 2 lemons
1 garlic clove, peeled and crushed
150 ml/¼ pint water
2 × 15 ml spoons/2 tablespoons seedless raisins

AMERICAN

1½ lb cod fillets, skinned and cut into large pieces, or 6 cod steaks
flour for coating
salt
freshly ground black pepper
2 tablespoons vegetable oil
1 teaspoon dried rosemary
2 tablespoons honey
juice of 2 lemons
1 garlic clove, peeled and crushed
⅔ cup water
2 tablespoons seedless raisins

Coat the fish in flour seasoned with salt and pepper. Heat the oil in a pan, add the rosemary and the fish and fry gently until lightly coloured on all sides. Transfer the fish to an ovenproof dish or foil container.
Put the remaining ingredients in a pan and bring to the boil. Pour over the fish, cover and bake in a preheated moderate oven (180°C/350°F or Gas Mark 4) for 15 to 20 minutes or until the fish is cooked.
To freeze: cool quickly, then cover with foil. Seal, label and freeze.
To thaw and serve: thaw at room temperature for 4 hours, then reheat in the covered dish in a preheated moderate oven (180°C/350°F or Gas Mark 4) for 25 minutes or until heated through.
SERVES 6

BABY FISH QUICHES

METRIC/IMPERIAL

basic shortcrust pastry dough made with 225 g/½ lb flour
225 g/½ lb cod fillets, poached, skinned and flaked
2 eggs
300 ml/½ pint milk
1 × 40 g/1½ oz can crabmeat, drained
salt
freshly ground black pepper

AMERICAN

basic pie dough made with 2 cups flour
½ lb cod fillets, poached, skinned and flaked
2 eggs
1¼ cups milk
1 × 1½ oz can crabmeat, drained
salt
freshly ground black pepper

Roll out the dough on a floured surface and use to line 4 individual flan dishes. Bake blind in a preheated moderately hot oven (200°C/400°F or Gas Mark 6) for 20 minutes.
Meanwhile, put the remaining ingredients in a bowl and stir well to mix. Divide the mixture equally between the baked pastry cases (pie shells), reduce the heat to 190°C/375°F or Gas Mark 5 and bake for 20 minutes or until the filling is set.
To freeze: cool quickly. Open (flash) freeze until firm, then wrap individually in freezer bags or foil. Seal, label and return to the freezer.
To thaw and serve: remove wrappings and thaw at room temperature for 4 hours. Reheat in a preheated moderate oven (180°C/350°F or Gas Mark 4) for 25 minutes or until heated through.
MAKES 4

CRUNCHY FISH BAKE

METRIC/IMPERIAL

75 g/3 oz butter
1 large onion, peeled and sliced
25 g/1 oz flour
300 ml/½ pint fish stock
salt
freshly ground black pepper
4 cod steaks, poached, skinned and flaked
2 tomatoes, peeled and quartered
1 small white loaf, crusts removed and bread diced
freshly chopped parsley, to garnish

AMERICAN

⅜ cup butter
1 large onion, peeled and sliced
¼ cup flour
1¼ cups fish stock
salt
freshly ground black pepper
4 cod steaks, poached, skinned and flaked
2 tomatoes, peeled and quartered
1 small white loaf, crusts removed and bread diced
freshly chopped parsley, to garnish

Melt 25 g/1 oz/2 tablespoons butter in a pan, add the onion and fry gently until soft. Stir in the flour and cook for 2 minutes, stirring constantly. Stir in the stock and salt and pepper to taste and bring to the boil, stirring. Simmer until thick.
Put the fish and tomatoes in an ovenproof dish or foil container and pour over the sauce. Melt the remaining butter in a pan, add the diced bread and fry briskly until golden brown and crisp on all sides. Pile on top of the fish and tomatoes and bake in a preheated moderate oven (180°C/350°F or Gas Mark 4) for 15 minutes.
To freeze: cool quickly, then cover with foil. Seal, label and freeze.
To thaw and serve: remove wrappings and thaw in the refrigerator overnight. Bake in a preheated moderate oven for 40 minutes or until heated through. Sprinkle with parsley.
SERVES 4

COD AND MUSHROOM SCALLOPS

METRIC/IMPERIAL

6 cod steaks
1 × 275 g/10 oz can condensed mushroom soup
1 × 15 ml spoon/1 tablespoon dry sherry
pinch of garlic salt
675 g/1½ lb potatoes, peeled, boiled and mashed with butter and milk
25 g/1 oz fresh white breadcrumbs, to finish

AMERICAN

6 cod steaks
1 × 10 oz can condensed mushroom soup
1 tablespoon dry sherry
pinch of garlic salt
1½ lb potatoes, peeled, boiled and mashed with butter and milk
½ cup fresh white breadcrumbs, to finish

Put the fish in a pan, cover with water and poach gently for 10 minutes. Drain and reserve the fish liquor. Discard any bones and skin from the cod, then divide the fish equally between 8 scallop shells or individual ovenproof dishes.
Put the soup in a pan, add 2 × 15 ml spoons/2 tablespoons fish liquor, the sherry and garlic salt and bring to the boil, stirring constantly. Remove from the heat and pour over the fish. Pipe the mashed potatoes around the edge.
To freeze: cool quickly. Open (flash) freeze until firm, then wrap individually in freezer bags or foil. Seal, label and return to the freezer.
To thaw and serve: remove wrappings and thaw in the refrigerator for 4 hours. Sprinkle with the breadcrumbs and reheat in a preheated moderately hot oven (190°C/375°F or Gas Mark 5) for 30 to 40 minutes or until heated through and golden brown on top.
MAKES 8

COD PROVENÇALE

METRIC/IMPERIAL

2 × 15 ml spoons/2 tablespoons olive oil
1 onion, peeled and finely chopped
1 garlic clove, peeled and crushed
50 g/2 oz mushrooms, sliced
1 × 225 g/8 oz can tomatoes
120 ml/4 fl oz dry white wine
1 × 5 ml spoon/1 teaspoon dried thyme
salt
freshly ground black pepper
50 g/2 oz butter
4 cod steaks

AMERICAN

2 tablespoons olive oil
1 onion, peeled and finely chopped
1 garlic clove, peeled and crushed
½ cup sliced mushrooms
1 × ½ lb can tomatoes
½ cup dry white wine
1 teaspoon dried thyme
salt
freshly ground black pepper
¼ cup butter
4 cod steaks

Heat the oil in a pan, add the onion and garlic and fry gently until soft. Stir in the mushrooms and cook gently for 4 minutes. Add the tomatoes, wine, thyme and salt and pepper to taste and bring to the boil. Simmer for 20 minutes, stirring occasionally.

Melt the butter in a pan, add the fish and fry gently for 4 minutes on each side. Pour over the sauce and simmer for 10 minutes.

To freeze: cool quickly, then transfer to a rigid container. Seal, label and freeze.

To thaw and serve: thaw at room temperature for 4 hours, then reheat gently on top of the stove, shaking the pan occasionally.

SERVES 4

COD GOUJONS

METRIC/IMPERIAL

1 kg/2 lb cod fillets, skinned and cut into thin strips
flour for coating
salt
freshly ground black pepper
2 eggs, beaten
2 × 15 ml spoons/2 tablespoons milk
fresh white breadcrumbs
vegetable oil for deep-frying
sauce Tartare, to serve

AMERICAN

2 lb cod fillets, skinned and cut into thin strips
flour for coating
salt
freshly ground black pepper
2 eggs, beaten
2 tablespoons milk
fresh white breadcrumbs
vegetable oil for deep-frying
sauce Tartare, to serve

Coat the strips of fish in flour seasoned with salt and pepper. Mix the eggs with the milk. Dip the strips of fish into the egg and milk mixture one at a time, then coat in breadcrumbs until the fish is thoroughly coated. Chill in the referigerator for 30 minutes.

Deep-fry the goujons in hot oil until golden brown and crisp. Drain on paper towels.

To freeze: cool quickly, then open (flash) freeze until firm. Pack in a rigid container, separating each layer with foil. Seal, label and return to the freezer.

To serve: put frozen goujons on a baking sheet and reheat in a preheated moderately hot oven (190°C/375°F or Gas Mark 5) for 20 to 25 minutes. Serve with sauce Tartare.

SERVES 6 to 8

COD AND TOMATO CASSEROLE

METRIC/IMPERIAL

50 g/2 oz butter
1 small onion, peeled and finely chopped
50 g/2 oz flour
600 ml/1 pint milk
100 g/4 oz Cheddar cheese, grated
2 × 15 ml spoons/2 tablespoons tomato purée
salt
freshly ground black pepper
450 g/1 lb cod fillets, poached, skinned and flaked
1 × 99 g/3½ oz can salmon, drained, skinned and flaked
3 × 15 ml spoons/3 tablespoons fresh white breadcrumbs
25 g/1 oz butter to finish

AMERICAN

¼ cup butter
1 small onion, peeled and finely chopped
½ cup flour
2½ cups milk
1 cup grated Cheddar cheese
2 tablespoons tomato paste
salt
freshly ground black pepper
1 lb cod fillets, poached, skinned and flaked
1 × 3½ oz can salmon, drained, skinned and flaked
3 tablespoons fresh white breadcrumbs
2 tablespoons butter, to finish

Melt the butter in a pan, add the onion and fry gently until soft. Stir in the flour and cook for 2 minutes, stirring constantly. Remove from the heat and gradually stir in the milk. Return to the heat and bring to the boil, stirring constantly. Simmer until thick, then stir in the tomato purée (paste), cheese and salt and pepper to taste. Fold in the flaked fish and salmon.

Pour the mixture into an ovenproof dish or foil container and sprinkle breadcrumbs over the top.

To freeze: cool quickly, then cover with foil. Seal, label and freeze.

To thaw and serve: thaw at room temperature for 4 hours then dot with butter. Reheat, uncovered, in a pre-heated moderate oven (180°C/350°F or Gas Mark 4) for 35 minutes or until heated through and golden brown on top.

SERVES 4

COLEY (COD) AND SWEETCORN BAKE

METRIC/IMPERIAL
20 g/¾ oz butter
20 g/¾ oz flour
450 ml/¾ pint milk
salt
freshly ground black pepper
1 × 425 g/15 oz can sweetcorn, drained
350 g/¾ lb fresh coley fillets, poached, skinned and flaked
350 g/¾ lb smoked coley fillets, poached, skinned and flaked
25 g/1 oz grated Parmesan cheese
25 g/1 oz dried breadcrumbs
To garnish:
225 g/½ lb tomatoes, peeled and chopped
freshly chopped parsley

AMERICAN
1½ tablespoons butter
3 tablespoons flour
2 cups milk
salt
freshly ground black pepper
1 × 15 oz can corn kernels, drained
¾ lb fresh cod fillets, poached, skinned and flaked
¾ lb smoked cod fillets, poached, skinned and flaked
¼ cup grated Parmesan cheese
¼ cup dried breadcrumbs
To garnish:
1 cup peeled and chopped tomatoes
freshly chopped parsley

Melt the butter in a pan, stir in the flour and cook for 2 minutes, stirring constantly. Remove from the heat and gradually stir in the milk. Return to the heat and bring to the boil, stirring constantly. Simmer until thick, then add salt and pepper to taste.

Remove from the heat and stir in the corn. Fold in the flaked fish and pour into an ovenproof dish or foil container. Mix the Parmesan cheese and breadcrumbs together and sprinkle over the top.

To freeze: cool quickly, then wrap in foil. Seal, label and freeze.

To thaw and serve: thaw at room temperature for 4 hours, then reheat, uncovered, in a preheated moderate oven (180°C/350°F or Gas Mark 4) for 35 minutes or until heated through. Put the chopped tomatoes around the edge of the dish or container and sprinkle parsley in the centre.

SERVES 4

FISH CURRY

METRIC/IMPERIAL
50 g/2 oz butter
1 small onion, peeled and finely chopped
675 g/1½ lb cod fillets
flour for coating
salt
freshly ground black pepper
For the sauce:
40 g/1½ oz butter
40 g/1½ oz flour
2 × 5 ml spoons/2 teaspoons curry powder
600 ml/1 pint milk
1 cooking apple, peeled, cored and chopped
75 g/3 oz pineapple, chopped
1 green pepper, cored, seeded and chopped
25 g/1 oz sultanas
juice of 1 lemon

AMERICAN
¼ cup butter
1 small onion, peeled and finely chopped
1½ lb cod fillets
flour for coating
salt
freshly ground black pepper
For the sauce:
3 tablespoons butter
⅜ cup flour
2 teaspoons curry powder
2½ cups milk
1 baking apple, peeled, cored and chopped
½ cup chopped pineapple
1 green pepper, cored, seeded and chopped
3 tablespoons seedless white raisins
juice of 1 lemon

Melt the butter in a frying pan (skillet), add the onion and fry gently until soft. Remove from the pan with a slotted spoon. Coat the fish in flour seasoned with salt and pepper, add to the pan and fry until golden. Remove from the pan and keep hot.

To make the sauce: melt the butter in a large pan, stir in the flour and curry powder and cook for 2 minutes, stirring constantly. Remove from the heat and gradually stir in the milk. Return to the heat and bring to the boil, stirring constantly. Simmer until thick, then add the remaining ingredients to the pan with the onion and fish. Simmer very gently for a further 5 minutes.

To freeze: cool quickly, then transfer to a rigid container. Seal, label and freeze.

To thaw and serve: thaw at room temperature for 4 hours, then reheat very gently on top of the stove, stirring occasionally.

SERVES 4

SEAFOOD HOT POT

METRIC/IMPERIAL

450 g/1 lb cod fillets, skinned and cut into cubes
150 ml/¼ pint dry white wine
300 ml/½ pint water
1 small onion, peeled and chopped
2 bay leaves
1 sprig of parsley
1 × 15 ml spoon/1 tablespoon tomato purée
100 g/4 oz peeled prawns
100 g/4 oz peeled shrimps
1 × 100 g/4 oz jar mussels in brine, drained
juice of ½ lemon
salt
freshly ground black pepper
3 × 15 ml spoons/3 tablespoons fresh white breadcrumbs
15 g/½ oz butter

AMERICAN

1 lb cod fillets, skinned and cut into cubes
⅔ cup dry white wine
1¼ cups water
1 small onion, peeled and chopped
2 bay leaves
1 sprig of parsley
1 tablespoon tomato paste
1⅓ cups shelled shrimp
1 × 4 oz jar mussels in brine, drained
juice of ½ lemon
salt
freshly ground black pepper
3 tablespoons fresh white breadcrumbs
1 tablespoon butter

Put the cod in a pan, add the wine, water, onion, bay leaves and parsley and simmer gently for 10 minutes or until the fish is tender.

Remove the fish with a slotted spoon and set aside. Discard the bay leaves and parsley. Stir the tomato purée (paste) into the fish liquor. Add the shellfish, lemon juice and salt and pepper to taste, then return the cod to the pan. Pour into an ovenproof dish or foil container, sprinkle the top with the breadcrumbs and dot with the butter.

To freeze: cool quickly, then cover with foil. Seal, label and freeze.

To thaw and serve: thaw overnight in the refrigerator, then reheat, uncovered, in a preheated hot oven (220°C/425°F or Gas Mark 7) for 30 minutes or until heated through and golden brown on top.

SERVES 6

SOMERSET FISH PIE

METRIC/IMPERIAL

50 g/2 oz butter
50 g/2 oz flour
300 ml/½ pint milk
450 ml/¾ pint cider
450 g/1 lb haddock fillets, poached, skinned and flaked
1 × 200 g/7 oz can sweetcorn, drained
225 g/½ lb tomatoes, peeled and chopped
salt
freshly ground black pepper
basic puff pastry dough made with 225 g/½ lb flour
beaten egg, to glaze

AMERICAN

¼ cup butter
½ cup flour
1¼ cups milk
2 cups hard cider
1 lb haddock fillets, poached, skinned and flaked
1 × 7 oz can corn kernels, drained
1 cup peeled and chopped tomatoes
salt
freshly ground black pepper
basic puff paste dough made with 2 cups flour
beaten egg, to glaze

Melt the butter in a pan, stir in the flour and cook for 2 minutes, stirring constantly. Remove from the heat and gradually stir in the milk and cider. Return to the heat and bring to the boil, stirring constantly. Simmer until thick, then add the flaked fish, corn, tomatoes, and salt and pepper to taste. Spoon the mixture into an ovenproof pie dish and leave to cool.

Roll out the dough on a floured surface to a shape slightly larger than the pie dish. Cut out a 'lid' to fit the dish and a narrow strip of dough to fit the rim of the dish. Moisten the rim with water and press on the strip of dough. Moisten the strip with water and place the 'lid' on the dish. Press firmly to seal, then trim and flute the edge.

Use any pastry trimmings to make leaves or fish shapes and use to decorate the top of the pie. Cut an air vent in the centre of the pie.

To freeze: open (flash) freeze until firm, then wrap in a freezer bag or foil. Seal, label and return to the freezer.

To thaw and serve: remove wrappings and place the dish on a baking sheet. Brush the dough with the beaten egg. Bake from frozen in a preheated moderately hot oven (200°C/400°F or Gas Mark 6) for 40 minutes or until heated through. Cover with foil if the pastry becomes too brown during cooking.

SERVES 6

CURRIED FISH PIES

METRIC/IMPERIAL
basic shortcrust pastry dough made with 450 g/1 lb flour
1 kg/2 lb white fish fillets, skinned and cut into thin strips
100 g/4 oz peeled shrimps
beaten egg, to glaze
For the sauce:
50 g/2 oz butter
2 onions, peeled and finely chopped
50 g/2 oz flour
1.5 × 15 ml spoons/1½ tablespoons curry powder
600 ml/1 pint fish stock or water
2 × 15 ml spoons/2 tablespoons tomato purée
1 × 15 ml spoon/1 tablespoon lemon juice
1 bay leaf
salt
freshly ground black pepper

AMERICAN
basic pie dough made with 4 cups flour
2 lb white fish fillets, skinned and cut into thin strips
⅔ cup shelled shrimp
beaten egg, to glaze
For the sauce:
¼ cup butter
2 onions, peeled and finely chopped
½ cup flour
1½ tablespoons curry powder
2½ cups fish stock or water
2 tablespoons tomato paste
1 tablespoon lemon juice
1 bay leaf
salt
freshly ground black pepper

Roll out half the dough on a floured surface, cut out 24 rounds and use to line 24 greased patty tins. Prick the bottom of the dough with a fork, then divide the white fish and shrimp(s) equally between the tins.
To make the sauce: melt the butter in a pan, add the onions and fry gently until soft. Stir in the flour and curry powder and cook for 2 minutes, stirring constantly. Stir in the stock or water and bring to the boil, stirring. Simmer until thick, then stir in the remaining sauce ingredients and simmer for a further 10 minutes, stirring occasionally. Remove the bay leaf, leave the sauce to cool, then pour into the patty tins to cover the fish.
Roll out the remaining dough on a floured surface and cut into 24 rounds for the lids. Moisten the edges of the dough in the tins and cover with the lids. Press firmly to seal, then trim and flute the edges. Cut an air vent in the centre of each pie.
To freeze: open (flash) freeze until firm, then remove the pies from the tins and pack in a rigid container, separating each layer with foil. Seal, label and return to the freezer.
To thaw and serve: return the frozen pies to the tins and brush with the beaten egg. Bake in a preheated moderately hot oven (200°C/400°F or Gas Mark 6) for 30 to 35 minutes or until heated through. Cover with foil if the pastry becomes too brown during cooking.
MAKES 24

HOMEMADE FISH FINGERS

METRIC/IMPERIAL
25 g/1 oz butter
25 g/1 oz flour
150 ml/¼ pint milk
1 × 5 ml spoon/1 teaspoon prepared English mustard
2 × 5 ml spoons/2 teaspoons freshly chopped parsley
salt
freshly ground black pepper
450 g/1 lb white fish fillets, poached, skinned and flaked
flour for coating
1 egg, beaten
100 g/4 oz fresh white breadcrumbs
vegetable oil for deep-frying, to finish

AMERICAN
2 tablespoons butter
¼ cup flour
⅔ cup milk
1 teaspoon prepared English mustard
2 teaspoons freshly chopped parsley
salt
freshly ground black pepper
1 lb white fish fillets, poached, skinned and flaked
flour for coating
1 egg, beaten
2 cups fresh white breadcrumbs
vegetable oil for deep-frying, to finish

Melt the butter in a pan, stir in the flour and cook for 2 minutes, stirring constantly. Remove from the heat and gradually stir in the milk. Return to the heat and bring to the boil, stirring constantly. Simmer until thick, stir in the mustard, parsley and salt and pepper to taste, then fold in the flaked fish.
Form the mixture into 12 finger shapes and coat in flour. Dip into the beaten egg one at a time, then coat in breadcrumbs. Repeat with more egg and breadcrumbs until thoroughly coated.

To freeze: open (flash) freeze until firm, then pack in a rigid container, separating each layer with foil. Seal, label and return to the freezer.
To thaw and serve: thaw in the refrigerator for 2 hours, then deep-fry in hot oil for 5 minutes or until golden on all sides. Drain on paper towels and serve with a hot tomato sauce.
MAKES 12

HOMEMADE FISH FINGERS WITH DEVILLED TOPPING

METRIC/IMPERIAL
12 homemade fish fingers (see previous recipe)
vegetable oil for deep-frying
40 g/1½ oz butter
2 × 15 ml spoons/2 tablespoons sweet chutney
1 × 15 ml spoon/1 tablespoon freshly chopped parsley
2 × 15 ml spoons/2 tablespoons tomato ketchup
1 × 5 ml spoon/1 teaspoon prepared mustard
salt
freshly ground black pepper
To finish:
25 g/1 oz potato crisps, crushed
4 lemon slices

AMERICAN
12 homemade fish fingers (see previous recipe)
vegetable oil for deep-frying
3 tablespoons butter
2 tablespoons sweet chutney
1 tablespoon freshly chopped parsley
2 tablespoons tomato ketchup
1 teaspoon prepared mustard
salt
freshly ground black pepper
To finish:
½ cup crushed potato chips
4 lemon slices

Deep-fry the fish fingers in hot oil for 5 minutes until golden on all sides. Drain on paper towels, then arrange in an ovenproof dish or foil container. Melt the butter in a pan, add the chutney, parsley, ketchup, mustard and salt and pepper to taste and heat through. Pour over the fish fingers.
To freeze: cool quickly, then cover with foil. Seal, label and freeze.
To thaw and serve: remove wrappings and thaw at room temperature for 4 hours. Sprinkle the crisps over the top and bake in a preheated moderate oven (180°C/350°F or Gas Mark 4) for 25 minutes or until heated through. Garnish with lemon slices just before serving.
SERVES 4

RUSSIAN FISH ROLL

METRIC/IMPERIAL
25 g/1 oz butter
1 medium onion, peeled and finely chopped
100 g/4 oz mushrooms, chopped
450 g/1 lb smoked fish fillets, poached, skinned and flaked
2 × 5 ml spoons/2 teaspoons prepared mustard
2 × 15 ml spoons/2 tablespoons freshly chopped parsley
a few thin strips of canned red pimento
freshly ground black pepper
basic puff pastry dough made with 225 g/½ lb flour
beaten egg, to glaze

AMERICAN
2 tablespoons butter
1 medium onion, peeled and finely chopped
1 cup chopped mushrooms
1 lb smoked fish fillets, poached, skinned and flaked
2 teaspoons prepared mustard
2 tablespoons freshly chopped parsley
a few thin strips of canned red pimiento
freshly ground black pepper
basic puff paste dough made with 2 cups flour
beaten egg, to glaze

Melt the butter in a pan, add the onion and fry gently until soft. Add the mushrooms, fry for 2 minutes, then transfer to a bowl. Add the flaked fish, mustard, parsley, pimento and pepper to taste. Stir well to mix.
Roll out the dough on a floured surface to a rectangular shape. Transfer to a baking sheet. Spread the mixture on the dough, moisten the edges with water, then roll up like a Swiss (jelly) roll, tucking under the ends. Use any trimmings from the dough to decorate the top of the roll.
Cut an air vent in the centre of the roll.
To freeze: open (flash) freeze until firm, then wrap in foil. Seal, label and return to the freezer.
To thaw and serve: remove wrappings, place the fish roll on a baking sheet and thaw in the refrigerator for 4 hours.
Brush the dough with beaten egg. Bake in a preheated moderately hot oven (200°C/400°F or Gas Mark 6) for 35 minutes or until heated through. Cover with foil if the pastry becomes too brown during cooking.
SERVES 4 to 6

SAVOURY FISH PLAIT

METRIC/IMPERIAL

1 × 375 g/13 oz packet frozen puff pastry, thawed
150 ml/¼ pint coating sauce
225 g/½ lb smoked haddock fillets, poached, skinned and flaked
1 × 5 ml spoon/1 teaspoon lemon juice
2 × 5 ml spoons/2 teaspoons tomato purée
freshly ground black pepper
beaten egg, to glaze

AMERICAN

1 × 13 oz package frozen puff pastry, thawed
⅔ cup white coating sauce
½ lb smoked haddock fillets, poached, skinned and flaked
1 teaspoon lemon juice
2 teaspoons tomato paste
freshly ground black pepper
beaten egg, to glaze

Roll out the dough on a floured surface to a rectangle 30 × 25 cm/12 × 10 inches. Place on a baking sheet and mark into 3 sections lengthways. Put the white sauce in a bowl and add the flaked fish, lemon juice, tomato purée (paste) and pepper to taste. Stir well to mix.

Spoon the fish mixture onto the centre section of the dough. Cut diagonal slits in the 2 outer sections of the dough, moisten the edges with water and plait alternately across the centre filling.

To freeze: open (flash) freeze until firm, then wrap in a freezer bag or foil. Seal, label and return to the freezer.

To thaw and serve: remove wrappings and place the fish plait on a baking sheet. Brush the dough with the beaten egg. Bake from frozen in a preheated moderately hot oven (200°C/400°F or Gas Mark 6) for 40 minutes or until heated through. Cover with foil if the pastry becomes too brown during cooking.

SERVES 4

SMOKED HADDOCK KEDGEREE

METRIC/IMPERIAL

225 g/½ lb patna or long-grain rice
salt
75 g/3 oz butter
1 small onion, peeled and finely chopped
450 g/1 lb smoked haddock fillets, poached, skinned and flaked
cayenne pepper
To finish:
2 × 15 ml spoons/2 tablespoons single cream
lemon wedges
parsley sprigs

AMERICAN

1⅓ cups patna or long-grain rice
salt
⅜ cup butter
1 small onion, peeled and finely chopped
1 lb smoked haddock fillets, poached, skinned and flaked
cayenne pepper
To finish:
2 tablespoons light cream
lemon wedges
parsley sprigs

Cook the rice in boiling salted water until tender, rinse under cold running water and drain. Melt the butter in a pan, add the onion and fry gently until soft. Remove from the heat and stir in the rice, fish and salt and cayenne pepper to taste. Stir well with a fork to mix.

To freeze: pack in a buttered foil container, then cover with foil. Seal, label and freeze.

To thaw and serve: reheat from frozen in the covered container in a preheated moderately hot oven (200°C/400°F or Gas Mark 6) for 45 minutes or until heated through. Stir occasionally with a fork during the reheating. Stir in the cream just before serving and garnish with lemon and parsley.

SERVES 8

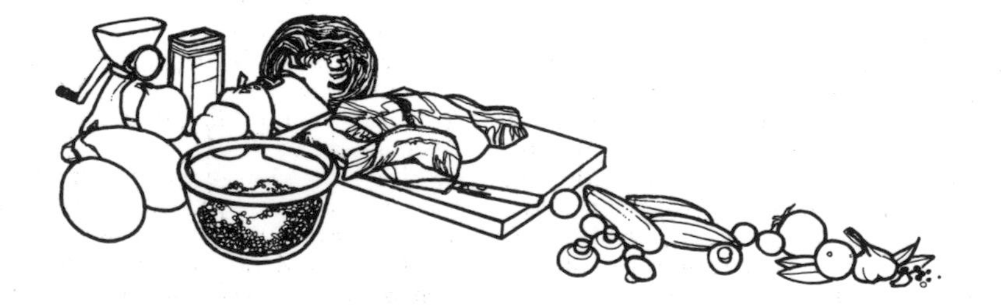

HADDOCK AND TOMATO PIE

METRIC/IMPERIAL

225 g/½ lb haddock fillets, skinned and cut into small pieces
3 tomatoes, peeled and sliced
100 g/4 oz button mushrooms, sliced
1 × 15 ml spoon/1 tablespoon freshly chopped parsley
juice of ½ lemon
25 g/1 oz butter
25 g/1 oz flour
300 ml/½ pint milk
salt
freshly ground black pepper
pinch of ground mace
basic flaky or puff pastry dough made with 225 g/½ lb flour
beaten egg, to glaze

AMERICAN

½ lb haddock fillets, skinned and cut into small pieces
3 tomatoes, peeled and sliced
1 cup sliced button mushrooms
1 tablespoon freshly chopped parsley
juice of ½ lemon
2 tablespoons butter
¼ cup flour
1¼ cups milk
salt
freshly ground black pepper
pinch of ground mace
basic flaky or puff paste dough made with 2 cups flour
beaten egg, to glaze

Arrange the fish, tomatoes and mushrooms in layers in an ovenproof pie dish. Sprinkle with the parsley and lemon juice. Melt the butter in a pan, stir in the flour and cook for 2 minutes, stirring constantly. Remove from the heat and gradually stir in the milk. Return to the heat and bring to the boil, stirring constantly. Simmer until thick, then add salt and pepper to taste and the mace. Pour over the fish and vegetables and leave to cool.

Roll out the dough on a floured surface to a shape slightly larger than the pie dish. Cut out a lid to fit the dish and a narrow strip of dough to fit the rim of the dish. Moisten the rim with water and press on the strip of dough. Moisten the strip with water and place the lid on the dish. Press firmly to seal, then trim and flute the edge. Use any trimmings to decorate the top of the pie. Cut an air vent in the centre of the pie.

To freeze: open (flash) freeze until firm, then wrap in a freezer bag or foil. Seal, label and return to the freezer.

To thaw and serve: remove wrappings and thaw in the refrigerator for 5 to 6 hours. Place on a baking sheet and brush the dough with beaten egg. Bake in a preheated moderately hot oven (200°C/400°F or Gas Mark 6) for 20 minutes, then reduce the heat to moderate (160°C/325°F or Gas Mark 3) and bake for a further 15 to 20 minutes or until heated through.

Cover with foil if the pastry becomes too brown during cooking.

SERVES 4

SMOKED HADDOCK CASSEROLE

METRIC/IMPERIAL

2 × 15 ml spoons/2 tablespoons olive oil
2 large onions, peeled and finely chopped
2 garlic cloves, peeled and chopped
1.25 kg/2½ lb smoked haddock fillets, poached and flaked
675 g/1½ lb boiled potatoes, peeled and sliced
freshly ground black pepper
To finish:
150 ml/¼ pint double cream
a few black olives, halved and stoned
2 hard-boiled eggs, quartered
freshly chopped parsley

AMERICAN

2 tablespoons olive oil
2 large onions, peeled and finely chopped
2 garlic cloves, peeled and chopped
2½ lb smoked haddock fillets, poached and flaked
1½ lb boiled potatoes, peeled and sliced
freshly ground black pepper
To finish:
⅔ cup heavy cream
a few black olives, halved and pitted
2 hard-cooked eggs, quartered
freshly chopped parsley

Heat the oil in a pan, add the onions and garlic and fry gently until soft. Put the fish, onions and potatoes in layers in a foil container, sprinkling each layer with pepper and finishing with a layer of potato.

To freeze: cool quickly, then wrap in foil. Seal, label and freeze.

To thaw and serve: thaw at room temperature for 4 hours, then pour over the cream and bake in a preheated moderately hot oven (200°C/400°F or Gas Mark 6) for 30 to 35 minutes until heated through. Garnish with the olives, eggs and parsley just before serving.

SERVES 6

SMOKED HADDOCK PANCAKES (CRÊPES)

METRIC/IMPERIAL

8 pancakes made from 300 ml/½ pint batter
For the filling:
1 kg/2 lb smoked haddock fillets
1 small onion, peeled and finely chopped
450 ml/¾ pint milk
freshly ground black pepper
50 g/2 oz butter
50 g/2 oz flour
2 × 15 ml spoons/2 tablespoons lemon juice
2 × 15 ml spoons/2 tablespoons single cream
For the topping:
25 g/1 oz butter, melted
2 × 15 ml spoons/2 tablespoons grated Gruyère cheese
1 × 15 ml spoon/1 tablespoon dried breadcrumbs

AMERICAN

8 crêpes made from 1¼ cups batter
For the filling:
2 lb smoked haddock fillets
1 small onion, peeled and finely chopped
2 cups milk
freshly ground black pepper
¼ cup butter
½ cup flour
1 tablespoon lemon juice
2 tablespoons light cream
For the topping:
2 tablespoons butter, melted
2 tablespoons grated Gruyère cheese
1 tablespoon dried breadcrumbs

To make the filling: put the fish in a pan with the onion, milk and pepper to taste. Cover and poach gently for 15 minutes. Strain the fish, skin and flake. Reserve the poaching liquid and onion.
Melt the butter in a separate pan, stir in the flour and cook for 2 minutes, stirring constantly. Remove from the heat and gradually stir in the reserved poaching liquid. Return to the heat and bring to the boil, stirring constantly. Simmer until thick, then fold in the flaked fish, reserved onion and the cream. Leave to cool.
Divide the filling equally between the pancakes (crêpes) and fold or roll up.
To freeze: put the pancakes (crêpes) in an ovenproof dish or foil container. Mix together the ingredients for the topping and sprinkle over the top. Wrap in foil, seal, label and freeze.
To thaw and serve: reheat from frozen, uncovered, in a preheated moderate oven (180°C/350°F or Gas Mark 4) for 35 to 40 minutes or until heated through and golden brown on top.
SERVES 4

HADDOCK EN CROÛTE

METRIC/IMPERIAL

2 large haddock fillets, skinned
25 g/1 oz butter
basic puff pastry dough made with 225 g/½ lb flour
beaten egg, to glaze
For the filling:
175 g/6 oz Gouda cheese, grated
100 g/4 oz button mushrooms, sliced
1 × 190 g/6½ oz can pimento, drained and sliced
2 × 15 ml spoons/2 tablespoons dry vermouth or sherry
1 × 15 ml spoon/1 tablespoon freshly chopped parsley
1 × 5 ml spoon/1 teaspoon dried oregano
salt
freshly ground black pepper
1 egg, beaten

AMERICAN

2 large haddock fillets, skinned
2 tablespoons butter
basic puff paste dough made with 2 cups flour
beaten egg, to glaze
For the filling:
1½ cups grated Gouda cheese
1 cup sliced button mushrooms
1 × 6½ oz can pimiento, drained and sliced
2 tablespoons dry vermouth or sherry
1 tablespoon freshly chopped parsley
1 teaspoon dried oregano
salt
freshly ground black pepper
1 egg, beaten

Put the fish in an ovenproof dish, dot with the butter and bake in a preheated moderately hot oven (190°C/375°F or Gas Mark 5) for 10 minutes. Leave to cool.
To make the filling: put all the ingredients in a bowl and stir well to mix.
Roll out the dough on a floured surface to a rectangle 33 × 30 cm/14 × 12 inches. Cut off a 2.5 cm/1 inch strip and reserve to decorate the top of the dough. Transfer the rectangle to a baking sheet.
Put one fish fillet on one half of the dough and spread half the filling over it. Put the second fish fillet on top, then spread with the remaining filling. Moisten the edges of the dough with water and fold over the fish and filling to enclose them completely. Tuck under the ends. Use the reserved strip of dough to make leaves to decorate the top. Cut an air vent in the centre of the pie.
To freeze: open (flash) freeze until firm, then wrap in foil. Seal, label and return to the freezer.
To thaw and serve: remove wrappings and place the pie on a baking sheet. Brush the dough with

the beaten egg. Bake from frozen in a preheated moderately hot oven (200°C/400°F or Gas Mark 6) for 40 minutes or until heated through. Cover with foil if the pastry becomes too brown during cooking.
SERVES 6

HADDOCK FISH CAKES

METRIC/IMPERIAL

450 g/1 lb potatoes, peeled, boiled and mashed with butter and milk
1 × 15 ml spoon/1 tablespoon freshly chopped parsley
1 × 15 ml spoon/1 tablespoon snipped chives
1 × 15 ml spoon/1 tablespoon lemon juice
salt
freshly ground black pepper
450 g/1 lb haddock fillets, poached, skinned and flaked
1 egg, beaten
flour for coating
vegetable oil for frying

AMERICAN

1 lb potatoes, peeled, boiled and mashed with butter and milk
1 tablespoon freshly chopped parsley
1 tablespoon snipped chives
1 tablespoon lemon juice
salt
freshly ground black pepper
1 lb haddock fillets, poached, skinned and flaked
1 egg, beaten
flour for coating
vegetable oil for frying

Put the mashed potatoes in a bowl with the parsley, chives, lemon juice and salt and pepper to taste. Stir well to mix, then fold in the flaked fish.
Bind the mixture with the beaten egg and chill in the refrigerator until firm. Form into six flat cakes and coat in flour seasoned with salt and pepper.
To freeze: open (flash) freeze until firm, then pack in a rigid container, separating each layer with foil. Seal, label and return to the freezer.
To thaw and serve: thaw in the refrigerator for 3 hours, then fry in hot oil for 5 minutes on each side until golden brown. Drain on paper towels.
MAKES 6

SUSSEX SMOKIES

METRIC/IMPERIAL

350 g/¾ lb smoked haddock fillets
300 ml/½ pint milk
2 × 5 ml spoons/2 teaspoons lemon juice
25 g/1 oz flour
25 g/1 oz butter
1 × 2.5 ml spoon/1 teaspoon mustard powder
75 g/3 oz Cheddar cheese, grated
2 × 15 ml spoons/2 tablespoons single cream
freshly ground black pepper
25 g/1 oz fresh white breadcrumbs

AMERICAN

¾ lb smoked haddock fillets
1¼ cups milk
2 teaspoons lemon juice
¼ cup flour
2 tablespoons butter
½ teaspoon mustard powder
¾ cup grated Cheddar cheese
2 tablespoons light cream
freshly ground black pepper
½ cup fresh white breadcrumbs

Put the haddock in a pan with a little of the milk and the lemon juice and poach gently for 8 to 10 minutes. Strain and reserve the poaching liquid, then skin and flake the fish.
Put the reserved poaching liquid, the remaining milk, flour and butter in a pan and beat over a medium heat until thick. Simmer for 2 to 3 minutes, stirring occasionally, then remove from the heat and stir in the mustard, 50 g/2 oz/½ cup cheese, the cream and pepper to taste. Fold in the flaked fish.

Divide the fish mixture equally between 4 individual ovenproof dishes. Mix the remaining cheese with the breadcrumbs and sprinkle on top. Put under a preheated grill (broiler) for 3 to 4 minutes until golden brown.
To freeze: cool quickly, then wrap in foil. Seal, label and freeze.
To thaw and serve: thaw at room temperature for 40 minutes, then reheat in the covered dishes in a preheated moderate oven (180°C/350°F or Gas Mark 4) for 20 minutes or until heated through.
MAKES 4

HADDOCK CASSEROLE

METRIC/IMPERIAL

575 g/1¼ lb haddock fillets, skinned and cut into cubes
350 g/¾ lb tomatoes, peeled and sliced
100 g/4 oz mushrooms, sliced
1 × 15 ml spoon/1 tablespoon freshly chopped parsley
salt
freshly ground black pepper
150 ml/¼ pint cider
50 g/2 oz Cheddar cheese, grated, to finish

AMERICAN

1¼ lb haddock fillets, skinned and cut into cubes
¾ lb tomatoes, peeled and sliced
1 cup sliced mushrooms
1 tablespoon freshly chopped parsley
salt
freshly ground black pepper
⅔ cup hard cider
½ cup grated Cheddar cheese, to finish

Put the haddock in a buttered ovenproof dish or foil container and arrange the tomatoes and mushrooms on top. Sprinkle with parsley and salt and pepper to taste.
Pour over the cider, cover with buttered greaseproof paper or non-stick parchment and bake in a preheated moderately hot oven (190°C/375°F or Gas Mark 5) for 20 minutes.
To freeze: cool quickly, then cover with foil. Seal, label and freeze.
To thaw and serve: thaw at room temperature for 4 hours, then sprinkle with the cheese and reheat in a preheated moderate oven (180°C/350°F or Gas Mark 4) for 25 minutes or until heated through. Put under a preheated grill (broiler) to brown before serving.
SERVES 4

HADDOCK WITH PAPRIKA

METRIC/IMPERIAL

25 g/1 oz butter
2 × 15 ml spoons/2 tablespoons vegetable oil
1 medium onion, peeled and sliced
1 garlic clove, peeled and crushed
1 × 5 ml spoon/1 teaspoon paprika pepper
1 kg/2 lb haddock fillets, skinned and cut into cubes
3 large tomatoes, peeled, seeded and chopped
150 ml/¼ pint tomato juice
salt
freshly ground black pepper

AMERICAN

2 tablespoons butter
2 tablespoons vegetable oil
1 medium onion, peeled and sliced
1 garlic clove, peeled and crushed
1 teaspoon paprika pepper
2 lb haddock fillets, skinned and cut into cubes
3 large tomatoes, peeled, seeded and chopped
⅔ cup tomato juice
salt
freshly ground black pepper

Heat the butter and oil in a pan, add the onion and garlic and fry gently until soft. Add the paprika and the haddock and fry gently for 5 minutes. Stir in the remaining ingredients, cover and simmer for 5 minutes.
To freeze: cool quickly, then pour into a rigid container. Seal label and freeze.
To thaw and serve: put the frozen haddock and sauce in the top of a double boiler and reheat.
SERVES 4 to 6

PLAICE (FLOUNDER) IN MUSTARD SAUCE

METRIC/IMPERIAL

8 small plaice fillets, skinned
1 small onion, peeled and finely chopped
25 g/1 oz butter
25 g/1 oz flour
300 ml/½ pint milk
1 × 15 ml spoon/1 tablespoon prepared French mustard
1 × 15 ml spoon/1 tablespoon freshly chopped parsley
salt
freshly ground black pepper

AMERICAN

8 small flounder fillets, skinned
1 small onion, peeled and finely chopped
2 tablespoons butter
2 tablespoons flour
1¼ cups milk
1 tablespoon prepared French mustard
1 tablespoon freshly chopped parsley
salt
freshly ground black pepper

Roll up the fish fillets and arrange in a buttered ovenproof dish or foil container. Sprinkle over the onion.
Melt the butter in a pan, stir in the flour and cook for 2 minutes, stirring constantly. Remove from the heat and gradually stir in the milk. Return to the heat and bring to the boil, stirring constantly. Simmer until thick, then stir in the mustard, parsley and salt and pepper to taste.

Pour over the fish and onion and bake in a preheated moderately hot oven (190°C/375°F or Gas Mark 5) for 10 minutes.
To freeze: cool quickly, then cover with foil. Seal, label and freeze.
To thaw and serve: thaw at room temperature for 4 hours, then reheat in the covered dish or container in a preheated moderately hot oven for 25 minutes or until heated through.
SERVES 4

TOMATO PLAICE (FLOUNDER) PANCAKES (CRÊPES)

METRIC/IMPERIAL
8 pancakes (crêpes) made from 300 ml/½ pint batter
For the filling:
20 g/¾ oz butter
20 g/¾ oz flour
300 ml/½ pint fish stock
4 × 15 ml spoons/4 tablespoons tomato purée
salt
freshly ground black pepper
225 g/½ lb plaice fillets, poached, skinned and flaked
1 × 225 g/8 oz packet frozen peas and sweetcorn, cooked

AMERICAN
8 crêpes made from 1¼ cups batter
For the filling:
1½ tablespoons butter
3 tablespoons flour
1¼ cups fish stock
¼ cup tomato paste
salt
freshly ground black pepper
½ lb flounder fillets, poached, skinned and flaked
1 × 8 oz package frozen peas and corn kernels, cooked

To make the filling: melt the butter in a pan, stir in the flour and cook for 2 minutes, stirring constantly. Stir in the stock and bring to the boil, stirring. Simmer until thick, then stir in the tomato purée (paste) and salt and pepper to taste. Leave to cool. Mix the fish and peas and corn into the sauce. Divide the sauce equally between the pancakes (crêpes) and fold or roll up.
To freeze: put the pancakes (crêpes) in a foil container. Cover with foil. Seal, label and freeze.
To thaw and serve: reheat from frozen in the covered dish or container in a preheated moderate oven (180°C/350°F or Gas Mark 4) for 35 to 40 minutes or until heated through.
SERVES 4

PLAICE (FLOUNDER) FLORENTINE

METRIC/IMPERIAL
2 × 350 g/12 oz packets frozen chopped spinach
salt
freshly ground black pepper
4 plaice fillets, skinned
flour for coating
50 g/2 oz butter
For the sauce:
25 g/1 oz butter
25 g/1 oz flour
300 ml/½ pint milk
100 g/4 oz Cheddar cheese, grated
2 × 15 ml spoons/2 tablespoons grated Parmesan cheese

AMERICAN
2 × 12 oz packages frozen chopped spinach
salt
freshly ground black pepper
4 flounder fillets, skinned
flour for coating
¼ cup butter
For the sauce:
2 tablespoons butter
¼ cup flour
1¼ cups milk
1 cup grated Cheddar cheese
2 tablespoons grated Parmesan cheese

Cook the spinach according to packet directions, put in an ovenproof dish or foil container and sprinkle with salt and pepper to taste.
Coat the fish in flour seasoned with salt and pepper. Melt the butter in a pan, add the fish and fry for 5 minutes on each side until golden. Remove from the pan with a slotted spoon and arrange on top of the spinach.
To make the sauce: melt the butter in a pan, stir in the flour and cook for 2 minutes, stirring constantly. Remove from the heat and gradually stir in the milk. Return to the heat and bring to the boil, stirring constantly. Simmer until thick, then stir in the Cheddar cheese and salt and pepper to taste. Pour the sauce over the fish and sprinkle with the Parmesan cheese.
To freeze: cool quickly, then wrap in foil. Seal, label and freeze.
To thaw and serve: thaw at room temperature for 4 hours, then reheat, uncovered, in a preheated moderately hot oven (200°C/400°F or Gas Mark 6) for 35 minutes or until heated through and golden brown on top.
SERVES 4

SWEET AND SOUR PLAICE (FLOUNDER)

METRIC/IMPERIAL

4 large plaice fillets, skinned
2 celery stalks, chopped
1 carrot, peeled and chopped
1 onion, peeled and sliced
salt
freshly ground black pepper
25–50 g/1–2 oz dried breadcrumbs
For the sauce:
15 g/½ oz butter
15 g/½ oz flour
25 g/1 oz sugar
25 g/1 oz sultanas
juice of 1 lemon
½ small onion, peeled and finely chopped

AMERICAN

4 large flounder fillets, skinned
2 celery stalks, chopped
1 carrot, peeled and chopped
1 onion, peeled and sliced
salt
freshly ground black pepper
¼–½ cup dried breadcrumbs
For the sauce:
1 tablespoon butter
2 tablespoons flour
2 tablespoons sugar
3 tablespoons seedless white raisins
juice of 1 lemon
½ small onion, peeled and finely chopped

Fold the fish fillets in half and place in a pan with the vegetables and salt and pepper to taste. Cover with water and simmer gently for 10 to 15 minutes or until the fish is tender. Strain the stock and reserve 150 ml/¼ pint/⅔ cup.

To make the sauce: melt the butter in a pan, stir in the flour and cook for 2 minutes, stirring constantly. Stir in the reserved fish stock and bring to the boil, stirring constantly. Simmer until thick, then add the remaining sauce ingredients with salt and pepper to taste and simmer for a further 10 minutes. Remove from the heat.

To freeze: cool the fish and sauce quickly. Put the fish in an ovenproof dish or foil container, then pour over the sauce and cover with breadcrumbs. Cover with foil, then wrap in a freezer bag. Seal, label and freeze.

To thaw and serve: thaw at room temperature for 4 hours, then reheat in a preheated moderate oven (180°C/350°F or Gas Mark 4) for 25 minutes or until heated through. Put under a preheated grill (broiler) to brown before serving.

SERVES 4

CRISPY PLAICE (FLOUNDER) PIE

METRIC/IMPERIAL

450 g/1 lb plaice fillets, skinned
25 g/1 oz butter
1 onion, peeled and sliced into rings
225 g/½ lb tomatoes, peeled and chopped
75 g/3 oz mushrooms, sliced
15 g/½ oz cheese, grated
15 g/½ oz fresh white breadcrumbs
2 eggs
300 ml/½ pint milk
salt
freshly ground black pepper
For the topping:
40 g/1½ oz fresh white breadcrumbs
40 g/1½ oz cheese, grated

AMERICAN

1 lb flounder fillets, skinned
2 tablespoons butter
1 onion, peeled and sliced into rings
1 cup peeled and chopped tomatoes
¾ cup sliced mushrooms
2 tablespoons grated cheese
¼ cup fresh white breadcrumbs
2 eggs
1¼ cups milk
salt
freshly ground black pepper
For the topping:
¾ cup fresh white breadcrumbs
6 tablespoons grated cheese

Fold the fish fillets in half and place in a buttered ovenproof dish or foil container. Melt the butter in a pan, add the onion and fry gently until soft. Add the tomatoes and mushrooms and fry for a further 3 to 4 minutes. Remove from the heat, stir in the cheese and breadcrumbs and spoon over the fish. Put the eggs, milk and salt and pepper to taste in a bowl and beat well to mix. Pour into the dish.

To make the topping: mix the cheese and breadcrumbs together and sprinkle over the dish. Bake in a preheated moderate oven (160°C/325°F or Gas Mark 3) for 30 minutes.

To freeze: cool quickly, then wrap in foil. Seal, label and freeze.

To thaw and serve: remove wrappings and thaw at room temperature for 4 hours. Reheat in a preheated moderate oven (160°C/325°F or Gas Mark 3) for 20 to 30 minutes or until heated through. Put under a preheated grill (broiler) to brown before serving.

SERVES 4

SOLE BONNE FEMME

METRIC/IMPERIAL

8 sole fillets, skinned
150 ml/¼ pint fish stock or water
150 ml/¼ pint dry white wine
juice of ½ lemon
1 bay leaf
salt
freshly ground black pepper
25 g/1 oz butter
50 g/2 oz mushrooms, sliced
For the sauce:
25 g/1 oz butter
25 g/1 oz flour
4 × 15 ml spoons/4 tablespoons single cream

AMERICAN

8 sole fillets, skinned
⅔ cup fish stock or water
⅔ cup dry white wine
juice of ½ lemon
1 bay leaf
salt
freshly ground black pepper
2 tablespoons butter
½ cup sliced mushrooms
For the sauce:
2 tablespoons butter
¼ cup flour
¼ cup light cream

Fold the fish fillets in half and place in a buttered ovenproof dish or foil container. Add the fish stock or water, the wine, the lemon juice, bay leaf and salt and pepper to taste. Cover and bake in a preheated moderate oven (180°C/350°F or Gas Mark 4) for 20 minutes. Remove the bay leaf, strain off the fish liquor and reserve 250 ml/8 fl oz/1 cup. Melt the butter in a pan, add the mushrooms and fry gently for 2 minutes then spoon over the fish.
To make the sauce: melt the butter in a pan, stir in the flour and cook for 2 minutes, stirring constantly. Stir in the reserved fish liquor and bring to the boil, stirring constantly. Simmer until thick, then remove from the heat and stir in the cream, with salt and pepper to taste. Pour the sauce over the mushrooms and fish.
To freeze: cool quickly, then wrap in foil. Seal, label and freeze.
To thaw and serve: reheat from frozen in the covered dish or container in a preheated moderate oven (160°C/325°F or Gas Mark 3) for 30 minutes or until heated through.
SERVES 4

MACKEREL WITH FRENCH MUSTARD STUFFING

METRIC/IMPERIAL

4 mackerel, cleaned and boned, with the heads removed
For the stuffing:
75 g/3 oz butter
1 medium onion, peeled and finely chopped
100 g/4 oz fresh white breadcrumbs
1 × 15 ml spoon/1 tablespoon prepared French mustard
1 × 5 ml spoon/1 teaspoon lemon juice
½ bunch of watercress leaves, finely chopped
salt
freshly ground black pepper
1 egg, beaten
To garnish:
lemon slices
gherkins

AMERICAN

4 mackerel, cleaned and boned out, with the heads removed
For the stuffing:
⅜ cup butter
1 medium onion, peeled and finely chopped
2 cups fresh white breadcrumbs
1 tablespoon prepared French mustard
1 teaspoon lemon juice
½ bunch of watercress leaves, finely chopped
salt
freshly ground black pepper
1 egg, beaten
To garnish:
lemon slices
small sweet dill pickles

To make the stuffing: melt 25 g/1 oz/2 tablespoons butter in a pan, add the onion and fry gently until soft. Transfer to a bowl, add the remaining stuffing ingredients and stir well to mix.
Spoon the stuffing into the cavity of each mackerel, dividing it equally between them. Place in an ovenproof dish or foil container. Melt the remaining butter, pour over the fish and sprinkle with salt and pepper to taste. Cover and bake in a preheated moderate oven (180°C/350°F or Gas Mark 4) for 25 minutes or until the fish is tender.
To freeze: cool quickly then wrap in foil. Seal, label and freeze.
To thaw and serve: reheat from frozen in the covered dish or container in a preheated moderate oven (180°C/350°F or Gas Mark 4) until heated through. Garnish with lemon and gherkins (small sweet dill pickles).
SERVES 4

DEVILLED MACKEREL

METRIC/IMPERIAL

4 mackerel, cleaned and boned, with the heads removed
flour for coating
For the stuffing:
2 × 15 ml spoons/2 tablespoons fresh white breadcrumbs
2 × 15 ml spoons/2 tablespoons grated onion
salt
pinch of cayenne pepper
1 × 15 ml spoon/1 tablespoon mustard powder
To finish:
50 g/2 oz butter
a few raw onion rings

AMERICAN

4 mackerel, cleaned and boned out, with the heads removed
flour for coating
For the stuffing:
2 tablespoons fresh white breadcrumbs
2 tablespoons grated onion
salt
pinch of cayenne pepper
1 tablespoon mustard powder
To finish:
¼ cup butter
a few raw onion rings

To make the stuffing: put the breadcrumbs, onion, salt, cayenne and half the mustard in a bowl and stir well to mix.
Lay the mackerel flat on a surface, skin side down. Put the stuffing near the tail end of each mackerel, dividing it equally between them. Roll up from the tail end and secure with wooden cocktail sticks (toothpicks). Coat the fish in flour mixed with the remaining mustard.
To freeze: open (flash) freeze until firm, then pack in a rigid container. Seal, label and return to the freezer.
To thaw and serve: thaw in the refrigerator for 5 hours. Melt the butter in a pan, add the mackerel and fry for 5 minutes on each side until golden brown. Remove the cocktail sticks (toothpicks) and garnish with onion rings.
SERVES 4

HUSS PIE

METRIC/IMPERIAL

450 g/1 lb cut macaroni
salt
450 g/1 lb huss fillets, poached, skinned and flaked
3 × 15 ml spoons/3 tablespoons vegetable oil
2 × 15 ml spoons/2 tablespoons flour
50 g/2 oz cooked ham, diced
1 × 225 g/8 oz can tomatoes
1 × 2.5 ml spoon/½ teaspoon dried mixed herbs
freshly ground black pepper
100 g/4 oz fresh white breadcrumbs

AMERICAN

4 cups cut macaroni
salt
1 lb huss fillets, poached, skinned and flaked
3 tablespoons vegetable oil
2 tablespoons flour
¼ cup diced cooked ham
1 × ½ lb can tomatoes
½ teaspoon dried mixed herbs
freshly ground black pepper
2 cups fresh white breadcrumbs

Cook the macaroni in boiling salted water until 'al dente'. Drain and mix with the fish, then arrange in an ovenproof dish or foil container. Put 2 × 15 ml spoons/2 tablespoons oil in a pan with the flour and cook for 1 minute, stirring constantly. Add the ham and tomatoes, simmer until thick, then add the herbs and salt and pepper to taste. Simmer the sauce for 30 minutes, adding a little water if it becomes too thick.
Pour the sauce over the macaroni and fish. Heat the remaining oil in a pan, add the breadcrumbs and fry until golden. Sprinkle on top of the sauce.
To freeze: cool quickly, then wrap in foil. Seal, label and freeze.
To thaw and serve: thaw at room temperature for 4 hours, then reheat, uncovered, in a preheated moderate oven (180°C/350°F or Gas Mark 4) for 35 minutes or until heated through.
SERVES 4

STARGAZY PIE

METRIC/IMPERIAL

approx 75 g/3 oz fresh white breadcrumbs
6 fresh pilchards or herrings, cleaned and boned, with the heads left on
freshly chopped parsley
salt
freshly ground black pepper
3 eggs
2–3 × 15 ml spoons/2–3 tablespoons single cream
basic shortcrust pastry dough made with 225 g/½ lb flour
a little milk, to glaze

AMERICAN

approx 1½ cups fresh white breadcrumbs
6 fresh pilchards or herrings, cleaned and boned out, with the heads left on

freshly chopped parsley
salt
freshly ground black pepper
3 eggs
2–3 tablespoons light cream
basic pie dough made with 2 cups flour
a little milk, to glaze

Line a buttered ovenproof dish with breadcrumbs and put in the fish with their heads facing inwards. Sprinkle with parsley and salt and pepper to taste. Beat the eggs and cream together and pour over the fish.
Roll out the dough on a floured surface and use to cover the dish. Make 6 holes in the dough through which the heads of the fish can protrude. Brush the dough with a little milk and bake in a preheated moderate oven (180°C/350°F or Gas Mark 4) for 40 minutes.
To freeze: cool quickly. Open (flash) freeze until firm, then wrap in a freezer bag or foil. Seal, label and return to the freezer.
To thaw and serve: remove wrappings and thaw at room temperature for 4 hours. Cover with foil and reheat in a preheated moderate oven for 30 to 40 minutes or until heated through. Remove the foil 5 minutes before the end of cooking time.
SERVES 6

CRAB PANCAKES (CRÊPES)

METRIC/IMPERIAL
8 pancakes (crêpes) made from 300 ml/½ pint batter
50 g/2 oz cheese, grated
For the filling:
25 g/1 oz butter
25 g/1 oz flour
300 ml/½ pint milk
100 g/4 oz crabmeat
salt
freshly ground black pepper

AMERICAN
8 crêpes made from 1¼ cups batter
½ cup grated cheese
For the filling:
2 tablespoons butter
¼ cup flour
1¼ cups milk
¼ lb crabmeat
salt
freshly ground black pepper

To make the filling: melt the butter in a pan, stir in the flour and cook for 2 minutes, stirring constantly. Remove from the heat and stir in the milk, then return to the heat and bring to the boil, stirring constantly. Simmer until the sauce thickens, then stir in the crabmeat and salt and pepper to taste.
Divide the filling equally between the pancakes (crêpes) and fold or roll up.
To freeze: put the pancakes (crêpes) in an ovenproof dish or foil container and cover with the cheese. Wrap in foil, seal, label and freeze.
To thaw and serve: reheat from frozen in the covered dish or container in a preheated moderate oven (180°C/350°F or Gas Mark 4) for 35 to 40 minutes or until heated through.
SERVES 4

KIPPER KEDGEREE

METRIC/IMPERIAL
50 g/2 oz butter
1 onion, peeled and chopped
2 × 200 g/7 oz packets frozen kipper fillets, thawed and cut into small pieces
300 g/11 oz boiled long-grain rice
freshly ground black pepper
5 × 15 ml spoons/5 tablespoons single cream
1 × 15 ml spoon/1 tablespoon prepared mustard
To garnish:
freshly chopped parsley
2 tomatoes, quartered

AMERICAN
¼ cup butter
1 onion, peeled and chopped
2 × 7 oz packages frozen kipper fillets, thawed and cut into small pieces
2 cups boiled long-grain rice
freshly ground black pepper
⅓ cup light cream
1 tablespoon prepared mustard
To garnish:
freshly chopped parsley
2 tomatoes, quartered

Melt the butter in a pan, add the onion and fry gently until soft. Add the kippers and heat through, shaking the pan constantly. Add the rice and pepper to taste and stir with a fork for 3 to 4 minutes. Beat the cream and mustard together, then stir into the kipper mixture and heat through, stirring occasionally.
To freeze: cool quickly, then pour into a rigid container. Seal, label and freeze.
To thaw and serve: thaw at room temperature for 4 hours, then reheat gently on top of the stove, stirring occasionally. Garnish with parsley and tomatoes just before serving.
SERVES 4

CORNISH KIPPERS

METRIC/IMPERIAL

1 × 275 g/10 oz packet frozen buttered kipper fillets
1 onion, peeled and finely chopped
100 g/4 oz mushrooms, sliced
100 g/4 oz tomatoes, peeled and chopped
freshly ground black pepper
basic puff pastry dough made with 225 g/½ lb flour
beaten egg, to glaze

AMERICAN

1 × 10 oz package frozen buttered kipper fillets
1 onion, peeled and finely chopped
1 cup sliced mushrooms
½ cup peeled and chopped tomatoes
freshly ground black pepper
basic puff paste dough made with 2 cups flour
beaten egg, to glaze

Cook the kippers according to packet directions, strain and reserve the liquor. Skin and flake the kippers.

Put the liquor in a pan, add the onion and cook gently for 5 minutes. Stir in the mushrooms, tomatoes, flaked fish and pepper to taste, then leave to cool.

Roll out the dough on a floured surface and cut out eight 13 cm/5 inch squares. Divide the fish mixture equally between the squares of dough, moisten the edges with water and fold the dough over to make oblong pasties. Press the edges firmly to seal.

To freeze: open (flash) freeze until firm, then wrap individually in foil and pack in a rigid container. Seal, label and return to the freezer.

To thaw and serve: remove the wrappings and place on a baking sheet. Brush the dough with beaten egg and bake from frozen in a preheated moderately hot oven (200°C/400°F or Gas Mark 6) for 45 minutes or until heated through. Cover with foil if the pastry becomes too brown during cooking.

MAKES 8

HERRING PARCELS

METRIC/IMPERIAL

75 g/3 oz butter, softened
1 small onion, peeled and finely chopped
finely grated rind and juice of ½ lemon
1 × 5 ml spoon/1 teaspoon prepared mustard
2 × 5 ml spoons/2 teaspoons freshly chopped parsley
salt
freshly ground black pepper
4 herrings, cleaned and boned, heads removed

AMERICAN

⅜ cup butter, softened
1 small onion, peeled and finely chopped
finely grated rind and juice of ½ lemon
1 teaspoon prepared mustard
2 teaspoons freshly chopped parsley
salt
freshly ground black pepper
4 herrings, cleaned and boned out, heads removed

Put the butter in a bowl and beat until light and fluffy. Add the onion, lemon rind and juice, mustard, parsley and salt and pepper to taste. Beat well to mix. Stuff the butter mixture into the cavity of each herring, dividing it equally between them, then wrap each fish in buttered foil to form a parcel.

Put the parcels in an ovenproof dish and bake in a preheated moderate oven (180°C/350°F or Gas Mark 4) for 20 minutes.

To freeze: cool quickly, then pack the foil parcels in a freezer bag. Seal, label and freeze.

To thaw and serve: reheat the foil parcels from frozen in a preheated moderate oven for 35 minutes or until heated through.

MAKES 4

STUFFED HERRING SALAD

METRIC/IMPERIAL

4 herrings, cleaned and boned, with the heads left on
For the stuffing:
175 g/6 oz fresh white breadcrumbs
1 medium onion, peeled and finely chopped
1 cooking apple, peeled, cored and finely chopped
2 × 15 ml spoons/2 tablespoons freshly chopped parsley
2 × 5 ml spoons/2 teaspoons dried mixed herbs
salt
freshly ground black pepper
1 egg, beaten
To garnish:
few lettuce leaves, shredded
tomato quarters
lemon wedges

AMERICAN

4 herrings, cleaned and boned out, with the heads left on
For the stuffing:
3 cups fresh white breadcrumbs
1 medium onion, peeled and finely chopped
1 baking apple, peeled, cored and finely chopped
2 tablespoons freshly chopped parsley
2 teaspoons dried mixed herbs
salt
freshly ground black pepper
1 egg, beaten
To garnish:
few lettuce leaves, shredded
tomato quarters
lemon wedges

To make the stuffing: put all the ingredients in a bowl and stir well to mix. Add a little water if the mixture seems dry.
Divide the stuffing equally between the herrings and place in a buttered ovenproof dish or foil container. Cover and bake in a preheated moderate oven (180°C/350°F or Gas Mark 4) for 25 minutes or until the fish is tender.
To freeze: cool quickly, then wrap in foil. Seal, label and freeze.
To thaw and serve: thaw in the refrigerator overnight, then serve cold. Arrange on a bed of shredded lettuce and garnish with tomatoes and lemon wedges.
SERVES 4

HERRINGS WITH HONEY

METRIC/IMPERIAL

4 herrings, cleaned and boned, with the heads removed
2 green dessert apples, cored and sliced
2 small onions, peeled and finely sliced
juice of ½ lemon
2 × 15 ml spoons/2 tablespoons honey
25 g/1 oz butter
1 × 5 ml spoon/1 teaspoon dried mixed herbs

AMERICAN

4 herrings, cleaned and boned out, with the heads removed
2 green dessert apples, cored and sliced
2 small onions, peeled and finely sliced
juice of ½ lemon
2 tablespoons honey
2 tablespoons butter
1 teaspoon dried mixed herbs

Put the herrings in a buttered ovenproof dish or foil container and arrange the apple and onion slices on top. Sprinkle with the lemon juice. Put the honey, butter and herbs in a pan and heat gently until the honey has dissolved. Pour into the dish, cover with buttered greaseproof paper or non-stick parchment and bake in a preheated moderately hot oven (190°C/375°F or Gas Mark 5) for 20 minutes.
To freeze: cool quickly, then cover with foil. Seal, label and freeze.
To thaw and serve: thaw at room temperature for 4 hours, then reheat in the covered dish or container in a preheated moderate oven (180°C/350°F or Gas Mark 4) for 25 minutes or until heated through.
SERVES 4

SOUSED HERRINGS

METRIC/IMPERIAL

6 herrings, cleaned and boned
For the marinade:
1 onion, peeled and sliced
1 bay leaf
250 ml/8 fl oz water
250 ml/8 fl oz malt vinegar
2 cloves
2 allspice
1 × 5 ml spoon/1 teaspoon brown sugar
2 × 5 ml spoons/2 teaspoons salt
6 black peppercorns

AMERICAN

6 herrings, cleaned and boned out
For the marinade:
1 onion, peeled and sliced
1 bay leaf
1 cup water
1 cup malt vinegar
2 cloves
2 allspice
1 teaspoon brown sugar
2 teaspoons salt
6 black peppercorns

Roll up the herrings from head to tail and place in an ovenproof dish or foil container. Put all the ingredients for the marinade in a pan, bring to the boil, then remove from the heat and leave to cool. Pour over the herrings and bake in a preheated moderate oven (160°C/325°F or Gas Mark 3) for 1 hour.
To freeze: cool quickly. Wrap in foil, then overwrap in a freezer bag. Seal, label and freeze.
To thaw and serve: remove wrappings and thaw at room temperature for 4 hours, then chill in the refrigerator before serving.
SERVES 6

STUFFED SOUSED HERRINGS

METRIC/IMPERIAL

4 herrings, cleaned and boned, with the heads removed
1 small onion, peeled and cut into rings
1 small blade of mace
3 cloves
8 peppercorns
150 ml/¼ pint water
150 ml/¼ pint vinegar
For the stuffing:
50 g/2 oz fresh white breadcrumbs
2 × 5 ml spoons/2 teaspoons chopped capers
finely grated rind of 1 small lemon
25 g/1 oz butter, melted
salt
freshly ground black pepper
1 egg, beaten

AMERICAN

4 herrings, cleaned and boned out, with the heads removed
1 small onion, peeled and cut into rings
1 small blade of mace
3 cloves
8 peppercorns
⅔ cup water
⅔ cup vinegar
For the stuffing:
1 cup fresh white breadcrumbs
2 teaspoons chopped capers
finely grated rind of 1 small lemon
2 tablespoons butter, melted
salt
freshly ground black pepper
1 egg, beaten

To make the stuffing: put all ingredients in a bowl and stir well to mix. Add a little water if the mixture seems dry.

Lay the herrings flat on a surface, skin side down. Sprinkle with salt and pepper, then put the stuffing near the tail end of each herring, dividing it equally between them. Roll up from the tail end and arrange in a single layer in a buttered ovenproof dish or foil container, with the joins underneath.

Cover with the onion rings, mace, cloves and peppercorns. Mix together the water and vinegar and pour over the herrings. Cover and bake in a preheated moderately hot oven (190°C/375°F or Gas Mark 5) for 20 minutes or until the fish is tender.

To freeze: cool quickly, then wrap in foil. Seal, label and freeze.

To thaw and serve: thaw in the refrigerator overnight, then serve cold.

SERVES 4

CANNELLONI WITH TUNA STUFFING

METRIC/IMPERIAL

12 cannelloni tubes
salt
15 g/½ oz butter
½ onion, peeled and chopped
25 g/1 oz mushrooms, chopped
1 × 200 g/7 oz can tuna fish, drained and flaked
15 g/½ oz fresh white breadcrumbs
1 × 5 ml spoon/1 teaspoon chopped capers
freshly ground black pepper
50 g/2 oz Cheddar cheese, grated
300 ml/½ pint hot white coating sauce
2 × 15 ml spoons/2 tablespoons grated Parmesan cheese

AMERICAN

12 canneloni tubes
salt
1 tablespoon butter
½ onion, peeled and chopped
¼ cup chopped mushrooms
1 × 7 oz can tuna fish, drained and flaked
¼ cup fresh white breadcrumbs
1 teaspoon chopped capers
freshly ground black pepper
½ cup grated Cheddar cheese
1¼ cups hot white coating sauce
2 tablespoons grated Parmesan cheese

Cook the cannelloni in boiling salted water until 'al dente'. Drain carefully and refresh in cold water. Melt the butter in a pan, add the onion and mushrooms and fry gently until soft. Transfer to a bowl and add the tuna, breadcrumbs, capers and salt and pepper to taste. Stir well to mix.

Spoon or pipe the tuna mixture into the cannelloni, then arrange in a single layer in a buttered ovenproof dish or foil container. Stir the Cheddar cheese into the hot white sauce, spoon over the cannelloni and sprinkle with the Parmesan.

To freeze: cool quickly, then cover with foil. Seal, label and freeze.

To thaw and serve: thaw at room temperature for 4 hours, then reheat in the covered dish or container in a preheated moderately hot oven (190°C/375°F or Gas Mark 5) for 30 to 40 minutes or until heated through. Put under a preheated grill (broiler) to brown before serving.

SERVES 4

SCAMPI (JUMBO SHRIMP) WITH MUSHROOM SAUCE

METRIC/IMPERIAL

25 g/1 oz butter
1 onion, peeled and chopped
1 garlic clove, peeled and crushed
175 g/6 oz mushrooms, sliced
2 × 5 ml spoons/2 teaspoons cornflour
150 ml/¼ pint dry white wine
150 ml/¼ pint chicken stock
salt
freshly ground black pepper
150 ml/¼ pint double cream
450 g/1 lb frozen prepared scampi
flour for coating
2 × 15 ml spoons/2 tablespoons vegetable oil

AMERICAN

2 tablespoons butter
1 onion, peeled and chopped
1 garlic clove, peeled and crushed
1½ cups sliced mushrooms
2 teaspoons cornstarch
⅔ cup dry white wine
⅔ cup chicken stock
salt
freshly ground black pepper
⅔ cup heavy cream
1 lb frozen prepared jumbo shrimp
flour for coating
2 tablespoons vegetable oil

Melt the butter in a pan, add the onion and garlic and fry gently until soft. Add the mushrooms and fry for 3 minutes. Blend the cornflour (cornstarch) with the wine and stir into the pan with the stock. Bring to the boil, stirring constantly, then cover and simmer for 15 minutes. Remove from the heat, add salt and pepper to taste and stir in the cream.
Toss the scampi (jumbo shrimp) in flour seasoned with salt and pepper. Heat the oil in a pan, add the scampi (jumbo shrimp) and fry for 5 minutes until lightly coloured on all sides.
To freeze: cool quickly. Put the scampi (jumbo shrimp) in a rigid container and pour over the sauce. Seal, label and freeze.
To thaw and serve: put the frozen scampi (jumbo shrimp) and sauce in the top of a double boiler and reheat gently, stirring occasionally.
SERVES 4 to 6

DEVILLED SEAFOOD SCALLOPS

METRIC/IMPERIAL

300 ml/½ pint white coating sauce
175 g/6 oz peeled prawns
1 × 2.5 ml spoons/½ teaspoon Worcestershire sauce
pinch of mustard powder
salt
cayenne pepper
25 g/1 oz Parmesan cheese, grated
For the topping:
675 g/1½ lb potatoes, peeled, boiled and mashed
25 g/1 oz butter
3–4 × 15 ml spoons/3–4 tablespoons milk
To garnish:
a few whole prawns
freshly chopped parsley

AMERICAN

1¼ cups white coating sauce
1 cup shelled shrimp
½ teaspoon Worcestershire sauce
pinch of mustard powder
salt
cayenne pepper
¼ cup grated Parmesan cheese
For the topping:
1½ lb potatoes, peeled, boiled and mashed
2 tablespoons butter
3–4 tablespoons milk
To garnish:
a few whole shrimp
freshly chopped parsley

Put the white sauce in a bowl and add the prawns (shrimp), Worcestershire sauce, mustard and salt and cayenne pepper to taste. Stir well to mix. Divide the mixture equally between 6 scallop shells or individual ovenproof dishes. Sprinkle with the Parmesan cheese.
Put the mashed potatoes in a bowl and add the butter and enough milk to mix to a creamy consistency. Pipe the creamed potatoes in a border around the shells or dishes.
To freeze: open (flash) freeze until firm, then wrap individually in freezer bags or foil. Seal, label and return to the freezer.
To thaw and serve: remove wrappings and thaw in the refrigerator for 4 hours. Reheat in a preheated moderately hot oven (190°C/375°F or Gas Mark 5) for 30 to 40 minutes or until heated through. Garnish with prawns (shrimp) and parsley just before serving.
MAKES 6

PRAWN (SHRIMP) CREOLE

METRIC/IMPERIAL

1 small onion, peeled and chopped
½ green pepper, cored, seeded and chopped
150 ml/¼ pint tomato juice
pinch of dried rosemary
1 × 5 ml spoon/1 teaspoon Worcestershire sauce
1 × 5 ml spoon/1 teaspoon prepared German mustard
175g/6 oz peeled prawns
salt
freshly ground black pepper
225 g/½ lb bean sprouts, to finish

AMERICAN

1 small onion, peeled and chopped
½ green pepper, cored, seeded and chopped
⅔ cup tomato juice
pinch of dried rosemary
1 teaspoon Worcestershire sauce
1 teaspoon prepared German mustard
1 cup shelled shrimp
salt
freshly ground black pepper
4 cups bean sprouts, to finish

Put the onion, green pepper, tomato juice, rosemary, Worcestershire sauce and mustard in a pan. Bring to the boil slowly, then cover and simmer for 15 minutes. Add the prawns (shrimp) and simmer for a further 5 minutes. Add salt and pepper to taste.
To freeze: cool quickly, then pour into a rigid container. Seal, label and freeze.
To thaw and serve: thaw in the refrigerator for 4 hours, then reheat gently on top of the stove. Add the bean sprouts and heat through.
SERVES 2 to 3

PRAWN (SHRIMP) PROVENÇALE

METRIC/IMPERIAL

40 g/1½ oz butter
1 onion, peeled and finely chopped
1 garlic clove, peeled and crushed
2 × 15 ml spoons/2 tablespoons cornflour
2 × 15 ml spoons/2 tablespoons tomato purée
300 ml/½ pint chicken stock
100 g/4 oz button mushrooms, sliced
2 tomatoes, peeled and sliced
salt
freshly ground black pepper
2 × 15 ml spoons/2 tablespoons dry white wine or cider
225 g/½ lb peeled prawns
freshly chopped parsley, to garnish

AMERICAN

3 tablespoons butter
1 onion, peeled and finely chopped
1 garlic clove, peeled and crushed
2 tablespoons cornstarch
2 tablespoons tomato paste
1¼ cups chicken stock
1 cup sliced button mushrooms
2 tomatoes, peeled and sliced
salt
freshly ground black pepper
2 tablespoons dry white wine or hard cider
1⅓ cups shelled shrimp
freshly chopped parsley, to garnish

Melt the butter in a pan, add the onion and garlic and fry gently until soft. Stir in the cornflour (cornstarch) and tomato purée (paste) and cook for 2 minutes. Stir in the stock and bring to the boil, stirring constantly.
Add the remaining ingredients, except the parsley, cover and simmer for 10 minutes.
To freeze: cool quickly, then pour into a rigid container. Seal, label and freeze.
To thaw and serve: thaw in the refrigerator for 4 hours, then reheat gently on top of the stove, stirring occasionally. Sprinkle with parsley just before serving.
SERVES 4

PAELLA

METRIC/IMPERIAL

120 ml/4 fl oz olive oil
2 garlic cloves, peeled and crushed
2 onions, peeled and chopped
1 green pepper, cored, seeded and chopped
675 g/1½ lb Valencia or long-grain rice
approx 900 ml/1½ pints chicken stock
4 tomatoes, peeled and chopped
pinch of saffron
salt
freshly ground black pepper
1 medium chicken, skinned, boned and cut into small pieces
100 g/4 oz streaky bacon rashers, rinds removed and chopped
225 g/½ lb peeled prawns
100 g/4 oz squid, prepared and cut into rings
150 g/5 oz frozen peas
100 g/4 oz cooked mussels
To garnish:
lemon wedges
a few whole prawns

AMERICAN

½ cup olive oil
2 garlic cloves, peeled and crushed
2 onions, peeled and chopped
1 green pepper, cored, seeded and chopped
4 cups Valencia or long-grain rice
approx 3¾ cups chicken stock
4 tomatoes, peeled and chopped
pinch of saffron
salt
freshly ground black pepper
1 medium chicken, skinned, boned and cut into small pieces
6 fatty bacon slices, chopped
1⅓ cups shelled shrimp
¼ lb squid, prepared and cut into rings
1 cup frozen peas
¼ lb cooked mussels
To garnish:
lemon wedges
a few whole shrimp

Heat half the oil in a pan, add the garlic and onions and fry gently until soft. Add the green pepper and the rice and fry gently for 3 minutes, stirring constantly with a fork. Stir in the stock, tomatoes, saffron and salt and pepper to taste, bring to the boil and simmer for 10 minutes.
Heat the remaining oil in a separate pan, add the chicken and fry gently for 10 minutes, then add the bacon and fry until crisp. Transfer to the pan with the rice and stir in the prawns (shrimp), squid, frozen peas and mussels. Simmer gently for 10 to 15 minutes until the rice has absorbed the stock, but the grains of rice are still separate. Add more stock if necessary to make the paella fairly moist.
To freeze: cool quickly, then turn into a rigid container. Seal, label and freeze.
To thaw and serve: put the paella in a buttered ovenproof dish, cover with buttered foil and reheat from frozen in a preheated moderately hot oven (190°C/375°F or Gas Mark 5) for 1 hour or until heated through, stirring with a fork occasionally. Garnish with lemon wedges and whole prawns (shrimp) just before serving.
SERVES 8

PRAWN (SHRIMP) CHOP SUEY

METRIC/IMPERIAL

2 × 15 ml spoons/2 tablespoons vegetable oil
5 spring onions, trimmed and sliced
small piece of fresh root ginger, peeled and chopped
1 small garlic clove, peeled and crushed
100 g/4 oz peeled prawns
2 × 5 ml spoons/2 teaspoons cornflour
5 × 15 ml spoons/5 tablespoons chicken stock
1.5 × 15 ml spoons/1½ tablespoons soy sauce
1 × 15 ml spoon/1 tablespoon honey
1 × 15 ml spoon/1 tablespoon dry sherry
1 × 15 ml spoon/1 tablespoon tomato ketchup
To finish:
225 g/½ lb bean sprouts
1 × 15 ml spoon/1 tablespoon vegetable oil
1 egg, beaten

AMERICAN

2 tablespoons vegetable oil
5 scallions, trimmed and sliced
1 small piece of fresh ginger root, peeled and chopped
1 small garlic clove, peeled and crushed
⅔ cup shelled shrimp
2 teaspoons cornstarch
⅓ cup chicken stock
1½ tablespoons soy sauce
1 tablespoon honey
1 tablespoon dry sherry
1 tablespoon tomato ketchup
To finish:
4 cups bean sprouts
1 tablespoon vegetable oil
1 egg, beaten

Heat the oil in a pan, add the onions (scallions) and fry gently for 1 minute. Add the ginger, garlic and prawns (shrimp) and stir-fry for 2 minutes. Mix the cornflour (cornstarch) to a paste with the stock and stir into the pan with the soy sauce, honey, sherry and tomato ketchup. Stir-fry for a further 2 minutes.
To freeze: cool quickly, then pour into a rigid container. Seal, label and freeze.
To thaw and serve: thaw in the refrigerator for 4 hours, then reheat gently on top of the stove, stirring occasionally. Add the bean sprouts and heat through. Heat the oil in a small pan, add the egg and cook as for an omelet. Arrange the chop suey on a hot serving dish and top with the omelet.
SERVES 2

HONEYED BEEF STEW

METRIC/IMPERIAL

2 × 15 ml spoons/2 tablespoons vegetable oil for frying
1 kg/2 lb chuck steak, trimmed of fat and cut into cubes
1 large onion, peeled and chopped
1 medium green pepper, cored, seeded and chopped
3 celery stalks, chopped
2 large carrots, peeled and sliced
2 × 15 ml spoons/2 tablespoons honey
2 × 15 ml spoons/2 tablespoons lemon juice
2 × 5 ml spoons/2 teaspoons mustard powder
175 ml/6 fl oz tomato ketchup
450 ml/¾ pint water
salt
freshly ground black pepper

AMERICAN

2 tablespoons vegetable oil for frying
2 lb chuck steak, trimmed of fat and cut into cubes
1 large onion, peeled and chopped
1 medium green pepper, cored, seeded and chopped
3 celery stalks, chopped
2 large carrots, peeled and sliced
2 tablespoons honey
2 tablespoons lemon juice
2 teaspoons mustard powder
¾ cup tomato ketchup
2 cups water
salt
freshly ground black pepper

Heat the oil in a flameproof casserole dish. Add the beef and fry briskly on all sides. Add the vegetables and fry for a further 5 minutes, stirring occasionally. Mix the remaining ingredients together in a bowl, and stir into the casserole.

Cover and cook in a preheated moderate oven (180°C/350°F or Gas Mark 4) for 2 to 2½ hours or until the meat is tender.

To freeze: cool quickly, leave in the casserole or pour into a rigid container. Cover, then wrap the casserole in a freezer bag or foil. Seal, label and freeze.

To thaw and serve: remove wrappings and thaw at room temperature for 4 hours. Reheat gently on top of the stove, stirring occasionally.

SERVES 4

CORNISH PASTIES

METRIC/IMPERIAL

basic shortcrust pastry dough made with 225 g/½ lb flour
2 × 15 ml spoons/2 tablespoons dripping or lard
225 g/½ lb lean minced beef
100 g/4 oz peeled and finely diced potatoes
1 small onion, peeled and finely chopped
1 small carrot, peeled and finely diced
1 × 15 ml spoon/1 tablespoon water
salt
freshly ground black pepper
milk, to glaze

AMERICAN

basic pie dough made with 2 cups flour
2 tablespoons drippings or lard
1 cup lean ground beef
⅔ cup peeled and finely diced potatoes
1 small onion, peeled and finely chopped
1 small carrot, peeled and finely diced
1 tablespoon water
salt
freshly ground black pepper
milk, to glaze

Roll out the dough on a floured surface, divide into 4 equal portions and roll each into a 15 cm/6 inch round.

Melt the fat in a pan, add the beef and fry for 5 minutes, stirring constantly to break up the meat. Transfer to a bowl and combine with the remaining ingredients, except the milk. Stir well to mix.

Divide the meat mixture between the rounds of dough, mounding it in the centre. Moisten the edges with water, fold in half and press and pinch the edges firmly together with the join on the top.

Place on a baking sheet and brush with milk. Bake in a preheated moderately hot oven (200°C/400°F or Gas Mark 6) for 15 minutes, then reduce the heat to moderate (160°C/325°F or Gas Mark 3) and bake for a further 30 minutes. Leave to cool on a wire rack.

To freeze: wrap individually in foil, then pack in a freezer bag. Seal, label and freeze.

To thaw and serve: reheat from frozen in foil wrappings in a preheated moderate oven (180°C/350°F or Gas Mark 4) for 20 minutes, then remove wrappings and bake for a further 10 minutes.

MAKES 4

CABBAGE AND MEAT CASSEROLE

METRIC/IMPERIAL

1 large green cabbage, finely shredded
salt
25 g/1 oz dripping
1 large onion, peeled and chopped
350 g/¾ lb lean minced beef
350 g/¾ lb lean minced pork
freshly ground black pepper
2 × 15 ml spoons/2 tablespoons freshly chopped parsley
75 g/3 oz long-grain rice
300 ml/½ pint tomato juice
1 × 5 ml spoon/1 teaspoon sugar
150 ml/¼ pint beef stock
150 ml/¼ pint soured cream, to finish

AMERICAN

1 large head green cabbage, finely shredded
salt
2 tablespoons drippings
1 large onion, peeled and chopped
1½ cups lean ground beef
1½ cups lean ground pork
freshly ground black pepper
2 tablespoons freshly chopped parsley
½ cup long-grain rice
1¼ cups tomato juice
1 teaspoon sugar
⅔ cup beef stock
⅔ cup sour cream, to finish

Blanch the cabbage in boiling salted water, then drain. Heat the dripping in a pan, add the onion and fry gently until golden. Add the beef and pork and fry briskly until well browned, stirring constantly to break up the meat. Add salt and pepper to taste, then add the parsley, rice, tomato juice and sugar. Cover and simmer for 15 minutes. Fill a deep foil container with alternate layers of cabbage and meat mixture, beginning and ending with cabbage. Pour in the stock. Cover with greased foil and bake in a preheated moderately hot oven (190°C/375°F or Gas Mark 5) for 45 minutes.

To freeze: cool quickly. Cover, seal, label and freeze.

To thaw and serve: thaw at room temperature for 4 hours. Add a little extra stock or water to the dish, then reheat in a preheated moderately hot oven (190°C/375°F or Gas Mark 5) for 45 minutes or until heated through. Top with the sour(ed) cream and heat through for a further 5 minutes.

SERVES 4

BEEF AND TOMATO CASSEROLE

METRIC/IMPERIAL

3 × 15 ml spoons/3 tablespoons vegetable oil
1 kg/2 lb chuck steak, trimmed of fat and cut into cubes
2 leeks, thickly sliced
2 carrots, peeled and sliced
1 large onion, peeled and sliced
25 g/1 oz flour
450 ml/¾ pint beef stock
1 × 400 g/14 oz can tomatoes
salt
freshly ground black pepper

AMERICAN

3 tablespoons vegetable oil
2 lb blade steak, trimmed of fat and cut into cubes
2 leeks, thickly sliced
2 carrots, peeled and sliced
1 large onion, peeled and sliced
¼ cup flour
2 cups beef stock
1 × 14 oz can tomatoes
salt
freshly ground black pepper

Heat half the oil in a pan, add the beef and fry briskly until browned on all sides. Drain and transfer to an ovenproof casserole dish. Add the leeks and carrots to the meat.

Heat the remaining oil in the pan, add the onion and fry gently until soft. Sprinkle the flour into the pan, cook for 2 minutes, then stir in the stock. Bring to the boil, stirring constantly, then add the tomatoes and salt and pepper to taste.

Pour the onion and tomato sauce into the casserole dish, cover and cook in a preheated cool oven (150°C/300°F or Gas Mark 2) for 2 to 2½ hours or until the meat is tender.

To freeze: cool quickly. Leave in the casserole or pour into a rigid container. Cover, then wrap the casserole in a freezer bag or foil. Seal, label and freeze.

To thaw and serve: remove wrappings and thaw at room temperature for 4 hours. Reheat gently on top of the stove, stirring occasionally.

SERVES 4 to 6

MEXICAN MEAT STEW

METRIC/IMPERIAL

2 × 15 ml spoons/2 tablespoons vegetable oil
675-900 g/1½-2 lb chuck steak, trimmed of fat and cut into cubes
1 large onion, peeled and sliced
1 green pepper, cored, seeded and cut into rings
3 celery stalks, chopped
1 × 2.5 ml spoon/½ teaspoon chilli powder
25 g/1 oz flour
1 × 400 g/14 oz can tomatoes
2 × 5 ml spoons/2 teaspoons tomato purée
2 × 5 ml spoons/2 teaspoons mustard powder
150 ml/¼ pint dry red wine
600 ml/1 pint beef stock
1 × 2.5 ml spoon/½ teaspoon brown sugar
salt
freshly ground black pepper

AMERICAN

2 tablespoons vegetable oil
1½-2 lb blade steak, trimmed of fat and cut into cubes
1 large onion, peeled and sliced
1 green pepper, cored, seeded and cut into rings
3 celery stalks, chopped
½ teaspoon chili powder
¼ cup flour
1 × 14 oz can tomatoes
2 teaspoons tomato paste
2 teaspoons mustard powder
⅔ cup dry red wine
2½ cups beef stock
½ teaspoon brown sugar
salt
freshly ground black pepper

Heat the oil in a flameproof casserole dish, add the meat and fry briskly until browned on all sides. Remove from the casserole, add the onion, green pepper and celery and fry gently for 10 minutes. Return the beef to the casserole, stir in the chilli powder and flour and cook for 2 minutes. Add the tomatoes.

Mix the tomato purée (paste) and mustard to a paste with a little water, then add to the casserole with the wine, stock, sugar and salt and pepper to taste. Cover and cook in a preheated moderate oven (160°C/325°F or Gas Mark 3) for 2 to 2½ hours or until the meat is tender.

To freeze: cool quickly. Leave in the casserole or transfer to a rigid container. Cover, then wrap in a freezer bag or foil. Seal, label and freeze.

To thaw and serve: thaw at room temperature for 4 hours, then reheat in the covered casserole in a preheated moderate oven (180°C/350°F or Gas Mark 4) for 1 hour or until heated through.

SERVES 4

BEEF AND BEAN POT

METRIC/IMPERIAL

1 kg/2 lb dried red kidney beans, soaked overnight in cold water
salt
2 × 15 ml spoons/2 tablespoons olive or corn oil
1 kg/2 lb chuck steak, trimmed of fat and cut into cubes
1–2 garlic cloves, peeled and crushed
1 × 175 g/6 oz can tomato purée
1 × 15 ml spoon/1 tablespoon soft brown sugar
2 small bay leaves
freshly ground black pepper

AMERICAN

3 cups dried red kidney beans, soaked overnight in cold water
salt
2 tablespoons olive or corn oil
2 lb blade steak, trimmed of fat and cut into cubes
1–2 garlic cloves, peeled and crushed
1 × 6 oz can tomato paste
1 tablespoon light brown sugar
2 small bay leaves
freshly ground black pepper

Drain the beans and rinse under cold running water. Place in a pan with a little salt and cover with cold running water. Bring to the boil, remove any scum, then cover and simmer for 1 hour or until tender. Strain the cooking liquid and reserve 300 ml/½ pint/1¼ cups.
Heat the oil in a pan, add the beef and fry briskly until browned on all sides. Add the garlic, tomato purée (paste), sugar, bay leaves and the reserved cooking liquid from the beans. Add salt and pepper to taste and simmer gently for 10 minutes.
Transfer to a casserole dish, add the beans and enough water to just cover. Cover and cook in a preheated moderate oven (160°C/325°F or Gas Mark 3) for 2 to 2½ hours or until the meat is tender.
To freeze: cool quickly. Leave in the casserole or pour into a rigid container. Cover, then wrap the casserole in a freezer bag or foil. Seal, label and freeze.
To thaw and serve: remove wrappings and thaw at room temperature for 4 hours. Reheat in the covered casserole dish in a preheated moderate oven (180°C/350°F or Gas Mark 4) for about 1 hour or until it is thoroughly heated through.
SERVES 8

BEEF AND VEGETABLE STEW

METRIC/IMPERIAL

800 g/1¾ lb chuck steak, trimmed of fat and cut into cubes
25 g/1 oz flour
salt
freshly ground black pepper
50 g/2 oz dripping
8 small pickling onions
600 ml/1 pint beef stock
8 small carrots
2–3 celery stalks, chopped
100 g/4 oz button mushrooms
1 bouquet garni
freshly chopped parsley, to garnish

AMERICAN

1¾ lb blade steak, trimmed of fat and cut into cubes
¼ cup flour
salt
freshly ground black pepper
¼ cup drippings
8 baby onions
2½ cups beef stock
8 baby carrots
2–3 celery stalks, chopped
1 cup button mushrooms
1 bouquet garni
freshly chopped parsley, to garnish

Toss the beef in the flour seasoned with salt and pepper. Melt the fat in a large pan, add the meat and onions and fry briskly for a few minutes until browned on all sides. Stir in the stock and bring to the boil, stirring constantly. Add the remaining vegetables and the bouquet garni. Add salt and pepper to taste, cover and simmer for 2 to 2½ hours or until the meat is tender. Remove the bouquet garni.
To freeze: cool quickly, then turn into a rigid container. Seal, label and freeze.
To thaw and serve: thaw at room temperature for 4 hours then reheat gently on top of stove, stirring occasionally. Sprinkle with parsley just before serving.
SERVES 4

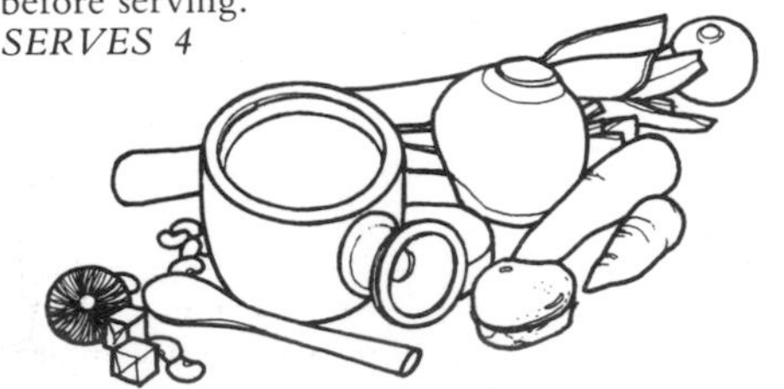

MOUSSAKA

METRIC/IMPERIAL

675 g/1½ lb aubergines, sliced
salt
approx 6 × 15 ml spoons/6 tablespoons olive oil
25 g/1 oz butter
2 onions, peeled and sliced
1 garlic clove, peeled and crushed
450 g/1 lb lean minced lamb or beef
1 × 5 ml spoon/1 teaspoon dried marjoram
pinch of ground mace
freshly ground black pepper
1 × 15 ml spoon/1 tablespoon tomato purée
1 × 400 g/14 oz can tomatoes
For the sauce:
25 g/1 oz butter
25 g/1 oz flour
300 ml/½ pint milk
1 egg yolk
25 g/1 oz Cheddar cheese, grated

AMERICAN

1½ lb eggplant, sliced
salt
approx 6 tablespoons olive oil
2 tablespoons butter
2 onions, peeled and sliced
1 garlic clove, peeled and crushed
2 cups lean ground lamb or beef
1 teaspoon dried marjoram
pinch of ground mace
freshly ground black pepper
1 tablespoon tomato paste
1 × 14 oz can tomatoes
For the sauce:
2 tablespoons butter
¼ cup flour
1¼ cups milk
1 egg yolk
¼ cup grated Cheddar cheese

Sprinkle the aubergines (eggplant) with salt and leave for 30 minutes. Drain off any liquid, rinse under cold running water, then dry on paper towels. Heat the oil in a large frying pan (skillet), add the aubergines (eggplant) and fry until soft, adding more oil if necessary. Remove from the pan. Melt the butter in the pan, add the onions and garlic and fry until soft. Stir in the meat, marjoram, mace and salt and pepper and fry briskly for 8 minutes, stirring constantly to break up the meat. Stir in the tomato purée (paste) and canned tomatoes, bring to the boil, then remove from the heat.
Put the aubergines (eggplant) and meat mixture in layers in a greased casserole dish, starting and ending with a layer of aubergines (eggplant).
To make the sauce: melt the butter in a pan, stir in the flour and cook for 2 minutes stirring constantly. Remove from the heat and gradually stir in the milk. Return to the heat and bring to the boil, stirring constantly, then simmer until the sauce thickens. Remove from the heat and stir in the egg yolk. Add salt and pepper to taste. Pour the sauce over the casserole and sprinkle with the grated cheese.
To freeze: cool quickly. Cover and wrap in a freezer bag or foil. Seal, label and freeze.
To thaw and serve: remove wrappings and reheat from frozen, covered, in a moderately hot oven (190°C/375°F or Gas Mark 5) for 1½ hours. Remove the lid 15 minutes before the end of cooking to brown the topping.
SERVES 6

NORFOLK STEW

METRIC/IMPERIAL

675–900 g/1½–2 lb chuck steak, trimmed of fat and cut into cubes
25 g/1 oz flour
2 × 5 ml spoons/2 teaspoons mustard powder
salt
freshly ground black pepper
40 g/1½ oz dripping or lard
2 onions, peeled and sliced
2 large carrots, peeled and sliced
2–3 celery stalks, chopped
450 ml/¾ pint beef stock
1 bay leaf

AMERICAN

1½–2 lb blade steak, trimmed of fat and cut into cubes
¼ cup flour
2 teaspoons mustard powder
salt
freshly ground black pepper
3 tablespoons drippings or lard
2 onions, peeled and sliced
2 large carrots, peeled and sliced
2–3 celery stalks, chopped
2 cups beef stock
1 bay leaf

Coat the beef in the flour seasoned with the mustard and salt and pepper to taste. Melt the fat in a pan, add the beef and fry briskly until browned on all sides. Add the vegetables to the pan and fry for a further few minutes. Stir in the stock and add the bay leaf. Cover and cook gently for 2 to 2½ hours or until the meat is tender. Remove the bay leaf.
To freeze: cool quickly, then pour into a rigid container. Seal, label and freeze.

To thaw and serve: thaw at room temperature for 4 hours, then reheat gently on top of the stove, stirring occasionally.
SERVES 4 to 6

SHEPHERD'S PIE

METRIC/IMPERIAL
25 g/1 oz butter
1 large onion, peeled and chopped
25 g/1 oz flour
450 g/1 lb lean minced beef
300 ml/½ pint beef stock
1 × 15 ml spoon/1 tablespoon tomato purée
salt
freshly ground black pepper
For the topping:
450 g/1 lb potatoes, peeled, boiled and mashed
25 g/1 oz butter
2 × 15 ml spoons/2 tablespoons milk

AMERICAN
2 tablespoons butter
1 large onion, peeled and chopped
¼ cup flour
2 cups lean ground beef
1¼ cups beef stock
1 tablespoon tomato paste
salt
freshly ground black pepper
For the topping:
1 lb potatoes, peeled, boiled and mashed
2 tablespoons butter
2 tablespoons milk

Melt the butter in a pan, add the onion and fry gently until soft. Stir in the flour and cook for 2 minutes, then add the beef and fry until browned, stirring constantly to break up the meat.
Stir in the remaining ingredients and bring to the boil. Cover and simmer for 30 minutes, stirring occasionally. Pour into a 900 ml/1½ pint/3¾ cup pie dish or foil container.
To make the topping: put all the ingredients in a bowl with salt and pepper to taste. Beat until thoroughly combined, then spread over the meat mixture and mark the top with the prongs of a fork.
To freeze: cool quickly, then wrap in foil. Seal, label and freeze.
To thaw and serve: remove wrappings and thaw at room temperature for 4 hours. Bake in a preheated moderately hot oven (190°C/375°F or Gas Mark 5) for 45 minutes or until heated through and golden brown on top.
SERVES 4

CHILLI CON CARNE

METRIC/IMPERIAL
225 g/½ lb dried red kidney beans, soaked overnight in cold water
salt
4 × 15 ml spoons/4 tablespoons corn oil
2 onions, peeled and chopped
2 garlic cloves, peeled and crushed
1 kg/2 lb lean minced beef
1 green pepper, cored, seeded and chopped
1 × 5 ml spoon/1 teaspoon chilli powder
1 × 5 ml spoon/1 teaspoon paprika pepper
1 × 5 ml spoon/1 teaspoon ground cumin
1 × 15 ml spoon/1 tablespoon tomato purée
1 × 15 ml spoon/1 tablespoon flour
freshly ground black pepper
2 × 400 g/14 oz cans tomatoes

AMERICAN
¾ cup dried red kidney beans, soaked overnight in cold water
salt
¼ cup corn oil
2 onions, peeled and chopped
2 garlic cloves, peeled and crushed
4 cups lean ground beef
1 green pepper, cored, seeded and chopped
1 teaspoon chili powder
1 teaspoon paprika pepper
1 teaspoon ground cumin
1 tablespoon tomato paste
1 tablespoon flour
freshly ground black pepper
2 × 14 oz cans tomatoes

Drain the beans and rinse under cold running water. Place in a pan with a little salt and cover with cold water. Bring to the boil, remove any scum, then cover and simmer for 1 hour or until tender. Strain the cooking liquid and reserve 150 ml/¼ pint/⅔ cup.
Heat the oil in a pan, add the onions and garlic and fry until golden. Add the beef and green pepper and fry for 5 minutes, stirring constantly to break up the meat. Stir in the chilli powder, paprika, cumin, tomato purée (paste), flour and salt and pepper to taste and cook for 2 minutes. Add the tomatoes and beans, stir thoroughly to mix, then bring to the boil.
Cover and simmer for 1½ hours, stirring occasionally. If the mixture becomes too dry, stir in the reserved cooking liquid from the beans.
To freeze: cool quickly, then pour into a rigid container. Seal, label and freeze.
To thaw and serve: thaw at room temperature for 4 hours, then reheat gently on top of the stove, stirring occasionally.
SERVES 6

BEEF OLIVES WITH YOGURT

METRIC/IMPERIAL

1 kg/2 lb rump steak, trimmed of fat and cut into 4 thin escalopes
25 g/1 oz flour
25 g/1 oz butter
2 × 15 ml spoons/2 tablespoons vegetable oil
2 × 15 ml spoons/2 tablespoons tomato purée
300 ml/½ pint beef stock
1 bay leaf
300 ml/½ pint natural yogurt, to finish
For the stuffing:
25 g/1 oz butter
1 small onion, peeled and finely chopped
50 g/2 oz mushrooms, finely chopped
2 × 15 ml spoons/2 tablespoons fresh white breadcrumbs
2 × 5 ml spoons/2 teaspoons freshly chopped parsley
1 × 5 ml spoon/1 teaspoon chopped fresh basil or thyme
salt
freshly ground black pepper
1 egg, beaten

AMERICAN

2 lb boneless sirloin steak, trimmed of fat and cut into 4 thin escalopes
¼ cup flour
2 tablespoons butter
2 tablespoons vegetable oil
2 tablespoons tomato paste
1¼ cups beef stock
1 bay leaf
1¼ cups unflavored yogurt, to finish
For the stuffing:
2 tablespoons butter
1 small onion, peeled and finely chopped
½ cup finely chopped mushrooms
2 tablespoons fresh white breadcrumbs
2 teaspoons freshly chopped parsley
1 teaspoon chopped fresh basil or thyme
salt
freshly ground black pepper
1 egg, beaten

To make the stuffing: melt the butter in a pan, add the onion and mushrooms and fry gently until soft. Transfer to a bowl, add the remaining stuffing ingredients and stir well to mix.
Divide the stuffing equally between the four escalopes, place at one end of the meat, then roll up and secure with string or wooden cocktail sticks (toothpicks). Coat in the flour seasoned with salt and pepper. Heat the butter and oil in a flameproof casserole dish, add the beef olives and fry until browned on all sides. Stir in the tomato purée (paste) and stock, then add the bay leaf and salt and pepper to taste.
Cover and cook in a preheated moderate oven (180°C/350°F or Gas Mark 4) for 1½ hours. Remove the bay leaf.
To freeze: cool quickly. Leave in the casserole or transfer to a rigid container. Cover, then wrap in a freezer bag or foil. Seal, label and freeze.
To thaw and serve: remove wrappings and thaw at room temperature for 4 hours. Reheat in the covered casserole in a preheated moderate oven (180°C/350°F or Gas Mark 4) for 1 hour or until heated through. Remove the string or cocktail sticks (toothpicks) from the beef olives, stir the yogurt into the sauce and heat through. Do not allow to boil.
SERVES 4

SWEET AND SOUR BEEF

METRIC/IMPERIAL

75 g/3 oz butter
1.5 kg/3 lb topside of beef, trimmed of fat and cut into thin strips
2 medium onions, peeled and chopped
4–6 celery stalks, chopped
1 × 800 g/1 lb 12 oz can pineapple chunks
600 ml/1 pint beef stock
salt
freshly ground black pepper
4 × 15 ml spoons/4 tablespoons cornflour
2 × 15 ml spoons/2 tablespoons soy sauce
2 × 15 ml spoons/2 tablespoons tomato ketchup
6 × 15 ml spoons/6 tablespoons vinegar

AMERICAN

⅜ cup butter
3 lb top round of beef, trimmed of fat and cut into thin strips
2 medium onions, peeled and chopped
4–6 celery stalks, chopped
1 × 1 lb 12 oz can pineapple chunks
2½ cups beef stock
salt
freshly ground black pepper
¼ cup cornstarch
2 tablespoons soy sauce
2 tablespoons tomato ketchup
6 tablespoons vinegar

Melt the butter in a pan, add the beef and fry briskly until browned on all sides. Add the onions and celery and fry gently for 5 minutes, stirring occasionally.
Drain the juice from the pineapple and make up to 600 ml/1 pint/2½ cups with water. Stir into the pan with the stock and salt and pepper to taste. Bring to the boil, then cover and simmer for about 1 hour or until the meat is tender.

Put the remaining ingredients in a jug (pitcher) and blend together. Pour into the beef mixture with the pineapple chunks and bring to the boil, stirring constantly. Simmer for 2 to 3 minutes until the mixture thickens.
To freeze: cool quickly, then pour into a rigid container. Seal, label and freeze.
To thaw and serve: thaw at room temperature for 4 hours, then reheat gently on top of the stove, stirring occasionally.
SERVES 12

CLEMENTINE BEEF

METRIC/IMPERIAL
675–900 g/1½–2 lb chuck steak, trimmed of fat and cut into cubes
40 g/1½ oz flour
40 g/1½ oz dripping
2 medium onions, peeled and sliced
2 medium carrots, peeled and sliced
thinly pared rind and juice of 1 large orange
150 ml/¼ pint dry cider
1 beef stock cube
salt
freshly ground black pepper

AMERICAN
1½–2 lb blade steak, trimmed of fat and cut into cubes
⅜ cup flour
3 tablespoons drippings
2 medium onions, peeled and sliced
2 medium carrots, peeled and sliced
thinly pared rind and juice of 1 large orange
⅔ cup hard cider
2 beef bouillon cubes
salt
freshly ground black pepper

Coat the beef in the flour. Melt the dripping in a pan, add the beef and fry briskly until browned on all sides. Stir in any remaining flour, then add the onions and carrots.
Mix the orange juice and cider together in a measuring jug and make up to 450 ml/¾ pint/ 2 cups with water. Stir into the pan with the orange rind, stock (bouillon) cube(s) and salt and pepper to taste. Bring to the boil, cover and simmer for 2 to 2½ hours or until the meat is tender.
To freeze: cool quickly, then pour into a rigid container. Seal, label and freeze.
To thaw and serve: thaw at room temperature for 4 hours, then reheat gently on top of the stove, stirring occasionally.
SERVES 4

POLPETTE

METRIC/IMPERIAL
2 thick slices of bread, crusts removed
3 eggs
450 g/1 lb lean minced beef
2 × 15 ml spoons/2 tablespoons freshly chopped parsley
pinch of grated nutmeg
finely grated rind of 1 lemon
2 garlic cloves, peeled and crushed
salt
freshly ground black pepper
flour for coating
50 g/2 oz dried breadcrumbs
vegetable oil for deep-frying

AMERICAN
2 thick slices of bread, crusts removed
3 eggs
2 cups lean ground beef
2 tablespoons freshly chopped parsley
pinch of grated nutmeg
finely grated rind of 1 lemon
2 garlic cloves, peeled and crushed
salt
freshly ground black pepper
flour for coating
½ cup dried breadcrumbs
vegetable oil for deep-frying

Put the bread in a bowl, beat 2 eggs and pour over the bread. Leave to soak until soft.
Put the beef, parsley, nutmeg and lemon rind in a separate bowl and stir well to mix. Mash the soaked bread and stir into the meat mixture with the garlic and salt and pepper to taste.
Shape the mixture into small balls with lightly floured hands. Beat the remaining egg, dip the meatballs into the egg one at a time, then coat with the breadcrumbs. Repeat with more egg and breadcrumbs until the meatballs are thoroughly coated.
Deep-fry in hot oil until cooked through and golden brown. Drain on paper towels.
To freeze: cool quickly, then pack in a rigid container. Seal, label and freeze.
To thaw and serve: thaw at room temperature for 4 hours, then put on a baking sheet and reheat in a preheated moderately hot oven (200°C/400°F or Gas Mark 6) for 20 to 30 minutes or until heated through. Serve with tomato sauce.
SERVES 4 to 6

LASAGNE WITH YOGURT TOPPING

METRIC/IMPERIAL

6 sheets (approx 100 g/4 oz) lasagne
1 × 15 ml spoon/1 tablespoon oil
For the meat sauce:
3 × 15 ml spoons/3 tablespoons vegetable oil
1 medium onion, peeled and finely chopped
450 g/1 lb lean minced beef
1 × 400 g/14 oz can tomatoes
1 × 15 ml spoon/1 tablespoon dried mixed herbs
salt
freshly ground black pepper
2 × 5 ml spoons/2 teaspoons cornflour
1 × 15 ml spoons/1 tablespoon Worcestershire sauce
For the cheese sauce:
25 g/1 oz butter
25 g/1 oz flour
300 ml/½ pint milk
50 g/2 oz Cheddar cheese, grated
pinch of mustard powder
For the topping:
300 ml/½ pint natural yogurt
2 eggs, beaten
25 g/1 oz flour
1 × 15 ml spoon/1 tablespoon grated Parmesan cheese, to finish

AMERICAN

6 sheets (approx ¼ lb) lasagne
1 tablespoon oil
For the meat sauce:
3 tablespoons vegetable oil
1 medium onion, peeled and finely chopped
2 cups lean ground beef
1 × 14 oz can tomatoes
1 tablespoon dried mixed herbs
salt
freshly ground black pepper
2 teaspoons cornstarch
1 tablespoon Worcestershire sauce
For the cheese sauce:
2 tablespoons butter
¼ cup flour
1¼ cups milk
½ cup grated Cheddar cheese
pinch of mustard powder
For the topping:
1¼ cups unflavored yogurt
2 eggs, beaten
¼ cup flour
1 tablespoon grated Parmesan cheese, to finish

To make the meat sauce: heat 2 × 15 ml spoons/2 tablespoons oil in a pan, add the onion and fry gently until soft. Add the beef and fry until browned, stirring constantly to break up the meat. Stir in the tomatoes, herbs and salt and pepper to taste. Bring to the boil, stirring constantly, then cover and simmer for 30 minutes. Mix the cornflour (cornstarch) and Worcestershire sauce to a paste, then stir into the meat sauce and bring to the boil, stirring constantly. Remove from the heat.

To make the cheese sauce: melt the butter in a pan, stir in the flour and cook for 2 minutes, stirring constantly. Remove from the heat and gradually stir in the milk. Return to the heat and bring to the boil, stirring constantly, then simmer until the sauce thickens. Stir in the cheese, mustard and salt and pepper to taste. Remove from the heat.

Put the lasagne in boiling salted water to which the oil has been added. Cook for about 11 minutes or until 'al dente', then drain.

Arrange the meat and cheese sauces and the lasagne in layers in an ovenproof casserole dish or foil container, finishing with a layer of lasagne. Mix the yogurt, eggs and flour together and spoon over the lasagne. Bake in a preheated moderately hot oven (190°C/375°F or Gas Mark 5) for 20 to 25 minutes or until the topping is set.

To freeze: cool quickly, then open (flash) freeze until firm. Wrap in foil, seal, label and return to the freezer.

To thaw and serve: loosen the foil, sprinkle the yogurt topping with the Parmesan cheese, then reheat from frozen in a preheated moderately hot oven (190°C/375°F or Gas Mark 5) for 1½ hours or until heated through. Remove the foil for the last 10 minutes to brown the topping.

SERVES 4 to 6

KOFTA CURRY

METRIC/IMPERIAL

For the meatballs:
450 g/1 lb lean minced beef
1 onion, peeled and finely minced
4 garlic cloves, peeled and finely minced
2 green chillis, seeds removed and finely minced
2 potatoes, peeled, boiled and mashed
0.5 × 2.5 ml spoon/¼ teaspoon each of freshly ground black pepper, ground cinnamon, ground cloves and ground cardamoms
1 × 5 ml spoon/1 teaspoon salt
1 egg, beaten
flour for coating
vegetable oil for frying
For the sauce:
1 large onion, peeled and finely chopped
3 tomatoes, peeled and chopped
1 × 5 ml spoon/1 teaspoon ground coriander
1 × 2.5 ml spoon/½ teaspoon ground turmeric

1 × 2.5 ml spoon/½ teaspoon chilli powder
1 × 2.5 ml spoon/½ teaspoon ground cumin
1 × 2.5 ml spoon/½ teaspoon ground ginger
1 × 5 ml spoon/1 teaspoon salt
150 ml/¼ pint natural yogurt
juice of ½ lemon

AMERICAN
For the meatballs:
2 cups lean ground beef
1 onion, peeled and finely ground
4 garlic cloves, peeled and finely ground
2 green chilis, seeds removed and finely ground
2 potatoes, peeled, boiled and mashed
¼ teaspoon each of freshly ground black pepper, ground cinnamon, ground cloves and ground cardamoms
1 teaspoon salt
1 egg, beaten
flour for coating
vegetable oil for frying
For the sauce:
1 large onion, peeled and finely chopped
3 tomatoes, peeled and chopped
1 teaspoon ground coriander
½ teaspoon ground turmeric
½ teaspoon chili powder
½ teaspoon ground cumin
½ teaspoon ground ginger
1 teaspoon salt
⅔ cup unflavored yogurt
juice of ½ lemon

To make the meatballs: put all the ingredients in a bowl, except the flour and oil, and stir well to mix. Shape into small balls with lightly floured hands. Heat 2 × 15 ml spoons/2 tablespoons of oil in a frying pan (skillet), put in some of the meatballs and fry until browned on all sides. Repeat with more oil and the remaining meatballs. Drain on paper towels.
To make the sauce: heat 2 × 15 ml spoons/2 tablespoons of oil in a pan, add the onion and tomatoes and cook gently for 5 minutes. Stir in the spices and salt and fry for a further 5 minutes, stirring occasionally. Stir in the yogurt and lemon juice. Add the meatballs to the sauce, cover and cook gently for 30 minutes. Shake the pan occasionally, but do not stir or the meatballs will break.
To freeze: cool quickly, then transfer to a rigid container. Overwrap in a freezer bag or foil. Seal, label and freeze.
To thaw and serve: remove wrappings and thaw at room temperature for 4 hours. Reheat gently on top of the stove, shaking the pan occasionally. Serve with plain boiled rice, mango chutney, peppers, onion rings and cucumber.
SERVES 4

BITKIS

METRIC/IMPERIAL
675 g/1½ lb lean minced beef
1 large onion, peeled and finely chopped
100 g/4 oz fresh brown breadcrumbs
1 × 15 ml spoon/1 tablespoon freshly chopped parsley
salt
freshly ground black pepper
1 egg, beaten
5 × 15 ml spoons/5 tablespoons vegetable oil
600 ml/1 pint tomato sauce
3 × 15 ml spoons/3 tablespoons soured cream, to finish

AMERICAN
3 cups lean ground beef
1 large onion, peeled and finely chopped
2 cups fresh brown breadcrumbs
1 tablespoon freshly chopped parsley
salt
freshly ground black pepper
1 egg, beaten
⅓ cup vegetable oil
2½ cups tomato sauce
3 tablespoons sour cream, to finish

Put the beef and onion in a bowl, stir well to mix, then stir in the breadcrumbs, parsley and salt and pepper to taste. Bind the mixture together with the egg, divide into 20 equal portions and shape into flat cakes with floured hands.
Heat the oil in a pan, add the bitkis and fry until golden on all sides, shaking the pan frequently. Remove from the pan with a slotted spoon and drain on paper towels.
Heat the tomato sauce in a large pan, add the bitkis and simmer for 20 minutes.
To freeze: cool quickly, then pack in rigid containers in usable quantities. Seal, label and freeze.
To thaw and serve: tip the frozen bitkis and sauce into an ovenproof dish. Cook in a preheated moderate oven (180°C/350°F or Gas Mark 4) for 1¼ hours or until heated through. Spoon the sour(ed) cream over the bitkis and cook for a further 10 minutes.
MAKES 20

POTATO THATCHED MEAT LOAF

METRIC/IMPERIAL

2 thick slices white bread, crusts removed
150 ml/¼ pint milk
1.5 kg/3 lb lean minced beef
2 bacon rashers, rinds removed and finely chopped
2 celery stalks, finely chopped
1 beef stock cube, crumbled
2 × 15 ml spoons/2 tablespoons Worcestershire sauce
2 × 15 ml spoons/2 tablespoons tomato ketchup
4 × 15 ml spoons/4 tablespoons fruit chutney
1 × 15 ml spoon/1 tablespoon salt
freshly ground black pepper
1.5 kg/3 lb potatoes, peeled, boiled and mashed with butter and milk

AMERICAN

2 thick slices white bread, crusts removed
⅔ cup milk
6 cups lean ground beef
2 bacon slices, rinds removed and finely chopped
2 celery stalks, finely chopped
2 beef bouillon cubes, crumbled
2 tablespoons Worcestershire sauce
2 tablespoons tomato ketchup
¼ cup fruit chutney
1 tablespoon salt
freshly ground black pepper
3 lb potatoes, peeled, boiled and mashed with butter and milk

Grease two 1 kg/2 lb loaf tins.
Put the bread in a large bowl, cover with the milk and leave to soak for 30 minutes. Add the remaining ingredients, except the potatoes, and stir well to mix.
Press the mixture lightly into the prepared tins then bake in a preheated moderate oven (180°C/350°F or Gas Mark 4) for 1 hour or until set. Drain off the liquor from the tins, then leave to cool. Turn the loaves out on to a baking sheet and spread thickly with the mashed potato using the prongs of a fork to give a 'thatched' effect.
To freeze: open (flash) freeze until firm, then pack in freezer bags. Seal, label and return to the freezer.
To thaw and serve: remove wrappings and thaw at room temperature for 4 hours. Reheat in a preheated moderate oven (180°C/350°F or Gas Mark 4) for 1 hour or until heated through and golden.
EACH LOAF SERVES 6

ALU KEEMA TIKKI

This is an Indian recipe for potato cutlets with a hot minced (ground) beef stuffing.

METRIC/IMPERIAL

For the potato dough:
450 g/1 lb potatoes, peeled, boiled and mashed
50 g/2 oz flour
25 g/1 oz butter
1 egg, beaten
1 × 2.5 ml spoon/½ teaspoon garam masala or freshly ground black pepper
pinch of paprika pepper
1.5 × 5 ml spoons/1½ teaspoons salt
flour for dredging
a little milk mixed with ½ beaten egg, to seal
vegetable oil for deep-frying, to finish
For the stuffing:
25 g/1 oz butter
1 onion, peeled and finely chopped
2 green chillis, seeds removed and finely chopped
225 g/½ lb cooked minced beef
2 × 5 ml spoons/2 teaspoons tomato purée
salt
freshly ground black pepper

AMERICAN

For the potato dough:
1 lb potatoes, peeled, boiled and mashed
½ cup flour
2 tablespoons butter
1 egg, beaten
½ teaspoon garam masala or freshly ground black pepper
pinch of paprika pepper
1½ teaspoons salt
flour for dredging
a little milk mixed with ½ beaten egg, to seal
vegetable oil for deep-frying, to finish
For the stuffing:
2 tablespoons butter
1 onion, peeled and finely chopped
2 green chilis, seeds removed and finely chopped
1 cup cooked ground beef
2 teaspoons tomato paste
salt
freshly ground black pepper

To make the potato dough: put all the ingredients in a bowl and mix together to make a firm paste. Transfer to a well-floured surface and dredge with flour. Roll out the dough and cut out 10 rounds or squares.
To make the stuffing: melt the butter in a pan, add the onion and fry gently until soft. Add the remaining ingredients and cook gently for 5 minutes, stirring occasionally. Leave to cool. Place a spoonful of stuffing on each piece of dough. Brush the edges of the dough with the

milk and egg mixture, then fold over and press firmly to seal. Dredge lightly with flour.
To freeze: open (flash) freeze until firm, then pack in a rigid container, separating each layer with foil. Seal, label and return to the freezer.
To thaw and serve: thaw at room temperature for 4 hours. Dredge lightly with flour, then deep-fry in hot oil until golden brown on all sides. Serve hot with tomato sauce.
MAKES 10

ORIENTAL CURRIED BEEF

METRIC/IMPERIAL
50 g/2 oz dripping or lard
1 medium onion, peeled and chopped
1 garlic clove, peeled and finely chopped
2 green dessert apples, cored and chopped
2 × 15 ml spoons/2 tablespoons curry powder
2 × 5 ml spoons/2 teaspoons mustard powder
1 × 5 ml spoon/1 teaspoon curry paste
1 × 15 ml spoon/1 tablespoon tomato purée
675 g/1½ lb lean minced beef
150 ml/¼ pint beef stock
1 × 2.5 ml spoon/½ teaspoon salt
2 × 15 ml spoons/2 tablespoons redcurrant jelly
2 × 15 ml spoons/2 tablespoons natural yogurt

AMERICAN
¼ cup drippings or lard
1 medium onion, peeled and chopped
1 garlic clove, peeled and finely chopped
2 green dessert apples, cored and chopped
2 tablespoons curry powder
2 teaspoons mustard powder
1 teaspoon curry paste
1 tablespoon tomato paste
3 cups lean ground beef
⅔ cup beef stock
½ teaspoon salt
2 tablespoons redcurrant jelly
2 tablespoons unflavored yogurt

Melt the fat in a pan, add the onion and garlic and fry for 5 minutes until soft. Add the apples and fry for a further 5 minutes. Stir in the curry powder, mustard, curry paste and tomato purée (paste). Add the beef and fry until evenly browned, stirring constantly to break up the meat. Stir in the stock and salt. Bring to the boil, cover and simmer for 40 minutes. Stir in the redcurrant jelly and yogurt and cook for 1 minute.
To freeze: cool quickly, then pour into a rigid container. Seal, label and freeze.
To thaw and serve: thaw at room temperature for 4 hours, then reheat gently on top of the stove, stirring occasionally.
SERVES 6

BEEF AND ONION CURRY

METRIC/IMPERIAL
150 ml/¼ pint vegetable oil
1 kg/2 lb onions, peeled and chopped
6 × 15 ml spoons/6 tablespoons curry powder
4 × 5 ml spoons/4 teaspoons paprika pepper
1 litre/1¾ pints beef stock
600 ml/1 pint tomato juice
4 celery stalks, chopped
75 g/3 oz dried apricots
1.25 kg/2½ lb chuck steak, trimmed of fat and cut into cubes
2 bay leaves
salt

AMERICAN
⅔ cup vegetable oil
2 lb onions, peeled and chopped
6 tablespoons curry powder
4 teaspoons paprika pepper
4¼ cups beef stock
2½ cups tomato juice
4 celery stalks, chopped
½ cup dried apricots
2½ lb blade steak, trimmed of fat and cut into cubes
2 bay leaves
salt

Heat the oil in a flameproof casserole dish, add the onions and fry gently until soft. Stir in the curry powder and paprika and cook gently for 2 minutes. Stir in the stock, tomato juice, celery and apricots and cook gently for 15 minutes. Add the beef, bay leaves and salt.
Cover and cook gently for 2 to 2½ hours or until the meat is tender. Remove the bay leaves.
To freeze: cool quickly, then pour into a rigid container. Seal, label and freeze.
To thaw and serve: thaw at room temperature for 4 hours, then reheat gently on top of the stove, stirring occasionally. Serve with plain boiled rice, mango chutney and side dishes of salted peanuts, pineapple chunks and desiccated (shredded) coconut.
SERVES 6 to 8

CARBONNADE OF BEEF

METRIC/IMPERIAL

1 × 15 ml spoon/1 tablespoon vegetable oil
675 g/1½ lb chuck steak, trimmed of fat and cut into cubes
1 medium onion, peeled and sliced
1 garlic clove, peeled and crushed
1 × 15 ml spoon/1 tablespoon flour
300 ml/½ pint brown ale
300 ml/½ pint beef stock
1 × 5 ml spoon/1 teaspoon vinegar
salt
freshly ground black pepper
To finish:
6 thick slices of French bread
a little prepared French mustard

AMERICAN

1 tablespoon vegetable oil
1½ lb blade steak, trimmed of fat and cut into cubes
1 medium onion, peeled and sliced
1 garlic clove, peeled and crushed
1 tablespoon flour
1¼ cups dark beer
1¼ cups beef stock
1 teaspoon vinegar
salt
freshly ground black pepper
To finish:
6 thick slices of French bread
a little prepared French mustard

Heat the oil in a flameproof casserole dish, add the beef and fry briskly until browned on all sides. Remove from the casserole with a slotted spoon, then add the onion, and garlic and fry gently until soft. Stir in the flour and cook for 2 minutes, then gradually stir in the brown ale (beer) and stock.

Return the beef to the casserole, then add the vinegar and salt and pepper to taste. Cover and cook in a preheated moderate oven (160°C/325°F or Gas Mark 3) for 2 to 2½ hours or until the meat is tender.

To freeze: cool quickly. Leave in the casserole or transfer to a rigid container. Cover, then wrap the casserole in a freezer bag or foil. Seal, label and freeze.

To thaw and serve: thaw at room temperature for 4 hours. Spread the bread with mustard, then place on top of the meat in the casserole, mustard side uppermost. Press the bread down slightly into the meat. Reheat, uncovered, in a preheated moderately hot oven (190°C/375°F or Gas Mark 5) for 1 hour or until the bread is crisp and the meat is heated through.

SERVES 4

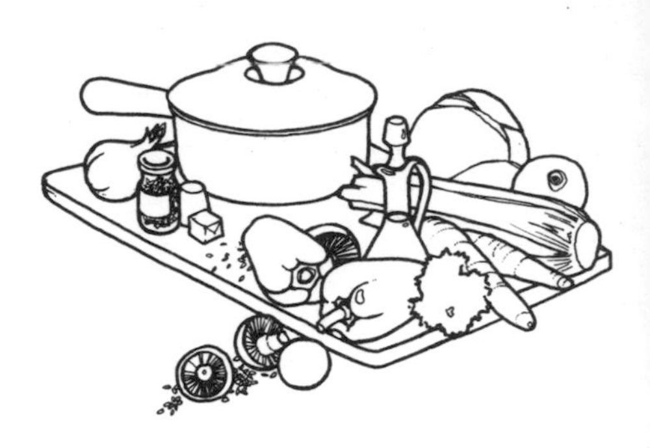

STUFFED AUBERGINES (EGGPLANTS)

METRIC/IMPERIAL

2 medium aubergines, stalks removed and halved lengthways
25 g/1 oz butter
1 medium onion, peeled and finely chopped
175 g/6 oz lean minced beef
1 garlic clove, peeled and crushed
1 × 15 ml spoon/1 tablespoon freshly chopped parsley
1 × 400 g/14 oz can tomatoes
1 × 5 ml spoon/1 teaspoon dried marjoram
salt
freshly ground black pepper
2 × 5 ml spoons/2 teaspoons cornflour
100 g/4 oz Cheddar cheese, grated

AMERICAN

2 medium eggplants, stalks removed and halved lengthwise
2 tablespoons butter
1 medium onion, peeled and finely chopped
¾ cup lean ground beef
1 garlic clove, peeled and crushed
1 tablespoon freshly chopped parsley
1 × 14 oz can tomatoes
1 teaspoon dried marjoram
salt
freshly ground black pepper
2 teaspoons cornstarch
1 cup grated Cheddar cheese

Scoop out the flesh from the aubergines (eggplants) and chop finely. Put the shells in an ovenproof dish.

Melt the butter in a pan, add the onion and aubergine (eggplant) flesh and fry gently until soft. Stir in the beef and fry until browned, stirring constantly to break up the meat. Add

the garlic, parsley, tomatoes, marjoram and salt and pepper to taste. Bring to the boil.
Mix the cornflour (cornstarch) to a paste with a little cold water, then stir into the pan. Cook for 3 minutes, stirring constantly, then remove from the heat and divide the mixture equally between the aubergine (eggplant) halves.
Top with grated cheese and cook in a preheated moderate oven (180°C/350°F or Gas Mark 4) for 30 minutes.
To freeze: cool quickly. Open (flash) freeze until firm, then wrap individually in foil and pack in a freezer bag. Seal, label and return to the freezer.
To thaw and serve: reheat from frozen in a covered casserole dish in a preheated moderate oven for 1¼ hours. Remove the lid and cook for a further 15 minutes until the aubergines (eggplants) are heated through and the cheese is brown and bubbling.
SERVES 4

BOEUF BOURGUIGNONNE

METRIC/IMPERIAL
4 × 15 ml spoons/4 tablespoons vegetable oil
1.25 kg/2½ lb topside of beef, trimmed of fat and cut into cubes
100 g/4 oz streaky bacon, rinds removed and diced
2 × 15 ml spoons/2 tablespoons flour
250 ml/8 fl oz red wine
250 ml/8 fl oz beef stock
2 bay leaves
1 garlic clove, peeled and crushed
pinch of dried mixed herbs
3 × 15 ml spoons/3 tablespoons brandy
salt
freshly ground black pepper
12 small pickling onions, peeled
freshly chopped parsley, to garnish

AMERICAN
¼ cup vegetable oil
2½ lb top round of beef, trimmed of fat and cut into cubes
¼ lb fatty bacon, diced
2 tablespoons flour
1 cup red wine
1 cup beef stock
2 bay leaves
1 garlic clove, peeled and crushed
pinch of dried mixed herbs
3 tablespoons brandy
salt
freshly ground black pepper
12 baby onions, peeled
freshly chopped parsley, to garnish

Heat 3 × 15 ml spoons/3 tablespoons oil in a pan, add the beef and fry briskly until browned on all sides. Drain and transfer to an ovenproof casserole dish. Add the bacon to the pan and fry until crisp and golden brown, then stir in the flour and fry for 2 minutes, stirring constantly. Stir in the wine, stock, bay leaves, garlic and herbs and simmer gently.
Put the brandy in a small pan, warm through, then ignite and pour over the meat while still flaming. Pour over the sauce, add salt and pepper to taste, then cover and cook in a preheated moderate oven (160°C/325°F or Gas Mark 3) for 1½ hours.
Heat the remaining oil in a pan, add the onions and fry gently until browned. Drain thoroughly, add to the casserole and cook for a further 1 hour or until the meat is tender. Remove the bay leaves.
To freeze: cool quickly. Leave in the casserole or pour into a rigid container. Cover, then wrap the casserole in a freezer bag or foil. Seal, label and freeze.
To thaw and serve: reheat from frozen in the covered casserole in a preheated moderate oven (160°C/325°F or Gas Mark 3) for 2 hours or until heated through. Sprinkle with parsley just before serving.
SERVES 6 to 8

POLDER PIE

METRIC/IMPERIAL

1 large aubergine, sliced
salt
50 g/2 oz butter
1 large onion, peeled and finely chopped
1 garlic clove, peeled and crushed
450 g/1 lb lean minced beef
1 × 5 ml spoon/1 teaspoon dried basil
25 g/1 oz flour
150 ml/¼ pint beef stock
freshly ground black pepper
225 g/½ lb tomatoes, peeled and sliced
450 g/1 lb potatoes, peeled, boiled and mashed
75 g/3 oz Edam cheese, grated
a little milk, to mix

AMERICAN

1 large eggplant, sliced
salt
¼ cup butter
1 large onion, peeled and finely chopped
1 garlic clove, peeled and crushed
2 cups lean ground beef
1 teaspoon dried basil
¼ cup flour
⅔ cup beef stock
freshly ground black pepper
1 cup peeled and sliced tomatoes
1 lb potatoes, peeled, boiled and mashed
¾ cup grated Edam cheese
a little milk, to mix

Sprinkle the aubergine (eggplant) with salt and leave for 30 minutes.
Meanwhile, melt half the butter in a pan, add the onion and garlic and fry gently until soft. Add the beef and fry briskly for 8 to 10 minutes, stirring constantly to break up the meat. Stir in the basil, flour and stock and continue cooking until the mixture thickens. Add salt and pepper to taste, then pour into a casserole dish or foil container.
Drain off any liquid from the aubergine (eggplant), rinse under cold running water, then dry on paper towels. Melt the remaining butter in the pan, add the aubergine (eggplant) and fry gently until golden. Place on top of the meat mixture, then cover with the tomatoes.
Put the potatoes and cheese in a bowl, beat well to mix and add enough milk to make the mixture soft. Pipe or spoon around the edge of the dish, then bake in a preheated moderately hot oven (200°C/400°F or Gas Mark 6) for 25 to 30 minutes or until golden brown.
To freeze: cool quickly. Cover, then wrap in a freezer bag or foil. Seal, label and freeze.
To thaw and serve: thaw at room temperature for 4 hours, then reheat in the covered casserole or container in a preheated moderate oven (180°C/350°F or Gas Mark 4) for 45 minutes or until heated through.
SERVES 4

SCOTCH MINCE

METRIC/IMPERIAL

1 × 15 ml spoon/1 tablespoon dripping
2 small onions, peeled and chopped
1 × 65 g/2½ oz can tomato purée
1 × 5 ml spoon/1 teaspoon salt
freshly ground black pepper
25 g/1 oz flour
450 ml/¾ pint beef stock
1 kg/2 lb lean minced beef

AMERICAN

1 tablespoon drippings
2 small onions, peeled and chopped
¼ cup tomato paste
1 teaspoon salt
freshly ground black pepper
¼ cup flour
2 cups beef stock
4 cups lean ground beef

Melt the dripping in a pan, add the onion and fry gently for 5 minutes until soft. Stir in the tomato purée (paste), salt, pepper and flour and cook for 2 minutes. Add the stock and beef and bring to the boil, stirring constantly to break up the meat.
Cover and simmer for 50 minutes to 1 hour until the beef is cooked, stirring occasionally.
To freeze: cool quickly, then pour into a rigid container. Seal, label and freeze.
To thaw and serve: thaw at room temperature for 4 hours, then reheat gently on top of the stove, stirring occasionally.
SERVES 4 to 6

HAMBURGERS

METRIC/IMPERIAL

1 kg/2 lb lean minced beef
50 g/2 oz fresh brown breadcrumbs
6 × 15 ml spoons/6 tablespoons water
1 × 2.5 ml spoon/½ teaspoon dried thyme
salt
freshly ground black pepper
flour for coating
vegetable oil for frying

AMERICAN

4 cups lean ground beef
1 cup fresh brown breadcrumbs
6 tablespoons water
½ teaspoon dried thyme
salt
freshly ground black pepper
flour for coating
vegetable oil for frying

Put all the ingredients in a bowl and stir well to mix. Divide the mixture into 8 equal portions and shape into rounds with lightly floured hands.
To freeze: open (flash) freeze until firm, then pack in a freezer bag. Seal, label and return to the freezer.
To thaw and serve: fry frozen hamburgers in hot oil for 6 to 8 minutes on each side.
MAKES 10

EGG AND BACON BURGER

Place a fried hamburger on a toasted bap (bun). Top with a rasher (slice) of lean (Canadian) bacon and a fried egg. Garnish with tomatoes and watercress.

PINEAPPLE BURGER

Place a fried hamburger on a toasted bap (bun). Top with a ring of pineapple and fill the centre with cream cheese. Sprinkle with snipped chives just before serving.

CURRYBURGERS

METRIC/IMPERIAL

450 g/1 lb lean minced beef
1 onion, peeled and finely chopped
1 × 5 ml spoon/1 teaspoon curry powder
1 × 5 ml spoon/1 teaspoon ground coriander
50 g/2 oz fresh brown breadcrumbs
salt
freshly ground black pepper
1 egg, beaten
flour for coating
vegetable oil for frying
To serve:
1 onion, peeled and sliced
3 tomatoes, sliced

AMERICAN

2 cups lean ground beef
1 onion, peeled and finely chopped
1 teaspoon curry powder
1 teaspoon ground coriander
1 cup fresh brown breadcrumbs
salt
freshly ground black pepper
1 egg, beaten
flour for coating
vegetable oil for frying
To serve:
1 onion, peeled and sliced
3 tomatoes, sliced

Put all the ingredients, except the flour and oil, in a bowl and stir well to mix. Divide the mixture into 8 equal portions and shape into 2.5 cm/1 inch thick flat rounds with floured hands.
To freeze: open (flash) freeze until firm, then wrap individually in foil and pack together in a freezer bag. Seal, label and return to the freezer.
To thaw and serve: fry from frozen in hot oil for 6 to 8 minutes on each side. Serve in baps (buns) with slices of onion and tomato.
MAKES 8

BOEUF EN CROÛTE

METRIC/IMPERIAL

1 kg/2 lb fillet of beef, trimmed of fat
freshly ground black pepper
50 g/2 oz butter
1 × 15 ml spoon/1 tablespoon vegetable oil
100 g/4 oz mushrooms, sliced
1 × 5 ml spoon/1 teaspoon dried mixed herbs
salt
basic flaky or puff pastry dough made with 225 g/½ lb flour
beaten egg, to glaze

AMERICAN

2 lb fillet of beef, trimmed of fat
freshly ground black pepper
¼ cup butter
1 tablespoon vegetable oil
1 cup sliced mushrooms
1 teaspoon dried mixed herbs
salt
basic flaky or puff paste dough made with 2 cups flour
beaten egg, to glaze

Tie the fillet in a neat shape and sprinkle with pepper.
Melt half the butter in a pan, put in the beef and fry briskly until browned on all sides. Transfer to a roasting tin and roast in a preheated moderately hot oven (200°C/400°F or Gas Mark 6) for 10 minutes. Leave to cool.
Heat the remaining butter and the oil in a pan, add the mushrooms and herbs and fry gently for 3 minutes. Add salt and pepper to taste, then leave to cool.
Roll out the dough on a floured surface to a thin rectangle large enough to cover the meat and overlap generously. Place the meat in the centre of the dough and spoon over the mushrooms. Moisten the edges of the dough, fold over the meat, then turn the ends upwards so that no juices escape. Use any trimmings to decorate the top of the dough.

To freeze: wrap in foil, then overwrap in a freezer bag. Seal, label and freeze.
To thaw and serve: thaw in the refrigerator for 6 hours. Remove wrappings, place on a baking sheet and brush with beaten egg. Bake in a preheated hot oven (220°C/425°F or Gas Mark 7) for 15 minutes, then reduce the heat to moderately hot (190°C/375°F or Gas Mark 5) and bake for a further 30 minutes until golden brown and heated through. Cut into thick slices and serve hot or cold.
SERVES 4 to 6

BOEUF STROGANOFF

METRIC/IMPERIAL

50 g/2 oz butter
2 × 15 ml spoons/2 tablespoons vegetable oil
575 g/1¼ lb beef fillet, cut into thin strips
1 medium onion, peeled and finely chopped
100 g/4 oz button mushrooms, sliced
150 ml/¼ pint dry white wine
2 × 5 ml spoons/2 teaspoons tomato purée
1 × 2.5 ml spoon/½ teaspoon Worcestershire sauce
salt
freshly ground black pepper
To finish:
300 ml/½ pint soured cream
freshly chopped parsley

AMERICAN

¼ cup butter
2 tablespoons vegetable oil
1¼ lb beef fillet, cut into thin strips
1 medium onion, peeled and finely chopped
1 cup sliced button mushrooms
⅔ cup dry white wine
2 teaspoons tomato paste
½ teaspoon Worcestershire sauce
salt
freshly ground black pepper
To finish:
1¼ cups sour cream
freshly chopped parsley

Heat the butter and half the oil in a pan, add the beef and fry briskly for about 1 minute until browned on all sides. Remove from the pan with a slotted spoon.
Heat the remaining oil in the pan, add the onion and fry gently until soft. Add the mushrooms and fry for 1 to 2 minutes. Stir in the remaining ingredients, bring to the boil and boil rapidly for 2 minutes. Remove from the heat, return the beef to the pan and stir well to mix.
To freeze: cool quickly, then pour into a rigid container. Seal, label and freeze.
To thaw and serve: thaw at room temperature for 4 hours, then reheat gently on top of the stove, stirring occasionally. Stir in 250 ml/8 fl oz/1 cup sour(ed) cream and heat through. Do not allow to boil. Sprinkle with parsley just before serving and top with the remaining sour(ed) cream.
SERVES 4

STEAK AND KIDNEY PUDDING

METRIC/IMPERIAL
450 g/1 lb chuck steak, trimmed of fat and cut into cubes
225 g/½ lb ox kidney, skin and cores removed and cut into cubes
1 × 15 ml spoon/1 tablespoon flour
salt
freshly ground black pepper
50 g/2 oz dripping or lard
1 large onion, peeled and chopped
150 ml/¼ pint beef stock
For the suet pastry:
225 g/½ lb self-raising flour
1 × 5 ml spoon/1 teaspoon salt
100 g/4 oz shredded suet
approx 150 ml/¼ pint water

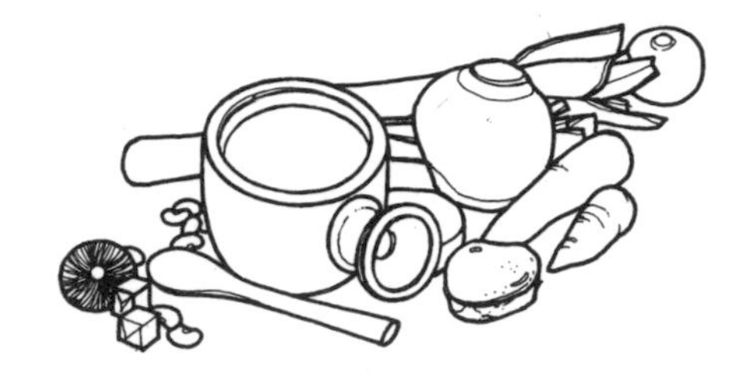

AMERICAN
1 lb blade steak, trimmed of fat and cut into cubes
½ lb beef kidney, skin and cores removed and cut into cubes
1 tablespoon flour
salt
freshly ground black pepper
¼ cup drippings or lard
1 large onion, peeled and chopped
⅔ cup beef stock
For the suet pastry:
2 cups self-rising flour
1 teaspoon salt
¾ cup shredded suet
approx ⅔ cup water

Coat the steak and kidney in the flour seasoned with salt and pepper. Melt the fat in a pan, add the meat and fry briskly until browned on all sides. Add the onion and cook for 2 minutes, then gradually stir in the stock. Bring to the boil, stirring constantly. Cover and cook gently for 2 to 2½ hours or until the meat is tender. Leave to cool.
To make the pastry: sift the flour and salt into a bowl, then stir in the suet. Add the water gradually, to give a soft, but not sticky, dough. Knead lightly until smooth. Roll out two-thirds of the dough on a floured board and use to line a lightly greased 1.2 litre/2 pint/5 cup pudding or foil basin (steaming mold).
Spoon in the meat and gravy mixture, moisten the edge of the dough with water, then cover with a lid made from the remaining dough. Press the edges firmly together to seal.
To freeze: wrap in foil, seal, label and freeze.
To thaw and serve: leave in wrappings overnight in the refrigerator. Remove wrappings and cover the top of the basin (mold) with buttered foil. Make a pleat in the centre of the foil to allow for expansion, then tie string around the basin (mold) to secure the foil. Steam for 2 hours. Serve from the basin with a napkin wrapped around the outside.
SERVES 4

SPICY BEEFBURGERS

METRIC/IMPERIAL

225 g/½ lb sausagemeat
400 g/14 oz lean minced beef
1 large onion, peeled and minced
1 egg, beaten
1.5 × 15 ml spoons/1½ tablespoons fruit sauce
salt
freshly ground black pepper
flour for coating
vegetable oil for frying

AMERICAN

1 cup sausagemeat
1¾ cups lean ground beef
1 large onion, peeled and ground
1 egg, beaten
1½ tablespoons fruit sauce
salt
freshly ground black pepper
flour for coating
vegetable oil for frying

Put all the ingredients in a bowl and stir well to mix. Divide the mixture into 8 equal portions and shape into rounds with lightly floured hands.
To freeze: open (flash) freeze until firm, then pack in a freezer bag. Seal, label and return to the freezer.
To thaw and serve: fry the frozen beefburgers in hot oil for 6 to 8 minutes on each side.
MAKES 8

STEAK AND KIDNEY PIE

METRIC/IMPERIAL

1 kg/2 lb chuck steak, trimmed of fat and cut into cubes
225 g/½ lb ox kidney, skin and cores removed and cut into cubes
50 g/2 oz flour
50 g/2 oz dripping or lard
2 large onions, peeled and sliced
300 ml/½ pint beef stock
1 × 2.5 ml spoon/½ teaspoon dried marjoram
1 bay leaf
salt
freshly ground black pepper
basic puff pastry dough made with 225 g/½ lb flour
beaten egg, to glaze

AMERICAN

2 lb blade steak, trimmed of fat and cut into cubes
½ lb beef kidney, skin and cores removed and cut into cubes
½ cup flour
¼ cup drippings or lard
2 large onions, peeled and sliced
1¼ cups beef stock
½ teaspoon dried marjoram
1 bay leaf
salt
freshly ground black pepper
basic puff paste dough made with 2 cups flour
beaten egg, to glaze

Coat the steak and kidney in the flour. Melt the fat in a pan, add the meat and fry briskly until browned on all sides. Add the onion and cook for 2 minutes, then gradually stir in the stock, marjoram, bay leaf and salt and pepper to taste. Bring to the boil, stirring constantly. Cover and cook gently for 2 to 2½ hours or until the meat is tender. Leave to cool, then remove the bay leaf and spoon the meat into an ovenproof pie dish or foil container.
Roll out the dough on a floured surface and use to cover the meat mixture, moistening the edge with water and pressing down firmly to seal. Flute the edge and use any trimmings to decorate the top of the pie. Cut an air vent.
To freeze: wrap in a freezer bag or foil. Seal, label and freeze.
To thaw and serve: remove wrappings and brush the dough with the beaten egg. Bake from frozen in a preheated hot oven (220°C/425°F or Gas Mark 7) for 30 minutes. Reduce the heat to moderate (180°C/350°F or Gas Mark 4) and bake for a further 30 minutes or until heated through. Cover with foil if the pastry becomes too brown during cooking.
SERVES 6

ENGLISH CLUB STEAK AND MUSHROOM PIE

METRIC/IMPERIAL

450 g/1 lb chuck steak, trimmed of fat and cut into thin strips
flour for coating
salt
freshly ground black pepper
100 g/4 oz button mushrooms, sliced
2 × 5 ml spoons/2 teaspoons prepared mustard
pinch of dried mixed herbs
6 × 15 ml spoons/6 tablespoons water
basic puff pastry dough made with 225 g/½ lb flour
a little milk, to glaze

AMERICAN

1 lb chuck steak, trimmed of fat and cut into thin strips
flour for coating
salt
freshly ground black pepper
1 cup sliced button mushrooms
2 teaspoons prepared mustard
pinch of dried mixed herbs
6 tablespoons water
basic puff paste dough made with 2 cups flour
a little milk, to glaze

Coat the beef in flour seasoned with salt and pepper. Place in a pan with the mushrooms, mustard, herbs and water. Cover and simmer for 2 to 2½ hours or until the meat is tender. Leave to cool, then spoon into an ovenproof pie dish or foil container.
Roll out the dough on a floured surface and use to cover the meat mixture, moistening the edge with water and pressing down firmly to seal. Flute the edge and use any trimmings to decorate the top of the pie. Cut an air vent in the centre.
To freeze: wrap in a freezer bag or foil. Seal, label and freeze.
To thaw and serve: remove wrappings and thaw at room temperature for 4 hours. Brush the dough with a little milk and bake in a preheated hot oven (220°C/425°F or Gas Mark 7) for 20 to 25 minutes or until golden brown and heated through.
SERVES 4

BEEF LOAF

METRIC/IMPERIAL

450 g/1 lb lean minced beef
225 g/½ lb sausagemeat
1 onion, peeled and chopped
25 g/1 oz fresh white breadcrumbs
1 × 15 ml spoon/1 tablespoon tomato purée
1 × 15 ml spoon/1 tablespoon Worcestershire sauce
1 × 5 ml spoon/1 teaspoon dried mixed herbs
salt
freshly ground black pepper
1 egg, beaten

AMERICAN

2 cups lean ground beef
1 cup sausagemeat
1 onion, peeled and chopped
½ cup fresh white breadcrumbs
1 tablespoon tomato paste
1 tablespoon Worcestershire sauce
1 teaspoon dried mixed herbs
salt
freshly ground black pepper
1 egg, beaten

Line a 675 g/1½ lb loaf tin with foil.
Put all the ingredients in a bowl and stir well to mix. Press the mixture lightly into the prepared tin and cover with foil.
To freeze: open (flash) freeze until firm, then remove the loaf from the tin in the foil lining. Overwrap in a freezer bag, seal, label and return to the freezer.
To thaw and serve: remove the freezer bag and leave to thaw in the refrigerator overnight. Replace in the tin and bake in a preheated moderate oven (180°C/350°F or Gas Mark 4) for 1 to 1½ hours or until the loaf shrinks away from the sides of the tin. Remove the foil wrapping and serve hot or cold.
SERVES 4 to 6

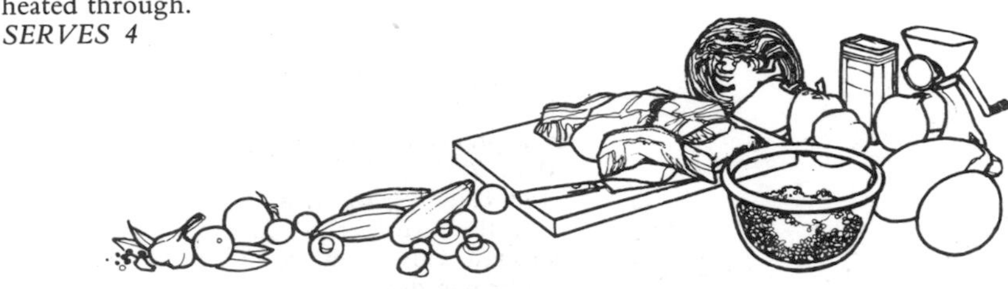

MEAT AND CHEESE LOAF

METRIC/IMPERIAL

4–6 streaky bacon rashers, rinds removed
100 g/4 oz dried breadcrumbs
120 ml/4 fl oz milk
1 × 15 ml spoon/1 tablespoon Worcestershire sauce
1 × 5 ml spoon/1 teaspoon dried mixed herbs
1 onion, peeled and chopped
2 celery stalks, chopped
450 g/1 lb lean minced beef
175 g/6 oz Edam or Gouda cheese, grated
salt
freshly ground black pepper
2 eggs, beaten

AMERICAN

4–6 fatty bacon slices
1 cup dried breadcrumbs
½ cup milk
1 tablespoon Worcestershire sauce
1 teaspoon dried mixed herbs
1 onion, peeled and chopped
2 celery stalks, chopped
2 cups lean ground beef
1½ cups grated Edam or Gouda cheese
salt
freshly ground black pepper
2 eggs, beaten

Line a 1 kg/2 lb loaf tin with foil.
Stretch the bacon with the back of a knife and use to line the bottom and sides of the prepared tin. Put the remaining ingredients in a bowl and stir well to mix. Press the mixture lightly into the prepared tin and cover with foil. Stand in a roasting tin half filled with water and bake in a preheated moderately hot oven (190°C/375°F or Gas Mark 5) for 1 to 1¼ hours or until set.
To freeze: cool quickly, chill in the refrigerator until firm, then turn out and wrap in foil. Seal, label and freeze.
To thaw and serve: remove wrappings, thaw at room temperature for 4 hours and serve cold, or reheat in the tin in a preheated moderate oven (160°C/325°F or Gas Mark 3) for 30 to 40 minutes and serve hot.
SERVES 4 to 6

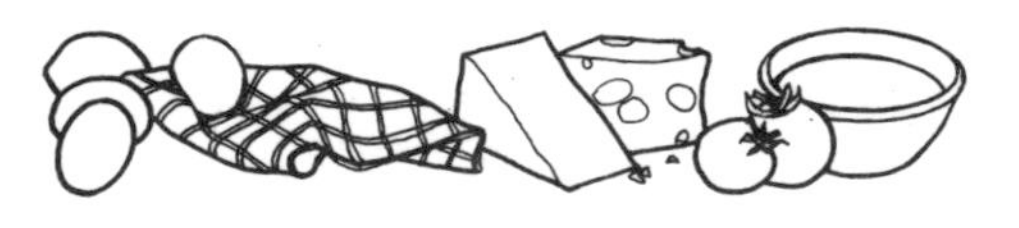

QUICK SAVOURY LOAF

METRIC/IMPERIAL

1 packet onion sauce mix
450 g/1 lb lean minced beef
100 g/4 oz streaky bacon, rinds removed and chopped
75 g/3 oz fresh brown breadcrumbs
1 × 15 ml spoon/1 tablespoon Worcestershire sauce
pinch of dried mixed herbs
salt
freshly ground black pepper
1 egg, beaten

AMERICAN

1 package onion sauce mix
2 cups lean ground beef
½ cup chopped fatty bacon
1½ cups fresh brown breadcrumbs
1 tablespoon Worcestershire sauce
pinch of dried mixed herbs
salt
freshly ground black pepper
1 egg, beaten

Put all the ingredients in a bowl and stir well to mix. Press the mixture lightly into a greased 675 g/1½ lb loaf tin. Cover with foil and bake in a preheated moderately hot oven (190°C/375°F or Gas Mark 5) for 1 to 1¼ hours or until set.
To freeze: cool quickly, chill in the refrigerator then wrap in foil. Seal, label and freeze.
To thaw and serve: remove wrappings, thaw at room temperature for 4 hours and serve cold, or reheat in the tin in a preheated moderate oven (160°C/325°F or Gas Mark 3) for 30 to 40 minutes and serve hot.
SERVES 4

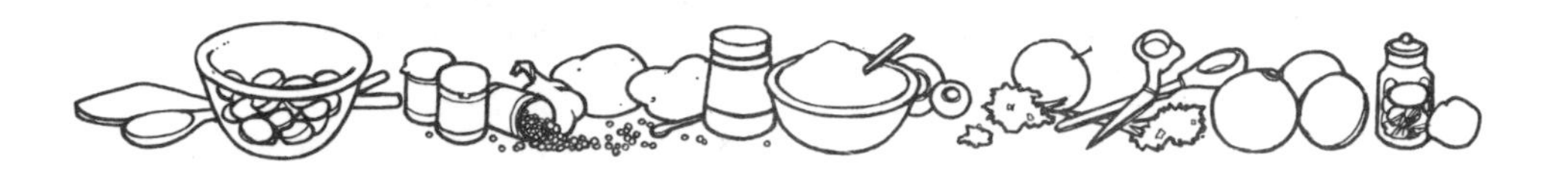

ROUNDY MEAT LOAF

METRIC/IMPERIAL

450 g/1 lb lean minced beef
175 g/6 oz fresh white breadcrumbs
2 large carrots, peeled and grated
1 small onion, peeled and finely chopped
½ green pepper, cored, seeded and finely chopped, or 6 stuffed olives, finely chopped
1 × 15 ml spoon/1 tablespoon Worcestershire sauce
1 × 15 ml spoon/1 tablespoon tomato purée
1 × 5 ml spoon/1 teaspoon prepared mustard
1 × 5 ml spoon/1 teaspoon dried mixed herbs
salt
freshly ground black pepper
1 egg, beaten

AMERICAN

2 cups lean ground beef
3 cups fresh white breadcrumbs
2 large carrots, peeled and grated
1 small onion, peeled and finely chopped
½ green pepper, cored, seeded and finely chopped, or 6 stuffed olives, finely chopped
1 tablespoon Worcestershire sauce
1 tablespoon tomato paste
1 teaspoon prepared mustard
1 teaspoon dried mixed herbs
salt
freshly ground black pepper
1 egg, beaten

Grease a 15 cm/6 inch cake tin and line the bottom with greaseproof paper or non-stick parchment.

Put all the ingredients in a bowl and stir well to mix. Press the mixture lightly into the prepared tin and cover with foil. Bake in a preheated moderate oven (180°C/350°F or Gas Mark 4) for 1¼ to 1½ hours or until set. Leave to cool in the tin, then put heavy weights on top of the loaf and chill in the refrigerator overnight.

To freeze: turn the loaf out and wrap in foil. Seal, label and freeze.

To thaw and serve: remove wrappings and thaw at room temperature for 4 hours. Serve cold.

SERVES 4 to 6

BEEF AND PORK LOAF

METRIC/IMPERIAL

1 kg/2 lb lean minced beef
225 g/½ lb lean minced pork
225 g/½ lb fresh white breadcrumbs
1 large onion, peeled and finely chopped
1 garlic clove, peeled and crushed
1 × 15 ml spoon/1 tablespoon Worcestershire sauce
2 × 15 ml spoons/2 tablespoons tomato ketchup
1 × 5 ml spoon/1 teaspoon dried mixed herbs
1 × 15 ml spoon/1 tablespoon freshly chopped parsley
salt
freshly ground black pepper
1 egg, beaten

AMERICAN

4 cups lean ground beef
1 cup lean ground pork
4 cups fresh white breadcrumbs
1 large onion, peeled and finely chopped
1 garlic clove, peeled and crushed
1 tablespoon Worcestershire sauce
2 tablespoons tomato ketchup
1 teaspoon dried mixed herbs
1 tablespoon freshly chopped parsley
salt
freshly ground black pepper
1 egg, beaten

Line two 675 g/1½ lb loaf tins with foil.

Put all the ingredients in a bowl and stir well to mix. Press the mixture lightly into the prepared tins and cover with foil.

To freeze: open (flash) freeze until firm, then remove the loaves from the tins in the foil linings. Overwrap in freezer bags, seal, label and return to the freezer.

To thaw and serve: remove wrappings and place the frozen loaves in greased tins. Cover with foil and bake in a preheated moderate oven (180°C/350°F or Gas Mark 4) for 2 hours or until the loaves shrink away from the sides of the tins. Serve hot with tomato sauce, or cold with a salad.

EACH LOAF SERVES 4 to 6

PAPRIKA GOULASH

METRIC/IMPERIAL

50 g/2 oz dripping or lard
1 kg/2 lb chuck steak, trimmed of fat and cut into cubes
2 large onions, peeled and finely sliced
1 small green pepper, cored, seeded and sliced
1 × 15 ml spoon/1 tablespoon flour
1 × 15 ml spoon/1 tablespoon paprika pepper
2 × 15 ml spoons/2 tablespoons tomato purée
salt
freshly ground black pepper
450 ml/¾ pint beef stock
To finish:
150 ml/¼ pint soured cream
freshly chopped parsley

AMERICAN

¼ cup drippings or lard
2 lb blade steak, trimmed of fat and cut into cubes
2 large onions, peeled and finely sliced
1 small green pepper, cored, seeded and sliced
1 tablespoon flour
1 tablespoon paprika pepper
2 tablespoons tomato paste
salt
freshly ground black pepper
2 cups beef stock
To finish:
⅔ cup sour cream
freshly chopped parsley

Melt the fat in a flameproof casserole dish, add the beef and fry briskly until browned on all sides. Remove from the dish. Add the onions and green pepper to the pan and fry gently until soft. Sprinkle in the flour and paprika and cook for 1 minute. Stir in the tomato purée (paste) and salt and pepper to taste, then gradually stir in the stock. Bring to the boil, stirring constantly. Return the beef to the dish, cover and cook in a preheated moderate oven (160°C/325°F or Gas Mark 3) for 2 to 2½ hours or until the meat is tender.

To freeze: cool quickly. Leave in the casserole or pour into a rigid container. Cover, then wrap the casserole in a freezer bag or foil. Seal, label and freeze.

To thaw and serve: remove wrappings and thaw at room temperature for 4 hours. Reheat in the covered casserole in a preheated moderate oven (180°C/350°F or Gas Mark 4) for about 1 hour or until heated through. Stir in the sour(ed) cream and sprinkle with parsley just before serving.

SERVES 4 to 6

BEEF VALENCIA

METRIC/IMPERIAL

675 g/1½ lb chuck steak, trimmed of fat and cut into cubes
25 g/1 oz cornflour
salt
freshly ground black pepper
2 × 15 ml spoons/2 tablespoons vegetable or corn oil
1 onion, peeled and chopped
1 garlic clove, peeled and crushed
2 oranges
150 ml/¼ pint cider
2 beef stock cubes
50 g/2 oz prunes, soaked overnight and stoned
few stoned olives

AMERICAN

1½ lb blade steak, trimmed of fat and cut into cubes
¼ cup cornstarch
salt
freshly ground black pepper
2 tablespoons vegetable or corn oil
1 onion, peeled and chopped
1 garlic clove, peeled and crushed
2 oranges
⅔ cup hard cider
4 beef bouillon cubes
⅓ cup prunes, soaked overnight and pitted
few pitted olives

Coat the beef in the cornflour (cornstarch) seasoned with salt and pepper. Heat the oil in a pan, add the beef, onion and garlic and fry for 5 minutes until browned. Meanwhile, peel one orange thinly, squeeze the juice from both the oranges, add to the cider and make up to 600 ml/1 pint/2½ cups with water.

Blanch the orange peel in boiling water for a few minutes, then cut into shreds. Add half to the meat and vegetables and reserve the remaining half for the garnish. Add the stock (bouillon) cubes and the cider mixture. Cover and cook gently for 1½ hours.

Stuff each prune with an olive, put in the pan and continue cooking for a further 30 minutes or until the meat is tender.

To freeze: cool quickly, then pour into a rigid container. Sprinkle the reserved orange shreds on top. Cover, then wrap in a freezer bag or foil. Seal, label and freeze.

To thaw and serve: thaw at room temperature for 4 hours, then remove the orange shreds. Reheat gently on top of the stove, stirring occasionally. Sprinkle with the orange shreds just before serving.

SERVES 4

BEEF FLAMENCO

METRIC/IMPERIAL

1 × 15 ml spoon/1 tablespoon vegetable oil
2 streaky bacon rashers, rinds removed and chopped
2 large onions, peeled and chopped
675 g/1½ lb chuck steak, trimmed of fat and cut into cubes
25 g/1 oz flour
1 × 400 g/14 oz can tomatoes
2 × 15 ml spoons/2 tablespoons Worcestershire sauce
600 ml/1 pint beef stock
salt
freshly ground black pepper
350 g/¾ lb potatoes, peeled and diced
8 stuffed olives

AMERICAN

1 tablespoon vegetable oil
2 fatty bacon slices, chopped
2 large onions, peeled and chopped
1½ lb blade steak, trimmed of fat and cut into cubes
¼ cup flour
1 × 14 oz can tomatoes
2 tablespoons Worcestershire sauce
2½ cups beef stock
salt
freshly ground black pepper
1⅓ cups peeled and diced potatoes
8 stuffed olives

Heat the oil in a flameproof casserole dish, add the bacon and onions and fry for 3 minutes. Add the beef and fry briskly until browned on all sides. Stir in the flour, then add the tomatoes, Worcestershire sauce, stock and salt and pepper to taste. Bring to the boil, stirring constantly.
Cover and cook in a preheated moderate oven (160°C/325°F or Gas Mark 3) for 2 hours. Add the potatoes and olives and cook for a further 30 minutes.
To freeze: cool quickly. Leave in the casserole or pour into a rigid container. Cover, then wrap the casserole in a freezer bag or foil. Seal, label and freeze.
To thaw and serve: reheat from frozen in the covered casserole in a preheated moderate oven (180°C/350°F or Gas Mark 4) for 1½ hours or until heated through.
SERVES 4

BEEF AND MUSHROOM PIE WITH POTATO TOPPING

METRIC/IMPERIAL

450 g/1 lb chuck steak, trimmed of fat and cut into thin strips
1 large onion, peeled and sliced
100 g/4 oz mushrooms, sliced
1 × 2.5 ml spoon/½ teaspoon mustard powder
pinch of dried mixed herbs
150 ml/¼ pint beef stock
salt
freshly ground black pepper
For the topping:
800 g/1¾ lb potatoes, peeled
100 g/4 oz Cheddar cheese, grated
pinch of mustard powder
a little milk, to mix

AMERICAN

1 lb blade steak, trimmed of fat and cut into thin strips
1 large onion, peeled and sliced
1 cup sliced mushrooms
½ teaspoon mustard powder
pinch of dried mixed herbs
⅔ cup beef stock
salt
freshly ground black pepper
For the topping:
1¾ lb potatoes, peeled
1 cup grated Cheddar cheese
pinch of mustard powder
a little milk, to mix

Put the beef in a casserole dish together with the onion, mushrooms, mustard and herbs. Pour over the stock and add salt and pepper to taste. Cover and cook in a preheated cool oven (150°C/300°F or Gas Mark 2) for 2 to 2½ hours or until the meat is tender.
Meanwhile, make the topping: cook the potatoes in boiling salted water for 20 minutes. Drain well, then mash together with the grated cheese and mustard. Add salt and pepper to taste and enough milk to give a smooth consistency.
Put the meat mixture into a pie dish or foil container, then spread the potato mixture over the top.
To freeze: cool quickly, cover with foil, then pack in a freezer bag. Seal, label and freeze.
To thaw and serve: remove wrappings and thaw at room temperature for 4 hours. Reheat in a preheated moderately hot oven (190°C/375°F or Gas Mark 5) for 45 minutes until golden brown and heated through.
SERVES 4

SAVOURY MEAT LOAF

METRIC/IMPERIAL

50 g/2 oz butter
3–4 celery stalks, finely chopped
1 small onion, peeled and finely chopped
2 × 15 ml spoons/2 tablespoons mustard powder
1 × 5 ml spoon/1 teaspoon caraway seeds
450 g/1 lb lean minced beef or pork
50 g/2 oz fresh breadcrumbs
salt
freshly ground black pepper
1 egg, beaten

AMERICAN

$\frac{1}{4}$ cup butter
3–4 celery stalks, finely chopped
1 small onion, peeled and finely chopped
2 tablespoons mustard powder
1 teaspoon caraway seeds
2 cups lean ground beef or pork
1 cup fresh breadcrumbs
salt
freshly ground black pepper
1 egg, beaten

Melt the butter in a pan, add the celery and onion and fry gently for about 10 minutes. Add the mustard and caraway seeds, then the beef or pork, breadcrumbs and salt and pepper to taste. Fry briskly for a few minutes, then remove from the heat and stir in the egg. Press the mixture lightly into a greased 450 g/1 lb loaf tin. Cover with foil and bake in a preheated moderate oven (180°C/350°F or Gas Mark 4) for 1 to $1\frac{1}{2}$ hours or until set.

To freeze: cool quickly, chill in the refrigerator. Turn out and wrap in foil. Seal, label and freeze.
To thaw and serve: remove wrappings and thaw at room temperature for 4 hours and serve cold. Alternatively, reheat in the tin in a preheated moderate oven (160°C/325°F or Gas Mark 3) for 30 to 40 minutes and serve hot.
SERVES 4

METRIC/IMPERIAL

350 g/$\frac{3}{4}$ lb cold cooked meat
1 medium onion, peeled
1 × 298 g/$10\frac{1}{2}$ oz can condensed oxtail soup
1 × 2.5 ml spoon/$\frac{1}{2}$ teaspoon dried mixed herbs
2 × 15 ml spoons/2 tablespoons fruit sauce
salt
freshly ground black pepper
450 g/1 lb potatoes, mashed
25 g/1 oz butter
75 g/3 oz Gouda cheese, grated

AMERICAN

$\frac{3}{4}$ lb cold cooked meat
1 medium onion, peeled
1 × $10\frac{1}{2}$ oz can condensed oxtail soup
$\frac{1}{2}$ teaspoon dried mixed herbs
2 tablespoons fruit sauce
salt
freshly ground black pepper
2 cups mashed potato
2 tablespoons butter
$\frac{3}{4}$ cup grated Gouda cheese

Mince (grind) the meat and onion together. Stir in the soup, herbs, sauce and salt and pepper to taste. Mix well, then turn into an ovenproof dish or foil container.
Mix the potato with the butter and cheese and spread over the meat. Rough up the potato with a fork.
To freeze: cover with foil, seal, label and freeze.
To thaw and serve: place the frozen pie, covered, on a baking sheet in a preheated moderately hot oven (200°C/400°F or Gas Mark 6) and reheat for 1 hour or until heated through. Remove the foil 15 minutes before the end of cooking to brown the potatoes.
SERVES 2 to 4

BEEF COBBLER

The scone (biscuit) topping can either be prepared and frozen unbaked, or prepared and baked and then frozen. If the scones (biscuits) are frozen unbaked the end result will look more attractive but they can only be stored for 2 to 3 weeks in the freezer. Baked scones (biscuits) can be stored for 2 months.

METRIC/IMPERIAL

450 g/1 lb chuck steak, trimmed of fat and cut into cubes
flour for coating
salt
freshly ground black pepper
3 × 15 ml spoons/3 tablespoons vegetable oil
1 large onion, peeled and chopped
1 large carrot, peeled and sliced
450 ml/$\frac{3}{4}$ pint beef stock
2 × 5 ml spoons/2 teaspoons prepared French or German mustard
1 × 2.5 ml spoon/$\frac{1}{2}$ teaspoon dried mixed herbs
For the topping:
225 g/$\frac{1}{2}$ lb flour
4 × 5 ml spoons/4 teaspoons baking powder
1 × 5 ml spoon/1 teaspoon salt
40 g/$1\frac{1}{2}$ oz butter
approx 150 ml/$\frac{1}{4}$ pint milk

AMERICAN

1 lb blade steak, trimmed of fat and cut into cubes
flour for coating
salt
freshly ground black pepper
3 tablespoons vegetable oil
1 large onion, peeled and chopped
1 large carrot, peeled and sliced
2 cups beef stock
2 teaspoons prepared French or German mustard
½ teaspoon dried mixed herbs
For the topping:
2 cups flour
4 teaspoons baking powder
1 teaspoon salt
3 tablespoons butter
approx ⅔ cup milk

Coat the beef in flour seasoned with salt and pepper. Heat the oil in a flameproof casserole dish, add the beef and fry briskly until browned on all sides. Add the onion and carrot and fry for 2 to 3 minutes, then slowly stir in the stock with the mustard and herbs. Cook in a preheated cool oven (150°C/300°F or Gas Mark 2) for 2 to 2½ hours or until the meat is tender.

To make the topping: sift the flour, baking powder and salt into a bowl, then rub in the butter. Add the milk gradually to give a soft, but not sticky, dough. Knead lightly until smooth. Roll out on a floured surface to 1 cm/½ inch thickness, then cut out rounds with a 5 cm/2 inch cutter. If freezing scones (biscuits) baked, place on a preheated baking sheet in the shape of the casserole dish, brush with milk and bake in a preheated hot oven (220°C/425°F or Gas Mark 7) for 10 to 15 minutes until well risen and golden.

To freeze: cool the beef quickly, cover the casserole with foil, then pack in a freezer bag. Seal, label and freeze. Cool baked scones (biscuits) quickly, pack in a rigid container, seal, label and freeze. Pack unbaked scones as for baked.

To thaw and serve: remove wrappings and thaw the beef and scones (biscuits) at room temperature for 4 hours. Reheat the beef in the covered casserole in a preheated moderate oven (180°C/350°F or Gas Mark 4) for 15 minutes. If baked scones (biscuits) have been made, arrange on top of the beef and bake for a further 10 minutes. If unbaked scones (biscuits) are used, arrange on top of the beef and brush with milk. Increase the heat to moderately hot (190°C/375°F or Gas Mark 5) and bake for about 15 minutes.

SERVES 4

SAVOURY BEEF ROLL

METRIC/IMPERIAL

For the suet pastry:
225 g/½ lb self-raising flour
1 × 5 ml spoon/1 teaspoon salt
100 g/4 oz shredded suet
approx 150 ml/¼ pint water
For the filling:
350 g/¾ lb lean minced beef
1 onion, peeled and finely chopped
50 g/2 oz mushrooms, sliced
pinch of dried mixed herbs
2 × 5 ml spoons/2 teaspoons prepared English mustard
1 × 15 ml spoon/1 tablespoon water
salt
freshly ground black pepper

AMERICAN

For the suet pastry:
2 cups self-rising flour
1 teaspoon salt
¾ cup shredded suet
approx ⅔ cup water
For the filling:
1½ cups lean ground beef
1 onion, peeled and finely chopped
½ cup sliced mushrooms
pinch of dried mixed herbs
2 teaspoons prepared English mustard
1 tablespoon water
salt
freshly ground black pepper

To make the pastry: sift the flour and salt into a bowl, then stir in the suet. Add the water gradually to give a soft, but not sticky, dough. Knead lightly until smooth. Roll out on a lightly floured sheet of foil to a rectangle approx 25 × 20 cm/10 × 8 inches.

To make the filling: combine all the filling ingredients together in a bowl and stir well to mix. Spread over the dough, leaving 1 cm/½ inch clear around the edges, then roll up from the long side like a Swiss (jelly) roll.

To freeze: wrap in the foil then overwrap in a freezer bag. Seal, label and freeze.

To thaw and serve: thaw at room temperature for 4 hours, then wrap in greased foil and steam for 2¾ hours. Serve with gravy or tomato sauce.

SERVES 4

OXTAIL RAGOÛT

METRIC/IMPERIAL

50 g/2 oz butter
1 oxtail, cut into serving pieces
4 streaky bacon rashers, rinds removed and diced
1 onion, peeled and sliced
1 garlic clove, peeled and crushed
25 g/1 oz flour
300 ml/½ pint beef stock
2 × 15 ml spoons/2 tablespoons red wine
salt
freshly ground black pepper
2 large carrots, peeled and sliced
4 celery stalks, chopped
1 × 2.5 ml spoon/½ teaspoon dried marjoram

AMERICAN

¼ cup butter
1 oxtail, cut into serving pieces
4 fatty bacon slices, diced
1 onion, peeled and sliced
1 garlic clove, peeled and crushed
¼ cup flour
1¼ cups beef stock
2 tablespoons red wine
salt
freshly ground black pepper
2 large carrots, peeled and sliced
4 celery stalks, chopped
½ teaspoon dried marjoram

Melt the butter in a pan, add the oxtail and fry until golden brown. Transfer to a casserole dish. Add the bacon, onion and garlic to the pan and cook for 2 minutes. Stir in the flour, then the stock and wine. Add salt and pepper to taste and bring to the boil. Pour over the oxtail, add the carrots, celery and marjoram and cook in a preheated moderate oven (180°C/350°F or Gas Mark 4) for 2 to 3 hours or until the oxtail is very tender.
To freeze: cool quickly. Leave in the casserole or transfer to a rigid container. Cover, then wrap the casserole in a freezer bag or foil. Seal, label and freeze.
To thaw and serve: remove wrappings and thaw in the refrigerator overnight. Reheat in the covered casserole in a preheated moderate oven (160°C/325°F or Gas Mark 3) for 1 hour or until heated through.
SERVES 4

OXTAIL AND TOMATO STEW

METRIC/IMPERIAL

50 g/2 oz dripping or lard
1 oxtail, cut into serving pieces
50 g/2 oz flour
salt
freshly ground black pepper
2 onions, peeled and sliced
2 carrots, peeled and sliced
2 celery stalks, chopped
450 ml/¾ pint beef stock
1 × 400 g/14 oz can tomatoes
1 × 5 ml spoon/1 teaspoon dried mixed herbs
1 bay leaf
juice of ½ lemon

AMERICAN

¼ cup drippings or lard
1 oxtail, cut into serving pieces
½ cup flour
salt
freshly ground black pepper
2 onions, peeled and sliced
2 carrots, peeled and sliced
2 celery stalks, chopped
2 cups beef stock
1 × 14 oz can tomatoes
1 teaspoon dried mixed herbs
1 bay leaf
juice of ½ lemon

Heat the fat in a flameproof casserole dish. Toss the oxtail in the flour seasoned with salt and pepper. Add the oxtail and fry until golden brown. Remove from the casserole. Add the onions, carrots and celery and cook for 2 minutes. Sprinkle in any leftover flour and cook until pale brown, stirring constantly. Stir in the remaining ingredients and bring to the boil. Add salt and pepper to taste and return the oxtail to the casserole. Cover and cook in a preheated moderately hot oven (190°C/375°F or Gas Mark 5) for 30 minutes, then reduce the heat to cool (150°C/300°F or Gas Mark 2) and cook for a further 2 hours or until the oxtail is very tender. Remove the bay leaf.
To freeze: cool quickly and leave in the casserole or pour into a rigid container. Cover, then wrap the casserole in a freezer bag or foil. Seal, label and freeze.
To thaw and serve: remove wrappings and thaw in the refrigerator overnight. Reheat in a covered casserole in a preheated moderate oven (180°C/350°F or Gas Mark 4) for 1 hour or until heated through.
SERVES 4

PORK MEATBALLS HONGROISE

METRIC/IMPERIAL

For the meatballs:

25 g/1 oz butter
1 large onion, peeled and finely chopped
100 g/4 oz fresh white breadcrumbs
450 g/1 lb lean minced pork belly
1 × 15 ml spoon/1 tablespoon freshly chopped parsley
salt
freshly ground black pepper
3 × 15 ml spoons/3 tablespoons water
1 egg, beaten
flour, for coating
25 g/1 oz butter
1 × 15 ml spoon/1 tablespoon vegetable oil

For the sauce:

1 onion, peeled and chopped
1 × 400 g/14 oz can tomatoes
1 × 15 ml spoon/1 tablespoon paprika

AMERICAN

For the meatballs:

2 tablespoons butter
1 large onion, peeled and finely chopped
2 cups fresh white breadcrumbs
2 cups lean ground pork belly
1 tablespoon freshly chopped parsley
salt
freshly ground black pepper
3 tablespoons water
1 egg, beaten
flour, for coating
2 tablespoons butter
1 tablespoon vegetable oil

For the sauce:

1 onion, peeled and chopped
1 × 14 oz can tomatoes
1 tablespoon paprika

Melt the butter in a pan, add the onion and fry gently until soft. Combine with the remaining ingredients, except the flour, remaining butter, and oil. Divide the mixture into 12 portions and shape into balls with lightly floured hands.

Heat the butter and oil in a pan, add the meatballs and fry until brown. Drain on paper towels. Add the onion to the pan and cook until soft. Stir in the paprika, tomatoes, and salt and pepper to taste. Bring to the boil, then return the meatballs to the pan, reduce the heat, cover and simmer for 40 minutes. Remove the meatballs from the pan. Purée the sauce in a blender or Mouli-légumes or rub through a sieve (strainer).

To freeze: cool quickly. Turn the meatballs into a rigid container and pour over the sauce. Seal, label and freeze.

To thaw and serve: reheat gently from frozen on top of the stove.

SERVES 2 to 4

PORKBURGERS WITH BARBECUE SAUCE

METRIC/IMPERIAL

For the porkburgers:

450 g/1 lb lean minced pork
1 onion, peeled and finely chopped
1 × 5 ml spoon/1 teaspoon freshly chopped parsley
1 × 5 ml spoon/1 teaspoon Worcestershire sauce
salt
freshly ground black pepper
vegetable oil for frying, to finish

For the sauce:

4 × 15 ml spoons/4 tablespoons wine vinegar
½ onion, peeled and finely chopped
300 ml/½ pint water
4 × 15 ml spoons/4 tablespoons tomato ketchup
2 × 5 ml spoons/2 teaspoons Worcestershire sauce
finely grated rind of 1 lemon
50 g/2 oz butter

AMERICAN

For the porkburgers:

2 cups lean ground pork
1 onion, peeled and finely chopped
1 teaspoon freshly chopped parsley
1 teaspoon Worcestershire sauce
salt
freshly ground black pepper
vegetable oil for frying, to finish

For the sauce:

¼ cup wine vinegar
½ cup onion, peeled and finely chopped
1¼ cups water
¼ cup tomato ketchup
2 teaspoons Worcestershire sauce
finely grated rind of 1 lemon
¼ cup butter

To make the porkburgers: put all the ingredients in a bowl and stir well to mix. Divide the mixture into 8 portions and shape into rounds.

To make the sauce: put all the ingredients in a pan, bring to the boil and simmer for 15 minutes.

To freeze: open (flash) freeze the porkburgers, then pack in freezer bags. Seal, label and return to the freezer. Cool the sauce quickly and pour into a rigid container. Seal, label and freeze.

To thaw and serve: fry the frozen porkburgers in hot oil for 6 to 8 minutes on each side. Reheat the sauce from frozen on top of the stove, stirring occasionally. Pour over the porkburgers.

MAKES 8

PORK AND APPLE HOT POT

METRIC/IMPERIAL

25 g/1 oz dripping or lard
4 thick slices of belly pork
1 garlic clove, peeled and crushed
2 medium onions, peeled and chopped
2 medium cooking apples, peeled, cored and chopped
salt
freshly ground black pepper
150 ml/¼ pint cider
1 kg/2 lb potatoes, peeled and finely sliced
15 g/½ oz butter

AMERICAN

2 tablespoons drippings or lard
4 thick slices of salt pork
1 garlic clove, peeled and crushed
2 medium onions, peeled and chopped
2 medium baking apples, peeled, cored and chopped
salt
freshly ground black pepper
⅔ cup hard cider
2 lb potatoes, peeled and finely sliced
1 tablespoon butter

Melt the fat in a pan, add the pork and fry until browned on all sides. Arrange in a shallow foil container. Mix together the garlic, onions and apples with salt and pepper to taste and spoon over the pork. Pour in the cider, then cover with overlapping potato slices. Dot with the butter, cover with foil and cook in a preheated moderate oven (160°C/325°F or Gas Mark 3) for 1½ hours. Remove the foil and cook for a further 30 minutes to brown the potatoes.

To freeze: cool quickly, cover with foil then wrap in a freezer bag. Seal, label and freeze.

To thaw and serve: remove the bag and thaw at room temperature for 4 hours. Reheat in the covered container in a preheated moderate oven (180°C/350°F or Gas Mark 4) for 1 hour or until heated through.

SERVES 4

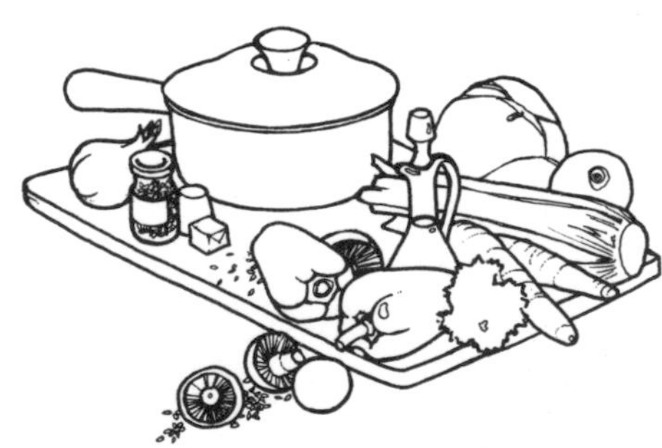

PORK AND LEMON PASTIES

METRIC/IMPERIAL

25 g/1 oz lard
1 onion, peeled and sliced
225 g/½ lb lean pork, finely diced
25 g/1 oz flour
1 × 15 ml spoon/1 tablespoon milk
finely grated rind and juice of ½ lemon
1 × 15 ml spoon/1 tablespoon sultanas
salt
freshly ground black pepper
basic shortcrust pastry dough made with 225 g/½ lb flour
beaten egg or milk, to glaze

AMERICAN

2 tablespoons lard
1 onion, peeled and sliced
½ lb lean pork, finely diced
¼ cup flour
1 tablespoon milk
finely grated rind and juice of ½ lemon
1 tablespoon seedless white raisins
salt
freshly ground black pepper
basic pie dough made with 2 cups flour
beaten egg or milk, to glaze

Melt the lard in a pan, add the onion and pork and fry until the pork is browned on all sides. Add the flour and stir well. Add the milk, lemon rind and juice, sultanas (seedless white raisins) and stir until the mixture thickens. Add salt and pepper to taste.

Roll out the dough on a floured surface, divide into 4 equal portions and roll each into a 15 cm/6 inch round. Divide the pork mixture between the rounds of dough, mounding it in the centre. Moisten the edges with water, fold in half and press and pinch the edges firmly together with the join on the top.

To freeze: open (flash) freeze until firm, then wrap in foil. Seal, label and return to freezer.

To thaw and serve: remove wrappings and place on a baking sheet. Brush the dough with egg or milk and bake from frozen in a preheated moderately hot oven (200°C/400°F or Gas Mark 6) for 35 to 40 minutes or until heated through. Cover with foil if the pastry becomes too brown.

MAKES 4

PORK AND LIVER PIE

METRIC/IMPERIAL

For the filling:

350 g/¾ lb pig's liver
a little milk
450 g/1 lb boned sparerib pork
25 g/1 oz lard
2 onions, peeled and chopped
2 × 15 ml spoons/2 tablespoons flour
150 ml/¼ pint beef stock
2 × 15 ml spoons/2 tablespoons Worcestershire sauce
salt
freshly ground black pepper

For the pastry:

275 g/10 oz flour
1 × 2.5 ml spoon/½ teaspoon salt
65 g/2½ oz butter
65 g/2½ oz lard
approx 4 × 15 ml spoons/4 tablespoons water
beaten egg or milk, to glaze

AMERICAN

For the filling:

¾ lb pork liver
a little milk
1 lb pork butterfly chop
2 tablespoons lard
2 onions, peeled and chopped
2 tablespoons flour
⅔ cup beef stock
2 tablespoons Worcestershire sauce
salt
freshly ground black pepper

For the pastry:

2½ cups flour
½ teaspoon salt
¼ cup plus 1 tablespoon butter
¼ cup plus 1 tablespoon shortening
approx ¼ cup water
beaten egg or milk, to glaze

Put the liver in a bowl and cover with milk. Leave for 30 minutes, then drain. Mince (grind) the liver with the pork.

Melt the lard in a pan, add the onion and fry until soft. Add the minced (ground) meats and cook until browned, stirring constantly to break up the meat. Stir in the remaining ingredients, cover and cook gently for 30 minutes. Leave to cool.

To make the pastry: Sift the flour and salt together into a bowl. Rub in the fats until the mixture resembles fine breadcrumbs. Add enough water to mix to a firm dough. Turn onto a floured surface and divide in half. Roll out one half and use to line a 20–23 cm/8–9 inch pie plate. Spoon the filling onto the dough. Roll out the remaining dough to form a lid. Moisten the edge of the dough on the plate with water, cover with the lid and press firmly together to seal. Trim and flute the edge. Use any trimmings to decorate the top of the pie. Cut an air vent in the centre.

To freeze: open (flash) freeze until firm, then wrap in foil. Seal, label and return to the freezer.

To thaw and serve: remove wrappings and brush the top of the pie with beaten egg or milk. Bake from frozen in a preheated moderately hot oven (200°C/400°F or Gas Mark 6) for 15 minutes. Reduce the heat to moderate (180°C/350°F or Gas Mark 4) and bake for a further 40 minutes or until heated through. Cover with foil if the pastry becomes too brown.

SERVES 6

PORK STROGANOFF

METRIC/IMPERIAL

50 g/2 oz butter
1 small onion, peeled and finely chopped
1 garlic clove, peeled and crushed
3 bacon rashers, rinds removed and chopped
0.5 × 2.5 ml spoon/¼ teaspoon caraway seeds
0.5 × 2.5 ml spoon/¼ teaspoon dried marjoram
freshly ground black pepper
225 g/½ lb button mushrooms, sliced
450 g/1 lb pork fillet, cut into very thin strips
150 ml/¼ pint soured cream, to finish

AMERICAN

¼ cup butter
1 small onion, peeled and finely chopped
1 garlic clove, peeled and crushed
3 bacon slices, chopped
¼ teaspoon caraway seeds
¼ teaspoon dried marjoram
freshly ground black pepper
2 cups sliced button mushrooms
1 lb pork tenderloin, cut into very thin strips
⅔ cup sour cream, to finish

Melt the butter in a pan, add the onion, garlic and bacon and fry gently for 5 minutes. Add the caraway seeds, marjoram and pepper to taste, cover and cook for a further 5 minutes.

Stir in the mushrooms, cover and cook for a further 5 minutes, then stir in the pork and cook, uncovered, for 20 minutes or until tender.

To freeze: cool quickly, then turn into a rigid container. Seal, label and freeze.

To thaw and serve: thaw at room temperature for 4 hours, then reheat gently on top of the stove, stirring occasionally. Add the sour(ed) cream and stir briskly. Do not allow to boil.

SERVES 4

HERBY SAUSAGE ROLL

METRIC/IMPERIAL

For the filling:

1 cooking apple, peeled, cored and chopped
225 g/½ lb sausagemeat
1 small onion, peeled and chopped
1 × 5 ml spoon/1 teaspoon chopped fresh mixed herbs
salt
freshly ground black pepper

For the pastry:

225 g/½ lb flour
1 × 2.5 ml spoon/½ teaspoon salt
2 × 5 ml spoons/2 teaspoons baking powder
100 g/4 oz shredded suet
beaten egg, to glaze

AMERICAN

For the filling:

1 baking apple, peeled, cored and chopped
1 cup sausagemeat
1 small onion, peeled and chopped
1 teaspoon chopped fresh mixed herbs
salt
freshly ground black pepper

For the pastry:

2 cups flour
½ teaspoon salt
2 teaspoons baking powder
¾ cup shredded suet
beaten egg, to glaze

To make the filling: put all the ingredients in a bowl and stir well to mix.

To make the pastry: sift the flour, salt and baking powder into a bowl. Mix in the suet lightly, then stir in sufficient cold water to make a soft dough. Roll out the dough on a floured surface into an oblong approx 23 × 18 cm/9 × 7 inches. Spread the sausage mixture over the dough, leaving a 2.5 cm/1 inch border all round. Moisten the border with water, then roll up the dough like a Swiss (jelly) roll. Seal the ends and the join.

Put the roll on a baking sheet with the join underneath and make 3 or 4 slits in the top of the dough to allow the steam to escape. Bake in a preheated moderately hot oven (200°C/400°F or Gas Mark 6) for 30 minutes.

To freeze: cool quickly. Open (flash) freeze until firm, then wrap in foil or a freezer bag. Seal, label and return to the freezer.

To thaw and serve: remove wrappings, then thaw at room temperature for 4 hours. Place on a baking sheet, brush the dough with beaten egg and bake in a preheated moderately hot oven (190°C/375°F or Gas Mark 5) for 20 minutes or until golden brown and heated through.

SERVES 4

SAUSAGE AND TOMATO PIE

METRIC/IMPERIAL

For the pastry:

225 g/½ lb flour
pinch of salt
100 g/4 oz butter
approx 2 × 15 ml spoons/2 tablespoons water
milk, to glaze

For the filling:

350 g/¾ lb sausagemeat
pinch of dried mixed herbs
salt
freshly ground black pepper
1 egg, beaten
3 large tomatoes, peeled and sliced

AMERICAN

For the pastry:

2 cups flour
pinch of salt
½ cup butter
approx 2 tablespoons water
milk, to glaze

For the filling:

1½ cups sausagemeat
pinch of dried mixed herbs
salt
freshly ground black pepper
1 egg, beaten
3 large tomatoes, peeled and sliced

To make the pastry: sift the flour and salt into a bowl. Add the butter in pieces and rub into the flour with the fingertips until the mixture resembles fine breadcrumbs. Stir in enough water to form a firm dough.

Divide the dough in two. Roll out one half on a floured surface and use to line a 20 cm/8 inch deep ovenproof or foil pie plate.

To make the filling: put the sausagemeat, herbs, salt and pepper to taste and the egg into a bowl. Stir well to mix. Put half the tomatoes in the bottom of the dough-lined plate. Cover with the sausage mixture, then top with the remaining tomatoes.

Roll out the remaining dough to form a lid. Moisten the edges of the dough, place the lid on top of the filling and press firmly to seal together. Trim and flute the edge and use any trimmings to decorate the top of the pie. Cut an air vent in the centre.

To freeze: open (flash) freeze until firm, then wrap in foil or a freezer bag. Seal, label and return to the freezer.

To thaw and serve: remove wrappings, then thaw at room temperature for 4 hours. Brush the dough with milk and bake in a preheated moderately hot oven (190°C/375°F or Gas

Mark 5) for 40 to 45 minutes or until golden brown and heated through. Cover with foil if the pastry becomes too brown.
SERVES 6 to 8

PORK FILLET IN SHERRY

METRIC/IMPERIAL
25 g/1 oz butter
675 g/1½ lb pork fillet, cut into cubes
1 garlic clove, peeled and crushed
100 g/4 oz mushrooms, sliced
2× 5 ml spoons/2 teaspoons paprika pepper
2× 5 ml spoons/2 teaspoons flour
150 ml/¼ pint sherry
120 ml/4 fl oz stock
salt
freshly ground black pepper
150 ml/¼ pint single cream, to finish

AMERICAN
2 tablespoons butter
1½ lb pork tenderloin, cut into cubes
1 garlic clove, peeled and crushed
1 cup sliced mushrooms
2 teaspoons paprika pepper
2 teaspoons flour
⅔ cup sherry
½ cup stock
salt
freshly ground black pepper
⅔ cup light cream, to finish

Melt the butter in a pan, add the pork and fry gently until lightly browned on all sides. Place in a casserole dish, then add the garlic and mushrooms.
Stir the paprika and flour into the juices in the pan and cook for 2 minutes, stirring constantly. Stir in the sherry, stock and salt and pepper to taste, then bring to the boil. Pour over the pork in the casserole. Cook in a preheated moderate oven (180°C/350°F or Gas Mark 4) for 1 hour or until the pork is tender.
To freeze: cool quickly. Leave in the casserole or pour into a rigid container. Cover, then wrap the casserole in a freezer bag or foil. Seal, label and freeze.
To thaw and serve: removing wrappings and thaw at room temperature for 4 hours. Reheat in the covered casserole in a preheated moderate oven (180°C/350°F or Gas Mark 4) for 30 minutes or until heated through. Pour the cream over the meat just before serving.
SERVES 4

SAUSAGE KEBABS

METRIC/IMPERIAL
For the meatballs:
450 g/1 lb pork sausagemeat
4× 15 ml spoons/4 tablespoons sage and onion stuffing mix
salt
freshly ground black pepper
For the barbecue sauce:
1× 400 g/14 oz can tomatoes
1× 15 ml spoon/1 tablespoon tomato purée
1× 15 ml spoon/1 tablespoon Worcestershire sauce
2× 5 ml spoons/2 teaspoons prepared French mustard
To finish:
8 button mushrooms
1 large red pepper, cored, seeded and cut into chunks
4× 15 ml spoons/4 tablespoons vegetable oil
2× 15 ml spoons/2 tablespoons beer

AMERICAN
For the meatballs:
2 cups pork sausagemeat
¼ cup sage and onion stuffing mix
salt
freshly ground black pepper
For the barbecue sauce:
1× 14 oz can tomatoes
1 tablespoon tomato paste
1 tablespoon Worcestershire sauce
2 teaspoons prepared French mustard
To finish:
8 button mushrooms
1 large red pepper, cored, seeded and cut into chunks
¼ cup vegetable oil
2 tablespoons beer

To make the meatballs: put the sausagemeat, stuffing mix and salt and pepper to taste in a bowl and stir well to mix. Shape the mixture into small balls with lightly floured hands.
To make the sauce: put all the ingredients in a pan and simmer for 5 minutes. Leave to cool, then purée in an electric blender or Mouli-légumes or work through a sieve (strainer).
To freeze: open (flash) freeze the meatballs until firm, then pack in a rigid container. Seal, label and return to freezer. Pour the sauce into a rigid container, seal, label and freeze.
To thaw and serve: thaw the meatballs and sauce in the refrigerator overnight. Thread the meatballs on to 4 skewers with the mushrooms and red pepper. Mix the oil and beer together and brush over the kebabs. Grill (broil) the kebabs until golden brown, basting and turning occasionally. Meanwhile, reheat the sauce on top of stove. Serve with the kebabs.
MAKES 4

FRANKFURTERS WITH RED CABBAGE

METRIC/IMPERIAL

50 g/2 oz butter or lard
1 large onion, peeled and sliced
1 kg/2 lb red cabbage, thinly sliced
2 large cooking apples, peeled, cored and sliced
4 × 15 ml spoons/4 tablespoons wine vinegar
4 × 15 ml spoons/4 tablespoons water
1 × 15 ml spoon/1 tablespoon sugar
salt
freshly ground black pepper
8 frankfurters

AMERICAN

¼ cup butter or lard
1 large onion, peeled and sliced
2 lb red cabbage, thinly sliced
2 large baking apples, peeled, cored and sliced
¼ cup wine vinegar
¼ cup water
1 tablespoon sugar
salt
freshly ground black pepper
8 frankfurters

Melt the butter or lard in a pan, add the onion and fry gently for 5 minutes until soft. Stir in the cabbage and apples and simmer for 10 minutes. Add the remaining ingredients, except the frankfurters, then bring to the boil. Cover and simmer for 30 minutes until all the liquid has been absorbed and the cabbage is tender. Slice each frankfurter into three and stir into the cabbage mixture.
To freeze: cool quickly, then transfer to a rigid container. Seal, label and freeze.
To thaw and serve: thaw at room temperature for 4 hours, then reheat in the covered casserole in a preheated moderate oven (180°C/350°F or Gas Mark 4) for 45 minutes until heated through.
SERVES 4

BARBECUED PORK CHOPS

METRIC/IMPERIAL

2 × 15 ml spoons/2 tablespoons vegetable oil
4 pork chops, trimmed of fat
1 medium onion, peeled and chopped
1 × 15 ml spoon/1 tablespoon tomato purée
3 × 15 ml spoons/3 tablespoons vinegar
2 × 15 ml spoons/2 tablespoons brown sugar
1 × 5 ml spoon/1 teaspoon prepared English mustard
2 × 5 ml spoons/2 teaspoons Worcestershire sauce
150 ml/¼ pint chicken stock

AMERICAN

2 tablespoons vegetable oil
4 pork chops, trimmed of fat
1 medium onion, peeled and chopped
1 tablespoon tomato paste
3 tablespoons vinegar
2 tablespoons brown sugar
1 teaspoon prepared English mustard
2 teaspoons Worcestershire sauce
⅔ cup chicken stock

Heat the oil in a flameproof casserole dish, add the chops and fry briskly until browned on both sides. Remove from the casserole with a slotted spoon, then add the onion and fry gently until soft. Return the chops to the casserole. Mix together the remaining ingredients and pour over the chops.
Cover and cook in a preheated moderate oven (180°C/350°F or Gas Mark 4) for 1 hour or until the chops are tender. *To freeze:* cool quickly. Leave in the casserole or transfer to a rigid container. Cover, then wrap the casserole in a freezer bag or foil. Seal, label and freeze.
To thaw and serve: thaw at room temperature for 4 hours, then reheat in the covered casserole in a preheated moderate oven (180°C/350°F or Gas Mark 4) for about 1 hour or until heated through.
SERVES 4

PORTUGUESE MARINATED PORK

METRIC/IMPERIAL

1 kg/2 lb boneless stewing pork, cut into cubes
150 ml/¼ pint dry white wine
4 × 15 ml spoons/4 tablespoons wine vinegar
3 garlic cloves, peeled and crushed
salt
freshly ground black pepper
1 × 2.5 ml spoon/½ teaspoon dried savory
1 × 2.5 ml spoon/½ teaspoon dried marjoram
4 cloves, crushed
2 × 5 ml spoons/2 teaspoons olive oil

AMERICAN

2 lb boneless stewing pork, cut into cubes
⅔ cup dry white wine
¼ cup wine vinegar
3 garlic cloves, peeled and crushed
salt
freshly ground black pepper
½ teaspoon dried savory
½ teaspoon dried marjoram
4 cloves, crushed
2 teaspoons olive oil

Put the pork in a bowl, add the remaining ingredients, except the oil, and stir well to mix. Cover and marinate in the refrigerator overnight, stirring the mixture once or twice.
Strain the pork and reserve the marinade. Heat the oil in a pan, add the meat and fry briskly until browned on all sides. Strain the marinade, stir into the pan and bring to the boil. Cover and simmer for 1 hour or until the meat is tender.
To freeze: cool quickly, then pour into a rigid container. Seal, label and freeze.
To thaw and serve: thaw at room temperature for 4 hours, then reheat gently on top of the stove, stirring occasionally.
SERVES 4 to 6

PORK CHOP PARCELS

METRIC/IMPERIAL
4 pork chops, trimmed of fat
1 × 15 ml spoon/1 tablespoon flour
salt
freshly ground black pepper
50 g/2 oz butter
2 onions, peeled and cut into rings
1 garlic clove, peeled and crushed
350 g/¾ lb tomatoes, peeled and chopped
1 × 5 ml spoon/1 teaspoon dried thyme
2 × 5 ml spoons/2 teaspoons Worcestershire sauce
2 × 5 ml spoons/2 teaspoons freshly chopped parsley

AMERICAN
4 pork chops, trimmed of fat
1 tablespoon flour
salt
freshly ground black pepper
¼ cup butter
2 onions, peeled and cut into rings
1 garlic clove, peeled and crushed
1½ cups peeled and chopped tomatoes
1 teaspoon dried thyme
2 teaspoons Worcestershire sauce
2 teaspoons freshly chopped parsley

Coat the chops in the flour seasoned with salt and pepper. Melt the butter in a pan, add the chops and fry briskly until browned on both sides. Remove from the pan and place each chop on a large square of foil.
Add the onions and garlic to the pan and fry for 2 minutes. Stir in the tomatoes, thyme and Worcestershire sauce, add salt and pepper to taste and cook gently for 5 minutes. Remove from the heat and stir in the parsley. Divide the mixture into four and spread over the chops. Leave to cool, then fold the foil loosely around the chops and seal the edges securely.

To freeze: overwrap the foil parcels in a freezer bag, seal, label and freeze.
To thaw and serve: thaw at room temperature for 4 hours, then cook in foil wrappings, in a preheated moderately hot oven (190°C/375°F or Gas Mark 5) for 45 minutes or until they are tender and heated through.
SERVES 4

PORK AND PEPPER CASSEROLE

METRIC/IMPERIAL
450 g/1 lb pork fillets, sliced
50 g/2 oz flour
salt
freshly ground black pepper
50 g/2 oz butter
2 onions, peeled and sliced
2 large green peppers, cored, seeded and sliced
225 g/½ lb tomatoes, peeled and chopped
150 ml/¼ pint tomato juice

AMERICAN
1 lb pork tenderloin, sliced
½ cup flour
salt
freshly ground black pepper
¼ cup butter
2 onions, peeled and sliced
2 large green peppers, cored, seeded and sliced
1 cup peeled and chopped tomatoes
⅔ cup tomato juice

Coat the pork slices in the flour seasoned with salt and pepper. Melt half the butter in a pan, add the pork and fry briskly until browned on all sides. Transfer to a casserole dish.
Melt the remaining butter in the pan, add the onion and peppers and fry gently until soft. Spoon over the pork together with the tomatoes. Season with salt and pepper to taste, then pour over the tomato juice. Cover and bake in a preheated moderate oven (180°C/350°F or Gas Mark 4) for 1 hour or until the pork is tender.
To freeze: cool quickly. Leave in the casserole or pour into a rigid container. Cover, then wrap the casserole in a freezer bag or foil. Seal, label and freeze.
To thaw and serve: remove wrappings and thaw at room temperature for 4 hours. Reheat gently on top of the stove, stirring occasionally, or in a preheated moderate oven (180°C/350°F or Gas Mark 4) for 1 hour or until heated through.
SERVES 3 to 4

SAUSAGE PLAIT

METRIC/IMPERIAL

1 × 215 g/7½ oz packet frozen puff pastry, thawed
225 g/½ lb pork chipolata sausages, sliced
1 onion, peeled and chopped
175 g/6 oz Gouda cheese, grated
100 g/4 oz mushrooms, sliced
3 × 15 ml spoons/3 tablespoons tomato chutney
1 × 15 ml spoon/1 tablespoon Worcestershire sauce
pinch of dried mixed herbs
salt
freshly ground black pepper
1 egg, beaten

AMERICAN

1 × 7½ oz package frozen puff paste, thawed
½ lb pork link sausages, sliced
1 onion, peeled and chopped
1½ cups grated Gouda cheese
1 cup sliced mushrooms
3 tablespoons tomato chutney
1 tablespoon Worcestershire sauce
pinch of dried mixed herbs
salt
freshly ground black pepper
1 egg, beaten

Roll out the dough on a floured surface to a rectangle 35 × 30 cm/14 × 12 inches. Mix the remaining ingredients together, reserving a little of the egg for glazing, then arrange down the centre third of the dough, leaving a margin at the top and bottom.

Using a sharp knife, cut diagonal slits 1 cm/½ inch wide down each side of the rectangle. Brush the edges with water. Fold in the dough, top and bottom, and plait the strips over the filling. Lift onto a baking sheet, and brush the plait with the reserved beaten egg. Bake in a preheated hot oven (220°C/425°F or Gas Mark 7) for 20 minutes, then reduce the heat to moderately hot (190°C/375°F or Gas Mark 5) and bake for a further 10 minutes.

To freeze: cool quickly, then wrap in foil, seal, label and freeze.

To thaw and serve: thaw in wrappings at room temperature for 4 hours, then reheat on a baking sheet in a preheated moderate oven (180°C/350°F or Gas Mark 4) for 25 to 30 minutes or until heated through.

SERVES 4

PORK RAGOÛT WITH GREEN BEANS

METRIC/IMPERIAL

25 g/1 oz butter
1 × 15 ml spoon/1 tablespoon vegetable oil
2 onions, peeled and sliced
4 boneless pork chops
2 × 15 ml spoons/2 tablespoons cornflour
150 ml/¼ pint chicken stock
150 ml/¼ pint red wine
2 garlic cloves, peeled and crushed
2 × 5 ml spoons/2 teaspoons paprika pepper
1 × 5 ml spoon/1 teaspoon celery salt
1 bay leaf
freshly ground black pepper
225 g/½ lb frozen French beans, to finish

AMERICAN

2 tablespoons butter
1 tablespoon vegetable oil
2 onions, peeled and sliced
4 boneless pork chops
2 tablespoons cornstarch
⅔ cup chicken stock
⅔ cup red wine
2 garlic cloves, peeled and crushed
2 teaspoons paprika pepper
1 teaspoon celery salt
1 bay leaf
freshly ground black pepper
½ lb frozen green beans, to finish

Heat the butter and oil in a pan, add the onions and fry gently for 5 minutes until soft. Drain and transfer to an ovenproof casserole dish. Add the chops to the pan, fry for 1 minute on each side, then add to the casserole. Mix the cornflour (cornstarch) to a paste with a little of the stock, then add to the pan with the remaining stock and the remaining ingredients except the beans. Bring to the boil, then pour over the chops. Cover and cook in a preheated moderate oven (180°C/350°F or Gas Mark 4) for 1¼ hours or until the meat is tender

To freeze: cool quickly. Leave in the casserole or transfer to a rigid container. Cover, then wrap the casserole in a freezer bag or foil. Seal, label and freeze.

To thaw and serve: remove wrappings and thaw at room temperature for 4 hours. Reheat in a preheated moderate oven (180°C/350°F or Gas Mark 4) for 45 minutes or until heated through. Stir the beans into the casserole 20 minutes before the end of the reheating time.

SERVES 4

PORK AND PINEAPPLE CRUNCH

METRIC/IMPERIAL

2 × 15 ml spoons/2 tablespoons vegetable oil
4 pork chops, trimmed of fat
1 small onion, peeled and chopped
1 × 219 g/7¾ oz can pineapple chunks
20 g/¾ oz cornflour
2 chicken stock cubes
1 green pepper, cored, seeded and sliced
50 g/2 oz salted peanuts

AMERICAN

2 tablespoons vegetable oil
4 pork chops, trimmed of fat
1 small onion, peeled and chopped
1 × 7¾ oz can pineapple chunks
3 tablespoons cornstarch
3 chicken bouillon cubes
1 green pepper, cored, seeded and sliced
½ cup salted peanuts

Heat the oil in a pan, add the chops and fry briskly until browned on both sides. Transfer to a foil container. Add the onion to the pan and fry gently for 5 minutes until soft.

Drain the pineapple chunks and make up the juice to 600 ml/1 pint/2½ cups with water. Mix the cornflour (cornstarch) to a paste with a little of the liquid, then stir into the pan with the remaining liquid and the stock cubes. Bring to the boil, stirring constantly.

Arrange the pineapple chunks, green pepper and peanuts over the chops and coat with the sauce. Cover with foil and bake in a preheated moderate oven (180°C/350°F or Gas Mark 4) for 30 minutes.

To freeze: cool quickly, then wrap in a freezer bag. Seal, label and freeze.

To thaw and serve: remove the freezer bag, then reheat from frozen in a preheated moderate oven (180°C/350°F or Gas Mark 4) for 1½ hours or until heated through.

SERVES 4

PORK IN ORANGE SAUCE

METRIC/IMPERIAL

1 boneless loin of pork (approx 675 g/1½ lb)
salt
freshly ground black pepper
1 large onion, peeled and sliced
150 ml/¼ pint orange juice
finely grated rind and juice of 1 orange
1 × 15 ml spoon/1 tablespoon wine vinegar
1 × 15 ml spoon/1 tablespoon redcurrant jelly
To garnish:
2 oranges, peeled and sliced
mustard and cress

AMERICAN

1 boneless loin of pork (approx 1½ lb)
salt
freshly ground black pepper
1 large onion, peeled and sliced
⅔ cup orange juice
finely grated rind and juice of 1 orange
1 tablespoon wine vinegar
1 tablespoon redcurrant jelly
To garnish:
2 oranges, peeled and sliced
garden cress

Roll the pork into a neat shape and secure with string. Score the skin with a sharp knife and rub salt and pepper into the surface. Place in a roasting tin and roast without basting in a preheated hot oven (220°C/425°F or Gas Mark 7) for 15 minutes. Add the onion to the fat in the tin and continue cooking for a further 20 minutes. Pour off any excess fat, add the orange juice, rind and juice of the orange and the vinegar. Reduce the heat to moderate (180°C/350°F or Gas Mark 4) and roast for a further 45 minutes. Remove from the oven, stir in the redcurrant jelly and add salt and pepper to taste.

To freeze: cool quickly, then transfer to a rigid container. Seal, label and freeze.

To thaw and serve: reheat from frozen in the roasting tin in a preheated moderate oven (180°C/350°F or Gas Mark 4) for 1½ hours or until heated through. Garnish with orange slices and cress.

SERVES 4

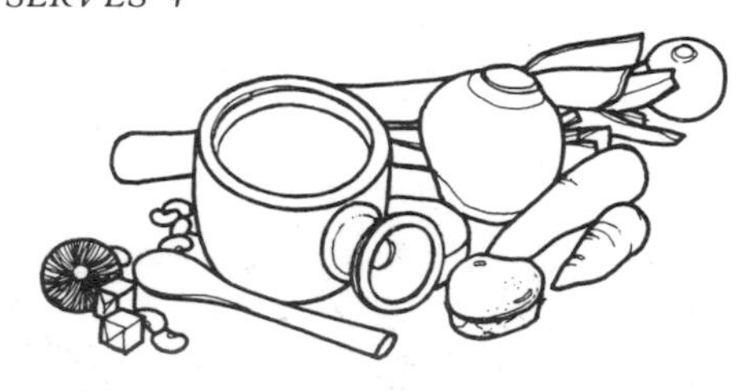

SWEET AND SOUR PORK KEBABS

METRIC/IMPERIAL

approx 1.5 kg/3 lb pork fillet, cut into cubes
salt
freshly ground black pepper
For the marinade:
6 × 15 ml spoons/6 tablespoons vegetable oil
finely grated rind and juice of 2 lemons
3 × 15 ml spoons/3 tablespoons dark brown sugar
3 × 15 ml spoons/3 tablespoons soy sauce
2 × 15 ml spoons/2 tablespoons black treacle
3 fresh green chillis, seeded and finely chopped
1 small piece of fresh root ginger, peeled, chopped and pounded
1 × 5 ml spoon/1 teaspoon Tabasco sauce

AMERICAN

approx 3 lb pork tenderloin, cut into cubes
salt
freshly ground black pepper
For the marinade:
6 tablespoons vegetable oil
finely grated rind and juice of 2 lemons
3 tablespoons dark brown sugar
3 tablespoons soy sauce
2 tablespoons molasses
3 fresh green chilis, seeded and finely chopped
1 small piece of fresh ginger root, peeled, chopped and pounded
1 teaspoon Tabasco sauce

Put the pork in bowl and sprinkle liberally with salt and pepper. Mix all the ingredients for the marinade together, pour over the pork and stir well to coat each cube of meat. Chill in the refrigerator for 24 hours, stirring occasionally.
Let the mixture stand at room temperature for 1 to 2 hours, then thread the cubes of pork onto 8 oiled kebab skewers. Place under a preheated grill (broiler) and cook for about 30 minutes, turning the skewers frequently during cooking and brushing the pork with the remaining marinade.
To freeze: cool quickly, then wrap the kebabs individually in foil. Pack in a freezer bag, seal, label and freeze.
To thaw and serve: thaw at room temperature for 4 hours, then place on a baking sheet and reheat in a preheated moderate oven (180°C/350°F or Gas Mark 4) for 30 minutes or until heated through.
MAKES 8

BAKERS PORK POT

METRIC/IMPERIAL

575 g/1¼ lb boneless shoulder of pork, cut into cubes
225 g/½ lb large pork sausages, chopped
1 onion, peeled and chopped
3 carrots, peeled and sliced
3 celery stalks, chopped
1 × 15 ml spoon/1 tablespoon flour
600 ml/1 pint chicken stock
1 × 2.5 ml spoon/½ teaspoon dried rosemary
1 × 5 ml spoon/1 teaspoon soy sauce
salt
freshly ground black pepper
To finish:
6 slices of French bread
a little prepared French mustard

AMERICAN

1¼ lb boneless shoulder of pork, cut into cubes
½ lb large pork sausages, chopped
1 onion, peeled and chopped
3 carrots, peeled and sliced
3 celery stalks, chopped
1 tablespoon flour
2½ cups chicken stock
½ teaspoon dried rosemary
1 teaspoon soy sauce
salt
freshly ground black pepper
To finish:
6 slices of French bread
a little prepared French mustard

Put the pork and sausages in a pan and fry gently in their own fat until lightly browned. Transfer to an ovenproof casserole dish. Add the vegetables to the pan and fry gently for 5 minutes. Stir in the flour, then the stock. Bring to the boil, stirring constantly, then add the remaining ingredients. Pour into the casserole, cover and cook in a preheated moderate oven (180°C/350°F or Gas Mark 4) for 45 minutes or until the pork is tender.
To freeze: cool quickly. Leave in the casserole or póur into a rigid container. Cover, then wrap the casserole in a freezer bag or foil. Seal, label and freeze.
To thaw and serve: remove wrappings and thaw at room temperature for 4 hours. Spread the bread with mustard, then place on top of the meat in the casserole, mustard side uppermost. Press the bread down slightly into the meat. Reheat, uncovered, in a preheated moderately hot oven (190°C/375°F or Gas Mark 5) for 1 hour or until the bread is crisp and the meat is heated through.
SERVES 4

PORK STEW WITH BEER

METRIC/IMPERIAL

25 g/1 oz butter
2 × 5 ml spoons/2 teaspoons vegetable oil
225 g/½ lb onions, peeled and finely chopped
1 large carrot, peeled and finely sliced
2 garlic cloves, peeled and chopped
1 kg/2 lb boneless stewing pork, trimmed of fat and cut into cubes
350 ml/12 fl oz light ale
salt
freshly ground black pepper
1 × 15 ml spoon/1 tablespoon cornflour
5 × 15 ml spoons/5 tablespoons water
freshly chopped parsley, to garnish

AMERICAN

2 tablespoons butter
2 teaspoons vegetable oil
2 cups finely chopped onions
1 large carrot, peeled and finely sliced
2 garlic cloves, peeled and chopped
2 lb boneless stewing pork, trimmed of fat and cut into cubes
1½ cups dark beer
salt
freshly ground black pepper
1 tablespoon cornstarch
⅓ cup water
freshly chopped parsley, to garnish

Heat the butter and oil in a pan, add the onions, carrot and garlic, then cover and fry gently for 15 minutes or until the vegetables are lightly coloured. Add the pork, increase the heat and fry briskly until browned on all sides.

Stir in the light ale (beer) and add salt and pepper to taste. Bring to the boil, stirring. Lower the heat, cover and simmer for 1 to 1¼ hours or until the pork is tender. Mix the cornflour (cornstarch) to a smooth paste with the water, then stir into the pan. Simmer for 5 minutes until the stew thickens.

To freeze: cool quickly, then pour into a rigid container. Cover, seal, label and freeze.

To thaw and serve: put the frozen pork into a casserole dish, cover and cook in a preheated moderate oven (180°C/350°F or Gas Mark 4) for 1½ hours or until heated through. Sprinkle with parsley just before serving.

SERVES 4 to 6

GAMMON (HAM) STEAKS EN CROÛTE

METRIC/IMPERIAL

4 bacon steaks
1 × 15 ml spoon/1 tablespoon flour
1 × 5 ml spoon/1 teaspoon soft brown sugar
pinch of mustard powder
freshly ground black pepper
few drops of Tabasco sauce
4 rings of fresh or canned pineapple
4 thin slices Gouda cheese
basic puff pastry dough made with 225 g/½ lb flour
a little milk
beaten egg, to glaze

AMERICAN

4 smoked ham slices
1 tablespoon flour
1 teaspoon light brown sugar
pinch of mustard powder
freshly ground black pepper
few drops of Tabasco sauce
4 rings fresh or canned pineapple
4 thin slices Gouda cheese
basic puff paste dough made with 2 cups flour
a little milk
beaten egg, to glaze

Coat the steaks in the flour mixed with the sugar, mustard and pepper, then sprinkle each one with a few drops of Tabasco sauce. Put a pineapple ring on each steak, then top each with a slice of cheese.

Roll out the dough on a floured surface, divide into 4 equal portions and roll each into a square large enough to enclose a steak. Put the steaks on the squares of dough, moisten the edges with a little milk and fold over to cover the steaks completely. Press down the edges firmly to seal. Use any trimmings to decorate the tops of the parcels.

To freeze: open (flash) freeze until firm, then wrap in foil. Seal, label and return to freezer.

To thaw and serve: remove wrappings and place the steaks on a baking sheet. Brush with beaten egg and bake from frozen in a moderately hot oven (200°C/400°F or Gas Mark 6) for 30 to 40 minutes or until heated through. Cover with foil if the pastry becomes too brown.

MAKES 4

GLAZED ROAST GAMMON

METRIC/IMPERIAL

1–1.5 kg/2–3 lb piece of corner or middle gammon
a few cloves
3–4 × 15 ml spoons/3–4 tablespoons marmalade
2 × 15 ml spoons/2 tablespoons demerara sugar
approx 150 ml/¼ pint dry cider

AMERICAN

2–3 lb smoked ham
a few cloves
3–4 tablespoons marmalade
2 tablespoons raw brown sugar
approx ⅔ cup hard cider

Weigh the gammon (ham) and calculate the cooking time as 20 minutes per 0.5 kg/1 lb plus 20 minutes over.
Put the gammon (ham) in a large pan and cover with cold water. Leave to stand for several hours, preferably overnight. Drain, cover with fresh cold water and bring to the boil. Simmer gently for half the total cooking time, adding more water if the level becomes low. Remove from the heat and drain off the water.
Cut the skin off the gammon (ham),score the fat and press in a few cloves. Place the gammon (ham) in a roasting tin. Mix the marmalade and sugar together and spread thickly over the cut surface of the gammon. Pour in sufficient cider to cover the bottom of the tin.
Roast in a preheated moderately hot oven (190°C/375°F or Gas Mark 5) for the remainder of the cooking time.
To freeze: cool quickly, then wrap in foil or cling film (saran wrap). Seal, label and freeze.
To thaw and serve: thaw in the refrigerator overnight. Serve cold, or reheat in a covered dish in a preheated moderate oven (180°C/350°F or Gas Mark 4) for 40 minutes or until heated through.
SERVES 6

HAM CROQUETTES

METRIC/IMPERIAL

225 g/½ lb cold mashed potato
100 g/4 oz cooked ham, finely chopped
1 small onion, peeled and chopped
1 egg, beaten
1 × 2.5 ml spoon/½ teaspoon salt
1 × 5 ml spoon/1 teaspoon prepared mustard
For the coating:
2 eggs, beaten
4 × 15 ml spoons/4 tablespoons milk
225 g/½ lb fresh white breadcrumbs
vegetable oil for deep-frying, to finish

AMERICAN

1 cup cold mashed potato
½ cup finely chopped cooked ham
1 small onion, peeled and chopped
1 egg, beaten
½ teaspoon salt
1 teaspoon prepared mustard
For the coating:
2 eggs, beaten
¼ cup milk
4 cups fresh white breadcrumbs
vegetable oil for deep-frying, to finish

Put all the ingredients for the croquettes in a bowl and stir well to mix. Divide the mixture into 14 equal portions, then shape into croquettes on a floured surface.
To make the coating: put the eggs and milk in a shallow dish and beat well to mix. Dip each croquette into the egg mixture, then into the breadcrumbs.
To freeze: open (flash) freeze until firm, then pack in a rigid container, separating each layer with foil. Seal, label and return to the freezer.
To thaw and serve: thaw in the refrigerator for 1 hour, then deep-fry in hot oil until golden brown. Drain on paper towels and serve hot with tomato sauce.
MAKES 14

PORK AND PÂTÉ PARCELS

METRIC/IMPERIAL

6 pork chops, trimmed of fat
a little vegetable oil
basic puff pastry dough made with 225 g/½ lb flour
100 g/4 oz pork liver pâté, softened
salt
freshly ground black pepper
a little milk
beaten egg, to glaze

AMERICAN

6 pork chops, trimmed of fat
a little vegetable oil
basic puff paste dough made with 2 cups flour
¼ lb pork liver pâté, softened
salt
freshly ground black pepper
a little milk
beaten egg, to glaze

Brush the chops with the oil and grill (broil) for 5 minutes on each side. Leave to cool.
Roll out the dough thinly on a floured surface, divide into 6 equal portions, then roll each piece into a square large enough to enclose a

chop. Spread each chop on both sides with the pâté and sprinkle with salt and pepper to taste. Put the chops on the squares of dough, moisten the edges with a little milk, then fold over to cover the chops completely, leaving any bones protruding. Press the edges firmly to seal. Use any trimmings to decorate the tops of the parcels.
To freeze: open (flash) freeze until firm, then wrap in a freezer bag or foil. Seal, label and return to the freezer.
To thaw and serve: remove wrappings and place the chops on a baking sheet. Brush with the beaten egg and bake from frozen in a preheated moderately hot oven (200°C/400°F or Gas Mark 6) for 30 to 40 minutes or until heated through. Cover with foil if the pastry becomes too brown during cooking.
MAKES 6

BACON AND EGG PIE

METRIC/IMPERIAL
basic shortcrust pastry dough made with 225 g/½ lb flour
4 bacon rashers, rinds removed and chopped
50 g/2 oz mushrooms, sliced
4 large eggs
5 × 15 ml spoons/5 tablespoons milk
1 × 15 ml spoon/1 tablespoon freshly chopped parsley
salt
freshly ground black pepper

AMERICAN
basic pie dough made with 2 cups flour
4 bacon slices, chopped
½ cup sliced mushrooms
4 large eggs
⅓ cup milk
1 tablespoon freshly chopped parsley
salt
freshly ground black pepper

Roll out half the dough on a floured surface and use to line a 20 cm/8 inch sandwich tin (layer cake pan). Put the bacon in the tin and cover with the mushrooms. Beat the eggs and milk together in a bowl, then add the parsley and salt and pepper to taste. Pour over the bacon and mushrooms.
Roll out the remaining dough to form a lid. Moisten the edges of the dough, place the lid on top of the filling and press firmly to seal together. Trim and flute the edge and use any trimmings to decorate the top of the pie. Brush the dough with the egg and milk mixture left in the bowl, then bake in a preheated moderately hot oven (200°C/400°F or Gas Mark 6) for 10 minutes. Reduce the heat to moderate (180°C/350°F or Gas Mark 4) and continue baking for a further 30 minutes.
To freeze: cool quickly. Open (flash) freeze until firm, then wrap in foil or a freezer bag. Seal, label and return to the freezer.
To thaw and serve: remove wrappings, then thaw at room temperature for 4 hours.
Serve cold with a green salad.
SERVES 4

GAMMON (HAM) AND APRICOT CASSEROLE

METRIC/IMPERIAL
25 g/1 oz lard
675 g/1½ lb lean gammon, cut into cubes
1 large onion, peeled and chopped
175 g/6 oz long-grain rice
600 ml/1 pint stock
75 g/3 oz dried apricots, chopped
1 bay leaf
salt
freshly ground black pepper

AMERICAN
2 tablespoons lard
1½ lb lean ham, cut into cubes
1 large onion, peeled and chopped
1 cup long-grain rice
2½ cups stock
½ cup dried apricots, chopped
1 bay leaf
salt
freshly ground black pepper

Melt the lard in a pan, add the gammon (ham) and fry until browned on all sides. Remove from the pan with a slotted spoon and transfer to a casserole dish. Add the onion to the pan and fry gently for 3 minutes. Stir in the rice, then add the stock and bring to the boil. Add the remaining ingredients, pour over the gammon and stir well. Cover and cook in a preheated moderate oven (180°C/350°F or Gas Mark 4) for 1 hour. Remove the bay leaf.
To freeze: cool quickly. Leave in the casserole or transfer to a rigid container. Cover, then wrap the casserole in a freezer bag or foil. Seal, label and freeze.
To thaw and serve: remove wrappings, then reheat from frozen in the covered casserole in a preheated moderate oven (180°C/350°F or Gas Mark 4) for 1 hour or until heated through. Fork the rice through occasionally during cooking.
SERVES 4 to 6

BACON STEW POT

METRIC/IMPERIAL

675 g/1½ lb piece collar bacon, rind and fat removed and diced
40 g/1½ oz butter
1 small onion, peeled and chopped
2–3 leeks, trimmed and sliced
2 × 15 ml spoons/2 tablespoons flour
450 ml/¾ pint ham or chicken stock
1 large carrot, peeled and chopped
freshly ground black pepper
1 × 200 g/7 oz can butter beans, drained
freshly chopped parsley, to garnish

AMERICAN

1½ lb piece collar bacon, rind and fat removed and diced
3 tablespoons butter
1 small onion, peeled and chopped
2–3 leeks, trimmed and sliced
2 tablespoons flour
2 cups ham or chicken stock
1 large carrot, peeled and chopped
freshly ground black pepper
1 × 7 oz can butter beans, drained
freshly chopped parsley, to garnish

Put the bacon in a pan, cover with water and bring slowly to the boil. Strain and leave to drain on paper towels. Melt the butter in a pan, add the onion and leeks and fry until soft. Stir in the flour and cook for 2 minutes, then stir in the stock. Bring to the boil, stirring constantly, then remove the pan from the heat and add the carrot, bacon and pepper to taste.
Cover and cook gently for 1¼ hours. Add the butter beans and heat through for 5 minutes.
To freeze: cool quickly, then turn into a rigid container. Seal, label and freeze.
To thaw and serve: thaw at room temperature for 4 hours, then reheat on top of the stove, stirring occasionally. Sprinkle with parsley.
SERVES 4

APPLE AND BACON CHARLOTTE

METRIC/IMPERIAL

225 g/½ lb streaky bacon rashers, rinds removed
a little prepared mustard
100 g/4 oz butter
225 g/½ lb fresh white breadcrumbs
3 large cooking apples, peeled, cored and grated
salt
freshly ground black pepper
225 g/½ lb Cheddar cheese, grated
parsley sprigs, to garnish

AMERICAN

½ lb fatty bacon slices
a little prepared mustard
½ cup butter
4 cups fresh white breadcrumbs
3 large baking apples, peeled, cored and grated
salt
freshly ground black pepper
2 cups grated Cheddar cheese
parsley sprigs, to garnish

Chop the bacon roughly, reserving 4 whole rashers (slices) for the topping. Put the chopped bacon in a lightly greased ovenproof dish or foil container and spread over a little mustard.
Melt the butter in a pan, then stir in the breadcrumbs, apples, 175 g/6 oz/1½ cups cheese and salt and pepper to taste. Put this mixture on top of the bacon, sprinkle with the remaining cheese and top with the reserved bacon rashers (slices). Bake in a preheated moderate oven (180°C/350°F or Gas Mark 4) for 45 minutes.
To freeze: cool quickly. Cover with foil, then wrap in a freezer bag. Seal, label and freeze.
To thaw and serve: remove wrappings and thaw at room temperature for 4 hours. Reheat in the covered dish or container in a preheated moderate oven for 1 hour or until heated through. Serve garnished with parsley sprigs.
SERVES 4

CHEESE AND BACON PIE

METRIC/IMPERIAL

675 g/1½ lb potatoes, peeled and finely sliced
225 g/½ lb bacon rashers, rinds removed and cut in half
parsley sprigs, to garnish
For the sauce:
50 g/2 oz butter
50 g/2 oz flour
600 ml/1 pint milk
100 g/4 oz Cheddar cheese, grated
1 large onion, peeled and finely chopped
freshly ground black pepper

AMERICAN

1½ lb potatoes, peeled and finely sliced
½ lb bacon slices, cut in half
parsley sprigs, to garnish
For the sauce:
¼ cup butter
½ cup flour
2½ cups milk
1 cup grated Cheddar cheese
1 large onion, peeled and finely chopped
freshly ground black pepper

To make the sauce: melt the butter in a pan, stir in the flour and cook for 2 minutes, stirring constantly. Remove from the heat and gradually stir in the milk. Return to the heat and bring to the boil, stirring constantly, then simmer until the sauce thickens. Stir in 75 g/3 oz/¾ cup cheese, the onion and pepper to taste. Cook until the cheese melts, stirring occasionally, then remove from the heat.
Put the sauce, potatoes and bacon in layers in a casserole dish or foil container, finishing with a layer of sauce. Sprinkle with the remaining cheese, cover with foil and bake in a preheated moderately hot oven (190°C/375°F or Gas Mark 5) for 1½ hours.
To freeze: cool quickly, then wrap in a freezer bag. Seal, label and freeze.
To thaw and serve: remove wrappings and reheat from frozen in a preheated moderate oven (180°C/350°F or Gas Mark 4) for 1 to 1½ hours or until heated through. Garnish with parsley just before serving.
SERVES 4

HAM AND SAUSAGE JAMBALAYA

METRIC/IMPERIAL
3 × 15 ml spoons/3 tablespoons vegetable oil
2 onions, peeled and chopped
1 green pepper, cored, seeded and sliced
1 red pepper, cored, seeded and sliced
175 g/6 oz long-grain rice
1 ham stock cube dissolved in 450 ml/¾ pint hot water
pinch of saffron or turmeric powder
4 sausages, grilled and sliced
100 g/4 oz cooked ham, cut into strips
75 g/3 oz peeled prawns
3 tomatoes, peeled and quartered
salt
freshly ground black pepper

AMERICAN
3 tablespoons vegetable oil
2 onions, peeled and chopped
1 green pepper, cored, seeded and sliced
1 red pepper, cored, seeded and sliced
1 cup long-grain rice
2 ham bouillon cubes dissolved in 2 cups hot water
pinch of saffron or turmeric powder
4 sausages, broiled and sliced
¼ lb cooked ham, cut into strips
½ cup shelled shrimp
3 tomatoes, peeled and quartered
salt
freshly ground black pepper

Heat the oil in a pan, add the onions, peppers and rice and fry for 5 minutes. Stir in the stock and saffron or turmeric and bring to the boil. Cover and simmer for 15 minutes.
Stir in the remaining ingredients and cook for a further 5 minutes until the liquid has been absorbed and the rice is tender.
To freeze: cool quickly, then pour into a foil container. Seal, label and freeze.
To thaw and serve: thaw at room temperature for 1 hour, then reheat in the covered container in a preheated moderate oven (180°C/350°F or Gas Mark 4) for 20 minutes or until heated through.
SERVES 4

BACON IN PASTRY

METRIC/IMPERIAL
2 × 15 ml spoons/2 tablespoons demerara sugar
2 × 5 ml spoons/2 teaspoons prepared French mustard
8 stuffed green olives, finely chopped
1 × 575 g/1¼ lb piece of cooked lean bacon or gammon, rind removed
basic puff pastry dough made with 225 g/½ lb flour
beaten egg, to glaze

AMERICAN
2 tablespoons raw brown sugar
2 teaspoons prepared French mustard
8 stuffed green olives, finely chopped
1 × 1¼ lb piece of cooked lean bacon or ham, rind and fat removed
basic puff paste dough made with 2 cups flour
beaten egg, to glaze

Mix together the sugar, mustard and olives and spread over the top of the bacon or gammon.
Roll out the dough on a floured surface to a circle large enough to enclose the meat. Put the meat in the centre of the dough, sugar side down. Fold the dough over the meat to enclose it completely, then brush the edges with a little beaten egg and press firmly to seal. Use any trimmings to decorate the top. Put on a baking sheet with the seams underneath and brush all over with beaten egg. Cut air vent in the top.
To freeze: open (flash) freeze until firm, then wrap in foil. Seal, label and return to the freezer.
To thaw and serve: remove wrappings and thaw in the refrigerator for 12 hours. Put on a baking sheet and bake in a preheated moderately hot oven (200°C/400°F or Gas Mark 6) for 40 to 45 minutes or until heated through. Cover with foil if the pastry becomes too brown during cooking.
SERVES 4

BEAN AND BACON HOT POT

METRIC/IMPERIAL

2 × 15 ml spoons/2 tablespoons vegetable oil
1 large onion, peeled and sliced
450 g/1 lb chipolata sausages
225 g/½ lb piece of bacon, rind removed and diced
1 × 425 g/15 oz can butter beans, drained
1 × 15 ml spoon/1 tablespoon tomato purée
150 ml/¼ pint beef stock
salt
freshly ground black pepper
75 g/3 oz Cheddar cheese, grated, to finish

AMERICAN

2 tablespoons vegetable oil
1 large onion, peeled and sliced
1 lb link sausages
½ lb piece of Canadian bacon, diced
1 × 15 oz can butter beans, drained
1 tablespoon tomato paste
⅔ cup beef stock
salt
freshly ground black pepper
¾ cup grated Cheddar cheese, to finish

Heat the oil in a flameproof casserole dish, add the onion and fry gently for 5 minutes until soft. Add the sausages and bacon and fry gently for a further 5 minutes, turning the sausages occasionally. Add the butter beans, tomato purée (paste), stock and salt and pepper to taste. Cover and cook in a preheated moderate oven (180°C/350°F or Gas Mark 4) for 40 minutes.

To freeze: cool quickly. Leave in the casserole or pour into a rigid container. Cover, than wrap the casserole in a freezer bag or foil. Seal, label and freeze.

To thaw and serve: remove wrappings and thaw at room temperature for 4 hours. Reheat in the covered casserole in a preheated moderate oven (180°C/350°F or Gas Mark 4) for 50 minutes. Sprinkle the cheese over the top, return to the oven, uncovered, for a further 10 minutes or until golden brown and heated through.

SERVES 4

PICNIC LOAF

METRIC/IMPERIAL

1 × 575 g/1¼ lb piece of collar bacon
1 small onion, peeled
50 g/2 oz fresh white breadcrumbs
4 × 15 ml spoons/4 tablespoons ham or chicken stock
finely grated rind of ½ lemon
1 × 15 ml spoon/1 tablespoon freshly chopped parsley
1 × 2.5 ml spoon/½ teaspoon dried mixed herbs
freshly ground black pepper
1 egg, beaten
3 streaky bacon rashers, rinds removed

AMERICAN

1 × 1¼ lb smoked shoulder roll
1 small onion, peeled
1 cup fresh white breadcrumbs
¼ cup ham or chicken stock
finely grated rind of ½ lemon
1 tablespoon freshly chopped parsley
½ teaspoon dried mixed herbs
freshly ground black pepper
1 egg, beaten
3 fatty bacon slices

Put the bacon (smoked shoulder roll) in a pan, cover with water and bring slowly to the boil. Remove from the heat and leave to soak for 3 hours. Remove the rind, fat and any gristle from the bacon (smoked shoulder roll), then mince (grind) the meat with the onion. Put the minced (ground) mixture in a bowl, add the remaining ingredients, except the bacon rashers (slices), and stir well to mix.

Stretch the bacon rashers (slices) with the blade of a knife and arrange crossways in a greased 450 g/1 lb loaf tin. Press the bacon mixture lightly into the tin, cover with foil and stand in a roasting tin half filled with water. Bake in a preheated moderate oven (160°C/325°F or Gas Mark 3) for 1½ hours or until set.

To freeze: cool quickly, chill in the refrigerator until firm, then turn out and wrap in foil. Seal, label and freeze.

To thaw and serve: thaw in the refrigerator overnight. Serve cold, cut into thick slices.

MAKES APPROX 12 SLICES

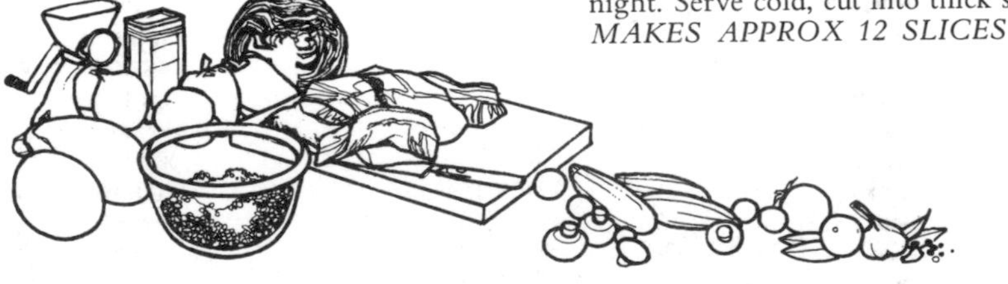

CORNISH HAM PIE

METRIC/IMPERIAL

40 g/1½ oz butter
40 g/1½ oz flour
150 ml/¼ pint milk
150 ml/¼ pint medium dry cider
225 g/½ lb cooked ham, diced
1 × 200 g/7 oz can sweetcorn, drained
1 × 15 ml spoon/1 tablespoon freshly chopped parsley
salt
freshly ground black pepper
basic puff pastry dough made with 225 g/½ lb flour
a little milk
beaten egg, to glaze

AMERICAN

3 tablespoons butter
⅜ cup flour
⅔ cup milk
⅔ cup hard cider
1 cup diced cooked ham
1 × 7 oz can corn kernels, drained
1 tablespoon freshly chopped parsley
salt
freshly ground black pepper
basic puff paste dough made with 2 cups flour
a little milk
beaten egg, to glaze

Melt the butter in a pan, stir in the flour and cook for 2 minutes, stirring constantly. Remove from the heat and gradually stir in the milk and cider. Return to the heat and bring to the boil, stirring constantly. Simmer until thick, then add the ham, corn, parsley and salt and pepper to taste. Leave to cool.

Roll out the dough on a floured surface. Cut into 2 pieces and roll out each piece into a circle, one slightly larger than the other. Put the smallest circle on a baking sheet and spread over the sauce mixture. leaving a border around the edge. Brush the edge of dough with milk, put the remaining piece of dough over and press firmly to seal the edge. Use any trimmings to decorate the top of the pie. Cut an air vent in the centre of the pie.

To freeze: open (flash) freeze until firm, then wrap in a freezer bag or foil. Seal, label and return to the freezer.

To thaw and serve: remove wrappings and place on a baking sheet. Brush with the beaten egg Bake from frozen in a preheated hot oven (220°C/425°F or Gas Mark 7) for 25 to 35 minutes or until heated through. Cover with foil if the pastry becomes too brown during cooking.

SERVES 6

OSSO BUCCO

METRIC/IMPERIAL

40 g/1½ oz butter
2 onions, peeled and sliced
4 thick slices shin of veal
25 g/1 oz flour
salt
freshly ground black pepper
2 carrots, peeled and sliced
2 celery stalks, chopped
2 garlic cloves, peeled and crushed
1 × 5 ml spoon/1 teaspoon dried basil
1 × 5 ml spoon/1 teaspoon dried thyme
1 bay leaf
450 ml/¾ pint chicken stock
650 ml/1¼ pint dry white wine
freshly chopped parsley, to finish

AMERICAN

3 tablespoons butter
2 onions, peeled and sliced
4 thick slices shin of veal
¼ cup flour
salt
freshly ground black pepper
2 carrots, peeled and sliced
2 celery stalks, chopped
2 garlic cloves, peeled and crushed
1 teaspoon dried basil
1 teaspoon dried thyme
1 bay leaf
2 cups chicken stock
⅔ cup dry white wine
freshly chopped parsley, to finish

Melt the butter in a flameproof casserole, add the onions and fry gently for 10 minutes. Coat the veal in the flour seasoned with salt and pepper. Add to the pan and fry until browned on all sides. Add the remaining ingredients except the parsley. Bring to the boil, stirring, then cook in a preheated moderate oven (180°C/350°F or Gas Mark 4) for 2½ to 3 hours or until the meat is tender. Remove the bay leaf.

To freeze: cool quickly, leave in the casserole or pour into a rigid container. Cover, then wrap the casserole in a freezer bag or foil. Seal, label and freeze.

To thaw and serve: remove wrappings and reheat from frozen, covered, in a preheated moderate oven (180°C/350°F or Gas Mark 4) for 1½ hours or until heated through. Sprinkle with parsley just before serving.

SERVES 4

VEAL CHOPS MAGYAR

METRIC/IMPERIAL

8 small veal chops, trimmed of fat
3 × 15 ml spoons/3 tablespoons flour
salt
freshly ground black pepper
25 g/1 oz butter
1 onion, peeled and sliced
175 g/6 oz mushrooms, sliced
1 × 15 ml spoon/1 tablespoon paprika pepper
3 × 15 ml spoons/3 tablespoons tomato purée
300 ml/½ pint chicken stock
juice of 1 lemon
To finish:
150 ml/¼ pint single cream
paprika pepper

AMERICAN

8 small veal chops, trimmed of fat
3 tablespoons flour
salt
freshly ground black pepper
2 tablespoons butter
1 onion, peeled and sliced
1½ cups sliced mushrooms
1 tablespoon paprika pepper
3 tablespoons tomato paste
1¼ cups chicken stock
juice of 1 lemon
To finish:
⅔ cup light cream
paprika pepper

Coat the chops in 2 × 15 ml spoons/2 tablespoons flour, seasoned with salt and pepper. Melt the butter in a flameproof casserole dish, put in the chops and fry until browned on both sides. Remove from the casserole. Add the onion and mushrooms and fry until soft. Sprinkle in the paprika and remaining flour and cook for 1 minute, stirring constantly. Stir in the tomato purée (paste), stock and lemon juice and bring to the boil. Return the chops to the casserole, cover and cook in a preheated moderate oven (180°C/350°F or Gas Mark 4) for 1 hour or until the chops are tender.

To freeze: cool quickly. Leave in the casserole or transfer to a rigid container. Cover, then wrap the casserole in a freezer bag or foil. Seal, label and freeze.

To thaw and serve: reheat from frozen, covered, in a preheated moderate oven (180°C/350°F or Gas Mark 4) for 1½ hours or until heated through. Pour over the cream and sprinkle with paprika just before serving.

SERVES 4

RUSSIAN VEAL BALLS

METRIC/IMPERIAL

For the veal balls:
3 × 15 ml spoons/3 tablespoons vegetable oil
1 large onion, peeled and finely chopped
100 g/4 oz fresh white breadcrumbs
350 g/¾ lb lean minced veal
1 × 2.5 ml spoon/½ teaspoon garlic powder
1 × 5 ml spoon/1 teaspoon crushed dill seeds
salt
freshly ground black pepper
flour for coating
25 g/1 oz butter
For the sauce:
175 g/6 oz mushrooms, sliced
25 g/1 oz flour
450 ml/¾ pint chicken stock
150 ml/¼ pint soured cream, to finish

AMERICAN

For the veal balls:
3 tablespoons vegetable oil
1 large onion, peeled and finely chopped
2 cups fresh white breadcrumbs
1½ cups lean ground veal
½ teaspoon garlic powder
1 teaspoon crushed dill seeds
salt
freshly ground black pepper
flour for coating
2 tablespoons butter
For the sauce:
1½ cups sliced mushrooms
¼ cup flour
2 cups chicken stock
⅔ cup sour cream, to finish

To make the veal balls: heat 1 × 15 ml spoon/1 tablespoon oil in a flameproof casserole dish, add the onion and fry gently until soft. Remove from the casserole with a slotted spoon and put in a bowl with the breadcrumbs, veal, garlic powder, dill and salt and pepper to taste. Stir well to mix.

Divide the mixture into 12 equal portions and shape into balls with lightly floured hands. Heat the remaining oil and the butter in the casserole, add the veal balls and fry until browned on all sides. Drain on paper towels.

To make the sauce: add the mushrooms to the casserole and fry for 2 to 3 minutes. Stir in the flour and cook for 2 minutes, stirring constantly, then gradually stir in the stock. Bring to the boil, stirring constantly, then simmer until the sauce thickens.

Return the veal balls to the casserole, cover and simmer for 15 minutes.

To freeze: cool quickly. Leave in the casserole

or transfer to a rigid container. Cover, then wrap the casserole in a freezer bag or foil. Seal, label and freeze.
To thaw and serve: remove wrappings and thaw at room temperature for 4 hours. Reheat in the covered casserole in a preheated moderate oven (180°C/350°F or Gas Mark 4) for 1 hour or until heated through. Serve with the sour(ed) cream.
SERVES 4

VEAL ZURICH

METRIC/IMPERIAL
450 g/1 lb boneless leg of veal, trimmed of fat, beaten and cut into thin strips
2 × 15 ml spoons/2 tablespoons flour
salt
freshly ground black pepper
50 g/2 oz butter
2 spring onions, trimmed and finely chopped
pinch of paprika pepper
4 × 15 ml spoons/4 tablespoons dry white wine
150 ml/¼ pint single cream
freshly chopped parsley, to garnish

AMERICAN
1 lb lean round steak of veal, trimmed of fat, beaten and cut into thin strips
2 tablespoons flour
salt
freshly ground black pepper
¼ cup butter
2 scallions, trimmed and finely chopped
pinch of paprika pepper
¼ cup dry white wine
⅔ cup light cream
freshly chopped parsley, to garnish

Coat the veal in the flour seasoned with salt and pepper. Melt the butter in a pan, add the onions (scallions) and fry gently until soft. Add the veal and fry briskly for 2 minutes, shaking the pan constantly.
Stir in the paprika, wine and cream, then cover and simmer for 5 minutes. Do not boil or the cream will separate.
To freeze: cool quickly, then pour into a rigid container. Seal, label and freeze.
To thaw and serve: thaw at room temperature for 4 hours, then reheat gently on top of the stove, stirring occasionally. Do not allow to boil. Sprinkle with parsley just before serving.
SERVES 4

BLANQUETTE OF VEAL

METRIC/IMPERIAL
100 g/4 oz butter
2 medium onions, peeled and sliced
1.5 kg/3 lb boneless shoulder of veal, cut into cubes
2 × 15 ml spoons/2 tablespoons flour
300 ml/½ pint dry white wine
600 ml/1 pint veal or chicken stock
2 bay leaves
salt
freshly ground black pepper
To finish:
4 egg yolks
4 × 15 ml spoons/4 tablespoons lemon juice
150 ml/¼ pint single cream
paprika pepper
freshly chopped parsley

AMERICAN
½ cup butter
2 medium onions, peeled and sliced
3 lb boneless shoulder of veal, cut into cubes
2 tablespoons flour
1¼ cups dry white wine
2½ cups veal or chicken stock
2 bay leaves
salt
freshly ground black pepper
To finish:
4 egg yolks
¼ cup lemon juice
⅔ cup light cream
paprika pepper
freshly chopped parsley

Melt the butter in a pan, add the onions and fry gently until soft. Add the veal and fry until browned on all sides. Stir in the flour, then gradually stir in the wine and stock. Add the bay leaves and salt and pepper to taste. Bring to the boil, then cover and simmer for 1½ hours or until tender. Remove the bay leaves.
To freeze: cool quickly, then pour into a rigid container. Seal, label and freeze.
To thaw and serve: thaw in the refrigerator for 24 hours. Reheat gently on top of the stove, stirring occasionally. Strain the sauce from the meat and vegetables. Transfer the meat and vegetables to a warmed serving dish and keep hot. Put the sauce in a clean pan and keep hot. Beat the egg yolks, lemon juice and cream in a bowl, stir in a spoonful of the hot sauce and beat until well blended. Pour this mixture into the sauce in the pan and bring just to boiling point, beating constantly until thick and creamy. Pour the sauce over the meat, then sprinkle with a little paprika and parsley just before serving.
SERVES 8

SPICY LAMB CHOP PIE

METRIC/IMPERIAL

25 g/1 oz butter
450 g/1 lb lamb chops, cut from the loin
1 large onion, peeled and sliced
25 g/1 oz flour
450 ml/¾ pint beef stock
1 × 15 ml spoon/1 tablespoon Worcestershire sauce
pinch of ground cinnamon
salt
freshly ground black pepper
1 medium cooking apple, peeled, cored and sliced
basic shortcrust pastry dough made with 175 g/6 oz flour
beaten egg or milk, to glaze

AMERICAN

2 tablespoons butter
1 lb lamb chops, cut from the loin
1 large onion, peeled and sliced
¼ cup flour
2 cups beef stock
1 tablespoon Worcestershire sauce
pinch of ground cinnamon
salt
freshly ground black pepper
1 medium baking apple, peeled, cored and sliced
basic pie dough made with 1½ cups flour
beaten egg or milk, to glaze

Melt the butter in a pan, add the chops and fry for 5 to 6 minutes until browned on both sides. Remove and drain on paper towels. Add the onion to the pan and fry until soft. Stir in the flour and cook for 1 minute. Stir in stock and Worcestershire sauce, bring to the boil, then simmer until thick and smooth, stirring constantly. Add the cinnamon and salt and pepper to taste. Put the chops and apple slices in layers in a 1.75 litre/3 pint/7½ cup freezerproof pie dish, pour over the sauce and leave to cool.

Roll out the dough on a floured surface to a shape 5 cm/2 inches larger than the pie dish. Cut off a 2.5 cm/1 inch strip all round. Put the strip around the edge of the dish, moisten with water, then put the remaining dough on top. Press the edges firmly together to seal. Trim and flute the edge and use any trimmings to decorate the top of the pie. Cut an air vent in the centre.

To freeze: open (flash) freeze until firm, then wrap in foil. Seal, label and return to freezer.

To thaw and serve: remove wrappings and brush the top of the pie with beaten egg or milk. Bake from frozen in a preheated moderately hot oven (200°C/400°F or Gas Mark 6) for 50 minutes to 1 hour or until heated through. Cover with foil if the pastry becomes too brown.

SERVES 4

LAMB CURRY

METRIC/IMPERIAL

1 kg/2 lb boneless stewing lamb, trimmed of fat and cut into cubes
175 g/6 oz onions, peeled
4 garlic cloves, peeled and crushed
25 g/1 oz ground almonds
25 g/1 oz ground coriander
2 × 5 ml spoons/2 teaspoons salt
100 g/4 oz butter
150 ml/¼ pint hot water
150 ml/¼ pint natural yogurt
150 ml/¼ pint single cream
pinch of ground saffron or turmeric
1 × 5 ml spoon/1 teaspoon paprika
2 × 5 ml spoons/2 teaspoons curry powder
juice of 1 lemon

AMERICAN

2 lb boneless stewing lamb, trimmed of fat and cut into cubes
6 oz onions, peeled
4 garlic cloves, peeled and crushed
¼ cup ground almonds
¼ cup ground coriander
2 teaspoons salt
¼ cup butter
⅔ cup hot water
⅔ cup unflavored yogurt
⅔ cup light cream
pinch of ground saffron or turmeric
1 teaspoon paprika
2 teaspoons curry powder
juice of 1 lemon

Put the lamb in a large bowl. Mince (grind) 50 g/2 oz onions, and mix to a paste with the garlic, almonds, coriander and salt. Add to the lamb and leave for 2 hours, stirring occasionally. Slice the remaining onions. Melt the butter in a large pan, add the onions and fry gently until soft. Remove from pan. Add the lamb to the pan and fry until the liquid has evaporated. Stir in the hot water, cover and cook until the lamb is almost tender. Remove the lid and continue cooking until the mixture becomes dry. Stir the yogurt into the pan and continue cooking until dry again. Return the fried onions to the pan with the remaining ingredients, except the coriander leaves. Continue cooking for 30 minutes or until the lamb is tender.

To freeze: cool quickly and turn into a rigid container. Cover, overwrap in a freezer bag or foil, seal, label and freeze.

To thaw and serve: thaw at room temperature for 4 hours, then reheat gently on top of the stove, stirring occasionally.

SERVES 4

DEVONSHIRE SQUAB PIE

METRIC/IMPERIAL

6 best end of neck lamb cutlets, trimmed of fat
4 cooking apples, peeled, cored and sliced
pinch of grated nutmeg
pinch of ground allspice
2 × 15 ml spoons/2 tablespoons sugar
6 leeks, finely sliced
salt
freshly ground black pepper
600 ml/1 pint cider
basic shortcrust pastry dough made with 225 g/½ lb flour
milk, to glaze

AMERICAN

6 rib chops of lamb, trimmed of fat
4 baking apples, peeled, cored and sliced
pinch of grated nutmeg
pinch of ground allspice
2 tablespoons sugar
6 leeks, finely sliced
salt
freshly ground black pepper
2½ cups hard cider
basic pie dough made with 2 cups flour
milk, to glaze

Put half the chops in the bottom of a large pie dish. Layer the apples, spices and sugar alternately with the leeks, salt and pepper to taste and the remaining chops until all the ingredients are used up. Pour in the cider.

Roll out the dough on a floured surface and use to cover the dish. Use any trimmings to decorate the top of the pie. Brush with a little milk and cut an air vent in the centre.

Bake in a preheated moderately hot oven (190°C/375°F or Gas Mark 5) for 15 minutes. Cover with foil, reduce the heat to cool (150°C/300°F or Gas Mark 2) and bake for a further 1¼ hours.

To freeze: cool quickly, then open (flash) freeze until firm. Wrap in foil, seal, label and return to the freezer.

To thaw and serve: remove wrappings and thaw at room temperature for 4 hours. Reheat in a preheated moderately hot oven (190°C/375°F or Gas Mark 5) for 30 minutes or until heated through.

SERVES 4 to 6

LAMB AND ORANGE PUFF

METRIC/IMPERIAL

2 × 15 ml spoons/2 tablespoons vegetable oil
½ shoulder of lamb, boned, trimmed of fat and cut into small cutlets
1 medium onion, peeled and finely chopped
1 × 2.5 ml spoon/½ teaspoon finely grated orange rind
juice of 1 orange
300 ml/½ pint stock
2 × 5 ml spoons/2 teaspoons cornflour
salt
freshly ground black pepper
basic puff pastry dough made with 350 g/¾ lb flour
beaten egg, to glaze

AMERICAN

2 tablespoons vegetable oil
½ shoulder of lamb, boned, trimmed of fat and cut into small cutlets
1 medium onion, peeled and finely chopped
½ teaspoon finely grated orange rind
juice of 1 orange
1¼ cups stock
2 teaspoons cornstarch
salt
freshly ground black pepper
basic puff paste dough made with 3 cups flour
beaten egg, to glaze

Heat the oil in a pan, add the lamb and fry briskly until browned on all sides. Add the onion and fry gently until soft. Stir in the orange rind, juice and stock, cover and simmer for 45 minutes or until the meat is tender. Mix the cornflour (cornstarch) to a paste with a little water, stir into the meat mixture and bring to the boil. Simmer for 2 to 3 minutes, stirring constantly. Add salt and pepper to taste and leave to cool.

Roll out the dough on a floured surface. Cut into 2 pieces and roll each piece into an oblong, one slightly larger than the other. Put the smallest oblong on a baking sheet and spread over the lamb mixture leaving a border around the edge. Brush the edge of dough with water, put the remaining dough over the top and press firmly to seal the edge. Use any trimmings to decorate and make diagonal slashes in the top of the pie.

To freeze: open (flash) freeze until firm, then wrap in a freezer bag or foil. Seal, label and return to freezer.

To thaw and serve: remove wrappings and place on a baking sheet. Brush with beaten egg and bake from frozen in a preheated moderately hot oven (200°C/400°F or Gas Mark 6) for 25 to 35 minutes or until heated through. Cover with foil if the pastry becomes too brown.

SERVES 4 to 6

AMERICAN LAMB CHOPS

METRIC/IMPERIAL

1 × 15 ml spoon/1 tablespoon olive oil
25 g/1 oz butter
1 large onion, peeled and sliced
1 garlic clove, peeled and crushed
8 lamb chops, trimmed of fat
300 ml/½ pint stock
2 × 15 ml spoons/2 tablespoons tomato purée
1 × 5 ml spoon/1 teaspoon dried thyme
1 × 5 ml spoon/1 teaspoon dried marjoram
salt
freshly ground black pepper
pinch of sugar
freshly chopped parsley, to garnish

AMERICAN

1 tablespoon olive oil
2 tablespoons butter
1 large onion, peeled and sliced
1 garlic clove, peeled and crushed
8 lamb chops, trimmed of fat
1¼ cups stock
2 tablespoons tomato paste
1 teaspoon dried thyme
1 teaspoon dried marjoram
salt
freshly ground black pepper
pinch of sugar
freshly chopped parsley, to garnish

Heat the oil and butter in a pan, add the onion and garlic and fry gently until soft. Add the chops, increase the heat and fry until golden brown on all sides. Add the remaining ingredients, except the parsley, and bring to the boil. Cover and simmer for 1½ hours, stirring occasionally.
To freeze: cool quickly, then transfer to a rigid container. Seal, label and freeze.
To thaw and serve: reheat from frozen on top of the stove for 30 to 40 minutes or until heated through, stirring occasionally. Sprinkle with parsley just before serving.
SERVES 4

CARAWAY LAMB

METRIC/IMPERIAL

225 g/½ lb cabbage, finely chopped
salt
40 g/1½ oz butter
1 onion, peeled and sliced
450 g/1 lb lean minced lamb
450 g/1 lb potatoes, peeled and thinly sliced
1 × 2.5 ml spoon/½ teaspoon caraway seeds
freshly ground black pepper
200 ml/⅓ pint stock

AMERICAN

3 cups finely chopped cabbage
salt
3 tablespoons butter
1 onion, peeled and sliced
2 cups lean ground lamb
1 lb potatoes, peeled and thinly sliced
½ teaspoon caraway seeds
freshly ground black pepper
⅞ cup stock

Plunge the cabbage into boiling salted water, boil for 2 minutes, then drain. Melt the butter in a pan, add the onion and lamb and fry gently for a few minutes, stirring constantly.
Arrange the potatoes, meat and cabbage in layers in a greased casserole dish or foil container, sprinkling with caraway seeds and salt and pepper between each layer. Finish with a layer of potatoes. Pour in the stock. Cover and cook in a preheated moderately hot oven (190°C/375°F or Gas Mark 5) for 1 hour. Remove the lid 15 minutes before the end of cooking.
To freeze: cool quickly, cover and wrap in a freezer bag or foil. Seal, label and freeze.
To thaw and serve: remove wrappings and thaw at room temperature for 4 hours. Reheat, covered, in a preheated moderate oven (180°C/350°F or Gas Mark 4) for 1 hour or until heated through.
SERVES 4

BIXLEY SPRING LAMB

METRIC/IMPERIAL

25 g/1 oz butter
4 lamb chops, trimmed of fat
1 large onion, peeled and finely chopped
25 g/1 oz flour
450 ml/¾ pint beef stock
2 × 15 ml spoons/2 tablespoons tomato purée
1 × 15 ml spoon/1 tablespoon prepared mustard
1 sprig of rosemary
salt
freshly ground black pepper

AMERICAN

2 tablespoons butter
4 lamb chops, trimmed of fat
1 large onion, peeled and finely chopped
¼ cup flour
2 cups beef stock
2 tablespoons tomato paste
1 tablespoon prepared mustard
1 sprig of rosemary
salt
freshly ground black pepper

Melt the butter in a flameproof casserole dish, add the chops and fry briskly until browned on both sides. Remove from the casserole. Add the onion and fry gently until soft. Stir in the flour and cook for 2 minutes, stirring constantly. Return the chops to the casserole, pour in the stock and stir in the remaining ingredients. Cover and cook in a preheated moderately hot oven (200°C/400°F or Gas Mark 6) for 30 minutes or until the chops are just tender. Remove the rosemary.
To freeze: cool quickly. Leave in the casserole or transfer to a rigid container. Cover, then wrap the casserole in a freezer bag or foil. Seal, label and freeze.
To thaw and serve: remove wrappings and thaw at room temperature for 4 hours. Reheat in the covered casserole in a preheated moderate oven (180°C/350°F or Gas Mark 4) for 1 hour or until heated through.
SERVES 4

FRENCH LAMB CUTLETS

METRIC/IMPERIAL
50 g/2 oz butter
8 lamb cutlets, trimmed of fat, boned and tied into noisettes
salt
freshly ground black pepper
2 medium onions, peeled and sliced
1 large green pepper, cored, seeded and sliced
225 g/½ lb tomatoes, peeled and sliced
100 g/4 oz mushrooms, sliced
3 × 15 ml spoons/3 tablespoons dry white wine
3 × 15 ml spoons/3 tablespoons stock
1 × 2.5 ml spoon/½ teaspoon dried mixed herbs

AMERICAN
¼ cup butter
8 lamb cutlets, trimmed of fat, boned and tied into noisettes
salt
freshly ground black pepper
2 medium onions, peeled and sliced
1 large green pepper, cored, seeded and sliced
1 cup peeled and sliced tomatoes
1 cup sliced mushrooms
3 tablespoons dry white wine
3 tablespoons stock
½ teaspoon dried mixed herbs

Melt the butter in a flameproof casserole dish, add the lamb and fry gently until browned on all sides. Sprinkle with salt and pepper to taste. Put the vegetables on top of the meat, pour over the wine and stock and sprinkle with the herbs. Cover and cook in a preheated moderate oven (180°C/350°F or Gas Mark 4) for 1¾ to 2 hours.
To freeze: cool quickly. Leave in the casserole or transfer to a rigid container. Cover, then wrap in a freezer bag or foil. Seal, label and freeze.
To thaw and serve: remove wrappings and thaw at room temperature for 4 hours. Reheat in the covered casserole in a preheated moderate oven for 1 hour or until heated through.
SERVES 4

ROAST LAMB WITH APRICOT AND NUT STUFFING

METRIC/IMPERIAL
1 kg/2 lb loin of lamb
40 g/1½ oz dripping, to finish
For the stuffing:
1 × 425 g/15 oz can apricots, drained and chopped
75 g/3 oz fresh breadcrumbs
50 g/2 oz walnuts, chopped
50 g/2 oz butter, softened
juice of 1 orange
juice of 1 lemon
salt
freshly ground black pepper
1 egg, beaten

AMERICAN
2 lb loin of lamb
3 tablespoons drippings, to finish
For the stuffing:
1 × 15 oz can apricots, drained and chopped
1½ cups fresh breadcrumbs
½ cup chopped walnuts
¼ cup butter, softened
juice of 1 orange
juice of 1 lemon
salt
freshly ground black pepper
1 egg, beaten

Combine all the ingredients for the stuffing, and moisten with a little juice from the apricots if the mixture seems dry. Spread the stuffing over the lamb, roll up and tie with string.
To freeze: wrap the lamb in a freezer bag, seal, label and freeze. Use within 1 month.
To thaw and serve: thaw in the refrigerator overnight, then put in a roasting tin and spread with the dripping. Cook in a preheated hot oven (220°C/425°F or Gas Mark 7) for 15 minutes, lower heat to moderately hot (190°C/375°F or Gas Mark 5) and cook for 1 to 1¼ hours.
SERVES 4

ARMENIAN LAMB WITH PILAFF

METRIC/IMPERIAL

1 × 15 ml spoon/1 tablespoon vegetable oil
2 large onions, peeled and chopped
675 g/1½ lb boneless shoulder of lamb, trimmed of fat and cut into cubes
150 ml/¼ pint beef stock
1 × 15 ml spoon/1 tablespoon tomato purée
1 × 15 ml spoon/1 tablespoon Worcestershire sauce
salt
freshly ground black pepper
2 × 5 ml spoons/2 teaspoons cornflour
1 × 15 ml spoon/1 tablespoon water
For the pilaff:
50 g/2 oz butter
1 onion, peeled and chopped
175 g/6 oz long-grain rice
600 ml/1 pint beef stock
50 g/2 oz frozen peas
50 g/2 oz seedless raisins
To finish:
50 g/2 oz shelled peanuts
25 g/1 oz butter

AMERICAN

1 tablespoon vegetable oil
2 large onions, peeled and chopped
1½ lb boneless shoulder of lamb, trimmed of fat and cut into cubes
⅔ cup beef stock
1 tablespoon tomato paste
1 tablespoon Worcestershire sauce
salt
freshly ground black pepper
2 teaspoons cornstarch
1 tablespoon water
For the pilaff:
¼ cup butter
1 onion, peeled and chopped
1 cup long-grain rice
2½ cups beef stock
⅓ cup frozen peas
⅓ cup seedless raisins
To finish:
⅓ cup shelled peanuts
2 tablespoons butter

Heat the oil in a pan, add the onions and fry gently for 5 minutes until soft. Add the lamb and fry briskly until browned on all sides. Stir in the stock and tomato purée (paste) and bring to boil. Add the Worcestershire sauce and salt and pepper to taste. Cover and cook gently for 45 minutes or until the meat is tender. Mix the cornflour (cornstarch) to a paste with the water, then stir into the lamb and cook for 3 minutes until thick, stirring constantly.

To make the pilaff: melt the butter in a pan, add the onion and fry for 5 minutes until soft. Stir in the rice and cook for 2 minutes, then add the stock and bring to the boil, stirring constantly. Simmer for 15 minutes uncovered. Add the peas and simmer for a further 10 minutes, adding a little more stock or water if necessary. Stir in the raisins and add salt and pepper to taste.
To freeze: cool the lamb and pilaff quickly. Pour the lamb into a rigid container, seal, label and freeze. Pack the pilaff in a freezer bag, seal, label and freeze. Squeeze the bag halfway through the freezing time to separate the grains.
To thaw and serve: thaw the lamb and pilaff at room temperature for 4 hours. Reheat the lamb gently on top of the stove, stirring occasionally. Transfer the pilaff to a shallow ovenproof dish, stir in the peanuts and dot with the butter. Cover and reheat in a preheated moderate oven (160°C/325°F or Gas Mark 3) for about 20 minutes or until heated through.
SERVES 4

MILD LAMB CURRY

METRIC/IMPERIAL

6 × 15 ml spoons/6 tablespoons vegetable oil
1 kg/2 lb onions, peeled and chopped
1.5 kg/3½ lb boneless lean shoulder of lamb, cut into cubes
50 g/2 oz flour
4 × 15 ml spoons/4 tablespoons curry powder
salt
1.5 litres/2½ pints chicken stock
To finish:
2 × 15 ml spoons/2 tablespoons mango chutney
2 bananas, peeled and sliced
50 g/2 oz sultanas
2 cooking apples, peeled, cored and chopped

AMERICAN

6 tablespoons vegetable oil
2 lb onions, peeled and chopped
3½ lb boneless lean shoulder of lamb, cut into cubes
½ cup flour
¼ cup curry powder
salt
6¼ cups chicken stock
To finish:
2 tablespoons mango chutney
2 bananas, peeled and sliced
⅓ cup seedless white raisins
2 baking apples, peeled, cored and chopped

Heat the oil in a pan, add the onions and fry gently until soft. Coat the meat in the flour, add to the pan and fry briskly until browned on all

sides. Stir in the curry powder and salt to taste and cook gently for 2 minutes. Stir in the stock, cover and cook gently for 1½ to 2 hours or until the meat is tender.
To freeze: cool quickly, then pour into a rigid container. Seal, label and freeze.
To thaw and serve: thaw at room temperature for 4 hours, then reheat gently on top of the stove, stirring occasionally. Add the chutney, bananas, sultanas (raisins) and apples.
SERVES 10

BARBECUED LAMB RIBS

METRIC/IMPERIAL
1 large best end of neck of lamb, cut into ribs with excess skin and fat removed
For the sauce:
1 × 15 ml spoon/1 tablespoon soy sauce
1 × 15 ml spoon/1 tablespoon clear honey
2 × 15 ml spoons/2 tablespoons fruit sauce
1 × 5 ml spoon/1 teaspoon malt vinegar
1 × 15 ml spoon/1 tablespoon Worcestershire sauce
1 × 2.5 ml spoon/½ teaspoon mustard powder
4 × 15 ml spoons/4 tablespoons tomato ketchup
4 × 15 ml spoons/4 tablespoons water
salt
freshly ground black pepper

AMERICAN
1 large rib roast of lamb, cut into ribs with excess skin and fat removed
For the sauce:
1 tablespoon soy sauce
1 tablespoon clear honey
2 tablespoons fruit sauce
1 teaspoon malt vinegar
1 tablespoon Worcestershire sauce
½ teaspoon mustard powder
¼ cup tomato ketchup
¼ cup water
salt
freshly ground black pepper

Put the lamb in a roasting tin and roast in a preheated moderately hot oven (200°C/400°F or Gas Mark 6) for 1 hour. Put all the ingredients for the sauce in a pan and simmer for 4 minutes, stirring constantly. Taste and adjust the seasoning if necessary. Pour the sauce over the meat and cook for a further 30 minutes.
To freeze: cool quickly, then transfer to a rigid container. Seal, label and freeze.
To thaw and serve: thaw at room temperature for 4 hours, then reheat in a preheated hot oven for 30 minutes or until heated through.
SERVES 4

LAMB AND PEPPER GOULASH

METRIC/IMPERIAL
3 × 15 ml spoons/3 tablespoons vegetable oil
1 large onion, peeled and sliced
2 green peppers, cored, seeded and chopped
1 large celery stalk, chopped
1 kg/2 lb boneless leg of lamb, cut into cubes
flour for coating
1 × 15 ml spoon/1 tablespoon paprika pepper
pinch of chilli powder
1 × 5 ml spoon/1 teaspoon sugar
1 bay leaf
salt
freshly ground black pepper
1 × 800 g/1 lb 12 oz can tomatoes
To serve:
150 ml/¼ pint soured cream
150 ml/¼ pint natural yogurt

AMERICAN
3 tablespoons vegetable oil
1 large onion, peeled and sliced
2 green peppers, cored, seeded and chopped
1 large celery stalk, chopped
2 lb boneless leg of lamb, cut into cubes
flour for coating
1 tablespoon paprika pepper
pinch of chili powder
1 teaspoon sugar
1 bay leaf
salt
freshly ground black pepper
1 × 1 lb 12 oz can tomatoes
To serve:
⅔ cup sour cream
⅔ cup unflavored yogurt

Heat the oil in a flameproof casserole dish, add the vegetables and fry gently until lightly browned, stirring occasionally. Remove from the casserole with a slotted spoon. Coat the lamb in flour, add to the pan and fry briskly until browned on all sides.
Return the vegetables to the casserole, then stir in the remaining ingredients. Cover and cook in a preheated moderate oven (180°C/350°F or Gas Mark 4) for about 1½ hours or until the meat is tender. Remove the bay leaf.
To freeze: cool quickly. Leave in the casserole or pour into a rigid container. Cover, then wrap in a freezer bag or foil. Seal, label and freeze.
To thaw and serve: remove wrappings and thaw at room temperature for 4 hours. Reheat in a preheated moderate oven for 1 hour or until heated through. Mix the sour(ed) cream and yogurt. Add to the goulash just before serving.
SERVES 4 to 6

CHICKEN AND HAM ROLL

METRIC/IMPERIAL

75 g/3 oz full fat cream cheese
100 g/4 oz cooked chicken meat, minced
50 g/2 oz cooked ham, minced
75 g/3 oz pineapple chunks, chopped
salt
freshly ground black pepper
basic puff pastry dough made with 225 g/½ lb flour
beaten egg, to glaze

AMERICAN

⅜ cup full fat cream cheese
½ cup ground cooked chicken meat
¼ cup ground cooked ham
⅓ cup pineapple chunks, chopped
salt
freshly ground black pepper
basic puff paste dough made with 2 cups flour
beaten egg, to glaze

Beat the cream cheese until smooth, then beat in the chicken, ham and pineapple. Add salt and pepper to taste.

Roll out the dough on a floured surface to an oblong 30 × 15 cm/12 × 6 inches. Put the mixture on the dough in a sausage shape, brush one of the long edges of the dough with egg and roll to enclose mixture, keeping the join underneath. Make diagonal cuts along the top of roll.

To freeze: open (flash) freeze until firm, then wrap in a freezer bag or foil. Seal, label and return to freezer.

To thaw and serve: remove wrappings and place on a baking sheet. Thaw at room temperature for 1 hour, then brush the top of dough with beaten egg. Bake in a preheated hot oven (230°C/450°F or Gas Mark 8) for 25 to 30 minutes or until heated through. Cover with foil if the pastry becomes too brown during cooking. Serve hot or cold.

SERVES 3 to 4

CHICKEN AND CHIPOLATA DRUMSTICKS

METRIC/IMPERIAL

8 pork chipolata sausages
8 chicken drumsticks, boned
1 × 15 ml spoon/1 tablespoon flour
salt
freshly ground black pepper
1 egg, beaten
1 × 15 ml spoon/1 tablespoon milk
approx 50 g/2 oz fresh white breadcrumbs
vegetable oil for frying

AMERICAN

8 pork link sausages
8 chicken drumsticks, boned
1 tablespoon flour
salt
freshly ground black pepper
1 egg, beaten
1 tablespoon milk
approx 1 cup fresh white breadcrumbs
vegetable oil for frying

Put one sausage inside each drumstick and reshape. Roll the stuffed drumsticks in flour seasoned with salt and pepper. Beat the egg and milk together and dip the drumsticks into the mixture, one at a time. Coat in the breadcrumbs. Repeat with more egg and breadcrumbs until the drumsticks are thoroughly coated. Fry in hot oil for 20 minutes until golden brown on all sides, turning frequently. Drain on paper towels.

To freeze: cool quickly. Open (flash) freeze until firm, then pack in a rigid container, separating each layer with foil. Seal, label and return to the freezer.

To thaw and serve: thaw at room temperature for 4 hours, then reheat in a preheated moderately hot oven (190°C/375°F or Gas Mark 5) for 30 minutes or until heated through.

MAKES 8

CHICKEN AND HAM PIE

METRIC/IMPERIAL

For the pastry:

350 g/¾ lb flour
pinch of salt
225 g/½ lb butter
approx 3 × 15 ml spoons/3 tablespoons water
milk, to glaze

For the filling:

1 cooked chicken leg, skinned, boned and cut into cubes
100 g/4 oz cooked ham, chopped
1 small onion, peeled and chopped
100 g/4 oz frozen sweetcorn, cooked and drained
salt
freshly ground black pepper
2 eggs, beaten

AMERICAN

For the pastry:

3 cups flour
pinch of salt
1 cup butter
approx 3 tablespoons water
milk, to glaze

For the filling:

1 cooked chicken leg, skinned, boned and cut into cubes
½ cup chopped cooked ham
1 small onion, peeled and chopped
¾ cup frozen corn kernels, cooked and drained
salt
freshly ground black pepper
2 eggs, beaten

To make the pastry: sift the flour and salt into a bowl. Add the butter in pieces and rub into the flour with the fingertips until the mixture resembles fine breadcrumbs. Stir in enough water to form a firm dough. Divide the dough in two. Roll out one half on a floured surface and use to line a 23 cm/9 in ovenproof or foil pie plate.

To make the filling: put all the ingredients in a bowl and stir well to mix. Spread over the dough-lined plate, leaving a small margin all round. Roll out the remaining dough to form a lid. Moisten the edges of the dough, place the lid on top of the filling and press firmly to seal together. Trim and flute the edge and use any trimmings to decorate the top of the pie. Cut an air vent in the centre.

To freeze: open (flash) freeze until firm, then wrap in foil or a freezer bag. Seal, label and return to the freezer.

To thaw and serve: remove wrappings, then thaw at room temperature for 4 hours. Brush the dough with milk and bake in a preheated moderately hot oven (190°C/375°F or Gas Mark 5) for 40 to 45 minutes. Cover with foil if the pastry becomes too brown.

SERVES 8

COQ AU VIN

METRIC/IMPERIAL

25 g/1 oz butter
1 × 15 ml spoon/1 tablespoon vegetable oil
4 chicken quarters, skinned
100 g/4 oz lean bacon, rinds removed and cut into thin strips
1 large onion, peeled and sliced
1 garlic clove, peeled and crushed
25 g/1 oz flour
300 ml/½ pint red wine
300 ml/½ pint chicken stock
salt
freshly ground black pepper
100 g/4 oz button mushrooms, sliced

AMERICAN

2 tablespoons butter
1 tablespoon vegetable oil
4 chicken quarters, skinned
¼ lb Canadian bacon, cut into thin strips
1 large onion, peeled and sliced
1 garlic clove, peeled and crushed
¼ cup flour
1¼ cups red wine
1¼ cups chicken stock
salt
freshly ground black pepper
1 cup sliced button mushrooms

Heat the butter and oil in a pan, add the chicken and fry until browned on all sides. Drain and transfer to a flameproof casserole dish. Add the bacon and onion to the pan, fry gently until lightly coloured, then transfer to the casserole. Add the garlic and flour to the pan and cook for 2 minutes, stirring constantly. Stir in the wine and stock, bring to the boil, then add salt and pepper to taste. Pour over the chicken, then cover and simmer for 45 minutes. Add the mushrooms to the casserole and cook for a further 15 minutes or until the chicken is tender.

To freeze: cool quickly. Leave in the casserole or transfer to a rigid container. Cover, then wrap the casserole in a freezer bag or foil. Seal, label and freeze.

To thaw and serve: remove wrappings and thaw at room temperature for 4 hours. Reheat in the covered casserole in a preheated moderate oven (180°C/350°F or Gas Mark 4) for 45 minutes or until heated through.

SERVES 4

SUMMER CHICKEN PIE

METRIC/IMPERIAL

For the filling:

1 × 1.5 kg/3½ lb roasting chicken
300 ml/½ pint water
2 × 15 ml spoons/2 tablespoons Worcestershire sauce
2 bay leaves
6 peppercorns
1 bouquet garni
1 onion, peeled and stuck with cloves
1 carrot, peeled and chopped
175 g/6 oz cooked ham, diced

For the pastry:

275 g/10 oz flour
pinch of salt
65 g/2½ oz butter
65 g/2½ oz lard
3–4 × 15 ml spoons/3–4 tablespoons water
milk or beaten egg, to glaze

AMERICAN

For the filling:

1 × 3½ lb roasting chicken
1¼ cups water
2 tablespoons Worcestershire sauce
2 bay leaves
6 peppercorns
1 bouquet garni
1 onion, peeled and stuck with cloves
1 carrot, peeled and chopped
¾ cup diced cooked ham

For the pastry:

2½ cups flour
pinch of salt
¼ cup plus 1 tablespoon butter
¼ cup plus 1 tablespoon shortening
3–4 tablespoons water
milk or beaten egg, to glaze

To make the filling: put the chicken in a large pan with all the other filling ingredients, except the ham. Bring to the boil, then cover and simmer gently for 50 minutes or until the chicken is tender. Strain and reserve the stock. Leave the chicken to cool, then remove the meat from the carcass and chop coarsely.

To make the pastry: sift the flour and salt into a bowl. Rub in the fats until the mixture resembles fine breadcrumbs, then add enough water to mix to a firm dough. Turn on to a floured surface and knead lightly until smooth. Cut off two-thirds of the dough and roll out to a 30 cm/12 inch circle. Use to line a 20 cm/8 inch loose-bottomed cake tin.

Put half the chicken in the bottom of the pie, add the ham and cover with the remaining chicken. Spoon over 3–4 × 15 ml spoons/3–4 tablespoons of the reserved stock. Roll out the reserved dough to a 20 cm/8 inch circle for the lid. Moisten the edges of the dough with water and cover the pie. Trim and seal the edges. Use any trimmings to decorate the top of the pie. Cut an air vent in the centre of the pie.

To freeze: open (flash) freeze until firm, then wrap in a freezer bag or foil. Seal label and return to the freezer.

To thaw and serve: remove wrappings and place on a baking sheet. Brush with milk or beaten egg and bake in a preheated moderately hot oven (200°C/400°F or Gas Mark 6) for 30 minutes, then reduce the heat to moderate (180°C/350°F or Gas Mark 4) and bake for a further 40 minutes. Cover with foil if the pastry becomes too brown. Serve hot or cold.

SERVES 6

CHICKEN PAPRIKA

METRIC/IMPERIAL

4 chicken quarters
1 onion, peeled and chopped
finely grated rind of 1 lemon
1 blade mace
6 peppercorns
1 fresh thyme sprig, or 0.5 × 2.5 ml spoon/ ¼ teaspoon dried thyme
few parsley stalks
salt
900 ml/1½ pints water

For the sauce:

75 g/3 oz butter
100 g/4 oz button mushrooms, sliced
25 g/1 oz flour
2 × 15 ml spoons/2 tablespoons paprika pepper
150 ml/¼ pint soured cream
freshly ground black pepper

AMERICAN

4 chicken quarters
1 onion, peeled and chopped
finely grated rind of 1 lemon
1 blade mace
6 peppercorns
1 fresh thyme sprig, or ¼ teaspoon dried thyme
few parsley stalks
salt
3¾ cups water

For the sauce:

⅜ cup butter
1 cup sliced button mushrooms
¼ cup flour
2 tablespoons paprika pepper
⅔ cup sour cream
freshly ground black pepper

Put the chicken, onion, lemon rind, mace, peppercorns, thyme, parsley and salt to taste in a pan. Cover with the water and bring to the boil. Cover and simmer for 1 to 1¼ hours.

Strain the chicken, reserving 600 ml/1 pint/ 2½ cups stock. Chill the stock in the refrigerator. Remove the skin and bones from the chicken and cut the meat into cubes.

To make the sauce: melt the butter in a pan, add the mushrooms and fry for a few minutes until soft. Remove from the pan. Stir in the flour and paprika, cook for 2 minutes, then remove from the heat. Skim off the excess fat from the reserved stock and gradually stir into the pan, beating well.

Return the pan to the heat, bring to the boil and simmer until the sauce thickens, stirring constantly. Add the chicken, mushrooms, sour(ed) cream and salt and pepper to taste. Do not allow to boil.

To freeze: cool quickly, then pour into a rigid container. Seal, label and freeze.

To thaw and serve: thaw at room temperature for 4 hours, then reheat gently on top of the stove, stirring occasionally. Do not allow to boil.

SERVES 4

CHICKEN AND WINE CASSEROLE

METRIC/IMPERIAL

25 g/1 oz butter
1 × 15 ml spoon/1 tablespoon vegetable oil
1 large onion, peeled and sliced
4 chicken quarters, skinned
50 g/2 oz flour
salt
freshly ground black pepper
300 ml/½ pint chicken stock
150 ml/¼ pint dry white wine
1 × 15 ml spoon/1 tablespoon Worcestershire sauce
finely grated rind and juice of 1 orange
50 g/2 oz sultanas

AMERICAN

2 tablespoons butter
1 tablespoon vegetable oil
1 large onion, peeled and sliced
4 chicken quarters, skinned
½ cup flour
salt
freshly ground black pepper
1¼ cups chicken stock
⅔ cup dry white wine
1 tablespoon Worcestershire sauce
finely grated rind and juice of 1 orange
⅓ cup seedless white raisins

Heat the butter and oil in a pan, add the onion and fry gently for 5 minutes until soft. Drain and transfer to a casserole dish. Coat the chicken in the flour seasoned with salt and pepper, add to the pan and fry gently until browned on all sides. Place in the casserole, pour in the stock, then add the remaining ingredients. Cover and cook in a preheated moderate oven (180°C/350°F or Gas Mark 4) for 1 hour or until the chicken is tender.

To freeze: cool quickly. Leave in the casserole or transfer to a rigid container. Cover, then wrap the casserole in a freezer bag or foil. Seal, label and freeze.

To thaw and serve: reheat from frozen in the covered casserole in a preheated hot oven (220°C/425°F or Gas Mark 7) for 45 minutes or until heated through.

SERVES 4

PIQUANT CHICKEN

METRIC/IMPERIAL

4 chicken quarters, skinned
1 large onion, peeled and sliced
1 × 400 g/14 oz can tomatoes
1 × 15 ml spoon/1 tablespoon paprika pepper
salt
freshly ground black pepper
150 ml/¼ pint natural yogurt, to finish

AMERICAN

4 chicken quarters, skinned
1 large onion, peeled and sliced
1 × 14 oz can tomatoes
1 tablespoon paprika pepper
salt
freshly ground black pepper
⅔ cup unflavored yogurt, to finish

Put the chicken, onion, tomatoes, paprika and salt and pepper to taste in a flameproof casserole dish and mix well together. Cover and cook for 50 minutes to 1 hour or until the chicken is tender.

To freeze: cool quickly. Leave in the casserole, or transfer to a rigid container. Cover, then wrap the casserole in a freezer bag or foil. Seal, label and freeze.

To thaw and serve: remove wrappings and thaw at room temperature for 4 hours. Reheat in the covered casserole in a preheated moderately hot oven (190°C/375°F or Gas Mark 5) for 45 minutes or until heated through. Stir in the yogurt and heat through, but do not allow to boil.

SERVES 4

DEVONSHIRE CHICKEN CASSEROLE

METRIC/IMPERIAL

2 × 15 ml spoons/2 tablespoons vegetable oil
4 chicken quarters, skinned
1 large onion, peeled and sliced
2 medium carrots, peeled and sliced
2 celery stalks, chopped
2 × 15 ml spoons/2 tablespoons flour
450 ml/¾ pint cider
2 × 15 ml spoons/2 tablespoons Worcestershire sauce
salt
freshly ground black pepper
100 g/4 oz frozen peas, to finish

AMERICAN

2 tablespoons vegetable oil
4 chicken quarters, skinned
1 large onion, peeled and sliced
2 medium carrots, peeled and sliced
2 celery stalks, chopped
2 tablespoons flour
2 cups hard cider
2 tablespoons Worcestershire sauce
salt
freshly ground black pepper
¾ cup frozen peas, to finish

Heat the oil in a pan, add the chicken and fry gently until browned on all sides. Drain and transfer to a casserole dish. Add the onion, carrots and celery to the pan and fry gently for 5 minutes until soft. Stir in the flour and cook for 2 minutes, stirring constantly, then stir in the cider, Worcestershire sauce and salt and pepper to taste. Bring to the boil, stirring constantly, then pour over the chicken in the casserole. Cover and cook in a preheated moderate oven (180°C/350°F or Gas Mark 4) for 1 hour or until the chicken is tender.

To freeze: cool quickly. Leave in the casserole or transfer to a rigid container. Cover, then wrap the casserole in a freezer bag or foil. Seal, label and freeze.

To thaw and serve: remove wrappings and thaw at room temperature for 4 hours. Reheat in the covered casserole in a preheated moderate oven (180°C/350°F or Gas Mark 4) for 45 minutes or until heated through. Stir in the peas 10 minutes before the end of the reheating time.

SERVES 4

TURKEY CHASSEUR

METRIC/IMPERIAL

25 g/1 oz butter
1 medium onion, peeled and chopped
1 garlic clove, peeled and crushed
100 g/4 oz mushrooms, sliced
2 × 15 ml spoons/2 tablespoons flour
2 × 15 ml spoons/2 tablespoons tomato purée
300 ml/½ pint turkey or chicken stock
1 × 2.5 ml spoon/½ teaspoon dried mixed herbs
salt
freshly ground black pepper
approx 350 g/¾ lb cooked turkey meat, sliced
To finish:
25 g/1 oz Cheddar cheese, grated
2 × 15 ml spoons/2 tablespoons fresh breadcrumbs

AMERICAN

2 tablespoons butter
1 medium onion, peeled and chopped
1 garlic clove, peeled and crushed
1 cup sliced mushrooms
2 tablespoons flour
2 tablespoons tomato paste
1¼ cups turkey or chicken stock
½ teaspoon dried mixed herbs
salt
freshly ground black pepper
approx 1½ cups sliced cooked turkey meat
To finish:
¼ cup grated Cheddar cheese
2 tablespoons fresh breadcrumbs

Melt the butter in a pan, add the onion and garlic and fry gently until soft. Add the mushrooms and fry gently for 5 to 6 minutes. Stir in the flour and cook for 1 minute, then add the tomato purée (paste) and stock. Bring to the boil, stirring constantly, then add the herbs and salt and pepper to taste and simmer for a few minutes.

Put the turkey in an ovenproof dish or foil container and pour over the sauce.

To freeze: cool quickly. Cover, then wrap in a freezer bag or foil. Seal, label and freeze.

To thaw and serve: remove wrappings and reheat from frozen in a covered dish in a preheated moderate oven (180°C/350°F or Gas Mark 4) for 1½ hours or until heated through. Sprinkle the cheese and breadcrumbs over the top and grill (broil) until brown.

SERVES 4

CHEESE AND CHICKEN CROQUETTES

METRIC/IMPERIAL

75 g/3 oz butter
65 g/2½ oz flour
300 ml/½ pint milk
100 g/4 oz Gouda cheese, grated
100 g/4 oz cooked chicken meat, chopped
1 × 15 ml spoon/1 tablespoon freshly chopped parsley or snipped chives
1 × 5 ml spoon/1 teaspoon Worcestershire sauce
salt
freshly ground black pepper
2 egg yolks
For the coating:
2 egg whites, lightly beaten
dried breadcrumbs
oil for deep-frying

AMERICAN

⅜ cup butter
½ cup plus 2 tablespoons flour
1¼ cups milk
1 cup grated Gouda cheese
½ cup chopped cooked chicken meat
1 tablespoon freshly chopped parsley or snipped chives
1 teaspoon Worcestershire sauce
salt
freshly ground black pepper
2 egg yolks
For the coating:
2 egg whites, lightly beaten
dried breadcrumbs
oil for deep-frying

Put the butter, flour and milk in a pan and whisk over a moderate heat until the sauce boils. Stir in the cheese, chicken, parsley or chives, Worcestershire sauce and salt and pepper to taste, then remove from the heat and leave to cool slightly. Beat in the egg yolks, then chill in the refrigerator overnight.
Divide the mixture into 12 equal portions, then shape into croquettes. Dip into the egg whites one at a time, then coat with breadcrumbs. Repeat with more egg white and breadcrumbs until thoroughly coated.
To freeze: open (flash) freeze until firm, then pack in a rigid container, separating the layers with foil. Seal, label and return to the freezer.
To thaw and serve: thaw in the refrigerator for 2 hours then deep-fry in hot oil for a few minutes until golden brown. Drain on paper towels. Serve with tomato sauce.
MAKES 12

TURKEY AND TOMATO CASSEROLE

METRIC/IMPERIAL

2 turkey legs, skinned and boned
2 × 15 ml spoons/2 tablespoons vegetable oil
1 large onion, peeled and chopped
3 bacon rashers, rinds removed and chopped
100 g/4 oz mushrooms, sliced
150 ml/¼ pint turkey or chicken stock
150 ml/¼ pint red wine
1 × 400 g/14 oz can tomatoes
1 × 2.5 ml spoon/½ teaspoon dried mixed herbs
2 celery stalks, chopped
salt
freshly ground black pepper

AMERICAN

2 turkey legs, skinned and boned
2 tablespoons vegetable oil
1 large onion, peeled and chopped
3 bacon slices, chopped
1 cup sliced mushrooms
⅔ cup turkey or chicken stock
⅔ cup red wine
1 × 14 oz can tomatoes
½ teaspoon dried mixed herbs
2 celery stalks, chopped
salt
freshly ground black pepper

Cut the turkey meat into bite-sized pieces. Heat the oil in a pan, add the turkey and fry gently until browned on all sides. Transfer to a casserole dish. Add the onion, bacon and mushrooms to the pan, fry for a few minutes, then transfer to the casserole.
Stir in the remaining ingredients, cover and cook in a preheated moderate oven (180°C/350°F or Gas Mark 4) for 1¼ hours or until the meat is tender.
To freeze: cool quickly. Leave in the casserole or pour into a rigid container. Cover, then wrap the casserole in a freezer bag or foil. Seal, label and freeze.
To thaw and serve: remove wrappings and thaw at room temperature for 4 hours. Reheat in a preheated moderate oven (180°C/350°F or Gas Mark 4) for 1 hour or until heated through.
SERVES 4

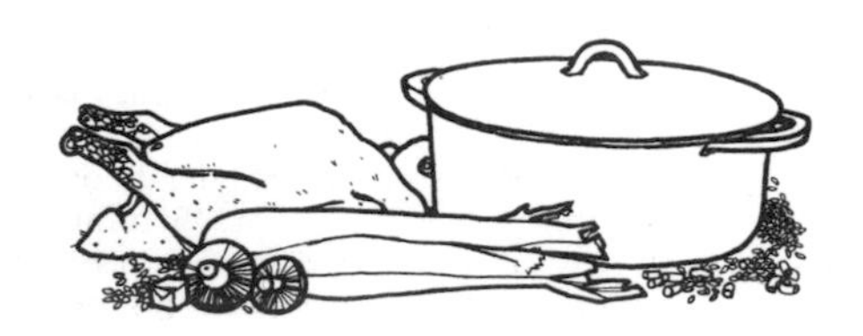

TURKEY TRANCHE

METRIC/IMPERIAL

basic shortcrust pastry dough made with 225 g/½ lb flour
50 g/2 oz butter
1 onion, peeled and chopped
50 g/2 oz mushrooms, sliced
225 g/½ lb streaky bacon, rinds removed and chopped
450 g/1 lb turkey meat, cut into cubes
pinch of dried mixed herbs
2 × 5 ml spoons/2 teaspoons freshly chopped parsley
2 × 5 ml spoons/2 teaspoons cornflour
150 ml/¼ pint water
salt
freshly ground black pepper
juice of ½ lemon
a little milk, to glaze

AMERICAN

basic pie dough made with 2 cups flour
¼ cup butter
1 onion, peeled and chopped
½ cup sliced mushrooms
½ lb fatty bacon, chopped
1 lb turkey meat, cut into cubes
pinch of dried mixed herbs
2 teaspoons freshly chopped parsley
2 teaspoons cornstarch
⅔ cup water
salt
freshly ground black pepper
juice of ½ lemon
a little milk, to glaze

Grease a 450 g/1 lb loaf tin and line with foil. Roll out two-thirds of the dough on a floured surface and use to line the base and sides of the prepared tin. Melt the butter in a pan, add the onion and fry gently until soft. Add the mushrooms, bacon, turkey and herbs. Mix the cornflour (cornstarch) and water together and stir into the pan. Cook until thick, stirring constantly. Add salt and pepper to taste and the lemon juice, then pour into the loaf tin. Roll out the remaining dough to form a lid. Moisten the edges of dough with water and cover the pie with the lid. Trim and seal the edges and cut an air vent.
To freeze: open (flash) freeze until firm, then remove the loaf from the tin. Wrap in a freezer bag, seal, label and return to freezer.
To thaw and serve: remove wrappings and replace the loaf in the tin. Brush the top of the pie with milk and reheat from frozen in a preheated moderately hot oven (200°C/400°F or Gas Mark 6) for 50 minutes to 1 hour. Cover with foil if the pastry becomes too brown.
SERVES 6 to 8

SPICED TURKEY PIES

METRIC/IMPERIAL

50 g/2 oz butter
25 g/1 oz flour
1 × 15 ml spoon/1 tablespoon mild curry powder
300 ml/½ pint turkey stock
150 ml/¼ pint milk
350 g/¾ lb cooked turkey meat, chopped
few pieces leftover stuffing (optional)
2 × 15 ml spoons/2 tablespoons finely chopped sweet chutney or pickle
1 × 15 ml spoon/1 tablespoon lemon juice
2 × 15 ml spoons/2 tablespoons double cream (optional)
salt
freshly ground black pepper
basic shortcrust pastry dough made with 350 g/¾ lb flour
beaten egg, to glaze

AMERICAN

¼ cup butter
¼ cup flour
1 tablespoon mild curry powder
1¼ cups turkey stock
⅔ cup milk
1½ cups chopped cooked turkey meat
few pieces leftover stuffing (optional)
2 tablespoons finely chopped sweet chutney or pickle
1 tablespoon lemon juice
2 tablespoons heavy cream (optional)
salt
freshly ground black pepper
basic pie dough made with 3 cups flour
beaten egg, to glaze

Melt the butter in a pan, add the flour and curry powder and cook for 2 minutes, stirring constantly. Remove from heat and gradually stir in the stock and milk, then return to the heat. Bring to the boil and simmer until the sauce thickens, stirring constantly. Remove pan from the heat, add the turkey, stuffing (if using), chutney or pickle, lemon juice, cream (if using) and salt and pepper to taste. Divide the mixture between 4 individual deep ovenproof dishes. Leave to cool.
Roll out the dough on a floured surface and cut out 4 pieces to cover the tops of the dishes. Cut some small strips of dough from the trimmings. Moisten the rims of the dishes with water and place the strips of dough around them. Brush the strips with beaten egg, then place the dough lids on top. Trim and flute the edges and press down firmly to seal. Use any trimmings to decorate the tops of the pies.
To freeze: open (flash) freeze, then pack in a freezer bag. Seal, label and return to freezer.

To thaw and serve: remove wrappings and place on a baking sheet. Brush with beaten egg and bake from frozen in a preheated hot oven (220°C/425°F or Gas Mark 7) for 15 minutes, then reduce heat to moderately hot (200°C/400°F or Gas Mark 6) and bake for a further 15 minutes until golden.
SERVES 4

SIMLA CHICKEN

METRIC/IMPERIAL
3 × 15 ml spoons/3 tablespoons vegetable oil
1 large onion, peeled and chopped
1 small garlic clove, peeled and crushed
1 × 5 ml spoon/1 teaspoon ground turmeric
0.5 × 2.5 ml spoon/¼ teaspoon ground ginger
0.5 × 2.5 ml spoon/¼ teaspoon crushed cardamoms
0.5 × 2.5 ml spoon/¼ teaspoon ground cinnamon
4 chicken quarters, skinned
1 × 15 ml spoon/1 tablespoon honey
2 × 15 ml spoons/2 tablespoons water
salt
freshly ground black pepper

AMERICAN
3 tablespoons vegetable oil
1 large onion, peeled and chopped
1 small garlic clove, peeled and crushed
1 teaspoon ground turmeric
¼ teaspoon ground ginger
¼ teaspoon crushed cardamoms
¼ teaspoon ground cinnamon
4 chicken quarters, skinned
1 tablespoon honey
2 tablespoons water
salt
freshly ground black pepper

Heat the oil in a pan, add the onion, garlic and spices and fry gently for 1 minute. Add the chicken and fry for 1 minute on each side. Stir in the honey and water and add salt and pepper to taste. Cover tightly and simmer for 40 minutes or until the chicken is tender.
To freeze: cool quickly, then transfer to a rigid container. Seal, label and freeze.
To thaw and serve: thaw at room temperature for 4 hours, then reheat gently on top of the stove, stirring occasionally.
SERVES 4

SPANISH CHICKEN

METRIC/IMPERIAL
25 g/1 oz butter
4 chicken quarters, skinned
12 small pickling onions, peeled
100 g/4 oz streaky bacon rashers, rinds removed and cut into strips
25 g/1 oz flour
150 ml/¼ pint dry white wine
150 ml/¼ pint stock or water
salt
freshly ground black pepper
To finish:
12 stuffed green olives
few fried bread croûtes
freshly chopped parsley

AMERICAN
2 tablespoons butter
4 chicken quarters, skinned
12 baby onions, peeled
¼ lb fatty bacon slices, cut into strips
¼ cup flour
⅔ cup dry white wine
⅔ cup stock or water
salt
freshly ground black pepper
To finish:
12 stuffed green olives
few fried bread croûtes
freshly chopped parsley

Melt the butter in a pan, add the chicken and fry until browned all over. Transfer to a casserole dish. Add the onions and bacon to the pan, fry until browned, then transfer to the casserole. Stir the flour into the butter remaining in the pan and cook for 2 minutes. Add the wine, stock or water and salt and pepper to taste and bring to the boil, stirring. Pour over the chicken and cook in a preheated moderate oven (180°C/350°F or Gas Mark 4) for 1 hour or until the chicken is tender.
To freeze: cool quickly. Leave in the casserole or transfer to a rigid container. Cover, then wrap the casserole in a freezer bag or foil. Seal, label and freeze.
To thaw and serve: remove wrappings and thaw in the refrigerator overnight. Reheat in the covered casserole in a preheated moderately hot oven (190°C/375°F or Gas Mark 5) for 45 minutes, or until heated through. Stir in the olives, sprinkle with parsley and garnish with croûtes just before serving.
SERVES 4

TANDOORI CHICKEN

METRIC/IMPERIAL

2 small pieces fresh root ginger, peeled and chopped
3 garlic cloves, peeled and chopped
3 black peppercorns
1 × 5 ml spoon/1 teaspoon chilli powder
2 × 5 ml spoons/2 teaspoons ground coriander
2 × 5 ml spoons/2 teaspoons ground cumin
1 × 5 ml spoon/1 teaspoon salt
finely grated rind and juice of 1 lemon
1–2 drops bright red food colouring
10 chicken breasts or drumsticks, skinned
150 ml/¼ pint natural yogurt
To serve:
1–2 lettuces, washed and separated into leaves
3 tomatoes, quartered
1 cucumber, sliced
salt
freshly ground black pepper

AMERICAN

2 small pieces fresh ginger root, peeled and chopped
3 garlic cloves, peeled and chopped
3 black peppercorns
1 teaspoon chili powder
2 teaspoons ground coriander
2 teaspoons ground cumin
1 teaspoon salt
finely grated rind and juice of 1 lemon
1–2 drops bright red food coloring
10 chicken breasts or drumsticks, skinned
⅔ cup unflavored yogurt
To serve:
1–2 heads lettuce, washed and separated into leaves
3 tomatoes, quartered
1 cucumber, sliced
salt
freshly ground black pepper

Pound the ginger, garlic and peppercorns in a mortar and pestle. Mix with the chilli powder, coriander, cumin, salt, lemon rind and juice and the food colouring.

Score the chicken flesh with the point of a very sharp knife, then rub in the pounded mixture. Brush each chicken portion with 1 × 15 ml spoon/1 tablespoon yogurt and chill in the refrigerator for 24 hours.

Let the chicken stand at room temperature for 1 to 2 hours, then place in a roasting tin and cook in a preheated moderately hot oven (200°C/400°F or Gas Mark 6) for 50 minutes to 1 hour or until the outside of the chicken is charred and the meat is cooked through, turning the portions frequently during cooking.

To freeze: cool quickly, then pack into a rigid container. Seal, label and freeze.

To thaw and serve: thaw at room temperature for 4 hours, then place in a roasting tin and reheat in a preheated moderate oven (180°C/350°F or Gas Mark 4) for 1 hour or until heated through. Serve on a bed of lettuce, tomatoes and cucumber, seasoned liberally with salt and pepper.

SERVES 10

CHICKEN WITH LEMON AND TARRAGON

METRIC/IMPERIAL

25 g/1 oz butter
4 chicken quarters, skinned
1 onion, peeled and chopped
25 g/1 oz flour
450 ml/¾ pint chicken stock
1 × 5 ml spoon/1 teaspoon dried tarragon
juice of 1 lemon
1 × 225 g/8 oz can butter beans, drained
2 × 15 ml spoons/2 tablespoons double cream
salt
freshly ground black pepper

AMERICAN

2 tablespoons butter
4 chicken quarters, skinned
1 onion, peeled and chopped
¼ cup flour
2 cups chicken stock
1 teaspoon dried tarragon
juice of 1 lemon
1 × 8 oz can butter beans, drained
2 tablespoons heavy cream
salt
freshly ground black pepper

Melt the butter in a pan, add the chicken and fry gently for 10 minutes, turning once. Remove from the pan with a slotted spoon and transfer to a casserole dish. Add the onion to the pan and fry gently for 5 minutes. Remove the pan from the heat, stir in the flour and blend in the stock. Add the tarragon and lemon juice and return the pan to the heat. Bring to the boil, stirring constantly, then pour over the chicken. Cover and cook in a preheated moderately hot oven (190°C/375°F or Gas Mark 5) for 50 minutes or until the chicken is tender. Stir in the butter beans, cream and salt and pepper to taste.

To freeze: cool quickly. Leave in the casserole, or transfer to a rigid container. Cover, then wrap the casserole in foil. Seal, label and freeze.

To thaw and serve: remove wrappings, then thaw at room temperature for 4 hours. Reheat in the covered casserole in a preheated moderate oven (180°C/350°F or Gas Mark 4) for 1 hour.

SERVES 4

CHICKEN PIE

METRIC/IMPERIAL

20 g/¾ oz butter
1 medium onion, peeled and chopped
1 medium green pepper, cored, seeded and cut into strips
50 g/2 oz button mushrooms, halved
20 g/¾ oz flour
150 ml/¼ pint dry white wine or dry cider
150 ml/¼ pint milk
pinch of dried thyme
salt
freshly ground black pepper
450 g/1 lb cooked chicken meat, diced
basic flaky or puff pastry dough made with 225 g/½ lb flour
beaten egg, to glaze

AMERICAN

1½ tablespoons butter
1 medium onion, peeled and chopped
1 medium green pepper, cored, seeded and cut into strips
½ cup halved button mushrooms
3 tablespoons flour
⅔ cup dry white wine or hard cider
⅔ cup milk
pinch of dried thyme
salt
freshly ground black pepper
2 cups diced cooked chicken meat
basic flaky or puff paste dough made with 2 cups flour
beaten egg, to glaze

Melt the butter in a pan, add the onion, pepper and mushrooms and fry gently until soft. Stir in the flour and cook for 1 minute. Remove from the heat and gradually stir in the wine or cider and milk. Return to the heat and bring to the boil, stirring constantly. Simmer for 1 minute. Add thyme, salt, pepper and chicken. Turn into a pie dish. Leave to cool.
Roll out the dough on a floured surface to a shape slightly larger than the pie dish. Cut out a lid to fit the dish and a narrow strip of dough to fit the rim of the dish. Moisten the rim with water and press on the strip of dough. Moisten the strip with water and place the lid on the dish. Press firmly to seal then flute the edge. Use any trimmings to decorate the top of the pie. Cut an air vent in the centre.
To freeze: open (flash) freeze until firm, then wrap in a freezer bag or foil. Seal, label and return to the freezer.
To thaw and serve: remove wrappings and thaw in the refrigerator for 12 hours. Place on a baking sheet, brush the dough with beaten egg. Bake in a preheated hot oven (220°C/425°F or Gas Mark 7) for 15 minutes, then reduce the heat to moderate (180°C/350°F or Gas Mark 4) and bake for a further 20 to 30 minutes. Cover with foil if the pastry becomes too brown.
SERVES 4

CHICKEN IN CIDER

METRIC/IMPERIAL

4–6 chicken quarters, skinned
flour for coating
salt
freshly ground black pepper
75 g/3 oz butter
12 small pickling onions, peeled
300 ml/½ pint cider
1 bouquet garni
100 g/4 oz button mushrooms, sliced

AMERICAN

4–6 chicken quarters, skinned
flour for coating
salt
freshly ground black pepper
⅜ cup butter
12 baby onions, peeled
1¼ cups hard cider
1 bouquet garni
1 cup sliced button mushrooms

Coat the chicken in flour seasoned with salt and pepper. Melt 50 g/2 oz/¼ cup butter in a flameproof casserole dish, add the chicken and fry until browned on all sides. Remove from the casserole and drain on paper towels.
Add the onions to the casserole and fry until browned. Return the chicken to the casserole, pour in the cider and add the bouquet garni and salt and pepper to taste. Cover and cook in a preheated moderately hot oven (190°C/375°F or Gas Mark 5) for 40 minutes.
Melt the remaining butter in a pan, add the mushrooms and fry for 1 minute. Stir into the casserole and cook for a further 10 minutes or until the chicken is tender. Remove the bouquet garni.
To freeze: cool quickly. Leave in the casserole or transfer to a rigid container. Cover, then wrap the casserole in a freezer bag or foil. Seal, label and freeze.
To thaw and serve: remove wrappings, then thaw in the refrigerator overnight. Reheat in the covered casserole in a preheated moderately hot oven (190°C/375°F or Gas Mark 5) for 45 minutes or until heated through.
SERVES 4 to 6

CURRIED CHICKEN WITH PINEAPPLE

METRIC/IMPERIAL
50 g/2 oz butter
2 × 15 ml spoons/2 tablespoons vegetable oil
4 chicken quarters, skinned
2 onions, peeled and sliced
1 garlic clove, peeled and crushed
25 g/1 oz flour
1 × 15 ml spoon/1 tablespoon curry powder
1 × 2.5 ml spoon/½ teaspoon ground ginger
1 × 2.5 ml spoon/½ teaspoon ground coriander
300 ml/½ pint chicken stock
1 × 2.5 ml spoon/½ teaspoon salt
1 × 15 ml spoon/1 tablespoon mango chutney
1 × 200 g/7 oz can pineapple pieces, drained
1 × 15 ml spoon/1 tablespoon vinegar

AMERICAN
¼ cup butter
2 tablespoons vegetable oil
4 chicken quarters, skinned
2 onions, peeled and sliced
1 garlic clove, peeled and crushed
¼ cup flour
1 tablespoon curry powder
½ teaspoon ground ginger
½ teaspoon ground coriander
1¼ cups chicken stock
½ teaspoon salt
1 tablespoon mango chutney
1 × 7 oz can pineapple pieces, drained
1 tablespoon vinegar

Heat the butter and oil in a pan, add the chicken and fry until browned on all sides. Remove from the pan with a slotted spoon and drain on paper towels.
Add the onions and garlic to the pan and fry until soft. Stir in the flour, curry powder, ginger and coriander and cook for 1 minute, stirring constantly. Stir in the chicken stock, bring to the boil and simmer until the sauce thickens. Add the salt and mango chutney and return the chicken to the pan. Cover and simmer for 40 minutes or until the chicken is tender. Stir in the pineapple pieces and the vinegar.
To freeze: cool quickly, then transfer to a rigid container. Seal, label and freeze.
To thaw and serve: reheat from frozen in a covered casserole in a preheated moderate oven (160°C/325°F or Gas Mark 3) for 40 minutes to 1 hour or until heated through.
SERVES 4

MANGO CHICKEN

METRIC/IMPERIAL
25 g/1 oz butter
4 chicken quarters, skinned
1 large onion, peeled and sliced
1 garlic clove, peeled and crushed
25 g/1 oz flour
1 × 15 ml spoon/1 tablespoon curry powder
2 × 5 ml spoons/2 teaspoons tomato purée
2 × 15 ml spoons/2 tablespoons mango chutney
juice of ½ lemon
300 ml/½ pint chicken stock
salt
freshly ground black pepper
1 × 100 g/4 oz packet frozen mixed vegetables

AMERICAN
2 tablespoons butter
4 chicken quarters, skinned
1 large onion, peeled and sliced
1 garlic clove, peeled and crushed
¼ cup flour
1 tablespoon curry powder
2 teaspoons tomato paste
2 tablespoons mango chutney
juice of ½ lemon
1¼ cups chicken stock
salt
freshly ground black pepper
1 × ¼ lb package frozen mixed vegetables

Melt the butter in a flameproof casserole dish, add the chicken and fry until browned on all sides. Remove from the casserole with a slotted spoon and drain on paper towels.
Add the onion and garlic to the casserole and fry gently until soft. Stir in the flour and curry powder and cook for 1 minute. Stir in the remaining ingredients, except the mixed vegetables, and cook until thick and smooth, stirring constantly.
Return the chicken to the casserole, cover and cook in a preheated moderate oven (180°C/350°F or Gas Mark 4) for 45 minutes. Stir in the mixed vegetables and cook for a further 15 minutes or until the chicken is tender.
To freeze: cool quickly. Leave in the casserole or transfer to a rigid container. Cover, then wrap the casserole in a freezer bag or foil. Seal, label and freeze.
To thaw and serve: remove wrappings, then reheat from frozen on top of the stove, stirring occasionally.
SERVES 4

GINGER CHICKEN WITH ALMONDS

METRIC/IMPERIAL

25 g/1 oz butter
1 × 15 ml spoon/1 tablespoon vegetable oil
4 chicken quarters, skinned
salt
freshly ground black pepper
1 medium onion, peeled and chopped
300 ml/½ pint chicken stock
1 × 5 ml spoon/1 teaspoon grated nutmeg
50 g/2 oz preserved ginger, chopped
100 g/4 oz button mushrooms, sliced
2 × 15 ml spoons/2 tablespoons cornflour
4 × 15 ml spoons/4 tablespoons water
To finish:
150 ml/¼ pint natural yogurt
50 g/2 oz slivered, blanched almonds

AMERICAN

2 tablespoons butter
1 tablespoon vegetable oil
4 chicken quarters, skinned
salt
freshly ground black pepper
1 medium onion, peeled and chopped
1¼ cups chicken stock
1 teaspoon grated nutmeg
¼ cup chopped, preserved stem ginger
1 cup sliced button mushrooms
2 tablespoons cornstarch
¼ cup water
To finish:
⅔ cup unflavored yogurt
½ cup slivered, blanched almonds

Heat the butter and oil in a pan. Sprinkle the chicken liberally with salt and pepper, add to the pan and fry for 5 minutes on each side. Remove from the pan.

Add the onion to the pan and fry gently for 3 minutes. Stir in the stock, nutmeg and ginger and bring to the boil, stirring constantly. Return the chicken to the pan, cover and simmer for 30 minutes. Add the mushrooms and cook for a further 10 minutes, or until the chicken is tender. Remove the chicken from pan and set aside to cool.

Mix the cornflour (cornstarch) and water to a paste and stir into the pan. Bring to the boil, stirring constantly, then simmer until the sauce thickens.

To freeze: cool quickly. Put the chicken in a rigid container and pour over the sauce. Seal, label and freeze.

To thaw and serve: thaw at room temperature for 4 hours, then reheat gently on top of the stove, stirring occasionally. Stir in the yogurt and heat through, but do not allow to boil. Transfer the chicken and sauce to a warmed serving dish and sprinkle with the almonds.

SERVES 4

CHICKEN AND SWEETCORN PIE

METRIC/IMPERIAL

25 g/1 oz butter
1 onion, peeled and chopped
50 g/2 oz mushrooms, sliced
25 g/1 oz flour
450 ml/¾ pint chicken stock
450 g/1 lb chicken meat, diced
1 × 200 g/7 oz can sweetcorn, drained
basic shortcrust pastry dough made with 225 g/½ lb flour
beaten egg, to glaze

AMERICAN

2 tablespoons butter
1 onion, peeled and chopped
½ cup sliced mushrooms
¼ cup flour
2 cups chicken stock
2 cups diced chicken meat
1 × 7 oz can corn kernels, drained
basic pie dough made with 2 cups flour
beaten egg, to glaze

Melt the butter in a pan, add the onion and mushrooms and fry gently for 1 minute. Stir in the flour, and cook for 2 minutes, then gradually stir in the stock. Bring to the boil and simmer until thick, stirring constantly. Add chicken and corn to the sauce. Pour into a 900 ml/1½ pint/3¾ cup pie dish. Leave to cool. Roll out the dough on a floured surface to a shape slightly larger than the pie dish. Cut out a lid to fit the dish and a narrow strip of dough to fit the rim of the dish. Moisten the rim with water and press on the strip of dough. Moisten the strip with water and place the lid on the dish. Press firmly to seal, then flute the edge. Use any trimmings to decorate the top of the pie. Cut an air vent in the centre.

To freeze: open (flash) freeze until firm, then wrap in a freezer bag or foil. Seal, label and return to the freezer.

To thaw and serve: remove wrappings and place on a baking sheet. Brush the dough with beaten egg and bake from frozen in a preheated moderately hot oven (200°C/400°F or Gas Mark 6) for 1¼ hours or until heated through. Cover with foil if the pastry becomes too brown.

SERVES 4

CHICKEN AND HAM LOAF

METRIC/IMPERIAL

350 g/¾ lb minced chicken meat
350 g/¾ lb minced ham, bacon or gammon
1 onion, peeled and finely chopped
1 small green pepper, cored, seeded and finely chopped
2 celery stalks, finely chopped
75 g/3 oz fresh white breadcrumbs
salt
freshly ground black pepper
2 eggs, beaten

AMERICAN

1½ cups ground chicken meat
1½ cups ground ham or bacon
1 onion, peeled and finely chopped
1 small green pepper, cored, seeded and finely chopped
2 celery stalks, finely chopped
1½ cups fresh white breadcrumbs
salt
freshly ground black pepper
2 eggs, beaten

Grease a 450 g/1 lb loaf tin.
Put all the ingredients in a bowl and stir well to mix. Press the mixture lightly into the prepared loaf tin, cover with foil and bake in a preheated moderate oven (180°C/350°F or Gas Mark 4) for 1 hour or until set. Remove the foil.
To freeze: cool quickly, chill in the refrigerator, then turn out. Wrap in foil, seal, label and freeze.
To thaw and serve: thaw in the refrigerator for about 6 hours or overnight.
SERVES 8

CHICKEN WITH CASHEW NUTS

METRIC/IMPERIAL

2 × 15 ml spoons/2 tablespoons vegetable oil
100 g/4 oz cashew nuts
1 large onion, peeled and chopped
1 slice fresh root ginger, chopped
350 g/¾ lb boned chicken breast, cut into thin strips
2 × 5 ml spoons/2 teaspoons cornflour
4 × 15 ml spoons/4 tablespoons chicken stock
1 × 15 ml spoon/1 tablespoon soy sauce
1 × 15 ml spoon/1 tablespoon honey
salt
freshly ground black pepper
225 g/½ lb bean sprouts, to finish

AMERICAN

2 tablespoons vegetable oil
1 cup cashew nuts
1 large onion, peeled and chopped
1 slice fresh ginger root, chopped
¾ lb boned chicken breast, cut into thin strips
2 teaspoons cornstarch
¼ cup chicken stock
1 tablespoon soy sauce
1 tablespoon honey
salt
freshly ground black pepper
½ lb bean sprouts, to finish

Heat half the oil in a pan, add the nuts and fry until golden brown. Remove from the pan, add the remaining oil and the onion and ginger and fry for 1 minute. Add the chicken and fry for 1 minute, stirring. Mix the cornflour (cornstarch) with the stock and stir into the pan with the soy sauce and honey. Cook for 1 to 2 minutes. Return the nuts to pan and add salt and pepper.
To freeze: cool quickly, then pour into a rigid container. Seal, label and freeze.
To thaw and serve: thaw at room temperature for 4 hours, then reheat gently on top of the stove, stirring occasionally. Stir in the bean sprouts and heat through.
SERVES 4

DEVILLED CHICKEN

METRIC/IMPERIAL

3 × 15 ml spoons/3 tablespoons chutney, chopped
1 × 15 ml spoon/1 tablespoon mustard powder
2 × 5 ml spoons/2 teaspoons Worcestershire sauce
1 × 15 ml spoon/1 tablespoon tomato ketchup
50 g/2 oz fresh white breadcrumbs
1 × 2.5 ml spoon/½ teaspoon ground mixed spice
0.5 × 2.5 ml spoon/¼ teaspoon cayenne pepper
1 × 2.5 ml spoon/½ teaspoon salt
8 chicken quarters, skinned
50 g/2 oz butter, melted
50 g/2 oz dried breadcrumbs

AMERICAN

3 tablespoons chutney, chopped
1 tablespoon mustard powder
2 teaspoons Worcestershire sauce
1 tablespoon tomato ketchup
1 cup fresh white breadcrumbs
½ teaspoon ground mixed spice
¼ teaspoon cayenne pepper
½ teaspoon salt
8 chicken quarters, skinned
¼ cup butter, melted
½ cup dried breadcrumbs

Put the chutney, mustard, Worcestershire sauce, tomato ketchup, fresh breadcrumbs, spice, cayenne and salt in a bowl and stir well to mix. Make 3 to 4 deep cuts in the flesh on each piece of chicken and fill each cut with a little of the mixture. Cover and leave in a cool place for at least 1 hour.
Put the chicken in a roasting tin, pour over the melted butter and sprinkle with the dried bread-crumbs. Cover and cook in a preheated moderately hot oven (200°C/400°F or Gas Mark 6) for 30 minutes. Remove the lid and cook for a further 10 minutes or until the chicken is tender.
To freeze: cool quickly, then open (flash) freeze until firm. Pack in a rigid container, seal, label and return to the freezer.
To thaw and serve: thaw at room temperature for 4 hours, then reheat in roasting tin in a preheated moderately hot oven (190°C/375°F or Gas Mark 5) for 45 minutes or until heated through.
SERVES 8

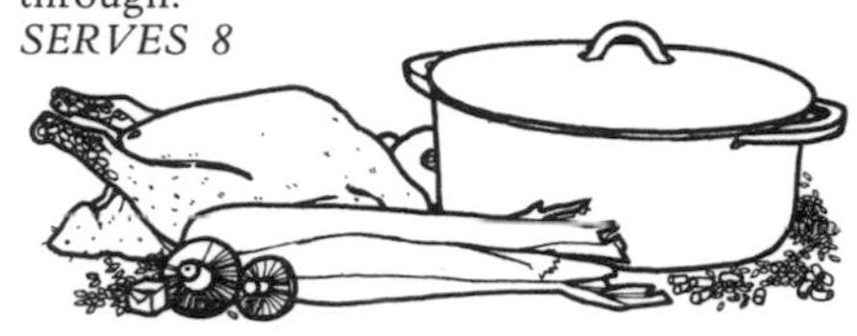

CHICKEN KIEV

METRIC/IMPERIAL
100 g/4 oz unsalted butter
1 garlic clove, peeled and crushed
1 × 15 ml spoon/1 tablespoon freshly chopped parsley
salt
freshly ground black pepper
4 large chicken breasts, skinned, boned and beaten thin
For the coating:
1 × 15 ml spoon/1 tablespoon flour
1 egg, beaten
100 g/4 oz fresh white breadcrumbs
oil for deep-frying, to finish

AMERICAN
½ cup unsalted butter
1 garlic clove, peeled and crushed
1 tablespoon freshly chopped parsley
salt
freshly ground black pepper
4 large chicken breasts, skinned, boned and beaten thin
For the coating:
1 tablespoon flour
1 egg, beaten
2 cups fresh white breadcrumbs
oil for deep-frying, to finish

Beat the butter, garlic and parsley together with salt and pepper to taste. Form into 4 cylindrical shapes, wrap in foil and chill until firm.
Put one piece of butter on each chicken breast, fold one end of the chicken over the butter, then fold the sides inwards to the centre and roll up to enclose the butter completely. Coat in the flour seasoned with salt and pepper, dip in the egg one at a time. Coat with breadcrumbs, then repeat with more egg and breadcrumbs until the breasts are thoroughly coated.
To freeze: open (flash) freeze until firm, then pack in a rigid container or freezer bag. Seal, label and return to the freezer.
To thaw and serve: thaw at room temperature for 1 to 2 hours, then deep-fry in hot oil for 15 minutes until golden brown on all sides. Drain on paper towels before serving.
SERVES 4

HONEYED CHICKEN WITH ALMONDS

METRIC/IMPERIAL
3 × 15 ml spoons/3 tablespoons vegetable oil
4 chicken quarters, skinned
1 onion, peeled and finely chopped
½ green pepper, cored, seeded and finely chopped
1.5 × 15 ml spoons/1½ tablespoons honey
150 ml/¼ pint chicken stock
salt
freshly ground black pepper
25 g/1 oz slivered, blanched almonds, to finish

AMERICAN
3 tablespoons vegetable oil
4 chicken quarters, skinned
1 onion, peeled and finely chopped
½ green pepper, cored, seeded and finely chopped
1½ tablespoons honey
⅔ cup chicken stock
salt
freshly ground black pepper
¼ cup slivered, blanched almonds, to finish

Heat the oil in a pan, add the chicken and fry for 5 minutes until browned on all sides. Add the onion, pepper, honey, stock and salt and pepper to taste, bring to the boil, cover tightly and simmer for 40 minutes or until the chicken is tender.
To freeze: cool quickly, then transfer to a rigid container. Seal, label and freeze.
To thaw and serve: thaw at room temperature for 4 hours, then reheat gently on top of the stove. Add the almonds just before serving.
SERVES 4

CHICKEN CURRY

METRIC/IMPERIAL

50 g/2 oz butter
2 medium onions, peeled and finely sliced
4 garlic cloves, peeled and slivered
2 cloves
2 cardamoms
1 × 5 cm/2 inch stick cinnamon
2 × 5 ml spoons/2 teaspoons ground coriander
1 × 2.5 ml spoon/½ teaspoon ground turmeric
1 × 2.5 ml spoon/½ teaspoon ground ginger
1 × 2.5 ml spoon/½ teaspoon ground cumin
a little paprika pepper
salt
4 chicken quarters, skinned
juice of 1 lemon, to finish

AMERICAN

¼ cup butter
2 medium onions, peeled and finely sliced
4 garlic cloves, peeled and slivered
2 cloves
2 cardamoms
1 × 2 inch stick cinnamon
2 teaspoons ground coriander
½ teaspoon ground turmeric
½ teaspoon ground ginger
½ teaspoon ground cumin
a little paprika pepper
salt
4 chicken quarters, skinned
juice of 1 lemon, to finish

Melt the butter in a pan, add the onions and garlic and fry gently until soft. Crush the cloves, cardamoms and cinnamon together and stir into the pan. Fry gently for 2 minutes, then stir in the remaining spices and salt to taste. Fry gently for a further 5 minutes.

Add the chicken to the pan and fry until browned on all sides, stirring constantly. Stir in enough water to make a thick gravy, then cover and simmer for 40 minutes or until the chicken is tender.

To freeze: cool quickly, then transfer to a rigid container. Seal, label and freeze.

To thaw and serve: thaw at room temperature for 4 hours, then reheat gently on top of the stove, stirring occasionally. Pour the lemon juice over the curry just before serving.

SERVES 4

CHICKEN TETRAZZINI

METRIC/IMPERIAL

350 g/¾ lb cooked chicken meat, diced
40 g/1½ oz butter
100 g/4 oz button mushrooms, sliced
175 g/6 oz spaghetti, cooked
1 × 225 g/8 oz can tomatoes, drained
For the sauce:
40 g/1½ oz butter
40 g/1½ oz flour
300 ml/½ pint chicken stock
300 ml/½ pint milk
4 × 15 ml spoons/4 tablespoons dry white wine
50 g/2 oz Cheddar cheese, grated
salt
freshly ground black pepper

AMERICAN

1½ cups diced cooked chicken meat
3 tablespoons butter
1 cup sliced button mushrooms
6 oz spaghetti, cooked until 'al dente'
1 × 8 oz can tomatoes, drained
For the sauce:
3 tablespoons butter
6 tablespoons flour
1¼ cups chicken stock
1¼ cups milk
¼ cup dry white wine
½ cup grated Cheddar cheese
salt
freshly ground black pepper

To make the sauce: melt the butter in a pan, stir in the flour and cook for 2 minutes, stirring constantly. Remove from the heat and gradually stir in the stock and milk. Return to the heat and bring to the boil, stirring constantly. Simmer until thick, then remove from the heat and stir in the wine, cheese and salt and pepper to taste. Mix half the sauce with the chicken and set aside. Melt the butter in a pan, add the mushrooms and fry gently for 5 minutes. Stir into the remaining sauce and mix with the spaghetti.

To freeze: cool quickly, then line a large ovenproof dish with foil. Spoon in the spaghetti mixture, top with the tomatoes, then cover with the chicken in sauce. Open (flash) freeze until firm, remove from the dish and overwrap with foil or a freezer bag. Seal, label and return to freezer.

To thaw and serve: remove wrappings and bake from frozen in covered ovenproof dish in preheated moderate oven (180°C/350°F or Gas Mark 4) for about 1 hour. Fork through during heating.

SERVES 4

CHICKEN AND TOMATO CASSEROLE

METRIC/IMPERIAL

8 chicken quarters, skinned
40 g/1½ oz flour
salt
freshly ground black pepper
75 g/3 oz butter
2 × 15 ml spoons/2 tablespoons vegetable oil
1 large onion, peeled and chopped
2 × 400 g/14 oz cans tomatoes
1 × 60 g/2¼ oz can tomato purée
300 ml/½ pint dry white wine
1 bay leaf
2 × 5 ml spoons/2 teaspoons dried mixed herbs
350 g/¾ lb button mushrooms, quartered

AMERICAN

8 chicken quarters, skinned
6 tablespoons flour
salt
freshly ground black pepper
6 tablespoons butter
2 tablespoons vegetable oil
1 large onion, peeled and chopped
2 × 14 oz cans tomatoes
1 × 2¼ oz can tomato paste
1¼ cups dry white wine
1 bay leaf
2 teaspoons dried mixed herbs
3 cups quartered button mushrooms

Coat the chicken in the flour seasoned with salt and pepper. Heat the butter and oil in a pan, add the chicken and fry until browned on all sides. Remove from the pan with a slotted spoon and drain on paper towels.

Add the onion to the pan and fry gently until soft. Stir in the remaining ingredients, except the mushrooms, and add salt and pepper to taste. Bring to the boil, stirring constantly, then return the chicken to the pan.

Cover and simmer for 30 minutes, then add the mushrooms and simmer for a further 10 minutes or until the chicken is tender. Remove the bay leaf.

To freeze: cool quickly, then transfer to a rigid container. Seal, label and freeze.

To thaw and serve: thaw at room temperature for 4 hours, then reheat gently on top of the stove, stirring occasionally.

SERVES 8

BARBECUED CHICKEN

METRIC/IMPERIAL

3 × 15 ml spoons/3 tablespoons vegetable oil
6 chicken quarters, skinned
1 × 5 ml spoon/1 teaspoon paprika pepper
3 × 15 ml spoons/3 tablespoons malt vinegar
3 × 15 ml spoons/3 tablespoons water
1 × 5 ml spoon/1 teaspoon brown sugar
1 × 5 ml spoon/1 teaspoon chilli sauce
1 × 5 ml spoon/1 teaspoon Worcestershire sauce
1 × 15 ml spoon/1 tablespoon mustard powder
approx 150 ml/¼ pint chicken stock

AMERICAN

3 tablespoons vegetable oil
6 chicken quarters, skinned
1 teaspoon paprika pepper
3 tablespoons malt vinegar
3 tablespoons water
1 teaspoon brown sugar
1 teaspoon chili sauce
1 teaspoon Worcestershire sauce
1 tablespoon mustard powder
approx ⅔ cup chicken stock

Heat the oil in a pan, add the chicken and fry until browned on all sides. Remove the chicken from the pan with a slotted spoon and transfer to a casserole dish. Sprinkle with the paprika.

Mix the remaining ingredients together, except the stock, and stir into the pan. Bring slowly to the boil, stirring constantly, then stir in half the stock. Pour over the chicken in the casserole and cook, uncovered, in a preheated moderate oven (160°C/325°F or Gas Mark 3) for 1 to 1¼ hours or until the chicken is tender. Baste frequently and add more stock to cover the chicken if it becomes dry during the cooking.

To freeze: cool quickly. Leave in the casserole or transfer to a rigid container. Cover, then wrap the casserole in a freezer bag or foil. Seal, label and freeze.

To thaw and serve: remove wrappings, then thaw at room temperature for 4 hours. Reheat in the covered casserole in a preheated moderate oven (180°C/350°F or Gas Mark 4) for 1 hour or until heated through.

SERVES 6

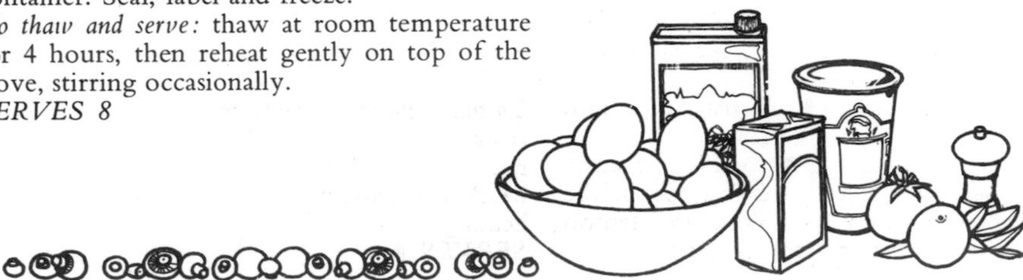

CHICKEN WITH CRANBERRIES AND RED WINE

METRIC/IMPERIAL

2 × 15 ml spoons/2 tablespoons vegetable oil
1 onion, peeled and finely chopped
4 chicken quarters, skinned
1 × 225 g/8 oz can cranberry sauce
1 × 298 g/10½ oz can condensed tomato soup
150 ml/¼ pint red wine
juice of 1 lemon
100 g/4 oz button mushrooms, sliced
salt
freshly ground black pepper

AMERICAN

2 tablespoons vegetable oil
1 onion, peeled and finely chopped
4 chicken quarters, skinned
1 × 8 oz can cranberry sauce
1 × 10½ oz can condensed tomato soup
⅔ cup red wine
juice of 1 lemon
1 cup sliced button mushrooms
salt
freshly ground black pepper

Heat the oil in a pan, add the onion and fry until golden. Add the chicken, fry until browned on all sides, then remove from pan. Add the cranberry sauce, soup and red wine gradually, then the lemon juice. Bring to the boil, stirring, and boil for 2 minutes. Add the mushrooms and salt and pepper to taste. Return the chicken to the pan, cover and simmer for 40 minutes or until chicken is tender.
To freeze: cool quickly, then transfer to a foil container. Seal, label and freeze.
To thaw and serve: reheat from frozen in the covered container in a preheated moderately hot oven (190°C/375°F or Gas Mark 5) for 1½ hours or until heated through.
SERVES 4

CHICKEN CACCIATORE

METRIC/IMPERIAL

75 g/3 oz butter
4 chicken quarters, skinned
1 large onion, peeled and chopped
1 medium green pepper, cored, seeded and chopped
1 clove garlic, peeled and crushed
1 × 396 g/14 oz can tomatoes
150 ml/¼ pint chicken stock
1 × 2.5 ml spoon/½ teaspoon sugar
salt
freshly ground black pepper

AMERICAN

75 g/3 oz butter
4 chicken quarters, skinned
1 large onion, peeled and chopped
1 medium green pepper, cored, seeded and chopped
1 clove garlic, peeled and crushed
1 × 14 oz can tomatoes
⅔ cup chicken stock
½ teaspoon sugar
salt
freshly ground black pepper

Melt 50 g/2 oz/¼ cup butter in a pan, add the chicken and fry for 15 minutes, turning once during cooking. Transfer to a casserole dish.
Melt the remaining butter in the pan add the onion, pepper and garlic and fry gently for 5 minutes. Stir in the tomatoes, stock, sugar and salt and pepper to taste. Bring to the boil, then pour over the chicken. Cover the casserole and bake in a preheated moderate oven (180°C/350°F or Gas Mark 4) for 1 hour, until tender.
To freeze: cool quickly. Leave in the casserole or transfer to a rigid container. Cover, then wrap in a freezer bag or foil. Seal, label and freeze.
To thaw and serve: remove wrappings, then thaw at room temperature for 4 hours. Reheat in the covered casserole in a preheated moderate oven (180°C/350°F or Gas Mark 4) for 1 hour or until heated through.
SERVES 4

CHICKEN A LA KING

METRIC/IMPERIAL

50 g/2 oz butter
1 small onion, peeled and finely chopped
1 small green pepper, cored, seeded and diced
225 g/½ lb button mushrooms, sliced
25 g/1 oz flour
300 ml/½ pint creamy milk
300 ml/½ pint chicken stock
450 g/1 lb cooked chicken meat, diced
salt
paprika pepper

AMERICAN

¼ cup butter
1 small onion, peeled and finely chopped
1 small green pepper, cored, seeded and diced
2 cups sliced button mushrooms
¼ cup flour
1¼ cups creamy milk
1¼ cups chicken stock
2 cups diced cooked chicken meat
salt
paprika pepper

Melt the butter in a pan, add the onion, green pepper and mushrooms and fry gently until soft. Stir in the flour and cook for 1 minute, stirring constantly. Stir in the milk and stock and simmer until the sauce thickens. Add the chicken and salt and paprika to taste, then simmer for 5 minutes.
To freeze: cool quickly, then pour into a rigid container. Seal, label and freeze.
To thaw and serve: reheat from frozen on top of the stove, stirring occasionally.
SERVES 4

PIGEONS IN TOMATO SAUCE

METRIC/IMPERIAL

50 g/2 oz bacon fat
1 garlic clove, peeled and finely chopped
4 wood pigeons
225 g/½ lb mushrooms, sliced
1 onion, peeled and chopped
1 bouquet garni
1 kg/2 lb tomatoes, peeled and chopped
150 ml/¼ pint water
1 × 15 ml spoon/1 tablespoon brown sugar
salt
freshly ground black pepper

AMERICAN

¼ cup bacon fat
1 garlic clove, peeled and finely chopped
4 wood pigeons
2 cups sliced mushrooms
1 onion, peeled and chopped
1 bouquet garni
4 cups peeled and chopped tomatoes
⅔ cup water
½ tablespoon brown sugar
salt
freshly ground black pepper

Melt the bacon fat in a flameproof casserole dish, add the garlic and pigeons and fry gently until browned. Add the remaining ingredients and bring to the boil. Cover and cook in a preheated moderate oven (180°C/350°F or Gas Mark 4) for 2 to 3 hours or until the pigeons are tender. Remove the bouquet garni.
To freeze: cool quickly. Leave in the casserole or transfer to a rigid container. Cover, then wrap in a freezer bag of foil. Seal, label and freeze.
To thaw and serve: thaw at room temperature for 4 hours, then reheat in the covered casserole in a preheated moderate oven (180°C/350°F or Gas Mark 4) for 1 hour or until heated through.
SERVES 4

PIGEON PIE

METRIC/IMPERIAL

3 wood pigeons
4 streaky bacon rashers, rinds removed and cut into thin strips
1 large onion, peeled and chopped
75 g/3 oz mushrooms, sliced
450 ml/¾ pint stock
2 × 5 ml spoons/2 teaspoons prepared mustard
basic puff pastry dough made with 225 g/½ lb flour
a little milk, to glaze

AMERICAN

3 wood pigeons
4 fatty bacon slices, cut into thin strips
1 large onion, peeled and chopped
¾ cup sliced mushrooms
2 cups stock
2 teaspoons prepared mustard
basic puff paste dough made with 2 cups flour
a little milk, to glaze

Remove the meat carefully from the pigeons and cut into strips. Put in a pan with the bacon, vegetables, stock and mustard. Cover and cook gently for 1 hour. Leave to cool, then spoon into an ovenproof pie dish or foil container.
Roll out the dough on a floured surface and use to cover the pigeon mixture, moistening the edge with water and pressing down firmly to seal. Flute the edge and use any trimmings to decorate the top of the pie. Cut an air vent in the centre.
To freeze: wrap in a freezer bag or foil. Seal, label and freeze.
To thaw and serve: remove wrappings, brush the dough with milk and bake from frozen in a preheated hot oven (220°C/425°F or Gas Mark 7) for 30 minutes. Reduce the heat to moderate (180°C/350°F or Gas Mark 4) and bake for a further 30 minutes or until heated through. Cover with foil if the pastry becomes too brown during cooking.
SERVES 4

WOODMANS CASSEROLE

METRIC/IMPERIAL

4 wood pigeons
150 ml/¼ pint red wine
1 bouquet garni
25 g/1 oz lard
4 smoked streaky bacon rashers, rinds removed and chopped
1 large onion, peeled and sliced
2 large carrots, peeled and sliced
50 g/2 oz mushrooms, sliced
salt
freshly ground black pepper

AMERICAN

4 wood pigeons
⅔ cup red wine
1 bouquet garni
2 tablespoons lard
4 fatty bacon slices, chopped
1 large onion, peeled and sliced
2 large carrots, peeled and sliced
½ cup sliced mushrooms
salt
freshly ground black pepper

Put the pigeons in a shallow dish, pour over the wine, add the bouquet garni and marinate for several hours, turning at least once.

Melt the lard in a pan, add the bacon and vegetables and fry gently until golden. Drain and transfer to a casserole dish. Drain and dry the pigeons, brown them in the hot fat, then transfer to the casserole. Pour over the marinade, add salt and pepper to taste, cover and cook in a preheated moderate oven (180°C/350°F or Gas Mark 4) for 2 to 3 hours or until the pigeons are tender. Remove the bouquet garni.

To freeze: cool quickly. Leave in the casserole or transfer to a rigid container. Cover, then wrap the casserole in a freezer bag or foil. Seal, label and freeze.

To thaw and serve: remove wrappings and thaw at room temperature for 4 hours. Reheat in the covered casserole in a preheated moderate oven (180°C/350°F or Gas Mark 4) for 45 minutes or until heated through.

SERVES 4

PHEASANT WITH FRUIT

METRIC/IMPERIAL

50 g/2 oz butter
2 pheasants, dressed, cleaned and cut into serving pieces
salt
freshly ground black pepper
4 × 15 ml spoons/4 tablespoons brandy
2 × 15 ml spoons/2 tablespoons stock or water
2 × 15 ml spoons/2 tablespoons lemon juice
2 × 15 ml spoons/2 tablespoons pineapple juice
a little arrowroot (optional)
To garnish:
1 orange, peeled and sliced
4 slices fresh or canned pineapple

AMERICAN

¼ cup butter
2 pheasants, dressed, cleaned and cut into serving pieces
salt
freshly ground black pepper
¼ cup brandy
2 tablespoons stock or water
2 tablespoons lemon juice
2 tablespoons pineapple juice
a little arrowroot (optional)
To garnish:
1 orange, peeled and sliced
4 slices fresh or canned pineapple

Melt the butter in a large pan, add the pheasant and fry gently until lightly coloured on all sides. Add salt and pepper to taste, then cover and cook gently for 30 to 40 minutes or until the pheasant is tender. Remove from the pan and set aside to cool.

Drain off half the butter from the pan, add the brandy and bring to the boil. Flame the brandy, then simmer for a few minutes, stirring constantly. Stir in the stock or water, the lemon and pineapple juices and bring to the boil. Thicken the sauce with a little arrowroot, if liked.

To freeze: cool quickly. Put the pheasant and sauce in a rigid container. Seal, label and freeze.

To thaw and serve: thaw at room temperature for 4 hours, then reheat in a covered casserole in a preheated moderate oven (180°C/350°F or Gas Mark 4) for 1 hour or until heated through. Garnish with orange and pineapple slices just before serving.

SERVES 6

PHEASANT ALSACIENNE

METRIC/IMPERIAL

1 large pheasant, dressed and cleaned
50 g/2 oz butter
1 eating apple, cored and sliced
150 ml/¼ pint dry white wine
300 ml/½ pint stock
a little arrowroot (optional)
For the stuffing:
2 frankfurters
50 g/2 oz butter
1 small onion, peeled and finely chopped
75 g/3 oz fresh white breadcrumbs
1 × 5 ml spoon/1 teaspoon dried thyme
1 × 5 ml spoon/1 teaspoon dried sage
salt
freshly ground black pepper
1 egg, beaten

AMERICAN

1 large pheasant, dressed and cleaned
¼ cup butter
1 eating apple, cored and sliced
⅔ cup dry white wine
1¼ cups stock
a little arrowroot (optional)
For the stuffing:
2 frankfurters
¼ cup butter
1 small onion, peeled and finely chopped
1½ cups fresh white breadcrumbs
1 teaspoon dried thyme
1 teaspoon dried sage
salt
freshly ground black pepper
1 egg, beaten

To make the stuffing: put the frankfurters in a bowl, cover with boiling water and leave to stand for 5 minutes. Meanwhile, melt the butter in a pan, add the onion and fry gently until soft. Transfer to a bowl and add the remaining stuffing ingredients. Drain the frankfurters, remove the skin and cut into small dice. Add to the stuffing and stir well to mix.

Cut the pheasant down the back and bone out the carcass, leaving in the leg and wing bones. Spoon the stuffing into the pheasant, then sew up with fine string. Put the bird in a roasting tin and brush all over with the butter. Add the apple and wine and roast in a preheated moderately hot oven (200°C/400°F or Gas Mark 6) for 45 minutes, basting and turning occasionally. Remove the pheasant and set aside to cool. Transfer the tin to the top of the stove. Stir in the stock and bring to the boil, stirring constantly. Strain the sauce and thicken with a little arrowroot, if liked.

To freeze: cool quickly, put pheasant and sauce in a rigid container. Seal, label and freeze.

To thaw and serve: thaw at room temperature for 4 hours, then reheat in a covered casserole in a preheated moderate oven (180°C/350°F or Gas Mark 4) for 1 hour or until heated through. Add more stock or water if necessary.

SERVES 4

RABBIT HOT POT

METRIC/IMPERIAL

4 rabbit portions
2 × 15 ml spoons/2 tablespoons flour
salt
freshly ground black pepper
2 large onions, peeled and sliced
2 large Carrots, peeled and sliced
300–450 ml/½–¼ pint chicken stock
2 × 5 ml spoons/2 teaspoons prepared mustard
1 × 15 ml spoon/1 tablespoon freshly chopped parsley
450 g/1 lb potatoes, peeled and finely sliced
25 g/1 oz dripping or lard, melted

AMERICAN

4 rabbit portions
2 tablespoons flour
salt
freshly ground black pepper
2 large onions, peeled and sliced
2 large carrots, peeled and sliced
1¼–2 cups chicken stock
2 teaspoons prepared mustard
1 tablespoon freshly chopped parsley
1 lb potatoes, peeled and finely sliced
2 tablespoons drippings or lard, melted

Coat the rabbit in the flour seasoned with salt and pepper, then place in a casserole dish. Add the onions, carrots, stock, mustard and parsley. Cover with the sliced potatoes, then brush with the melted fat. Cover and cook in a preheated moderate oven (160°C/325°F or Gas Mark 3) for 1½ to 2 hours, then remove the lid and increase the heat to hot (220°C/425°F or Gas Mark 7). Cook for a further 15 minutes or until the potatoes are brown.

To freeze: cool quickly. Cover the casserole, then wrap in a freezer bag or foil. Seal, label and freeze.

To thaw and serve: remove wrappings and thaw at room temperature for 4 hours. Reheat in the covered casserole in a preheated moderate oven (180°C/350°F or Gas Mark 4) for about 1 hour or until heated through.

SERVES 4

RABBIT CASSEROLE

METRIC/IMPERIAL

50 g/2 oz butter
1 rabbit, cut into serving pieces
2 onions, peeled and chopped
salt
freshly ground black pepper
1 × 15 ml spoon/1 tablespoon flour
450 ml/¾ pint stock or water
3 × 15 ml spoons/3 tablespoons tomato purée
1 × 5 ml spoon/1 teaspoon dried mixed herbs
freshly chopped parsley, to garnish

AMERICAN

¼ cup butter
1 rabbit, cut into serving pieces
2 onions, peeled and chopped
salt
freshly ground black pepper
1 tablespoon flour
2 cups stock or water
3 tablespoons tomato paste
1 teaspoon dried mixed herbs
freshly chopped parsley, to garnish

Melt the butter in a pan, add the rabbit and fry briskly until browned on all sides. Transfer to a casserole dish, put the onions on top and add salt and pepper to taste. Stir the flour into the pan and cook for 2 minutes, stirring constantly. Stir in the stock or water. Bring to the boil and simmer for 2 to 3 minutes. Stir in the tomato purée (paste) and mixed herbs, then pour over the rabbit in the casserole.

Cover and cook in a preheated moderate oven (180°C/350°F or Gas Mark 4) for 1½ to 2 hours or until the rabbit is tender.

To freeze: cool quickly. Leave in the casserole or transfer to a rigid container. Cover, then wrap the casserole in a freezer bag or foil. Seal, label and freeze.

To thaw and serve: remove wrappings and thaw at room temperature for 4 hours. Reheat in the covered casserole in a preheated moderately hot oven (190°C/375°F or Gas Mark 5) for 40 to 45 minutes or until heated through. Sprinkle with parsley just before serving.

SERVES 4

RABBIT CHASSEUR

METRIC/IMPERIAL

1 rabbit, cut into serving pieces
½ lemon
50 g/2 oz butter
1 × 15 ml spoon/1 tablespoon corn or olive oil
1 onion, peeled and chopped
2 carrots, peeled and sliced
100 g/4 oz button mushrooms
25 g/1 oz flour
200 ml/⅓ pint dry white wine
200 ml/⅓ pint chicken stock
2 × 5 ml spoons/2 teaspoons tomato purée
1 × 5 ml spoon/1 teaspoon dried thyme
1 bay leaf
salt
freshly ground black pepper

AMERICAN

1 rabbit, cut into serving pieces
½ lemon
¼ cup butter
1 tablespoon corn or olive oil
1 onion, peeled and chopped
2 carrots, peeled and sliced
1 cup button mushrooms
¼ cup flour
⅞ cup dry white wine
⅞ cup chicken stock
2 teaspoons tomato paste
1 teaspoon dried thyme
1 bay leaf
salt
freshly ground black pepper

Put the rabbit in a large bowl with the lemon, cover with cold water and leave overnight. Drain, rinse under cold running water, then dry on paper towels.

Heat the butter and oil in a pan, add the rabbit and cook gently until golden brown on all sides. Add the onion, carrots and mushrooms and cook for a further 2 minutes. Sprinkle in the flour and cook for 2 minutes, stirring constantly. Stir in the wine, stock and tomato purée (paste), then bring to the boil. Add the thyme, bay leaf and salt and pepper to taste, then cover and simmer for 1½–2 hours or until the rabbit is tender. Remove the bay leaf.

To freeze: cool quickly, then transfer to a rigid container. Seal, label and freeze.

To thaw and serve: thaw at room temperature for 4 hours, then reheat gently on top of the stove, stirring occasionally.

SERVES 4

SWEET AND SOUR RABBIT WITH PRUNES

METRIC/IMPERIAL

1 × 1 kg/2 lb rabbit, cut into serving pieces
1 large onion, peeled and sliced
300 ml/½ pint dry white wine
300 ml/½ pint chicken stock
1 bay leaf
2 × 15 ml spoons/2 tablespoons redcurrant jelly
8 prunes, stoned
50 g/2 oz seedless raisins
To finish:
2 × 5 ml spoons/2 teaspoons cornflour
1 × 15 ml spoon/1 tablespoon malt vinegar
salt
freshly ground black pepper
fried almonds

AMERICAN

1 × 2 lb rabbit, cut into serving pieces
1 large onion, peeled and sliced
1¼ cups dry white wine
1¼ cups chicken stock
1 bay leaf
2 tablespoons redcurrant jelly
8 prunes, pitted
⅓ cup seedless raisins
To finish:
2 teaspoons cornstarch
1 tablespoon malt vinegar
salt
freshly ground black pepper
fried almonds

Put the rabbit and onion in a bowl, pour in the wine and leave to marinate overnight. Discard the onion and transfer the rabbit and wine to a flameproof casserole dish. Add the stock, bay leaf and redcurrant jelly and bring to the boil. Add the prunes and raisins, cover and cook in a preheated moderate oven (180°C/350°F or Gas Mark 4) for 1½ hours or until the rabbit is tender. Remove the rabbit from the pan and discard the bones.

To freeze: cool quickly. Put the meat in a foil container and cover with the contents of the casserole. Seal, label and freeze.

To thaw and serve: reheat from frozen in the covered container in a preheated moderate oven (180°C/350°F or Gas Mark 4) for 1 hour or until heated through. Arrange the rabbit, prunes and raisins on a warm serving dish and keep hot. Mix the cornflour (cornstarch) and vinegar to a paste and stir into the sauce. Pour into a saucepan and boil for 1 to 2 minutes. Add salt and pepper to taste then pour over the rabbit. Garnish with almonds.

SERVES 4 to 6

RABBIT IN MUSTARD SAUCE

METRIC/IMPERIAL

1 rabbit cut into serving pieces
salt
4 × 15 ml spoons/4 tablespoons prepared French mustard
25 g/1 oz flour
freshly ground black pepper
50 g/2 oz butter
100 g/4 oz salt pork, rind removed and diced
1 medium onion, peeled and chopped
1 garlic clove, peeled and crushed
300 ml/½ pint chicken stock
To finish:
150 ml/¼ pint single cream
8 large bread croûtes, fried in butter

AMERICAN

1 rabbit, cut into serving pieces
salt
¼ cup prepared French mustard
¼ cup flour
freshly ground black pepper
¼ cup butter
½ cup diced salt pork
1 medium onion, peeled and chopped
1 garlic clove, peeled and crushed
1¼ cups chicken stock
To finish:
⅔ cup light cream
8 large bread croûtes, fried in butter

Put the rabbit in a large bowl, cover with lightly salted water and leave overnight. Drain, rinse under cold running water, then dry on paper towels.

Spread the mustard over the rabbit, cover and chill in the refrigerator for 4 hours, then coat with the flour seasoned with salt and pepper. Melt the butter in a flameproof casserole dish, add the rabbit and fry on all sides until browned. Add the salt pork, onion and garlic, then cover and cook for 20 minutes, stirring occasionally. Stir in the stock, then cover and cook in a preheated moderate oven (160°C/325°F or Gas Mark 3) for 45 minutes.

To freeze: cool quickly. Leave in the casserole or pour into a rigid container. Cover, then wrap the casserole in a freezer bag or foil. Seal, label and freeze.

To thaw and serve: thaw at room temperature for 4 hours then reheat, covered, in a preheated moderate oven (180°C/350°F or Gas Mark 4) for 1 hour or until heated through. Stir in the cream just before serving and garnish with the croûtes.

SERVES 4

SAVOURY DUCKS

METRIC/IMPERIAL

450 g/1 lb pig's liver
2 large onions, peeled
175 g/6 oz fresh white breadcrumbs
50 g/2 oz shredded suet
1 × 2.5 ml spoon/½ teaspoon dried sage
1 × 15 ml spoon/1 tablespoon Worcestershire sauce
salt
freshly ground black pepper
For the gravy:
25 g/1 oz lard
1 onion, peeled and sliced
2 carrots, peeled and grated
25 g/1 oz flour
450 ml/¾ pint beef stock
2 × 5 ml spoons/2 teaspoons Worcestershire sauce

AMERICAN

1 lb pork liver
2 large onions, peeled
3 cups fresh white breadcrumbs
6 tablespoons shredded suet
½ teaspoon dried sage
1 tablespoon Worcestershire sauce
salt
freshly ground black pepper
For the gravy:
2 tablespoons lard
1 onion, peeled and sliced
2 carrots, peeled and grated
¼ cup flour
2 cups beef stock
2 teaspoons Worcestershire sauce

Mince (grind) the liver and onions, then put in a bowl with the remaining ingredients and stir well to mix. Divide the mixture into 8 equal portions and shape into balls. Place in a greased casserole dish and bake, uncovered, in a preheated moderate oven (180°C/350°F or Gas Mark 4) for 30 minutes. Remove from the oven, then turn each savoury duck over.

Meanwhile, make the gravy. Melt the lard in a pan, add the onion and carrots and fry gently for 5 minutes. Stir in the flour and cook for 2 minutes, stirring constantly. Remove from the heat and stir in the stock and Worcestershire sauce. Return to the heat and bring to the boil, stirring constantly. Simmer for 10 minutes, then strain and add salt and pepper to taste. Pour the gravy over the savoury ducks, return to the oven and cook for a further 20 minutes.

To freeze: cool quickly. Leave in the casserole or transfer to a rigid container. Cover, then wrap the casserole in a freezer bag or foil. Seal, label and freeze.

To thaw and serve: remove wrappings and thaw at room temperature for 4 hours. Reheat in the covered casserole in a preheated moderate oven (180°C/350°F or Gas Mark 4) for 30 to 40 minutes or until heated through.

SERVES 4

LAMBS' TONGUES WITH SWEET AND SOUR SAUCE

METRIC/IMPERIAL
6 fresh lambs' tongues
salt
approx 600 ml/1 pint hot stock
1 bouquet garni
1 bay leaf
few black peppercorns
For the sauce:
25 g/1 oz butter
2 onions, peeled and finely sliced
2 × 15 ml spoons/2 tablespoons flour
3 × 15 ml spoons/3 tablespoons vinegar
3 × 15 ml spoons/3 tablespoons honey
freshly ground black pepper
25 g/1 oz seedless raisins, to finish

AMERICAN
6 fresh lamb tongues
salt
approx 2½ cups hot stock
1 bouquet garni
1 bay leaf
few black peppercorns
For the sauce:
2 tablespoons butter
2 onions, peeled and finely sliced
2 tablespoons flour
3 tablespoons vinegar
3 tablespoons honey
freshly ground black pepper
3 tablespoons seedless raisins, to finish

Put the tongues in a large bowl, cover with cold salted water and leave to soak for 1 hour. Drain and rinse well under cold running water. Put the tongues in a pan, cover with the stock and add the bouquet garni, bay leaf and peppercorns. Bring to the boil, then simmer for 1 to 1½ hours. Strain the cooking liquid and reserve 600 ml/1 pint/2½ cups. Remove the skin and gristle from the tongues while still hot, then cut the flesh into thin strips and leave to cool.
To make the sauce: melt the butter in a pan, add the onions and fry gently until soft. Stir in the flour, cook for 2 minutes, stirring constantly, then stir in the reserved cooking liquid. Bring to the boil, stirring constantly, then simmer until the sauce thickens. Stir in the vinegar, honey and salt and pepper to taste.
To freeze: cool the sauce quickly. Put the cold tongues in a rigid container and pour over the sauce. Seal, label and freeze.
To thaw and serve: thaw at room temperature for 4 hours, then reheat gently on top of the stove, stirring occasionally. Stir in the raisins.
SERVES 4 to 6

LAMBS' TONGUES WITH MUSTARD SAUCE

METRIC/IMPERIAL
8 fresh lambs' tongues
salt
approx 900 ml/1½ pints hot stock
1 bouquet garni
1 bay leaf
few black peppercorns
For the sauce:
25 g/1 oz butter
25 g/1 oz flour
300 ml/½ pint milk
2 × 5 ml spoons/2 teaspoons prepared mustard
salt
freshly ground black pepper

AMERICAN
8 fresh lamb tongues
salt
approx 3¾ cups hot stock
1 bouquet garni
1 bay leaf
few black peppercorns
For the sauce:
2 tablespoons butter
¼ cup flour
1¼ cups milk
2 teaspoons prepared mustard
salt
freshly ground black pepper

Put the tongues in a large bowl, cover with cold salted water and leave to soak for 1 hour. Drain and rinse well under cold running water. Put the tongues in a large pan, cover with the stock and add the bouquet garni, bay leaf and peppercorns. Bring to the boil, then simmer for 1 to 1½ hours. Remove the skin and gristle from the tongues while still hot, then cut the flesh into thin strips and leave to cool.
To make the sauce: melt the butter in a pan, stir in the flour and cook for 2 minutes, stirring constantly. Remove from the heat and gradually stir in the milk. Add the mustard and salt and pepper to taste, then return to the heat. Bring to the boil, stirring constantly, then simmer until the sauce thickens.
To freeze: cool the sauce quickly. Put the cold tongues into a rigid container and pour over the sauce. Seal, label and freeze.
To thaw and serve: thaw at room temperature for 4 hours, then reheat on top of stove, stirring occasionally.
SERVES 6

ROMAN LIVER

METRIC/IMPERIAL

675 g/1½ lb pig's liver, sliced
25 g/1 oz flour
salt
freshly ground black pepper
25 g/1 oz butter
1 medium onion, peeled and sliced
1 × 400 g/14 oz can tomatoes
1 × 2.5 ml spoon/½ teaspoon dried oregano

AMERICAN

1½ lb pork liver, sliced
¼ cup flour
salt
freshly ground black pepper
2 tablespoons butter
1 medium onion, peeled and sliced
1 × 14 oz can tomatoes
½ teaspoon dried oregano

Coat the liver in the flour seasoned with salt and pepper. Melt the butter in a pan, add the liver and fry until browned on all sides. Transfer to a casserole dish.

Add the sliced onion to the pan and fry gently for 5 minutes, until soft. Add to the casserole with the tomatoes and oregano, cover and cook in a preheated moderate oven (180°C/350°F or Gas Mark 4) for 1 hour.

To freeze: cool quickly. Leave in the casserole or pour into a rigid container. Cover, then wrap the casserole in a freezer bag or foil. Seal, label and freeze.

To thaw and serve: remove wrappings and thaw at room temperature for 4 hours. Reheat in the covered casserole in a preheated moderate oven (160°C/325°F or Gas Mark 3) for 1 hour or until heated through.

SERVES 4 to 6

LIVER HOT POT

METRIC/IMPERIAL

450 g/1 lb ox liver, cut into thin strips
50 g/2 oz flour
salt
freshly ground black pepper
50 g/2 oz butter
1 large onion, peeled and sliced
4 bacon rashers, rinds removed and chopped
2 tomatoes, peeled and chopped
1 × 2.5 ml spoon/½ teaspoon dried mixed herbs (optional)
1 kg/2 lb potatoes, peeled and finely sliced
2 × 15 ml spoons/2 tablespoons water
freshly chopped parsley, to garnish

AMERICAN

1 lb beef liver, cut into thin strips
½ cup flour
salt
freshly ground black pepper
¼ cup butter
1 large onion, peeled and sliced
4 bacon slices, chopped
2 tomatoes, peeled and chopped
½ teaspoon dried mixed herbs (optional)
2 lb potatoes, peeled and finely sliced
2 tablespoons water
freshly chopped parsley, to garnish

Coat the liver in the flour seasoned with salt and pepper. Melt the butter in a flameproof casserole dish, add the liver and onions and fry for 3 to 4 minutes until browned, stirring occasionally.

Add the bacon, tomatoes and herbs (if using), then cover with the sliced potatoes. Pour in the water.

Cover and cook in a preheated moderate oven (180°C/350°F or Gas Mark 4) for 1¼ to 1½ hours, then remove the lid and cook for a further 20 to 25 minutes to brown the potatoes.

To freeze: cool quickly, cover with the lid or foil, then wrap in a freezer bag. Seal, label and freeze.

To thaw and serve: remove wrappings and thaw at room temperature for 4 hours. Reheat in the covered casserole in a preheated moderate oven for 1 hour or until heated through. Sprinkle with parsley just before serving.

SERVES 6

LIVER AND BACON

METRIC/IMPERIAL

450 g/1 lb lambs' liver, sliced
25 g/1 oz flour
salt
freshly ground black pepper
1 × 15 ml spoon/1 tablespoon vegetable oil
6 bacon rashers, rinds removed
1 small onion, peeled and chopped
150 ml/¼ pint stock

AMERICAN

1 lb lamb liver, sliced
¼ cup flour
salt
freshly ground black pepper
1 tablespoon vegetable oil
6 bacon slices
1 small onion, peeled and chopped
⅔ cup stock

Coat the liver in the flour seasoned with salt and pepper. Heat the oil in a flameproof casserole dish, add the bacon and onion and fry gently until lightly coloured. Remove from the casserole with a slotted spoon, then add the liver and any remaining flour. Fry gently for a few minutes, then stir in the stock with salt and pepper to taste. Return the bacon and onion to the casserole, cover and cook in a preheated moderate oven (180°C/350°F or Gas Mark 4) for 1 hour or until the liver is tender.
To freeze: cool quickly. Leave in the casserole or transfer to a rigid container. Cover, then wrap the casserole in a freezer bag or foil. Seal, label and freeze.
To thaw and serve: remove wrappings and thaw at room temperature for 4 hours. Reheat in the covered casserole in a preheated moderate oven (180°C/350°F or Gas Mark 4) for 1 hour.
SERVES 4

LIVER AND ONION CASSEROLE

METRIC/IMPERIAL
450 g/1 lb lambs' liver, sliced
flour for coating
salt
freshly ground black pepper
25 g/1 oz butter
100 g/4 oz fresh breadcrumbs
2 × 5 ml spoons/2 teaspoons mustard powder
3 onions, peeled and finely sliced
300 ml/½ pint stock
freshly chopped parsley, to garnish

AMERICAN
1 lb lamb liver, sliced
flour for coating
salt
freshly ground black pepper
2 tablespoons butter
2 cups fresh breadcrumbs
2 teaspoons mustard powder
3 onions, peeled and finely sliced
1¼ cups stock
freshly chopped parsley, to garnish

Coat the liver in the flour seasoned with salt and pepper. Melt the butter in a pan, add the liver and brown quickly on all sides – do not overcook.
Mix the breadcrumbs with the mustard powder. Place a layer of liver at the bottom of a foil container, cover with a layer of breadcrumbs, then a layer of onion. Repeat these layers, sprinkling with salt and pepper between each layer and finishing with a layer of breadcrumbs. Pour in the stock, cover and cook in a preheated moderate oven (180°C/350°F or Gas Mark 4) for 45 minutes.
To freeze: cool quickly, seal, label and freeze.
To thaw and serve: uncover and reheat from frozen in a preheated moderate oven for 1½ hours or until heated through. Sprinkle with parsley just before serving.
SERVES 4

LAMBS' LIVER IN CREAM SAUCE

METRIC/IMPERIAL
450 g/1 lb lambs' liver, thinly sliced
15 g/½ oz flour
salt
freshly ground black pepper
25 g/1 oz butter
1 × 15 ml spoon/1 tablespoon vegetable oil
2 large onions, peeled and finely sliced
2 × 5 ml spoons/2 teaspoons tomato purée
150 ml/¼ pint beef stock
2 × 5 ml spoons/2 teaspoons mustard powder
300 ml/½ pint single cream
freshly chopped parsley, to garnish

AMERICAN
1 lb lamb liver, thinly sliced
2 tablespoons flour
salt
freshly ground black pepper
2 tablespoons butter
1 tablespoon vegetable oil
2 large onions, peeled and sliced
2 teaspoons tomato paste
⅔ cup beef stock
2 teaspoons mustard powder
1¼ cups light cream
freshly chopped parsley, to garnish

Coat the liver in the flour, seasoned with salt and pepper. Heat the butter and oil in a pan, add the onions and fry gently until soft. Add the liver and fry for 1 minute each side. Stir in the tomato purée (paste), stock and salt and pepper to taste. Cover and simmer for 20 minutes, then blend the mustard with the cream and stir into the pan.
To freeze: cool quickly and turn into a rigid container. Seal, label and freeze.
To thaw and serve: reheat gently from frozen on top of stove, stirring occasionally.
Sprinkle generously with freshly chopped parsley just before serving.
SERVES 4

DEVILLED KIDNEYS

METRIC/IMPERIAL

8 lambs' kidneys, skin and cores removed and cut into thick slices
1 × 15 ml spoon/1 tablespoon mustard powder
1 × 5 ml spoon/1 teaspoon curry powder
1 × 15 ml spoon/1 tablespoon flour
50 g/2 oz butter
2 × 15 ml spoons/2 tablespoons tomato ketchup
150 ml/¼ pint beef stock
salt
freshly ground black pepper
freshly chopped parsley, to garnish

AMERICAN

8 lamb kidneys, skin and cores removed and cut into thick slices
1 tablespoon mustard powder
1 teaspoon curry powder
1 tablespoon flour
¼ cup butter
2 tablespoons tomato ketchup
⅔ cup beef stock
salt
freshly ground black pepper
freshly chopped parsley, to garnish

Sift the mustard and curry powders together with the flour and use to coat the kidneys. Melt the butter in a pan, add the kidneys and cook for about 5 minutes until lightly browned on all sides, stirring constantly. Stir in the tomato ketchup, stock and salt and pepper to taste. Cover and simmer for about 20 minutes until the kidneys are tender.
To freeze: cool quickly, then pour into a rigid container. Seal, label and freeze.
To thaw and serve: thaw at room temperature for 4 hours. Reheat gently on top of the stove, stirring occasionally. Sprinkle with parsley just before serving.
SERVES 4

CREAMY KIDNEYS IN ALE

METRIC/IMPERIAL

50 g/2 oz butter
8 lambs' kidneys, skin and cores removed and sliced
1 large onion, peeled and chopped
4 streaky bacon rashers, rinds removed and chopped
100 g/4 oz button mushrooms, sliced
2 × 15 ml spoons/2 tablespoons flour
300 ml/½ pint brown ale or stout
1 × 15 ml spoon/1 tablespoon tomato purée
salt
freshly ground black pepper
300 ml/½ pint soured cream

AMERICAN

¼ cup butter
8 lamb kidneys, skin and cores removed and sliced
1 large onion, peeled and chopped
4 fatty bacon slices, chopped
1 cup sliced button mushrooms
2 tablespoons flour
1¼ cups dark beer
1 tablespoon tomato paste
salt
freshly ground black pepper
1¼ cups sour cream

Melt half the butter in a pan, add the kidneys and fry gently for 5 minutes, stirring occasionally. Remove from the pan with a slotted spoon and keep warm. Melt the remaining butter in the pan, add the onion, bacon and mushrooms and fry for 5 minutes.
Stir in the flour and cook for 2 minutes, stirring constantly. Stir in the ale or stout (beer), the tomato purée (paste) and salt and pepper to taste. Bring to the boil and boil rapidly for 5 minutes to reduce the sauce.
Return the kidneys to the pan, then gradually stir in the sour(ed) cream, and heat through gently. Do not allow to boil.
To freeze: cool quickly, then pour into a rigid container. Seal, label and freeze.
To thaw and serve: thaw at room temperature for 4 hours, then reheat gently on top of the stove until heated through, occasionally. Do not allow to boil.
SERVES 4

OXFORD KIDNEYS

METRIC/IMPERIAL

12 lambs' kidneys, skin and cores removed and cut into thick slices
75 g/3 oz butter
1 × 15 ml spoon/1 tablespoon finely chopped onion
150 ml/¼ pint dry white wine
1 × 15 ml spoon/1 tablespoon lemon juice
1 × 15 ml spoon/1 tablespoon prepared French mustard
freshly chopped parsley, to garnish

AMERICAN

12 lamb kidneys, skin and cores removed and cut into thick slices
⅜ cup butter
1 tablespoon finely chopped onion
⅔ cup dry white wine
1 tablespoon lemon juice
1 tablespoon prepared French mustard
freshly chopped parsley, to garnish

Melt 50 g/2 oz/$\frac{1}{4}$ cup butter in a pan, add the kidneys and fry for 5 minutes, turning frequently. Remove from the pan, cool, then transfer to a rigid container.

Add the onion to the pan and cook for 2 minutes until soft. Stir in the wine and lemon juice, increase the heat and boil until the liquid has reduced by about one-third. Remove from the heat. Mix the mustard with the remaining butter and swirl this into the sauce in small pieces.

To freeze: cool quickly, then pour over the kidneys. Seal, label and freeze.

To thaw and serve: thaw at room temperature for 4 hours, then reheat gently on top of the stove, stirring occasionally. Sprinkle with parsley just before serving.

SERVES 4 to 6

SAUTÉ OF KIDNEYS AND MUSHROOMS

METRIC/IMPERIAL

8 lambs' kidneys, skin and cores removed and cut into thick slices
75 g/3 oz butter
1 onion, peeled and finely chopped
100 g/4 oz mushrooms, sliced
25 g/1 oz flour
300 ml/$\frac{1}{2}$ pint beef stock
2 × 15 ml spoons/2 tablespoons medium dry sherry
120 ml/4 fl oz red wine
salt
freshly ground black pepper
freshly chopped parsley, to garnish

AMERICAN

8 lamb kidneys, skin and cores removed and cut into thick slices
$\frac{3}{8}$ cup butter
1 onion, peeled and finely chopped
1 cup sliced mushrooms
$\frac{1}{4}$ cup flour
1$\frac{1}{4}$ cups beef stock
2 tablespoons medium dry sherry
$\frac{1}{2}$ cup red wine
salt
freshly ground black pepper
freshly chopped parsley, to garnish

Melt the butter in a pan, add the kidneys and fry briskly for 5 minutes. Remove from the pan. Add the onion and mushrooms and fry gently until soft. Stir in the flour and cook for 2 minutes, stirring constantly. Stir in the stock, sherry and wine, bring to the boil and simmer until the sauce is smooth. Return the kidneys to the pan and simmer for 10 minutes.

To freeze: cool quickly, then pour into a rigid container. Seal, label and freeze.

To thaw and serve: reheat from frozen on top of the stove, stirring occasionally. Sprinkle with parsley just before serving.

SERVES 4

KIDNEYS WITH MUSTARD SAUCE

METRIC/IMPERIAL

8 lambs' kidneys, skin and cores removed and cut into thick slices
25 g/1 oz butter
1 small onion, peeled and sliced
225 g/$\frac{1}{2}$ lb mushrooms, sliced
1 × 15 ml spoon/1 tablespoon prepared French mustard
4 × 15 ml spoons/4 tablespoons milk
4 × 15 ml spoons/4 tablespoons single cream
1 × 2.5 ml spoon/$\frac{1}{2}$ teaspoon grated nutmeg
salt
freshly ground black pepper

AMERICAN

8 lamb kidneys, skin and cores removed and cut into thick slices
2 tablespoons butter
1 small onion, peeled and sliced
2 cups sliced mushrooms
1 tablespoon prepared French mustard
$\frac{1}{4}$ cup milk
$\frac{1}{4}$ cup light cream
$\frac{1}{2}$ teaspoon grated nutmeg
salt
freshly ground black pepper

Melt the butter in a pan, add the kidneys and cook until tender. Remove from the pan and keep warm.

Add the onion and mushrooms to the pan, cook for 5 minutes, then stir in the mustard, milk and cream. Return the kidneys to the pan, add nutmeg and salt and pepper to taste, then reheat to just below boiling point.

To freeze: cool quickly, then pour into a rigid container. Seal, label and freeze.

To thaw and serve: thaw at room temperature for 4 hours then reheat gently on top of the stove,

SERVES 4

KIDNEY AND SAUSAGE SAUTÉ

METRIC/IMPERIAL

2 × 15 ml spoons/2 tablespoons vegetable oil
225 g/½ lb chipolata sausages, halved
4 lambs' kidneys, skin and cores removed and halved
1 onion, peeled and sliced
25 g/1 oz flour
150 ml/¼ pint red wine
300 ml/½ pint beef stock
salt
freshly ground black pepper
2 celery stalks, chopped
2 tomatoes, peeled and chopped
1 bouquet garni

AMERICAN

2 tablespoons vegetable oil
½ lb link sausages, halved
4 lamb kidneys, skin and cores removed and halved
1 onion, peeled and sliced
¼ cup flour
⅔ cup red wine
1¼ cups beef stock
salt
freshly ground black pepper
2 celery stalks, chopped
2 tomatoes, peeled and chopped
1 bouquet garni

Heat the oil in a pan, add the sausages and fry gently until lightly browned. Remove from the pan with a slotted spoon. Add the kidneys to the pan and fry until lightly browned on all sides. Remove from the pan with a slotted spoon. Add the onion and fry gently until soft.

Stir in the flour and cook for 2 minutes, then gradually stir in the wine and stock. Bring to the boil, stirring constantly. Add salt and pepper to taste, then add the celery and tomatoes. Return the sausages and kidneys to the pan, add the bouquet garni, cover and simmer for 20 to 30 minutes or until the sausages and kidneys are cooked. Remove the bouquet garni.

To freeze: cool quickly, then pour into a rigid container. Seal, label and freeze.

To thaw and serve: thaw at room temperature for 4 hours, then reheat gently on top of the stove.

SERVES 4

KIDNEYS IN RED WINE

METRIC/IMPERIAL

50 g/2 oz butter
1 onion, peeled and chopped
10 lambs' kidneys, skin and cores removed and cut into thick slices
3 × 15 ml spoons/3 tablespoons flour
150 ml/¼ pint red wine
150 ml/¼ pint stock
1 bouquet garni
1 × 15 ml spoon/1 tablespoon tomato purée
salt
freshly ground black pepper
100 g/4 oz button mushrooms, quartered
100 g/4 oz seedless raisins
freshly chopped parsley, to garnish

AMERICAN

¼ cup butter
1 onion, peeled and chopped
10 lamb kidneys, skin and cores removed and cut into thick slices
3 tablespoons flour
⅔ cup red wine
⅔ cup stock
1 bouquet garni
1 tablespoon tomato paste
salt
freshly ground black pepper
1 cup quartered button mushrooms
⅔ cup seedless raisins
freshly chopped parsley, to garnish

Melt the butter in a pan, add the onion and fry until golden brown. Add the kidneys to the pan and cook for 5 minutes, stirring occasionally. Stir in the flour, then add the wine and stock and bring to the boil. Add the bouquet garni, tomato purée (paste) and salt and pepper to taste and simmer for 5 minutes. Add the mushrooms and raisins and simmer for a further 10 minutes. Remove the bouquet garni.

To freeze: cool quickly, then pour into a rigid container. Seal, label and freeze.

To thaw and serve: reheat from frozen in a covered casserole in a preheated moderate oven (180°C/350°F or Gas Mark 4) for 1½ hours or until heated through. Garnish with parsley just before serving.

SERVES 4 to 6

SWEETBREAD CASSEROLE

METRIC/IMPERIAL
675 g/1½ lb sweetbreads
75 g/3 oz butter
2 carrots, peeled and sliced
4 celery stalks, chopped
1 onion, peeled and finely sliced
1 × 15 ml spoon/1 tablespoon prepared mustard
300 ml/½ pint chicken stock
salt
freshly ground black pepper
25 g/1 oz flour

AMERICAN
1½ lb sweetbreads
⅜ cup butter
2 carrots, peeled and sliced
4 celery stalks, chopped
1 onion, peeled and finely sliced
1 tablespoon prepared mustard
1¼ cups chicken stock
salt
freshly ground black pepper
¼ cup flour

Soak the sweetbreads in cold water for several hours, then rinse under cold running water. Put in a small pan, cover with fresh cold water and bring to the boil. Simmer for 15 minutes, then drain. When cool, remove any fat and gristle and cut into small pieces.

Melt 25 g/1 oz/2 tablespoons of the butter in a flameproof casserole dish, add the sweetbreads and fry until light brown. Remove from the casserole and keep warm. Melt 25 g/1 oz/2 tablespoons of the remaining butter, add the vegetables, cover with greaseproof (waxed) paper and allow to sweat for several minutes. Remove the paper and stir in the mustard. Return the sweetbreads to the casserole and stir in the stock. Add salt and pepper to taste.

Cover the casserole and cook in a preheated moderate oven (180°C/350°F or Gas Mark 4) for 40 minutes. Remove the sweetbreads and vegetables from the casserole and set aside to cool.

Transfer the casserole to the top of the stove and boil to reduce the sauce. Work the remaining butter and flour together with a wooden spoon until smooth, then stir into the sauce and cook until thick. Cool quickly.

To freeze: put the cooled sweetbreads and vegetables into a rigid container and cover with the sauce. Seal, label and freeze.

To thaw and serve: thaw in the refrigerator for 24 hours, then reheat gently on top of the stove, stirring occasionally.

SERVES 4 to 6

STUFFED HEARTS

METRIC/IMPERIAL
4 lambs' hearts
450 ml/¾ pint beef stock
1 × 400 g/14 oz can tomatoes
4 celery stalks, chopped
1 large carrot, peeled and chopped
For the stuffing:
15 g/½ oz butter
1 small onion, peeled and finely chopped
50 g/2 oz fresh white breadcrumbs
1 × 5 ml spoon/1 teaspoon dried mixed herbs
2 × 5 ml spoons/2 teaspoons finely chopped celery
salt
freshly ground black pepper
1 egg, beaten

AMERICAN
4 lamb hearts
2 cups beef stock
1 × 14 oz can tomatoes
4 celery stalks, chopped
1 large carrot, peeled and chopped
For the stuffing:
1 tablespoon butter
1 small onion, peeled and finely chopped
1 cup fresh white breadcrumbs
1 teaspoon dried mixed herbs
2 teaspoons finely chopped celery
salt
freshly ground black pepper
1 egg, beaten

To make the stuffing: melt the butter in a pan, add the onion and fry gently until soft. Stir in the breadcrumbs, herbs, celery and salt and pepper to taste. Bind the mixture with the egg. Trim the hearts and remove all blood vessels and membranes from the outside. Divide the stuffing equally between the hearts and sew up the openings. Place in a casserole dish and pour over the stock and tomatoes. Cover and cook in a preheated moderate oven (160°C/325°F or Gas Mark 3) for 1 hour. Add the celery and carrots, cover and continue cooking for a further 1 hour or until the hearts are tender.

To freeze: cool quickly. Leave in the casserole or transfer to a rigid container. Cover, and wrap in a freezer bag or foil. Seal, label and freeze.

To thaw and serve: thaw at room temperature for 4 hours, then reheat in the covered casserole in a preheated moderate oven (180°C/350°F or Gas Mark 4) for 1 hour or until heated through.

SERVES 4

APPLE AND PEACH SOUFFLÉ

METRIC/IMPERIAL

575 g/1¼ lb cooking apples, peeled, cored and sliced
1 × 440 g/15½ oz can peach slices
6 eggs, separated
275 g/10 oz caster sugar
2 × 15 ml spoons/2 tablespoons lemon juice
5 × 5 ml spoons/5 teaspoons gelatine
3 × 15 ml spoons/3 tablespoons water
2 × 15 ml spoons/2 tablespoons orange-flavoured liqueur
150 ml/¼ pint single cream
300 ml/½ pint double cream
To finish:
a few peach slices
150 ml/¼ pint double cream, stiffly whipped

AMERICAN

1¼ lb baking apples, peeled, cored and sliced
1 × 15½ oz can peach slices
6 eggs, separated
1¼ cups sugar
2 tablespoons lemon juice
5 teaspoons unflavored gelatin
3 tablespoons water
2 tablespoons orange-flavored liqueur
⅔ cup light cream
1¼ cups heavy cream
To finish:
a few peach slices
⅔ cup heavy cream, stiffly whipped

Prepare a 1.5 litre/2½ pint/6¼ cup soufflé dish: cut a strip of doubled greaseproof (waxed) paper long enough to go around the outside of the dish (overlapping) and 5 to 7.5 cm/2 to 3 inches higher than the dish. Tie this securely around the outside of the dish with string and brush the inside of the paper lightly with melted butter or oil.

Put the apples in a pan with 6 × 15 ml spoons/6 tablespoons peach syrup (from the can) and poach gently until the apples are soft. Leave to cool slightly, then work to a smooth purée with the drained peaches in an electric blender or Mouli-légumes (food mill), or rub through a sieve (strainer).

Put the egg yolks, sugar and lemon juice in a heatproof bowl and stand over a pan of gently simmering water. Beat until thick and creamy, then remove from the heat and beat until cool.

Sprinkle the gelatin over the water in a heatproof bowl. Leave until spongy, then place the bowl in a pan of hot water and stir over a low heat until the gelatin has dissolved. Leave to cool slightly, stir into the fruit purée, then beat into the egg mixture with the liqueur.

Beat the creams together until they hold their shape, then fold into the fruit mixture. Beat the egg whites until stiff and fold into the mixture. Spoon into the prepared soufflé dish and chill in the refrigerator until set.

To freeze: open (flash) freeze until firm, then pack in a freezer bag. Seal, label and return to the freezer.

To thaw and serve: remove wrappings and paper collar. Thaw in the refrigerator for 4 to 5 hours, then decorate with the peach slices and rosettes of whipped cream.

SERVES 8

SUMMER PUDDING

METRIC/IMPERIAL

½ large white loaf, crusts removed and sliced
450 g/1 lb cooking apples, peeled, cored and sliced
3 × 15 ml spoons/3 tablespoons water
175 g/6 oz caster sugar, or to taste
225 g/½ lb raspberries
350 g/¾ lb redcurrants
whipped cream, to serve

AMERICAN

½ large white loaf, crusts removed and sliced
1 lb baking apples, peeled, cored and sliced
3 tablespoons water
¾ cup sugar, or to taste
½ lb raspberries
½ lb redcurrants
whipped cream, to serve

Cut the bread into triangles or fingers, then use about one-third to line a 1.2 litre/2 pint/5 cup pudding basin (mold), making sure there are no gaps between the pieces.
Put the apples, water and the sugar in a pan, cover and cook gently until reduced to a purée. Add the raspberries and redcurrants and heat through. Leave to cool slightly, then taste for sweetness and add more sugar if liked.
Spoon some of the fruit mixture into the lined basin (mold), then cover with a layer of bread. Add two more layers of fruit and bread, finishing with a layer of bread, then cover with a saucer and put heavy weights on top. Chill in the refrigerator overnight.
To freeze: remove the weights and saucer, cover the basin (mold) with foil, then pack in a freezer bag. Seal, label and freeze.
To thaw and serve: remove wrappings and thaw at room temperature for 4 hours. Turn out onto a serving platter and serve with whipped cream.
SERVES 6 to 8

BAKEWELL PUDDING

METRIC/IMPERIAL

225 g/½ lb stale sponge cake crumbs
4 × 15 ml spoons/4 tablespoons red jam
3 large eggs, beaten
600 ml/1 pint milk
75 g/3 oz butter
25 g/1 oz ground almonds or hazelnuts

AMERICAN

4 cups stale sponge cake crumbs
¼ cup red jam
3 large eggs, beaten
2½ cups milk
⅜ cup butter
¼ cup ground almonds or hazelnuts

Put the cake crumbs in a buttered 900 ml/1½ pint/3¾ cup ovenproof pie dish and spoon over the jam. Melt the butter in a pan, stir in the ground nuts, then mix with the beaten eggs and milk. Pour the mixture into the pie dish and smooth the top. Bake in a preheated moderate oven (180°C/350°F or Gas Mark 4) for 1 hour.
To freeze: cool quickly, then pack in a freezer bag. Seal, label and freeze.
To thaw and serve: remove wrappings and thaw at room temperature for 2 hours.
SERVES 4 to 6

QUICK RASPBERRY MOUSSE

METRIC/IMPERIAL

1 packet of raspberry jelly
225 g/½ lb raspberries
1 small can evaporated milk, chilled
1 × 15 ml spoon/1 tablespoon kirsch (optional)
whipped cream, to finish

AMERICAN

1 package of raspberry flavored gelatin
½ lb raspberries
1 small can evaporated milk, chilled
1 tablespoon kirsch (optional)
whipped cream, to finish

Put the jelly cubes (gelatin crystals) in a measuring jug (pitcher) and make up to 300 ml/½ pint/1¼ cups with boiling water. Stir to dissolve, then leave until just beginning to set.
Work the raspberries to a purée in an electric blender, then work through a nylon sieve (strainer). Beat into the jelly (gelatin) and continue beating until fluffy. Beat the evaporated milk until thick and creamy, then fold into the raspberry mixture until evenly blended. Stir in the kirsch (if using). Spoon the mixture into a freezerproof serving dish and chill in the refrigerator until set.
To freeze: cover with foil, then pack in a freezer bag. Seal, label and freeze.
To thaw and serve: remove wrappings and thaw the mousse at room temperature for 3 hours. Decorate with rosettes of whipped cream piped over the top.
SERVES 4

MINCEMEAT AND APPLE TART

METRIC/IMPERIAL

basic shortcrust pastry dough made with 175 g/6 oz flour
175 g/6 oz mincemeat
1 medium cooking apple, peeled, cored and grated
To finish:
150 ml/¼ pint double cream, lightly whipped
25 g/1 oz blanched almonds, toasted and chopped

AMERICAN

basic pie dough made with 1½ cups flour
¾ cup mincemeat
1 medium baking apple, peeled, cored and grated
To finish:
⅔ cup heavy cream, lightly whipped
¼ cup blanched almonds, toasted and chopped

Roll out the dough on a floured surface and use to line a 20 cm/8 inch fluted flan ring set on a baking sheet. Mix the mincemeat and apple and spoon into the pastry case (pie shell).
Bake in a preheated moderately hot oven (200°C/400°F or Gas Mark 6) for 15 minutes, then reduce the heat to moderate (160°C/325°F or Gas Mark 3) and bake for a further 10 minutes. Cool quickly, then remove the flan ring.
To freeze: open (flash) freeze until firm, then pack in a freezer bag. Seal, label and return to the freezer.
To thaw and serve: remove wrappings and thaw at room temperature for 2 hours. Cover with cream and scatter the almonds on the top.
SERVES 4 to 6

RUM BABA

METRIC/IMPERIAL

For the dough:
100 g/4 oz flour
pinch of salt
10 g/¼ oz fresh yeast, or 1 × 5 ml spoon/1 teaspoon dried yeast
2 × 15 ml spoons/2 tablespoons caster sugar
4 × 15 ml spoons/4 tablespoons warm milk
2 eggs, beaten
65 g/2½ oz butter, creamed
For the rum syrup:
100 g/4 oz sugar
175 ml/6 fl oz water
120 ml/4 fl oz rum
To finish:
100 g/4 oz apricot jam, sieved
1 × 400 g/14 oz can apricot halves, drained
25 g/1 oz toasted slivered almonds
150 ml/¼ pint double cream, stiffly whipped

AMERICAN

For the dough:
1 cup flour
pinch of salt
¼ cake of compressed fresh yeast, or ½ package active dry yeast
2 tablespoons sugar
¼ cup warm milk
2 eggs, beaten
5 tablespoons butter, creamed
For the rum syrup:
½ cup sugar
¾ cup water
½ cup rum
To finish:
⅓ cup apricot jam, strained
1 × 14 oz can apricot halves, drained
¼ cup toasted slivered almonds
⅔ cup heavy cream, stiffly whipped

To make the dough: sift the flour and salt into a warm bowl and put in a warm place. Cream the yeast with the sugar, add the milk and the eggs, then gradually stir into the flour and beat to a smooth batter. Cover the bowl with a cloth and leave in a warm place for 45 minutes or until the dough has doubled in bulk.
Beat the butter into the dough a little at a time, then put into a greased 18 cm/7 inch baba ring. Leave in warm place until the dough has risen to the rim. Bake in a preheated moderately hot oven (200°C/400°F or Gas Mark 6) for 10 minutes, then reduce the heat to moderate (180°C/350°F or Gas Mark 4) and bake for a further 30 minutes or until a skewer inserted in the centre of the baba comes out clean. Remove from the oven, allow to shrink for 5 to 10 minutes, then loosen with a knife and turn out upside-down.
To make the rum syrup: put the sugar and water in a pan and heat gently until the sugar has dissolved. Boil rapidly until reduced to a syrup, leave to cool slightly, then stir in the rum. Prick the baba and spoon over the syrup. Baste frequently until all the syrup has been absorbed.
To freeze: open (flash) freeze until firm, then wrap in soil. Seal, label and return to the freezer.
To thaw and serve: remove wrappings, place the baba on a serving platter and thaw at room temperature for 4 hours. Heat the jam in a pan, thin with a little water if necessary, then brush over the baba. Arrange 8 apricot halves around the edge of the baba and brush with more apricot jam. Insert the almonds between the apricots. Chop the remaining apricots, fold into the whipped cream and pile into the centre of the baba.
SERVES 4 to 6

ALMOND MACAROON FLAN

METRIC/IMPERIAL

basic sweet shortcrust pastry dough made with 175 g/6 oz flour
50 g/2 oz unsalted butter
50 g/2 oz flour
1 egg
1 egg yolk
275 g/10 oz caster sugar
150 ml/¼ pint milk
2 × 5 ml spoons/2 teaspoons finely grated lemon rind
50 g/2 oz macaroons, crushed
0.5 × 2.5 ml spoon/¼ teaspoon almond essence
2–3 × 15 ml spoons/2–3 tablespoons raspberry jam
To finish:
5 × 15 ml spoons/5 tablespoons whipped cream
a few toasted slivered almonds

AMERICAN

basic sweet pie dough made with 1½ cups flour
¼ cup sweet butter
½ cup flour
1 egg
1 egg yolk
1¼ cups sugar
⅔ cup milk
2 teaspoons finely grated lemon rind
½ cup crushed macaroons
¼ teaspoon almond extract
2–3 tablespoons raspberry jam
To finish:
⅓ cup whipped cream
a few toasted slivered almonds

Roll out the dough on a floured surface and use to line a 20 cm/8 inch flan dish (pie pan). Chill in the refrigerator, then bake blind in a preheated moderately hot oven (200°C/400°F or Gas Mark 6) for 20 to 30 minutes.

Melt the butter in a pan, remove from the heat and stir in the flour. Beat the egg and egg yolk together, then gradually stir into the pan. Add the sugar and stir in the milk. Return to the heat and cook gently until the mixture thickens and begins to leave the sides of the pan, stirring constantly. Remove from the heat and stir in the lemon rind, macaroons and almond essence (extract). Spread the jam in the bottom of the pastry case (pie shell), pour in the almond cream and smooth the top.

To freeze: cool quickly. Open (flash) freeze until firm, then wrap in foil. Seal, label and return to the freezer.

To thaw and serve: remove wrappings and thaw in the refrigerator for 5 hours. Decorate with rosettes of whipped cream and slivered almonds.

SERVES 6

CARAMEL FLAN

METRIC/IMPERIAL

basic shortcrust pastry dough made with 175 g/6 oz flour
100 g/4 oz butter, softened
100 g/4 oz soft brown sugar
1 large egg, beaten
50 g/2 oz walnuts, finely chopped
100 g/4 oz self-raising flour
1 × 2.5 ml spoon/½ teaspoon ground cinnamon
1 × 15 ml spoon/1 tablespoon milk
For the icing:
50 g/2 oz icing sugar, sifted
1 × 5 ml spoon/1 teaspoon coffee essence
8 walnut halves, to decorate

AMERICAN

basic pie dough made with 1½ cups flour
½ cup butter, softened
⅔ cup light brown sugar
1 large egg, beaten
½ cup finely chopped walnuts
1 cup self-rising flour
½ teaspoon ground cinnamon
1 tablespoon milk
For the icing:
½ cup sifted confectioners' sugar
1 teaspoon strong black coffee
8 walnut halves, to decorate

Roll out the dough on a floured surface and use to line a 20 cm/8 inch flan dish (pie pan).

Put the butter and sugar in a bowl, beat together until light and fluffy, then beat in the egg a little at a time. Stir in the walnuts, sift together the flour and cinnamon and fold into the mixture alternately with the milk.

Spoon the mixture into the pastry case (pie shell) and smooth the top. Bake in a preheated hot oven (220°C/425°F or Gas Mark 7) for 15 minutes, reduce the heat to moderate (160°C/325°F or Gas Mark 3) and bake for a further 25 minutes. Leave to cool.

To make the icing: put the icing (confectioners') sugar in a bowl and beat in the coffee until the mixture is smooth. Spread over the top of the flan, decorate with the walnut halves and leave to set.

To freeze: open (flash) freeze until firm, then pack in a freezer bag, seal, label and return to the freezer.

To thaw and serve: remove wrappings and thaw the flan at room temperature for 4 hours.

SERVES 6

ORANGE CHEESECAKE

METRIC/IMPERIAL

For the biscuit crust:
50 g/2 oz butter
finely grated rind of 2 oranges
50 g/2 oz caster sugar
175 g/6 oz digestive biscuits, crushed
For the filling:
50 g/2 oz butter
finely grated rind of 1 orange
75 g/3 oz caster sugar
2 eggs, separated
25 g/1 oz cornflour
350 g/¾ lb cottage cheese, sieved
2 × 15 ml spoons/2 tablespoons orange juice
To finish:
a little sifted icing sugar
1 × 300 g/11 oz can mandarin oranges, drained

AMERICAN

For the crumb crust:
¼ cup butter
finely grated rind of 2 oranges
¼ cup sugar
1½ cups crushed Graham crackers
For the filling:
¼ cup butter
finely grated rind of 1 orange
⅜ cup sugar
2 eggs, separated
¼ cup cornstarch
1½ cups cottage cheese, strained
2 tablespoons orange juice
To finish:
a little sifted confectioners' sugar
1 × 11 oz can mandarin oranges, drained

To make the crust: put the butter, orange rind and sugar in a bowl and beat until creamy. Stir in the biscuits (crackers) and press into a 20 cm/8 inch loose-bottomed cake tin. Chill until set.
To make the filling: put the butter, orange rind and sugar in a bowl and beat until creamy. Stir in the egg yolks, cornflour (cornstarch), cottage cheese and orange juice. Beat the egg whites until stiff, then fold into the mixture. Spoon into the crust and bake in a preheated moderate oven (160°C/325°F or Gas Mark 3) for about 1¼ hours until firm and golden. Turn off the heat, leave to cool in the oven, then remove from the tin. Chill in the refrigerator.
To freeze: open (flash) freeze until firm, then pack in a freezer bag. Seal, label and return to the freezer.
To thaw and serve: thaw in the refrigerator for 4 hours, then sprinkle with icing (confectioners') sugar and decorate with mandarin oranges.
SERVES 6 to 8

PEACH TART

METRIC/IMPERIAL

basic rich shortcrust pastry dough made with 225 g/½ lb flour
1 × 411 g/14½ oz can peach halves, drained
a little egg white, to glaze
caster sugar for sprinkling
150 ml/¼ pint double cream, stiffly whipped, to finish

AMERICAN

basic rich pie dough made with 2 cups flour
1 × 14½ oz can peach halves, drained
a little egg white, to glaze
sugar for sprinkling
⅔ cup heavy cream, stiffly whipped, to finish

Roll out half the dough on a floured surface and use to line a 20 cm/8 inch flan ring set on a baking sheet. Prick the dough and arrange the peaches in the bottom of the pastry case (pie shell). Roll out the remaining dough on a floured surface to a circle large enough to cover the tart. Cut a hole in the centre using a 7.5 cm/3 inch plain cutter, then put the dough over the peaches and seal the edges well. Brush with the egg white, then sprinkle with sugar. Bake in a preheated moderately hot oven (190°C/375°F or Gas Mark 5) for about 35 minutes or until pastry is lightly browned. Cool quickly on a wire rack, then remove the flan ring.
To freeze: open (flash) freeze until firm, then pack in a freezer bag. Seal, label and return to the freezer.
To thaw and serve: remove wrappings and thaw at room temperature for 4 hours. Spoon some of the whipped cream into the centre of the tart and serve the remainder separately.
SERVES 6

APRICOT SPONGE FLAN

METRIC/IMPERIAL

2 eggs
50 g/2 oz caster sugar
50 g/2 oz flour, sifted
1 × 400 g/14 oz can apricot halves, drained
100 g/4 oz apricot jam, sieved
whipped cream, to finish

AMERICAN

2 eggs
¼ cup sugar
½ cup flour, sifted
1 × 14 oz can apricot halves, drained
⅓ cup apricot jam, strained
whipped cream, to finish

Put the eggs and sugar in a bowl and beat until thick and creamy and the mixture leaves a trail from the beater. Fold in the flour quickly and lightly, then pour the mixture into a well greased 20 cm/8 inch flan dish.

Bake in a preheated moderately hot oven (200°C/400°F or Gas Mark 6) for 20 minutes or until well risen and golden. Leave to shrink, then turn out onto a wire rack and arrange the apricot halves in the flan. Heat the jam in a pan, thin with a little water if necessary, then spoon over the apricots.

To freeze: cool quickly. Open (flash) freeze until firm, then pack in a freezer bag. Seal, label and return to the freezer.

To thaw and serve: remove wrappings and thaw in the refrigerator overnight. Decorate with rosettes of whipped cream.

SERVES 4 to 6

WALNUT PUDDING

METRIC/IMPERIAL

225 g/½ lb walnuts, ground
0.5 × 2.5 ml spoon/¼ teaspoon ground mixed spice
4 eggs, separated
225 g/½ lb caster sugar
To finish:
whipped cream
50 g/2 oz walnut halves

AMERICAN

2 cups ground walnuts
¼ teaspoon ground allspice and cloves, mixed
4 eggs, separated
1 cup sugar
To finish:
whipped cream
½ cup walnut halves

Mix together the walnuts and spice(s). Beat the egg yolks and sugar together until pale and creamy, Beat the egg whites until stiff, then fold into the egg yolk mixture alternately with the ground walnuts.

Turn into a buttered 600 ml/1 pint/2½ cup pudding basin (steaming mold) leaving room for the pudding to rise. Cover with greased foil and steam for 1½ hours or until set and springy to the touch. Allow to shrink slightly then unmold.

To freeze: cool quickly. Open (flash) freeze until firm, then wrap in foil. Seal, label and return to the freezer.

To thaw and serve: remove wrappings and thaw in the refrigerator overnight. Decorate with rosettes of whipped cream and the walnut halves.

SERVES 4 to 6

COFFEE CREAM FLAN

METRIC/IMPERIAL

225 g/½ lb digestive biscuits, crushed
75 g/3 oz butter, melted
2 eggs, separated
75 g/3 oz caster sugar
2 × 15 ml spoons/2 tablespoons instant coffee powder
4 × 15 ml spoons/4 tablespoons water
2 × 15 ml spoons/2 tablespoons coffee-flavoured liqueur
2 × 5 ml spoons/2 teaspoons gelatine
To finish:
150 ml/¼ pint double cream, stiffly whipped
50 g/2 oz hazelnuts, toasted and skinned

AMERICAN

2 cups crushed Graham crackers
⅜ cup butter, melted
2 eggs, separated
⅜ cup sugar
2 tablespoons instant coffee powder
¼ cup water
2 tablespoons coffee-flavored liqueur
2 teaspoons unflavored gelatin
To finish:
⅔ cup heavy cream, stiffly whipped
½ cup hazelnuts, toasted and skinned

Put the biscuits in a bowl with the butter, stir well to mix, then press into the bottom and sides of a 20 cm/8 inch fluted flan ring set on a baking sheet. Chill in the refrigerator until set.

Put the egg yolks and sugar in a bowl and beat together until thick and creamy. Blend together the coffee, half the water and the liqueur and gradually beat into the egg mixture.

Sprinkle the gelatin over the remaining water in a heatproof bowl, leave for 5 minutes until spongy, then stand the bowl in a pan of hot water and stir gently until dissolved. Leave to cool, then stir into the coffee mixture and leave until just beginning to set. Beat the egg whites until stiff, fold into the coffee mixture until evenly blended, then spoon into the biscuit (crumb) base.

To freeze: open (flash) freeze until firm, remove the flan ring, then pack in a freezer bag. Seal, label and return to the freezer.

To thaw and serve: remove wrappings and place the flan on a serving platter. Thaw at room temperature for 4 hours, then pipe swirls of cream around the top edge of the flan and decorate with hazelnuts.

SERVES 6 to 8

PINEAPPLE CHARLOTTE RUSSE

METRIC/IMPERIAL

1 packet of lemon jelly
1 × 300 g/11 oz can pineapple pieces
a few strips of candied angelica, cut into diamond shapes
18 Boudoir biscuits or sponge fingers
1–2 × 15 ml spoons/1–2 tablespoons orange-flavoured liqueur
300 ml/½ pint whipping cream, stiffly whipped
To finish:
whipped cream
a few strips of candied angelica

AMERICAN

1 package of lemon-flavored gelatin
1 × 11 oz can pineapple pieces
a few strips of candied angelica, cut into diamond shapes
18 ladyfingers
1–2 tablespoons orange-flavored liqueur
1¼ cups whipping cream, stiffly whipped
To finish:
whipped cream
a few strips of candied angelica

Put the jelly cubes (gelatin crystals) in a bowl, make up to 300 ml/½ pint/1¼ cups with boiling water and stir to dissolve. Add the syrup from the pineapple, making the liquid up to 450 ml/¾ pint/2 cups with water if necessary. Pour a thin layer of liquid jelly (gelatin) into the bottom of a wetted 600 ml/1 pint/2½ cup charlotte mould. Chill in the refrigerator until set.
Cut off the ends of the biscuits (ladyfingers) to 1 cm/½ inch shorter than the mould.
Dip the pineapple pieces and angelica diamonds in the liquid jelly (gelatin), then arrange in an attractive pattern on top of the jelly (gelatin) in the mould. Chill in the refrigerator until set. Cover with another layer of liquid jelly (gelatin) and chill in the refrigerator until set. Dip the sugared side of the biscuits (ladyfingers) one at a time in the liquid jelly (gelatin), then stand them close together all round the sides of the mould. Fold the remaining pineapple and the liqueur into the cream and spoon into the mould. Spoon the remaining liquid jelly (gelatin) slowly down the sides of the mould between the biscuits (ladyfingers), until it shows at the rim of the mould. Chill in the refrigerator until set.
To freeze: cover with foil, then pack in a freezer bag. Seal, label and freeze.
To thaw and serve: thaw in the refrigerator overnight, then unmould and decorate with the whipped cream and angelica.
SERVES 4 to 6

RASPBERRY MERINGUE BASKETS

METRIC/IMPERIAL

For the Swiss meringue:
4 egg whites
225 g/½ lb icing sugar, sifted
0.5 × 2.5 ml spoon/¼ teaspoon vanilla essence
For the filling:
1 × 15 ml spoon/1 tablespoon Kirsch
2 × 5 ml spoons/2 teaspoons caster sugar
150 ml/¼ pint double cream, stiffly whipped
225 g/½ lb raspberries, hulled

AMERICAN

For the Swiss meringue:
4 egg whites
1 cup sifted confectioners' sugar
¼ teaspoon vanilla extract
For the filling:
1 tablespoon Kirsch
2 teaspoons sugar
⅔ cup heavy cream, stiffly whipped
½ lb raspberries, hulled

Put the egg whites and icing (confectioners') sugar in a heatproof bowl over a pan of gently simmering water. Beat until the mixture is very thick and will hold its shape. Beat in the vanilla essence (extract), then spoon into a piping (pastry) bag fitted with a large rose nozzle (tube).
Line 2 baking sheets with non-stick parchment paper and draw 18 circles 7.5 cm/3 inches in diameter. Pipe rings just inside the circles. Fill in 6 of the rings with more meringue to make flat discs, reserving a little meringue for making the baskets.
Bake in a preheated very cool oven (120°C/250°F or Gas Mark ½) for 1½ to 2 hours or until crisp and delicately coloured. Remove from the oven, leave to cool, then loosen the meringues from the parchment paper.
Mount 2 meringue rings on each disc, sticking them together with the reserved meringue. Return to the very cool oven and bake for a further 20 minutes or until firm. Remove from the oven and leave to cool.
Fold the Kirsch and sugar into the whipped cream, then fold in the raspberries and pile into the meringue baskets.
To freeze: open (flash) freeze until frozen, then pack in a rigid container, separating each layer with foil. Seal, label and return to the freezer.
To thaw and serve: transfer to a serving platter and thaw in the refrigerator for 5 to 6 hours.
MAKES 6

PAVLOVA CAKE

METRIC/IMPERIAL

For the meringue:
3 egg whites
175 g/6 oz icing sugar, sifted
1 × 5 ml spoon/1 teaspoon cornflour
0.5 × 2.5 ml spoon/¼ teaspoon vanilla essence
1 × 5 ml spoon/1 teaspoon distilled vinegar
For the filling:
100 g/4 oz strawberries or raspberries, hulled and sliced
100 g/4 oz stoned cherries, roughly chopped
4 ripe apricots, halved, stoned and roughly chopped
2 ripe peaches, halved, stoned and sliced
3 passion fruit (if available), skinned and roughly chopped
300 ml/½ pint double cream, stiffly whipped

AMERICAN

For the meringue:
3 egg whites
1⅓ cups sifted confectioners' sugar
1 teaspoon cornstarch
¼ teaspoon vanilla extract
1 teaspoon distilled vinegar
For the filling:
¼ lb strawberries or raspberries, hulled and sliced
¼ lb roughly chopped pitted cherries
4 ripe apricots, halved, pitted and roughly chopped
2 ripe peaches, halved, pitted and sliced
3 passion fruit (if available), skinned and roughly chopped
1¼ cups heavy cream, stiffly whipped

Line a baking sheet with non-stick parchment paper and draw a circle 18 cm/7 inches in diameter. Put the egg whites in a bowl and beat until very stiff and dry. Beat in half the sugar, then continue beating until the mixture is stiff and shiny. Mix the remaining sugar with the cornflour (cornstarch) and fold into the mixture with the vanilla essence (extract) and vinegar.
Spread the meringue on the circle and build up into a bowl-shaped shell, swirling the meringue around the outside of the shell. Bake in the centre of a preheated cool oven (150°C/300°F or Gas Mark 2) for 1½ hours or until crisp and delicately coloured. Remove from the oven, leave to cool, then peel off the parchment paper.
Fold the fruit into the whipped cream and pile into the centre of the meringue, arranging the passion fruit on the top.
To freeze: open (flash) freeze until firm, then pack in a rigid container. Cover with foil, seal, label and return to the freezer.
To thaw and serve: transfer to a serving platter and thaw in the refrigerator for 5 to 6 hours.
SERVES 4 to 6

PRUNE AND APRICOT SHORTCAKE

METRIC/IMPERIAL

For the shortcake:
100 g/4 oz unsalted butter
50 g/2 oz caster sugar
0.5 × 2.5 ml spoon/¼ teaspoon vanilla essence
175 g/6 oz flour
For the topping:
100 g/4 oz prunes, soaked in cold water overnight, drained and stoned
50 g/2 oz dried apricots, soaked in cold water overnight and drained
2–3 × 15 ml spoons/2–3 tablespoons lemon juice
soft brown sugar for sprinkling
300 ml/½ pint double cream, stiffly whipped, to serve

AMERICAN

For the shortcake:
½ cup sweet butter
¼ cup sugar
¼ teaspoon vanilla extract
1½ cups flour
For the topping:
⅔ cup prunes, soaked in cold water overnight, drained and pitted
⅓ cup dried apricots, soaked in cold water overnight and drained
2–3 tablespoons lemon juice
light brown sugar for sprinkling
1¼ cups heavy cream, stiffly whipped, to serve

Put the butter and sugar in a bowl and beat until light and fluffy. Add the vanilla essence (extract) and the flour and mix to a smooth dough. Knead lightly on a floured surface, pat out to a 5 mm/¼ inch thick circle and place in a 20 cm/8 inch loose-bottomed sandwich tin (layer cake pan). Chill in the refrigerator for 30 minutes, then bake in a preheated moderate oven 180°C/350°F or Gas Mark 4) for 20 minutes.
Arrange the prunes and apricots on top of the shortcake in an attractive pattern and sprinkle with the lemon juice. Cover the fruit with brown sugar, then bake in a preheated moderately hot oven (200°C/400°F or Gas Mark 6) for 10 minutes to caramelize the sugar. Cool quickly on a wire rack, then remove from the tin.
To freeze: open (flash) freeze until firm, then wrap in foil. Seal, label and return to the freezer.
To thaw and serve: remove wrappings and thaw the shortcake in the refrigerator for 5 hours. Serve with whipped cream.
SERVES 4 to 6

MOCHA POTS

METRIC/IMPERIAL

6 eggs, separated
25 g/1 oz butter
175 g/6 oz plain chocolate, broken into pieces
1.5 × 15 ml spoons/1½ tablespoons rum
3 × 15 ml spoons/3 tablespoons coffee essence
To finish:
150 ml/¼ pint double cream, stiffly whipped
50 g/2 oz plain chocolate, grated

AMERICAN

6 eggs, separated
2 tablespoons butter
1 cup semi-sweet chocolate pieces
1½ tablespoons rum
3 tablespoons strong black coffee
To finish:
⅔ cup heavy cream, stiffly whipped
⅓ cup semi-sweet chocolate pieces, grated

Put the egg yolks, butter and chocolate in a heatproof bowl, stand over a pan of gently simmering water and allow to melt. Remove from the heat, then beat in the rum and coffee. Beat the egg whites until stiff, then fold into the chocolate mixture. Pour into 8 small ramekin dishes or pots and leave in a cool place to set.
To freeze: cover with foil, seal, label and freeze.
To thaw and serve: thaw in the refrigerator for 2 hours. Decorate with cream and chocolate.
SERVES 8

POTS-AU-CHOCOLAT WITH GINGER

METRIC/IMPERIAL

100 g/4 oz plain chocolate, broken into pieces
300 ml/½ pint double cream
3 eggs, beaten
2 pieces of stem ginger, finely chopped

AMERICAN

⅔ cup semi-sweet chocolate pieces
1¼ cups heavy cream
3 eggs, beaten
2 pieces of preserved ginger, finely chopped

Put the chocolate in a heatproof bowl, stand over a pan of gently simmering water and allow to melt. Remove from the heat and beat in the cream. Strain the eggs and stir into the chocolate cream with the ginger.
Spoon into 4 individual ovenproof ramekins and place in a roasting tin half-filled with water. Cook in a preheated moderate oven (180°C/350°F or Gas Mark 4) for 30 minutes or until set.
To freeze: cool quickly. Wrap individually in foil, seal, label and freeze.
To thaw and serve: remove wrappings and thaw in the refrigerator overnight.
SERVES 4

YOGURT AND APPLE FLAN

METRIC/IMPERIAL

basic sweet shortcrust pastry dough made with 175 g/6 oz flour
For the filling:
2 medium dessert apples, peeled, cored and sliced
65 g/2½ oz caster sugar
1 × 15 ml spoon/1 tablespoon water
300 ml/½ pint natural yogurt
2 eggs
For the topping (to finish):
2 red-skinned dessert apples
1 × 15 ml spoon/1 tablespoon lemon juice
1 × 15 ml spoon/1 tablespoon liquid honey

AMERICAN

basic sweet pie dough made with 1½ cups flour
For the filling:
2 medium dessert apples, peeled, cored and sliced
5 tablespoons sugar
1 tablespoon water
1¼ cups unflavored yogurt
2 eggs
For the topping (to finish):
2 red-skinned dessert apples
1 tablespoon lemon juice
1 tablespoon liquid honey

Roll out the dough on a floured surface and use to line a 20 cm/8 inch fluted flan ring set on a baking sheet. Bake blind in a preheated moderately hot oven (190°C/375°F or Gas Mark 5) for 15 minutes.
To make the filling: put the apples, 15 g/½ oz/1 tablespoon sugar and the water in a pan, cover and cook gently for 8 to 10 minutes until the apples are soft. Arrange on the bottom of the pastry case (pie shell). Put the yogurt, eggs and remaining sugar in a bowl, beat well to mix, then spoon over the apples. Bake in a preheated moderate oven (180°C/350°F or Gas Mark 4) for 25 to 30 minutes or until the filling is set. Cool quickly, then remove the flan ring.
To freeze: open (flash) freeze until firm, then wrap in foil. Seal, label and return to the freezer.
To thaw and serve: remove wrappings and thaw at room temperature for 4 hours. Core and slice the apples, arrange on top of the flan, sprinkle with the lemon juice and brush with the honey.
SERVES 4 to 6

LATTICE CHEESECAKE

METRIC/IMPERIAL

For the pastry:

225 g/½ lb flour
0.5 × 2.5 ml spoon/¼ teaspoon salt
100 g/4 oz butter
40 g/1½ oz caster sugar
1 egg yolk
1–2 × 15 ml spoons/1–2 tablespoons water

For the filling:

4 eggs
50 g/2 oz sugar
finely grated rind of 2 lemons
juice of 1 lemon
225 g/½ lb cottage cheese, sieved
300 ml/½ pint soured cream
1 × 15 ml spoon/1 tablespoon flour
40 g/1½ oz currants
50 g/2 oz chopped mixed peel

AMERICAN

For the pastry:

2 cups flour
¼ teaspoon salt
½ cup butter
3 tablespoons sugar
1 egg yolk
1–2 tablespoons water

For the filling:

4 eggs
¼ cup sugar
finely grated rind of 2 lemons
juice of 1 lemon
1 cup cottage cheese, strained
1¼ cups sour cream
1 tablespoon flour
4½ tablespoons currants
6 tablespoons chopped candied peel

To make the pastry: sift the flour and salt into a bowl, add the butter in pieces and rub into the flour until the mixture resembles fine breadcrumbs. Stir in the sugar and egg yolk and enough water to give a stiff dough. Wrap in foil and chill in the refrigerator for 1 hour.
Roll out the dough on a floured surface and use to line a 20 cm/8 inch flan ring set on a baking sheet. Reserve the trimmings for the lattice. Bake blind in a preheated moderately hot oven (200°C/400°F or Gas Mark 6) for 15 minutes.
To make the filling: put the eggs and sugar in a bowl and beat well to mix. Beat in the remaining ingredients, then pour into the pastry case (pie shell). Bake in a preheated moderate oven (180°C/350°F or Gas Mark 4) for 25 minutes, then remove from the oven.

Roll out the reserved trimmings of dough into 5 mm/¼ inch strips. Arrange on top of the cheesecake in a lattice pattern, then return to the moderate oven and bake for a further 20 minutes. Turn off the heat and leave to cool in the oven, then remove the flan ring.
To freeze: open (flash) freeze until firm, then wrap in foil. Seal, label and return to the freezer.
To thaw and serve: remove wrappings and thaw at room temperature for 4 hours.
SERVES 8

INDIVIDUAL CURRANT CHEESECAKES

METRIC/IMPERIAL

basic sweet shortcrust pastry dough made with 225 g/½ lb flour
75 g/3 oz currants
225 g/½ lb cottage cheese, sieved
300 ml/½ pint soured cream
50 g/2 oz caster sugar
2 eggs
1 egg white
2 × 5 ml spoons/2 teaspoons finely grated lemon rind

AMERICAN

basic sweet pie dough made with 2 cups flour
½ cup currants
1 cup cottage cheese, strained
1¼ cups sour cream
¼ cup sugar
2 eggs
1 egg white
2 teaspoons finely grated lemon rind

Roll out the dough on a floured surface, cut out 24 circles with a 7.5 cm/3 inch fluted cutter and use to line 24 deep patty tins. Prick the dough, then chill in the refrigerator for at least 30 minutes.
Scatter the currants over the bottom of each pastry case (pie shell). Put the remaining ingredients in a bowl and beat well to mix. Divide the mixture equally between the pastry cases (pie shells) and bake in a preheated hot oven (220°C/425°F or Gas Mark 7) for 5 minutes. Reduce the heat to moderate (160°C/325°F or Gas Mark 3) and bake for a further 10 minutes.
To freeze: cool quickly. Open (flash) freeze until firm, then remove from the patty tins. Pack in a rigid container, separating each layer with foil. Seal, label and return to the freezer.
To thaw and serve: transfer the cheesecakes to a serving platter and thaw at room temperature for 1 to 2 hours.
MAKES 24

CHILLED ORANGE AND LEMON CHEESECAKE

METRIC/IMPERIAL

For the filling:

2 egg yolks
100 g/4 oz sugar
finely grated rind of 1 orange
finely grated rind of 1 lemon
3 × 15 ml spoons/3 tablespoons orange juice
3 × 15 ml spoons/3 tablespoons lemon juice
15 g/½ oz gelatine
2 × 15 ml spoons/2 tablespoons water
350 g/¾ lb cottage cheese, sieved
150 ml/¼ pint soured cream
4 egg whites

For the biscuit crust:

8 digestive biscuits, crushed
25 g/1 oz demerara sugar
50 g/2 oz butter, melted

To finish:

a few orange slices
whipped cream
chopped nuts

AMERICAN

For the filling:

2 egg yolks
½ cup sugar
finely grated rind of 1 orange
finely grated rind of 1 lemon
3 tablespoons orange juice
3 tablespoons lemon juice
2 envelopes unflavored gelatin
2 tablespoons water
1½ cups cottage cheese, strained
⅔ cup sour cream
4 egg whites

For the crumb crust:

8 Graham crackers, crushed
2 tablespoons raw brown sugar
¼ cup butter, melted

To finish:

a few orange slices
whipped cream
chopped nuts

To make the filling: put the egg yolks and 50 g/2 oz/¼ cup sugar in a heatproof bowl and beat well to mix. Stir in the orange and lemon rinds and the juices. Stand the bowl over a pan of gently simmering water and stir until the mixture coats the back of a spoon.

Sprinkle the gelatine over the water in a heatproof bowl. Leave until spongy, then place the bowl in a pan of hot water and stir over a low heat until the gelatine has dissolved. Stir into the egg yolk mixture, then leave to cool slightly. Fold in the cottage cheese and soured cream.

Beat the egg whites until stiff, fold in the remaining sugar, then stir into the cheese mixture. Pour into a 20 cm/8 inch cake tin and chill in the refrigerator until set.

To make the crust: put all the ingredients in a bowl and stir well to mix. Scatter over the cheesecake and press down lightly. Chill in the refrigerator until the crust is firm.

To freeze: open (flash) freeze until firm, then remove the tin and wrap the cheesecake in a freezer bag. Seal, label and return to the freezer.

To thaw and serve: remove wrappings and place the cheesecake on a serving platter, crust side down. Thaw in the refrigerator overnight, then decorate with orange slices, cream and nuts.

SERVES 6 to 8

RASPBERRY CHEESECAKE

METRIC/IMPERIAL

Basic sweet shortcrust pastry dough made with 100 g/4 oz flour

For the filling:

3 egg yolks
100 g/4 oz caster sugar
finely grated rind and juice of ½ lemon
150 ml/¼ pint soured cream
350 g/¾ lb cottage cheese, sieved
15 g/½ oz gelatine
2 × 15 ml spoons/2 tablespoons water
3 egg whites

To finish:

whipped cream
225 g/½ lb raspberries, hulled

AMERICAN

basic sweet pie dough made with 1 cup flour

For the filling:

3 egg yolks
½ cup sugar
finely grated rind and juice of ½ lemon
⅔ cup sour cream
1½ cups cottage cheese, strained
2 envelopes unflavored gelatin
2 tablespoons water
3 egg whites

To finish:

whipped cream
½ lb raspberries, hulled

Roll out the dough on a floured surface and use to line the bottom of a 20 cm/8 inch loose-bottomed cake tin. Bake blind in a preheated moderately hot oven (190°C/375°F or Gas Mark 5) for 15 minutes, then remove the foil and beans. Return to the oven, bake for a further 10 minutes, then leave to cool in the tin.

To make the filling: put the egg yolks and sugar in a heatproof bowl, stand over a pan of gently simmering water and beat until thick and creamy. Remove from the heat and stir in the lemon rind and juice, sour(ed) cream and cheese.

Sprinkle the gelatine over the water in a heatproof bowl, leave until spongy, then place the bowl in a pan of hot water and stir over a low heat until the gelatine has dissolved. Fold into the cheese mixture and leave until just beginning to set.

Beat the egg whites until stiff, fold into the cheese mixture, then pour into the pastry case (pie shell). Chill in the refrigerator until set, then remove from the cake tin.

To freeze: open (flash) freeze until firm, then pack in a freezer bag. Seal, label and return to the freezer.

To thaw and serve: remove wrappings and thaw in the refrigerator overnight. Decorate the top of the cheesecake with rosettes of whipped cream and the raspberries.

SERVES 6 to 8

ORANGE CHOCOLATE MOUSSE

METRIC/IMPERIAL

100 g/4 oz plain chocolate, broken into pieces
15 g/½ oz butter
finely grated rind and juice of 1 orange
2 eggs, separated
150 ml/¼ pint double cream, whipped

AMERICAN

⅔ cup semi-sweet chocolate pieces
1 tablespoon butter
finely grated rind and juice of 1 orange
2 eggs, separated
⅔ cup heavy cream, whipped

Put the chocolate in a heatproof bowl, stand over a pan of gently simmering water and allow to melt. Remove from the heat and beat in the butter, orange rind and juice and the egg yolks. Leave to cool, then fold in half the cream.

Beat the egg whites until stiff, then fold into the chocolate mixture. Pour into 4 individual freezerproof serving dishes and chill in the refrigerator until set. Decorate with the remaining whipped cream.

To freeze: open (flash) freeze until firm, then pack individually in freezer bags. Seal, label and return to the freezer.

To thaw and serve: remove wrappings and thaw in the refrigerator for 6 hours.

SERVES 4

YOGURT AND APRICOT ALMOND FLAN

METRIC/IMPERIAL

For the pastry:
100 g/4 oz flour
75 g/3 oz butter
75 g/3 oz ground almonds
50 g/2 oz caster sugar
1 egg yolk
2 × 5 ml spoons/2 teaspoons water
For the filling:
300 ml/½ pint natural yogurt
2 egg yolks
50 g/2 oz sugar
1 × 800 g/1 lb 13 oz can apricot halves, drained

AMERICAN

For the pastry:
1 cup flour
⅜ cup butter
¾ cup ground almonds
¼ cup sugar
1 egg yolk
2 teaspoons water
For the filling:
1¼ cups unflavored yogurt
2 egg yolks
¼ cup sugar
1 × 1 lb 13 oz can apricot halves, drained

To make the pastry: sift the flour into a bowl, add the butter in pieces and rub into the flour until the mixture resembles fine breadcrumbs. Stir in the almonds and sugar, then add the egg yolk and water. Mix to a firm dough. Knead lightly until smooth, then wrap in foil and chill in the refrigerator for 1 hour.

Roll out the dough on a floured surface and use to line a 20 cm/8 inch fluted flan ring set on a baking sheet. Bake blind in a preheated moderately hot oven (190°C/375°F or Gas Mark 5) for 15 minutes.

To make the filling: put the yogurt, egg yolks and sugar in a bowl and stir well to mix. Spoon half of the mixture into the pastry case (pie shell) and bake in a preheated moderate oven (180°C/350°F or Gas Mark 4) for 20 minutes. Arrange the apricots on top, cut sides down, then spoon the remaining yogurt mixture around them. Return to the moderate oven and bake for a further 10 to 15 minutes or until the filling is set. Cool quickly, then remove the flan ring.

To freeze: open (flash) freeze until firm, then wrap in foil. Seal, label and return to the freezer.

To thaw and serve: remove wrappings and thaw in the refrigerator overnight.

SERVES 4 to 6

APRICOT AND RAISIN CHEESECAKE

METRIC/IMPERIAL

For the sponge base:

50 g/2 oz soft tub margarine
50 g/2 oz caster sugar
1 egg
50 g/2 oz self-raising flour
1 × 2.5 ml spoon/½ spoon baking powder

For the filling:

350 g/¾ lb cottage cheese, sieved
150 ml/¼ pint double cream
25 g/1 oz desiccated coconut
25 g/1 oz flour
50 g/2 oz sugar
3 eggs, beaten
75 g/3 oz dried apricots, finely chopped
25 g/1 oz seedless raisins

To finish:

1 × 15 ml spoon/1 tablespoon sifted icing sugar
2 × 15 ml spoons/2 tablespoons apricot jam, warmed and sieved
1 packet of sponge fingers, cut in half

AMERICAN

For the sponge base:

¼ cup soft margarine
¼ cup sugar
1 egg
½ cup self-rising flour
½ teaspoon baking powder

For the filling:

1½ cups cottage cheese, strained
⅔ cup heavy cream
⅔ cup shredded coconut
¼ cup flour
¼ cup sugar
3 eggs, beaten
½ cup dried apricots, finely chopped
3 tablespoons seedless raisins

To finish:

1 tablespoon sifted confectioners' sugar
2 tablespoons apricot jam, warmed and strained
1 package of ladyfingers, cut in half

Grease an 18 cm/7 inch square cake tin and line with greased greaseproof paper or non-stick parchment.

To make the sponge base: put all the ingredients in a bowl and beat with a wooden spoon for 2 to 3 minutes or until smooth. Put into the bottom of the prepared tin and bake in a preheated moderate oven (160°C/325°F or Gas Mark 3) for 15 minutes or until firm to the touch.

To make the filling: put all the ingredients in a bowl and beat well to mix. Pour over the sponge and bake in the moderate oven for 1½ hours. Turn off the heat and leave the cheesecake in the oven for 30 minutes, then remove from the tin and cool quickly on a wire rack.

To freeze: open (flash) freeze until firm, then pack in a freezer bag. Seal, label and return to the freezer.

To thaw and serve: remove wrappings, place on a serving platter, and thaw at room temperature for 4 hours. Sprinkle the top of the cheesecake with the icing (confectioners') sugar. Brush the sides with the apricot jam, then press the sponge fingers (ladyfingers) around the sides, rounded ends uppermost.

MAKES 14 SLICES

CRÈME DE MENTHE SOUFFLÉ

METRIC/IMPERIAL

3 egg yolks
50 g/2 oz sugar
2 × 5 ml spoons/2 teaspoons gelatine
4 × 15 ml spoons/4 tablespoons water
2 × 15 ml spoons/2 tablespoons Crème de Menthe liqueur
2–3 drops of green food colouring
150 ml/¼ pint double cream
150 ml/¼ pint single cream
3 egg whites

To finish:

a little melted butter or vegetable oil
25 g/1 oz walnuts, finely chopped
whipped cream
chocolate curls

AMERICAN

3 egg yolks
¼ cup sugar
2 teaspoons unflavored gelatin
¼ cup water
2 tablespoons Crème de Menthe liqueur
2–3 drops of green food coloring
⅔ cup heavy cream
⅔ cup light cream
3 egg whites

To finish:

a little melted butter or vegetable oil
¼ cup finely chopped walnuts
whipped cream
chocolate curls

Prepare a 750 ml/1¼ pint/3 cup soufflé dish: cut a strip of doubled greaseproof (waxed) paper long enough to go around the outside of the dish (overlapping) and 5 to 7.5 cm/2 to 3 inches higher than the dish. Tie this securely around the outside of the dish and brush the inside of the paper lightly with melted butter or oil.

Put the egg yolks and sugar in a heatproof bowl and stand over a pan of gently simmering water. Beat until thick and creamy, then remove from the heat and beat until cool.

Sprinkle the gelatine over the water in a heatproof bowl, leave until spongy, then place the bowl in a pan of hot water and stir over a low heat until the gelatine has dissolved. Leave to cool slightly, then stir into the egg yolk mixture with the liqueur and food colouring.

Beat the creams together until they hold their shape, then fold into the egg yolk mixture. Beat the egg whites until stiff and fold into the mixture. Spoon into the prepared soufflé dish and chill in the refrigerator until set.

To freeze: open (flash) freeze until firm, then wrap in a freezer bag. Seal, label and return to the freezer.

To thaw and serve: remove wrappings and paper collar. Thaw the soufflé in the refrigerator for 4 to 5 hours, then brush the exposed edge lightly with the melted butter or oil and press the walnuts around the edge. Decorate the top with rosettes of whipped cream and chocolate curls.

SERVES 6

STRAWBERRY HAZELNUT SHORTCAKE

METRIC/IMPERIAL

For the shortcake:

225 g/½ lb flour
pinch of salt
75 g/3 oz roasted hazelnuts, finely chopped
175 g/6 oz butter
75 g/3 oz icing sugar, sifted
2 egg yolks

To finish

300 ml/½ pint double cream
4 × 15 ml spoons/4 tablespoons single cream or creamy milk
50 g/2 oz icing sugar, sifted
350 g/¾ lb strawberries, hulled

AMERICAN

For the shortcake:

2 cups flour
pinch of salt
¾ cup finely chopped roasted hazelnuts
¾ cup butter
¾ cup sifted confectioners' sugar
2 egg yolks

To finish:

1¼ cups heavy cream
¼ cup light cream or half-and-half
½ cup sifted confectioners' sugar
¾ lb strawberries, hulled

To make the shortcake: sift the flour and salt into a bowl and stir in the hazelnuts. Add the butter in pieces and rub into the flour until the mixture resembles fine breadcrumbs. Stir in the icing (confectioners') sugar and the egg yolks and mix to a firm dough. Cover with foil and chill in the refrigerator for 1 hour.

Divide the dough in two and roll out each piece on a floured surface to a 20 cm/8 inch circle. Press into the bottom of 2 greased 20 cm/8 inch flan rings set on a baking sheet. Prick the dough, then bake in a preheated moderate oven (180°C/350°F or Gas Mark 4) for 15 to 20 minutes until the shortcake is firm but not browned. Mark one circle into 6 to 8 triangles, leave until just cool, then cut through.

To freeze: open (flash) freeze until firm, then pack in a rigid container, separating each layer with foil. Seal, label and return to the freezer.

To thaw and serve: remove from the container and thaw at room temperature for 2 hours. Beat the creams together until stiff, then fold in the icing (confectioners') sugar. Put in a piping (pastry) bag fitted with a large star nozzle (fluted tube) and pipe over the circle of shortcake.

Slice the strawberries and put on top of the cream. Sprinkle 3 or 4 shortcake triangles with a little icing (confectioners') sugar, then arrange on top, alternating them with the 3 or 4 plain shortcake triangles.

SERVES 6 to 8

CHESTNUT DESSERT

METRIC/IMPERIAL

150 ml/¼ pint double cream
2 × 15 ml spoons/2 tablespoons milk
225 g/½ lb sweetened chestnut purée
5 × 15 ml spoons/5 tablespoons single cream, to serve

AMERICAN

⅔ cup heavy cream
2 tablespoons milk
scant 1 cup sweetened chestnut purée
⅓ cup light cream, to serve

Put the cream and milk in a bowl and beat until thick. Fold in the chestnut purée until evenly blended, then spoon or pipe into individual freezerproof dishes.

To freeze: cover with foil, then pack in freezer bags. Seal, label and freeze.

To thaw and serve: remove wrappings and thaw in the refrigerator for 6 hours. Pour a little single (light) cream over the top of each dessert before serving.

SERVES 4

YOGURT AND BANANA GINGERNUT (GINGERSNAP)

METRIC/IMPERIAL

For the flan case:

175 g/6 oz gingernut biscuits, crushed
50 g/2 oz caster sugar
50 g/2 oz butter, melted

For the filling:

5–6 medium ripe bananas, peeled
2 × 15 ml spoons/2 tablespoons lemon juice
½ small can evaporated milk, chilled
150 ml/¼ pint natural yogurt
2 × 5 ml spoons/2 teaspoons gelatine
2 × 15 ml spoons/2 tablespoons water

To finish:

1 small ripe banana, peeled and sliced
whipped cream

AMERICAN

For the flan case:

1½ cups crushed gingersnap cookies
¼ cup sugar
¼ cup butter, melted

For the filling:

5–6 medium ripe bananas, peeled
2 tablespoons lemon juice
½ can evaporated milk, chilled
⅔ cup unflavored yogurt
2 teaspoons unflavored gelatin
2 tablespoons water

To finish:

1 small ripe banana, peeled and sliced
whipped cream

Grease a 20 cm/8 inch flan ring set on a baking sheet and line with greased greaseproof (waxed) paper.

To make the flan case: put all the ingredients in a bowl and stir well to mix. Press into the prepared flan ring, then chill in the refrigerator until set.

To make the filling: work the bananas to a smooth purée in an electric blender or rub through a sieve (strainer). Stir in the lemon juice immediately to prevent discoloration. Beat the evaporated milk until thick, then fold into the banana purée with the yogurt.

Sprinkle the gelatine over the water in a heatproof bowl. Leave until spongy, then place the bowl in a pan of hot water and stir over a low heat until the gelatine has dissolved. Leave to cool slightly, then stir into the banana mixture. Pour into the flan case and chill until set.

To freeze: open (flash) freeze until firm, then remove the flan ring and paper. Pack in a freezer bag, seal, label and return to the freezer.

To thaw and serve: remove wrappings and thaw at room temperature for 4 hours. Decorate with the banana slices and rosettes of whipped cream.

SERVES 6

MARRONS MONT BLANC

METRIC/IMPERIAL

For the sponge base:

100 g/4 oz soft tub margarine
100 g/4 oz caster sugar
2 large eggs
100 g/4 oz self-raising flour
1 × 5 ml spoon/1 teaspoon baking powder

For the filling:

1 × 425 g/15 oz can unsweetened chestnut purée
2 × 15 ml spoons/2 tablespoons rum
50 g/2 oz caster sugar
300 ml/½ pint double cream, whipped

AMERICAN

For the sponge base:

½ cup soft margarine
½ cup sugar
2 large eggs
1 cup self-rising flour
1 teaspoon baking powder

For the filling:

1 × 15 oz can unsweetened chestnut purée
2 tablespoons rum
¼ cup sugar
1¼ cups heavy cream, whipped

To make the sponge base: put all the ingredients in a bowl and beat with a wooden spoon for 2 to 3 minutes or until smooth. Put into a greased 20 cm/8 inch flan tin and bake in a preheated moderate oven (160°C/325°F or Gas Mark 3) for 30 to 35 minutes or until a skewer inserted in the centre of the sponge comes out clean. Turn out onto a wire rack and leave to cool.

To make the filling: put all the ingredients, except the cream, in a bowl and beat well to mix. Put into a piping (pastry) bag fitted with a large star nozzle (fluted tube) and pipe over the flan base, finishing with a row of stars around the edge. Pile the whipped cream in the centre.

To freeze: open (flash) freeze until firm, then pack in a rigid container. Seal, label and return to the freezer.

To thaw and serve: remove from the container and place on a serving platter. Thaw in the refrigerator overnight.

SERVES 6

APPLE SUNSHINE TART

METRIC/IMPERIAL

basic shortcrust pastry dough made with 100 g/4 oz flour
3 large cooking apples, peeled, cored and sliced
3 × 15 ml spoons/3 tablespoons sugar
1 × 15 ml spoon/1 tablespoon water
1 × 15 ml spoon/1 tablespoon mincemeat
15 g/½ oz butter
1 × 15 ml spoon/1 tablespoon fresh white breadcrumbs

AMERICAN

basic pie dough made with 1 cup flour
3 large baking apples, peeled, cored and sliced
3 tablespoons sugar
1 tablespoon water
1 tablespoon mincemeat
1 tablespoon butter
1 tablespoon fresh white breadcrumbs

Roll out the dough on a floured surface and use to line a 20 cm/8 inch ovenproof pie plate. Make small cuts around the edge of the dough 1.5 cm/¾ inch apart. Moisten the edge with water, then fold one corner of the cut dough over diagonally. Press firmly, then continue this process to make a sunray pattern.
Prick the dough and bake in a preheated moderately hot oven (200°C/400°F or Gas Mark 6) for 20 to 25 minutes until golden and set.
Put the apples, sugar and water in a pan and cook gently until soft. Stir in the mincemeat, then spread over the centre of the pastry.
Melt the butter in a pan, add the breadcrumbs and fry gently until golden brown. Remove from the pan with a slotted spoon, then scatter over the apple mixture.
To freeze: open (flash) freeze until firm, then pack in a freezer bag. Seal, label and return to the freezer.
To thaw and serve: remove wrappings and thaw at room temperature for 4 hours.
SERVES 4 to 6

REDCURRANT TART

METRIC/IMPERIAL

basic shortcrust pastry dough made with 100 g/4 oz flour
450 g/1 lb redcurrants, stalks removed
3 × 15 ml spoons/3 tablespoons sugar
4 × 15 ml spoons/4 tablespoons water
2 × 5 ml spoons/2 teaspoons arrowroot
15 g/½ oz butter
1 × 15 ml spoon/1 tablespoon fresh white breadcrumbs

AMERICAN

basic pie dough made with 1 cup flour
1 lb redcurrants, stalks removed
3 tablespoons sugar
¼ cup water
2 teaspoons arrowroot flour
1 tablespoon butter
1 tablespoon fresh white breadcrumbs

Make and bake the pastry as for Apple Sunshine Tart.
Put the redcurrants, sugar and water in a pan and cook gently until soft. Strain the juice and measure 150 ml/¼ pint/⅔ cup, making up the quantity with water if necessary. Return to the rinsed-out pan.
Mix the arrowroot to a paste with a little water and stir into the juice. Bring to the boil and simmer for 2 to 3 minutes until thick, stirring constantly. Add the redcurrants to the thickened juice and pour into the centre of the pastry.
Fry the breadcrumbs in the butter, freeze, thaw and serve as for Apple Sunshine Tart.
SERVES 4 to 6

DAMSON AND APPLE TART

METRIC/IMPERIAL

basic shortcrust pastry dough made with 100 g/4 oz flour
225 g/½ lb damsons
2 medium cooking apples, peeled, cored and sliced
3 × 15 ml spoons/3 tablespoons sugar
4 × 15 ml spoons/4 tablespoons water
15 g/½ oz butter
1 × 15 ml spoon/1 tablespoon fresh white breadcrumbs

AMERICAN

basic pie dough made with 1 cup flour
½ lb damsons
2 medium baking apples, peeled, cored and sliced
3 tablespoons sugar
¼ cup water
1 tablespoon butter
1 tablespoon fresh white breadcrumbs

Make and bake the pastry as for Apple Sunshine Tart.
Put the damsons, apples, sugar and water in a pan and cook gently until soft. Remove the stones (seeds) from the damsons, then spread the mixture over the centre of the pastry and smooth the top.
Fry the breadcrumbs in the butter, freeze, thaw and serve as for Apple Sunshine Tart.
SERVES 4 to 6

AUSTRIAN COFFEE CAKE

METRIC/IMPERIAL

For the cake:

100 g/4 oz butter
100 g/4 oz caster sugar
2 × 15 ml spoons/2 tablespoons coffee essence
2 eggs, beaten
100 g/4 oz self-raising flour
pinch of salt

For the coffee syrup:

150 ml/¼ pint water
100 g/4 oz sugar
5 × 15 ml spoons/5 tablespoons very strong black coffee
1–2 × 15 ml spoons/1–2 tablespoons brandy

To finish:

300 ml/½ pint double cream, stiffly whipped
50 g/2 oz toasted slivered almonds

AMERICAN

For the cake:

½ cup butter
½ cup sugar
2 tablespoons strong black coffee
2 eggs, beaten
1 cup self-rising flour
pinch of salt

For the coffee syrup:

⅔ cup water
½ cup sugar
⅓ cup very strong black coffee
1–2 tablespoons brandy

To finish:

1¼ cups heavy cream, stiffly whipped
½ cup toasted slivered almonds

To make the cake: put the butter and sugar in a bowl and beat together until light and fluffy. Beat in the coffee, then the eggs a little at a time. Sift the flour and salt together, then beat 1 × 15 ml spoon/1 tablespoon flour into the creamed mixture. Fold in the remaining flour.

Put the mixture in a buttered and floured savarin tin and smooth the top. Bake in a preheated moderate oven (160°C/325°F or Gas Mark 3) for 30 to 35 minutes or until well risen and golden. Turn out onto a wire rack, leave to cool, then prick all over the cake with a skewer.

To make the coffee syrup: put the water and sugar in a pan and heat gently until the sugar has dissolved. Bring to the boil and boil rapidly for 2 to 3 minutes. Remove from the heat and leave to cool slightly, then stir in the coffee and brandy. Spoon slowly over the cake.

To freeze: cool quickly. Open (flash) freeze until firm, then wrap in foil. Seal, label and return to the freezer.

To thaw and serve: remove wrappings and place the cake on a serving platter. Thaw at room temperature for 4 hours, then cover the cake with some of the whipped cream. Decorate with the almonds and the remaining cream piped into rosettes.

SERVES 6

APRICOT AND PRUNE CREAM TART

METRIC/IMPERIAL

basic shortcrust pastry dough made with 175 g/6 oz flour
50 g/2 oz dried apricots, soaked in cold water overnight, drained and chopped
50 g/2 oz prunes, soaked in cold water overnight, drained, stoned and chopped
1 egg
150 ml/¼ pint soured cream
25 g/1 oz caster sugar
6 walnut halves

AMERICAN

basic pie dough made with 1½ cups flour
⅓ cup dried apricots, soaked in cold water overnight, drained and chopped
⅓ cup prunes, soaked in cold water overnight, drained, pitted and chopped
1 egg
⅔ cup sour cream
2 tablespoons sugar
6 walnut halves

Roll out the dough on a floured surface and use to line an 18 cm/7 inch fluted flan ring set on a baking sheet. Bake blind in a preheated moderately hot oven (200°C/400°F or Gas Mark 6) for 15 minutes.

Pack the apricots and prunes tightly into the bottom of the pastry case (pie shell). Put the egg, sour(ed) cream and sugar in a bowl, beat well to mix, then pour over the fruit. Bake in a preheated moderately hot oven (190°C/375°F or Gas Mark 5) for 40 minutes or until set. Decorate with the walnuts, cool quickly on a wire rack, then remove the flan ring.

To freeze: open (flash) freeze until firm, then pack in a freezer bag. Seal, label and return to the freezer.

To thaw and serve: remove wrappings and thaw at room temperature for 4 hours.

SERVES 4

TREACLE TART

METRIC/IMPERIAL

basic shortcrust pastry dough made with 225 g/½ lb flour
3 × 15 ml spoons/3 tablespoons golden syrup
3 × 15 ml spoons/3 tablespoons fresh white breadcrumbs
finely grated rind of 1 lemon (optional)

AMERICAN

basic pie dough made with 2 cups flour
3 tablespoons light corn syrup
3 tablespoons fresh white breadcrumbs
finely grated rind of 1 lemon (optional)

Roll out the dough thinly on a floured surface and cut out a 20 to 23 cm/8 to 9 inch circle. Roll out the trimmings of dough and cut a 2.5 cm/1 inch strip long enough to go around the outside of a 20 to 23 cm/8 to 9 inch ovenproof pie plate. Moisten the rim of the plate with water and press the strip firmly in position. Moisten the strip with water, then place the circle of dough over the plate and press down gently. Trim and flute the edge.
Put the syrup, breadcrumbs and lemon rind (if using) in a pan and cook gently until the syrup has melted. Leave to cool slightly, then spread over the dough, leaving the edge clear.
Roll out the remaining dough and cut into strips long enough to criss-cross the filling. Moisten the ends of the strips with water and arrange over the filling in a criss-cross pattern, twisting them if liked. Press the wetted ends against the outside edge of the plate. Bake in a preheated moderately hot oven (200°C/400°F or Gas Mark 6) for 30 to 35 minutes.
To freeze: cool quickly. Open (flash) freeze until firm, then pack in a freezer bag. Seal, label and return to the freezer.
To thaw and serve: remove wrappings and thaw at room temperature for 4 hours.
SERVES 6

LEMON CURD (CHEESE) TART

Make as for Treacle Tart, substituting 2–3 × 15 ml spoons/2–3 tablespoons lemon curd (cheese) for the golden (light corn) syrup.
Freeze, thaw and serve as for Treacle Tart.
SERVES 6

MARMALADE TART

METRIC/IMPERIAL

basic shortcrust pastry dough made with 175 g/6 oz flour
50 g/2 oz butter
25 g/1 oz caster sugar
1 egg, beaten
1 × 15 ml spoon/1 tablespoon flour
2 × 15 ml spoons/2 tablespoons marmalade

AMERICAN

basic pie dough made with 1½ cups flour
¼ cup butter
2 tablespoons sugar
1 egg, beaten
1 tablespoon flour
2 tablespoons marmalade

Roll out the dough on a floured surface and use to line an 18 cm/7 inch fluted flan ring set on a baking sheet. Reserve the trimmings. Bake blind in a preheated moderately hot oven (190°C/375°F or Gas Mark 5) for 15 minutes.
Put the butter and sugar in a bowl and beat together until light and fluffy. Beat in the egg a little at a time, then fold in the flour and marmalade. Spoon into the pastry case (pie shell).
Roll out the reserved trimmings of dough and cut out 4 thin strips. Moisten the ends of the strips with water and arrange over the filling in a criss-cross pattern. Return to the moderately hot oven and bake for a further 25 to 30 minutes or until the filling is set. Cool quickly on a wire rack, then remove the flan ring.
To freeze: open (flash) freeze until firm, then pack in a freezer bag. Seal, label and return to the freezer.
To thaw and serve: remove wrappings and thaw at room temperature for 4 hours.
SERVES 4 to 6

LEMON AND LIME SOUFFLÉ

METRIC/IMPERIAL

15 g/½ oz gelatine
1 × 15 ml spoon/1 tablespoon water
2 × 15 ml spoons/2 tablespoons undiluted lime juice
4 eggs, separated
100 g/4 oz caster sugar
finely grated rind and juice of 2 lemons
To finish:
a little melted butter or vegetable oil
chopped nuts
whipped cream

AMERICAN

2 envelopes unflavored gelatin
1 tablespoon water
2 tablespoons undiluted lime juice
4 eggs, separated
½ cup sugar
finely grated rind and juice of 2 lemons
To finish:
a little melted butter or vegetable oil
chopped nuts
whipped cream

Prepare a 600 ml/1 pint/2½ cup soufflé dish: cut a strip of doubled greaseproof (waxed) paper long enough to go around the outside of the dish (overlapping) and 5 to 7.5 cm/2 to 3 inches higher than the dish. Tie this securely around the outside of the dish and brush the inside of the paper lightly with melted butter or oil.

Sprinkle the gelatine over the water and lime juice in a heatproof bowl. Leave until spongy, then place the bowl in a pan of hot water and stir over a low heat until the gelatine has dissolved. Leave to cool slightly.

Meanwhile, put the egg yolks, sugar, lemon rind and juice in a heatproof bowl and stand over a pan of gently simmering water. Beat until thick and creamy, then remove from the heat and beat until cool. Stir in the gelatine and leave until just beginning to set.

Beat the egg whites until stiff, then fold into the lemon and lime mixture until evenly blended. Pour into the prepared soufflé dish and chill in the refrigerator until set.

To freeze: open (flash) freeze until firm, then pack in a freezer bag. Seal, label and return to the freezer.

To thaw and serve: remove wrappings and paper collar. Thaw the soufflé in the refrigerator for 4 to 5 hours, then brush the exposed edge lightly with the melted butter or oil and press chopped nuts around the edge to coat it completely. Decorate the top of the soufflé with rosettes of whipped cream.

SERVES 4 to 6

GALA RING

METRIC/IMPERIAL

For the choux pastry:
50 g/2 oz butter
150 ml/¼ pint water
pinch of salt
65 g/2½ oz flour, sifted
2–3 eggs, beaten
0.5 × 2.5 ml spoon/¼ teaspoon vanilla essence (optional)
For the filling:
300 ml/½ pint double cream, stiffly whipped
To finish:
225 g/½ lb icing sugar, sifted
1–2 × 15 ml spoons/1–2 tablespoons warm water
a few glacé cherries
a few strips of candied angelica

AMERICAN

For the choux paste:
¼ cup butter
⅔ cup water
pinch of salt
⅔ cup flour, sifted
2–3 eggs, beaten
¼ teaspoon vanilla extract (optional)
For the filling:
1¼ cups heavy cream, stiffly whipped
To finish:
2 cups sifted confectioners' sugar
1–2 tablespoons warm water
a few candied cherries
a few strips of candied angelica

To make the choux pastry (paste): put the butter, water and salt in a pan and heat gently until the butter has melted. Bring to the boil. Immediately remove the pan from the heat and quickly beat in the flour all at once. Continue beating for 2 minutes until the mixture draws away from the sides of the pan and forms a ball. Leave to cool slightly, then beat in the eggs one at a time and the vanilla essence (extract), if using. Beat until the dough is smooth and shiny. Add enough egg to make a mixture that just falls from the spoon.

Put the mixture into a large piping (pastry) bag fitted with a 1.5 cm/¾ inch plain nozzle (tube) and pipe a 15 to 18 cm/6 to 7 inch circle on a greased baking sheet. Bake in a preheated hot oven (220°C/425°F or Gas Mark 7) for 15 minutes, then reduce the heat to moderately hot (190°C/375°F or Gas Mark 5) and bake for a further 20 to 25 minutes. Cool quickly on a wire rack, then cut into 2 thin layers. Spread the whipped cream over one layer, then place the second layer on top.

To freeze: open (flash) freeze until firm, then

pack carefully in a rigid container. Seal, label and return to the freezer.
To thaw and serve: arrange on a serving platter and thaw in the refrigerator overnight. Put the icing (confectioners') sugar in a bowl and gradually beat in the water until smooth and glossy. Pour over the pastry ring, letting it run down the sides. Decorate with glacé (candied) cherries and angelica 'leaves' before the icing sets.
SERVES 8

APPLE AND ORANGE FLAN

METRIC/IMPERIAL
basic sweet shortcrust pastry dough made with 225 g/½ lb flour
675 g/1½ lb unsweetened thick apple purée
100 g/4 oz sugar
25 g/1 oz butter, softened
finely grated rind of 1 lemon
2 oranges, peeled and sliced into thin rings
For the glaze:
2 × 15 ml spoons/2 tablespoons apricot jam
1 × 15 ml spoon/1 tablespoon water
2 × 5 ml spoons/2 teaspoons lemon juice

AMERICAN
basic sweet pie dough made with 2 cups flour
3 cups apple sauce
½ cup sugar
2 tablespoons butter, softened
finely grated rind of 1 lemon
2 oranges, peeled and sliced into thin rings
For the glaze:
2 tablespoons apricot jam
1 tablespoon water
2 teaspoons lemon juice

Roll out the dough on a floured surface and use to line a 20 cm/8 inch flan ring set on a baking sheet. Bake blind in a preheated moderately hot oven (200°C/400°F or Gas Mark 6) for 15 minutes, then remove the foil and beans. Bake for a further 10 to 15 minutes.
Put the apple purée (apple sauce), sugar, butter and lemon rind in a bowl and stir well to mix. Spoon into the pastry case (pie shell), then arrange the orange slices on top.
To make the glaze: put the jam, water and lemon juice in a pan, heat gently until syrupy, then sieve (strain) and brush over the oranges.
To freeze: cool quickly. Open (flash) freeze until firm, then remove the flan ring and wrap the flan in foil. Seal, label and return to the freezer.
To thaw and serve: remove wrappings and thaw at room temperature for 4 hours.
SERVES 4 to 6

LEMON ICE BOX PIE

METRIC/IMPERIAL
For the biscuit crust:
100 g/4 oz digestive biscuits, crushed
75 g/3 oz butter, melted
100 g/4 oz soft brown sugar
1 × 5 ml spoon/1 teaspoon ground cinnamon
pinch of ground ginger
pinch of ground cloves
1 × 2.5 ml spoon/½ teaspoon grated nutmeg
For the filling:
2 eggs, separated
100 g/4 oz caster sugar
finely grated rind and juice of 2 large lemons
1 × 425 g/15 oz can evaporated milk, chilled
a few slices of lemon, to finish

AMERICAN
For the crumb crust:
1 cup crushed Graham crackers
⅜ cup butter, melted
⅔ cup light brown sugar
1 teaspoon ground cinnamon
pinch of ground ginger
pinch of ground cloves
½ teaspoon grated nutmeg
For the filling:
2 eggs, separated
½ cup sugar
finely grated rind and juice of 2 large lemons
1 × 15 oz can evaporated milk, chilled
a few slices of lemon, to finish

To make the crust: put all the ingredients in a bowl and stir well to mix. Press into a greased 28 × 15 cm/11 × 7 inch oblong tin and chill in the refrigerator until set.
To make the filling: put the egg yolks, sugar, lemon rind and juice in a bowl and stir well to mix. Beat the egg whites until stiff, then fold into the lemon mixture. Beat the evaporated milk until thick, then fold into the mixture. Pour into the tin and chill in the refrigerator until set.
To freeze: pack in a freezer bag, seal, label and freeze.
To thaw and serve: remove wrappings and thaw at room temperature for 4 hours. Decorate with lemon slices before serving.
SERVES 12

REFRIGERATOR HONEY FLAN

METRIC/IMPERIAL

100 g/4 oz butter, softened
2 × 15 ml spoons/2 tablespoons honey
1 × 15 ml spoon/1 tablespoon cocoa powder
1 × 15 ml spoon/1 tablespoon sherry
225 g/½ lb digestive biscuits, crushed
To finish:
150 ml/¼ pint double cream, whipped
1 × 800 g/1 lb 13 oz can peach, pear or apricot halves, drained

AMERICAN

½ cup butter, softened
2 tablespoons honey
1 tablespoon unsweetened cocoa powder
1 tablespoon sherry
2 cups crushed Graham crackers
To finish:
⅔ cup heavy cream, whipped
1 × 1 lb 13 oz can peach, pear or apricot halves, drained

Put the butter in a bowl and beat until creamy. Beat in the honey, cocoa and sherry, then add the crushed biscuits (crackers) and stir well to mix. Press into a greased 20 cm/8 inch flan ring set on a baking sheet and chill in the refrigerator until set.
To freeze: open (flash) freeze until firm, then remove the flan ring and wrap in foil. Pack in a freezer bag, seal, label and return to the freezer.
To thaw and serve: remove wrappings and place the flan case on a serving platter. Spread a little of the whipped cream in the bottom of the flan case, then arrange the fruit on top. Decorate with rosettes of the remaining whipped cream.
SERVES 4 to 6

CHOCOLATE AND ORANGE TART

METRIC/IMPERIAL

For the base:
basic shortcrust pastry dough made with 175 g/6 oz flour
1.5 × 15 ml spoons/1½ tablespoons marmalade
For the sponge:
50 g/2 oz soft tub margarine
50 g/2 oz caster sugar
1 egg, beaten
40 g/1½ oz self-raising flour
1.5 × 15 ml spoons/1½ tablespoons sifted cocoa powder
2 × 15 ml spoons/2 tablespoons undiluted concentrated orange juice

AMERICAN

For the base:
basic pie dough made with 1½ cups flour
1½ tablespoons marmalade
For the sponge:
¼ cup soft margarine
¼ cup sugar
1 egg, beaten
6 tablespoons self-rising flour
1½ tablespoons sifted unsweetened cocoa powder
2 tablespoons undiluted concentrated orange juice

To make the base: roll out the dough on a floured surface and use to line an 18 cm/7 inch flan ring set on a baking sheet. Reserve the trimmings. Spread the marmalade in the bottom.
To make the sponge: put all the ingredients in a bowl and beat well to mix. Pour into the pastry case (pie shell). Roll out the reserved trimmings of dough and cut into 5 mm/¼ inch strips long enough to criss-cross the top of the tart. Moisten the ends of the strips with water and arrange over the sponge in a criss-cross pattern.
Bake in a preheated moderately hot oven (190°C/375°F or Gas Mark 5) for 30 to 35 minutes or until the sponge is firm to the touch. Cool quickly on a wire rack, then remove the flan ring.
To freeze: open (flash) freeze until firm, then pack in a freezer bag. Seal, label and return to the freezer.
To thaw and serve: remove wrappings and thaw at room temperature for 4 hours.
SERVES 4 to 6

CONTINENTAL LEMON FLAN

METRIC/IMPERIAL

basic shortcrust pastry dough made with 175 g/6 oz flour
50 g/2 oz butter
100 g/4 oz caster sugar
25 g/1 oz self-raising flour, sifted
1 large egg, separated
100 g/4 oz cottage cheese, sieved
25 g/1 oz sultanas
finely grated rind of 1 lemon

AMERICAN

basic pie dough made with 1½ cups flour
¼ cup butter
½ cup sugar
¼ cup self-rising flour, sifted
1 large egg, separated
½ cup cottage cheese, strained
3 tablespoons seedless white raisins
finely grated rind of 1 lemon

Roll out the dough on a floured surface and use to line an 18 cm/7 inch flan ring set on a baking sheet, reserving the trimmings of dough.
Put the butter and sugar in a bowl and beat until light and fluffy. Add the flour, egg yolk, cheese, sultanas (raisins) and lemon rind and beat well. Beat the egg white until stiff, then fold into the mixture until evenly blended.
Pour the mixture into the pastry case (pie shell). Roll out the trimmings of dough and cut into thin strips long enough to criss-cross the top of the flan. Moisten the ends of the strips with water and arrange over the filling in a criss-cross pattern, pressing the ends firmly to seal.
Bake in a preheated moderately hot oven (190°C/375°F or Gas Mark 5) for 45 to 50 minutes or until the filling is set. Cool quickly on a wire rack, then remove the flan ring.
To freeze: open (flash) freeze until firm, then pack in a freezer bag. Seal, label and return to the freezer.
To thaw and serve: remove wrappings and thaw at room temperature for 4 hours.
SERVES 4 to 6

GOOSEBERRY FOOL

METRIC/IMPERIAL
450 g/1 lb gooseberries, topped and tailed
3 × 15 ml spoons/3 tablespoons water
caster sugar, according to taste
a few drops of green food colouring
300 ml/½ pint double cream
2 × 15 ml spoons/2 tablespoons milk
25 g/1 oz toasted or slivered almonds, to finish

AMERICAN
1 lb gooseberries, cleaned
3 tablespoons water
sugar, according to taste
a few drops of green food coloring
1¼ cups heavy cream
2 tablespoons milk
¼ cup toasted or slivered almonds, to finish

Put the gooseberries and water in a pan, bring slowly to the boil, then simmer until soft. Leave to cool slightly, then add sugar to taste. Work to a smooth purée in an electric blender or rub through a sieve (strainer), then stir in the food colouring. Leave to cool.
Beat the cream and milk together until thick, then fold into the gooseberry purée. Spoon into 4 to 6 individual freezerproof serving dishes and chill in the refrigerator until set.
To freeze: cover with foil, then pack in freezer bags. Seal, label and freeze.
To thaw and serve: remove wrappings and thaw in the refrigerator for 6 hours. Sprinkle with almonds before serving.
SERVES 4 to 6

STRAWBERRY FOOL

METRIC/IMPERIAL
450 g/1 lb strawberries, hulled
300 ml/½ pint double cream
1 × 15 ml spoon/1 tablespoon honey

AMERICAN
1 lb strawberries, hulled
1¼ cups heavy cream
1 tablespoon honey

Work 350 g/¾ lb strawberries through a wire sieve (strainer) and slice the remainder. Put the cream and honey in a bowl and beat until thick. Fold in the strawberry purée and the slices and pour into a freezerproof glass serving dish. Chill in the refrigerator until firm.
To freeze: cover with foil, then pack in a freezer bag. Seal, label and freeze.
To thaw and serve: remove wrappings and thaw in the refrigerator overnight. If liked, sprinkle with almonds to serve.
SERVES 4

SUMMER FRUIT FOOL

METRIC/IMPERIAL
225 g/½ lb puréed fruit (apricots, blackberries, blackcurrants, gooseberries, raspberries)
300 ml/½ pint thick custard
150 ml/¼ pint double cream, whipped
8 sponge fingers, to serve

AMERICAN
1 cup puréed fruit (apricots, blackberries, blackcurrants, gooseberries, raspberries)
1¼ cups thick custard
⅔ cup heavy cream, whipped
8 ladyfingers, to serve

Put the fruit and custard in a bowl and stir well to mix. Fold in the whipped cream until evenly blended, then spoon into individual freezerproof ramekins or serving dishes.
To freeze: cover with foil, then pack in freezer bags. Seal, label and freeze.
To thaw and serve: remove wrappings and thaw in the refrigerator for 6 hours. Serve with sponge fingers (ladyfingers).
SERVES 4

PROFITEROLES WITH HOT CHOCOLATE SAUCE

METRIC/IMPERIAL

For the choux pastry:

50 g/2 oz butter
150 ml/¼ pint water
pinch of salt
65 g/2½ oz flour, sifted
2 large eggs, beaten

For the chocolate sauce:

100 g/4 oz plain chocolate, broken into pieces
2 × 15 ml spoons/2 tablespoons honey
1 × 15 ml spoon/1 tablespoon lemon juice
1 × 15 ml spoon/1 tablespoon cornflour
150 ml/¼ pint water
50 g/2 oz butter

To finish:

150 ml/¼ pint double cream
1 × 15 ml spoon/1 tablespoon honey

AMERICAN

For the choux paste:

¼ cup butter
⅔ cup water
pinch of salt
⅔ cup flour, sifted
2 large eggs, beaten

For the chocolate sauce:

⅔ cup semi-sweet chocolate pieces
2 tablespoons honey
1 tablespoon lemon juice
1 tablespoon cornstarch
⅔ cup water
¼ cup butter

To finish:

⅔ cup heavy cream
1 tablespoon honey

To make the choux pastry (paste): put the butter, water and salt in a pan and heat gently until the butter has melted. Bring to the boil, then immediately remove the pan from the heat and quickly beat in the flour all at once. Continue beating for 2 minutes until the mixture draws away from the sides of the pan and forms a ball. Leave to cool slightly, then beat in the eggs a little at a time until the dough is smooth and shiny. Add enough to give a mixture that just falls from the spoon.

Put the mixture into a large piping (pastry) bag fitted with a 1 cm/½ inch plain nozzle (tube). Pipe about 20 mounds on a wetted baking sheet, allowing room for expansion. Bake in a preheated moderately hot oven (200°C/400°F or Gas Mark 6) for 20 minutes or until the profiteroles are golden brown. Make a slit in the side of each profiterole so that the steam can escape, then cool quickly on a wire rack.

To make the chocolate sauce: put all the ingredients in a pan and heat gently until the chocolate has melted. Stir briskly until the mixture boils and is thick and smooth. Remove from the heat and leave to cool, stirring occasionally.

To freeze: open (flash) freeze the profiteroles until firm, then pack in a rigid container, separating each layer with foil. Seal, label and return to the freezer. Pour the chocolate sauce into a separate rigid container. Seal, label and freeze.

To thaw and serve: transfer the profiteroles to a serving platter and thaw at room temperature for 2 hours. Beat the cream and honey together until thick, and use to fill the profiteroles. Pile them up into a pyramid shape. Put the frozen chocolate sauce in a heatproof bowl over a pan of gently simmering water and reheat gently. Pour over the profiteroles and serve immediately.

SERVES 4 to 6

TURINOIS

METRIC/IMPERIAL

100 g/4 oz unsalted butter
100 g/4 oz caster sugar
225 g/½ lb plain chocolate, broken into pieces
1 × 440 g/15½ oz can unsweetened chestnut purée
a few drops of vanilla essence

To decorate:

whipped cream
chocolate curls

AMERICAN

½ cup sweet butter
½ cup sugar
1⅓ cups semi-sweet chocolate pieces
1 × 15½ oz can unsweetened chestnut purée
a few drops of vanilla extract

To decorate:

whipped cream
chocolate curls

Grease a 450 g/1 lb loaf tin and line the bottom with greased greaseproof (waxed) paper.

Put the butter and sugar in a bowl and beat together until light and fluffy. Put the chocolate in a heatproof bowl, stand over a pan of gently simmering water and allow to melt. Leave to cool slightly.

Beat the melted chocolate into the creamed butter and sugar with the chestnut purée and vanilla essence (extract). Turn into the prepared tin, chill until set, then unmould.

To freeze: open (flash) freeze until firm, then pack in a freezer bag. Seal, label and return to the freezer.

To thaw and serve: remove wrappings and place on a serving platter. Thaw in the refrigerator for 4 to 5 hours, then decorate with whipped cream and chocolate curls.

SERVES 8 to 10

STRAWBERRY CREAM

METRIC/IMPERIAL

675 g/1½ lb strawberries, hulled
approx 100 g/4 oz caster sugar, or to taste
3 × 15 ml spoons/3 tablespoons brandy
15 g/½ oz gelatine
3 × 15 ml spoons/3 tablespoons water
600 ml/1 pint double cream, lightly whipped
To finish:
whipped cream
crisp biscuits

AMERICAN

1½ lb strawberries, hulled
approx ½ cup sugar, or to taste
3 tablespoons brandy
2 envelopes unflavored gelatin
3 tablespoons water
2½ cups heavy cream, lightly whipped
To finish:
whipped cream
crisp cookies

Put 225 g/½ lb strawberries and 50 g/2 oz/¼ cup sugar in an electric blender and work to a smooth purée. Transfer to a bowl and stir in the brandy. Slice the remaining strawberries, put in a shallow bowl and sprinkle with more sugar, according to taste.

Sprinkle the gelatine over the water in a heatproof bowl. Leave until spongy, then place the bowl in a pan of hot water and stir over a low heat until the gelatine has dissolved. Leave to cool slightly, then stir into the strawberry purée. Leave until just beginning to set, then fold the cream into the purée until evenly blended. Stir in the sliced strawberries, then pour into a freezerproof glass serving dish. Chill in the refrigerator until set.

To freeze: cover with foil, then pack in a freezer bag. Seal, label and freeze.

To thaw and serve: remove wrappings and thaw in the refrigerator overnight. Decorate with rosettes of whipped cream and serve with crisp biscuits (cookies).

SERVES 6

NÜSS TORTE

METRIC/IMPERIAL

For the base:
250 g/9 oz flour
pinch of salt
175 g/6 oz butter
75 g/3 oz caster sugar
50 g/2 oz roasted hazelnuts, finely ground
For the chocolate cream:
15 marshmallows
1 × 15 ml spoon/1 tablespoon cocoa powder
1 knob of butter
4 × 15 ml spoons/4 tablespoons milk
150 ml/¼ pint double cream, whipped
To finish:
whipped cream
a few whole roasted hazelnuts

AMERICAN

For the base:
2¼ cups flour
pinch of salt
¾ cup butter
⅜ cup sugar
½ cup finely ground roasted hazelnuts
For the chocolate cream:
15 marshmallows
1 tablespoon unsweetened cocoa powder
1 knob of butter
¼ cup milk
⅔ cup heavy cream, whipped
To finish:
whipped cream
a few whole roasted hazelnuts

Sift the flour and salt into a bowl, add the butter in pieces and rub into the flour until the mixture resembles fine breadcrumbs. Stir in the sugar and hazelnuts and knead well until the mixture holds together.

Divide the dough into 4 equal portions and roll each portion into an 18 cm/7 inch circle. Place on baking sheets and bake in a preheated moderately hot oven (190°C/375°F or Gas Mark 5) for 10 minutes.

Put the marshmallows, cocoa, butter and milk in a pan and cook gently until the marshmallows have dissolved and the mixture is smooth, stirring constantly. Leave to cool. Fold the cream into the chocolate mixture, then use to sandwich together the layers of shortbread.

To freeze: open (flash) freeze until firm, then pack carefully in a rigid container. Seal, label and return to the freezer.

To thaw and serve: transfer to a serving platter and thaw at room temperature for 2 hours. Decorate with whipped cream and hazelnuts.

SERVES 6

STRAWBERRY SOUFFLÉ

METRIC/IMPERIAL

1 × 15 ml spoon/1 tablespoon gelatine
4 × 15 ml spoons/4 tablespoons water
3 eggs, separated
75 g/3 oz caster sugar
150 ml/¼ pint strawberry purée
150 ml/¼ pint double cream, whipped
To finish:
a little melted butter or vegetable oil
grated chocolate
whipped cream

AMERICAN

1 tablespoon unflavored gelatin
¼ cup water
3 eggs, separated
⅜ cup sugar
⅔ cup strawberry purée
⅔ cup heavy cream, whipped
To finish:
a little melted butter or vegetable oil
grated chocolate
whipped cream

Prepare a 600 ml/1 pint/2½ cup soufflé dish: cut a strip of doubled greaseproof (waxed) paper long enough to go around the outside of the dish (overlapping) and 5 to 7.5 cm/2 to 3 inches higher than the dish. Tie this securely around the outside of the dish and brush the inside of the paper lightly with melted butter or oil.

Sprinkle the gelatine over half the water in a heatproof bowl. Leave until spongy, then place the bowl in a pan of hot water and stir over a low heat until the gelatine has dissolved. Leave to cool slightly.

Meanwhile, put the egg yolks, sugar and the remaining water in a heatproof bowl and stand over a pan of gently simmering water. Beat until thick and creamy, then remove from the heat and beat until cool. Stir in the gelatine, then fold in the strawberry purée and the whipped cream.

Beat the egg whites until stiff, then fold into the strawberry mixture until evenly blended. Spoon into the prepared soufflé dish and chill in the refrigerator until set.

To freeze: open (flash) freeze until firm, then pack in a freezer bag. Seal, label and return to the freezer.

To thaw and serve: remove wrappings and paper collar. Thaw the soufflé in the refrigerator for 4 to 5 hours, then brush the exposed edge lightly with the melted butter or oil and press grated chocolate around the edge to coat it completely. Decorate the top with rosettes of whipped cream.

SERVES 4 to 6

ITALIAN DESSERT

METRIC/IMPERIAL

1 large packet of sponge fingers
1 × 425 g/15 oz can cherries
1 × 15 ml spoon/1 tablespoon cherry brandy
450 ml/¾ pint milk
25 g/1 oz cocoa powder
50 g/2 oz caster sugar
2 eggs, separated
15 g/½ oz gelatine
2 × 15 ml spoons/2 tablespoons water
To finish:
150 ml/¼ pint double cream, whipped
a few strips of candied angelica
a few glacé cherries, halved

AMERICAN

1 large packet of ladyfingers
1 × 15 oz can cherries
1 tablespoon cherry brandy
2 cups milk
¼ cup unsweetened cocoa powder
¼ cup sugar
2 eggs, separated
2 envelopes unflavored gelatin
2 tablespoons water
To finish:
⅔ cup heavy cream, whipped
a few strips of candied angelica
a few candied cherries, halved

Arrange the sponge fingers (ladyfingers) in the bottom of a 1 kg/2 lb loaf tin. Drain the cherries and measure 150 ml/¼ pint/⅔ cup juice. Stir in the liqueur, then pour over the fingers. Remove the stones (seeds) from the cherries.

Put the milk, cocoa and sugar in a pan and heat gently until well blended, stirring occasionally. Beat in the egg yolks and cook gently for 1 minute or until thickened, stirring constantly. Leave to cool.

Sprinkle the gelatine over the water in a heatproof bowl. Leave until spongy, then stand the bowl in a pan of hot water and stir until the gelatine has dissolved. Leave to cool slightly, then stir into the custard mixture. Leave until just beginning to set, then stir in the cherries.

Beat the egg whites until stiff, fold into the mixture, then pour into the tin. Chill in the refrigerator until set.

To freeze: cover with foil, then pack in a freezer bag. Seal, label and freeze.

To thaw and serve: remove wrappings and thaw in the refrigerator for 1 hour. Turn out onto a serving platter and thaw in the refrigerator for a further 4 hours. Decorate with whipped cream, angelica 'leaves' and glacé (candied) cherries.

SERVES 4 to 6

CHOCOLATE SOUFFLÉ

METRIC/IMPERIAL

450 ml/¾ pint milk
40 g/1½ oz cocoa powder
75 g/3 oz caster sugar
3 large eggs, separated
15 g/½ oz gelatine
4 × 15 ml spoons/4 tablespoons water
150 ml/¼ pint double cream, lightly whipped
To finish:
a little melted butter or vegetable oil
50 g/2 oz plain chocolate, grated
whipped cream

AMERICAN

2 cups milk
⅓ cup unsweetened cocoa powder
⅜ cup sugar
3 large eggs, separated
2 envelopes unflavored gelatin
¼ cup water
⅔ cup heavy cream, lightly whipped
To finish:
a little melted butter or vegetable oil
⅓ cup semi-sweet chocolate pieces, grated
whipped cream

Prepare a 600 ml/1 pint/2½ cup soufflé dish: cut a strip of doubled greaseproof (waxed) paper long enough to go around the outside of the dish (overlapping) and 5 to 7.5 cm/2 to 3 inches higher than the dish. Tie this securely around the outside of the dish with string and brush the inside of the paper lightly with melted butter or oil.

Put the milk and cocoa in a pan, bring slowly to the boil, then remove from the heat. Put the sugar and egg yolks in a bowl and beat together until creamy. Pour the milk mixture slowly into the bowl, stirring constantly. Return to the heat and cook gently until thick. Do not allow to boil. Leave to cool.

Sprinkle the gelatine over the water in a heatproof bowl. Leave until spongy, then place the bowl in a pan of hot water and stir over a low heat until the gelatine has dissolved. Leave to cool slightly, then stir into the custard.

Fold the cream into the custard until evenly blended, then leave until just beginning to set. Beat the egg whites until stiff, then fold into the mixture until evenly blended. Pour into the prepared soufflé dish and chill in the refrigerator until set.

To freeze: open (flash) freeze until firm, then pack in a freezer bag. Seal, label and return to the freezer.

To thaw and serve: remove wrappings and paper collar. Thaw the soufflé in the refrigerator for 4 to 5 hours, then brush the exposed edge lightly with melted butter or oil and press the grated chocolate around the edge to coat it completely. Decorate the top with rosettes of whipped cream.

SERVES 4 to 6

APRICOT MOUSSE

METRIC/IMPERIAL

1 × 800 g/1 lb 13 oz can apricot halves, drained
3 × 15 ml spoons/3 tablespoons cornflour
25 g/1 oz sugar
2 × 5 ml spoons/2 teaspoons gelatine
2 × 15 ml spoons/2 tablespoons water
juice of ½ lemon
150 ml/¼ pint double cream, lightly whipped

AMERICAN

1 × 1 lb 13 oz can apricot halves, drained
3 tablespoons cornstarch
2 tablespoons sugar
2 teaspoons unflavored gelatin
2 tablespoons water
juice of ½ lemon
2 teaspoons unflavored gelatin
2 tablespoons water
juice of ½ lemon
⅔ cup heavy cream, lightly whipped

Rub the apricots through a wire sieve (strainer), reserving a few halves for decoration. Measure the purée and make up to 450 ml/¾ pint/2 cups with water, if necessary.

Mix the cornflour (cornstarch) with the sugar and a little of the apricot purée. Put the remaining purée in a pan and heat gently. Stir in the cornflour (cornstarch) mixture, bring to the boil and boil rapidly for 3 minutes, stirring constantly. Remove from the heat.

Sprinkle the gelatine over the water in a heatproof bowl. Leave until spongy, then place the bowl in a pan of hot water and stir until the gelatine has dissolved. Stir into the apricot purée with the lemon juice. Leave to cool.

Fold in the whipped cream until evenly blended, then pour the mousse into a wetted 450 g/1 lb loaf tin. Chill until set, then unmould.

To freeze: open (flash) freeze until firm, then pack in a freezer bag. Seal, label and return to the freezer. Pack the reserved apricot halves in a rigid container. Seal, label and freeze.

To thaw and serve: remove wrappings and place on a serving platter. Thaw in the refrigerator for 4 hours, then decorate with the reserved apricot halves.

SERVES 4 to 6

CHESTNUT ROLL

METRIC/IMPERIAL

For the Swiss roll:

75 g/3 oz caster sugar
3 eggs, beaten
75 g/3 oz flour
50 g/2 oz ground almonds
25 g/1 oz plain chocolate, grated

For the filling:

50 g/2 oz butter, softened
100 g/4 oz icing sugar, sifted
2 egg yolks
1 × 15 ml spoon/1 tablespoon brandy
1 × 225 g/8 oz can sweetened chestnut purée

AMERICAN

For the jelly roll:

⅜ cup sugar
3 eggs, beaten
¾ cup flour
½ cup ground almonds
1 square semi-sweet chocolate, grated

For the filling:

¼ cup butter, softened
1 cup sifted confectioners' sugar
2 egg yolks
1 tablespoon brandy
1 × ½ lb can sweetened chestnut purée

Grease a 33 × 23cm/13 × 9 inch Swiss (jelly) roll tin and line with greaseproof paper or non-stick parchment.

To make the Swiss (jelly) roll: put the sugar and eggs in a bowl and beat until thick and creamy. Sift the flour and ground almonds and fold into the egg mixture with the chocolate. Turn into the prepared tin and bake in a preheated moderately hot oven (190°C/375°F or Gas Mark 5) for 20 minutes or until firm to the touch. Turn out onto a piece of sugared greaseproof paper or non-stick parchment and roll up with the paper inside. Wrap in a damp tea (dish) towel and leave to cool.

To make the filling: put the butter and icing (confectioners') sugar in a bowl and beat together until light and fluffy. Add the egg yolks, brandy and chestnut purée and beat well to mix. Unwrap the Swiss (jelly) roll and discard the paper. Spread the cake with the filling, then roll up again.

To freeze: open (flash) freeze until firm, then wrap carefully in foil. Pack in a freezer bag, seal, label and return to the freezer.

To thaw and serve: remove wrappings and place the roll on a serving platter. Thaw at room temperature for 4 hours.

SERVES 8

HONEY AND FRUIT TIPSY PUDDING

METRIC/IMPERIAL

350 g/¾ lb stale Madeira or sponge cake, broken into small pieces
6 × 15 ml spoons/6 tablespoons sweet white wine
2 × 15 ml spoons/2 tablespoons honey
1 × 225 g/8 oz can raspberries
2 × 15 ml spoons/2 tablespoons honey
1 × 225 g/8 oz can raspberries

To finish:

300 ml/½ pint double cream, whipped
25 g/1 oz blanched almonds, toasted and shredded
grated chocolate

AMERICAN

¾ lb stale Madeira or sponge cake, broken into small pieces
6 tablespoons sweet white wine
2 tablespoons honey
1 × ½ lb can raspberries

To finish:

1¼ cups heavy cream, whipped
¼ cup blanched almonds, toasted and shredded
grated chocolate

Put the cake in a bowl and pour in the wine. Put the honey in a pan, heat gently, then add to the cake mixture with the raspberries. Stir well to mix. Spoon into a buttered 600 ml/1 pint/2½ cup pudding basin (slope-sided mold) pressing down firmly. Cover with a saucer that just fits inside the rim, then put weights on top and leave in the refrigerator overnight.

To freeze: remove the saucer and weights and cover with foil. Pack in a freezer bag, seal, label and freeze.

To thaw and serve: remove wrappings and thaw at room temperature for 3 hours. Turn out onto a serving platter, then spread the cream over the pudding to cover it completely. Decorate with the almonds and grated chocolate.

SERVES 4 to 6

CHESTNUT SLICE

METRIC/IMPERIAL

300 ml/½ pint double cream
75 g/3 oz caster sugar
1 × 440 g/15½ oz can sweetened chestnut purée
4 eggs, separated

AMERICAN

1¼ cups heavy cream
⅜ cup sugar
1 × 15½ oz can sweetened chestnut purée
4 eggs, separated

Put the cream and 25 g/1 oz/2 tablespoons sugar in a bowl, beat until thick and fluffy, then use to line the bottom and sides of a 900 ml/1½ pint/3¾ cup charlotte mould. Freeze until firm.
Put the chestnut purée, egg yolks and remaining sugar in a bowl and beat well to mix. Beat the egg whites until stiff, then fold into the chestnut mixture until evenly blended. Pour into the charlotte mould, then chill in the refrigerator until set.
To freeze: cover with foil, then pack in a freezer bag. Seal, label and freeze.
To thaw and serve: remove wrappings. Stand the mould in a bowl of warm water for 10 seconds, then loosen the edge of the cream with a palette knife and turn out onto a serving platter. Chill in the refrigerator before serving and use within 2 hours of unmoulding.
SERVES 8

DRIED FRUIT COMPOTE

METRIC/IMPERIAL
225 g/½ lb prunes, stoned
225 g/½ lb dried apricots
225 g/½ lb figs
100 g/4 oz seedless raisins
100 g/4 oz dried apple rings
450 ml/¾ pint water
150 ml/¼ pint white wine
To finish:
50 g/2 oz walnut pieces
50 g/2 oz blanched almonds
soured cream or natural yogurt

AMERICAN
1⅓ cups prunes, pitted
1⅓ cups dried apricots
1¼ cups figs
⅔ cup seedless raisins
⅔ cup dried apple rings
2 cups water
⅔ cup white wine
To finish:
½ cup walnut pieces
scant ½ cup whole blanched almonds
sour cream or unflavored yogurt

Put the fruit, water and wine in a casserole dish and cook in a preheated moderate oven (160°C/325°F or Gas Mark 3) for 1 hour.
To freeze: cool quickly, then pour into a rigid container. Seal, label and freeze.
To thaw and serve: thaw at room temperature for 4 hours, then stir in the nuts. Serve with sour(ed) cream or yogurt handed separately.
SERVES 6

PINEAPPLE GÂTEAU

METRIC/IMPERIAL
4 eggs
225 g/½ lb caster sugar
50 g/2 oz flour
50 g/2 oz potato flour
2 × 5 ml spoons/2 teaspoons baking powder
1 large can pineapple slices
2 × 15 ml spoons/2 tablespoons Kirsch
300 ml/½ pint double cream, stiffly whipped
1 × 15 ml spoon/1 tablespoon chopped pistachio nuts

AMERICAN
4 eggs
1 cup sugar
½ cup flour
⅓ cup potato flour
2 teaspoons baking powder
1 large can pineapple slices
2 tablespoons Kirsch
1¼ cups heavy cream, stiffly whipped
1 tablespoon chopped pistachio nuts

Grease a 20 cm/8 inch round cake tin and line with greased greaseproof paper or non-stick parchment.
Put the eggs and sugar in a bowl and beat until the mixture is thick enough to fall in ribbons from the beater. Sift together the flour, potato flour and baking powder and fold into the egg and sugar mixture a little at a time.
Spoon the mixture into the prepared tin and bake in a preheated moderately hot oven (200°C/400°F or Gas Mark 6) for 20 to 30 minutes or until well risen and springy to the touch. Leave to cool in the tin until the cake shrinks slightly, then turn out onto a wire rack and cool completely.
Meanwhile, drain the pineapple slices. Cut half the pineapple into wedges and halve the remainder. Mix 2 × 15 ml spoons/2 tablespoons pineapple syrup with the Kirsch.
Split the cake in half. Place one half on a dish, then prick all over with a skewer. Spoon the syrup and Kirsch mixture slowly over the cake, then arrange the pineapple wedges on top. Cover with half the whipped cream, then with the top half of the cake. Arrange the pineapple halves in a circle on top of the cake, then pipe rosettes with the remaining cream and sprinkle with the nuts.
To freeze: open (flash) freeze until firm, then pack in a rigid container. Seal, label and return to the freezer.
To thaw and serve: transfer to a serving platter and thaw in the refrigerator for 6 hours.
SERVES 6 to 8

APPLE AND ALMOND FLAN

METRIC/IMPERIAL

basic shortcrust pastry dough made with 225 g/½ lb flour
2 large cooking apples, peeled, cored and sliced
50 g/2 oz soft brown sugar
1 × 15 ml spoon/1 tablespoon water
1 × 5 ml spoon/1 teaspoon ground cinnamon
50 g/2 oz ground almonds
300 ml/½ pint soured cream
To serve:
sifted icing sugar
whipped cream

AMERICAN

basic pie dough made with 2 cups flour
2 large baking apples, peeled, cored and sliced
⅓ cup light brown sugar
1 tablespoon water
1 teaspoon ground cinnamon
½ cup ground almonds
1¼ cups sour cream
To serve:
sifted confectioners' sugar
whipped cream

Roll out the dough on a floured surface and use to line a 20 cm/8 inch flan ring set on a baking sheet, reserving the trimmings of dough. Bake blind in a preheated moderately hot oven (190°C/375°F or Gas Mark 5) for 15 minutes.
Meanwhile put the apples, sugar, water, cinnamon and almonds in a pan and cook gently until the apples are soft. Spoon into the pastry case (pie shell) and pour over the sour(ed) cream.
Roll out the reserved trimmings of dough and cut out 8 thin strips long enough to criss-cross the top of the flan. Moisten the ends of the strips with water and arrange over the cream in a criss-cross pattern, pressing the wetted ends firmly to seal. Bake in the moderately hot oven for 25 to 30 minutes or until the filling is set. Cool quickly on a wire rack, then remove the flan ring.
To freeze: open (flash) freeze until firm, then pack carefully in a freezer bag. Seal, label and return to the freezer.
To thaw and serve: remove wrappings and place on a serving platter. Thaw at room temperature for 4 hours, then sprinkle with icing (confectioners') sugar and serve with whipped cream.
SERVES 4 to 6

APPLE AND HAZELNUT FLAN

Make as for Apple and Almond Flan, substituting 50 g/2 oz/½ cup ground roasted hazelnuts for the ground almonds. Freeze, thaw and serve as for Apple and Almond Flan.
SERVES 4 to 6

TRADITIONAL CHEESECAKE

METRIC/IMPERIAL

basic sweet shortcrust pastry dough made with 175 g/6 oz flour
50 g/2 oz butter
75 g/3 oz caster sugar
2 eggs, separated
40 g/1½ oz ground almonds
25 g/1 oz semolina
225 g/½ lb cottage cheese, sieved
finely grated rind and juice of 1 lemon

AMERICAN

basic sweet pie dough made with 1½ cups flour
¼ cup butter
⅜ cup sugar
2 eggs, separated
⅓ cup ground almonds
3 tablespoons semolina flour
1 cup cottage cheese, strained
finely grated rind and juice of 1 lemon

Roll out the dough on a floured surface and line a 20 cm/8 inch sandwich tin (layer cake pan). Put the butter and sugar in a bowl and cream together until light and fluffy. Add the egg yolks and the remaining ingredients, except the egg whites, and beat well to mix.
Beat the egg whites until stiff, then fold into the mixture until evenly blended. Pour into the pastry case (pie shell) and bake in a preheated moderate oven (180°C/350°F or Gas Mark 4) for 50 minutes.
To freeze: cool quickly. Open (flash) freeze until firm, remove from the tin, then pack in a freezer bag. Seal, label and return to the freezer.
To thaw and serve: remove wrappings and thaw at room temperature for 4 hours.
SERVES 6

CHOCOLATE AND RUM CHEESECAKE

METRIC/IMPERIAL

For the base:
175 g/6 oz digestive biscuits, crushed
75 g/3 oz caster sugar
75 g/3 oz butter, melted

For the filling:
100 g/4 oz cottage cheese, sieved
100 g/4 oz cream cheese
100 g/4 oz caster sugar
100 g/4 oz plain chocolate, broken into pieces
15 g/½ oz gelatine
6 × 15 ml spoons/6 tablespoons water
2 × 15 ml spoons/2 tablespoons rum
150 ml/¼ pint double cream, lightly whipped
To finish:
whipped cream
chocolate curls
sifted icing sugar

AMERICAN
For the base:
1½ cups crushed Graham crackers
⅜ cup sugar
⅜ cup butter, melted
For the filling:
½ cup cottage cheese, strained
½ cup cream cheese
½ cup sugar
⅔ cup semi-sweet chocolate pieces
2 envelopes unflavored gelatin
6 tablespoons water
2 tablespoons rum
⅔ cup heavy cream, lightly whipped
To finish:
whipped cream
chocolate curls
sifted confectioners' sugar

To make the base: put the biscuits (crackers), sugar and butter in a bowl and stir well to mix. Press into the bottom and around the sides of a 20 cm/8 inch fluted flan dish. Chill until set.
To make the filling: put the cheeses in a bowl, beat together until creamy, then beat in the sugar. Put the chocolate in a heatproof bowl, stand over a pan of gently simmering water and allow to melt. Stir into the cheese mixture.
Sprinkle the gelatine over the water in a heatproof bowl. Leave until spongy, then place the bowl in a pan of hot water and stir over a low heat until the gelatine has dissolved. Leave to cool slightly, then stir into the cheese mixture and beat well. Leave until just beginning to set, then stir in the rum and fold in the cream until evenly blended. Pour into the flan dish and chill in the refrigerator until set.
To freeze: cover with foil, then pack in a freezer bag. Seal, label and freeze.
To thaw and serve: remove wrappings and thaw at room temperature for 4 hours. Decorate with swirls of whipped cream and chocolate curls sprinkled with icing (confectioners') sugar.
SERVES 8

BAKED FRUIT CHEESECAKE

METRIC/IMPERIAL
For the base:
25 g/1 oz butter, melted
150 g/5 oz cake crumbs
For the filling:
1 × 234 g/8¼ oz can pineapple rings, drained
50 g/2 oz butter
50 g/2 oz caster sugar
225 g/½ lb full fat cream cheese
150 ml/¼ pint soured cream
2 eggs, separated
For the topping:
150 ml/¼ pint natural yogurt
50 g/2 oz caster sugar

AMERICAN
For the base:
2 tablespoons butter, melted
2½ cups cake crumbs
For the filling:
1 × 8¼ oz can pineapple rings, drained
¼ cup butter
¼ cup sugar
1 cup full fat cream cheese
⅔ cup sour cream
2 eggs, separated
For the topping:
⅔ cup unflavored yogurt
¼ cup sugar

To make the base: put the butter and cake crumbs in a bowl and stir well to mix. Press into the bottom of a 23 cm/9 inch loose-bottomed cake tin and chill in the refrigerator until set.
To make the filling: arrange the pineapple rings on the cake crumb base. Put the butter and sugar in a bowl, beat together until light and fluffy, then gradually beat in the cream cheese, sour(ed) cream and egg yolks.
Beat the egg whites until stiff, then fold into the cold cheese mixture. Pour over the pineapple, smooth the top and bake in a preheated moderate oven (180°C/350°F or Gas Mark 4) for 1 hour or until the filling is set and golden brown. Reduce the heat to cool (150°C/300°F or Gas Mark 2). Remove the cheesecake from the oven.
To make the topping: put the yogurt and sugar in a bowl and beat well to mix. Pour over the cheesecake filling and smooth the top. Bake in the cool oven for 15 minutes or until the topping is set. Leave to cool, then remove the cake tin.
To freeze: open (flash) freeze until firm, then remove the bottom of the cake tin. Pack in a freezer bag. Seal, label and return to the freezer.
To thaw and serve: remove wrappings and thaw in the refrigerator overnight.
SERVES 4 to 6

COOKED CHEESECAKE

METRIC/IMPERIAL

For the base:
6 digestive biscuits, crushed
40 g/1½ oz butter, melted
For the filling:
3 eggs
175 g/6 oz caster sugar
15 g/½ oz cornflour
450 g/1 lb curd cheese
1 × 5 ml spoon/1 teaspoon lemon juice
75 g/3 oz sultanas
For the topping:
150 ml/¼ pint soured cream
1 × 15 ml spoon/1 tablespoon caster sugar

AMERICAN

For the base:
¾ cup crushed Graham crackers
3 tablespoons butter, melted
For the filling:
3 eggs
¾ cup sugar
2 tablespoons cornstarch
2 cups curd cheese
1 teaspoon lemon juice
½ cup seedless white raisins
For the topping:
⅔ cup sour cream
1 tablespoon sugar

To make the base: put the biscuits (crackers) and butter in a bowl and stir well to mix. Press into the bottom of a 20 cm/8 inch loose-bottomed cake tin, then chill in the refrigerator until set. Meanwhile, make the filling: put the eggs, sugar and cornflour (cornstarch) in a bowl and beat well to mix, then stir in the cheese and lemon juice.

Scatter the sultanas (seedless white raisins) over the bottom of the biscuit (crumb) base, then pour in the cheese mixture. Bake in preheated moderate oven (160°C/325°F or Gas Mark 3) for 30 to 40 minutes or until the filling is set. Leave to cool, then mix the sour(ed) cream and sugar together and spread over the filling. Bake in a preheated moderately hot oven (200°C/400°F or Gas Mark 6) for 5 minutes.

To freeze: cool quickly. Open (flash) freeze until firm, then remove the cheesecake from the tin and pack in a freezer bag. Seal, label and return to the freezer.

To thaw and serve: remove wrappings and thaw at room temperature for 4 hours.

SERVES 6

CURDCAKE

METRIC/IMPERIAL

For the base:
100 g/4 oz digestive biscuits, crushed
50 g/2 oz butter, melted
50 g/2 oz soft brown sugar
For the filling:
15 g/½ oz gelatine
2 × 15 ml spoons/2 tablespoons water
350 g/¾ lb curd cheese
75 g/3 oz caster sugar
finely grated rind and juice of 1 lemon
300 ml/½ pint double cream, stiffly whipped
To finish:
sifted icing sugar
whipped cream

AMERICAN

For the base:
1 cup crushed Graham crackers
¼ cup butter, melted
⅓ cup light brown sugar
For the filling:
2 envelopes unflavored gelatin
2 tablespoons water
1½ cups curd cheese
6 tablespoons sugar
finely grated rind and juice of 1 lemon
1¼ cups heavy cream, stiffly whipped
To finish:
sifted confectioners' sugar
whipped cream

To make the base: put the biscuits (crackers), butter and sugar in a bowl and stir well to mix. Press half the mixture into the bottom of a 20 cm/8 inch springform pan and chill in the refrigerator until set.

Meanwhile, make the filling: sprinkle the gelatine over the water in a heatproof bowl. Leave until spongy, then place the bowl in a pan of hot water and stir over a low heat until the gelatine has dissolved. Leave to cool slightly. Meanwhile, put the cheese, sugar, lemon rind and juice in a bowl and beat well to mix. Stir in the gelatine, then fold in the whipped cream until evenly blended. Pour the mixture into the pan, chill until set, then scatter the remaining biscuit (cracker) mixture over the top.

To freeze: open (flash) freeze until firm, then remove the pan and pack the cheesecake in a freezer bag. Seal, label and return to the freezer.

To thaw and serve: remove wrappings and place on a serving platter. Thaw at room temperature for 4 hours or in the refrigerator overnight, then sprinkle with the icing (confectioners') sugar and decorate with whipped cream.

SERVES 6

GOOSEBERRY CHEESECAKE

METRIC/IMPERIAL

For the base:

100 g/4 oz ginger biscuits, crushed
50 g/2 oz butter, melted
50 g/2 oz demerara sugar

For the filling:

15 g/½ oz gelatine
2 × 15 ml spoons/2 tablespoons water
450 g/1 lb frozen gooseberries, thawed
75 g/3 oz sugar
275 g/10 oz cream cheese, softened
150 ml/¼ pint double cream, lightly whipped

AMERICAN

For the base:

1 cup crushed ginger cookies
¼ cup butter, melted
⅓ cup raw brown sugar

For the filling:

2 envelopes unflavored gelatin
2 tablespoons water
1 lb frozen gooseberries, thawed
⅜ cup sugar
1¼ cups cream cheese, softened
⅔ cup heavy cream, lightly whipped

To make the base: put the biscuits (cookies), butter and sugar in a bowl and stir well to mix. Press into a greased 20 cm/8 inch loose-bottomed cake tin and chill in the refrigerator until set.

To make the filling: sprinkle the gelatine over the water in a heatproof bowl. Leave until spongy, then place the bowl in a pan of hot water and stir over a low heat until the gelatine has dissolved. Leave to cool slightly.

Meanwhile, work the gooseberries to a smooth purée in an electric blender or rub through a sieve (strainer). Stir in the sugar, then the gelatine. Beat in the cream cheese, then fold in the cream. Spread the mixture over the biscuit (crumb) base, then chill in the refrigerator until set.

To freeze: open (flash) freeze until firm, then remove the cheesecake from the tin and pack in a freezer bag. Seal, label and return to the freezer.

To thaw and serve: remove wrappings and thaw in the refrigerator overnight.

SERVES 8

GRAPEFRUIT CHEESECAKE

METRIC/IMPERIAL

For the base:

75 g/3 oz butter
2 × 5 ml spoons/2 teaspoons golden syrup
100 g/4 oz digestive biscuits, crushed

For the filling:

1 × 450 g/16 oz can grapefruit segments, drained
15 g/½ oz gelatine
225 g/½ lb cottage cheese, sieved
150 ml/¼ pint soured or double cream, lightly whipped
1 small can sweetened condensed milk
2 eggs, separated

AMERICAN

For the base:

⅜ cup butter
2 teaspoons light corn syrup
1 cup crushed Graham crackers

For the filling:

1 × 16 oz can grapefruit segments, drained
2 envelopes unflavored gelatin
1 cup cottage cheese, strained
⅔ cup sour or heavy cream, lightly whipped
1 small can sweetened condensed milk
2 eggs, separated

To make the base: put the butter and syrup in a pan and heat gently until melted. Stir in the biscuits (crackers), then press into the bottom of a greased 23 cm/9 inch loose-bottomed cake tin. Chill in the refrigerator until set.

To make the filling: chop the grapefruit roughly and arrange half on the biscuit (crumb) base. Sprinkle the gelatine over 3 × 15 ml spoons/ 3 tablespoons grapefruit juice in a heatproof bowl. Leave until spongy, then place the bowl in a pan of hot water and stir over a low heat until the gelatine has dissolved. Leave to cool slightly.

Meanwhile, put the cottage cheese in a bowl and beat in the sour(ed) cream, or fold in the double (heavy) cream. Stir in the condensed milk, the remaining grapefruit, the gelatine and the egg yolks.

Beat the egg whites until stiff, then fold into the mixture until evenly blended. Pour into the tin and chill in the refrigerator until set.

To freeze: open (flash) freeze until firm, then remove the cheesecake from the tin and pack in a freezer bag. Seal, label and return to the freezer.

To thaw and serve: remove wrappings and thaw in the refrigerator overnight.

SERVES 6 to 8

TIPSY CAKE

METRIC/IMPERIAL

225 g/½ lb stale sponge cake, crumbled
100 g/4 oz ground almonds
25 g/1 oz slivered almonds
6 × 15 ml spoons/6 tablespoons port
6 × 15 ml spoons/6 tablespoons brandy
225 g/½ lb raspberries, puréed
2 × 15 ml spoons/2 tablespoons black cherry jam
To decorate:
175 ml/6 fl oz double cream, stiffly whipped
a few whole raspberries
a few mint leaves

AMERICAN

4 cups crumbled stale sponge cake
1 cup ground almonds
¼ cup slivered almonds
6 tablespoons port
6 tablespoons brandy
½ lb raspberries, puréed
2 tablespoons bing cherry jam
To decorate:
¾ cup heavy cream, stiffly whipped
a few whole raspberries
a few mint leaves

Put the cake, ground almonds, slivered almonds, port and brandy in a bowl and beat well to mix. Put the raspberries and jam in a pan and heat gently until well mixed. Add to the sponge mixture and stir thoroughly.
Spoon the mixture into a 15 cm/6 inch cake tin, cover with a saucer and place heavy weights on top. Leave overnight.
Remove the weights and saucer and run a palette knife around the sides of the tin. Turn the cake onto a baking sheet, cover with the whipped cream, then decorate with whole raspberries and mint leaves.
To freeze: open (flash) freeze until firm, then pack in a rigid container. Seal, label and return to the freezer.
To thaw and serve: place on a serving platter and thaw in the refrigerator overnight.
SERVES 6

PINEAPPLE CHEESECAKE

METRIC/IMPERIAL

For the base:
100 g/4 oz digestive biscuits, crushed
50 g/2 oz butter, melted
For the filling:
75 g/3 oz cream cheese
50 g/2 oz icing sugar, sifted
1 × 300 g/11 oz can crushed pineapple, drained
250 ml/8 fl oz double cream, lightly whipped
chopped nuts, to decorate

AMERICAN

For the base:
1 cup crushed Graham crackers
¼ cup butter, melted
For the filling:
⅓ cup cream cheese
½ cup sifted confectioners' sugar
1 × 11 oz can crushed pineapple, drained
1 cup heavy cream, lightly whipped
chopped nuts, to decorate

To make the base: put the biscuits (crackers) and butter in a bowl and stir well to mix. Press into the bottom of a greased 20 cm/8 inch loose-bottomed cake tin. Chill in the refrigerator until set.
To make the filling: put the cream cheese and icing (confectioners') sugar in a bowl and beat until light and fluffy. Stir in the pineapple, reserving a little for decoration, then fold in the cream. Spread the mixture over the biscuit (crumb) base, then chill in the refrigerator until set. Arrange the reserved pineapple and chopped nuts on top of the cheesecake.
To freeze: open (flash) freeze until firm, then remove the cheesecake from the tin and pack in a rigid container. Seal, label and return to the freezer.
To thaw and serve: transfer the cheesecake to a serving platter and thaw in the refrigerator overnight.
SERVES 8

QUICK CHOCOLATE MOUSSE

METRIC/IMPERIAL

225 g/½ lb plain chocolate, broken into pieces
4 eggs, separated
1 × 15 ml spoon/1 tablespoon rum
1 knob of butter
150 ml/¼ pint double cream, lightly whipped
To finish:
whipped cream
grated chocolate

AMERICAN

1⅓ cups semi-sweet chocolate pieces
4 eggs, separated
1 tablespoon rum
1 knob of butter
⅔ cup heavy cream, lightly whipped
To finish:
whipped cream
grated chocolate

Put the chocolate in a heatproof bowl, stand over a pan of gently simmering water and allow to melt. Remove from the heat and stir in the egg yolks one at a time. Add the rum and butter, then fold in the cream until evenly blended.
Beat the egg whites until stiff, then fold into the chocolate mixture until evenly blended. Pour into a freezerproof glass serving dish and chill in the refrigerator until set.
To freeze: cover with foil, then pack in a freezer bag. Seal, label and freeze.
To thaw and serve: remove wrappings and thaw in the refrigerator for 4 hours. Decorate with whipped cream and grated chocolate.
SERVES 6

CHOCOLATE FLUFF

METRIC/IMPERIAL

175 g/6 oz plain chocolate, broken into pieces
5 × 15 ml spoons/5 tablespoons very strong black coffee
75 g/3 oz caster sugar
4 egg whites
whipped cream, to serve

AMERICAN

1 cup semi-sweet chocolate pieces
⅓ cup very strong black coffee
6 tablespoons sugar
4 egg whites
whipped cream, to serve

Put the chocolate and coffee in a pan and heat very gently until the chocolate has melted, stirring once or twice. Add the sugar, stir until smooth, then cook gently for 4 to 5 minutes.
Put the egg whites in a bowl and beat until stiff. Pour the hot chocolate sauce into the bowl, mix gently, then pour into a freezerproof glass serving dish. Chill in the refrigerator until firm.
To freeze: cover with foil, then pack in a freezer bag. Seal, label and freeze.
To thaw and serve: remove wrappings and thaw in the refrigerator for 6 hours. Serve with whipped cream.
SERVES 4

BLACK FOREST GÂTEAU

METRIC/IMPERIAL

4 eggs
100 g/4 oz caster sugar
100 g/4 oz flour
25 g/1 oz cocoa powder
450 ml/¾ pint double cream, stiffly whipped
50 g/2 oz plain chocolate, coarsely grated
To finish:
1 × 400 g/14 oz can black cherries
1 × 15 ml spoon/1 tablespoon arrowroot
2 × 15 ml spoons/2 tablespoons Kirsch
150 ml/¼ pint double cream, stiffly whipped

AMERICAN

4 eggs
½ cup sugar
1 cup flour
¼ cup unsweetened cocoa powder
2 cups heavy cream, stiffly whipped
⅓ cup semi-sweet chocolate pieces, coarsely grated
To finish:
1 × 14 oz can bing cherries
1 tablespoon arrowroot flour
2 tablespoons Kirsch
⅔ cup heavy cream, stiffly whipped

Grease two 20 cm/8 inch sandwich tins (layer cake pans) and dust with flour.
Put the eggs and sugar in a heatproof bowl, stand over a pan of gently simmering water and beat until thick and creamy. Remove from the heat and beat until cold. Sift together the flour and cocoa and fold carefully into the egg mixture.
Divide the mixture between the prepared tins and bake in a preheated moderately hot oven (190°C/375°F or Gas Mark 5) for 25 to 30 minutes until firm to the touch. Turn out onto a wire rack and leave to cool.
Cut the cakes in half, then sandwich together with some of the whipped cream. Spread the remaining cream around the sides of the gâteau, then roll in the grated chocolate until the cream is completely covered.
To freeze: open (flash) freeze until firm, then pack in a rigid container. Seal, label and return to the freezer.
To thaw and serve: remove wrappings and thaw at room temperature for 2 to 3 hours. Drain the cherries thoroughly and arrange on top of the gâteau.
Blend the arrowroot with the cherry juice in a pan and boil until thick, stirring constantly. Add the Kirsch, leave to cool slightly, then spoon over the cherries. Leave until completely cold, then pipe the whipped cream round the edge of the gâteau.
SERVES 6 to 8

BLACK CHERRY FLAN

METRIC/IMPERIAL

1 × 20 cm/8 inch baked pastry case

For the custard:

25 g/1 oz soft tub margarine
3 × 15 ml spoons/3 tablespoons flour
120 ml/4 fl oz milk
25 g/1 oz caster sugar
1 egg yolk
1 × 15 ml spoon/1 tablespoon cream
1 × 15 ml spoon/1 tablespoon Kirsch or sherry

For the topping:

1 × 440 g/15½ oz can black cherries
1 × 5 ml spoon/1 teaspoon arrowroot

To finish:

whipped cream
chopped roasted hazelnuts
a few black cherries

AMERICAN

1 × 8 inch baked pie shell

For the custard:

2 tablespoons soft margarine
3 tablespoons flour
½ cup milk
2 tablespoons sugar
1 egg yolk
1 tablespoon cream
1 tablespoon Kirsch or sherry

For the topping:

1 × 15½ oz can bing cherries
1 teaspoon arrowroot flour

To finish:

whipped cream
chopped roasted hazelnuts
a few black cherries

To make the custard: put the margarine, flour and milk in a pan and bring slowly to the boil, beating constantly. Simmer for 2 to 3 minutes, then remove from the heat and leave to cool. Beat in the remaining custard ingredients, then spread in the bottom of the pastry case (pie shell).
Drain the cherries, remove the stones (pits) and reserve 150 ml/¼ pint/⅔ cup syrup. Arrange the cherries in circles on top of the custard. Put the reserved syrup and arrowroot in a pan, stir well to mix, then bring to the boil and simmer for 2 to 3 minutes until thick. Leave to cool slightly, then spoon over the cherries.
To freeze: open (flash) freeze until firm, then pack in a freezer bag. Seal, label and return to the freezer.
To thaw and serve: remove wrappings and thaw in the refrigerator overnight. Decorate with swirls of whipped cream, chopped hazelnuts and a few black cherries.
SERVES 4 to 6

CHERRY LATTICE FLAN

METRIC/IMPERIAL

basic rich shortcrust pastry dough made with 175 g/6 oz flour
1 small beaten egg
1 × 389 g/13¾ oz can cherry pie filling
whipped cream, to serve

AMERICAN

basic rich pie dough made with 1½ cups flour
1 small beaten egg
1 × 13¾ oz can cherry pie filling
whipped cream, to serve

Roll out the dough on a floured surface and use to line an 18 cm/7 inch fluted flan ring set on a baking sheet, reserving the trimmings of dough. Prick the dough, then brush with a little beaten egg. Chill in the refrigerator for 10 minutes, then spread the pie filling in the bottom of the pastry case (pie shell).
Roll out the trimmings of dough and cut into thin strips long enough to criss-cross the top of the flan. Moisten the ends of the strips with water and arrange over the filling in a criss-cross pattern, pressing the wetted ends firmly to seal. Brush the strips with beaten egg.
Bake the flan in a preheated hot oven (220°C/425°F or Gas Mark 7) for 15 minutes, then reduce the heat to moderate (180°C/350°F or Gas Mark 4) and bake for a further 15 minutes. Cool quickly, then remove the flan ring.
To freeze: open (flash) freeze until firm, then pack carefully in a freezer bag. Seal, label and return to the freezer.
To thaw and serve: remove wrappings and thaw at room temperature for 4 hours. Serve with whipped cream.
SERVES 4 to 6

DANISH APPLE CAKE

METRIC/IMPERIAL

675 g/1½ lb cooking apples, peeled, cored and sliced
75 g/3 oz butter
approx 150 g/5 oz sugar
100 g/4 oz fresh white breadcrumbs
150 ml/¼ pint double cream, stiffly whipped
2 × 15 ml spoons/2 tablespoons redcurrant jelly

AMERICAN

1½ lb baking apples, peeled, cored and sliced
⅜ cup butter
approx ⅔ cup sugar
2 cups fresh white breadcrumbs
⅔ cup heavy cream, stiffly whipped
2 tablespoons redcurrant jelly

Put the apples in a pan with a little water and cook gently until soft. Remove from the heat and mash to a purée with 25 g/1 oz/2 tablespoons butter and 50 g/2 oz/¼ cup sugar, according to taste. Leave to cool.
Melt the remaining butter in a pan, add the breadcrumbs and the remaining sugar and fry until golden brown and crisp, turning frequently. Leave to cool.
Arrange the apples and breadcrumbs in layers in a freezerproof glass serving dish, finishing with a layer of breadcrumbs. Spread or pipe the whipped cream over the top and spoon the redcurrant jelly in the centre.
To freeze: cover with foil, then pack in a freezer bag. Seal, label and freeze.
To thaw and serve: remove wrappings and thaw in the refrigerator overnight.
SERVES 4

RASPBERRY AND HONEY MOUSSE

METRIC/IMPERIAL
1 packet of raspberry jelly
1 × 15 ml spoon/1 tablespoon honey
150 ml/¼ pint boiling water
2 × 5 ml spoons/2 teaspoons lemon juice
150 ml/¼ pint double cream
100 g/4 oz raspberries
To finish:
whipped cream
a few whole raspberries

AMERICAN
1 package of raspberry-flavored gelatin
1 tablespoon honey
⅔ cup boiling water
2 teaspoons lemon juice
⅔ cup heavy cream
¼ lb raspberries
To finish:
whipped cream
a few whole raspberries

Put the jelly cubes (gelatin crystals) and honey in a heatproof bowl, add the boiling water and stir to dissolve. Leave to cool, then stir in the lemon juice and cream and beat thoroughly.
Fold in the raspberries and, when just beginning to set, turn into a wetted 600 ml/1 pint/2½ cup mould. Chill in the refrigerator until set.
To freeze: cover with foil, seal, label and freeze.
To thaw and serve: thaw in the refrigerator overnight, then unmould onto a serving platter and decorate with cream and raspberries.
SERVES 3 to 4

LEMON SWEETHEART FLAN

METRIC/IMPERIAL
basic shortcrust pastry dough made with 175 g/6 oz flour
100 g/4 oz butter
100 g/4 oz caster sugar
100 g/4 oz semolina or ground rice
1 × 2.5 ml spoon/½ teaspoon almond essence
finely grated rind of 1 lemon
1 large egg
2 × 15 ml spoons/2 tablespoons apricot jam
1 × 15 ml spoon/1 tablespoon sifted icing sugar

AMERICAN
basic pie dough made with 1½ cups flour
½ cup butter
½ cup sugar
⅔ cup semolina flour or ground rice
½ teaspoon almond extract
finely grated rind of 1 lemon
1 large egg
2 tablespoons apricot jam
1 tablespoon sifted confectioners' sugar

Roll out the dough on a floured surface and use to line a 20 cm/8 inch flan ring set on a baking sheet, reserving the trimmings of dough. Prick the bottom of the dough and chill in the refrigerator.
Meanwhile, melt the butter in a pan, stir in the sugar and cook for 1 minute. Stir in the semolina or ground rice, the almond essence (extract) and the lemon rind. Crack the egg in a bowl, take out 2 × 5 ml spoons/2 teaspoons of the white and reserve for the topping. Beat the remaining egg, then stir into the semolina mixture.
Spread the jam in the bottom of the pastry case (pie shell), then pour in the filling. Blend together the icing (confectioners') sugar with the reserved egg white and brush over the filling. Roll out the trimmings of dough, cut into heart shapes and place around the edge of the filling. Bake in a preheated moderately hot oven (200°C/400°F or Gas Mark 6) for 30 minutes or until the filling is set. Cool quickly on a wire rack, then remove the flan ring.
To freeze: open (flash) freeze until firm, then pack in a freezer bag. Seal, label and return to the freezer.
To thaw and serve: remove wrappings and thaw at room temperature for 4 hours.
SERVES 4 to 6

MANCHESTER PUDDING PIE

METRIC/IMPERIAL

300 ml/½ pint milk
2 bay leaves
15 g/½ oz butter
2 × 15 ml spoons/2 tablespoons sugar
1 × 2.5 ml spoons/½ teaspoon vanilla essence
1 thick slice of bread, crusts removed and broken into small pieces
basic shortcrust pastry dough made with 175 g/6 oz flour
3 × 15 ml spoons/3 tablespoons red jam
2 eggs, beaten

AMERICAN

1¼ cups milk
2 bay leaves
1 tablespoon butter
2 tablespoons sugar
½ teaspoon vanilla extract
1 thick slice of bread, crusts removed and broken into small pieces
basic pie dough made with 1½ cups flour
3 tablespoons red jam
2 eggs, beaten

Put the milk, bay leaves, butter and sugar in a pan and heat to just below boiling point. Stir in the vanilla essence (extract), then strain over the bread in a bowl. Leave to cool.

Meanwhile, roll out the dough on a floured surface and use to line a 20 cm/8 inch flan ring set on a baking sheet. Spread the jam in the bottom of the pastry case (pie shell).

Add the eggs to the milk and bread mixture and beat until smooth. Pour into the pastry case (pie shell) and bake in a preheated moderate oven (160°C/325°F or Gas Mark 3) for 50 minutes or until the filling is set. Cool quickly on a wire rack, then remove the flan ring.

To freeze: open (flash) freeze until firm, then pack in a freezer bag. Seal, label and return to the freezer.

To thaw and serve: remove wrappings and thaw at room temperature for 4 hours.

SERVES 4 to 6

CHERRY SHORTCAKE

METRIC/IMPERIAL

For the shortcake:
175 g/6 oz butter
75 g/3 oz caster sugar
250 g/9 oz flour
For the filling:
225 g/½ lb cherries, stoned
150 ml/¼ pint double cream, stiffly whipped
3 × 15 ml spoons/3 tablespoons honey
To decorate:
1 × 15 ml spoon/1 tablespoon honey
25 g/1 oz walnuts, chopped

AMERICAN

For the shortcake:
¾ cup butter
⅜ cup sugar
2¼ cups flour
For the filling:
½ lb cherries, pitted
⅔ cup heavy cream, stiffly whipped
3 tablespoons honey
To decorate:
1 tablespoon honey
¼ cup chopped walnuts

To make the shortcake: put the butter and sugar in a bowl and beat until light and fluffy. Add the flour and mix to a smooth dough. Knead lightly on a floured surface, then roll out two-thirds of the dough and cut out a 20 cm/8 inch circle. Roll out the remaining dough and cut out an 18 cm/7 inch circle.

Place the circles of dough on a baking sheet, prick all over with a fork and flute the edges. Cut the small circle into 6 triangles. Bake in a preheated moderate oven (180°C/350°F or Gas Mark 4) for 20 to 25 minutes, then cool quickly on a wire rack.

To make the filling: put the cherries, cream and honey in a bowl and stir well to mix. Spread on top of the large circle of shortcake.

Brush the triangles of shortcake with the honey, then sprinkle with the walnuts. Arrange the triangles on top of the filling.

To freeze: open (flash) freeze until firm, then pack in a rigid container. Seal, label and return to the freezer.

To thaw and serve: transfer to a serving platter and thaw in the refrigerator for 5 hours.

SERVES 6

CIDER SYLLABUB

METRIC/IMPERIAL

600 ml/1 pint double cream
finely grated rind and juice of 2 lemons
150 ml/¼ pint cider
2 egg whites
50 g/2 oz caster sugar
a few glacé cherries, to finish

AMERICAN

2½ cups heavy cream
finely grated rind and juice of 2 lemons
⅔ cup hard cider
2 egg whites
¼ cup sugar
a few candied cherries, to finish

Put the cream and lemon rind in a bowl, beat until thick, then beat in the lemon juice and cider.
Put the egg whites in a separate bowl and beat until stiff. Add the sugar and beat again, then fold into the cream mixture.
To freeze: spoon into a rigid container, seal, label and freeze.
To thaw and serve: thaw in the refrigerator for 12 to 15 hours, then beat thoroughly and spoon into 6 individual glass bowls.
Decorate with glacé (candied) cherries and chill before serving.
SERVES 6

MONTELIMAR PUDDING

METRIC/IMPERIAL

1 × 225 g/8 oz can red cherries
½ packet of lemon jelly
1 small can evaporated milk, chilled
10 marshmallows, chopped
juice of ½ lemon
25 g/1 oz caster sugar
To finish:
whipped cream
a few glacé cherries, halved
a few strips of candied angelica

AMERICAN

1 × 1½ lb can red cherries
½ package lemon-flavored gelatin
1 small can evaporated milk, chilled
10 marshmallows, chopped
juice of ½ lemon
2 tablespoons sugar
To finish:
whipped cream
a few candied cherries, halved
a few strips of candied angelica

Drain the cherries, remove the stones (pits) and chop roughly. Measure 150 ml/¼ pint/⅔ cup cherry juice, making the quantity up with water, if necessary. Heat the cherry juice to boiling point, then pour over the jelly cubes (gelatin crystals) in a heatproof bowl and stir to dissolve. Leave until cold and just beginning to set.
Beat the evaporated milk until thick, then fold into the jelly with the chopped cherries, marshmallows, lemon juice and sugar. Turn into a wetted 900 ml/1½ pint/3¾ cup mould and chill in the refrigerator until set.
To freeze: cover with foil, then pack in a freezer bag. Seal, label and freeze.
To thaw and serve: thaw in the refrigerator overnight, then turn out onto a serving platter and decorate with whipped cream, cherries and angelica 'leaves'.
SERVES 6

MERINGUES

METRIC/IMPERIAL

4 egg whites
225 g/½ lb icing sugar, sifted
a few drops of vanilla essence
a few drops of cochineal food colouring (optional)
whipped cream, to finish

AMERICAN

4 egg whites
2 cups sifted confectioners' sugar
a few drops of vanilla extract
a few drops of cochineal food coloring (optional)
whipped cream, to finish

Put the egg whites and sugar in a large heatproof bowl, stand over a pan of gently simmering water and beat until the mixture is very thick and will hold its shape. Stir in the vanilla essence (extract) and food colouring (if using).
Put the mixture into a piping (pastry) bag fitted with a large rose nozzle (fluted tube). Pipe about 40 rosettes onto a baking sheet lined with non-stick parchment, then bake on the bottom shelf of a preheated very cool oven (120°C/250°F or Gas Mark ½) for 3 to 4 hours or until the meringues are quite dry. Cool quickly on a wire rack.
To freeze: open (flash) freeze until frozen, then pack carefully in a rigid container, separating each meringue with foil or cardboard to prevent breakages during storage. Seal, label and return to the freezer.
To thaw and serve: transfer to a serving platter and thaw at room temperature for 3 to 4 hours. Sandwich the meringues together with cream.
MAKES 20

BRAZILIAN MERINGUES

METRIC/IMPERIAL

For the meringue nests:
6 egg whites
350 g/12 oz caster sugar
To finish:
75 g/3 oz plain chocolate, broken into pieces
75 g/3 oz milk chocolate, broken into pieces
1.5 × 5 ml spoons/1½ teaspoons olive or corn oil
50 g/2 oz blanched almonds, chopped
a few drops of green food colouring
150 ml/¼ pint double cream
150 ml/¼ pint single cream
1 × 15 ml spoon/1 tablespoon caster sugar
1 × 15 ml spoon/1 tablespoon rum (optional)

AMERICAN

For the meringue nests:
6 egg whites
1½ cups superfine sugar
To finish:
½ cup semi-sweet chocolate pieces
½ cup sweet chocolate pieces
1½ teaspoons olive or corn oil
½ cup chopped blanched almonds
a few drops of green food coloring
⅔ cup heavy cream
⅔ cup light cream
1 tablespoon sugar
1 tablespoon rum (optional)

Draw eight 10 cm/4 inch circles on a piece of non-stick parchment placed on a baking sheet. Put the egg whites in a bowl and beat until very stiff and standing in peaks. Add 1 × 15 ml spoon/1 tablespoon sugar and beat again until smooth and stiff. Beat in half the remaining sugar, then fold in the remainder.

Put the mixture into a piping (pastry) bag fitted with a 5 mm/¼ inch plain nozzle (tube) and pipe nest shapes on the circles drawn on the parchment. Pipe 8 small circles separately for the 'lids'. Sprinkle with a little extra sugar, then bake on the bottom shelf of a preheated very cool oven (110°C/225°F or Gas Mark ¼) for 2½ to 3 hours or until the meringues are quite dry. Leave to cool on the paper, then carefully peel the paper off the meringues.

To freeze: open (flash) freeze until firm, then pack carefully in a rigid container, separating each meringue with foil or cardboard to prevent breakages during storage. Seal, label and return to the freezer.

To thaw and serve: transfer to a serving platter and thaw at room temperature for 3 to 4 hours. Put the chocolate and oil in a heatproof bowl, stand over a pan of gently simmering water and allow the chocolate to melt. Use to coat the edges of the meringue nests and the tops of the lids. Put the almonds and food colouring in a bowl and mix well together until the almonds are evenly coloured. Scatter over the chocolate. Beat the creams together until thick, then add the sugar and rum (if using). Divide equally between the meringue nests and place the lids on top.

MAKES 8

SNOWBALL PUDDING

METRIC/IMPERIAL

1 × 300 g/11 oz can mandarin oranges
50 g/2 oz sultanas
50 g/2 oz seedless raisins
75 g/3 oz glacé cherries, quartered
2 × 15 ml spoons/2 tablespoons sherry
100 g/4 oz butter
100 g/4 oz icing sugar, sifted
50 g/2 oz ground almonds
1 large packet of trifle sponges, crumbled
To finish:
150 ml/¼ pint double cream
2 × 15 ml spoons/2 tablespoons milk

AMERICAN

1 × 11 oz can mandarin oranges
⅓ cup seedless white raisins
⅓ cup seedless raisins
⅓ cup quartered candied cherries
2 tablespoons sherry
½ cup butter
1 cup sifted confectioners' sugar
½ cup ground almonds
½ lb sponge cake, crumbled
To finish:
⅔ cup heavy cream
2 tablespoons milk

Drain the mandarins and reserve the syrup. Put the mandarins in a bowl with the dried fruit, cherries and sherry. Leave to soak, stirring occasionally.

Put the butter and sugar in a bowl and beat together until light and fluffy. Fold in the ground almonds, trifle sponges and the soaked fruit, then spoon into a buttered 600 ml/1 pint/2½ cup pudding basin (slope-sided mold). Moisten with a little of the reserved mandarin syrup and press firmly.

Cover with a saucer that just fits inside the rim, then put weights on top and leave in the refrigerator overnight.

To freeze: remove the saucer and weights and cover with foil. Pack in a freezer bag, seal, label and freeze.

To thaw and serve: remove wrappings, thaw in the refrigerator overnight, then turn out onto a serving platter. Beat the cream and milk until thick, then spread over the pudding to cover it completely.
SERVES 4 to 6

TIPSY CHOCOLATE AND ORANGE RING

METRIC/IMPERIAL
1 × 15 ml spoon/1 tablespoon cocoa powder
3 × 15 ml spoons/3 tablespoons boiling water
100 g/4 oz soft tub margarine
100 g/4 oz caster sugar
100 g/4 oz self-raising flour
2 eggs
5 × 15 ml spoons/5 tablespoons frozen concentrated orange juice, thawed
3 × 15 ml spoons/3 tablespoons rum
To finish:
150 ml/¼ pint double cream, stiffly whipped
1 × 300 g/11 oz can mandarin oranges, drained

AMERICAN
1 tablespoon unsweetened cocoa powder
3 tablespoons boiling water
½ cup soft margarine
½ cup water
1 cup self-rising flour
2 eggs
⅓ cup frozen concentrated orange juice, thawed
3 tablespoons rum
To finish:
⅔ cup heavy cream, stiffly whipped
1 × 11 oz can mandarin oranges, drained

Mix the cocoa to a paste with the water, then leave to cool. Put in a bowl with the margarine, sugar, flour and eggs and beat well together to mix.
Pour the mixture into a greased 1.75 litre/3 pint/7½ cup ring mould and bake in a preheated moderate oven (160°C/325°F or Gas Mark 3) for 30 to 35 minutes until well risen and firm to the touch.
Turn out onto a dish, leave to cool, then spoon over the orange juice and rum and allow to soak into the cake.
To freeze: wrap in foil, then pack in a freezer bag. Seal, label and freeze.
To thaw and serve: remove wrappings and thaw at room temperature for 4 hours. Pipe the cream over the cake, then fill the centre with the mandarin oranges and arrange a few on the cream.
SERVES 4 to 6

APRICOT AND ALMOND RING

METRIC/IMPERIAL
For the cake:
100 g/4 oz self-raising flour
1 × 5 ml spoon/1 teaspoon baking powder
100 g/4 oz caster sugar
100 g/4 oz soft tub margarine
2 large eggs
For the sauce (to finish):
1 × 425 g/15 oz can apricot halves, drained
1 × 15 ml spoon/1 tablespoon cornflour
25 g/1 oz blanched slivered almonds
For the filling (to finish):
4 scoops soft ice cream
whipped cream

AMERICAN
For the cake:
1 cup self-rising flour
1 teaspoon baking powder
½ cup sugar
½ cup soft margarine
2 large eggs
For the sauce (to finish):
1 × 15 oz can apricot halves, drained
1 tablespoon cornstarch
¼ cup blanched slivered almonds
For the filling (to finish):
4 scoops of soft ice cream
whipped cream

To make the cake: put all the ingredients in a bowl and beat for about 3 minutes until light and fluffy. Spoon the mixture into a greased and floured 18 cm/7 inch ring mould and bake in a preheated moderate oven (160°C/325°F or Gas Mark 3) for 30 minutes or until well risen and firm to the touch. Turn out and cool quickly on a wire rack.
To freeze: wrap in foil, seal, label and freeze.
To thaw and serve: remove wrappings and thaw at room temperature for 4 hours.
To make the sauce: drain the apricots and reserve the juice and 5 apricot halves for decoration. Work the remaining apricots to a purée through a sieve (strainer), then put the purée in a pan with the reserved juice. Bring slowly to the boil. Mix the cornflour (cornstarch) to a paste with a little water and stir into the pan. Simmer until thick and smooth, stirring constantly, then stir the almonds into the sauce, reserving 5 for decoration. Leave to cool.
Put the cake on a serving platter and fill the centre with the ice cream. Pour over the sauce and decorate the cake with the reserved apricot halves and almonds and whipped cream.
SERVES 4 to 6

TARTE NÖEL

METRIC/IMPERIAL

For the pastry:
100 g/4 oz flour
50 g/2 oz butter
50 g/2 oz caster sugar
2 egg yolks
For the filling:
6 × 15 ml spoons/6 tablespoons mincemeat
100 g/4 oz ground almonds
100 g/4 oz caster sugar
2 egg whites
a few drops of almond essence
50 g/2 oz slivered blanched almonds
4 × 15 ml spoons/4 tablespoons sieved apricot jam, to glaze

AMERICAN

For the pastry:
1 cup flour
¼ cup butter
¼ cup sugar
2 egg yolks
For the filling:
6 tablespoons mincemeat
1 cup ground almonds
½ cup sugar
2 egg whites
a few drops of almond extract
½ cup slivered blanched almonds
¼ cup strained apricot jam, to glaze

To make the pastry: sift the flour onto a board or surface, make a well in the centre and put in the butter, sugar and egg yolks. Pinch and work the ingredients together to give a well-blended dough, using the fingertips. Chill in the refrigerator for 1 hour. Roll out the dough on a floured surface and use to line a 20 cm/8 inch loose-bottomed fluted flan ring set on a baking sheet.
To make the filling: spread the mincemeat over the bottom of the pastry case (pie shell). Put the ground almonds, sugar, egg whites and almond essence (extract) in a bowl and stir well to mix. Spread over the mincemeat, then cover with the almonds. Bake in a preheated moderately hot oven (190°C/375°F or Gas Mark 5) for about 1 hour or until firm in the centre. Cool quickly on a wire rack, then remove the flan ring.
To freeze: open (flash) freeze until firm, then wrap in foil. Seal, label and return to the freezer.
To thaw and serve: remove wrappings and thaw at room temperature for 4 hours.
Heat the apricot jam in a pan and brush over the almonds to glaze. Leave to set before serving cut into wedges.
SERVES 6 to 8

TARTE FRANÇAISE

METRIC/IMPERIAL

For the pastry:
175 g/6 oz flour
pinch of salt
75 g/3 oz butter
2 egg yolks
1 × 15 ml spoon/1 tablespoon caster sugar
For the filling:
675 g/1½ lb cooking apples
juice of 1 lemon
50 g/2 oz caster sugar, or to taste
50 g/2 oz butter, cut into small pieces
To finish:
4 × 15 ml spoons/4 tablespoons apricot jam
2 × 15 ml spoons/2 tablespoons lemon juice
whipped cream, to serve

AMERICAN

For the pastry:
1½ cups flour
pinch of salt
⅜ cup butter
2 egg yolks
1 tablespoon sugar
For the filling:
1½ lb baking apples
juice of 1 lemon
¼ cup sugar, or to taste
¼ cup butter, cut into small pieces
To finish:
¼ cup apricot jam
2 tablespoons lemon juice
whipped cream, to serve

Sift the flour and salt onto a marble slab or board and make a well in the centre. Add the butter in pieces, the egg yolks and sugar and draw the flour into the centre with the fingertips, working all the ingredients together to give a soft dough. Knead lightly on a floured surface until smooth, then wrap in foil and chill in the refrigerator for at least 30 minutes. Press into a buttered 23 cm/9 inch fluted flan ring set on a baking sheet, prick the base with a fork and chill in the refrigerator for a further 15 minutes.
Meanwhile, peel and core the apples and slice finely. Sprinkle immediately with the lemon juice to prevent discoloration, then arrange the apple slices, overlapping, in the flan case. Sprinkle with sugar to taste, then dot with the butter.
Bake in a preheated moderately hot oven (190°C/375°F or Gas Mark 5) for 30 minutes or until the apples are cooked through and the pastry is golden. Cool quickly on a wire rack, then remove the flan ring.
To freeze: open (flash) freeze until firm, then wrap in foil. Seal, label and return to the freezer.

To thaw and serve: remove wrappings and return the tart to the flan ring set on a baking sheet. Reheat from frozen in a preheated moderately hot oven (200°C/400°F or Gas Mark 6) for 20 minutes or until heated through. Cover with foil if the pastry becomes too brown during cooking. Leave to cool slightly, then remove the flan ring. Put the jam and lemon juice in a pan, heat gently, stirring constantly, then sieve (strain) and brush over the apples. Leave until set, then serve with whipped cream.
SERVES 6

ORANGE CREAMS

METRIC/IMPERIAL
finely grated rind and juice of 2 oranges
1 packet of lemon jelly
2 × 15 ml spoons/2 tablespoons boiling water
2 eggs, separated
4 × 15 ml spoons/4 tablespoons double cream, lightly whipped

AMERICAN
finely grated rind and juice of 2 oranges
1 package of lemon-flavored gelatin
2 tablespoons boiling water
2 eggs, separated
¼ cup heavy cream, lightly whipped

Measure the orange juice and make up to 150 ml/¼ pint/⅔ cup with water, if necessary.
Put the jelly cubes (gelatin crystals) in a heatproof bowl, add the water and stir well until dissolved. Add the orange juice, rind and egg yolks. Stir well to mix, then leave in a cool place until almost set.
Fold in the cream, then beat the egg whites until stiff and fold in until evenly blended. Spoon into 4 individual freezerproof serving dishes and chill in the refrigerator until set.
To freeze: cover with foil, then pack in freezer bags. Seal, label and freeze.
To thaw and serve: remove wrappings and thaw at room temperature for 4 hours.
SERVES 4

OLD ENGLISH CREAMS

METRIC/IMPERIAL
1 packet of lemon jelly
2 × 15 ml spoons/2 tablespoons lemon juice
4 × 15 ml spoons/4 tablespoons old English marmalade
150 ml/¼ pint single cream
450 ml/¾ pint double cream
whipped cream, to finish

AMERICAN
1 package of lemon-flavored gelatin
2 tablespoons lemon juice
¼ cup old English marmalade
⅔ cup light cream
2 cups heavy cream
whipped cream, to finish

Put the jelly cubes (gelatin crystals) in a heatproof bowl, make up to 300 ml/½ pint/1¼ cups with boiling water and stir to dissolve. Mix 2 × 15 ml spoons/2 tablespoons cold water with 4 × 15 ml spoons/4 tablespoons of the jelly (gelatin) and spoon into a wetted 900 ml/1½ pint/3¾ cup mold. Leave to set. Stir the lemon juice into the remaining jelly (gelatin) and chill in the refrigerator until half set.
Fold the marmalade into the half-set jelly (gelatin). Beat the creams together until they hold their shape, then fold into the marmalade mixture. Spoon into the mould and leave to set.
To freeze: cover with foil, seal, label and freeze.
To thaw and serve: thaw in the refrigerator overnight, then unmould onto a serving platter and decorate with rosettes of whipped cream.
SERVES 4 to 6

MINCEMEAT PLAIT

METRIC/IMPERIAL

225 g/½ lb mincemeat
50 g/2 oz glacé cherries, chopped
50 g/2 oz blanched almonds, chopped
350 g/¾ lb frozen puff pastry, thawed
beaten egg, to glaze
For the topping:
100 g/4 oz icing sugar, sifted
1 × 15 ml spoon/1 tablespoon lemon juice
a few glacé cherries, chopped
a few blanched almonds, chopped

AMERICAN

1 cup mincemeat
¼ cup candied cherries, chopped
½ cup chopped blanched almonds
¾ lb frozen puff paste, thawed
beaten egg, to glaze
For the topping:
1 cup sifted confectioners' sugar
1 tablespoon lemon juice
a few candied cherries, chopped
a few blanched almonds, chopped

Put the mincemeat, cherries and almonds in a bowl and beat well to mix.

Roll out the dough on a floured surface and cut into an oblong about 35 × 30 cm/14 × 12 inches. Mark the dough into 3 lengthways, then moisten the edges with water. Make diagonal slits along the outer sections of the dough 2.5 cm/1 inch apart and 7.5 cm/3 inches deep.

Spread the mincemeat mixture over the centre section of the dough and fold over the outer sections, arranging the cut strips to give a plaited (braid) effect. Press the ends firmly to seal. Put the plait on a baking sheet and brush all over with the beaten egg. Bake in a preheated hot oven (220°C/425°F or Gas Mark 7) for 20 minutes until golden brown. Leave to cool.

To make the topping: put the icing (confectioners') sugar in a bowl and gradually beat in the lemon juice with a few drops of boiling water. Beat until smooth and glossy, then spoon over the plait and sprinkle immediately with the cherries and almonds.

To freeze: open (flash) freeze until firm, then pack in a rigid container. Seal, label and return to the freezer.

To thaw and serve: remove wrappings and thaw at room temperature for 3 to 4 hours.

SERVES 6

APPLE AND DATE PLAIT

Make as for Mincemeat Plait substituting 450 g/1 lb dessert apples, peeled, cored and chopped, plus 75 g/3 oz stoned dates (⅓ cup pitted dates) for the mincemeat, cherries and almonds. Decorate the icing with finely chopped dates or nuts. Freeze, thaw and serve as for Mincemeat Plait.

SERVES 6

CHOCOLATE CREAM PIE

METRIC/IMPERIAL

For the base:
25 g/1 oz butter
1 × 15 ml spoon/1 tablespoon golden syrup
2 × 5 ml spoons/2 teaspoons brown sugar
175 g/6 oz digestive biscuits, crushed
For the filling:
100 g/4 oz plain chocolate, broken into pieces
2 × 15 ml spoons/2 tablespoons water
300 ml/½ pint double cream, stiffly whipped
chocolate curls, to decorate

AMERICAN

For the base:
2 tablespoons butter
1 tablespoon light corn syrup
2 teaspoons brown sugar
1½ cups crushed Graham crackers
For the filling:
⅔ cup semi-sweet chocolate pieces
2 tablespoons water
1¼ cups heavy cream, stiffly whipped
chocolate curls, to decorate

To make the base: melt the butter and syrup in a pan, remove from the heat, add the sugar and crushed biscuits (crackers) and stir well to mix. Press into the bottom and sides of a 20 cm/8 inch flan ring set on a baking sheet, then chill in the refrigerator until set.

Put the chocolate and water in a heatproof bowl, stand over a pan of gently simmering water and allow to melt. Remove from the heat and leave to cool, then carefully fold in the whipped cream and spoon into the flan case (pie shell). Smooth the top and decorate with chocolate curls.

To freeze: open (flash) freeze until firm, then remove the flan ring and pack the chocolate pie in a rigid container. Seal, label and return to the freezer.

To thaw and serve: transfer to a serving platter and thaw in the refrigerator overnight.

SERVES 6

SCOTCH TART

METRIC/IMPERIAL

basic shortcrust pastry dough made with 150 g/5 oz flour
2 × 15 ml spoons/2 tablespoons apricot jam
25 g/1 oz sultanas
25 g/1 oz glacé cherries, sliced
50 g/2 oz butter
50 g/2 oz caster sugar
1 egg, beaten
1 × 2.5 ml spoon/½ teaspoon almond essence
40 g/1½ oz ground rice
40 g/1½ oz stale cake crumbs
a few blanched slivered almonds
a few glacé cherries, quartered, to decorate

AMERICAN

basic pie dough made with 1¼ cups flour
2 tablespoons apricot jam
3 tablespoons seedless white raisins
1½ tablespoons sliced candied cherries
¼ cup butter
¼ cup sugar
1 egg, beaten
½ teaspoon almond extract
¼ cup ground rice
¾ cup stale cake crumbs
a few blanched slivered almonds
a few candied cherries, quartered, to decorate

Roll out the dough on a floured surface and use to line an 18 cm/7 inch flan ring set on a baking sheet. Spread the jam in the bottom of the pastry case (pie shell), then scatter over the sultanas (seedless white raisins) and glacé (candied) cherries.

Put the butter and sugar in a bowl and beat together until light and fluffy. Beat in the egg a little at a time, then fold in the almond essence (extract), ground rice and cake crumbs. Spoon the cake mixture into the pastry case (pie shell) and smooth the top. Scatter over the almonds, then bake in a preheated moderately hot oven (190°C/375°F or Gas Mark 5) for about 30 minutes or until the cake filling is firm to the touch. Decorate with glacé (candied) cherries, cool quickly on a wire rack, then remove the flan ring.

To freeze: open (flash) freeze until firm, then pack in a freezer bag. Seal, label and return to the freezer.

To thaw and serve: remove wrappings and thaw at room temperature for 4 hours.

SERVES 4 to 6

CHOCOLATE BAKEWELL TART

METRIC/IMPERIAL

basic shortcrust pastry dough made with 175 g/6 oz flour
3 × 15 ml spoons/3 tablespoons strawberry jam
50 g/2 oz butter
50 g/2 oz caster sugar
1 large egg, beaten
40 g/1½ oz self-raising flour
2 × 15 ml spoons/2 tablespoons cocoa powder
25 g/1 oz ground almonds
1 × 2.5 ml spoon/½ teaspoon almond essence
finely grated rind of ½ lemon

AMERICAN

basic pie dough made with 1½ cups flour
3 tablespoons strawberry jam
¼ cup butter
¼ cup sugar
1 large egg, beaten
6 tablespoons self-rising flour
2 tablespoons unsweetened cocoa powder
¼ cup ground almonds
½ teaspoon almond extract
finely grated rind of ½ lemon

Roll out the dough on a floured surface and use to line an 18 cm/7 inch fluted flan ring set on a baking sheet, reserving the trimmings of dough for the lattice. Spread the jam in the bottom of the pastry case (pie shell).

Put the butter and sugar in a bowl and beat together until light and fluffy. Beat in the egg a little at a time, then fold in the flour and cocoa. Add the almonds, almond essence (extract) and the lemon rind and stir well to mix.

Spoon the cake mixture into the pastry case (pie shell) and smooth the top. Roll out the reserved trimmings of dough and cut into thin strips long enough to criss-cross the top of the tart. Moisten the ends of the strips with water and arrange over the filling in a criss-cross pattern, pressing the wetted ends firmly to seal.

Bake in a preheated moderately hot oven (200°C/400°F or Gas Mark 6) for 15 minutes, then reduce the heat to moderate (180°C/350°F or Gas Mark 4) and bake for a further 15 minutes or until the cake filling is firm to the touch. Cool quickly on a wire rack, then remove the flan ring.

To freeze: open (flash) freeze until firm, then pack in a freezer bag. Seal, label and return to the freezer.

To thaw and serve: remove wrappings and thaw at room temperature for 4 hours.

SERVES 4 to 6

BREAD AND BUTTER PUDDING

METRIC/IMPERIAL

8 to 10 slices of white bread, crusts removed
75 g/3 oz butter
100 g/4 oz mixed dried fruit
2 eggs
50 g/2 oz caster sugar
600 ml/1 pint milk
1 × 2.5 ml spoon/½ teaspoon grated nutmeg

AMERICAN

8 to 10 slices of white bread, crusts removed
⅜ cup butter
¾ cup mixed dried fruit
2 eggs
¼ cup sugar
2½ cups milk
½ teaspoon grated nutmeg

Spread the slices of bread with the butter on one side only, then cut each slice into 4 triangles. Arrange some of the triangles around the sides of a buttered deep ovenproof dish or foil container, then put a layer of fruit in the bottom. Continue with these layers until all the bread and fruit have been used, finishing with a layer of bread.

Put the eggs, sugar and milk in a bowl and beat well to mix. Pour over the bread and leave to soak for 30 minutes, then sprinkle with the nutmeg. Bake in a preheated moderately hot oven (200°C/400°F or Gas Mark 6) for 35 to 40 minutes until the top of the pudding is golden brown.

To freeze: cool quickly, wrap in foil, then pack in a freezer bag. Seal, label and freeze.

To thaw and serve: remove the freezer bag and thaw at room temperature for 4 hours. Reheat in the covered dish or container in a preheated moderate oven (180°C/350°F or Gas Mark 4) for 1 hour or until heated through.

SERVES 4 to 6

MARMALADE AND GINGER PUDDING

METRIC/IMPERIAL

2 × 15 ml spoons/2 tablespoons marmalade
2 pieces of stem ginger, chopped
100 g/4 oz butter
100 g/4 oz caster sugar
2 eggs, beaten
150 g/5 oz flour
25 g/1 oz cornflour
2 × 5 ml spoons/2 teaspoons baking powder
2 × 5 ml spoons/2 teaspoons ground ginger
1 × 15 ml spoon/1 tablespoon milk

AMERICAN

2 tablespoons marmalade
2 pieces of preserved ginger, chopped
½ cup butter
½ cup sugar
2 eggs, beaten
1¼ cups flour
¼ cup cornstarch
2 teaspoons baking powder
2 teaspoons ground ginger
1 tablespoon milk

Put the marmalade and ginger in the bottom of a well-greased 1.2 litre/2 pint/5 cup pudding basin (steaming mold). Put the butter and sugar in a bowl and beat together until light and fluffy. Beat in the eggs a little at a time, then fold in the dry ingredients. Stir in the milk, then spoon the mixture into the basin (mold). Cover with greased foil, making a pleat in the centre, then secure with string. Steam for 2 hours until well risen, then leave to shrink slightly.

To freeze: turn out and cool. Wrap in foil, pack in a freezer bag, seal, label and freeze.

To thaw and serve: remove the freezer bag. Reheat from frozen in the foil wrapping in a preheated moderate oven (180°C/350°F or Gas Mark 4) for 40 to 45 minutes.

SERVES 6

CUSTARD TART

METRIC/IMPERIAL

basic shortcrust pastry dough made with 275 g/10 oz flour
3 large eggs
40 g/1½ oz caster sugar
600 ml/1 pint milk
1 × 2.5 ml spoon/½ teaspoon grated nutmeg

AMERICAN

basic pie dough made with 2½ cups flour
3 large eggs
3 tablespoons sugar
2½ cups milk
½ teaspoon grated nutmeg

Roll out the dough on a floured surface and use to line two 20 cm/8 inch fluted flan dishes (pie pans). Put the eggs and sugar in a bowl and beat lightly to mix. Stir in the milk, then strain into the pastry cases (pie shells). Sprinkle with nutmeg.
To freeze: open (flash) freeze until firm, then wrap in freezer bags. Seal, label and return to the freezer.
To thaw and serve: remove wrappings and bake from frozen in a preheated moderately hot oven (190°C/375°F or Gas Mark 5) for 1 hour or until the custard is set.
EACH TART SERVES 4

STEAMED APRICOT PUDDING

METRIC/IMPERIAL

25 g/1 oz dried apricots
300 ml/½ pint water
100 g/4 oz cake crumbs
50 g/2 oz ground almonds
5 × 15 ml spoons/5 tablespoons single cream or creamy milk
5 × 15 ml spoons/5 tablespoons milk
50 g/2 oz butter
50 g/2 oz caster sugar
finely grated rind of 1 lemon
2 eggs, separated

AMERICAN

3 tablespoons dried apricots
1¼ cups water
2 cups cake crumbs
½ cup ground almonds
⅓ cup light cream or half-and-half
⅓ cup milk
¼ cup butter
¼ cup sugar
finely grated rind of 1 lemon
2 eggs, separated

Put the apricots and water in a pan, bring to the boil, then simmer until soft.
Meanwhile, put the cake crumbs and ground almonds in a bowl, pour over the cream and milk and leave to soak, stirring occasionally. Put the butter, sugar and lemon rind in a separate bowl and beat together until light and fluffy. Beat in the egg yolks alternately with the soaked cake crumbs. Drain the apricots, chop them roughly, then stir into the mixture.
Beat the egg whites until stiff but not dry, then fold into the mixture. Spoon into a well-greased 900 ml/1½ pint/3¾ cup pudding basin (steaming mold). Cover with greased foil, making a pleat in the centre, then secure with string. Steam for 1¾ to 2 hours, then leave to shrink slightly.
To freeze: turn out and cool. Wrap in foil, then pack in a freezer bag. Seal, label and freeze.
To thaw and serve: remove the freezer bag and thaw at room temperature for 3 hours. Return to the basin (mold) in the foil wrapping and steam for 1 hour or until heated through.
SERVES 4 to 6

PLUM CRUMBLE

METRIC/IMPERIAL

450 g/1 lb plums, halved and stoned
100 g/4 oz caster sugar
For the topping:
225 g/½ lb flour
75 g/3 oz butter
100 g/4 oz caster sugar

AMERICAN

1 lb plums, halved and pitted
½ cup sugar
For the topping:
2 cups flour
⅜ cup butter
½ cup sugar

Put the plums and sugar in layers in a 900 ml/1½ pint/3¾ cup ovenproof pie dish.
To make the topping: sift the flour into a bowl, add the butter in pieces and rub into the flour until the mixture resembles fine breadcrumbs. Stir in the sugar, then scatter the mixture over the plums and press down lightly.
To freeze: cover with foil, then pack in a freezer bag. Seal, label and freeze.
To thaw and serve: remove wrappings and bake the crumble from frozen in a preheated hot oven (220°C/425°F or Gas Mark 7) for 20 minutes. Reduce the heat to 190°C/375°F or Gas Mark 5 and bake for a further 45 minutes.
SERVES 4

APPLE PIE

METRIC/IMPERIAL

basic shortcrust pastry dough made with 225 g/½ lb flour
450 g/1 lb cooking apples, peeled, cored and thinly sliced
100 g/4 oz caster sugar
finely grated rind of ½ lemon (optional)
a little milk, to glaze
extra caster sugar for sprinkling, to finish

AMERICAN

basic pie dough made with 2 cups flour
1 lb baking apples, peeled, cored and thinly sliced
½ cup sugar
finely grated rind of ½ lemon (optional)
a little milk, to glaze
extra sugar for sprinkling, to finish

Divide the dough in two, then roll out one half on a floured surface and use to line a 20 cm/8 inch ovenproof plate. Put the apples, sugar and lemon rind in a bowl, stir gently to mix, then pile onto the dough. Moisten the edge with water, roll out the remaining dough and use to cover the filling. Brush the top of the dough with milk and make a slit in the centre.
Bake in a preheated hot oven (220°C/425°F or Gas Mark 7) for 20 minutes, then reduce the heat to moderate (180°C/350°F or Gas Mark 4) and bake for a further 35 minutes.
To freeze: cool quickly, then pack carefully in a freezer bag. Seal, label and freeze.
To thaw and serve: remove wrappings and reheat the pie from frozen in a preheated hot oven (220°C/425°F or Gas Mark 7) for 20 minutes. Reduce the heat to moderate (180°C/350°F or Gas Mark 4) and bake for a further 20 minutes until heated through. Cover with foil if the pastry becomes too brown during cooking. Sprinkle with (caster) sugar while still hot.
SERVES 4 to 6

CHOCOLATE MERINGUE SURPRISE

METRIC/IMPERIAL

For the sponge base:
50 g/2 oz caster sugar
2 eggs
25 g/1 oz flour
25 g/1 oz cocoa powder
10 scoops of chocolate ice cream
For the meringue:
2 egg whites
100 g/4 oz caster sugar
25 g/1 oz slivered almonds, lightly toasted

AMERICAN

For the sponge base:
¼ cup sugar
2 eggs
¼ cup flour
¼ cup unsweetened cocoa powder
10 scoops of chocolate ice cream
For the meringue:
2 egg whites
½ cup superfine sugar
¼ cup slivered almonds, lightly toasted

Grease an 18 cm/7 inch sandwich tin (layer cake pan) and line the bottom with greased greaseproof paper or non-stick parchment.
To make the sponge: put the sugar and eggs in a bowl and beat together until thick and creamy. Sift the flour and cocoa together and fold into the mixture until evenly blended. Pour into the prepared tin and bake in a preheated moderately hot oven (190°C/375°F or Gas Mark 5) for 20 minutes until firm. Turn out onto a wire rack, remove the paper lining and leave to cool.
To make the meringue: beat the egg whites until stiff, then beat in the sugar. Arrange scoops of ice cream on the sponge, spread the meringue over the top and sides to enclose the sponge and ice cream completely, then scatter the almonds over the top. Bake in a preheated hot oven (230°C/450°F or Gas Mark 8) for 5 minutes.
To freeze: cool quickly. Open (flash) freeze until frozen, then pack in a rigid container. Seal, label and return to the freezer.
To thaw and serve: place the frozen dessert on a baking sheet and reheat in a preheated hot oven (230°C/450°F or Gas Mark 8) for 5 minutes.
SERVES 6

BAKED APPLE DUMPLINGS

METRIC/IMPERIAL

basic suet crust pastry dough made with 225 g/½ lb flour
4 medium cooking apples, peeled and cored
approx 4 × 5 ml spoons/4 teaspoons brown sugar or mincemeat
To glaze:
1 egg white, lightly beaten
4 × 5 ml spoons/4 teaspoons caster sugar

AMERICAN

basic suet crust dough made with 2 cups flour
4 medium baking apples, peeled and cored
approx 4 teaspoons brown sugar or mincemeat
To glaze:
1 egg white, lightly beaten
4 teaspoons sugar

Roll out the dough on a floured surface and cut out 4 squares large enough to enclose the apples. Put one apple on each square of dough and fill the centres with the brown sugar or mincemeat. Moisten the edges of the dough with water, draw the corners up to meet at the centre of each apple and press firmly to seal. Use any trimmings to decorate the top of the dumplings.

Put the dumplings in a greased roasting tin, brush with the egg white and sprinkle with the sugar. Bake in a preheated moderately hot oven (200°C/400°F or Gas Mark 6) for 30 minutes, then cool quickly on a wire rack.

To freeze: wrap individually in foil, then pack in a freezer bag. Seal, label and freeze.

To thaw and serve: remove wrappings, replace the apples in roasting tin and thaw at room temperature for 3 hours. Reheat in a preheated moderate oven (180°C/350°F or Gas Mark 4) for 20 to 30 minutes or until heated through.

MAKES 4

GUARDS' PUDDING

METRIC/IMPERIAL

175 g/6 oz fresh breadcrumbs
75 g/3 oz caster sugar
2 eggs, beaten
75 g/3 oz butter, melted
4 × 15 ml spoons/4 tablespoons raspberry jam
0.5 × 2.5 ml spoon/¼ teaspoon bicarbonate of soda

AMERICAN

3 cups fresh breadcrumbs
⅜ cup sugar
2 eggs, beaten
⅜ cup butter, melted
¼ cup raspberry jam
¼ teaspoon baking soda

Put the breadcrumbs and sugar in a bowl and stir well to mix. Stir in the eggs, butter and jam. Mix the bicarbonate of soda (baking soda) to a paste with a little water, then stir into the breadcrumb mixture until evenly blended.

Spoon the mixture into a well-greased 900 ml/1½ pint/3¾ cup pudding basin (steaming mold). Cover with greased foil, making a pleat in the centre, then secure with string. Steam for 2 hours until well-risen. Leave to shrink slightly.

To freeze: turn out and cool. Wrap in foil, pack in a freezer bag, seal, label and freeze.

To thaw and serve: remove the freezer bag and thaw at room temperature for 3 hours. Return to the basin (mold) in the foil wrapping and steam for 1 hour or until heated through.

SERVES 4 to 6

CHOCOLATE MARMALADE PUDDING

METRIC/IMPERIAL

75 g/3 oz butter
100 g/4 oz caster sugar
1 egg, beaten
25 g/1 oz cocoa powder
100 g/4 oz self-raising flour
1 × 5 ml spoon/1 teaspoon baking powder
a little milk
For the sauce:
2 × 5 ml spoons/2 teaspoons cornflour
300 ml/½ pint water
6 × 15 ml spoons/6 tablespoons marmalade

AMERICAN

⅜ cup butter
½ cup sugar
1 egg, beaten
¼ cup unsweetened cocoa powder
1 cup self-rising flour
1 teaspoon baking powder
a little milk
For the sauce:
2 teaspoons cornstarch
1¼ cups water
6 tablespoons marmalade

Put the butter and sugar in a bowl and beat together until light and fluffy. Beat in the egg a little at a time, then fold in the cocoa, flour and baking powder. Stir in enough milk to give a soft dropping consistency, then spoon into a well-greased 600 ml/1 pint/2½ cup pudding basin (steaming mold). Cover with greased foil, making a pleat in the centre, then secure with string. Steam for 1¼ hours or until well-risen, leave to shrink slightly, then unmould. Leave to cool.

Meanwhile, make the sauce: mix the cornflour (cornstarch) to a paste with a little of the water, then put in a pan with the remaining water and the marmalade. Bring to the boil, then simmer until the sauce is thick and clear, stirring constantly. Leave to cool.

To freeze: wrap the pudding in foil, then pack in a freezer bag. Seal, label and freeze. Pour the sauce into a rigid container, seal, label and freeze.

To thaw and serve: remove the freezer bag and thaw at room temperature for 3 hours. Return to the basin (mold) in the foil wrapping and steam for 1 hour or until heated through.

Thaw the sauce at room temperature for 3 hours, then reheat gently on top of the stove, stirring constantly.

SERVES 4 to 6

MINCEMEAT ROLY-POLY

METRIC/IMPERIAL

For the pastry:
225 g/½ lb self-raising flour
pinch of salt
112 g/4 oz shredded suet
water, to mix
For the filling:
6 × 15 ml spoons/6 tablespoons mincemeat
1 cooking apple, peeled, cored and grated
0.5 × 2.5 ml spoon/¼ teaspoon ground cinnamon

AMERICAN

For the pastry:
2 cups self-rising flour
pinch of salt
¾ cup shredded suet
water, to mix
For the filling:
6 tablespoons mincemeat
1 baking apple, peeled, cored and grated
¼ teaspoon ground cinnamon

To make the pastry: sift the flour and salt into a bowl, then stir in the suet and enough water to give a soft dough. Knead until smooth on a floured surface, then roll out to a rectangle about 35 × 25 cm/14 × 10 inches.
To make the filling: put all the ingredients in a bowl and stir well to mix. Spread the mixture over the dough, leaving a 2.5 cm/1 inch margin around the edge. Moisten the edges with water, then roll up the dough like a Swiss (jelly) roll, pinching and sealing the edges. Wrap loosely in greased foil, then steam for 1½ hours.
To freeze: cool quickly, wrap in clean foil, then pack in a freezer bag. Seal, label and freeze.
To thaw and serve: remove the freezer bag and thaw the roly-poly at room temperature for 4 hours. Steam for 1 hour or until heated through.
SERVES 4 to 5

STEAMED FRUIT PUDDING

METRIC/IMPERIAL

100 g/4 oz flour
pinch of salt
1 × 5 ml spoon/1 teaspoon baking powder
1 × 2.5 ml spoon/½ teaspoon mixed spice
1 × 2.5 ml spoon/½ teaspoon ground cinnamon
100 g/4 oz soft brown sugar
100 g/4 oz fresh white breadcrumbs
75 g/3 oz shredded suet
225 g/½ lb mixed dried fruit
finely grated rind of 1 orange
2 eggs, beaten
90–120 ml/3–4 fl oz milk

AMERICAN

1 cup flour
pinch of salt
1 teaspoon baking powder
½ teaspoon ground nutmeg and cloves, mixed
½ teaspoon ground cinnamon
⅔ cup light brown sugar
2 cups fresh white breadcrumbs
⅔ cup shredded suet
1½ cups mixed dried fruit
finely grated rind of 1 orange
2 eggs, beaten
⅓–½ cup milk

Sift the flour, salt, baking powder and spices into a bowl. Add the sugar, breadcrumbs, suet, dried fruit and orange rind and stir well to mix. Stir in the eggs and enough milk to give a soft dropping consistency.
Spoon the mixture into a well-greased 900 ml/1½ pint/3¾ cup pudding basin (steaming mold). Cover with greased foil, making a pleat in the centre, then secure with string. Steam for 2½ hours until well risen. Leave to shrink slightly, then turn out and leave to cool.
To freeze: wrap in foil, then pack in a freezer bag. Seal, label and freeze.
To thaw and serve: remove the freezer bag and thaw at room temperature for 3 hours. Return to the basin (mold) in the foil wrapping and steam for 1 hour or until heated through. Serve with brandy sauce or brandy butter.
SERVES 4 to 6

PLUM DOWDY

METRIC/IMPERIAL

6–8 slices of stale bread, crusts removed
75 g/3 oz butter
675 g/1½ lb cooking plums, halved and stoned
2 × 15 ml spoons/2 tablespoons golden syrup
2 × 15 ml spoons/2 tablespoons water
50 g/2 oz soft brown sugar

AMERICAN

6–8 slices of stale bread, crusts removed
⅜ cup butter
1½ lb baking plums, halved and pitted
2 tablespoons light corn syrup
2 tablespoons water
⅓ cup light brown sugar

Spread the slices of bread thickly with the butter on one side only. Use half to line the bottom and sides of a buttered deep ovenproof dish or foil container.
Put the plums in the centre of the dish, cut sides

uppermost. Put the syrup and water in a pan and heat gently until the syrup has dissolved, stirring constantly. Pour over the plums.
Cover the plums with the remaining buttered bread, sprinkle with the sugar, then bake in a preheated moderately hot oven (190°C/375°F or Gas Mark 5) for 1½ hours.
To freeze: cool quickly, cover with foil, then pack in a freezer bag. Seal, label and freeze.
To thaw and serve: remove the freezer bag and thaw at room temperature for 4 hours. Reheat in the covered dish or container in a preheated moderate oven (180°C/350°F or Gas Mark 4) for 1 hour or until heated through.
SERVES 4 to 6

EVE'S CRUMBLE

METRIC/IMPERIAL
675 g/1½ lb cooking apples, peeled, cored and finely sliced
2 × 15 ml spoons/2 tablespoons demerara sugar
0.5 × 2.5 ml spoon/¼ teaspoon ground cinnamon
pinch of salt
For the topping:
175 g/6 oz flour
75 g/3 oz butter
75 g/3 oz demerara sugar

AMERICAN
1½ lb baking apples, peeled, cored and finely sliced
2 tablespoons raw brown sugar
¼ teaspoon ground cinnamon
pinch of salt
For the topping:
1½ cups flour
⅜ cup butter
½ cup raw brown sugar

Put the apples in the bottom of a buttered ovenproof dish or foil container, then mix together the sugar, cinnamon and salt and scatter over the apples.
To make the topping: sift the flour into a bowl, add the butter in pieces and rub into the flour until the mixture resembles fine breadcrumbs. Stir in the sugar, then scatter over the apple mixture to cover it completely.
To freeze: cover with foil, then pack in a freezer bag. Seal, label and freeze.
To thaw and serve: remove wrappings and bake from frozen in a preheated hot oven (220°C/425°F or Gas Mark 7) for 20 minutes. Reduce the heat to moderately hot (190°C/375°F or Gas Mark 5) and bake for a further 45 minutes or until golden brown and heated through.
SERVES 4 to 6

NUTTY APPLE CRUMBLE

Make as for Eve's Crumble, substituting the following ingredients for the topping:

METRIC/IMPERIAL
150 g/5 oz flour
75 g/3 oz butter
75 g/3 oz demerara sugar
1 × 15 ml spoon/1 tablespoon rolled oats
1 × 15 ml spoon/1 tablespoon chopped walnuts

AMERICAN
1¼ cups flour
⅜ cup butter
½ cup raw brown sugar
1 tablespoon rolled oats
1 tablespoon chopped walnuts

Freeze, thaw and serve as for Eve's Crumble.
SERVES 4 to 5

BROWN BETTY

METRIC/IMPERIAL
675 g/1½ lb cooking apples, peeled, cored and sliced
175 g/6 oz stale white breadcrumbs
100 g/4 oz soft brown sugar
1 × 5 ml spoon/1 teaspoon ground cinnamon
50 g/2 oz butter

AMERICAN
1½ lb baking apples, peeled, cored and sliced
3 cups stale white breadcrumbs
⅔ cup light brown sugar
1 teaspoon ground cinnamon
¼ cup butter

Put a layer of apples in the bottom of a buttered deep ovenproof dish or foil container.
Put the breadcrumbs, sugar and cinnamon in a bowl, stir well to mix, then scatter a little over the apples to coat them lightly. Continue with these layers until all the ingredients have been used, finishing with a layer of the breadcrumb mixture. Dot with the butter.
Bake in a preheated moderately hot oven (190°C/375°F or Gas Mark 5) for 40 to 45 minutes until the apples are tender when pierced with a skewer.
To freeze: cool quickly, cover with foil, then pack in a freezer bag. Seal, label and freeze.
To thaw and serve: remove the freezer bag and thaw at room temperature for 4 hours. Reheat in the covered dish or container in a preheated moderate oven (180°C/350°F or Gas Mark 4) for 1 hour or until heated through.
SERVES 4 to 6

STRAWBERRY BAKED ALASKA

METRIC/IMPERIAL

100 g/4 oz trifle sponges, cut in half
2 × 15 ml spoons/2 tablespoons sherry
3 egg whites
175 g/6 oz caster sugar
600 ml/1 pint strawberry ice cream

AMERICAN

¼ lb pound cake, cut into 8 pieces
2 tablespoons sherry
3 egg whites
¾ cup superfine sugar
2½ cups strawberry ice cream

Line a shallow ovenproof dish or foil container with the sponges (cake pieces), then moisten with the sherry. Beat the egg whites until stiff, add half the sugar and continue beating for 1 minute, then fold in the remaining sugar. Pile the ice cream on top of the sponge, leaving a 1 cm/½ inch margin around the edge. Swirl the meringue over the ice cream and cake to cover them.
To freeze: open (flash) freeze immediately, then wrap loosely in freezer wrap once frozen. Seal, label and return to the freezer.
To thaw and serve: remove from the freezer 5 minutes before serving time and remove wrappings. Place in a preheated hot oven (220°C/425°F or Gas Mark 7) for 5 minutes.
SERVES 6

BAKED APPLES WITH CREAM AND GINGER

METRIC/IMPERIAL

4 large cooking apples, cored
50 g/2 oz seedless raisins
25 g/1 oz stoned dates, chopped
25 g/1 oz soft brown sugar
1 × 2.5 ml spoon/½ teaspoon ground cinnamon
4 × 15 ml spoons/4 tablespoons water
To finish:
300 ml/½ pint soured cream
4 pieces of stem ginger, coarsely chopped

AMERICAN

4 large baking apples, cored
⅓ cup seedless raisins
3 tablespoons chopped pitted dates
2 tablespoons light brown sugar
½ teaspoon ground cinnamon
¼ cup water
To finish:
1¼ cups sour cream
4 pieces of preserved ginger, coarsely chopped

Score a line around the centre of each apple with a sharp knife to prevent the skin bursting during baking. Put them in a shallow ovenproof dish. Put the raisins, dates, sugar and cinnamon in a bowl, stir well to mix, then use to fill the centres of the apples, pressing down well. Pour the water into the dish, then bake in a preheated moderate oven (180°C/350°F or Gas Mark 4) for 45 minutes or until the apples are tender, basting frequently.
To freeze: cool quickly. Open (flash) freeze until firm, wrap individually in foil, then pack in a rigid container. Seal, label and return to the freezer.
To thaw and serve: thaw in the refrigerator for 4 hours, then reheat in a preheated moderate oven (180°C/350°F or Gas Mark 4) for 30 minutes or until heated through.
Put the sour(ed) cream in a bowl, add the ginger and beat well to mix. Spoon on top of the apples just before serving.
SERVES 4

BAKED APPLES

METRIC/IMPERIAL

4 large cooking apples, cored
75 g/3 oz brown sugar
3 × 15 ml spoons/3 tablespoons seedless raisins
120 ml/4 fl oz cider
25 g/1 oz butter

AMERICAN

4 large baking apples, cored
⅜ cup brown sugar
3 tablespoons seedless raisins
½ cup hard cider
2 tablespoons butter

Score a line around the centre of each apple with a sharp knife to prevent the skin bursting during baking. Put them in a shallow ovenproof dish. Put the sugar and raisins in a bowl, stir well to mix, then use to fill the centres of the apples, pressing down well. Pour the cider into the dish and top each apple with a little butter. Bake in a preheated moderate oven (180°C/350°F or Gas Mark 4) for 45 minutes or until the apples are tender, basting frequently.
To freeze: cool quickly. Open (flash) freeze until firm, then pack in a rigid container. Seal, label and return to the freezer.
To thaw and serve: thaw in the refrigerator for 4 hours, then reheat in a preheated moderate oven (180°C/350°F or Gas Mark 4) for 30 minutes or until heated through.
SERVES 4

PEAR PIE

METRIC/IMPERIAL

basic shortcrust pastry dough made with 225 g/½ lb flour
1 kg/2 lb ripe dessert pears, peeled, quartered and cored
25 g/1 oz brown sugar
1 × 5 ml spoon/1 teaspoon ground cinnamon
a little milk, to glaze
icing sugar for sprinkling, to finish

AMERICAN

basic pie dough made with 2 cups flour
2 lb ripe dessert pears, peeled, quartered and cored
2 tablespoons brown sugar
1 teaspoon ground cinnamon
a little milk, to glaze
confectioners' sugar for sprinkling, to finish

Divide the dough in two, then roll out one half on a floured surface and use to line a 20 cm/8 inch flan dish (pie pan). Put the pears on the dough and sprinkle with the sugar and cinnamon. Moisten the edge with water, roll out the remaining dough and use to cover the filling. Press firmly to seal, then trim and flute the edge. Cut an air vent in the centre.
To freeze: open (flash) freeze until firm, then pack in a freezer bag. Seal, label and return to the freezer.
To thaw and serve: remove wrappings and bake the pie from frozen in a preheated moderately hot oven (200°C/400°F or Gas Mark 6) for 40 minutes. Brush with milk, then reduce the heat to moderate (180°C/350°F or Gas Mark 4) and bake for a further 15 minutes. Cover with foil if the pastry becomes too brown. Sprinkle with icing (confectioners') sugar while still hot.
SERVES 4 to 6

HOT APRICOT DESSERT

METRIC/IMPERIAL

100 g/4 oz butter
100 g/4 oz brown sugar
4 × 15 ml spoons/4 tablespoons sweet white wine
1 cinnamon stick
450 g/1 lb apricots, peeled, halved and stoned
1 × 15 ml spoon/1 tablespoon brandy

AMERICAN

½ cup butter
⅔ cup brown sugar
¼ cup sweet white wine
1 cinnamon stick
1 lb apricots, peeled, halved and pitted
1 tablespoon brandy

Put the butter, sugar, wine and cinnamon in a pan and heat gently until the sugar has dissolved, stirring constantly. Bring slowly to simmering point, add the apricots and simmer for 6 minutes. Remove the fruit from the pan with a slotted spoon and place in a rigid container. Boil the sauce for 6 minutes or until thick, then stir in the brandy and pour over the fruit.
To freeze: cool quickly. Cover, seal, label and freeze.
To thaw and serve: thaw at room temperature for 3 hours, then reheat gently in the top of a double boiler.
SERVES 4

EVE'S PUDDING

METRIC/IMPERIAL

450 g/1 lb cooking apples, peeled, cored and sliced
75 g/3 oz demerara sugar
finely grated rind of 1 lemon
100 g/4 oz butter
100 g/4 oz caster sugar
a few drops of vanilla essence
2 eggs, beaten
100 g/4 oz self-raising flour
sugar for sprinkling, to finish

AMERICAN

1 lb baking apples, peeled, cored and sliced
½ cup raw brown sugar
finely grated rind of 1 lemon
½ cup butter
½ cup sugar
a few drops vanilla extract
2 eggs, beaten
1 cup self-rising flour
sugar for sprinkling, to finish

Put the apples and demerara (raw) sugar in a buttered 900 ml/1½ pint/3¾ cup pudding basin (steaming mold).
Put the butter and (caster) sugar in a bowl and beat together until light and fluffy. Beat in the vanilla essence (extract) and the eggs, adding a little flour if the mixture begins to separate. Fold in the remaining flour, then spread the mixture evenly over the fruit.
To freeze: cover with a double thickness of greased foil, making a pleat in the centre, then secure with string. Pack in a freezer bag, seal, label and freeze.
To thaw and serve: remove the freezer bag. Steam from frozen in the foil wrapping for about 1¾ hours or until heated through. Turn out and sprinkle with sugar before serving.
SERVES 4 to 6

BREAD PUDDING

METRIC/IMPERIAL

8 slices of bread, crusts removed
300 ml/½ pint milk
350 g/¾ lb mixed dried fruit
50 g/2 oz chopped candied peel
1 medium cooking apple, peeled, cored and grated
25 g/1 oz soft brown sugar
3 × 15 ml spoons/3 tablespoons marmalade
2 eggs, beaten
1 × 5 ml spoon/1 teaspoon lemon juice
1 × 5 ml spoon/1 teaspoon ground cinnamon
100 g/4 oz butter, melted

AMERICAN

8 slices of bread, crusts removed
1¼ cups milk
2¼ cups mixed dried fruit
⅓ cup chopped candied peel
1 medium baking apple, peeled, cored and grated
2 tablespoons light brown sugar
3 tablespoons marmalade
2 eggs, beaten
1 teaspoon lemon juice
1 teaspoon ground cinnamon
½ cup butter, melted

Break the bread into small pieces and put in a bowl. Pour over the milk and leave to soak for about 45 minutes. Add the remaining ingredients and beat well to mix.

Pour the mixture into a buttered deep 18 cm/7 inch cake tin and smooth the top. Bake in a preheated cool oven (150°C/300°F or Gas Mark 2) for 1½ hours. Increase the heat to moderate (180°C/350°F or Gas Mark 4) and bake for a further 30 minutes. Cover with foil if the pudding becomes too brown during cooking.

To freeze: cool quickly, then remove the cake tin and wrap in foil. Pack in a freezer bag, seal, label and freeze.

To thaw and serve: remove the freezer bag and thaw at room temperature for 4 hours. Reheat in the foil wrapping in a preheated moderate oven (180°C/350°F or Gas Mark 4) for 35 minutes or until heated through.

SERVES 6

CRANBERRY AND APPLE PIE

METRIC/IMPERIAL

basic shortcrust pastry dough made with 225 g/½ lb flour
450 g/1 lb cooking apples, peeled, cored and sliced
1 × 185 g/6½ oz jar cranberry sauce
1 × 2.5 ml spoon/½ teaspoon ground cinnamon
75 g/3 oz sugar
a little milk, to glaze

AMERICAN

basic pie dough made with 2 cups flour
1 lb baking apples, peeled, cored and sliced
1 × 6½ oz jar cranberry sauce
½ teaspoon ground cinnamon
⅜ cup sugar
a little milk, to glaze

Roll out half the dough on a floured surface and use to line a lightly greased 18 cm/7 inch ovenproof pie plate. Put the apples and cranberries in layers on top of the dough, sprinkling each layer with cinnamon and sugar.

Roll out the remaining dough to a circle for the 'lid' and place on top of the filling. Moisten the edges with water, press firmly to seal, then trim and flute the edge. Make a slit in the centre, brush with milk, then bake in a preheated moderately hot oven (200°C/400°F or Gas Mark 6) for 30 to 35 minutes or until the pastry is golden.

To freeze: cool quickly. Open (flash) freeze until firm, remove the pie from the plate, then pack in a freezer bag. Seal, label and return to the freezer.

To thaw and serve: remove wrappings and replace the pie on the plate. Reheat from frozen in a preheated moderate oven (180°C/350°F or Gas Mark 4) for 25 minutes or until heated through. Cover with foil if the pastry becomes too brown during cooking.

SERVES 4 to 6

APPLE AND RAISIN PIE

METRIC/IMPERIAL

basic shortcrust pastry dough made with 225 g/½ lb flour
450 g/1 lb cooking apples, peeled, cored and sliced
75 g/3 oz seedless raisins
25 g/1 oz sugar
1 × 5 ml spoon/1 teaspoon ground cinnamon
a little milk, to glaze
extra sugar, for sprinkling

AMERICAN

basic pie dough made with 2 cups flour
1 lb baking apples, peeled, cored and sliced
½ cup seedless raisins
2 tablespoons sugar
1 teaspoon ground cinnamon
a little milk, to glaze
extra sugar, for sprinkling

Roll out half the dough on a floured surface and use to line a lightly greased 20 cm/8 inch oven-proof pie plate. Put the apples, raisins, sugar and cinnamon in a bowl, stir well to mix, then put on top of the dough.

Roll out the remaining dough to a circle for the 'lid' and place on top of the filling. Moisten the edges with water, press firmly to seal, then trim and flute the edge. Make a slit in the centre, brush with milk and sprinkle with sugar. Bake in a preheated moderately hot oven (200°C/400°F or Gas Mark 6) for 30 to 35 minutes or until the pastry is golden.

To freeze: cool quickly. Open (flash) freeze until firm, remove the pie from the plate, then pack in a freezer bag. Seal, label and return to the freezer.

To thaw and serve: remove wrappings and replace the pie on the plate. Reheat from frozen in a preheated moderate oven (180°C/350°F or Gas Mark 4) for 25 minutes or until heated through. Cover with foil if the pastry becomes too brown during cooking.

SERVES 4 to 6

SEVILLE PUDDING

METRIC/IMPERIAL

100 g/4 oz flour
1.5 × 5 ml spoons/1½ teaspoons baking powder
1 × 2.5 ml spoon/½ teaspoon salt
100 g/4 oz fresh white breadcrumbs
75 g/3 oz shredded suet
75 g/3 oz caster sugar
finely grated rind of 2 oranges
1 egg, beaten
120 ml/4 fl oz milk
3 oranges, peeled and sliced
For the sauce:
2 × 5 ml spoons/2 teaspoons cornflour
150 ml/¼ pint water
4 × 15 ml spoons/4 tablespoons marmalade
2 × 5 ml spoons/2 teaspoons lemon juice

AMERICAN

1 cup flour
1½ teaspoons baking powder
½ teaspoon salt
2 cups fresh white breadcrumbs
⅔ cup shredded suet
⅜ cup sugar
finely grated rind of 2 oranges
1 egg, beaten
½ cup milk
3 oranges, peeled and sliced
For the sauce:
2 teaspoons cornstarch
⅔ cup water
¼ cup marmalade
2 teaspoons lemon juice

Sift the flour, baking powder and salt into a bowl. Add the remaining ingredients, except the orange slices, and beat well to mix. Put one-third of the orange slices in the bottom of a greased 1.75 litre/3 pint/7½ cup pudding basin (steaming mold). Cover with one-third of the pudding mixture, then repeat these layers until all the ingredients have been used, finishing with a layer of the pudding mixture. Cover with greased foil, making a pleat in the centre, then secure with string. Steam for 2¾ to 3 hours until well risen. Leave to shrink slightly, then turn out and leave to cool.

To make the sauce: mix the cornflour (cornstarch) to a paste with a little of the water, then put in a pan with the remaining water, marmalade and lemon juice. Bring to the boil, then simmer for 5 minutes until thick and smooth, stirring constantly.

To freeze: wrap the pudding in foil, then pack in a freezer bag. Seal, label and freeze. Cool the sauce quickly, then pour into a rigid container. Seal, label and freeze.

To thaw and serve: remove wrappings from the pudding, then replace in the greased basin (mold). Cover with foil and steam from frozen for 1 hour or until heated through. Reheat the sauce gently from frozen on top of the stove, stirring occasionally. Turn the pudding out onto a warmed serving platter and pour over the sauce.

SERVES 6

BASIC PANCAKES (CRÊPES)

METRIC/IMPERIAL
100 g/4 oz flour
pinch of salt
1 egg, beaten
300 ml/½ pint milk
1 × 15 ml spoon/1 tablespoon vegetable oil

AMERICAN
1 cup flour
pinch of salt
1 egg, beaten
1¼ cups milk
1 tablespoon vegetable oil

To make the batter: sift the flour and salt into a bowl, make a well in the centre and add the egg. Gradually beat in half the milk, mix until smooth, then stir in the remaining milk and the 1 × 15 ml spoon/1 tablespoon of oil.
Put a little oil in a 15 cm/6 inch pancake (crêpe) pan and heat until just smoking. Pour off any excess fat, then pour in about 2 × 15 ml spoons/2 tablespoons batter and swirl around the pan until the bottom is evenly covered. Cook until golden brown, then toss or flip over and cook the other side. Cool on a wire rack, then repeat until 8 pancakes (crêpes) have been made.
To freeze: pack the pancakes (crêpes) in layers, interleaving each one with waxed paper. Pack in a freezer bag, seal, label and freeze.
To thaw and serve: unpack and spread out on a baking sheet. Cover with foil and reheat from frozen in a preheated moderately hot oven (200°C/400°F or Gas Mark 6) for 10 minutes or until heated through.
MAKES 8

CRÊPES SUZETTE

METRIC/IMPERIAL
8 basic crêpes (see above)
For the sauce:
100 g/4 oz butter
100 g/4 oz caster sugar
finely grated rind of 1 orange
juice of 2 oranges
4 × 15 ml spoons/4 tablespoons brandy

AMERICAN
8 basic crêpes (see above)
For the sauce:
½ cup butter
½ cup sugar
finely grated rind of 1 orange
juice of 2 oranges
¼ cup brandy

To make the sauce: put the butter, sugar and orange rind and juice in a pan and stir over a low heat until the butter has melted and the sugar has dissolved. Increase the heat and simmer for 5 minutes, then stir in half the brandy. Fold each crêpe into 4 to form a triangular shape, put in the pan and coat with the sauce.
To freeze: cool quickly, then arrange in a single layer in a buttered ovenproof dish or foil container. Cover with foil, then pack in a freezer bag. Seal, label and freeze.
To thaw and serve: remove the freezer bag, then reheat the crêpes from frozen in the covered dish or container in a preheated moderate oven (180°C/350°F or Gas Mark 4) for 15 to 20 minutes or until heated through. Transfer to a chafing dish, warm the remaining brandy in a separate pan, then pour over the crêpes. Set alight and serve immediately.
SERVES 4

LEMON CHEESE PANCAKES (CRÊPES)

METRIC/IMPERIAL
For the batter:
175 g/6 oz flour
pinch of salt
1 egg, beaten
1 × 175 ml/6 fl oz can pure lemon juice
vegetable oil for frying
For the filling:
1 × 425 g/15 oz can apricots, drained and sieved
225 g/½ lb cottage cheese, sieved
25–50 g/1–2 oz caster sugar, or to taste

AMERICAN
For the batter:
1½ cups flour
pinch of salt
1 egg, beaten
1 × 6 fl oz can pure lemon juice
vegetable oil for frying
For the filling:
1 × 15 oz can apricots, drained and strained
1 cup strained cottage cheese
2–4 tablespoons sugar, or to taste

To make the batter: sift the flour and salt into a bowl, make a well in the centre and add the egg. Make the lemon juice up to 300 ml/½ pint/1¼ cups with water, then gradually pour half onto the egg. Mix until smooth, then stir in the remaining lemon juice and water.
Use the batter and oil to make 8 thin pancakes (crêpes) (see above). Leave to cool.
To make the filling: put the apricots and cottage

cheese in a bowl, add sugar to taste and beat well to mix. Divide the mixture equally between the pancakes (crêpes) and roll up around the filling. Place in a single layer in an ovenproof dish or foil container.
To freeze: cover with foil, then pack in a freezer bag. Seal, label and freeze.
To thaw and serve: remove wrappings and thaw at room temperature for 2 hours. Reheat in a preheated moderately hot oven (200°C/400°F or Gas Mark 6) for 20 minutes or until heated through.
SERVES 4

RHUBARB LATTICE FLAN

METRIC/IMPERIAL
basic shortcrust pastry dough made with 225 g/½ lb flour
1 × 575 g/1 lb 3 oz can rhubarb, drained and mashed to a purée
50 g/2 oz butter
50 g/2 oz caster sugar
1 egg, beaten
50 g/2 oz self-raising flour
25 g/1 oz ground almonds
a little milk, to glaze
sugar, for sprinkling

AMERICAN
basic pie dough made with 2 cups flour
1 × 1 lb 3 oz can rhubarb, drained and mashed to a purée
¼ cup butter
¼ cup sugar
1 egg, beaten
½ cup self-rising flour
¼ cup ground almonds
a little milk, to glaze
sugar, for sprinkling

Roll out the dough on a floured surface and use to line a 23 cm/9 inch flan dish (pie pan), reserving the trimmings of dough for the lattice. Spread the rhubarb purée in the bottom of the flan.
Put the butter and sugar in a bowl and beat together until light and fluffy. Beat in the egg a little at a time, then fold in the flour and ground almonds. Spread the mixture over the rhubarb. Roll out the reserved trimmings of dough and cut into thin strips long enough to criss-cross the top of the flan. Moisten the ends of the strips with water and arrange over the filling, pressing the wetted ends to seal. Brush the lattice with milk, then sprinkle with sugar. Bake in a preheated moderate oven (180°C/350°F or Gas Mark 4) for 35 minutes.
To freeze: cool quickly. Open (flash) freeze until firm, remove the flan from the dish (pan), then pack in a freezer bag. Seal, label and return to the freezer.
To thaw and serve: remove the freezer bag and replace the flan in the dish (pan). Thaw at room temperature for 3 hours, then reheat in a preheated moderate oven (180°C/350°F or Gas Mark 4) for 25 minutes or until heated through. Cover with foil if the pastry becomes too brown.
SERVES 4 to 6

PEAR CHARLOTTE

METRIC/IMPERIAL
450 g/1 lb cooking pears, peeled, cored and sliced
5 × 15 ml spoons/5 tablespoons brown sugar
4 × 15 ml spoons/4 tablespoons apricot jam
6 slices of white bread, crusts removed
100 g/4 oz butter, melted

AMERICAN
1 lb baking pears, peeled, cored and sliced
⅓ cup brown sugar
¼ cup apricot jam
6 slices of white bread, crusts removed
½ cup butter, melted

Put half the pears in a buttered 1.2 litre/2 pint/5 cup ovenproof dish or foil container. Scatter 2 × 15 ml spoons/2 tablespoons sugar over the pears, then put in half the jam. Repeat these 3 layers once more.
Cut each slice of bread into 4 triangles. Brush with the melted butter, then arrange on top of the jam to cover it completely. Sprinkle the remaining sugar on top. Bake in a preheated moderately hot oven (190°C/375°F or Gas Mark 5) for 30 to 40 minutes until crisp and golden.
To freeze: cool quickly, cover with foil, then pack in a freezer bag. Seal, label and freeze.
To thaw and serve: remove the freezer bag and thaw the Charlotte at room temperature for 3 hours. Reheat in a preheated moderate oven (180°C/350°F or Gas Mark 4) for 25 minutes or until heated through.
SERVES 4

APPLE CHARLOTTE

Make as for Pear Charlotte (see above), substituting 450 g/1 lb cooking (baking) apples for the pears, and the finely grated rind of 1 lemon for the apricot jam.
Freeze, thaw and serve as for Pear Charlotte.
SERVES 4

COCONUT TART

METRIC/IMPERIAL

basic shortcrust pastry dough made with 150 g/5 oz flour
3 × 15 ml spoons/3 tablespoons red jam
50 g/2 oz butter
25 g/1 oz caster sugar
1 × 15 ml spoon/1 tablespoon golden syrup
100 g/4 oz desiccated coconut
1 egg, beaten

AMERICAN

basic pie dough made with 1¼ cups flour
3 tablespoons red jam
¼ cup butter
2 tablespoons sugar
1 tablespoon light corn syrup
1⅓ cups shredded coconut
1 egg, beaten

Roll out the dough on a floured surface and use to line an 18 cm/7 inch flan ring set on a baking sheet. Spread the jam in the bottom of the pastry case (pie shell).

Put the butter, sugar and syrup in a pan and heat gently until melted. Stir in the coconut and egg, then spoon into the pastry case (pie shell).

Bake in a preheated moderately hot oven (190°C/375°F or Gas Mark 5) for 25 minutes. Cover with foil if the top of the tart becomes too brown during cooking. Cool quickly on a wire rack, then remove the flan ring.

To freeze: open (flash) freeze until firm, then pack in a freezer bag. Seal, label and return to the freezer.

To thaw and serve: remove wrappings and place the tart on a baking sheet. Reheat from frozen in a preheated moderate oven (180°C/350°F or Gas Mark 4) for 25 minutes.

SERVES 4 to 5

YORKSHIRE APPLE PUDDING

METRIC/IMPERIAL

225 g/½ lb self-raising flour
0.5 × 2.5 ml spoon/¼ teaspoon salt
100 g/4 oz caster sugar
100 g/4 oz butter, melted
350 g/¾ lb cooking apples, peeled, cored and grated
1 egg, beaten
3 × 15 ml spoons/3 tablespoons milk
For the topping:
350 g/¾ lb cooking apples, cored and sliced
25 g/1 oz butter, softened
pinch of ground cinnamon
50 g/2 oz soft brown sugar

AMERICAN

2 cups self-rising flour
¼ teaspoon salt
½ cup sugar
½ cup butter, melted
¾ lb baking apples, peeled, cored and grated
1 egg, beaten
3 tablespoons milk
For the topping:
¾ lb baking apples, cored and sliced
2 tablespoons butter, softened
pinch of ground cinnamon
⅓ cup light brown sugar

Sift the flour and salt into a bowl, then stir in the sugar and melted butter. Add the grated apples, egg and milk and beat well to mix. Spread the mixture in a buttered 23 cm/9 inch cake tin.

To make the topping: arrange the apple slices in closely overlapping circles on top of the cake mixture. Brush the apples with the softened butter, then sprinkle with cinnamon and sugar. Bake in a preheated moderately hot oven (190°C/375°F or Gas Mark 5) for 45 minutes.

To freeze: open (flash) freeze until firm, then pack in a freezer bag. Seal, label and return to the freezer.

To thaw and serve: remove wrappings and thaw at room temperature for 3 hours. Reheat in a preheated moderate oven (180°C/350°F or Gas Mark 4) for 25 minutes or until heated through.

SERVES 8 to 10

SYRUP AND CORNFLAKE TART

METRIC/IMPERIAL

basic shortcrust pastry dough made with 175 g/6 oz flour
25 g/1 oz butter
3 × 15 ml spoons/3 tablespoons golden syrup
1 × 2.5 ml spoon/½ teaspoon finely grated lemon rind
½ egg, beaten
1 × 15 ml spoon/1 tablespoon creamy milk
75 g/3 oz cornflakes, crushed
a little milk, to glaze

AMERICAN

basic pie dough made with 1½ cups flour
2 tablespoons butter
3 tablespoons light corn syrup
½ teaspoon finely grated lemon rind
½ egg, beaten
1 tablespoon half-and-half
3 cups cornflakes, crushed
a little milk, to glaze

Roll out the dough on a floured surface and use to line a greased 20 cm/8 inch ovenproof pie plate, reserving the trimmings for the lattice. Put the butter and syrup in a pan and heat gently until melted. Remove from the heat, then add the remaining ingredients and stir well to mix. Spoon over the dough, then smooth the top.
Roll out the reserved trimmings of dough and cut into thin strips long enough to criss-cross the top of the tart. Moisten the ends of the strips with water and arrange over the filling, pressing the wetted ends firmly to seal.
To freeze: open (flash) freeze until firm, remove the tart from the plate, then pack in a freezer bag. Seal, label and return to the freezer.
To thaw and serve: remove wrappings and replace the tart on the plate. Brush the lattice lightly with milk, then bake the tart from frozen in a preheated moderately hot oven (190°C(375°F or Gas Mark 5) for about 40 minutes or until heated through.
SERVES 5 to 6

ORANGE AND HONEY ROLY-POLY

METRIC/IMPERIAL
basic suet crust pastry dough made with 225 g/½ lb flour
50 g/2 oz butter
50 g/2 oz caster sugar
finely grated rind and chopped flesh of 2 oranges
2 × 15 ml spoons/2 tablespoons honey
a little milk, to glaze

AMERICAN
basic suet crust pastry dough made with 2 cups flour
¼ cup butter
¼ cup sugar
finely grated rind and chopped flesh of 2 oranges
2 tablespoons honey
a little milk, to glaze

Roll out the dough on a floured surface to an oblong about 35 × 25 cm/14 × 10 inches.
Put the butter and sugar in a bowl and beat together until light and fluffy. Add the orange rind and honey and beat well to mix, then spread the mixture over the dough, leaving a 2.5 cm/1 inch margin around the edge.
Scatter the chopped orange flesh over the filling. Moisten the edges of the dough with water, then roll up like a Swiss (jelly) roll, pinching and sealing the edges. Place on a baking sheet, brush the dough with a little milk, then bake in a preheated moderately hot oven (200°C/400°F or Gas Mark 6) for 20 minutes.
To freeze: cool quickly, wrap loosely in foil, then pack in a freezer bag. Seal, label and freeze.
To thaw and serve: remove the freezer bag and thaw at room temperature for 4 hours. Place on a baking sheet and reheat in the foil wrapping in a preheated moderate oven (180°C/350°F or Gas Mark 4) for 25 minutes or until heated through. Serve with a honey and cinnamon sauce.
SERVES 4 to 5

BLACKBERRY AND APPLE PIE

METRIC/IMPERIAL
basic shortcrust pastry dough made with 225 g/½ lb flour
225 g/½ lb blackberries, stalks removed
450 g/1 lb cooking apples, peeled, cored and sliced
finely grated rind and juice of ½ lemon
100 g/4 oz caster sugar, or to taste
2 × 15 ml spoons/2 tablespoons flour

AMERICAN
basic pie dough made with 2 cups flour
½ lb blackberries, stalks removed
1 lb baking apples, peeled, cored and sliced
finely grated rind and juice of ½ lemon
½ cup sugar, or to taste
2 tablespoons flour

Roll out half the dough on a floured surface and use to line a shallow 20 cm/8 inch pie dish lined with foil. Chill in the refrigerator for 15 minutes.
Meanwhile, put the blackberries and apples in a bowl and fold in the remaining ingredients. Spoon the mixture on top of the dough. Roll out the remaining dough to a circle for the lid and place on top of the filling. Moisten the edges with water, press firmly to seal, then trim and flute the edge. Make a slit in the top of the pie.
To freeze: open (flash) freeze until firm, then remove the pie from the dish and pack in a freezer bag. Seal, label and return to the freezer.
To thaw and serve: remove wrappings and replace the pie in the dish. Bake from frozen in a preheated hot oven (220°C/425°F or Gas Mark 7) for 30 minutes, then cover the pie with foil. Reduce the heat to moderately hot (190°C/375°F or Gas Mark 5) and bake for a further 40 minutes. Remove the foil from the pie for the last 10 to 15 minutes of cooking to crisp up the pastry.
SERVES 4 to 6

PEAR UPSIDE-DOWN PUDDING

METRIC/IMPERIAL

3 × 15 ml spoons/3 tablespoons marmalade
1 × 440 g/15½ oz can pear halves, drained
175 g/6 oz butter
175 g/6 oz caster sugar
2 eggs, beaten
150 ml/¼ pint milk
175 g/6 oz fresh white breadcrumbs
0.5 × 2.5 ml spoon/¼ teaspoon ground mixed spice

AMERICAN

3 tablespoons marmalade
1 × 15½ oz can pear halves, drained
¾ cup butter
¾ cup sugar
2 eggs, beaten
⅔ cup milk
3 cups fresh white breadcrumbs
¼ teaspoon ground cinnamon and cloves, mixed

Spread the marmalade in the bottom of a greased 20 cm/8 inch round cake tin.
Put the butter and sugar in a bowl, beat together until light and fluffy, then beat in the eggs a little at a time. Stir in the milk, breadcrumbs and spice(s), then spoon on top of the marmalade. Bake in a preheated moderate oven (180°C/350°F or Gas Mark 4) for 1 hour. Leave to cool slightly, then turn out onto a foil plate.
To freeze: cool quickly. Open (flash) freeze until firm, wrap in foil, then pack in a freezer bag. Seal, label and return to the freezer.
To thaw and serve: remove wrappings and thaw at room temperature for 4 hours. Reheat on a foil plate in a preheated moderate oven for 25 minutes or until heated through.
SERVES 6 to 8

QUICK FRUIT CRUMBLE

METRIC/IMPERIAL

450–675 g/1–1½ lb cooked fruit
100 g/4 oz muesli
2 × 15 ml spoons/2 tablespoons honey
0.5 × 2.5 ml spoon/¼ teaspoon ground cinnamon
0.5 × 2.5 ml spoon/¼ teaspoon ground mixed spice
0.5 × 2.5 ml spoon/¼ teaspoon ground ginger

AMERICAN

1–1½ lb cooked fruit
1 cup muesli
2 tablespoons honey
¼ teaspoon ground cinnamon
¼ teaspoon grated nutmeg and ground cloves, mixed
¼ teaspoon ground ginger

Put the fruit in the bottom of an ovenproof dish or foil container. Mix the muesli, honey and spices in a bowl, then spread over the fruit.
To freeze: cover with foil, then pack in a freezer bag. Seal, label and freeze.
To thaw and serve: remove wrappings and thaw at room temperature for 3 hours. Bake in a preheated moderately hot oven (190°C/375°F or Gas Mark 5) for 25 minutes or until heated through. Serve with whipped cream.
SERVES 4

LEMON AND HONEY SPONGE PUDDING

METRIC/IMPERIAL

75 g/3 oz butter
75 g/3 oz caster sugar
2 eggs, beaten
175 g/6 oz flour
1 × 2.5 ml spoon/½ teaspoon baking powder
pinch of salt
finely grated rind and juice of 1 lemon
a little milk
2 × 15 ml spoons/2 tablespoons honey

AMERICAN

⅜ cup butter
⅜ cup sugar
2 eggs, beaten
1½ cups flour
¼ teaspoon baking powder
pinch of salt
finely grated rind and juice of 1 lemon
a little milk
2 tablespoons honey

Put the butter and sugar in a bowl, beat together until light and fluffy, then beat in the eggs a little at a time. Sift the flour with the baking powder and salt, then fold into the butter and sugar mixture. Add the lemon rind and juice, and enough milk to give a dropping consistency. Put the honey in the bottom of a buttered 900 ml/1½ pint/3¾ cup pudding basin (steaming mold). Spoon the sponge mixture on top of the honey. Cover with buttered foil, making a pleat in the centre, then secure with string.
Steam for 1½ hours or until well risen. Leave to shrink slightly, then turn out and leave to cool.
To freeze: wrap in foil, then pack in a freezer bag. Seal, label and freeze.
To thaw and serve: remove the freezer bag and thaw at room temperature for 3 hours. Return to the basin (mold) in the foil wrapping and steam for 1 hour or until heated through.
SERVES 4

PLUM AND DATE PIE

METRIC/IMPERIAL

basic shortcrust pastry dough made with 225 g/½ lb flour
1 × 575 g/1 lb 4 oz can red plums
100 g/4 oz stoned dates, chopped
finely grated rind of 1 lemon
sugar for sprinkling, to finish

AMERICAN

basic pie dough made with 2 cups flour
1 × 1 lb 4 oz can red plums
⅔ cup pitted dates, chopped
finely grated rind of 1 lemon
sugar for sprinkling, to finish

Roll out half the dough on a floured surface and use to line an 18 cm/7 inch ovenproof pie plate. Put the plums, dates and lemon rind in a bowl and stir well to mix. Spoon the mixture on top of the dough.

Roll out the remaining dough to a circle for the 'lid' and place on top of the filling. Moisten the edges with water, press firmly to seal, then trim and flute. Cut an air vent in the centre.

To freeze: pack in a freezer bag, seal, label and freeze.

To thaw and serve: remove wrappings, place the pie on a baking sheet and bake from frozen in a preheated moderately hot oven (200°C/400°F or Gas Mark 6) for 40 minutes or until heated through and golden. Sprinkle with sugar before serving.

SERVES 4 to 6

FLITTIN' DUMPLIN'

METRIC/IMPERIAL

350 g/¾ lb flour
1 × 2.5 ml spoon/½ teaspoon salt
100 g/4 oz walnuts, chopped
225 g/½ lb stoned dates, chopped
8 × 15 ml spoons/8 tablespoons golden syrup
1 × 178 g/6¼ oz can frozen concentrated orange juice, thawed and made up to 300 ml/½ pint with water
1 × 5 ml spoon/1 teaspoon bicarbonate of soda

AMERICAN

3 cups flour
½ teaspoon salt
1 cup chopped walnuts
1¼ cups pitted dates, chopped
8 tablespoons light corn syrup
1 × 6¼ oz can frozen concentrated orange juice, thawed and made up to 1¼ cups with water
1 teaspoon baking soda

Sift the flour and salt into a bowl, add the walnuts and dates and stir well to mix. Put the syrup in a pan and warm through. Remove from the heat and stir in the orange juice and the bicarbonate of soda (baking soda). Make a well in the centre of the dry ingredients, pour in the liquid and beat well to mix. Spoon into a well-greased 1.2 litre/2 pint/5 cup pudding basin (steaming mold). Cover with greased foil, making a pleat in the centre, then secure with string.

Steam for 2 to 3 hours until well risen, leave to shrink slightly, then turn out and leave to cool.

To freeze: wrap in foil, then pack in a freezer bag. Seal, label and freeze.

To thaw and serve: remove the freezer bag and thaw at room temperature for 3 hours. Return to the basin (mold) in the foil wrapping and steam for 1 hour or until heated through.

SERVES 10 to 12

APPLE AND BLACKBERRY CRUMBLE

METRIC/IMPERIAL

225 g/½ lb cooking apples, peeled, cored and sliced
225 g/½ lb blackberries, stalks removed
100 g/4 oz sugar
For the topping:
225 g/½ lb flour
75 g/3 oz butter
100 g/4 oz caster sugar

AMERICAN

½ lb baking apples, peeled, cored and sliced
½ lb blackberries, stalks removed
½ cup sugar
For the topping:
2 cups flour
⅜ cup butter
½ cup sugar

Put the fruit and sugar in layers in a buttered 900 ml/1½ pint/3¾ cup ovenproof dish or foil container.

To make the topping: sift the flour into a bowl, add the butter in pieces and rub into the flour until the mixture resembles fine breadcrumbs. Stir in the sugar, then scatter over the fruit.

To freeze: wrap in foil, then pack in a freezer bag. Seal, label and freeze.

To thaw and serve: remove wrappings and bake from frozen in a preheated hot oven (220°C/425°F or Gas Mark 7) for 20 minutes. Reduce the heat to moderately hot (190°C/375°F or Gas Mark 5) and bake for a further 45 minutes or until heated through.

SERVES 4

APPLE AND REDCURRANT FLAN

METRIC/IMPERIAL

basic shortcrust pastry dough made with 175 g/6 oz flour
4 × 15 ml spoons/4 tablespoons redcurrant jelly
450 g/1 lb cooking apples, peeled, cored and sliced
2 × 15 ml spoons/2 tablespoons white wine
1 × 15 ml spoon/1 tablespoon sugar
1 egg, beaten
For the topping:
50 g/2 oz butter
50 g/2 oz fresh white breadcrumbs
2 × 15 ml spoons/2 tablespoons demerara sugar

AMERICAN

basic pie dough made with 1½ cups flour
¼ cup redcurrant jelly
1 lb baking apples, peeled, cored and sliced
2 tablespoons white wine
1 tablespoon sugar
1 egg, beaten
For the topping:
¼ cup butter
1 cup fresh white breadcrumbs
2 tablespoons raw brown sugar

Roll out the dough on a floured surface and use to line a 20 cm/8 inch flan ring set on a baking sheet. Spread half the redcurrant jelly in the bottom of the pastry case (pie shell).

Put the apples, wine and sugar in a pan and cook gently until the apples are soft. Beat to a pulp, then stir in the egg and the remaining redcurrant jelly and pour the mixture into the pastry case (pie shell).

To make the topping: melt the butter in a pan, add the breadcrumbs and sugar and fry gently until golden, stirring frequently. Scatter over the apple filling.

To freeze: cool quickly. Open (flash) freeze until firm, remove the flan ring, then pack the flan in a freezer bag. Seal, label and return to the freezer.

To thaw and serve: remove wrappings and replace the flan in the flan ring. Place on a baking sheet and bake from frozen in a preheated moderately hot oven (190°C/375°F or Gas Mark 5) for 50 minutes to 1 hour or until heated through.

SERVES 6

APPLE PANCAKES (CRÊPES)

METRIC/IMPERIAL

8 basic pancakes (see page 254)
2 × 15 ml spoons/2 tablespoons apricot jam, warmed and sieved, to finish
For the filling:
25 g/1 oz butter
675 g/1½ lb cooking apples, peeled, cored and sliced
1 × 15 ml spoon/1 tablespoon brown sugar
1 × 2.5 ml spoon/½ teaspoon ground cinnamon

AMERICAN

8 basic crêpes (see page 254)
2 tablespoons apricot jam, warmed and strained, to finish
For the filling:
2 tablespoons butter
1½ lb baking apples, peeled, cored and sliced
1 tablespoon brown sugar
½ teaspoon ground cinnamon

To make the filling: melt the butter in a pan, add the apples, sugar and cinnamon, cover and cook gently until the apples are soft.

Put one pancake (crêpe) on an ovenproof or foil plate and spread with a little of the filling. Continue these layers until all the ingredients have been used, finishing with a pancake (crêpe).

To freeze: cool quickly. Open (flash) freeze until firm, cover with foil, then pack in a freezer bag. Seal, label and freeze.

To thaw and serve: remove wrappings and thaw at room temperature for 3 hours. Spoon the jam over the top, then reheat on the plate in a preheated moderate oven (180°C/350°F or Gas Mark 4) for 15 minutes or until heated through.

SERVES 4

DEVIL'S FOOD

METRIC/IMPERIAL

100 g/4 oz butter
75 g/3 oz soft brown sugar
2 eggs, beaten
175 g/6 oz self-raising flour
50 g/2 oz cocoa powder
2 × 15 ml spoons/2 tablespoons black treacle
2 × 15 ml spoons/2 tablespoons milk

AMERICAN

½ cup butter
½ cup light brown sugar
2 eggs, beaten
1½ cups self-rising flour
½ cup unsweetened cocoa powder
2 tablespoons molasses
2 tablespoons milk

Put the butter and sugar in a bowl, beat together until light and fluffy, then beat in the eggs a little at a time. Fold in the flour and cocoa, then stir in the black treacle (molasses) and milk.
Spoon the mixture into a greased 900 ml/1½ pint/ 3¾ cup pudding basin (steaming mold). Cover with greased foil, making a pleat in the centre, then secure with string. Steam for 2 hours or until well risen. Leave to shrink slightly, then turn out and leave to cool.
To freeze: wrap in foil, then pack in a freezer bag. Seal, label and freeze.
To thaw and serve: remove the freezer bag and thaw at room temperature for 3 hours. Steam for 1 hour or until heated through.
SERVES 6

FRUIT AND NUT PLAIT

METRIC/IMPERIAL
basic shortcrust pastry dough made with 225 g/½ lb flour
1 × 440 g/15½ oz can apricot halves, drained and chopped
1 dessert apple, peeled, cored and chopped
50 g/2 oz sultanas
50 g/2 oz chopped nuts
beaten egg, to glaze

AMERICAN
basic pie dough made with 2 cups flour
1 × 15½ oz can apricot halves, drained and chopped
1 dessert apple, peeled, cored and chopped
6 tablespoons seedless white raisins
½ cup chopped nuts
beaten egg, to glaze

Roll out the dough on a floured surface and cut out a rectangle about 30 × 25 cm/12 × 10 inches. Mark the dough into 3 lengthways, then moisten the edges with water. Make diagonal slits along the outer sections of the dough 2.5 cm/1 inch apart and 7.5 cm/3 inches deep.
Put the apricots, apple, sultanas (seedless white raisins) and nuts in a bowl and stir well to mix. Spread the mixture over the central section of the dough and fold over the outer sections, to give a plaited (braid) effect. Seal the ends.
To freeze: open (flash) freeze until firm, then pack in a freezer bag. Seal, label and return to the freezer.
To thaw and serve: remove wrappings and place on a baking sheet. Brush with beaten egg, then bake from frozen in a preheated moderately hot oven (200°C/400°F or Gas Mark 6) for 40 minutes or until heated through and golden brown.
SERVES 6

LEMON CHEESE MERINGUE

METRIC/IMPERIAL
For the custard:
2 egg yolks
50 g/2 oz sugar
25 g/1 oz flour
200 ml/⅓ pint milk
finely grated rind and juice of 1 lemon
225 g/½ lb cottage cheese, sieved
For the meringue topping (to finish):
2 egg whites
50 g/2 oz caster sugar
4 slices of crystallized lemon, to decorate

AMERICAN
For the custard:
2 egg yolks
¼ cup sugar
¼ cup flour
⅞ cup milk
finely grated rind and juice of 1 lemon
1 cup strained cottage cheese
For the meringue topping (to finish):
2 egg whites
¼ cup superfine sugar
4 slices of candied lemon, to decorate

To make the custard: put the egg yolks, sugar, flour and 1 × 15 ml spoon/1 tablespoon milk in a bowl and beat well to mix. Put the remaining milk in a pan and bring to the boil. Pour slowly over the egg mixture, stirring constantly. Return to the rinsed-out pan and bring slowly to the boil, stirring constantly.
Remove from the heat, leave to cool slightly, then stir in the remaining custard ingredients until evenly blended. Spoon into an ovenproof dish or foil container and bake in a preheated moderate oven (180°C/350°F or Gas Mark 4) for 15 minutes.
To freeze: cool quickly, then pack in a freezer bag. Seal, label and freeze.
To thaw and serve: remove wrappings and thaw the custard at room temperature for 4 hours. To make the meringue topping: beat the egg whites until stiff and dry. Add half the sugar and beat again until smooth. Fold in the remaining sugar, then spoon or pipe the meringue on top of the custard. Bake in a preheated moderate oven (180°C/350°F or Gas Mark 4) for 10 minutes until golden brown, then decorate with the lemon slices.
SERVES 4

BUTTERSCOTCH ICE CREAM

METRIC/IMPERIAL

50 g/2 oz butter
50 g/2 oz golden syrup
50 g/2 oz dark soft brown sugar
1 egg
40 g/$1\frac{1}{2}$ oz caster sugar
150 ml/$\frac{1}{4}$ pint milk, warmed
1 × 2.5 ml spoon/$\frac{1}{2}$ teaspoon vanilla essence
150 ml/$\frac{1}{4}$ pint double cream, lightly whipped

AMERICAN

$\frac{1}{4}$ cup butter
3 tablespoons light corn syrup
$\frac{1}{3}$ cup dark brown sugar
1 egg
3 tablespoons sugar
$\frac{2}{3}$ cup milk, warmed
$\frac{1}{2}$ teaspoon vanilla extract
$\frac{2}{3}$ cup heavy cream, lightly whipped

Put the butter, syrup and brown sugar in a pan and heat gently until melted. Leave to cool. Put the egg and (caster) sugar in a bowl, then stir in the milk and vanilla essence (extract). Strain into a pan and heat gently until the custard thickens, stirring constantly. Stir in the syrup mixture, leave to cool, then fold in the cream.
To freeze: pour into a rigid container, seal, label and freeze.
To thaw and serve: transfer to the refrigerator for 1 hour to soften slightly before serving.
SERVES 4 to 5

LEMON FREEZE

METRIC/IMPERIAL

For the base:
50 g/2 oz cornflakes, crushed
2 × 15 ml spoons/2 tablespoons caster sugar
25 g/1 oz butter
For the filling:
2 eggs, separated
1 small can sweetened condensed milk
4 × 15 ml spoons/4 tablespoons lemon juice
3 × 15 ml spoons/3 tablespoons caster sugar

AMERICAN

For the base:
2 cups cornflakes, crushed
2 tablespoons sugar
2 tablespoons butter
For the filling:
2 eggs, separated
1 small can sweetened condensed milk
$\frac{1}{4}$ cup lemon juice
3 tablespoons sugar

To make the base: put all the ingredients in a bowl and stir well to mix. Press into the base of a 900 ml/$1\frac{1}{2}$ pint/$3\frac{3}{4}$ cup freezing tray or shallow rigid container, reserving 4 × 15 ml spoons/4 tablespoons/$\frac{1}{4}$ cup for the topping.
To make the filling: beat the egg yolks until thick and creamy, then combine with the condensed milk and lemon juice and stir until thick.
Beat the egg whites until stiff but not dry, gradually beat in the sugar, then fold into the lemon mixture. Spoon over the cornflake base and sprinkle with the reserved topping.
To freeze: cover with foil, seal, label and freeze.
To thaw and serve: transfer to the refrigerator for 30 minutes to soften slightly before serving, then cut into bars.
SERVES 8

GRAPE ICE CREAM

METRIC/IMPERIAL

100 g/4 oz caster sugar
6 × 15 ml spoons/6 tablespoons water
5 egg yolks
450 g/1 lb green grapes, peeled and seeded
2 × 15 ml spoons/2 tablespoons lemon juice
300 ml/½ pint double cream, lightly whipped

AMERICAN

½ cup sugar
6 tablespoons water
5 egg yolks
4 cups green grapes, peeled and pitted
2 tablespoons lemon juice
1¼ cups heavy cream, lightly whipped

Put the sugar and water in a pan and heat gently until the sugar has dissolved. Bring to the boil and boil rapidly until syrupy, then leave to cool slightly. Beat the egg yolks until pale, then gradually pour in the syrup, beating constantly. Continue beating until frothy, thick and cold, then work to a smooth purée in an electric blender with the grapes and lemon juice. Fold the cream into the purée.
To freeze: pour into a rigid container, seal, label and freeze.
To thaw and serve: transfer to the refrigerator for 1 hour to soften slightly before serving.
SERVES 8

FROZEN ATHOL BROSE

METRIC/IMPERIAL

600 ml/1 pint double cream
4 × 15 ml spoons/4 tablespoons honey
2 × 15 ml spoons/2 tablespoons whisky
To finish:
whipped cream
chocolate curls

AMERICAN

2½ cups heavy cream
¼ cup honey
2 tablespoons whisky
To finish:
whipped cream
chocolate curls

Put all the ingredients in a bowl and beat until thick. Spoon into a 750 ml/1¼ pint/3 cup pudding basin or charlotte mould.
To freeze: cover with foil, seal, label and freeze.
To thaw and serve: turn out onto a serving dish and decorate with cream and chocolate curls.
SERVES 6

MARRON PARFAIT

METRIC/IMPERIAL

50 g/2 oz candied peel, chopped
50 g/2 oz glacé cherries, chopped
50 g/2 oz currants
50 g/2 oz sultanas
4 × 15 ml spoons/4 tablespoons maraschino liqueur or rum
4 egg yolks
225 g/½ lb icing sugar, sifted
600 ml/1 pint double cream
100 g/4 oz unsweetened chestnut purée
To finish:
whipped cream
marrons glacé

AMERICAN

⅓ cup chopped candied peel
¼ cup chopped candied cherries
⅓ cup currants
⅓ cup seedless white raisins
¼ cup maraschino liqueur or rum
4 egg yolks
1¾ cups confectioners' sugar
2½ cups heavy cream
scant ½ cup unsweetened chestnut purée
To finish:
whipped cream
marrons glacé

Put the peel and fruits in a bowl, stir in the liqueur or rum and leave to marinate for 1 hour, turning occasionally.
Put the egg yolks and sugar in a heatproof bowl and beat until light and fluffy. Heat 450 ml/¾ pint/2 cups cream, then beat gradually into the egg yolk mixture. Place the bowl over a pan of gently simmering water and stir constantly until the mixture just coats the back of the spoon. Do not allow to boil. Remove from the heat.
In a separate bowl, beat the chestnut purée with a little of the egg custard, then stir into the bulk of the custard. Leave to cool, then turn into a freezing tray or rigid shallow container and freeze until thick and slushy. Beat the remaining cream until stiff, then fold into the frozen custard with the marinated fruits. Spoon into a 1.5 litre/2½ pint/6¼ cup pudding basin or mould.
To freeze: cover with foil, seal, label and freeze.
To thaw and serve: turn out onto a serving dish and leave at room temperature for 1 hour to soften slightly before serving. Decorate with whipped cream and marrons glacé.
SERVES 10

CHOCOLATE AND RUM ICE CREAM

METRIC/IMPERIAL

For the ice cream:

2 eggs, separated
50 g/2 oz icing sugar, sifted
150 ml/¼ pint double cream, stiffly whipped

For the flavouring:

50 g/2 oz plain chocolate, broken into pieces
25 g/1 oz cocoa powder
2 × 15 ml spoons/2 tablespoons boiling water
2 × 5 ml spoons/2 teaspoons rum

AMERICAN

For the ice cream:

2 eggs, separated
½ cup sifted confectioners' sugar
⅔ cup heavy cream, stiffly whipped

For the flavoring:

⅓ cup semi-sweet chocolate pieces
¼ cup unsweetened cocoa powder
2 tablespoons boiling water
2 teaspoons rum

To make the ice cream: beat the egg whites until stiff, then beat in the icing (confectioners') sugar. Fold in half the whipped cream, then the egg yolks. Turn into a freezing tray or shallow rigid container and freeze for 30 minutes.
To make the flavouring: put the chocolate in a heatproof bowl, stand over a pan of gently simmering water and allow to melt. Remove from the heat. Dissolve the cocoa in the boiling water, stir in the melted chocolate, then fold into the remaining cream with the rum.
Turn the ice cream out of the tray or container and beat lightly. Fold in the flavoured cream.
To freeze: spoon into a rigid container, then cover with foil. Seal, label and freeze.
To thaw and serve: transfer to the refrigerator for 30 minutes to soften slightly before serving.
SERVES 4

COCONUT AND BRANDY ICE CREAM

Make as for Chocolate and Rum Ice Cream (see above), substituting 50 g/2 oz/⅔ cup desiccated (shredded) coconut and 2 × 5 ml spoons/2 teaspoons brandy for the chocolate, cocoa and rum. Add to the whipped cream before beating into the ice cream.
Freeze, thaw and serve as for Chocolate and Rum Ice Cream.
SERVES 4

HAZELNUT AND BRANDY ICE CREAM

Make as for Chocolate and Rum Ice Cream, substituting 50 g/2 oz/½ cup finely chopped roasted hazelnuts and 1 × 15 ml spoon/1 tablespoon brandy for the chocolate, cocoa and rum. Add to the whipped cream before beating into the ice cream.
Freeze, thaw and serve as for Chocolate and Rum Ice Cream.
SERVES 4

COFFEE AND TIA MARIA ICE CREAM

Make as for Chocolate and Rum Ice Cream, substituting 2 × 5 ml spoons/2 teaspoons instant coffee powder dissolved in 2 × 5 ml spoons/2 teaspoons boiling water and 2 × 5 ml spoons/2 teaspoons Tia Maria for the chocolate, cocoa and rum. Add to the whipped cream before beating into the ice cream.
Freeze, thaw and serve as for Chocolate and Rum Ice Cream.
SERVES 4

ORANGE SORBET (SHERBET)

METRIC/IMPERIAL

175 g/6 oz sugar
450 ml/¾ pint water
1 × 185 ml/6½ oz can concentrated frozen orange juice, thawed
2 egg whites

AMERICAN

¾ cup sugar
2 cups water
1 × 6½ oz can concentrated frozen orange juice, thawed
2 egg whites

Put the sugar and water in a pan and heat gently until the sugar has dissolved. Bring to the boil, then boil uncovered for 10 minutes. Put the orange juice in a bowl, pour in the syrup, then leave to cool. Pour into a 600 ml/1 pint/2½ cup freezing tray or shallow rigid container and freeze until thick and slushy.
Beat the egg whites until stiff but not dry, then fold into the orange mixture until evenly mixed.
To freeze: pour into a rigid container, seal, label and freeze.
To thaw and serve: transfer to the refrigerator for 5 minutes to soften slightly before serving.
SERVES 4 to 6

GOOSEBERRY AND ORANGE SORBET (SHERBET)

METRIC/IMPERIAL
1 kg/2 lb gooseberries, topped and tailed
150 ml/$\frac{1}{4}$ pint water
approx 100 g/4 oz sugar, or to taste
finely grated rind of 1 orange
juice of 2 oranges

AMERICAN
2 lb gooseberries, cleaned
$\frac{2}{3}$ cup water
approx $\frac{1}{2}$ cup sugar, or to taste
finely grated rind of 1 orange
juice of 2 oranges

Put the gooseberries, water and sugar in a pan, bring to the boil, then simmer for about 10 minutes until the gooseberries are soft. Taste for sweetness and add more sugar if liked. Leave to cool slightly, then work to a smooth purée through a sieve (strainer) and stir in the orange rind.
Measure the orange juice and make up to 600 ml/1 pint/2$\frac{1}{2}$ cups with water. Stir into the gooseberry purée.
To freeze: pour into a rigid container, seal, label and freeze.
To thaw and serve: transfer to the refrigerator for 2 hours to soften slightly before serving.
SERVES 6

LEMON ICE CREAM

METRIC/IMPERIAL
6 egg yolks
175 g/6 oz caster sugar
3 × 15 ml spoons/3 tablespoons lemon juice
300 ml/$\frac{1}{2}$ pint double cream

AMERICAN
6 egg yolks
$\frac{3}{4}$ cup sugar
3 tablespoons lemon juice
1$\frac{1}{4}$ cups heavy cream

Put the egg yolks and sugar in a bowl and beat until thick and light. Put the lemon juice and cream in a separate bowl and beat until the cream forms soft peaks. Fold in the egg mixture.
To freeze: pour into a rigid container, seal, label and freeze.
To thaw and serve: stand at room temperature for 10 minutes to soften slightly before serving.
SERVES 4 to 6

GRAPE SORBET (SHERBET)

METRIC/IMPERIAL
450 g/1 lb green grapes
600 ml/1 pint dry cider
100 g/4 oz sugar
2 egg whites

AMERICAN
1 lb green grapes
2$\frac{1}{2}$ cups hard cider
$\frac{1}{2}$ cup sugar
2 egg whites

Work the grapes to a purée in an electric blender, then rub through a sieve (strainer). Stir in 450 ml/$\frac{3}{4}$ pint/2 cups cider. Put the remaining cider in a pan with the sugar, heat gently until the sugar has dissolved, then stir into the grape mixture. Pour into a freezing tray or shallow rigid container and freeze until thick and slushy. Beat the egg whites until stiff but not dry, then fold into the grape mixture until evenly mixed.
To freeze: pour into a rigid container, seal, label and freeze.
To thaw and serve: transfer to the refrigerator for 15 minutes to soften slightly before serving.
SERVES 6 to 8

CIDER SORBET (SHERBET)

METRIC/IMPERIAL
600 ml/1 pint dry cider
200 ml/$\frac{1}{3}$ pint water
225 g/$\frac{1}{2}$ lb sugar
a few drops of vanilla essence
finely grated rind and juice of 1 lemon

AMERICAN
2$\frac{1}{2}$ cups hard cider
$\frac{7}{8}$ cup water
1 cup sugar
a few drops of vanilla extract
finely grated rind and juice of 1 lemon

Put the cider in a pan and boil rapidly until reduced by half. Leave to cool. Put the water, sugar, vanilla essence (extract) and lemon rind in a separate pan, bring to the boil, then add the lemon juice and leave to cool. Pass the mixture through a fine sieve (strainer), then pour into a freezing tray or shallow rigid container. Freeze until thick and slushy, then beat in the cider.
To freeze: pour into a rigid container, seal, label and freeze.
To thaw and serve: transfer to the refrigerator for 20 minutes to soften slightly before serving.
SERVES 6

ICED ZABAGLIONE

METRIC/IMPERIAL

6 egg yolks
75 g/3 oz caster sugar
finely grated rind of 1 orange
2 × 15 ml spoons/2 tablespoons Marsala
4 × 15 ml spoons/4 tablespoons double cream, lightly whipped
chopped pistachio nuts, to finish

AMERICAN

6 egg yolks
⅜ cup sugar
finely grated rind of 1 orange
2 tablespoons Marsala
¼ cup heavy cream, lightly whipped
chopped pistachio nuts, to finish

Put the egg yolks, sugar and orange rind in a heatproof bowl, beat until thick and light, then beat in the Marsala. Put the bowl over a pan of gently simmering water and beat until the mixture is thick. Remove from the heat and place the bowl in a bowl of iced water. Continue beating until cold, then fold in the cream.
To freeze: pour into individual ramekin dishes, cover with foil, seal, label and freeze.
To thaw and serve: remove wrappings and leave to stand at room temperature for 10 minutes to soften slightly before serving. Decorate with chopped pistachio nuts.
SERVES 4

BLACKCURRANT ICE CREAM

METRIC/IMPERIAL

1 packet of instant blackcurrant drink powder
300 ml/½ pint water
3 egg yolks
300 ml/½ pint double cream, lightly whipped

AMERICAN

1 package of instant blackcurrant drink powder
1¼ cups water
3 egg yolks
1¼ cups heavy cream, lightly whipped

Put the drink powder, water and egg yolks in a pan and beat well to mix. Cook gently until the custard thickens, stirring constantly, then strain. Cool, then fold in the cream until evenly mixed.
To freeze: pour into a rigid container, seal, label and freeze.
To thaw and serve: stand at room temperature for 10 to 15 minutes to soften slightly before serving.
SERVES 4

ICED STRAWBERRY MOUSSE

METRIC/IMPERIAL

225 g/½ lb strawberries, hulled
25 g/1 oz caster sugar
4 egg yolks
150 ml/¼ pint double cream, lightly whipped
2 egg whites

AMERICAN

½ lb strawberries, hulled
2 tablespoons sugar
4 egg yolks
⅔ cup heavy cream, lightly whipped
2 egg whites

Purée the strawberries in blender, then work through a nylon sieve (strainer). Transfer to a bowl, add the sugar and egg yolks and beat until thick. Fold in the cream. Beat the egg whites until stiff, then fold into the strawberry mixture.
To freeze: spoon the mixture into individual soufflé dishes, cover with foil, then pack in freezer bags. Seal, label and freeze.
To thaw and serve: remove wrappings and thaw in the refrigerator for 30 minutes.
SERVES 4

RASPBERRY SORBET (SHERBET)

METRIC/IMPERIAL

450 g/1 lb raspberries
175 g/6 oz sugar
2 egg whites

AMERICAN

1 lb raspberries
¾ cup sugar
2 egg whites

Work the raspberries through a sieve (strainer) and measure the purée. Make up to 600 ml/1 pint/2½ cups with water in a separate measure, then put the water in a pan with the sugar and heat gently until the sugar has dissolved. Bring to the boil, then boil uncovered for 10 minutes. Stir into the raspberry purée and leave to cool, then pour into a 600 ml/1 pint/2½ cup freezing tray or shallow rigid container and freeze until thick and slushy. Beat the egg whites until stiff but not dry, then fold into the raspberry purée.
To freeze: pour into a rigid container, seal, label and freeze.
To thaw and serve: transfer to the refrigerator for 5 minutes to soften slightly before serving.
SERVES 4 to 6

BLACKBERRY SORBET (SHERBET)

METRIC/IMPERIAL
1 kg/2 lb blackberries
175 g/6 oz caster sugar
900 ml/1½ pints water
2 × 15 ml spoons/2 tablespoons lemon juice

AMERICAN
2 lb blackberries
¾ cup sugar
3¾ cups water
2 tablespoons lemon juice

Put the blackberries, sugar and water in a pan and cook gently until the blackberries are soft. Add the lemon juice, then work to a purée through a sieve (strainer). Pour into a freezing tray or shallow rigid container, freeze until thick and slushy, then turn the mixture into a bowl and beat thoroughly.
To freeze: pour into a rigid container, seal, label and freeze.
To thaw and serve: transfer to the refrigerator for 5 minutes to soften slightly before serving.
SERVES 8 to 10

VANILLA SEMI-FREDO

METRIC/IMPERIAL
1 egg white
200 ml/⅓ pint double cream
40 g/1½ oz icing sugar, sifted
0.5 × 2.5 ml spoon/¼ teaspoon vanilla essence
fruit, fruit sauce or lightly toasted nuts, to serve

AMERICAN
1 egg white
⅞ cup heavy cream
⅜ cup sifted confectioners' sugar
¼ teaspoon vanilla extract
fruit, fruit sauce or lightly toasted nuts, to serve

Beat the egg white until stiff. Put the cream in a separate bowl and beat until thick and light, adding the sugar and vanilla essence (extract) during beating. Fold the egg white into the cream mixture.
To freeze: spoon into a rigid container, then cover with foil. Seal, label and freeze.
To thaw and serve: transfer to the refrigerator for about 1 hour to soften slightly. Serve topped with fruit, fruit sauce or nuts.
SERVES 4

APRICOT ICE CREAM

METRIC/IMPERIAL
450 g/1 lb stoned apricots
175 g/6 oz sugar
juice of 1 lemon
300 ml/½ pint double cream, stiffly whipped

AMERICAN
1 lb pitted apricots
¾ cup sugar
juice of 1 lemon
1¼ cups heavy cream, stiffly whipped

Put the apricots, sugar and lemon juice in an ovenproof dish, cover and cook in a preheated moderate oven (160°C/325°F or Gas Mark 3) for about 30 minutes or until the apricots are soft. Leave to cool slightly, then work to a smooth purée in an electric blender or rub through a sieve (strainer).
Fold the cream into the fruit purée until evenly mixed, then pour into a freezing tray or shallow rigid container. Freeze until thick and slushy, then turn into a bowl and beat thoroughly.
To freeze: pour into a rigid container, seal, label and freeze.
To thaw and serve: transfer to the refrigerator for 30 minutes to soften slightly before serving.
SERVES 4

CELEBRATION CREAM

METRIC/IMPERIAL
350 g/¾ lb sugar
300 ml/½ pint water
juice of 1 lemon
1 miniature bottle of brandy
300 ml/½ pint champagne cider
300 ml/½ pint double cream, stiffly whipped

AMERICAN
1½ cups sugar
1¼ cups water
juice of 1 lemon
1 miniature bottle of brandy
1¼ cups champagne cider
1¼ cups heavy cream, stiffly whipped

Put the sugar and water in a pan and heat gently until the sugar has dissolved. Bring to the boil, simmer for 15 minutes, then leave to cool.
Add the lemon juice, brandy and champagne cider, stir well to mix, then pour into a freezing tray or shallow rigid container. Freeze until thick and slushy, then fold in the cream until evenly mixed.
To freeze: pour into a rigid container, seal, label and freeze.
To thaw and serve: serve straight from the freezer.
SERVES 4 to 5

RASPBERRY ICE CREAM

METRIC/IMPERIAL
100 g/4 oz caster sugar
2 eggs
15 g/½ oz cornflour
600 ml/1 pint milk
450 g/1 lb fresh or frozen raspberries, or 1 × 375 g/13 oz can raspberries
150 ml/¼ pint double cream, lightly whipped

AMERICAN
½ cup sugar
2 eggs
2 tablespoons cornstarch
2½ cups milk
1 lb fresh or frozen raspberries, or 1 × 13 oz can raspberries
⅔ cup heavy cream, lightly whipped

Put the sugar and eggs in a bowl and beat well to mix. Mix the cornflour (cornstarch) to a paste with a little of the milk, then stir into the sugar and egg mixture.
Heat the remaining milk in a pan, then stir into the sugar and egg mixture. Return to the pan, then bring to the boil and simmer for 3 minutes until thick, stirring constantly. Pour into a bowl and leave to cool, stirring occasionally to prevent a skin forming.
If using fresh or frozen raspberries, put in a pan with 1 × 15 ml spoon/1 tablespoon water and sugar to taste. Bring slowly to the boil, leave to cool, then work to a purée through a sieve (strainer). If using canned raspberries, work the fruit and juice through the sieve (strainer).
Add the raspberry purée to the custard mixture and stir well to mix. Pour into a freezing tray or shallow rigid container and freeze until thick and slushy. Transfer to a chilled bowl, beat thoroughly then fold in the cream until evenly mixed.
To freeze: pour into a rigid container, seal, label and freeze.
To thaw and serve: stand at room temperature for 10 to 15 minutes to soften slightly before serving.
SERVES 6

VANILLA ICE CREAM

METRIC/IMPERIAL
100 g/4 oz caster sugar
2 eggs
15 g/½ oz cornflour
600 ml/1 pint milk
a few drops of vanilla essence
150 ml/¼ pint double cream, lightly whipped

AMERICAN
½ cup sugar
2 eggs
2 tablespoons cornstarch
2½ cups milk
a few drops of vanilla extract
⅔ cup heavy cream, lightly whipped

Put the sugar and eggs in a bowl and beat well to mix. Mix the cornflour (cornstarch) to a paste with a little of the milk, then stir into the sugar and egg mixture.
Heat the remaining milk in a pan, then stir into the sugar and egg mixture. Return to the pan, then bring to the boil and simmer for 3 minutes until thick, stirring constantly. Pour into a bowl and leave to cool, stirring occasionally to prevent a skin forming.
Stir in the vanilla essence (extract), pour into a freezing tray or shallow rigid container and freeze until thick and slushy. Transfer to a chilled bowl, beat thoroughly, then fold in the cream until evenly mixed.
To freeze: pour into a rigid container, seal, label and freeze.
To thaw and serve: stand at room temperature for 10 to 15 minutes to soften slightly before serving.
SERVES 6

LEMON GRANITA

METRIC/IMPERIAL
100 g/4 oz sugar
450 ml/¾ pint water
thinly pared rind of 1 lemon
pinch of salt
juice of 4 lemons

AMERICAN
½ cup sugar
2 cups water
thinly pared rind of 1 lemon
pinch of salt
juice of 4 lemons

Put the sugar and water in a pan and heat gently until the sugar has dissolved. Add the lemon rind, boil for 5 minutes, then add the salt and strain into a bowl. Leave to cool, then stir in the lemon juice.
To freeze: pour into a rigid container, then cover with foil. Seal, label and freeze.
To thaw and serve: transfer to the refrigerator for about 30 minutes to soften slightly before serving.
SERVES 4

STRAWBERRY SORBETO

METRIC/IMPERIAL
150 g/5 oz sugar
6 × 15 ml spoons/6 tablespoons water
450 ml/¾ pint unsweetened strawberry purée
1 × 15 ml spoon/1 tablespoon lemon juice
1 × 15 ml spoon/1 tablespoon orange juice

AMERICAN
⅝ cup sugar
6 tablespoons water
2 cups unsweetened strawberry purée
1 tablespoon lemon juice
1 tablespoon orange juice

Put the sugar and water in a pan and heat gently until the sugar has dissolved. Boil for 1 minute, then pour into a bowl and leave to cool. Add the remaining ingredients and stir well to mix. Pour the mixture into a shallow freezing tray, freeze until slushy, then turn into a bowl and beat thoroughly.
To freeze: spoon the mixture into a rigid container, then cover with foil. Seal, label and freeze.
To thaw and serve: transfer to the refrigerator for about 30 minutes to soften slightly.
SERVES 4

HAZELNUT ICE CREAM

METRIC/IMPERIAL
50 g/2 oz hazelnuts
150 ml/¼ pint evaporated milk, chilled
150 ml/¼ pint double cream, whipped
40 g/1½ oz caster sugar

AMERICAN
½ cup hazelnuts
⅔ cup evaporated milk, chilled
⅔ cup heavy cream, whipped
3 tablespoons sugar

Spread the nuts on a baking sheet and toast in a preheated moderate oven (180°C/350°F or Gas Mark 4) for 10 minutes. Leave to cool, then rub off the skins and grind the nuts finely in a nut mill.
Beat the evaporated milk until thick and creamy, fold into the whipped cream, then fold in the nuts and sugar until evenly blended.
To freeze: spoon the mixture into a rigid container, then cover with foil. Seal, label and freeze.
To thaw and serve: transfer to the refrigerator for about 1 hour to soften slightly.
SERVES 4

BANANA ICE CREAM

METRIC/IMPERIAL
4 ripe bananas, peeled and roughly chopped
2 × 15 ml spoons/2 tablespoons icing sugar, sifted
2 × 15 ml spoons/2 tablespoons lemon juice
300 ml/½ pint double cream, whipped

AMERICAN
4 ripe bananas, peeled and roughly chopped
2 tablespoons sifted confectioners' sugar
2 tablespoons lemon juice
1¼ cups heavy cream, whipped

Put the bananas, icing (confectioners') sugar and lemon juice in an electric blender and work to a smooth purée. Fold in the whipped cream until evenly blended.
To freeze: spoon the mixture into a rigid container, then cover with foil. Seal, label and freeze.
To thaw and serve: transfer to the refrigerator for about 1 hour to soften slightly.
SERVES 6

RUM AND CITRUS SORBET (SHERBET)

METRIC/IMPERIAL
100 g/4 oz sugar
300 ml/½ pint water
thinly pared rind and juice of 1 large lemon
juice of 1 orange
1 × 15 ml spoon/1 tablespoon rum
1 large egg white

AMERICAN
½ cup sugar
1¼ cups water
thinly pared rind and juice of 1 large lemon
juice of 1 orange
1 tablespoon rum
1 large egg white

Put the sugar and water in a pan and heat gently until the sugar has dissolved. Add the lemon rind and boil for 10 minutes, then strain into a bowl and leave to cool. Stir in the lemon and orange juices and pour into a shallow freezing tray. Freeze until slushy, then turn into a bowl, add the rum and beat thoroughly. Beat the egg white until stiff, then fold into the syrup mixture.
To freeze: spoon the mixture into a rigid container, then cover and freeze until firm, stirring from time to time if the ice shows signs of separating. Seal, label and freeze.
To thaw and serve: transfer to the refrigerator for about 30 minutes to soften slightly.
SERVES 4

BOMBE NÖEL

METRIC/IMPERIAL

3 egg yolks
25 g/1 oz cornflour
100 g/4 oz caster sugar
300 ml/½ pint milk
50 g/2 oz glacé cherries, chopped
50 g/2 oz candied angelica, chopped
50 g/2 oz walnuts, chopped
50 g/2 oz crystallized pineapple, chopped
50 g/2 oz sultanas
2 × 15 ml spoons/2 tablespoons brandy
2 × 15 ml spoons/2 tablespoons Madeira
150 ml/¼ pint double cream, whipped

AMERICAN

3 egg yolks
¼ cup cornstarch
½ cup sugar
1¼ cups milk
¼ cup chopped candied cherries
⅓ cup chopped candied angelica
½ cup chopped walnuts
⅓ cup chopped candied pineapple
⅓ cup seedless white raisins
2 tablespoons brandy
2 tablespoons Madeira
⅔ cup heavy cream, whipped

Put the egg yolks, cornflour (cornstarch) and sugar in a bowl and beat together until creamy. Heat the milk and pour onto the egg mixture, stirring constantly. Transfer the mixture to the top of a double boiler and stir over a gentle heat until thick. Leave to cool, then chill in the refrigerator.
Meanwhile, put the fruits and nuts in a bowl, stir in the brandy and Madeira and leave to marinate for 1 hour.
Fold the whipped cream into the chilled custard, then fold in the marinated mixture until evenly blended.
To freeze: spoon the mixture into a rigid container, then cover with foil. Seal, label and freeze.
To thaw and serve: transfer to the refrigerator for about 30 minutes to soften slightly.
SERVES 6

ICED LEMON MOUSSE

METRIC/IMPERIAL

2 eggs, separated
100 g/4 oz caster sugar
finely grated rind and juice of 1 lemon
1 small can evaporated milk, chilled

AMERICAN

2 eggs, separated
½ cup sugar
finely grated rind and juice of 1 lemon
1 small can evaporated milk, chilled

Put the egg yolks, sugar, lemon rind and juice in a bowl and beat together until light.
Put the evaporated milk in a separate bowl, beat until thick and creamy, then fold into the egg yolk mixture. Beat the egg whites until stiff but not dry, then fold in lightly until evenly blended.
To freeze: spoon the mixture into a rigid container, then cover with foil. Seal, label and freeze.
To thaw and serve: transfer to the refrigerator for about 30 minutes to soften slightly.
SERVES 4

MELON WATER ICE

METRIC/IMPERIAL

100 g/4 oz sugar
150 ml/¼ pint water
1–1.25 kg/2–2½ lb ripe melon, rind and seeds removed
juice of 1 lemon

AMERICAN

½ cup sugar
⅔ cup water
2–2½ lb ripe melon, rind and seeds removed
juice of 1 lemon

Put the sugar and water in a pan and heat gently until the sugar has dissolved. Boil for 5 minutes, then pour into a bowl. Leave to cool, then chill in the refrigerator.
Work the melon flesh to a smooth purée in an electric blender, or rub through a nylon sieve (strainer). Stir in the lemon juice, then the chilled syrup. Pour into a shallow freezing tray, freeze until slushy, then turn into a bowl and beat thoroughly.
To freeze: spoon the mixture into a rigid container, then cover with foil. Seal, label and freeze.
To thaw and serve: transfer to the refrigerator for 10 minutes to soften slightly.
SERVES 4

RICH CHOCOLATE ICE CREAM

METRIC/IMPERIAL

300 ml/½ pint milk
75 g/3 oz sugar
2 eggs, beaten
75 g/3 oz plain chocolate, melted
300 ml/½ pint double cream, lightly whipped

AMERICAN

1¼ cups milk
⅜ cup sugar
2 eggs, beaten
½ cup semi-sweet chocolate pieces, melted
1¼ cups heavy cream, lightly whipped

Put the milk and sugar in a pan, heat gently until the sugar has dissolved, then pour onto the eggs, stirring constantly. Return the mixture to the rinsed-out pan and heat gently until the custard thickens, stirring constantly. Strain into a bowl, then stir in the melted chocolate. Leave to cool, then fold in the whipped cream until evenly blended.

To freeze: spoon the mixture into a rigid container, then cover with foil. Seal, label and freeze.

To thaw and serve: transfer to the refrigerator for about 30 minutes to soften slightly.

SERVES 4

ORANGE ICE CREAM

METRIC/IMPERIAL

300 ml/½ pint double cream, whipped
300 ml/½ pint orange juice
50 g/2 oz caster sugar

AMERICAN

1¼ cups heavy cream, whipped
1¼ cups orange juice
¼ cup sugar

Put the cream in a bowl, add half the orange juice and stir until evenly blended, then stir in the remaining orange juice a little at a time. Fold in the sugar.

To freeze: spoon the mixture into a rigid container, cover and freeze for about 1 hour. Stir well, then seal, label and return to the freezer.

To thaw and serve: transfer to the refrigerator for 15 minutes to soften slightly.

SERVES 4

GOOSEBERRY ICE CREAM

METRIC/IMPERIAL

450 g/1 lb gooseberries, topped and tailed
100 g/4 oz sugar
2 × 15 ml spoons/2 tablespoons water
3 eggs, separated
75 g/3 oz icing sugar, sifted
150 ml/¼ pint double cream
4 × 15 ml spoons/4 tablespoons single cream

AMERICAN

1 lb gooseberries, cleaned
½ cup sugar
2 tablespoons water
3 eggs, separated
¾ cup sifted confectioners' sugar
⅔ cup heavy cream
¼ cup light cream

Put the gooseberries, sugar and water in a pan, cover and cook gently until the gooseberries are soft, shaking the pan occasionally. Work to a purée through a sieve (strainer), then leave to cool.

Put the egg yolks in a bowl and beat until well blended. Put the egg whites in a separate bowl, beat until stiff, then fold in the egg yolks and icing (confectioners') sugar. Beat the creams together until thick, then fold into the egg mixture with the gooseberry purée.

To freeze: pour into a rigid container, seal, label and freeze.

To thaw and serve: transfer to the refrigerator for 30 minutes to soften slightly before serving.

SERVES 8

YOGURT AND ORANGE SORBET (SHERBET)

METRIC/IMPERIAL

300 ml/½ pint natural yogurt
1 × 178 ml/6¼ oz can concentrated frozen orange juice, thawed
sugar to taste
15 g/½ oz gelatine
3 × 15 ml spoons/3 tablespoons water
2 egg whites

AMERICAN

1¼ cups unflavored yogurt
1 × 6¼ oz can concentrated frozen orange juice, thawed
sugar to taste
2 envelopes unflavored gelatin
3 tablespoons water
2 egg whites

Put the yogurt, orange juice and sugar to taste in a bowl and stir well to mix.
Sprinkle the gelatine over the water in a heatproof bowl. Leave until spongy, then place the bowl in a pan of hot water and stir over a low heat until the gelatine has dissolved. Leave to cool slightly, then stir into the yogurt mixture and leave until just beginning to set.
Beat the egg whites until stiff, then fold into the yogurt mixture.
To freeze: pour into a rigid container, seal, label and freeze.
To thaw and serve: transfer to the refrigerator for 30 minutes to soften slightly before serving.
SERVES 6

GRAPEFRUIT SORBET (SHERBET)

METRIC/IMPERIAL

50 g/2 oz sugar
300 ml/½ pint water
2 × 5 ml spoons/2 teaspoons gelatine
1 × 178 ml/6¼ oz can frozen concentrated grapefruit juice, thawed
2 egg whites

AMERICAN

¼ cup sugar
1¼ cups water
2 teaspoons unflavored gelatin
1 × 6¼ oz can frozen concentrated grapefruit juice, thawed
2 egg whites

Put the sugar and half the water in a pan, heat gently until thc sugar has dissolved, then leave to cool.
Sprinkle the gelatine over 2 × 15 ml spoons/2 tablespoons of the remaining water in a heatproof bowl and leave until spongy, then place the bowl in a pan of hot water and stir over a low heat until the gelatine has dissolved. Stir into the sugar syrup with the remaining water and the grapefruit juice.
Pour into a freezing tray or shallow rigid container and freeze until thick and slushy. Beat the egg whites until stiff but not dry, then fold into the grapefruit mixture until evenly mixed.
To freeze: pour into a rigid container, seal, label and freeze.
To thaw and serve: transfer to the refrigerator for 15 minutes to soften slightly before serving.
SERVES 6

LEMON THYME SORBET (SHERBET)

METRIC/IMPERIAL

thinly pared rind and juice of 2 lemons
600 ml/1 pint water
2 × 5 ml spoons/2 teaspoons gelatine
150 g/5 oz sugar
6 sprigs of fresh thyme
2 egg whites

AMERICAN

thinly pared rind and juice of 2 lemons
2½ cups water
2 teaspoons unflavored gelatin
⅔ cup sugar
6 sprigs of fresh thyme
2 egg whites

Put all the ingredients, except the egg whites, in a bowl and heat gently until the gelatine and sugar have dissolved, stirring constantly. Bring to the boil and boil for 5 minutes, then cover and leave to cool.
Strain into a freezing tray or shallow rigid container and freeze until thick and slushy. Beat the egg whites until stiff, then fold into the lemon mixture.
To freeze: pour into a rigid container, seal, label and freeze.
To thaw and serve: transfer to the refrigerator for 15 minutes to soften slightly before serving.
SERVES 6 to 8

MINT SORBET (SHERBET)

METRIC/IMPERIAL
150 ml/¼ pint water
100 g/4 oz sugar
1 handful of fresh mint leaves
juice of 1 lemon
2 egg whites

AMERICAN
⅔ cup water
½ cup sugar
1 handful of fresh mint leaves
juice of 1 lemon
2 egg whites

Put the water and sugar in a pan and heat gently until the sugar has dissolved. Bring to the boil, then boil rapidly for 3 minutes. Leave to cool. Put the mint leaves in an electric blender, add the syrup and blend to a smooth purée. Strain through a nylon sieve (strainer), pressing as much of the mint through as possible. Stir in the lemon juice, pour into a freezing tray or shallow rigid container and freeze for about 1 hour until soft frozen. Beat the egg whites until stiff but not dry then fold into the mint ice until evenly mixed.
To freeze: pour into a rigid container, seal, label and freeze.
To thaw and serve: transfer to the refrigerator for 10 to 15 minutes to soften slightly before serving.
SERVES 6

SOURED STRAWBERRIES

METRIC/IMPERIAL
675 g/1½ lb strawberries
900 ml/1½ pints soured cream
225 g/½ lb caster sugar
4 × 15 ml spoons/4 tablespoons brandy

AMERICAN
1½ lb strawberries
3¾ cups sour cream
1 cup sugar
¼ cup brandy

Put the strawberries, sour(ed) cream and sugar in an electric blender and work to a smooth purée. Stir in the brandy, then freeze until thick and slushy.
Turn the mixture into a bowl and beat thoroughly. Return to the freezer and freeze again until thick and slushy. Beat and freeze again several times to break up the ice crystals.
To freeze: pour into a rigid container, seal, label and freeze.
To thaw and serve: transfer to the refrigerator for 1 hour to soften slightly before serving.
SERVES 4 to 6

MINT ICE CREAM

METRIC/IMPERIAL
150 ml/¼ pint water
100 g/4 oz sugar
1 handful of fresh mint leaves
juice of 1 lemon
150 ml/¼ pint double cream, lightly whipped

AMERICAN
⅔ cup water
½ cup sugar
1 handful of fresh mint leaves
juice of 1 lemon
⅔ cup heavy cream, lightly whipped

Put the water and sugar in a pan and heat gently until the sugar has dissolved. Bring to the boil, then boil for 3 minutes. Leave to cool.
Put the mint leaves in an electric blender (reserving 6 mint leaves for the decoration), add the syrup, then blend to a smooth purée. Strain through a nylon sieve (strainer), pressing as much of the mint through as possible. Stir in the lemon juice, pour into a freezing tray or shallow rigid container and freeze for about 1 hour until soft frozen. Fold the mint ice into the cream until evenly mixed.
To freeze: pour into a rigid container, seal, label and freeze.
To thaw and serve: transfer to the refrigerator for 1 hour to soften slightly before serving.
SERVES 6

FROZEN CRUNCHY APPLE WHIP

METRIC/IMPERIAL

2 large cooking apples, peeled, cored and sliced
2 × 15 ml spoons/2 tablespoons water
50 g/2 oz sugar
1 × 15 ml spoon/1 tablespoon lemon juice
1 egg white
150 ml/¼ pint natural yogurt
100 g/4 oz gingernut biscuits, crushed
whipped cream, to finish

AMERICAN

2 large baking apples, peeled, cored and sliced
2 tablespoons water
¼ cup sugar
1 tablespoon lemon juice
1 egg white
⅔ cup unflavored yogurt
1 cup crushed gingernut cookies
whipped cream, to finish

Put the apples, water and sugar in a pan, then cover and cook gently for 10 minutes until the apples are soft. Work to a smooth purée through a sieve (strainer), then chill in the refrigerator.
Beat the egg white until stiff, fold into the apple purée with the yogurt and biscuits (cookies).
To freeze: pour into individual ramekin dishes, then cover with foil. Seal, label and freeze.
To thaw and serve: remove wrappings and thaw in the refrigerator for 1 hour. Decorate with whipped cream before serving.
SERVES 4

STRAWBERRY ICE CREAM

METRIC/IMPERIAL

225 g/½ lb strawberries, hulled
50 g/2 oz sugar
2 eggs, separated
50 g/2 oz caster sugar
1 small can evaporated milk, chilled

AMERICAN

½ lb strawberries, hulled
¼ cup sugar
2 eggs, separated
¼ cup superfine sugar
1 small can evaporated milk, chilled

Put the strawberries in a pan with the sugar and cook gently for about 5 minutes until soft. Work to a purée through a sieve (strainer), then leave to cool.
Put the egg yolks in a bowl and beat until well blended. Put the egg whites in a separate bowl, beat until stiff but not dry then beat in the caster (superfine) sugar a little at a time. Beat the egg yolks into the meringue slowly.
Put the evaporated milk in a bowl and beat until thick, then fold into the egg mixture with the strawberry purée.
To freeze: pour into a rigid container, seal, label and freeze.
To thaw and serve: stand at room temperature for 5 minutes to soften slightly before serving.
SERVES 4

CARAMEL AND HAZELNUT ICE CREAM

METRIC/IMPERIAL

75 g/3 oz fresh brown breadcrumbs
50 g/2 oz demerara sugar
50 g/2 oz roasted hazelnuts, skinned and ground
4 eggs, separated
100 g/4 oz caster sugar
300 ml/½ pint double cream, lightly whipped

AMERICAN

1½ cups fresh brown breadcrumbs
⅓ cup raw brown sugar
⅓ cup hazelnuts skinned and ground
4 eggs, separated
½ cup superfine sugar
1¼ cups heavy cream, lightly whipped

Put the breadcrumbs, demerara (raw) sugar and hazelnuts on a heatproof plate. Put under a hot grill (broiler) for 5 to 8 minutes until golden brown and caramelized, stirring occasionally. Leave to cool.
Put the egg yolks in a bowl and beat until well blended. Put the egg whites in a separate bowl, beat until stiff, then beat in the sugar a little at a time. Fold the cream into the meringue with the egg yolks and breadcrumb mixture.
To freeze: pour into a rigid container, seal, label and freeze.
To thaw and serve: stand at room temperature for 5 minutes to soften slightly before serving.
SERVES 6 to 8

RUM AND RAISIN ICE CREAM

METRIC/IMPERIAL

100 g/4 oz seedless raisins
4 × 15 ml spoons/4 tablespoons rum
4 eggs, separated
100 g/4 oz icing sugar, sifted
300 ml/½ pint double cream, whipped

AMERICAN

⅔ cup seedless raisins
¼ cup rum
4 eggs, separated
scant 1 cup sifted confectioners' sugar
1¼ cups heavy cream, whipped

Put the raisins and rum in a bowl and leave to marinate for 30 minutes.

Put the egg yolks and sugar in a separate bowl, beat together until thick and fluffy, then fold in the whipped cream until evenly blended. Stir in the marinated raisins, then beat the egg whites until stiff and fold into the mixture.

To freeze: spoon the mixture into a rigid container, then cover and freeze for about 1 hour. Stir well, then seal, label and return to the freezer.

To thaw and serve: transfer to the refrigerator for about 30 minutes to soften slightly.

SERVES 6 to 8

CASSATA

METRIC/IMPERIAL

600 ml/1 pint chocolate ice cream, slightly softened
450 ml/¾ pint strawberry ice cream or water ice, slightly softened
150 ml/¼ pint fresh double cream
15 g/½ oz icing sugar
25 g/1 oz sultanas, chopped
15 g/½ oz candied angelica, chopped
50 g/2 oz glacé cherries, chopped
15 g/½ oz almonds, blanched and cut into slivers

AMERICAN

1¼ pints chocolate ice cream, slightly softened
1 pint strawberry ice cream or sherbet, slightly softened
⅔ cup heavy cream
1¼ tablespoons confectioners' sugar
2 tablespoons chopped seedless white raisins
1 tablespoon candied angelica
¼ cup candied red cherries, chopped
2 tablespoons slivered almonds

Line a chilled 1 litre/2 pint/5 cup metal bowl or pudding basin (slope-sided mold) with the chocolate ice cream. Put in the freezer until hard, then smooth in the strawberry ice cream or water ice (sherbet) to form another layer, approximately 1 cm/½ inch thick, leaving a well in the centre. Return to the freezer until hard. Lightly whip the cream with the icing (confectioners') sugar, fold in the chopped fruit and nuts, then fill the centre well of the mould.

To freeze: cover with foil, then overwrap in a freezer bag. Seal, label and freeze.

To thaw and serve: wrap the mould briefly in a towel that has been wrung out in hot water, then unmould onto a chilled platter.

SERVES 6 to 8

BROWN BREAD ICE CREAM

METRIC/IMPERIAL

50 g/2 oz butter
75 g/3 oz stale brown breadcrumbs
175 g/6 oz sugar
4 egg yolks
300 ml/½ pint milk or single cream
2 × 15 ml spoons/2 tablespoons sweet sherry
300 ml/½ pint double cream, lightly whipped

AMERICAN

¼ cup butter
1 cup stale wholewheat breadcrumbs
¾ cup sugar
4 egg yolks
1¼ cups milk or light cream
2 tablespoons cream sherry
1¼ cups heavy cream, lightly whipped

Melt the butter in a pan, add the breadcrumbs and fry until crisp. Sprinkle on half the sugar and continue to fry until the sugar has caramelized, stirring constantly. Pour onto a wooden board leave to cool then crush into fine crumbs. Beat the egg yolks with the remaining sugar until light and fluffy. Scald the milk or single (light) cream and pour slowly onto the yolk and sugar mixture, beating constantly. Return to the pan and heat gently without allowing to boil. Stir constantly until the mixture has thickened enough to coat the back of a spoon. Remove from the heat and leave to cool. Stir in the breadcrumbs and sherry, then fold in the cream.

To freeze: pour into a rigid container and freeze for 1 hour, or until the mixture begins to set. Stir well with a fork. Cover with foil, seal, label and return to the freezer.

To thaw and serve: remove from freezer, wrap the dish with a towel that has been wrung out in hot water, then unmould onto a chilled platter. Smooth the sides with a metal spatula and return to freezer for 10 minutes, then transfer to the refrigerator for 30 minutes.

BASIC ALL-IN-ONE VICTORIA SANDWICH (LAYER CAKE)

METRIC/IMPERIAL

For the cake:

175 g/6 oz self-raising flour
1.5 × 5 ml spoons/1½ teaspoons baking powder
175 g/6 oz soft tub margarine
175 g/6 oz caster sugar
3 large eggs, beaten

To finish:

3 × 15 ml spoons/3 tablespoons jam
caster or icing sugar for sprinkling

AMERICAN

For the cake:

1½ cups self-rising flour
1½ teaspoons baking powder
¾ cup soft margarine
¾ cup sugar
3 large eggs, beaten

To finish:

3 tablespoons jam
sugar or confectioners' sugar for sprinkling

Grease two 18 cm/7 inch sandwich tins (layer cake pans) and line the bottoms with greased greaseproof paper or non-stick parchment.
Sift the flour and baking powder into a bowl. Add the remaining ingredients and beat for 2 to 3 minutes until well mixed.
Divide the mixture between the prepared tins and bake in a preheated moderate oven (180°C/350°F or Gas Mark 4) for 30 to 35 minutes until firm to the touch. Turn out onto a wire rack,

remove the paper linings, then leave to cool.
To freeze: wrap the cakes individually in cling film, then pack in a freezer bag. Seal, label and freeze.
To thaw and serve: remove wrappings and thaw at room temperature for 4 hours. Sandwich the cakes together with the jam, then sprinkle sugar over the top of the cake.
SERVES 6 to 8

CITRUS DRIZZLE CAKE

Prepare the mixture for an All-in-One Victoria Sandwich (Layer Cake). Grease a 1 kg/2 lb loaf tin, line the bottom with greased greaseproof paper or non-stick parchment and pour in the prepared cake mixture. Bake in a preheated moderate oven (180°C/350°F or Gas Mark 4) for 1 hour, turn out and cool on a wire rack, then remove the lining paper.
Prepare a citrus syrup and topping with the following ingredients:

METRIC/IMPERIAL
For the syrup:
juice of 1 orange
juice of 1 lemon
100 g/4 oz caster sugar
For the topping:
100 g/4 oz plain chocolate, broken into pieces
15 g/½ oz butter

AMERICAN
For the syrup:
juice of 1 orange
juice of 1 lemon
½ cup sugar
For the topping:
⅔ cup semi-sweet chocolate pieces
1 tablespoon butter

To make the syrup: put the fruit juices and sugar in a pan and heat gently until the sugar has dissolved. Make slits across the top of the cake, then spoon over the syrup.
To make the topping: put the chocolate and butter in a heatproof bowl, stand over a pan of gently simmering water and allow to melt, stirring once or twice. Spread over the top of the cake in swirls.
To freeze: open (flash) freeze until firm, then pack in a freezer bag. Seal, label and return to the freezer.
To thaw and serve: remove wrappings and place the cake on a serving platter. Thaw at room temperature for 4 hours.
SERVES 8

VICTORIA SANDWICH

METRIC/IMPERIAL
For the cake:
225 g/½ lb butter
225 g/½ lb caster sugar
4 eggs, beaten
225 g/½ lb self-raising flour
pinch of salt
approx 3–4 × 15 ml spoons/3–4 tablespoons warm water
To finish:
3 × 15 ml spoons/3 tablespoons jam
150 ml/¼ pint double cream, whipped
icing sugar, for sprinkling

AMERICAN
For the cake:
1 cup butter
1 cup sugar
4 eggs, beaten
2 cups self-rising flour
pinch of salt
approx 3–4 tablespoons warm water
To finish:
3 tablespoons jam
⅔ cup heavy cream, whipped
confectioners' sugar, for sprinkling

Grease two 20 cm/8 inch sandwich tins (layer cake pans) and line the bottoms with greased greaseproof paper or non-stick parchment.
Put the butter and sugar in a bowl, beat together until light and fluffy, then beat in the eggs a little at a time. Sift the flour and salt together, then beat 1 × 15 ml spoon/1 tablespoon flour into the creamed mixture. Fold in the remaining flour and stir in enough water to give a soft dropping consistency.
Divide the mixture equally between the two prepared tins. Bake in a preheated moderately hot oven (190°C/375°F or Gas Mark 5) for 25 minutes or until well risen and golden. Turn out onto a wire rack, remove the paper linings and leave to cool.
To freeze: wrap the cakes individually in cling film, then pack in a freezer bag. Seal, label and freeze.
To thaw and serve: remove wrappings and thaw at room temperature for 4 hours. Sandwich the cakes together with the jam and whipped cream, then sprinkle icing (confectioners') sugar over the top of the cake before serving.
SERVES 8 to 10

CHOCOLATE VICTORIA SANDWICH (LAYER CAKE)

Make as for plain Victoria Sandwich (see page 277),substituting 25 g/1 oz cocoa powder (¼ cup unsweetened cocoa) for 25 g/1 oz/¼ cup flour. Omit the jam from filling.

Freeze, thaw and serve as for plain Victoria Sandwich.

SERVES 8 to 10

CHOCOLATE WHISKED SPONGE

Make as for Whisked Sponge Cake, using 50 g/2 oz/½ cup flour and 25 g/1 oz/¼ cup cocoa powder (unsweetened cocoa) instead of the 75 g/3 oz/¾ cup flour.

Freeze, thaw and serve as for Whisked Sponge Cake.

SERVES 6

WHISKED SPONGE CAKE

METRIC/IMPERIAL

3 eggs
100 g/4 oz caster sugar
75 g/3 oz flour
3 × 15 ml spoons/3 tablespoons jam
150 ml/¼ pint double cream, whipped
sugar for sprinkling, to finish

AMERICAN

3 eggs
½ cup superfine sugar
¾ cup flour
3 tablespoons jam
⅔ cup heavy cream, whipped
sugar for sprinkling, to finish

Grease two 18 cm/7 inch sandwich tins (layer cake pans) and line with greased greaseproof paper on non-stick parchment.

Put the eggs and sugar in a heatproof bowl, stand over a pan of gently simmering water and beat until thick and creamy. Remove from the heat, beat for a further 2 minutes, then sift in the flour and fold in carefully.

Divide the mixture between the prepared tins and bake in a preheated moderately hot oven (190°C/375°F or Gas Mark 5) for 25 to 30 minutes until firm to the touch. Turn out onto a wire rack, remove the paper linings and leave the cakes to cool.

Sandwich the cakes together with the jam and whipped cream.

To freeze: open (flash) freeze until firm, wrap in cling film, then pack in a freezer bag. Seal, label and return to the freezer.

To thaw and serve: remove wrappings and place the cake on a serving platter. Thaw overnight in the refrigerator, then sprinkle the top of the cake with sugar.

SERVES 6

LEMON CREAM SPONGE

METRIC/IMPERIAL

For the cake:
6 eggs, separated
175 g/6 oz sugar
2 × 15 ml spoons/2 tablespoons water
finely grated rind of 1 lemon
pinch of salt
75 g/3 oz flour
25 g/1 oz cornflour
For the cream topping:
1 egg
150 g/5 oz sugar
25 g/1 oz cornflour
juice of 1½ lemons
300 ml/½ pint double cream, lightly whipped

AMERICAN

For the cake:
6 eggs, separated
¾ cup sugar
2 tablespoons water
finely grated rind of 1 lemon
pinch of salt
¾ cup flour
¼ cup cornstarch
For the cream topping:
1 egg
⅔ cup sugar
¼ cup cornstarch
juice of 1½ lemons
1¼ cups heavy cream, lightly whipped

Put the egg yolks, sugar, water, lemon rind and salt in a bowl and beat together until thick, white and fluffy. Sift the flour and cornflour (cornstarch) together, then stir lightly into the egg and sugar mixture. Beat the egg whites until stiff and fold in until evenly blended.

Divide the mixture equally between three buttered and floured 20 cm/8 inch round cake tins. Bake in a preheated moderate oven (180°C/350°F or Gas Mark 4) for 40 to 50 minutes or until well risen and light golden brown. Leave to cool in the tins for 15 minutes, then turn out onto a wire rack and leave to cool completely.

To make the cream topping: put the egg, sugar and cornflour (cornstarch) in a heatproof bowl and beat until light and fluffy. Beat in the lemon juice, then stand the bowl over a pan of gently simmering water and stir until the mixture thickens and becomes clear. Remove from the heat, leave until cold and thick, then beat into the whipped cream. Sandwich the cakes together with some of the cream mixture, then cover the top of the cake with the remainder.
To freeze: open (flash) freeze until firm, then pack in a rigid container. Seal, label and return to the freezer.
To thaw and serve: remove wrappings and place the cake on a serving platter. Thaw at room temperature for 4 hours.
SERVES 8

GENOESE SPONGE

METRIC/IMPERIAL
75 g/3 oz flour
1 × 2.5 ml spoon/½ teaspoon baking powder
3 eggs
75 g/3 oz caster sugar
25 g/1 oz butter, melted
3 × 15 ml spoons/3 tablespoons raspberry jam
150 ml/¼ pint double cream, whipped
icing sugar for sprinkling, to finish

AMERICAN
¾ cup flour
½ teaspoon baking powder
3 eggs
⅜ cup sugar
2 tablespoons butter, melted
3 tablespoons raspberry jam
⅔ cup heavy cream, whipped
confectioners' sugar for sprinkling, to finish

Grease two 18 cm/7 inch sandwich tins (layer cake pans), line with greased greaseproof paper or non-stick parchment and dust lightly with flour.
Sift together the flour and baking powder. Put the eggs in a heatproof bowl, stand over a pan of gently simmering water and beat to mix. Add the sugar and beat again for 10 to 15 minutes until the mixture is thick and creamy. Remove from the heat and continue beating for 5 minutes. Fold in the melted butter and the sifted mixture a little at a time, until evenly blended.
Pour the mixture into the prepared tins. Bake in a preheated moderate oven (180°C/350°F or Gas Mark 4) for 20 to 25 minutes until golden brown and firm to the touch. Turn out onto a wire rack, remove the paper linings and leave the cakes to cool. Sandwich the cakes together with the jam and whipped cream.
To freeze: open (flash) freeze until firm, wrap in cling film, then pack in a freezer bag. Seal, label and return to the freezer.
To thaw and serve: remove wrappings and place on a serving platter. Thaw at room temperature for 4 hours. Sprinkle icing (confectioners') sugar over the top of the cake before serving.
SERVES 6

ORANGE SANDWICH (LAYER) CAKE

METRIC/IMPERIAL
112 g/4 oz butter, softened
112 g/4 oz caster sugar
finely grated rind and juice of 1 orange
2 eggs, beaten
112 g/4 oz self-raising flour
orange butter cream made with 100 g/4 oz icing sugar (see page 411)
extra caster sugar for sprinkling, to finish

AMERICAN
½ cup butter, softened
½ cup sugar
finely grated rind and juice of 1 orange
2 eggs, beaten
1 cup self-rising flour
orange butter cream made with scant 1 cup confectioners' sugar (see page 411)
extra sugar for sprinkling, to finish

Grease two 18 cm/7 inch sandwich tins (layer cake pans) and line the bottoms with greased greaseproof paper or non-stick parchment.
Put the butter, sugar and orange rind in a bowl, beat together until light and fluffy, then beat in the eggs a little at a time. Fold in the flour and the orange juice until evenly blended.
Spoon the mixture into the prepared tins and bake in a preheated moderate oven (180°C/350°F or Gas Mark 4) for 25 to 30 minutes until well risen and golden. Leave to cool in the tins for a few minutes, then turn out onto a wire rack. Remove the paper lining and leave to cool. Sandwich the cakes together with the butter cream.
To freeze: wrap in foil, then pack in a freezer bag. Seal, label and freeze.
To thaw and serve: thaw in the wrappings at room temperature for 4 hours, then remove wrappings and sprinkle (caster) sugar over the top of the cake.
SERVES 4

LEMON SWISS (JELLY) ROLL

METRIC/IMPERIAL
112 g/4 oz butter, softened
112 g/4 oz caster sugar
2 large eggs, beaten
112 g/4 oz self-raising flour
2 × 15 ml spoons/2 tablespoons lemon curd, warmed
icing sugar for sprinkling, to finish

AMERICAN
½ cup butter, softened
½ cup sugar
2 large eggs, beaten
1 cup self-rising flour
2 tablespoons lemon cheese, warmed
confectioners' sugar for sprinkling, to finish

Grease a 28 × 18 cm/11 × 7 inch Swiss roll tin (jelly roll pan) and line with greased greaseproof paper or non-stick parchment to come 1 cm/½ inch above the sides.
Put the butter and sugar in a bowl, beat together until light and fluffy, then beat in the eggs a little at a time. Fold in the flour until evenly blended, then spoon into the prepared tin.
Bake on the shelf above the centre of a preheated moderately hot oven (200°C/400°F or Gas Mark 6) for 10 minutes until firm to the touch.
Place a large sheet of greaseproof (waxed) paper on a damp tea (dish) towel and sprinkle with caster (superfine) sugar. Turn the cake out upside-down onto the paper and carefully peel off the paper lining. Trim 5 mm/¼ inch off the cake around the edges, then spread the lemon curd (cheese) over evenly. Roll up, then hold in position for a few minutes. Cool on a wire rack.
To freeze: wrap in cling film, then pack in a freezer bag. Seal, label and freeze.
To thaw and serve: remove wrappings and place the cake on a serving platter with the join underneath. Thaw at room temperature for 3 to 4 hours. Sprinkle lightly with icing (confectioners') sugar before serving.
SERVES 6

CHOCOLATE SWISS (JELLY) ROLL

METRIC/IMPERIAL
3 large eggs
75 g/3 oz caster sugar
a few drops of vanilla essence
65 g/2½ oz flour
1 × 15 ml spoon/1 tablespoon cocoa powder
1 × 15 ml spoon/1 tablespoon warm water
butter cream icing made with 100 g/4 oz butter
sugar, for sprinkling

AMERICAN
3 large eggs
⅜ cup superfine sugar
a few drops of vanilla extract
⅝ cup flour
1 tablespoon unsweetened cocoa powder
1 tablespoon warm water
butter cream icing made with ½ cup butter
sugar, for sprinkling

Grease a 35 × 25 cm/14 × 10 inch Swiss roll tin (jelly roll pan) and line with greased greaseproof paper of non-stick parchment to come 1 cm/½ inch above the sides.
Put the eggs, sugar and vanilla essence (extract) in a heatproof bowl, stand over a pan of gently simmering water and beat until thick and creamy. Remove from the heat, beat for a further 2 minutes, then sift in the flour and cocoa and fold in carefully with the warm water.
Spoon the mixture into the prepared tin and bake in a preheated moderately hot oven (200°C/400°F or Gas Mark 6) for 10 to 12 minutes until firm to the touch.
Place a large sheet of greaseproof (waxed) paper on a damp tea (dish) towel and sprinkle with caster (superfine) sugar. Turn the cake out upside-down onto the paper and carefully peel off the paper lining. Trim 5 mm/¼ inch off the cake around the edges, then fold over and roll up with the paper inside. Hold in position for a few minutes, leave to cool on a wire rack, then unroll the cake and remove the paper.
Spread the cake with the icing, roll up with the join underneath and sprinkle with sugar.
To freeze: wrap in cling film, then pack in a freezer bag. Seal, label and freeze.
To thaw and serve: remove wrappings and place on a serving platter. Thaw at room temperature for 2 hours.
SERVES 6 to 8

RASPBERRY AND CREAM SWISS (JELLY) ROLL

METRIC/IMPERIAL
For the cake:
3 eggs, beaten
75 g/3 oz caster sugar
75 g/3 oz flour
1 × 15 ml spoon/1 tablespoon warm water
a few drops of vanilla essence
caster sugar for sprinkling
For the filling:
175 g/6 oz raspberries, crushed
150 ml/¼ pint double cream, whipped
2 × 15 ml spoons/2 tablespoons caster sugar

AMERICAN

For the cake:

3 eggs, beaten

$\frac{3}{8}$ cup sugar

$\frac{3}{4}$ cup flour

1 tablespoon warm water

a few drops of vanilla extract

sugar for sprinkling

For the filling:

6 oz raspberries, crushed

$\frac{2}{3}$ cup heavy cream, whipped

2 tablespoons sugar

Grease a 30 × 23 cm/12 × 9 inch Swiss roll tin (jelly roll pan) and line with greased greaseproof paper or non-stick parchment to come 1 cm/$\frac{1}{2}$ inch above the sides.

Put the eggs and sugar in a bowl and beat together until light and fluffy and the mixture falls away from the beater in ribbons. Sift in the flour, then fold in with the water and vanilla essence (extract) until evenly blended.

Spoon the mixture into the prepared tin. Bake on the shelf above the centre of a preheated hot oven (220°C/425°F or Gas Mark 7) for 8 to 10 minutes until springy to the touch.

Place a large sheet of greaseproof (waxed) paper on a damp tea (dish) towel and sprinkle with (caster) sugar. Turn the cake out upside-down onto the paper and carefully peel off the paper lining. Trim 5 mm/$\frac{1}{4}$ inch off the cake around the edges, then fold over and roll up with the paper inside. Hold in position for a few minutes, leave to cool on a wire rack, then unroll the cake and remove the paper.

To make the filling: put all the ingredients in a bowl and fold together lightly. Spread over the cake, then roll up carefully, keeping the join underneath.

To freeze: open (flash) freeze until firm, wrap in cling film, then pack in a freezer bag. Seal, label and return to the freezer.

To thaw and serve: remove wrappings and place on a serving platter. Thaw in the refrigerator overnight.

SERVES 6

PINK CLOUD BIRTHDAY CAKE

METRIC/IMPERIAL

175 g/6 oz butter, softened

175 g/6 oz caster sugar

3 eggs, beaten

175 g/6 oz self-raising flour

a few drops of pink food colouring

1 × 15 ml spoon/1 tablespoon cocoa powder

1 × 15 ml spoon/1 tablespoon milk

40 marshmallows

5 × 15 ml spoons/5 tablespoons strawberry jam, warmed and sieved

2 × 5 ml spoons/2 teaspoons lemon juice

cake candles, to finish

AMERICAN

$\frac{3}{4}$ cup butter, softened

$\frac{3}{4}$ cup sugar

3 eggs, beaten

$1\frac{1}{2}$ cups self-rising flour

a few drops of pink food coloring

1 tablespoon unsweetened cocoa powder

1 tablespoon milk

40 marshmallows

$\frac{1}{3}$ cup strawberry jam, warmed and strained

2 teaspoons lemon juice

cake candles, to finish

Grease two 18 cm/7 inch sandwich tins (layer cake pans) and line the bottoms with greased greaseproof paper or non-stick parchment.

Put the butter and sugar in a bowl and beat together until light and fluffy. Beat in the eggs a little at a time, then fold in the flour. Divide the cake mixture into two equal halves and beat the food colouring into one half. Mix the cocoa and milk together, then beat into the other half. Spoon into the prepared tins, alternating spoonfuls of pink mixture with spoonsfuls of chocolate. Bake in a preheated moderately hot oven (190°C/375°F or Gas Mark 5) for 20 minutes. Turn out onto a wire rack, remove the paper linings, then leave the cake to cool completely.

Put the marshmallows in a pan, reserving a few for the decoration, add 3 × 15 ml spoons/3 tablespoons jam and the lemon juice and heat gently until the marshmallows have melted, stirring constantly. Leave until cool and just beginning to set, then spread about half of the mixture on top of one of the cakes and spread the remaining jam on top of the other.

Sandwich the two cakes together, then spread the top of the cake with the remaining marshmallow mixture. Cut the reserved marshmallows into pieces according to the age of the child, then press around the edge of the cake.

To freeze: open (flash) freeze until firm, then pack in a rigid container. Seal, label and return to the freezer.

To thaw and serve: place the cake on a serving platter and thaw at room temperature for 4 hours. Press a candle into the centre of each piece of marshmallow.

SERVES 8 to 10

SHAGGY DOG BIRTHDAY CAKE

METRIC/IMPERIAL

butter cream icing made with 225 g/½ lb butter
1 chocolate Swiss roll (see page 280)
1 chocolate mini Swiss roll
2 chocolate buttons
1 glacé cherry
1 chocolate finger biscuit
cake candles, to finish

AMERICAN

butter cream icing made with 1 cup butter
1 chocolate jelly roll (see page 280)
1 chocolate mini jelly roll
2 chocolate buttons
1 candied cherry
1 chocolate finger cookie
cake candles, to finish

Spread a little butter cream on an oblong cake board and on one end of the large Swiss (jelly) roll. Stick the mini roll onto the creamed end to form the head, then place on the cake board.
Cover both the rolls with butter cream and cover 2.5 cm/1 inch of the board on both sides of the dog. Mark lines with a fork from the top of the roll down to the board, flicking up the ends for the dog's coat. Press the chocolate buttons into position for the eyes and the glacé (candied) cherry for the nose. Stick the finger biscuit (cookie) in position for the tail.
To freeze: open (flash) freeze until firm, then pack in a rigid container. Seal, label and return to the freezer.
To thaw and serve: place on a serving platter and thaw at room temperature for 2 hours. Press the candles along the dog's back.
SERVES 8 to 10

MOCHA CAKE

METRIC/IMPERIAL

For the cake:
1 × 15 ml spoon/1 tablespoon cocoa powder
2 × 15 ml spoons/2 tablespoons hot water
112 g/4 oz butter, softened
150 g/5 oz caster sugar
2 eggs, beaten
112 g/4 oz self-raising flour
1 × 15 ml spoon/1 tablespoon milk

To decorate:
225 g/½ lb almond paste
75 g/3 oz butter, softened
225 g/½ lb icing sugar, sifted
1 × 15 ml spoon/1 tablespoon milk
2 × 5 ml spoons/2 teaspoons coffee essence
25 g/1 oz walnuts, chopped
5 walnut halves

AMERICAN

For the cake:
1 tablespoon unsweetened cocoa powder
2 tablespoons hot water
½ cup butter, softened
⅔ cup sugar
2 eggs, beaten
½ cup self-rising flour
1 tablespoon milk
To decorate:
½ lb almond paste
⅜ cup butter, softened
scant 2 cups confectioners' sugar
1 tablespoon milk
2 teaspoons strong black coffee
¼ cup chopped walnuts
5 walnut halves

Grease a 20 cm/8 inch cake tin and line the bottom with greased greaseproof paper or non-stick parchment.
Mix the cocoa to a paste with the hot water, then leave to cool. Put the butter and sugar in a bowl, beat together until light and fluffy, then beat in the cocoa paste. Beat in the eggs a little at a time, then fold in the flour and the milk.
Spoon the mixture into the prepared tin and bake in a preheated moderate oven (160°C/325°F or Gas Mark 3) for 35 to 40 minutes. Turn out onto a wire rack, remove the paper and leave to cool.
To decorate: roll out the almond paste until thin, then cut half into 10 × 7.5 cm/3 inch triangles. Form the remaining half into small balls. Leave to dry for 2 to 3 hours.
Put the butter and half the icing (confectioners') sugar in a bowl, beat together until light and fluffy, then add the remaining sugar, the milk and coffee and beat until smooth and creamy. Spread the icing over the cake to cover it completely, then roll the sides in the chopped walnuts. Decorate the top of the cake with the almond triangles and balls, the walnut halves and any remaining icing piped into star shapes.
To freeze: open (flash) freeze until firm, then pack in a rigid container. Seal, label and return to the freezer.
To thaw and serve: place on a serving platter and thaw at room temperature for 4 hours.
SERVES 6

PINEAPPLE AND GINGER UPSIDE-DOWN CAKE

METRIC/IMPERIAL

For the topping:

25 g/1 oz butter, softened
25 g/1 oz brown sugar
1 × 275 g/10 oz can pineapple rings, drained
4 glacé cherries, halved

For the cake:

112 g/4 oz butter
112 g/4 oz soft brown sugar
2 eggs, beaten
112 g/4 oz self-raising flour
2 × 5 ml spoons/2 teaspoons ground ginger
a little pineapple juice

AMERICAN

For the topping:

2 tablespoons butter, softened
2 tablespoons brown sugar
1 × 10 oz can pineapple rings, drained
4 candied cherries, halved

For the cake:

½ cup butter
⅔ cup light brown sugar
2 eggs, beaten
1 cup self-rising flour
2 teaspoons ground ginger
a little pineapple juice

Grease a 20 cm/8 inch sandwich tin (layer cake pan) and line the bottom with greased greaseproof paper or non-stick parchment.

To make the topping: put the butter and sugar in a bowl, beat together until light and fluffy, then spread over the paper lining. Arrange the pineapple rings on top of the creamed mixture and place a cherry half in the centre of each ring.

To make the cake: put the butter and sugar in a bowl, beat together until light and fluffy, then beat in the eggs a little at a time. Sift the flour and ginger together and fold into the creamed mixture until evenly blended, adding a little pineapple juice to give a soft dropping consistency.

Spread the cake mixture over the pineapple rings and smooth the top. Bake in a preheated moderately hot oven (190°C/375°F or Gas Mark 5) for 30 to 40 minutes until firm to the touch. Turn out onto a wire rack, remove the paper lining, then leave to cool.

To freeze: open (flash) freeze until firm, wrap in cling film, then pack in a freezer bag. Seal, label and return to the freezer.

To thaw and serve: remove wrappings and place on a serving platter. Thaw at room temperature for 4 hours.

SERVES 6 to 8

LEMON MIMOSA CAKE

METRIC/IMPERIAL

For the cake:

100 g/4 oz butter, softened
100 g/4 oz caster sugar
7 × 15 ml spoons/7 tablespoons lemon curd
finely grated rind of ½ lemon
2 large eggs, beaten
225 g/½ lb self-raising flour

For the icing (to finish):

100 g/4 oz icing sugar, sifted
approx 2 × 5 ml spoons/2 teaspoons lemon juice
mimosa balls and candied angelica, to decorate

AMERICAN

For the cake:

½ cup butter, softened
½ cup sugar
7 tablespoons lemon cheese
finely grated rind of ½ lemon
2 large eggs, beaten
2 cups self-rising flour

For the icing (to finish):

scant 1 cup sifted confectioners' sugar
approx 2 teaspoons lemon juice
mimosa balls and candied angelica, to decorate

Grease an 18 cm/7 inch round cake tin and line the bottom with greased greaseproof paper or non-stick parchment.

Put the butter and sugar in a bowl and beat together until light and fluffy. Beat in 3 × 15 ml spoons/3 tablespoons lemon curd (cheese) and the lemon rind, then beat in the eggs a little at a time. Fold in the flour until evenly blended, then spoon the mixture into the prepared cake tin and smooth the top.

Bake in a preheated moderate oven (160°C/325°F or Gas Mark 3) for 55 minutes until a skewer inserted in the centre of the cake comes out clean. Leave to cool in the tin for 5 minutes, then turn out onto a wire rack. Remove the paper lining, then leave the cake to cool completely. Slice the cake in half and spread one half with the remaining lemon curd (cheese). Sandwich the two halves together.

To freeze: open (flash) freeze until firm, wrap in cling film, then pack in a freezer bag. Seal, label and return to the freezer.

To thaw and serve: remove wrappings, place the cake on a serving platter and thaw at room temperature for 4 hours.

Mix the icing (confectioners') sugar with enough lemon juice to give a fairly stiff consistency, then spread over the cake and decorate immediately with mimosa balls and diamonds of candied angelica. Leave to set before serving.

SERVES 6

SIMNEL CAKE

METRIC/IMPERIAL

For the cake:

225 g/½ lb flour
3 × 5 ml spoons/3 teaspoons ground mixed spice
1 × 2.5 ml spoon/½ teaspoon baking powder
175 g/6 oz butter, softened
175 g/6 oz soft brown sugar
3 large eggs
225 g/½ lb mixed dried fruit
50 g/2 oz glacé cherries, quartered
50 g/2 oz chopped candied peel
25 g/1 oz blanched almonds, chopped
1 × 15 ml spoon/1 tablespoon milk
100 g/4 oz almond paste

For the topping:

1 × 15 ml spoon/1 tablespoon apricot jam, warmed and sieved
225 g/½ lb almond paste
a little egg white, lightly beaten
25 g/1 oz icing sugar, sifted
a little water
coloured eggs, chicks and ribbon, to finish

AMERICAN

For the cake:

2 cups flour
1½ teaspoons grated nutmeg
1½ teaspoons ground allspice and cloves, mixed
½ teaspoon baking powder
¾ cup butter, softened
1 cup light brown sugar
3 large eggs
1½ cups mixed dried fruit
¼ cup quartered candied cherries
¼ cup chopped candied peel
¼ cup chopped blanched almonds
1 tablespoon milk
¼ lb almond paste

For the topping:

1 tablespoon apricot jam, warmed and strained
½ lb almond paste
a little egg white, lightly beaten
¼ cup sifted confectioners' sugar
a little water
colored eggs, chicks and ribbon, to finish

Grease a deep 18 cm/7 inch round cake tin and line with greased greaseproof paper or non-stick parchment.

Sift the flour, spice(s) and baking powder into a bowl, add the remaining cake ingredients, except the almond paste, and beat for 2 to 3 minutes until well mixed. Spoon half the mixture into the prepared tin.

Roll out the almond paste to an 18 cm/7 inch circle and place on top of the mixture in the tin. Spoon the remaining cake mixture on top of the almond paste and smooth the surface. Bake in a preheated moderate oven (160°C/325°F or Gas Mark 3) for 2 to 2½ hours until a skewer inserted in the centre of the cake comes out clean. Leave to cool in the tin, then turn out onto a wire rack and remove the paper lining.

To make the topping: brush the top of the cake with the apricot jam. Roll out half the almond paste to an 18 cm/7 inch circle and place on top of the cake. Form the remaining almond paste into 11 small balls and place around the edge of the cake, securing them with egg white. Put the cake under a medium grill (broiler) and brown the almond paste lightly. Mix the icing (confectioners') sugar with water and pour carefully over the centre of the cake. Leave until set.

To freeze: open (flash) freeze until firm, then pack in a rigid container. Seal, label and return to the freezer.

To thaw and serve: remove wrappings and place on a serving platter. Thaw at room temperature for at least 4 hours, then decorate the top of the cake with coloured eggs and chicks and tie a ribbon around the middle.

SERVES 8

SOMERSET APPLE CAKE

METRIC/IMPERIAL

225 g/½ lb flour
1 × 2.5 ml spoon/½ teaspoon ground mixed spice
75 g/3 oz butter
75 g/3 oz caster sugar
450 g/1 lb cooking apples, peeled, cored and finely chopped
1 egg, beaten
a little milk
sugar for sprinkling, to finish

AMERICAN

2 cups flour
¼ teaspoon grated nutmeg
¼ teaspoon ground allspice and cloves, mixed
⅜ cup butter
⅜ cup sugar
1 lb baking apples, peeled, cored and finely chopped
1 egg, beaten
a little milk
sugar for sprinkling, to finish

Grease a 20 cm/8 inch cake tin and line with greased greaseproof paper or non-stick parchment.
Sift the flour and spice(s) into a bowl, add the butter in pieces and rub into the flour until the mixture resembles fine breadcrumbs. Stir in the sugar and apples, then stir in the egg and enough milk to give a soft dropping consistency.
Spoon the mixture into the prepared tin and bake in a preheated moderately hot oven (190°C/375°F or Gas Mark 5) for 1 to 1¼ hours until firm to the touch. Turn out onto a wire rack, remove the paper lining and leave to cool.
To freeze: wrap in cling film, then pack in a freezer bag. Seal, label and freeze.
To thaw and serve: remove wrappings and place on a serving platter. Thaw at room temperature for 4 hours, then sprinkle sugar over the top of the cake.
SERVES 6 to 8

DARK CHOCOLATE CAKE

METRIC/IMPERIAL
For the cake:
112 g/4 oz butter, softened
112 g/4 oz caster sugar
112 g/4 oz self-raising flour
75 g/3 oz ground almonds
50 g/2 oz cocoa powder
25 g/1 oz drinking chocolate powder
2 eggs, lightly beaten
2 × 15 ml spoons/2 tablespoons coffee essence
For the butter cream icing:
50 g/2 oz butter
100 g/4 oz icing sugar, sifted
50 g/2 oz plain chocolate, melted
2 × 5 ml spoons/2 teaspoons coffee essence
To finish:
chocolate glacé icing made with 100 g/4 oz icing sugar
a few walnut halves

AMERICAN
For the cake:
½ cup butter, softened
½ cup sugar
1 cup self-rising flour
¾ cup ground almonds
½ cup unsweetened cocoa powder
3 tablespoons sweetened cocoa powder
2 eggs, lightly beaten
2 tablespoons strong black coffee
For the butter cream icing:
¼ cup butter
scant 1 cup sifted confectioners' sugar
⅓ cup semi-sweet chocolate pieces, melted
2 teaspoons strong black coffee
To finish:
chocolate glacé icing made with scant 1 cup confectioners' sugar
a few walnut halves

Put the butter and sugar in a bowl and beat together until light and fluffy. Blend together the dry ingredients, fold a little at a time into the creamed mixture alternately with the eggs, then stir in the coffee. Spoon the mixture into a greased 20 cm/8 inch loose-bottomed cake tin or springform pan. Bake in a preheated moderate oven (180°C/350°F or Gas Mark 4) for 45 minutes. Leave to cool in the tin for 10 minutes, then turn out onto a wire rack to cool completely.
To make the icing: put the butter and icing (confectioners') sugar in a bowl, beat together until light and fluffy, then beat in the chocolate and coffee. Slice the cooled cake in half and sandwich together with the butter cream icing.
To freeze: open (flash) freeze until firm, wrap in cling film, then pack in a freezer bag. Seal, label and return to the freezer.
To thaw and serve: remove wrappings, place on a serving platter and thaw at room temperature for 4 hours. Spread the glacé icing over the top of the cake and smooth the surface with a palette knife. Decorate with the nuts, then leave to set before serving.
SERVES 4 to 6

PARKIN

METRIC/IMPERIAL

450 g/1 lb flour
1 × 5 ml spoon/1 teaspoon bicarbonate of soda
1 × 5 ml spoon/1 teaspoon salt
2 × 5 ml spoons/2 teaspoons ground ginger
450 g/1 lb rolled oats
225 g/$\frac{1}{2}$ lb butter
250 ml/8 fl oz black treacle
250 ml/8 fl oz golden syrup
4 × 15 ml spoons/4 tablespoons clear honey
2 × 15 ml spoons/2 tablespoons soft brown sugar
350 ml/12 fl oz milk

AMERICAN

4 cups flour
1 teaspoon baking soda
1 teaspoon salt
2 teaspoons ground ginger
4$\frac{1}{2}$ cups rolled oats
1 cup butter
1 cup molasses
1 cup light corn syrup
$\frac{1}{4}$ cup clear honey
2 tablespoons light brown sugar
1$\frac{1}{2}$ cups milk

Sift the flour, soda, salt and ginger into a bowl and stir in the rolled oats. Put the butter, treacle (molasses), syrup, honey and sugar in a pan and heat gently until melted, stirring constantly. Remove from the heat, add to the flour mixture with the milk and beat well to mix.

Pour the mixture into two greased 23 cm/9 inch square cake tins. Bake in a preheated moderate oven (180°C/350°F or Gas Mark 4) for 45 to 50 minutes or until firm to the touch. Leave to cool in the tins for 15 minutes, then turn out onto a wire rack to cool completely. Store the parkins in an airtight tin for 1 week before freezing.

To freeze: wrap individually in cling film, then pack in a freezer bag. Seal, label and freeze.

To thaw and serve: thaw in the wrappings at room temperature for 4 hours.

SERVES 10

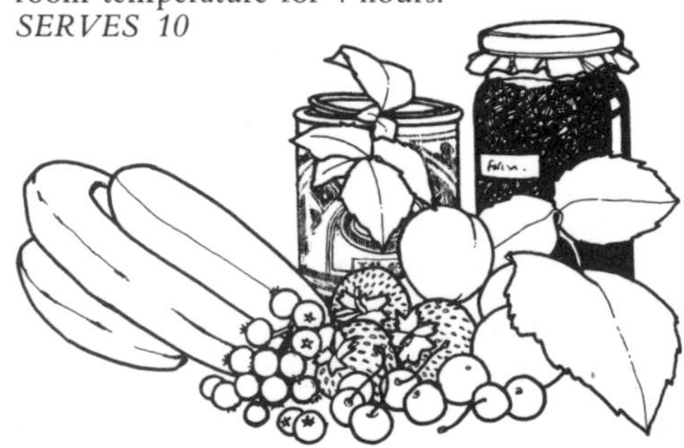

RICH FRUIT CAKE

METRIC/IMPERIAL

225 g/$\frac{1}{2}$ lb butter, softened
225 g/$\frac{1}{2}$ lb dark brown sugar
1 × 15 ml spoon/1 tablespoon black treacle
4 eggs, beaten
275 g/10 oz flour
2 × 5 ml spoons/2 teaspoons ground mixed spice
225 g/$\frac{1}{2}$ lb seedless raisins
100 g/4 oz currants
225 g/$\frac{1}{2}$ lb sultanas
100 g/4 oz glacé cherries, chopped
3 × 15 ml spoons/3 tablespoons undiluted orange squash

AMERICAN

1 cup butter, softened
1$\frac{1}{3}$ cups dark brown sugar
1 tablespoon molasses
4 eggs, beaten
2$\frac{1}{2}$ cups flour
1 teaspoon grated nutmeg
1 teaspoon ground allspice and cloves, mixed
1$\frac{1}{2}$ cups seedless raisins
$\frac{3}{4}$ cup currants
1$\frac{1}{2}$ cups seedless white raisins
$\frac{1}{2}$ cup chopped candied cherries
3 tablespoons undiluted orange squash

Grease a deep 23 cm/9 inch round cake tin and line with greased greaseproof paper or non-stick parchment.

Put the butter and sugar in a bowl, beat together until light and fluffy, then beat in the black treacle (molasses). Beat in the eggs a little at a time. Sift the flour and spice(s) together and fold into the creamed mixture, reserving 1 × 15 ml spoon/1 tablespoon.

Put the dried fruit in a bowl with the reserved flour and turn well so that the fruits remain separate and do not stick together. Stir into the cake mixture with the orange squash, then spoon into the prepared tin.

Bake in a preheated moderate oven (160°C/325°F or Gas Mark 3) for 1 hour, then reduce the heat to cool (150°C/300°F or Gas Mark 2) and bake for a further 2 hours. Leave to cool in the tin for 10 minutes. Turn out onto a wire rack, remove the paper lining and leave the cake to cool completely.

To freeze: wrap in cling film, then pack in a freezer bag. Seal, label and freeze.

To thaw and serve: thaw in the wrappings at room temperature for 6 hours.

SERVES 8 to 10

MARBLE RING CAKE

METRIC/IMPERIAL

112 g/4 oz butter, softened
112 g/4 oz caster sugar
2 × 5 ml spoons/2 teaspoons honey
2 large eggs, beaten
0.5 × 2.5 ml spoon/¼ teaspoon vanilla essence
200 g/7 oz self-raising flour
25 g/1 oz cornflour
1 × 2.5 ml spoon/½ teaspoon baking powder
75 g/3 oz icing sugar, sifted
120 ml/4 fl oz milk
a few drops of pink food colouring
2 × 5 ml spoons/2 teaspoons cocoa powder mixed to a paste with 1 × 5 ml spoon/1 teaspoon milk
chocolate glacé icing made with 100 g/4 oz icing sugar, to finish

AMERICAN

½ cup butter, softened
½ cup sugar
2 teaspoons honey
2 large eggs, beaten
¼ teaspoon vanilla extract
1¾ cups self-rising flour
¼ cup cornstarch
½ teaspoon baking powder
¾ cup sifted confectioners' sugar
½ cup milk
a few drops pink food coloring
2 teaspoons unsweetened cocoa powder mixed to a paste with 1 teaspoon milk
chocolate glacé icing made with scant 1 cup confectioners' sugar, to finish

Put the butter in pieces in a warm bowl. Add the sugar and honey and beat together until light and fluffy. Beat in the eggs a little at a time, then stir in the vanilla essence (extract). Sift together the flour, cornflour (cornstarch), baking powder and icing (confectioners') sugar and fold half into the creamed mixture with half the milk. Fold in the remaining sifted mixture and enough milk to give a soft batter.

Divide the batter into 3 equal portions. Stir the pink food colouring into one portion, the cocoa paste into another portion and leave the third portion white. Spoon into a greased and floured 18 cm/7 inch ring mould, alternating spoonfuls of pink mixture with spoonfuls of chocolate and white.

Bake in a preheated moderate oven (180°C/350°F or Gas Mark 4) for 40 minutes or until a skewer inserted in the centre of the cake comes out clean. Turn out onto a wire rack and leave to cool.

To freeze: wrap in cling film, then pack in a freezer bag. Seal, label and freeze.

To thaw and serve: remove wrappings and place on a serving platter. Thaw at room temperature for 4 hours. Spread the glacé icing over the cake and smooth the surface with a palette knife. Leave to set before serving.

SERVES 8

FUDGE CAKE

METRIC/IMPERIAL

150 g/5 oz butter, softened
400 g/14 oz caster sugar
2 eggs, beaten
1 × 5 ml spoon/1 teaspoon vanilla essence
75 g/3 oz plain chocolate, melted
225 g/½ lb flour
1.5 × 5 ml spoons/1½ teaspoons baking powder
pinch of salt
300 ml/½ pint water
chocolate butter cream icing made with 100 g/4 oz icing sugar, for the filling

AMERICAN

⅝ cup butter, softened
1¾ cups sugar
2 eggs, beaten
1 teaspoon vanilla extract
½ cup semi-sweet chocolate pieces, melted
2 cups flour
1½ teaspoons baking powder
pinch of salt
1¼ cups water
chocolate butter cream icing made with scant 1 cup confectioners' sugar, for the filling

Grease two 23 cm/9 inch sandwich tins (layer cake pans) and line with greased greaseproof paper or non-stick parchment.

Put the butter, sugar and eggs in a bowl, beat together until light and fluffy, then stir in the melted chocolate. Sift together the flour, baking powder and salt and beat into the creamed mixture alternately with the water.

Spoon the mixture into the prepared tins and bake in a preheated moderate oven (180°C/350°F or Gas Mark 4) for 30 minutes.

Turn out onto a wire rack and remove the paper linings. Leave to cool completely, then sandwich the cakes together with the chocolate butter cream icing.

To freeze: open (flash) freeze until firm, wrap in cling film, then pack in a freezer bag. Seal, label and return to the freezer.

To thaw and serve: remove wrappings and place on a serving platter. Thaw at room temperature for 4 hours.

SERVES 8 to 10

YULETIDE CHOCOLATE LOG

METRIC/IMPERIAL

For the cake:

100 g/4 oz self-raising flour
1 × 15 ml spoon/1 tablespoon drinking chocolate powder
100 g/4 oz butter, softened
100 g/4 oz caster sugar
2 large eggs, beaten

For the icing:

2 × 15 ml spoons/2 tablespoons cocoa powder
2 × 15 ml spoons/2 tablespoons water
100 g/4 oz butter, softened
250 g/9 oz icing sugar, sifted
1 × 15 ml spoon/1 tablespoon milk

To finish:

icing sugar, for dusting
a few sprigs of holly
plastic robins, etc

AMERICAN

For the cake:

1 cup self-rising flour
1 tablespoon sweetened cocoa powder
½ cup butter, softened
½ cup sugar
2 large eggs, beaten

For the icing:

2 tablespoons unsweetened cocoa powder
2 tablespoons water
½ cup butter, softened
2 cups sifted confectioners' sugar
1 tablespoon milk

To finish:

confectioners' sugar, for dusting
a few sprigs of holly
plastic robins, etc

Grease a 28 × 18 cm/11 × 7 inch Swiss roll tin (jelly roll pan) and line with greased greaseproof paper or non-stick parchment to come 1 cm/½ inch above the sides.

Sift the flour and cocoa into a bowl. Add the remaining cake ingredients and beat for 2 to 3 minutes until well mixed. Spread the mixture evenly in the prepared tin, then bake on the shelf above the centre of a preheated moderately hot oven (200°C/400°F or Gas Mark 6) for 10 to 12 minutes until firm to the touch.

Place a large sheet of greaseproof (waxed) paper on a damp tea (dish) towel and sprinkle with (caster) sugar. Turn the cake out upside down onto the paper and carefully peel off the paper lining. Trim 5 mm/¼ inch off the cake around the edges, then fold over and roll up with the paper inside. Hold in position for a few minutes, leave to cool on a wire rack, then unroll the cake and remove the paper.

To make the icing: put all the ingredients in a bowl and beat well together until very smooth. Spread the cake with a quarter of the icing, then roll up to form a log shape with the join underneath. Spread the remaining icing over the log to cover it completely and roughen the surface with the prongs of a fork.

To freeze: open (flash) freeze until firm, wrap in cling film, then pack in a freezer bag. Seal, label and return to the freezer.

To thaw and serve: remove wrappings and place on a silver cake board. Thaw at room temperature for 3 to 4 hours, then dust lightly with icing (confectioners') sugar and decorate with holly and robins as liked.

SERVES 6

YULETIDE MOCHA ROLL

Make as for Yuletide Chocolate Log (see above), substituting 3 × 15 ml spoons/3 tablespoons very strong black coffee for the cocoa and water in the icing.

Freeze, thaw and serve as for Yuletide Chocolate Log.

SERVES 6

YULETIDE ORANGE ROLL

Make as for Yuletide Chocolate Log (see above), substituting the finely grated rind of 1 orange for the drinking chocolate powder (sweetened cocoa) in the cake, and 2 × 15 ml spoons/ 2 tablespoons orange juice for the cocoa, water and milk in the icing. Decorate with slices of crystallized (candied) orange instead of the holly and robins.

Freeze, thaw and serve as for Yuletide Chocolate Log.

SERVES 6

COFFEE AND CHOCOLATE MARBLE CAKE

METRIC/IMPERIAL

225 g/½ lb butter, softened
225 g/½ lb caster sugar
1 × 2.5 ml spoon/½ teaspoon vanilla essence
3 eggs, beaten
275 g/10 oz self-raising flour
75 g/3 oz plain chocolate, melted
1 × 15 ml spoon/1 tablespoon instant coffee powder
chocolate butter cream icing made with 100 g/4 oz butter, to finish

AMERICAN

1 cup butter, softened
1 cup sugar
½ teaspoon vanilla extract
3 eggs, beaten
2½ cups self-rising flour
½ cup semi-sweet chocolate pieces, melted
1 tablespoon instant coffee powder
chocolate butter cream icing made with ½ cup butter, to finish

Grease a deep 20 cm/8 inch round cake tin with greased greaseproof paper or non-stick parchment.

Put the butter, sugar and vanilla essence (extract) in a bowl and beat together until light and fluffy. Beat in the eggs a little at a time, then gradually fold in the flour until evenly blended. Divide the cake mixture into two equal halves. Stir the melted chocolate into one half and the instant coffee powder into the other. Spoon into the prepared cake tin, alternating spoonfuls of chocolate mixture with spoonsfuls of coffee.

Bake in a preheated moderate oven (180°C/350°F or Gas Mark 4) for 40 minutes or until well risen and firm to the touch. Leave to cool in the tin for 5 minutes, then turn out onto a wire rack to cool completely. Slice the cake in half and sandwich together with the chocolate butter cream.

To freeze: wrap in foil, then pack in a freezer bag. Seal, label and freeze.

To thaw and serve: remove wrappings and thaw at room temperature for 2 to 3 hours.

SERVES 8

CRUNCHY CIDER CAKE

METRIC/IMPERIAL

For the cake:
225 g/½ lb self-raising flour
1 × 5 ml spoon/1 teaspoon baking powder
75 g/3 oz butter
75 g/3 oz caster sugar
finely grated rind of 1 lemon
1 egg, beaten
150 ml/¼ pint sweet cider
For the topping:
25 g/1 oz self-raising flour
50 g/2 oz soft brown sugar
25 g/1 oz butter, melted

AMERICAN

For the cake:
2 cups self-rising flour
1 teaspoon baking powder
⅜ cup butter
⅜ cup sugar
finely grated rind of 1 lemon
1 egg, beaten
⅔ cup cider
For the topping:
¼ cup self-rising flour
⅓ cup light brown sugar
2 tablespoons butter, melted

Grease a 20 cm/8 inch loose-bottomed cake tin and line the bottom with greased greaseproof paper or non-stick parchment.

Sift the flour and baking powder into a bowl, add the butter in pieces and rub into the flour until the mixture resembles fine breadcrumbs. Stir in the sugar and lemon rind, then add the egg and cider and stir well to mix. Spoon the mixture into the prepared tin and smooth the top.

To make the topping: put the flour and sugar in a bowl, then stir in the melted butter until the mixture is crumbly. Scatter over the top of the cake and bake in a preheated moderately hot oven (190°C/375°F or Gas Mark 5) for about 40 minutes until well risen and golden brown. Leave to cool in the tin for 5 minutes, then turn out onto a wire rack and remove the paper lining. Leave to cool completely.

To freeze: wrap in cling film, then pack in a freezer bag. Seal, label and freeze.

To thaw and serve: remove wrappings and place the cake on a serving platter. Thaw at room temperature for 4 hours.

SERVES 6 to 8

SPICY FRUIT CAKE

METRIC/IMPERIAL

225 g/½ lb self-raising flour
pinch of salt
175 g/6 oz butter
175 g/6 oz dark brown sugar
175 g/6 oz currants
175 g/6 oz sultanas
50 g/2 oz candied peel, chopped
50 g/2 oz glacé cherries, quartered
1 × 2.5 ml spoon/½ teaspoon ground ginger
1 × 2.5 ml spoon/½ teaspoon ground mixed spice
1 × 2.5 ml spoon/½ teaspoon ground cinnamon
3 eggs, beaten
2 × 15 ml spoons/2 tablespoons black treacle
a little milk, if necessary

AMERICAN

2 cups self-rising flour
pinch of salt
¾ cup butter
1 cup dark brown sugar
1 cup currants
1 cup seedless white raisins
⅓ cup chopped candied peel
¼ cup quartered candied cherries
½ teaspoon ground ginger
½ teaspoon ground allspice and cloves, mixed
½ teaspoon ground cinnamon
3 eggs, beaten
2 tablespoons molasses
a little milk, if necessary

Grease an 18 cm/7 inch square cake tin and line with greased greaseproof paper or non-stick parchment.

Sift the flour and salt into a bowl, add the butter in pieces and rub into the flour until the mixture resembles fine breadcrumbs. Stir in the sugar, dried fruit, candied peel and cherries, then the spices. Beat in the eggs and treacle (molasses) and a little milk to give a soft dropping consistency.

Spoon the mixture into the prepared tin. Bake in a preheated moderate oven (160°C/325°F or Gas Mark 3) for about 2 hours or until a skewer inserted in the centre of the cake comes out clean. Cover the top of the cake with greaseproof paper or foil if it becomes too brown during cooking. Cool in the tin for 10 minutes, then turn out onto a wire rack. Remove the paper lining and leave to cool completely.

To freeze: wrap in cling film, then pack in a freezer bag. Seal, label and freeze.

To thaw and serve: remove wrappings and place the cake on a serving platter. Thaw at room temperature for at least 4 hours.

SERVES 8

COCONUT CAKE

METRIC/IMPERIAL

175 g/6 oz butter, softened
175 g/6 oz sugar
3 eggs, beaten
225 g/½ lb self-raising flour
75 g/3 oz desiccated coconut
pinch of salt
2 × 15 ml spoons/2 tablespoons milk
4 × 15 ml spoons/4 tablespoons jam, for the filling
To finish:
2 × 15 ml spoons/2 tablespoons jam
2 × 15 ml spoons/2 tablespoons desiccated coconut
caster sugar, for sprinkling

AMERICAN

¾ cup butter, softened
¾ cup sugar
3 eggs, beaten
2 cups self-rising flour
1 cup shredded coconut
pinch of salt
2 tablespoons milk
¼ cup jam, for the filling
To finish:
2 tablespoons jam
2 tablespoons shredded coconut
sugar, for sprinkling

Grease a 20 cm/8 inch round cake tin and line with greased greaseproof paper or non-stick parchment.

Put the butter and sugar in a bowl and beat together until light and fluffy. Beat in the eggs a little at a time, then fold in the flour, coconut, salt and milk until evenly mixed.

Spoon the mixture into the prepared tin. Bake in a preheated moderate oven (180°C/350°F or Gas Mark 4) for 30 to 35 minutes or until well risen and golden brown. Turn out onto a wire rack, remove the paper lining, then leave the cake to cool. Slice the cake in half and sandwich together with the jam.

To freeze: wrap in cling film, then pack in a freezer bag. Seal, label and freeze.

To thaw and serve: remove wrappings and place on a serving platter. Thaw at room temperature for 4 hours. Spread the top of the cake with the jam, then scatter the coconut around the edge and sprinkle the centre with sugar.

SERVES 6

COFFEE CAKE

METRIC/IMPERIAL

For the cake:

112 g/4 oz butter, softened
112 g/4 oz caster sugar
1 × 15 ml spoon/1 tablespoon instant coffee powder dissolved in scant 1 × 15 ml spoon/1 tablespoon boiling water
75 g/3 oz flour
1 × 5 ml spoon/1 teaspoon baking powder
pinch of salt
2 eggs, well beaten
50 g/2 oz ground almonds

For the icing:

50 g/2 oz unsalted butter
100 g/4 oz icing sugar, sifted
1 × 15 ml spoon/1 tablespoon instant coffee powder dissolved in scant 1 × 15 ml spoon/1 tablespoon boiling water

AMERICAN

For the cake:

½ cup butter, softened
½ cup sugar
1 tablespoon instant coffee powder dissolved in scant 1 tablespoon boiling water
¾ cup flour
1 teaspoon baking powder
pinch of salt
2 eggs, well beaten
½ cup ground almonds

For the icing:

¼ cup sweet butter
scant 1 cup sifted confectioners' sugar
1 tablespoon instant coffee powder dissolved in scant 1 tablespoon boiling water

Put the butter and sugar in a bowl, beat together until light and fluffy, then beat in the dissolved coffee. Sift the flour with the baking powder and salt, then beat 2 × 15 ml spoons/2 tablespoons into the creamed mixture. Beat in the eggs a little at a time, then fold in the remaining flour and the ground almonds.

Divide the mixture between two buttered 18 cm/7 inch sandwich tins (layer cake pans). Bake in a preheated moderately hot oven (190°C/375°F or Gas Mark 5) for 25 minutes or until the cakes have shrunk away from the sides of the tins. Leave in the tins for 10 minutes, then turn out onto a wire rack to cool completely.

To make the icing: put the butter and icing (confectioners') sugar in a bowl and beat together until light and fluffy. Beat in the dissolved coffee. Sandwich the cakes together with half the icing, then spread the remaining icing on top of the cake. Draw a fork through the icing to make a wavy line pattern.

To freeze: open (flash) freeze until firm, then pack in a rigid container. Seal, label and return to the freezer.

To thaw and serve: place on a serving platter and thaw at room temperature for 2 to 3 hours.

SERVES 8

ZIKA CAKE

METRIC/IMPERIAL

175 g/6 oz butter, softened
175 g/6 oz caster sugar
3 eggs, beaten
finely grated rind and juice of 1 lemon
175 g/6 oz self-raising flour
50 g/2 oz walnuts, chopped
2 dessert apples, quartered and cored
7 walnut halves
3 × 15 ml spoons/3 tablespoons apricot ham, warmed and sieved

AMERICAN

¾ cup butter, softened
¾ cup sugar
3 eggs, beaten
finely grated rind and juice of 1 lemon
1½ cups self-rising flour
½ cup chopped walnuts
2 dessert apples, quartered and cored
7 walnut halves
3 tablespoons apricot jam, warmed and strained

Grease an 18 cm/7 inch round cake tin and line with greased greaseproof paper or non-stick parchment.

Put the butter and sugar in a bowl, beat together until light and fluffy, then beat in the eggs a little at a time with the lemon rind and juice. Fold in the flour and chopped nuts until evenly blended. Peel and chop one of the apple quarters and stir into the mixture.

Spoon the mixture into the prepared tin and smooth the top. Score each remaining apple quarter into three lengthways, then arrange on top of the cake, rounded side upwards. Arrange a walnut half between each apple quarter. Bake in a preheated moderate oven (180°C/350°F or Gas Mark 4) for 20 minutes until golden brown. Turn out onto a wire rack, brush the top of the cake with the apricot jam and leave to cool.

To freeze: open (flash) freeze until firm, wrap in cling film, then pack in a freezer bag. Seal, label and return to the freezer.

To thaw and serve: remove wrappings and place the cake on a serving platter. Thaw at room temperature for 4 hours.

SERVES 8 to 10

TIPSY DRIZZLE CAKE

METRIC/IMPERIAL

For the cake:

175 g/6 oz self-raising flour
1.5 × 5 ml spoons/1½ teaspoons baking powder
175 g/6 oz soft tub margarine
175 g/6 oz caster sugar
3 large eggs
2 × 15 ml spoons/2 tablespoons milk
finely grated rind of 2 oranges

For the orange syrup:

100 g/4 oz caster sugar
juice of 2 oranges
1–2 × 5 ml spoons/1–2 teaspoons Cointreau (optional)

To finish:

100 g/4 oz plain chocolate, broken into pieces
15 g/½ oz butter

AMERICAN

For the cake:

1½ cups self-rising flour
1½ teaspoons baking powder
¾ cup soft margarine
¾ cup sugar
3 large eggs
2 tablespoons milk
finely grated rind of 2 oranges

For the orange syrup:

½ cup sugar
juice of 2 oranges
1–2 teaspoons Cointreau (optional)

To finish:

⅔ cup semi-sweet chocolate pieces
1 tablespoon butter

Grease a 1 kg/2 lb loaf tin and line with greased greaseproof paper or non-stick parchment.
Sift the flour and baking powder into a bowl, add the remaining cake ingredients and beat for 2 to 3 minutes until well mixed. Spoon the mixture into the prepared tin and bake in a preheated moderate oven (180°C/350°F or Gas Mark 4) for 1 to 1¼ hours. Turn out onto a wire rack, remove the paper lining and leave to cool.
To make the orange syrup: put the sugar and orange juice in a pan and beat gently until the sugar has dissolved. Add the Cointeau (if using). Make diagonal slits across the top of the cake and slowly pour over the syrup until absorbed.
To freeze: wrap in cling film, then pack in a freezer bag. Seal, label and freeze.
To thaw and serve: remove wrappings, place the cake on a serving platter and thaw at room temperature for 4 hours. Put the chocolate and butter in a heatproof bowl, stand over a pan of gently simmering water and allow to melt, stirring once or twice. Pour over the top of the cake, letting it drip down the sides, then leave to set before serving.
SERVES 8

GÂTEAU AU CHOCOLAT NANCY

METRIC/IMPERIAL

For the cake:

150 g/5 oz butter, softened
100 g/4 oz bitter chocolate, melted
4 eggs, separated
1 × 15 ml spoon/1 tablespoon flour
40 g/1½ oz ground almonds
1 × 5 ml spoon/1 teaspoon vanilla essence

To finish:

150 ml/¼ pint double cream, whipped
icing sugar for sprinkling

AMERICAN

For the cake:

⅝ cup butter, softened
4 squares (¼ lb) unsweetened baking chocolate, melted
4 eggs, separated
1 tablespoon flour
⅓ cup ground almonds
1 teaspoon vanilla extract

To finish:

⅔ cup heavy cream, whipped
confectioners' sugar for sprinkling

Put the butter and melted chocolate in a bowl and blend together. Add the egg yolks and stir well to mix. Beat in the remaining ingredients, except the egg whites, until evenly blended.
Beat the egg whites until stiff, then fold into the cake mixture. Spoon into a buttered 20 cm/8 inch cake tin and bake in a preheated moderate oven (180°C/350°F or Gas Mark 4) for 30 minutes. Leave to cool slightly in the tin then turn out onto a wire rack to cool completely.
To freeze: open (flash) freeze until firm, wrap in cling film, then pack in a freezer bag. Seal, label and return to the freezer.
To thaw and serve: remove wrappings and thaw in the refrigerator overnight. Slice the cake in half, then sandwich together with the whipped cream. Sprinkle the icing (confectioners') sugar over the top of the cake.
SERVES 6 to 8

GINGER RING CAKE

METRIC/IMPERIAL

For the cake:

225 g/$\frac{1}{2}$ lb flour
1 × 2.5 ml spoon/$\frac{1}{2}$ teaspoon ground mixed spice
2 × 5 ml spoons/2 teaspoons ground ginger
1 × 2.5 ml spoon/$\frac{1}{2}$ teaspoon bicarbonate of soda
112 g/4 oz butter, softened
175 g/6 oz black treacle
50 g/2 oz golden syrup
150 ml/$\frac{1}{4}$ pint milk
2 eggs, beaten
50 g/2 oz caster sugar

To finish:

glacé icing made with 100 g/4 oz icing sugar
a few slices of crystallized ginger, chopped
candied angelica

AMERICAN

For the cake:

2 cups flour
$\frac{1}{2}$ teaspoon ground allspice and cloves, mixed
2 teaspoons ground ginger
$\frac{1}{2}$ teaspoon baking soda
$\frac{1}{2}$ cup butter, softened
$\frac{1}{2}$ cup molasses
3 tablespoons light corn syrup
$\frac{2}{3}$ cup milk
2 eggs, beaten
$\frac{1}{4}$ cup sugar

To finish:

glacé icing made with 1 cup confectioners' sugar
a few slices of candied ginger, chopped
candied angelica

Grease a 23 cm/9 inch ring mould and dust lightly with flour.

Sift the flour, spices and bicarbonate of soda (baking soda) into a bowl. Add the remaining ingredients and beat for 2 to 3 minutes until well mixed.

Spoon the mixture into the prepared mould and bake in a preheated cool oven (150°C/300°F or Gas Mark 2) for 1 to $1\frac{1}{4}$ hours until firm to the touch. Leave to cool in the tin for a few minutes, then turn out onto a wire rack to cool completely.

To freeze: wrap in cling film, then pack in a freezer bag. Seal, label and freeze.

To thaw and serve: remove wrappings and thaw at room temperature for 4 hours.

Pour the icing over the top of the cake and let it run down the sides. Decorate immediately with crystallized (candied) ginger and angelica and leave to set before serving.

SERVES 8

GINGERBREAD

METRIC/IMPERIAL

100 g/4 oz butter, softened
175 g/6 oz black treacle
50 g/2 oz golden syrup
100 g/4 oz dark brown sugar
6 × 15 ml spoons/6 tablespoons milk
2 eggs, lightly beaten
225 g/$\frac{1}{2}$ lb flour
0.5 × 2.5 ml spoon/$\frac{1}{4}$ teaspoon salt
1 × 5 ml spoon/1 teaspoon bicarbonate of soda
1 × 15 ml spoon/1 tablespoon ground ginger
1 × 5 ml spoon/1 teaspoon ground cinnamon

AMERICAN

$\frac{1}{2}$ cup butter, softened
$\frac{1}{2}$ cup molasses
3 tablespoons light corn syrup
$\frac{2}{3}$ cup dark brown sugar
6 tablespoons milk
2 eggs, lightly beaten
2 cups flour
$\frac{1}{4}$ teaspoon salt
1 teaspoon baking soda
1 tablespoon ground ginger
1 teaspoon ground cinnamon

Grease a 20 cm/8 inch square cake tin and line with greased greaseproof paper or non-stick parchment.

Put the butter, treacle (molasses), syrup and sugar in a pan and heat gently until melted, stirring constantly. Remove from the heat and leave to cool slightly, then stir in the milk and eggs.

Sift the dry ingredients into a bowl, make a well in the centre and gradually pour in the melted mixture, beating constantly until smooth.

Pour the mixture into the prepared tin. Bake in a preheated moderate oven (160°C/325°F or Gas Mark 3) for 1 hour or until a skewer inserted in the centre of the cake comes out clean. Leave to cool in the tin for 10 minutes, then turn out onto a wire rack and remove the paper lining. Leave to cool completely.

To freeze: wrap in cling film, then pack in a freezer bag. Seal, label and freeze.

To thaw and serve: remove wrappings and place on a serving platter. Thaw at room temperature for 4 hours.

SERVES 8 to 10

CHRISTMAS RING CAKE

METRIC/IMPERIAL

For the cake:

112 g/4 oz soft tub margarine
112 g/4 oz caster sugar
2 × 5 ml spoons/2 teaspoons honey
2 eggs
150 g/5 oz self-raising flour
1 × 2.5 ml spoon/½ teaspoon baking powder
3 × 15 ml spoons/3 tablespoons milk

For the icing:

175 g/6 oz sugar
1 egg white
3 × 15 ml spoons/3 tablespoons water
3–4 drops of vanilla essence

To finish:

1 tall red candle
1 holly sprig

AMERICAN

For the cake:

½ cup soft margarine
½ cup sugar
2 teaspoons honey
2 eggs
1¼ cups self-rising flour
½ teaspoon baking powder
3 tablespoons milk

For the icing:

¾ cup sugar
1 egg white
3 tablespoons water
3–4 drops of vanilla extract

To finish:

1 tall red candle
1 holly sprig

Put the margarine in pieces in a warm bowl. Add the remaining ingredients and beat well together for 1 minute until smooth. Spoon the mixture into a greased 20 cm/8 inch ring mould. Bake in a preheated moderate oven (180°C/350°F or Gas Mark 4) for 30 to 35 minutes. Turn out onto a wire rack and leave to cool.

To make the icing: put all the ingredients in a heatproof bowl, stand over a pan of boiling water and beat until thick and light and the mixture falls in a ribbon trail from the beater when lifted. Swirl over the cake with a palette knife and leave to set.

To freeze: open (flash) freeze until firm, then pack in a rigid container. Seal, label and return to the freezer.

To thaw and serve: place the cake on a serving platter and thaw at room temperature for 4 hours. Stand the candle in the centre of the cake and decorate with the holly.

SERVES 6 to 8

MARMALADE CAKE

METRIC/IMPERIAL

For the cake:

112 g/4 oz butter, softened
112 g/4 oz caster sugar
2 eggs, lightly beaten
3 × 15 ml spoons/3 tablespoons marmalade
finely grated rind of 1 orange
finely grated rind of 1 lemon
225 g/½ lb self-raising flour

For the icing (to finish):

100 g/4 oz icing sugar, sifted
juice of ½ orange
juice of ½ lemon

AMERICAN

For the cake:

½ cup butter, softened
½ cup sugar
2 eggs, lightly beaten
3 tablespoons marmalade
finely grated rind of 1 orange
finely grated rind of 1 lemon
2 cups self-rising flour

For the icing (to finish):

scant 1 cup confectioners' sugar
juice of ½ orange
juice of ½ lemon

Grease a 20 cm/8 inch cake tin and line with greased greaseproof paper or non-stick parchment.

Put the butter and sugar in a bowl, beat together until light and fluffy, then beat in the eggs a little at a time. Beat in the marmalade and orange and lemon rinds, then fold in the flour until evenly blended.

Spoon the mixture into the prepared tin. Bake in a preheated moderately hot oven (190°C/375°F or Gas Mark 5) for 50 minutes to 1 hour or until a skewer inserted in the centre of the cake comes out clean. Leave to cool in the tin for 5 minutes, turn out onto a wire rack, then remove the paper lining. Leave to cool completely.

To freeze: wrap in cling film, then pack in a freezer bag. Seal, label and freeze.

To thaw and serve: remove wrappings and place on a serving platter. Thaw at room temperature for 4 hours.

Put the icing (confectioners') sugar in a bowl and gradually beat in the orange and lemon juices until smooth. The consistency should be fairly stiff so that the icing does not trickle down the sides of the cake. Spread over the top of the cake and smooth the surface with a palette knife. Leave to set before serving.

SERVES 4 to 6

CHOCOLATE TREACLE CAKE

METRIC/IMPERIAL

175 g/6 oz flour
1 × 15 ml spoon/1 tablespoon cocoa powder
1 × 5 ml spoon/1 teaspoon bicarbonate of soda
1 × 5 ml spoon/1 teaspoon baking powder
2 eggs, beaten
2 × 15 ml spoons/2 tablespoons black treacle
120 ml/4 fl oz corn oil
120 ml/4 fl oz milk
chocolate or vanilla-flavoured butter cream icing made with 100 g/4 oz icing sugar, for the filling
icing sugar for sprinkling, to finish

AMERICAN

1½ cups flour
1 tablespoon unsweetened cocoa powder
1 teaspoon baking soda
1 teaspoon baking powder
2 eggs, beaten
2 tablespoons molasses
½ cup corn oil
½ cup milk
chocolate or vanilla-flavored butter cream icing made with scant 1 cup confectioners' sugar, for the filling
confectioners' sugar for sprinkling, to finish

Grease two 18 cm/7 inch sandwich tins (layer cake pans) and line with greased greaseproof paper, or non-stick parchment.

Put all the ingredients in a bowl, except the butter, cream and icing (confectioners') sugar, and beat well for 2 minutes. Pour the mixture into the prepared tins and bake in a preheated moderate oven (160°C/325°F or Gas Mark 3) for 45 minutes. Leave to cool in the tins for 5 minutes, turn out onto a wire rack and remove the paper linings. Leave to cool completely, then sandwich the cakes together with the butter cream icing.

To freeze: open (flash) freeze until firm, wrap in cling film, then pack in a freezer bag. Seal, label and return to the freezer.

To thaw and serve: remove wrappings and place the cake on a serving platter. Thaw at room temperature for 2 hours. Sprinkle icing (confectioners') sugar over the top of the cake before serving.

SERVES 6

RAISIN GINGERBREAD

METRIC/IMPERIAL

450 g/1 lb flour
pinch of salt
3 × 5 ml spoons/3 teaspoons ground ginger
100 g/4 oz sugar
225 g/½ lb seedless raisins
100 g/4 oz butter
225 g/½ lb clear honey
1 × 5 ml spoon/1 teaspoon bicarbonate of soda
a little milk, to mix
1 egg, beaten
approx 2 × 15 ml spoons/2 tablespoons brown sugar

AMERICAN

4 cups flour
pinch of salt
3 teaspoons ground ginger
½ cup sugar
1½ cups seedless raisins
½ cup butter
⅔ cup clear honey
1 teaspoon baking soda
a little milk, to mix
1 egg, beaten
approx 2 tablespoons brown sugar

Grease a 23 cm/9 inch square cake tin and line with greased greaseproof paper or non-stick parchment.

Sift the flour, salt and ginger into a bowl, then stir in the sugar and raisins. Put the butter and honey in a pan and heat gently until melted. Mix the bicarbonate of soda (baking soda) to a paste with a little milk, then stir into the melted mixture.

Make a well in the centre of the flour, pour in the melted mixture and the egg and beat well to mix. Add a little milk to give a soft dropping consistency, then pour the mixture into the prepared tin and sprinkle the top with brown sugar.

Bake in a preheated moderate oven (160°C/325°F or Gas Mark 3) for 1 to 1½ hours until a skewer inserted in the centre of the cake comes out cleam. Turn out onto a wire rack, remove the paper lining, then leave the cake to cool. Store the gingerbread in an airtight tin for 3 days before freezing.

To freeze: wrap in cling film, then pack in a freezer bag. Seal, label and freeze.

To thaw and serve: thaw in the wrappings at room temperature for 4 hours.

SERVES 8 to 10

HONEY CRUNCH REFRIGERATOR CAKE

METRIC/IMPERIAL

For the cake:

100 g/4 oz butter, softened
75 g/3 oz icing sugar, sifted
2 × 15 ml spoons/2 tablespoons clear honey
1 × 15 ml spoon/1 tablespoon drinking chocolate powder
1 × 15 ml spoon/1 tablespoon sherry
225 g/½ lb semi-sweet biscuits, crushed

To finish:

1 × 15 ml spoon/1 tablespoon clear honey
150 ml/¼ pint double cream, stiffly whipped
25 g/1 oz plain chocolate, grated

AMERICAN

For the cake:

½ cup butter, softened
¾ cup sifted confectioners' sugar
2 tablespoons clear honey
1 tablespoon sweetened cocoa powder
1 tablespoon sherry
2 cups crushed Graham crackers

To finish:

1 tablespoon clear honey
⅔ cup heavy cream, stiffly whipped
1 square (1 oz) semi-sweet chocolate, grated

Put the butter in a bowl and gradually beat in the icing (confectioners') sugar and honey until light and fluffy. Beat in the remaining ingredients. Spoon the mixture into a well-greased 18 cm/7 inch sandwich tin (layer cake pan), smoothing the top and pressing down well.

Chill in the refrigerator for at least 2 hours or overnight, then remove the cake from the tin.

To freeze: wrap in cling film, then pack in a freezer bag. Seal, label and freeze.

To thaw and serve: remove wrappings and thaw at room temperature for 3 hours. Stir the honey into the cream and spread over the top of the cake, then decorate with the grated chocolate.

SERVES 6

HONEY CAKE

METRIC/IMPERIAL

225 g/½ lb flour
1 × 5 ml spoon/1 teaspoon ground ginger
1 × 2.5 ml spoon/½ teaspoon ground mixed spice
50 g/2 oz butter, cut into small pieces
225 g/½ lb honey
1 egg, beaten
1 × 5 ml spoon/1 teaspoon bicarbonate of soda
7 × 15 ml spoons/7 tablespoons warm milk
50 g/2 oz blanched almonds, shredded

AMERICAN

2 cups flour
1 teaspoon ground ginger
¼ teaspoon grated nutmeg
¼ teaspoon ground allspice and cloves, mixed
¼ cup butter, cut into small pieces
⅔ cup honey
1 egg, beaten
1 teaspoon baking soda
7 tablespoons warm milk
½ cup blanched almonds, shredded

Sift together the flour, ginger and spice(s). Put the butter and honey in a heatproof bowl, stand over a pan of gently simmering water and allow to melt. Remove from the heat, then stir in the egg and the flour mixture. Dissolve the bicarbonate of soda (baking soda) in the warm milk, add to the mixture and stir well to mix.

Spoon the mixture into a greased 20 cm/8 inch cake tin and smooth the top. Scatter over the almonds, then bake in a preheated moderate oven (180°C/350°F or Gas Mark 4) for 1 to 1¼ hours. Turn onto a wire rack and leave to cool.

To freeze: wrap in cling film, then pack in a freezer bag. Seal, label and freeze.

To thaw and serve: thaw in the wrappings at room temperature for 4 hours.

SERVES 6

POLKA DOT CAKE

METRIC/IMPERIAL

For the cake:

225 g/½ lb lard, softened
225 g/½ lb caster sugar
4 eggs, beaten
225 g/½ lb self-raising flour
75 g/3 oz chocolate buttons

For the chocolate fudge icing:

50 g/2 oz cocoa powder
100 g/4 oz butter
6 × 15 ml spoons/6 tablespoons water
350 g/¾ lb icing sugar, sifted

AMERICAN

For the cake:

1 cup lard, softened
1 cup sugar
4 eggs, beaten
2 cups self-rising flour
½ cup chocolate chips

For the chocolate fudge icing:

½ cup unsweetened cocoa powder
½ cup butter
6 tablespoons water
2⅔ cups sifted confectioners' sugar

Put the lard and sugar in a bowl, beat together until light and fluffy, then beat in the eggs a little at a time. Fold in the flour, then stir in the chocolate buttons (chips).
Divide the mixture equally between two lightly greased 20 cm/8 inch sandwich tins (layer cake pans). Bake in a preheated moderate oven (180°C/350°F or Gas Mark 4) for 55 minutes. Cool in the tins, then turn out onto a wire rack.
To make the icing: put the cocoa, butter and water in a heatproof bowl, stand over a pan of gently simmering water and stir until the butter has melted. Remove from the heat and gradually beat in the icing (confectioners') sugar until thick. Swirl over the tops of the cakes, then leave to set.
To freeze: open (flash) freeze until firm, then pack in freezer bags. Seal, label and return to the freezer.
To thaw and serve: remove wrappings and thaw at room temperature for 4 hours. Turn out onto a serving platter.
EACH CAKE SERVES 6

UNCOOKED CHOCOLATE GÂTEAU

METRIC/IMPERIAL
For the cake:
225 g/½ lb plain chocolate, broken into pieces
2 eggs, beaten
25 g/1 oz caster sugar
225 g/½ lb butter, melted
225 g/½ lb digestive biscuits, crushed
25 g/1 oz glacé cherries
25 g/1 oz walnuts, chopped
1–2 × 15 ml spoons/1–2 tablespoons rum (optional)
To finish:
whipped cream
a few glacé cherries
a few strips of candied angelica

AMERICAN
For the cake:
1⅓ cups semi-sweet chocolate pieces
2 eggs, beaten
2 tablespoons sugar
1 cup butter, melted
2 cups crushed Graham crackers
2 tablespoons chopped candied cherries
¼ cup chopped walnuts
1–2 tablespoons rum (optional)
To finish:
whipped cream
a few candied cherries
a few strips of candied angelica

Put the chocolate in a heatproof bowl, stand over a pan of gently simmering water and allow to melt. Put the eggs and sugar in a separate bowl, beat well to mix, then pour in the melted butter in a steady stream, beating constantly. Stir in the melted chocolate and the biscuits (crackers) until evenly blended. Spoon the mixture into a greased 15 cm/6 inch loose-bottomed tin.
To freeze: pack in a freezer bag, seal, label and freeze.
To thaw and serve: remove the cake from the tin by dipping in hot water, then thaw at room temperature for 4 hours. Decorate with whipped cream, cherries and angelica.
SERVES 6 to 8

DATE AND SULTANA (SEEDLESS WHITE RAISIN) CAKE

METRIC/IMPERIAL
200 g/7 oz soft tub margarine
200 g/7 oz soft brown sugar
4 eggs, beaten
3 × 15 ml spoons/3 tablespoons milk
100 g/4 oz stoned dates, chopped
100 g/4 oz sultanas
350 g/¾ lb self-raising flour
1 × 2.5 ml spoon/½ teaspoon ground mixed spice

AMERICAN
⅞ cup soft margarine
1 cup light brown sugar, firmly packed
4 eggs, beaten
3 tablespoons milk
⅝ cup pitted dates, chopped
⅔ cup seedless white raisins
3 cups self-rising flour
½ teaspoon ground allspice, nutmeg and cloves, mixed

Grease a deep 20 cm/8 inch cake tin and line with greased greaseproof paper or non-stick parchment.
Put all the ingredients in a bowl and beat together for 2 to 3 minutes or until well mixed. Spoon the mixture into the prepared tin and bake in a preheated moderate oven (180°C/350°F or Gas Mark 4) for 1¼ hours. Leave to cool in the tin for 5 minutes, then turn out onto a wire rack and remove the paper lining.
To freeze: when cool, wrap in cling film, then pack in a freezer bag. Seal, label and freeze.
To thaw and serve: remove wrappings and thaw at room temperature for 4 hours.
SERVES 6

BANANA AND WALNUT FROSTED CAKE

METRIC/IMPERIAL

For the cake:

112 g/4 oz butter, softened
112 g/4 oz dark brown sugar
2 eggs, beaten
112 g/4 oz self-raising flour
1 × 2.5 ml spoon/½ teaspoon ground ginger
2 bananas, peeled and mashed
25 g/1 oz walnuts, chopped

For the frosting:

50 g/2 oz butter
1 × 15 ml spoon/1 tablespoon milk
175 g/6 oz icing sugar, sifted
1 × 2.5–5 ml spoon/½–1 teaspoon ground ginger, according to taste

AMERICAN

For the cake:

½ cup butter, softened
⅔ cup dark brown sugar
2 eggs, beaten
1 cup self-rising flour
½ teaspoon ground ginger
2 bananas, peeled and mashed
¼ cup chopped walnuts

For the frosting:

¼ cup butter
1 tablespoon milk
1⅓ cups sifted confectioners' sugar
½–1 teaspoon ground ginger, according to taste

Put the butter and sugar in a bowl, beat together until light and fluffy, then beat in the eggs a little at a time. Fold in the flour, then add the ground ginger, bananas and walnuts and stir well to mix.

Spoon the mixture into a lightly greased 18 cm/7 inch cake tin. Bake in a preheated moderate oven (180°C/350°F or Gas Mark 4) for 40 to 45 minutes. Turn out onto a wire rack and leave to cool.

To make the frosting: put the butter and milk in a heatproof bowl, stand over a pan of gently simmering water and allow to melt. Remove from the heat, then gradually beat in the icing (confectioners') sugar and ginger until thick and smooth. Spread over the top of the cake and mark the surface with the prongs of a fork. Leave to set.

To freeze: open (flash) freeze until firm, wrap in cling film, then pack in a freezer bag. Seal, label and return to the freezer.

To thaw and serve: remove wrappings and place the cake on a serving platter. Thaw at room temperature for 4 hours.

SERVES 6

GINGER SPICE CAKE

METRIC/IMPERIAL

100 g/4 oz butter
175 g/6 oz golden syrup
50 g/2 oz black treacle
50 g/2 oz brown sugar
150 ml/¼ pint milk
2 eggs, beaten
225 g/½ lb flour
2 × 5 ml spoons/2 teaspoons ground mixed spice
2 × 5 ml spoons/2 teaspoons ground ginger
1 × 5 ml spoon/1 teaspoon bicarbonate of soda

AMERICAN

½ cup butter
½ cup light corn syrup
3 tablespoons molasses
⅓ cup brown sugar
⅔ cup milk
2 eggs, beaten
2 cups flour
1 teaspoon grated nutmeg
1 teaspoon ground allspice and cloves, mixed
2 teaspoon ground ginger
1 teaspoon baking soda

Grease a deep 20 cm/8 inch square cake tin and line with greased greaseproof paper or non-stick parchment.

Put the butter, syrup, treacle (molasses) and sugar in a pan and heat gently until melted, stirring occasionally. Stir in the milk, leave to cool, then stir in the eggs.

Sift the dry ingredients into a bowl, add the melted mixture and beat well to mix. Pour into the prepared tin and bake in a preheated moderate oven (160°C/325°F or Gas Mark 3) for 1 to 1½ hours or until firm to the touch. Turn out and cool quickly on a wire rack.

To freeze: wrap in foil, then pack in a freezer bag. Seal, label and freeze.

To thaw and serve: remove wrappings and thaw at room temperature for 4 to 5 hours.

SERVES 6 to 8

CONTINENTAL CHOCOLATE CAKE

METRIC/IMPERIAL

For the cake:

112 g/4 oz butter, softened
112 g/4 oz icing sugar, sifted
100 g/4 oz plain chocolate, melted
4 eggs, separated
112 g/4 oz ground almonds
25 g/1 oz flour

For the chocolate icing:

50 g/2 oz plain chocolate, broken into pieces
1 × 15 ml spoon/1 tablespoon water
25 g/1 oz butter
2 × 15 ml spoons/2 tablespoons sifted icing sugar
1 × 15 ml spoon/1 tablespoon cocoa powder
25 g/1 oz blanched almonds, chopped (optional)

AMERICAN

For the cake:

½ cup butter, softened
scant 1 cup sifted confectioners' sugar
⅔ cup semi-sweet chocolate pieces, melted
4 eggs, separated
1 cup ground almonds
¼ cup flour

For the chocolate icing:

⅓ cup semi-sweet chocolate pieces
1 tablespoon water
2 tablespoons butter
2 tablespoons sifted confectioners' sugar
1 tablespoon unsweetened cocoa powder
¼ cup chopped blanced almonds (optional)

Grease a 20 × 15 cm/8 × 6 inch oblong cake tin and line the bottom with greased greaseproof paper or non-stick parchment.

Put the butter and sugar in a bowl, beat together until light and fluffy, then stir in the melted chocolate and egg yolks. Fold in the ground almonds and flour until evenly blended. Beat the egg whites until stiff, then fold into the creamed mixture.

Spoon the mixture into the prepared tin and smooth the top. Bake in a preheated moderate oven (160°C/325°F or Gas Mark 3) for 1¾ to 2 hours until a skewer inserted in the centre of the cake comes out clean. Turn out onto a wire rack, remove the paper lining, then leave the cake to cool.

To make the icing: put the chocolate, water and butter in a heatproof bowl, stand over a pan of gently simmering water and stir until melted. Remove from the heat and beat in the icing (confectioners') sugar and cocoa until smooth. Leave to cool, then spread the icing over the top of the cake and scatter over the chopped almonds, if liked.

To freeze: open (flash) freeze until firm, then pack in a rigid container. Seal, label and return to the freezer.

To thaw and serve: place the cake on a serving platter and thaw at room temperature for 4 hours.

SERVES 8 to 10

FAMILY FRUIT CAKE

METRIC/IMPERIAL

175 g/6 oz mixed dried fruit
50 g/2 oz chopped candied peel
1 × 178 ml/6¼ fl oz can frozen concentrated orange juice, thawed
120 ml/4 fl oz water
finely grated rind of 1 lemon
175 g/6 oz butter, softened
175 g/6 oz caster sugar
3 large eggs, beaten
450 g/1 lb flour
a few drops of vanilla essence

AMERICAN

1 cup mixed dried fruit
⅓ cup chopped candied peel
1 × 6¼ oz can frozen concentrated orange juice, thawed
½ cup water
finely grated rind of 1 lemon
¾ cup butter, softened
¾ cup sugar
3 large eggs, beaten
4 cups flour
a few drops of vanilla extract

Grease a deep 18 cm/7 inch round cake tin and line with greased greaseproof paper or non-stick parchment.

Put the dried fruit, candied peel, orange juice and water in a bowl and stir well to mix. Leave to soak overnight.

Put the butter and sugar in a bowl, beat together until light and fluffy, then beat in the eggs a little at a time. Fold in the fruit mixture alternately with the flour and vanilla essence (extract).

Spoon the mixture into the prepared tin. Bake in a preheated moderate oven (160°C/325°F or Gask Mark 3) for 2 hours or until a skewer inserted in the centre of the cake comes out clean. Leave to cool in the tin, then turn out and remove the paper lining.

To freeze: wrap in cling film, then pack in a freezer bag. Seal, label and freeze.

To thaw and serve: thaw in the wrappings at room temperature for 6 hours.

SERVES 6 to 8

CRYSTALLIZED (CANDIED) FRUIT CAKE

METRIC/IMPERIAL

For the cake:

225 g/½ lb flour
1 × 5 ml spoon/1 teaspoon ground mixed spice
175 g/6 oz soft tub margarine
175 g/6 oz caster sugar
3 large eggs, beaten
225 g/½ lb seedless raisins
finely grated rind of 1 orange
25 g/1 oz candied angelica, chopped
100 g/4 oz glacé cherries, chopped
100 g/4 oz blanched almonds, chopped
25 g/1 oz crystallized ginger, chopped
1–2 × 15 ml spoons/1–2 tablespoons brandy or milk

To decorate:

a few glacé cherries, halved
a few walnuts, halved
a few strips of candied angelica
apricot jam, warmed and sieved, to glaze

AMERICAN

For the cake:

2 cups flour
½ teaspoon grated nutmeg
½ teaspoon ground allspice and cloves, mixed
¾ cup soft margarine
¾ cup sugar
3 large eggs, beaten
1½ cups seedless raisins
finely grated rind of 1 orange
3 tablespoons chopped candied angelica
½ cup candied cherries, chopped
1 cup chopped blanched almonds
3 tablespoons chopped candied ginger
1–2 tablespoons brandy or milk

To decorate:

a few candied cherries, halved
a few walnuts, halved
a few strips of candied angelica
apricot jam, warmed and strained, to glaze

Grease a deep 18 cm/7 inch round cake tin and line with greased greaseproof paper or non-stick parchment.

Sift the flour and spice(s) into a bowl, add the remaining ingredients and beat for 2 to 3 minutes until well mixed.

Spoon the mixture into the prepared tin, smooth the top, then press in the cherries, walnuts and angelica. Bake in a preheated cool oven (140°C/275°F or Gas Mark 1) for 2½ to 3 hours until a skewer inserted in the centre of the cake comes out clean. Leave to cool in the tin for 10 minutes, then turn out onto a wire rack, remove the paper lining and brush the top of the cake with the apricot jam. Leave to cool.

To freeze: open (flash) freeze until firm, wrap in cling film, then pack in a freezer bag. Seal, label and return to the freezer.

To thaw and serve: remove wrappings and place the cake on a serving platter. Thaw at room temperature for 6 hours.

SERVES 8 to 10

WHOLEMEAL (WHOLE-WHEAT) DATE AND GINGER CAKE

METRIC/IMPERIAL

175 g/6 oz butter, softened
175 g/6 oz caster sugar
2 eggs, beaten
50 g/2 oz golden syrup
100 g/4 oz stoned dates, chopped
100 g/4 oz crystallized ginger, chopped
100 g/4 oz flour
275 g/10 oz wholemeal flour
1 × 2.5 ml spoon/½ teaspoon bicarbonate of soda
150 ml/¼ pint milk

AMERICAN

¾ cup butter, softened
¾ cup sugar
2 eggs, beaten
3 tablespoons light corn syrup
⅝ cup pitted dates, chopped
⅔ cup chopped candied ginger
1 cup flour
2½ cups wholewheat flour
½ teaspoon baking soda
⅔ cup milk

Grease a deep 20 cm/8 inch cake tin and line with greased greaseproof paper or non-stick parchment

Put the butter and sugar in a bowl, beat together until light and fluffy, then beat in the eggs a little at a time. Stir in the syrup, dates and ginger, then fold in the flours and bicarbonate of soda (baking soda) alternately with the milk.

Spoon the mixture into the prepared tin. Bake in a preheated moderate oven (160°C/325°F or Gas Mark 3) for 1½ to 1¾ hours until a skewer inserted in the centre of the cake comes out clean.

Turn out onto a wire rack, remove the paper lining and leave the cake to cool.

To freeze: wrap in cling film, then pack in a freezer bag. Seal, label and freeze.

To thaw and serve: remove wrappings and place the cake on a serving platter. Thaw at room temperature for 4 hours.

SERVES 6

BOILED FRUIT CAKE

METRIC/IMPERIAL

150 g/5 oz butter
6 × 15 ml spoons/6 tablespoons golden syrup
225 g/½ lb seedless raisins
225 g/½ lb currants
100 g/4 oz sultanas
100 g/4 oz stoned dates, chopped
100 g/4 oz chopped candied peel
175 ml/6 fl oz milk
225 g/½ lb flour
1 × 5 ml spoon/1 teaspoon ground mixed spice
1 × 5 ml spoon/1 teaspoon grated nutmeg
pinch of salt
2 eggs, beaten
1 × 2.5 ml spoon/½ teaspoon bicarbonate of soda

AMERICAN

⅝ cup butter
6 tablespoons light corn syrup
1½ cups seedless raisins
1½ cups currants
¾ cup seedless white raisins
⅝ cup pitted dates, chopped
⅔ cup chopped candied peel
¾ cup milk
2 cups flour
½ teaspoon ground cinnamon
½ teaspoon ground allspice and cloves, mixed
1 teaspoon grated nutmeg
pinch of salt
2 eggs, beaten
½ teaspoon baking soda

Grease a deep 18 cm/7 inch round cake tin and line with greased greaseproof paper or non-stick parchment.
Put the butter, syrup, dried fruit, dates, peel and milk in a pan and heat gently until the butter has melted. Simmer for 5 minutes, stirring occasionally, then remove from the heat and leave until lukewarm.
Sift the dry ingredients, except the soda, into a bowl. Make a well in the centre and put in the eggs. Stir the soda quickly into the melted mixture, then pour into the dry ingredients and beat well to mix.
Spoon the mixture into the prepared tin. Bake in a preheated cool oven (150°C/300°F or Gas Mark 2) for 1¾ hours to 2 hours until a skewer inserted in the centre of the cake comes out clean. Turn out onto a wire rack, remove the paper lining and leave the cake to cool.
To freeze: wrap in cling film, then pack in a freezer bag. Seal, label and freeze.
To thaw and serve: thaw in the wrappings at room temperature for 6 hours.
SERVES 8 to 10

EASTER FRUIT CAKE

METRIC/IMPERIAL

For the cake:
112 g/4 oz butter, softened
112 g/4 oz caster sugar
2 eggs, beaten
75 g/3 oz sultanas
2 × 15 ml spoons/2 tablespoons marmalade
175 g/6 oz self-raising flour
1 × 2.5 ml spoon/½ teaspoon ground mixed spice
1 × 15 ml spoon/1 tablespoon milk
To finish:
4 × 15 ml spoons/4 tablespoons sifted icing sugar
1 × 15 ml spoon/1 tablespoon orange juice
coloured eggs and chicks, to decorate

AMERICAN

For the cake:
½ cup butter, softened
½ cup sugar
2 eggs, beaten
½ cup seedless white raisins
2 tablespoons marmalade
1½ cups self-rising flour
¼ teaspoon grated nutmeg
¼ teaspoon ground allspice and cloves, mixed
1 tablespoon milk
To finish:
¼ cup sifted confectioners' sugar
1 tablespoon orange juice
colored eggs and chicks, to decorate

Grease an 18 cm/7 inch round cake tin and line with greased greaseproof paper or non-stick parchment.
Put the butter and sugar in a bowl, beat together until light and fluffy, then beat in the eggs a little at a time. Stir in the sultanas (seedless white raisins) and the marmalade, then fold in the flour and spice(s) and the milk.
Spoon the mixture into the prepared tin. Bake in a preheated moderate oven (180°C/350°F or Gas Mark 4) for 1 hour. Leave to cool in the tin for 5 minutes, then turn out onto a wire rack and remove the paper lining. Leave to cool completely.
To freeze: wrap in cling film, then pack in a freezer bag. Seal, label and freeze.
To thaw and serve: remove wrappings and place the cake on a serving platter. Thaw at room temperature for 4 hours. Put the icing (confectioners') sugar in a bowl and beat in the orange juice until thick and smooth. Spread over the top of the cake and decorate with coloured eggs and chicks. Leave to set before serving.
SERVES 6

DEVIL'S FOOD CAKE

METRIC/IMPERIAL

For the cake:

40 g/1½ oz cocoa powder
150 ml/¼ pint milk
1 × 2.5 ml spoon/½ teaspoon vanilla essence
100 g/4 oz lard
225 g/½ lb soft brown sugar
3 eggs, beaten
225 g/½ lb flour
1 × 5 ml spoon/1 teaspoon bicarbonate of soda
0.5 × 2.5 ml spoon/¼ teaspoon baking powder
0.5 × 2.5 ml spoon/¼ teaspoon salt

For the frosting:

350 g/¾ lb sugar
4 × 15 ml spoons/4 tablespoons water
2 egg whites
0.5 × 2.5 ml spoon/¼ teaspoon cream of tartar
grated chocolate, to decorate

AMERICAN

For the cake:

⅓ cup unsweetened cocoa powder
⅔ cup milk
½ teaspoon vanilla extract
1⅓ cups shortening
1⅓ cups light brown sugar
3 eggs, beaten
2 cups flour
1 teaspoon baking soda
¼ teaspoon baking powder
¼ teaspoon salt

For the frosting:

1¼ cups sugar
¼ cup water
2 egg whites
¼ teaspoon cream of tartar
grated chocolate, to decorate

Grease two 18 cm/7 inch sandwich tins (layer cake pans) and line the bottoms with greased greaseproof paper or non-stick parchment.
Mix the cocoa to a paste with a little of the milk, then stir in the remaining milk and the vanilla essence (extract). Put the lard (shortening) and sugar in a bowl, beat together until light and fluffy, then beat in the eggs a little at a time. Sift together the dry ingredients, then fold into the creamed mixture alternately with the liquid. Divide the mixture equally between the prepared tins. Bake in a preheated moderate oven (180°C/350°F or Gas Mark 4) for 35 to 40 minutes. Leave to cool in the tins for 5 minutes, then turn out onto a wire rack, remove the paper linings and leave to cool completely.
To make the frosting: put all the ingredients in a heatproof bowl, stand over a pan of boiling water and stir for about 10 minutes until the sugar has dissolved. Beat the mixture with an electric or rotary beater until very thick and stiff enough to hold its shape, then remove from the heat. Sandwich the cakes together with some of the frosting, then spread the remainder over the top of the cake and peak the surface with a palette knife. Scatter grated chocolate over the top and leave to set.
To freeze: open (flash) freeze until firm, then pack in a rigid container. Seal, label and return to the freezer.
To thaw and serve: place the cake on a serving platter and thaw at room temperature for 4 hours.
SERVES 6

LIGHT FRUIT CAKE

METRIC/IMPERIAL

225 g/½ lb flour
1 × 5 ml spoon/1 teaspoon baking powder
175 g/6 oz butter, softened
175 g/6 oz caster sugar
3 eggs, beaten
1 × 15 ml spoon/1 tablespoon milk
100 g/4 oz mixed dried fruit
50 g/2 oz glacé cherries, chopped

AMERICAN

2 cups flour
1 teaspoon baking powder
¾ cup butter, softened
¾ cup sugar
3 eggs, beaten
1 tablespoon milk
⅔ cup mixed dried fruit
¼ cup chopped candied cherries

Grease a deep 18 cm/7 inch cake tin and line with a double thickness of greased greaseproof paper or non-stick parchment.
Sift together the flour and baking powder. Put the butter and sugar in a bowl, beat together until light and fluffy, then beat in the eggs a little at a time. Fold in the sifted mixture, then stir in the remaining ingredients until evenly blended.
Spoon the mixture into the prepared tin and smooth the top. Bake in a preheated moderate oven (160°C/325°F or Gas Mark 3) for 1¾ to 2 hours until a skewer inserted in the centre of the cake comes out clean. Leave to cool in the tin for 5 minutes, then turn out onto a wire rack. Remove the paper lining and leave the cake to cool completely.
To freeze: wrap in cling film, then pack in a freezer bag. Seal, label and freeze.

To thaw and serve: thaw in the wrappings at room temperature for 6 hours.
SERVES 8

SPICED SULTANA (SEEDLESS WHITE RAISIN) CAKE

Make as for Light Fruit Cake (see opposite), adding 1 × 5 ml spoon/1 teaspoon ground mixed spice (ground cinnamon, allspice and cloves, mixed) to the flour and baking powder before sifting. Substitute 175 g/6 oz sultanas (1 cup seedless white raisins) for the mixed dried fruit and glacé (candied) cherries.
Freeze, thaw and serve as for Light Fruit Cake.
SERVES 8

DATE AND WALNUT CAKE

Make as for Light Fruit Cake (see opposite), substituting 100 g/4 oz/⅝ cup chopped stoned (pitted) dates and 50 g/2 oz/½ cup chopped walnuts for the mixed dried fruit and glacé (candied) cherries.
Freeze, thaw and serve as for Light Fruit Cake.
SERVES 8

CHOCOLATE CHESTNUT GÂTEAU

METRIC/IMPERIAL
For the cake:
2 × 15 ml spoons/2 tablespoons cocoa powder
2 × 15 ml spoons/2 tablespoons hot milk
50 g/2 oz flour
1 × 2.5 ml spoon/½ teaspoon baking powder
112 g/4 oz butter, softened
112 g/4 oz caster sugar
50 g/2 oz ground almonds
0.5 × 2.5 ml spoon/¼ teaspoon almond essence
50 g/2 oz plain chocolate, melted
2 × 15 ml spoons/2 tablespoons coffee essence
1 × 15 ml spoon/1 tablespoon water
2 eggs, separated
To finish:
1 × 225 g/8 oz can sweetened chestnut spread
300 ml/½ pint double cream, whipped
1 × 15 ml spoon/1 tablespoon brandy
grated chocolate

AMERICAN
For the cake:
2 tablespoons unsweetened cocoa powder
2 tablespoons hot milk
½ cup flour
½ teaspoon baking powder
½ cup butter, softened
½ cup sugar
½ cup ground almonds
¼ teaspoon almond extract
⅓ cup semi-sweet chocolate pieces, melted
2 tablespoons strong black coffee
1 tablespoon water
2 eggs, separated
To finish:
1 × ½ lb can sweetened chestnut spread
1¼ cups heavy cream, whipped
1 tablespoon brandy
grated chocolate

Grease a deep 20 cm/8 inch round cake tin and line the bottom with greased greaseproof paper or non-stick parchment. Dust the inside of the tin lightly with sifted flour.
Blend the cocoa and milk together and leave to cool.
Meanwhile, sift the flour and baking powder into a bowl. Add the remaining ingredients, except the egg whites, then add the cooled cocoa mixture. Beat for 2 to 3 minutes until all the ingredients are well mixed.
Beat the egg whites until stiff, then fold into the cake mixture until evenly blended. Spoon into the prepared tin and bake in a preheated moderate oven (180°C/350°F or Gas Mark 4) for 30 to 40 minutes or until firm to the touch. Turn out and cool on a wire rack, then remove the paper lining and slice the cake in half.
Put half the chestnut spread in a bowl and fold in half the whipped cream and the brandy. Use to sandwich together the two halves of the cake. Spread the remaining cream over the top and sides of the cake, then pipe whirls of chestnut spread around the top edge. Scatter the grated chocolate in the centre.
To freeze: open (flash) freeze until firm, wrap in cling film, then pack in a freezer bag. Seal, label and return to the freezer.
To thaw and serve: remove wrappings, place the cake on a serving platter and thaw in the refrigerator overnight.
SERVES 8

LEMON AND CHOCOLATE BATTENBURG

METRIC/IMPERIAL

For the cake:

175 g/6 oz self-raising flour
1.5 × 5 ml spoons/1½ teaspoons baking powder
175 g/6 oz soft tub margarine
175 g/6 oz caster sugar
3 large eggs
1 × 15 ml spoon/1 tablespoon cocoa powder
1 × 15 ml spoon/1 tablespoon hot water
finely grated rind of 1 lemon

To decorate:

6 × 15 ml spoons/6 tablespoons lemon curd
450 g/1 lb almond paste

AMERICAN

For the cake:

1½ cups self-rising flour
1½ teaspoons baking powder
¾ cup soft margarine
¾ cup sugar
3 large eggs
1 tablespoon unsweetened cocoa powder
1 tablespoon hot water
finely grated rind of 1 lemon

To decorate:

6 tablespoons lemon cheese
1 lb almond paste

Grease an 18 cm/7 inch square cake tin, line with greased greaseproof paper or non-stick parchment and divide down the centre with a double thickness of greaseproof paper or non-stick parchment.

Sift the flour and baking powder into a bowl. Add the margarine, sugar and eggs and beat for 2 to 3 minutes until all the ingredients are well mixed. Divide into two equal halves.

Mix the cocoa to a paste with the hot water, then beat into half of the mixture. Beat the lemon rind into the other half of the mixture. Spoon the cocoa mixture into one half of the tin and the lemon into the other half. Bake in a preheated moderate oven (160°C/325°F or Gas Mark 3) for 40 to 45 minutes. Turn out onto a wire rack, remove the paper lining and leave to cool.

Trim the edges of the cake and cut each half into two lengthways. Join alternate colours together with some of the lemon curd (cheese) to make a square. Roll out the almond paste to an oblong about 38 × 20 cm/15 × 8 inches. Spread the cake all over with the remaining lemon curd (cheese), then press the almond paste around the cake to cover it completely, sealing it underneath. Trim the ends, crimp the edges and make an 18 cm/7 inch plait (braid) with the almond paste trimmings to place on the top.

To freeze: wrap in cling film, then pack in a freezer bag. Seal, label and freeze.

To thaw and serve: remove wrappings and place the cake on a serving platter. Thaw at room temperature for 4 hours.

SERVES 6

WALNUT CREAM CAKE

METRIC/IMPERIAL

For the cake:

3 eggs
75 g/3 oz caster sugar
75 g/3 oz self-raising flour
2 × 5 ml spoons/2 teaspoons cocoa powder
50 g/2 oz walnuts, very finely chopped

For the filling:

300 ml/½ pint double cream
1 × 15 ml spoon/1 tablespoon caster sugar
1 × 5 ml spoon/1 teaspoon vanilla essence

AMERICAN

For the cake:

3 eggs
⅜ cup sugar
¾ cup self-rising flour
2 teaspoons unsweetened cocoa powder
½ cup very finely chopped walnuts

For the filling:

1¼ cups heavy cream
1 tablespoon sugar
1 teaspoon vanilla extract

Grease two 20 cm/8 inch sandwich tins (layer cake pans) and line the bottoms with greased greaseproof paper or non-stick parchment. Put the eggs and sugar in a bowl, beat together until light, then sift together the flour and cocoa and fold in alternately with the walnuts.

Divide the mixture equally between the prepared tins and bake in a preheated moderate oven (160°C/325°F or Gas Mark 5) for 25 minutes. Turn out onto a wire rack, remove the paper lining and leave to cool. Whip the cream, sugar and vanilla essence (extract) until thick, then use to sandwich the cakes together.

To freeze: open (flash) freeze until firm, then pack in a rigid container. Seal, label and return to the freezer.

To thaw and serve: place on a serving platter and thaw at room temperature for 3 hours.

SERVES 8

HAZELNUT CAROUSEL

METRIC/IMPERIAL

For the cake:

225 g/½ lb self-raising flour
1 × 2.5 ml spoon/½ teaspoon bicarbonate of soda
1 × 5 ml spoon/1 teaspoon baking powder
100 g/4 oz soft tub margarine
175 g/6 oz soft brown sugar
2 large eggs
120 ml/4 fl oz milk
1 × 15 ml spoon/1 tablespoon coffee essence
75 g/3 oz roasted hazelnuts, finely chopped
75 g/3 oz seedless raisins

For the coffee icing:

75 g/3 oz butter, softened
225 g/½ lb icing sugar, sifted
2 × 5 ml spoons/2 teaspoons milk
2 × 5 ml spoons/2 teaspoons coffee essence
25–50 g/1–2 oz chopped roasted hazelnuts, to decorate

AMERICAN

For the cake:

2 cups self-rising flour
½ teaspoon baking soda
1 teaspoon baking powder
½ cup soft tub margarine
1 cup light brown sugar
2 large eggs
½ cup milk
1 tablespoon strong black coffee
¾ cup finely chopped roasted hazelnuts
½ cup seedless raisins

For the coffee icing:

⅜ cup butter, softened
scant 2 cups sifted confectioners' sugar
2 teaspoons milk
2 teaspoons strong black coffee
¼–½ cup chopped roasted hazelnuts, to decorate

Grease two 20 cm/8 inch sandwich tins (layer cake pans) and line with greased greaseproof paper or non-stick parchment.
Sift the flour, soda and baking powder into a bowl, add the remaining cake ingredients and beat for 2 to 3 minutes until well mixed.
Spoon the mixture into the prepared tins. Bake in a preheated moderate oven (160°C/325°F or Gas Mark 3) for 30 to 35 minutes. Leave to cool in the tins for a few minutes, then turn out onto a wire rack, remove the paper linings and leave to cool completely.
To make the coffee icing: put all the ingredients in a bowl and beat until smooth and creamy. Sandwich the cakes together with one-third of the icing, then spread the remainder over the top and sides and pipe stars or rosettes around the edge. Decorate with hazelnuts.
To freeze: open (flash) freeze until firm, then pack in a rigid container. Seal, label and return to the freezer.
To thaw and serve: place cake on a serving platter and thaw at room temperature for 4 hours.
SERVES 6 to 8

ORANGE MARMALADE CAKE

METRIC/IMPERIAL

112 g/4 oz butter or margarine
112 g/4 oz caster sugar
2 eggs, lightly beaten
3 × 15 ml spoons/3 tablespoons coarse-cut marmalade
finely grated rind of 1 orange
finely grated rind of 1 lemon
225 g/½ lb self-raising flour, sifted

For the icing:

juice of ½ orange
juice of ½ lemon
100 g/4 oz icing sugar, sifted

AMERICAN

½ cup butter or margarine
½ cup sugar
2 eggs, lightly beaten
3 tablespoons coarse-cut marmalade
finely grated rind of 1 orange
finely grated rind of 1 lemon
2 cups self-rising flour, sifted

For the icing:

juice of ½ orange
juice of ½ lemon
⅔ cup sifted confectioners' sugar

Cream the butter or margarine and sugar together until light and fluffy, then beat in the eggs a little at a time, the marmalade and the orange and lemon rinds. Fold in the flour. Butter a 23 × 13 × 7.5 cm/9 × 5 × 3 inch loaf tin and pour in the mixture. Bake in a moderately hot oven (190°C/375°F or Gas Mark 5) for 60 to 70 minutes or until a skewer inserted in centre of cake comes out clean. Cool for 20 minutes in the tin, then turn out onto a wire rack.
To make the icing: stir the orange and lemon juices into the icing (confectioners') sugar and beat well with a wooden spoon. Spread smoothly over the top of the cake. Leave to dry.
To freeze: open (flash) freeze until firm, then wrap in cling film and overwrap in foil or a freezer bag. Seal, label and return to freezer.
To thaw and serve: unwrap, and leave for 4 to 5 hours at room temperature.
SERVES 6 to 8

FRANGIPANE FLAN

METRIC/IMPERIAL

basic sweet shortcrust pastry dough made with 100 g/4 oz flour
1 × 15 ml spoon/1 tablespoon lemon curd
50 g/2 oz butter, softened
25 g/1 oz caster sugar
1 × 15 ml spoon/1 tablespoon clear honey
1 egg, beaten
75 g/3 oz ground almonds
4 drops of almond essence
15 g/½ oz self-raising flour
To finish:
glacé icing
a few glacé cherries, halved
a few strips of candied angelica

AMERICAN

basic sweet pie dough made with 1 cup flour
1 tablespoon lemon cheese
¼ cup butter, softened
2 tablespoons sugar
1 tablespoon clear honey
1 egg, beaten
¾ cup ground almonds
4 drops of almond extract
2 tablespoons self-rising flour
To finish:
glacé icing
a few candied cherries, halved
a few strips of candied angelica

Roll out the dough on a floured surface and use to line an 18 cm/7 inch flan ring set on a baking sheet. Prick the bottom of the dough and spread with the lemon curd (cheese).

Put the butter, sugar and honey in a bowl, beat together until light and fluffy, then gradually beat in the egg and almond essence (extract). Stir in the ground almonds, then fold in the flour until evenly blended.

Spoon the mixture into the pastry case (pie shell) and smooth the top. Bake in a preheated moderately hot oven (190°C/375°F or Gas Mark 5) for 25 to 30 minutes until firm and golden. Cool quickly on a wire rack, then remove the flan ring.

To freeze: open (flash) freeze until firm, then pack in a freezer bag. Seal, label and return to the freezer.

To thaw and serve: remove wrappings and place on a serving platter. Thaw at room temperature for 4 hours. Spread the top of the cake with glacé icing and decorate with glacé (candied) cherries and diamonds of candied angelica. Leave to set before serving.

SERVES 4 to 6

CARAMEL RING CAKE

METRIC/IMPERIAL

For the cake:
225 g/½ lb flour
1 × 5 ml spoon/1 teaspoon ground mixed spice
1 × 2.5 ml spoon/½ teaspoon bicarbonate of soda
50 g/2 oz caster sugar
2 eggs, beaten
100 g/4 oz soft tub margarine
150 g/5 oz black treacle
75 g/3 oz golden syrup
120 ml/4 fl oz milk
For the caramel icing (to finish):
175 g/6 oz icing sugar
1 × 15 ml spoon/1 tablespoon black treacle

AMERICAN

For the cake:
2 cups flour
½ teaspoon grated nutmeg
½ teaspoon ground allspice and cloves, mixed
½ teaspoon baking soda
¼ cup sugar
2 eggs, beaten
½ cup soft margarine
scant ½ cup molasses
¼ cup light corn syrup
½ cup milk
For the caramel icing (to finish):
1⅓ cups confectioners' sugar
1 tablespoon molasses

Grease a 23 cm/9 inch ring mould and dust with flour.

Sift the flour, spice(s) and soda into a bowl and stir in the sugar. Add the remaining ingredients and beat for 2 to 3 minutes until well mixed.

Spoon the mixture into the prepared mould. Bake in a preheated cool oven (150°C/300°F or Gas Mark 2) for 1 to 1½ hours or until a skewer inserted in the centre of the cake comes out clean. Leave to cool in the tin for a few minutes, then turn out onto a wire rack and leave to cool.

To freeze: wrap in foil, then pack in a freezer bag. Seal, label and freeze.

To thaw and serve: thaw in the wrapping at room temperature for 2 to 3 hours.

To make the caramel icing: sift the icing (confectioners') sugar into a bowl, add the black treacle (molasses) and beat until smooth, adding a little water if necessary. Spread over the cake, then leave to set before serving.

SERVES 6

COFFEE WALNUT CAKE

METRIC/IMPERIAL

For the cake:

225 g/½ lb flour
1.5 × 5 ml spoons/1½ teaspoons baking powder
175 g/6 oz butter, softened
175 g/6 oz caster sugar
3 eggs, beaten
2 × 15 ml spoons/2 tablespoons milk
75 g/3 oz walnuts, chopped

For the coffee glacé icing (to finish):

350 g/¾ lb icing sugar, sifted
1 × 15 ml spoon/1 tablespoon coffee essence
1.5 × 15 ml spoons/1½ tablespoons warm water
5 walnut halves, to decorate

AMERICAN

For the cake:

2 cups flour
1½ teaspoons baking powder
¾ cup butter, softened
¾ cup sugar
3 eggs, beaten
2 tablespoons milk
¾ cup chopped walnuts

For the coffee glacé icing (to finish):

2⅔ cups sifted confectioners' sugar
1 tablespoon strong black coffee
1½ tablespoons warm water
5 walnut halves, to decorate

Grease an 18 cm/7 inch round cake tin and line with greased greaseproof paper or non-stick parchment.
Sift together the flour and baking powder. Put the butter and sugar in a bowl, beat together until light and fluffy, then beat in the eggs a little at a time. Fold in the sifted mixture, then the milk and walnuts.
Spoon the mixture into the prepared tin. Bake in a preheated moderate oven (160°C/325°F or Gas Mark 3) for 1½ to 2 hours until a skewer inserted in the centre of the cake comes out clean. Leave to cool in the tin for a few minutes, turn out onto a wire rack, then remove the paper lining. Leave to cool completely.
To freeze: wrap in cling film, then pack in a freezer bag. Seal, label and freeze.
To thaw and serve: remove wrappings and place on a serving platter. Thaw at room temperature for 4 hours.
To make the coffee glacé icing: put the icing (confectioners') sugar in a heatproof bowl, then gradually beat in the coffee and water. Stand the bowl in a pan of hot water to come halfway up the sides of the bowl. Heat very gently for 1 to 2 minutes, beating constantly until the icing coats the back of the spoon. Pour over the top of the cake, letting it run down the sides, then quickly swirl the surface with a palette knife. Decorate with the walnut halves, then leave to set before serving.
SERVES 8

MADEIRA CAKE

METRIC/IMPERIAL

175 g/6 oz butter, softened
175 g/6 oz caster sugar
3 eggs, beaten
225 g/½ lb flour
1.5 × 5 ml spoons/1½ teaspoons baking powder
2 × 15 ml spoons/2 tablespoons milk
2 thin strips of lemon rind, to decorate

AMERICAN

¾ cup butter, softened
¾ cup sugar
3 eggs, beaten
2 cups flour
1½ teaspoons baking powder
2 tablespoons milk
2 thin strips of lemon rind, to decorate

Grease an 18 cm/7 inch round cake tin and line with greased greaseproof paper or non-stick parchment.
Put the butter and sugar in a bowl, beat together until light and fluffy, then beat in the eggs a little at a time. Sift together the flour and baking powder, then fold into the creamed mixture with the milk.
Spoon the mixture into the prepared tin, smooth the top and place the lemon rind in the centre. Bake in a preheated moderate oven (160°C/325°F or Gas Mark 3) for 1½ to 1¾ hours until a skewer inserted in the centre of the cake comes out clean.
Leave to cool in the tin for 5 minutes, turn out onto a wire rack then remove the paper lining. Leave to cool completely.
To freeze: wrap in foil, then pack in a freezer bag. Seal, label and freeze.
To thaw and serve: thaw in the wrappings at room temperature for 4 hours.
SERVES 6

SEED CAKE

Make as for Madeira Cake (see above), folding in 2 × 15 ml spoons/2 tablespoons caraway seeds with the flour. Omit the lemon rind decoration. Freeze, thaw and serve as for Madeira Cake.
SERVES 6

CHOCOLATE FRUITY CAKE

METRIC/IMPERIAL

1 × 15 ml spoon/1 tablespoon cocoa powder
2 × 15 ml spoons/2 tablespoons hot water
112 g/4 oz butter, softened
112 g/4 oz caster sugar
2 eggs, beaten
112 g/4 oz self-raising flour
50 g/2 oz sultanas
icing sugar, for sprinkling, to finish

AMERICAN

1 tablespoon unsweetened cocoa powder
2 tablespoons hot water
½ cup butter, softened
½ cup sugar
2 eggs, beaten
1 cup self-rising flour
⅓ cup seedless white raisins
confectioners' sugar, for sprinkling, to finish

Grease a 20 cm/8 inch cake tin and line the bottom with greased greaseproof paper or non-stick parchment.

Mix the cocoa to a paste with the hot water, then leave to cool. Put the butter and sugar in a bowl, beat together until light and fluffy, then beat in the cocoa paste. Beat in the eggs a little at a time, then fold in the flour and sultanas (seedless white raisins) until evenly blended.

Spoon the mixture into the prepared tin and smooth the top. Bake in a preheated moderate oven (160°C/325°F or Gas Mark 3) for 35 to 40 minutes, turn out and cool on a wire rack.

To freeze: wrap in cling film, then pack in a freezer bag. Seal, label and freeze.

To thaw and serve: remove wrappings and thaw at room temperature for 3 to 4 hours. Sprinkle with icing (confectioners') sugar to serve.

SERVES 4 to 6

APRICOT UPSIDE-DOWN CAKE

METRIC/IMPERIAL

For the topping:
50 g/2 oz butter, melted
50 g/2 oz soft brown sugar
1 × 5 ml spoon/1 teaspoon ground cinnamon
225 g/½ lb apricot halves
15–20 whole roasted hazelnuts
For the cake:
112 g/4 oz self-raising flour
1 × 5 ml spoon/1 teaspoon baking powder
112 g/4 oz soft tub margarine
112 g/4 oz caster sugar
2 eggs

AMERICAN

For the topping:
¼ cup butter, melted
⅓ cup light brown sugar
1 teaspoon ground cinnamon
½ lb apricot halves
15–20 whole roasted hazelnuts
For the cake:
1 cup self-rising flour
1 teaspoon baking powder
½ cup soft margarine
½ cup sugar
2 eggs

To make the topping: put the melted butter, sugar and cinnamon in a bowl, stir well to mix, then spread in the bottom of a greased 20 cm/8 inch cake tin. Place a hazelnut in the centre of each apricot half, then arrange the apricots, cut side down, on the butter and sugar mixture.

To make the cake: sift the flour and baking powder into a bowl. Add the remining ingredients and beat for 2 to 3 minutes until well mixed. Spread the mixture over the apricots, then smooth the top. Bake in a preheated moderately hot oven (190°C/375°F or Gas Mark 5) for 30 minutes. Reduce the heat to moderate (180°C/350°F or Gas Mark 4) and bake for a further 30 minutes until well risen and golden brown. Leave to cool in the tin for 5 minutes, then turn out onto a wire rack and leave to cool completely.

To freeze: open (flash) freeze until firm, then pack in a freezer bag. Seal, label and return to the freezer.

To thaw and serve: remove wrappings and thaw at room temperature for 3 to 4 hours.

SERVES 6

GOLDEN GRILLED (BROILED) SPONGE

METRIC/IMPERIAL

25 g/1 oz butter, softened
25 g/1 oz demerara sugar
25 g/1 oz walnuts, chopped
1 × 255 g/9 oz can pineapple chunks, drained and finely chopped
1 × 20 cm/8 inch Victoria Sandwich (see page 277)

AMERICAN

2 tablespoons butter, softened
2 tablespoons raw brown sugar
¼ cup chopped walnuts
1 × 9 oz can pineapple chunks, drained and finely chopped
1 × 8 inch layer cake (see page 277)

Put the butter and sugar in a bowl and beat together until well mixed. Stir in the nuts and the pineapple, then spread the mixture on top of the cake. Put under a preheated hot grill (broiler) for 5 minutes or until the top is golden brown.
To freeze: cool quickly. Open (flash) freeze until firm, then pack in a freezer bag. Seal, label and return to the freezer.
To thaw and serve: remove wrappings and place on a serving platter. Thaw at room temperature for 3 to 4 hours.
SERVES 5 to 6

GENOA CAKE

METRIC/IMPERIAL
275 g/10 oz flour
1 × 2.5 ml spoon/½ teaspoon baking powder
50 g/2 oz ground almonds
225 g/½ lb butter, softened
225 g/½ lb caster sugar
4 eggs, beaten
225 g/½ lb sultanas
100 g/4 oz glacé cherries, halved
50 g/2 oz chopped candied peel
2 × 15 ml spoons/2 tablespoons milk

AMERICAN
2½ cups flour
½ teaspoon baking powder
½ cup ground almonds
1 cup butter, softened
1 cup sugar
4 eggs, beaten
1½ cups seedless white raisins
½ cup candied cherries, halved
⅓ cup chopped candied peel
2 tablespoons milk

Grease a deep 20 cm/8 inch round cake tin and line with a double thickness of greased greaseproof paper or non-stick parchment. Tie several thicknesses of brown paper around the outside of the tin, then stand on a wad of paper on a baking sheet.
Sift together the flour and baking powder, then stir in the ground almonds. Put the butter and sugar in a bowl, beat together until light and fluffy, then beat in the eggs a little at a time. Fold in the flour mixture and the remaining ingredients a little at a time until evenly blended. Spoon the mixture into the prepared tin and smooth the top. Bake in a preheated cool oven (150°C/300°F or Gas Mark 2) for 3¼ to 3¾ hours until a skewer inserted in the centre of the cake comes out clean. Leave to cool in the tin for a few minutes, turn out onto a wire rack, then remove the paper lining. Leave to cool completely.
To freeze: wrap in cling film, then pack in a freezer bag. Seal, label and freeze.
To thaw and serve: thaw in the wrappings at room temperature for 4 to 6 hours.
SERVES 8

GÂTEAU PITHIVIERS

METRIC/IMPERIAL
40 g/1½ oz butter, softened
75 g/3 oz caster sugar
75 g/3 oz ground almonds
finely grated rind and juice of ½ lemon
1 egg, beaten
2 × 15 ml spoons/2 tablespoons flour
basic puff pastry dough made with 225 g/½ lb flour
1 egg white, lightly beaten
caster sugar, for sprinkling

AMERICAN
3 tablespoons butter, softened
⅜ cup sugar
¾ cup ground almonds
finely grated rind and juice of ½ lemon
1 egg, beaten
2 tablespoons flour
basic puff paste dough made with 2 cups flour
1 egg white, lightly beaten
sugar, for sprinkling

Put the butter and sugar in a bowl, beat together until light and fluffy, then beat in the ground almonds, lemon rind and juice. Beat in the egg a little at a time, then fold in the flour.
Roll out the dough on a floured surface and cut out two 20 cm/8 inch circles. Put one circle on a baking sheet and spread with the creamed mixture to within 1 cm/½ inch of the edge. Moisten the edge with water, then cover with the remaining circle of dough, pressing the edge firmly to seal. Brush the dough with the egg white and sprinkle with (caster) sugar. Score crescent shapes in the dough with the point of a knife, then bake in a preheated hot oven (220°C/425°F or Gas Mark 7) for about 25 minutes until golden.
To freeze: cool quickly, then pack in a freezer bag. Seal, label and freeze.
To thaw and serve: remove wrappings and return the gâteau to the baking sheet. Reheat from frozen in a preheated moderately hot oven (190°C/375°F or Gas Mark 5) for 25 minutes or until heated through. Cover with foil if the pastry becomes too brown during cooking.
SERVES 4 to 6

DUNDEE CAKE

METRIC/IMPERIAL

175 g/6 oz flour
1 × 5 ml spoon/1 teaspoon ground mixed spice
100 g/4 oz butter, softened
100 g/4 oz caster sugar
finely grated rind of ½ orange
3 eggs, beaten
100 g/4 oz currants
100 g/4 oz sultanas
100 g/4 oz seedless raisins
50 g/2 oz chopped candied peel
25 g/1 oz glacé cherries, chopped
50 g/2 oz whole blanched almonds

AMERICAN

1½ cups flour
½ teaspoon grated nutmeg
½ teaspoon ground allspice and cloves, mixed
½ cup butter, softened
½ cup sugar
finely grated rind of ½ orange
3 eggs, beaten
¾ cup currants
¾ cup seedless white raisins
¾ cup seedless raisins
⅓ cup chopped candied peel
3 tablespoons chopped candied cherries
scant ½ cup whole blanched almonds

Grease a deep 15 cm/6 inch round cake tin and line with a double thickness of greased greaseproof paper or non-stick parchment. Tie several thicknesses of brown paper around the outside of the tin, then stand on a wad of paper on a baking sheet.

Sift together the flour and spice(s). Put the butter and sugar in a bowl, beat together until light and fluffy, then beat in the orange rind. Beat in the eggs a little at a time, then fold in the sifted mixture and the dried fruit, peel and cherries. Chop half the almonds and fold in until all the ingredients are evenly blended.

Spoon the mixture into the prepared tin, smooth the top, then arrange the whole almonds in a circular pattern on top of the cake. Bake in a preheated cool oven (140°C/275°F or Gas Mark 1) for 2¾ to 3¼ hours until a skewer inserted in the centre of the cake comes out clean.

Leave to cool in the tin for a few minutes, turn out onto a wire rack, then remove the paper lining. Leave to cool completely.

To freeze: wrap in cling film, then pack in a freezer bag. Seal, label and freeze.

To thaw and serve: thaw in the wrappings at room temperature for 4 to 6 hours.

SERVES 8 to 10

REDCURRANT LAYER CAKE

METRIC/IMPERIAL

For the cake:
112 g/4 oz butter, softened
112 g/4 oz caster sugar
2 eggs, beaten
112 g/4 oz self-raising flour
For the filling:
300 ml/½ pint milk
1 vanilla pod
1 egg
1 egg yolk
50 g/2 oz caster sugar
25 g/1 oz flour
225 g/½ lb fresh redcurrants, crushed
To finish:
150 ml/¼ pint double cream, whipped
100 g/4 oz fresh redcurrants

AMERICAN

For the cake:
½ cup butter, softened
½ cup sugar
2 eggs, beaten
1 cup self-rising flour
For the filling:
1¼ cups milk
1 vanilla bean
1 egg
1 egg yolk
¼ cup sugar
¼ cup flour
½ lb fresh redcurrants, crushed
To finish:
⅔ cup heavy cream, whipped
¼ lb fresh redcurrants

Grease two 18 cm/7 inch sandwich tins (layer cake pans) and line the bottoms with greased greaseproof paper or non-stick parchment.

Put the butter and sugar in a bowl, beat together until light and fluffy, then beat in the eggs a little at a time. Fold in the flour until evenly blended, then divide the mixture equally between the prepared tins.

Bake in a preheated moderately hot oven (190°C/375°F or Gas Mark 5) for 20 to 25 minutes, turn out onto a wire rack, then remove the paper linings. Leave to cool.

To make the filling: put the milk and vanilla pod (bean) in a pan, bring to the boil, then turn off the heat. Put the egg, egg yolk and sugar in a bowl and beat together until well mixed. Beat in the flour, then strain in the milk. Return to the rinsed-out pan, bring to the boil and simmer for 2 minutes until thick, stirring constantly. Remove from the heat and leave to cool.

Cut the two sponge cakes in half, then sandwich together with the crushed redcurrants and filling, dividing them equally between the layers.
To freeze: open (flash) freeze until firm, then pack in a rigid container. Seal, label and return to the freezer.
To thaw and serve: place on a serving platter and thaw at room temperature for 4 hours. Spread the top of the cake with the whipped cream and scatter over the redcurrants before serving.
SERVES 6 to 8

COFFEE FINGERS

METRIC/IMPERIAL
For the cake:
112 g/4 oz butter, softened
112 g/4 oz caster sugar
1 × 15 ml spoon/1 tablespoon coffee essence
2 eggs, beaten
112 g/4 oz self-raising flour
For the coffee cream:
112 g/4 oz butter, softened
1 × 15 ml spoon/1 tablespoon caster sugar
2 × 15 ml spoons/2 tablespoons hot water
1 × 15 ml spoon/1 tablespoon creamy milk
1 × 15 ml spoon/1 tablespoon coffee essence

AMERICAN
For the cake:
$\frac{1}{2}$ cup butter, softened
$\frac{1}{2}$ cup sugar
1 tablespoon strong black coffee
2 eggs, beaten
1 cup self-rising flour
For the coffee cream:
$\frac{1}{2}$ cup butter, softened
1 tablespoon sugar
2 tablespoons hot water
1 tablespoon creamy milk
1 tablespoon strong black coffee

Grease a 30 × 20 cm/12 × 8 inch Swiss roll tin (jelly roll pan) and line with greased greaseproof paper or non-stick parchment to come 1 cm/$\frac{1}{2}$ inch above the sides.
Put the butter and sugar in a bowl, beat together until light and fluffy, then beat in the coffee. Beat in the eggs a little at a time, then fold in the flour until evenly blended.
Spoon the mixture into the prepared tin and bake in a preheated moderate oven (180°C/350°F or Gas Mark 4) for 25 minutes until well risen and golden. Turn out onto a wire rack, remove the paper lining and leave to cool.
To make the coffee cream: put the butter and sugar in a bowl and beat together until light. Beat in half the water and the milk and continue beating until fluffy, then beat in the remaining water and the coffee.
Trim 5 mm/$\frac{1}{4}$ inch off the cake around the edges, then cut in two lengthways. Sandwich the cakes together with half the coffee cream, then spread the remaining coffee cream over the top and swirl with a palette knife. Leave to set, then cut into 12 fingers.
To freeze: open (flash) freeze until firm, then pack in a rigid container, separating each layer with foil. Seal, label and return to the freezer.
To thaw and serve: place on a serving platter and thaw at room temperature for 2 hours.
MAKES 12

CHOCOLATE FINGERS

Make as for Coffee Fingers (see above), substituting 50–75 g/2–3 oz plain chocolate ($\frac{1}{3}$–$\frac{1}{2}$ cup semi-sweet chocolate pieces), melted, for the coffee in the coffee cream.
Freeze, thaw and serve as for Coffee Fingers.
MAKES 12

FROSTED BUNS

METRIC/IMPERIAL

112 g/4 oz butter, softened
112 g/4 oz caster sugar
2 eggs, beaten
112 g/4 oz self-raising flour
1 × 15 ml spoon/1 tablespoon cocoa powder
2 × 15 ml spoons/2 tablespoons milk
22 marshmallows

AMERICAN

½ cup butter, softened
½ cup sugar
2 eggs, beaten
1 cup self-rising flour
1 tablespoon unsweetened cocoa powder
2 tablespoons milk
22 marshmallows

Put the butter and sugar in a bowl, beat together until light and fluffy, then beat in the eggs a little at a time. Fold in the flour until evenly blended.

Divide half the mixture equally between 11 paper bun cases. Mix the cocoa to a paste with the milk, beat into the remaining mixture, then divide equally between 11 separate paper bun cases.

Bake in a preheated moderate oven (180°C/ 350°F or Gas Mark 4) for 15 minutes, then place a marshmallow on top of each bun and bake for a further 5 minutes.

To freeze: cool quickly. Open (flash) freeze until firm, then pack in a rigid container. Seal, label and return to the freezer.

To thaw and serve: place the buns on a serving platter and thaw at room temperature for 1 to 2 hours.

MAKES 22

GINGERBREAD MEN

METRIC/IMPERIAL

450 g/1 lb flour
1 × 5 ml spoon/1 teaspoon salt
1 × 15 ml spoon/1 tablespoon ground ginger
1 × 5 ml spoon/1 teaspoon baking powder
1 × 5 ml spoon/1 teaspoon bicarbonate of soda
225 g/½ lb brown sugar
175 g/6 oz butter
100 g/4 oz black treacle
225 g/½ lb golden syrup
300 ml/½ pint milk
1 egg, beaten

AMERICAN

4 cups flour
1 teaspoon salt
1 tablespoon ground ginger
1 teaspoon baking powder
1 teaspoon baking soda
1⅓ cups brown sugar
¾ cup butter
⅓ cup molasses
⅔ cup light corn syrup
1¼ cups milk
1 egg, beaten

Grease two 30 × 20 cm/12 × 8 inch Swiss roll tins (jelly roll pans) and line with greased greaseproof paper or non-stick parchment.

Sift the dry ingredients into a bowl. Put the sugar, butter, treacle (molasses) and syrup in a pan and heat gently until melted. Remove from the heat and stir in the milk and egg.

Make a well in the centre of the sifted mixture, pour in the melted ingredients and beat well to mix. Pour the mixture into the prepared tins and bake in a preheated moderate oven (160°C/ 325°F or Gas Mark 3) for 1½ hours until risen and firm to the touch. Cool on a wire rack, then cut into about 12 shapes using a gingerbread man cutter.

To freeze: pack in a rigid container, separating each layer with foil. Seal, label and freeze.

To thaw and serve: place on a serving platter and thaw at room temperature for 1 to 2 hours.

MAKES 12

GINGERBREAD HEARTS

METRIC/IMPERIAL

100 g/4 oz butter, softened
175 g/6 oz caster sugar
1 egg, beaten
175 g/6 oz flour
50 g/2 oz cornflour
1 × 5 ml spoon/1 teaspoon baking powder
1 × 5 ml spoon/1 teaspoon ground ginger
pinch of salt
To decorate:
chocolate glacé icing made with 100 g/4 oz icing sugar
8–10 glacé cherries, halved

AMERICAN

½ cup butter, softened
⅔ cup sugar
1 egg, beaten
1½ cups flour
½ cup cornstarch
1 teaspoon baking powder
1 teaspoon ground ginger
pinch of salt
To decorate:
chocolate glacé icing made with scant 1 cup confectioners' sugar
8–10 candied cherries, halved

Put the butter and sugar in a bowl, beat together until smooth, then beat in the egg a little at a time. Sift together the dry ingredients, fold into the creamed mixture, then knead to a smooth dough. Chill in the refrigerator for 1 to 2 hours.
Roll out the dough thinly on a floured surface, then cut out 15 to 20 heart shapes. Place on a baking sheet, allowing room for expansion. Bake in a preheated moderately hot oven (190°C/375°F or Gas Mark 5) for about 15 minutes until golden brown. Transfer to a wire rack and leave to cool.
Spread a little glacé icing on each heart, decorate with a cherry half and leave to set.
To freeze: open (flash) freeze until firm, then pack in a rigid container, separating each layer with foil. Seal, label and return to the freezer.
To thaw and serve: place on a serving platter and thaw at room temperature for 1 to 2 hours.
MAKES 15 to 20

APRICOT ALMOND SLICES

METRIC/IMPERIAL

basic shortcrust pastry dough made with 225 g/½ lb flour
4 × 15 ml spoons/4 tablespoons apricot jam
112 g/4 oz butter, softened
112 g/4 oz caster sugar
2 eggs, beaten
112 g/4 oz ground almonds
25 g/1 oz flour
a few drops of almond essence

AMERICAN

basic pie dough made with 2 cups flour
¼ cup apricot jam
½ cup butter, softened
½ cup sugar
2 eggs, beaten
1 cup ground almonds
¼ cup flour
a few drops of almond extract

Roll out the dough on a floured surface and cut out an oblong about 30 × 20 cm/12 × 8 inches. Place on a Swiss roll tin (jelly roll pan). Reserve the trimmings of dough. Warm the jam and spread evenly over the dough.
Put the butter and sugar in a bowl, beat together until light and fluffy, then beat in the eggs a little at a time. Fold in the remaining ingredients then spread the mixture over the jam.
Roll out the reserved trimmings of dough and cut into thin strips long enough to criss-cross the dough. Moisten the ends of the strips with water and arrange over the dough in a criss-cross pattern, pressing the ends firmly to seal.
Bake in a preheated moderate oven (180°C/350°F or Gas Mark 4) for 30 to 35 minutes until golden. Cut into 16 slices while still warm, then leave to cool on a wire rack.
To freeze: open (flash) freeze until firm, then pack in a rigid container, separating each layer with foil. Seal, label and return to the freezer.
To thaw and serve: place on a serving platter and thaw at room temperature for 1 to 2 hours.
MAKES 16

MINCEMEAT AND ORANGE TURNOVERS

METRIC/IMPERIAL

1 × 375 g/13 oz packet frozen puff pastry, thawed
100 g/4 oz mincemeat
½ × 300 g/11 oz can mandarin oranges, drained
caster sugar for sprinkling, to finish

AMERICAN

1 × 13 oz package frozen puff paste, thawed
½ cup mincemeat
½ × 11 oz can mandarin oranges, drained
sugar for sprinkling, to finish

Roll out the dough thinly on a floured surface and cut out 6 to 8 rounds. Mix together the mincemeat and mandarins and divide equally between the rounds of dough. Moisten the edges with water, fold the rounds in half, then press and pinch the edges firmly to seal.
To freeze: open (flash) freeze until firm, wrap individually in foil, then pack in a freezer bag. Seal, label and return to the freezer.
To thaw and serve: remove wrappings and place the turnovers on a baking sheet. Brush with a little water and sprinkle with (caster) sugar. Bake from frozen in a preheated hot oven (230°C/450°F or Gas Mark 8) for 15 to 20 minutes until golden and heated through. Leave to cool on a wire rack before serving.
MAKES 6 to 8

CHOCOLATE ÉCLAIRS

METRIC/IMPERIAL

For the choux pastry:

50 g/2 oz butter
150 ml/¼ pint water
pinch of salt
65 g/2½ oz flour, sifted
2 large eggs, beaten

To finish:

150 ml/¼ pint double cream, stiffly whipped
chocolate glacé icing made with 100 g/4 oz icing sugar

AMERICAN

For the choux paste:

¼ cup butter
⅔ cup water
pinch of salt
⅔ cup flour, sifted
2 large eggs, beaten

To finish:

⅔ cup heavy cream, stiffly whipped
chocolate glacé icing made with scant 1 cup confectioners' sugar

Put the butter, water and salt in a pan and heat gently until the butter has melted. Bring to the boil, then immediately remove the pan from the heat and quickly beat in the flour all at once. Continue beating for 2 minutes until the mixture draws away from the sides of the pan and forms a ball. Leave to cool slightly, then beat in the eggs a little at a time until the dough is smooth and shiny. Add enough egg to give a mixture that just falls from the spoon.

Put the mixture into a large piping (pastry) bag fitted with a 1 cm/½ inch plain nozzle (tube). Pipe ten to twelve 10 cm/4 inch lengths on wetted baking sheets, allowing room for expansion. Bake in a preheated hot oven (220°C/425°F or Gas Mark 7) for 15 minutes, then reduce the heat to moderately hot (190°C/375°F or Gas Mark 5) and bake for a further 20 minutes. Make a slit in the side of each éclair so that the steam can escape, then cool quickly on a wire rack.

To freeze: open (flash) freeze until firm, then pack in a rigid container, separating each layer with foil. Seal, label and return to the freezer.

To thaw and serve: put the éclairs on a baking sheet and reheat from frozen in a preheated moderately hot oven (200°C/400°F or Gas Mark 6) for 5 to 10 minutes until crisp. Transfer to a wire rack and leave to cool, then fill with the whipped cream and coat with the glacé icing. Leave to set before serving.

MAKES 10 to 12

CREAM BUNS

Make the choux pastry (paste) as for Chocolate Eclairs, then put the mixture into a large piping (pastry) bag fitted with a large star nozzle (fluted tube). Pipe small round raised shapes onto wetted baking sheets, allowing room for expansion, then bake as for Chocolate Eclairs.

Make a small hole in the base of each bun so that the steam can escape, then cool quickly on a wire rack.

Freeze and thaw as for Chocolate Eclairs, fill with cream and sprinkle with icing (confectioners') sugar.

MAKES 10 to 12

MALTED SQUARES

METRIC/IMPERIAL

200 g/7 oz flour
100 g/4 oz butter
100 g/4 oz soft brown sugar
1 × 2.5 ml spoon/½ teaspoon baking powder
1 × 15 ml spoon/1 tablespoon malted drinking chocolate powder
65 g/2½ oz caster sugar
2 large eggs
1 × 5 ml spoon/1 teaspoon vanilla essence
50 g/2 oz desiccated coconut
50 g/2 oz walnuts, chopped

For the icing:

2 × 15 ml spoons/2 tablespoons malted drinking chocolate powder
1 × 2.5 ml spoon/½ teaspoon instant coffee powder
2 × 15 ml spoons/2 tablespoons hot water
15 g/½ oz soft tub margarine
225 g/½ lb icing sugar, sifted
1 × 2.5 ml spoon/½ teaspoon vanilla essence

AMERICAN

1¾ cups flour
½ cup butter
⅔ cup light brown sugar
½ teaspoon baking powder
1 tablespoon malted drinking chocolate powder
5 tablespoons sugar
2 large eggs
1 teaspoon vanilla extract
⅔ cup shredded coconut
½ cup chopped walnuts

For the icing:

2 tablespoons malted drinking chocolate powder
½ teaspoon instant coffee powder
2 tablespoons hot water
1 tablespoon soft margarine
scant 2 cups sifted confectioners' sugar
½ teaspoon vanilla extract

Sift 175 g/6 oz/1½ cups flour into a bowl, add the butter in pieces and rub into the flour until the mixture resembles fine breadcrumbs. Stir in the brown sugar, then press the mixture into a shallow 19 cm/7½ inch square cake tin. Prick the surface and bake in a preheated moderate oven (180°C/350°F or Gas Mark 4) for 20 minutes. Remove from the oven.

Sift together the remaining flour and the baking powder, then blend well with the remaining ingredients. Spread evenly over the pastry in the tin and bake in the moderate oven for 25 to 35 minutes until firm to the touch. Leave to cool in the tin.

To make the icing: mix the malted drinking chocolate and instant coffee powders to a paste with the hot water. Beat in the margarine and icing (confectioners') sugar until smooth, then beat in the vanilla essence (extract). Add a little water if necessary to give a spreading consistency. Spread over the cake, then leave to set. Cut into 16 squares and remove carefully from the tin.

To freeze: open (flash) freeze until firm, then pack in a rigid container, separating each layer with foil. Seal, label and return to the freezer.

To thaw and serve: place the squares on a serving platter and thaw at room temperature for 1 to 2 hours.

MAKES 16

CURRANT TURNOVERS

METRIC/IMPERIAL

basic shortcrust pastry dough made with 100 g/4 oz flour
75 g/3 oz currants
1 × 15 ml spoon/1 tablespoon sugar
1 × 15 ml spoon/1 tablespoon honey
2 × 5 ml spoons/2 teaspoons lemon juice
2 × 5 ml spoons/2 teaspoons melted butter

AMERICAN

basic pie dough made with 1 cup flour
½ cup currants
1 tablespoon sugar
1 tablespoon honey
2 teaspoons lemon juice
2 teaspoons melted butter

Roll out the dough on a floured surface and cut out 4 × 10 cm/4 inch rounds.

Put the currants in a pan with a little water and simmer until plump and tender. Drain well, then mix with the remaining ingredients. Divide the mixture equally between the rounds of dough. Moisten the edges with water, fold the rounds in half, then pinch and press the edges firmly to seal. Place on a baking sheet and bake in a preheated hot oven (220°C/425°F or Gas Mark 7) for 15 minutes until golden.

To freeze: cool quickly. Open (flash) freeze until firm, wrap individually in foil, then pack in a freezer bag. Seal, label and return to the freezer.

To thaw and serve: remove wrappings and place on a serving platter. Thaw at room temperature for 2 to 3 hours.

MAKES 4

SPITZBUBEN

METRIC/IMPERIAL

175 g/6 oz butter, softened
150 g/5 oz icing sugar, sifted
1 egg yolk
1 × 2.5 ml spoon/½ teaspoon vanilla essence
275 g/10 oz flour
100 g/4 oz ground almonds
approx 175 g/6 oz redcurrant jelly, warmed
extra icing sugar for sprinkling, to finish

AMERICAN

¾ cup butter, softened
1¼ cups sifted confectioners' sugar
1 egg yolk
½ teaspoon vanilla extract
2½ cups flour
1 cup ground almonds
approx ½ cup redcurrant jelly, warmed
extra confectioners' sugar for sprinkling, to finish

Put the butter, icing (confectioners') sugar, egg yolk and vanilla essence (extract) in a bowl and beat together until light and fluffy. Sift in the flour, then fold in with the ground almonds until evenly blended. Knead to a smooth dough, then chill in the refrigerator for 1 to 2 hours.

Roll out the dough thinly on a floured surface and cut out about 40 rounds using a 2.5 to 3.75 cm/1 to 1½ inch cutter. Place on a baking sheet, allowing room for expansion. Bake in a preheated moderately hot oven (190°C/375°F or Gas Mark 5) for about 15 minutes until golden. Transfer to a wire rack and leave to cool, then sandwich together in pairs with the warm redcurrant jelly.

To freeze: open (flash) freeze until firm, then pack in a rigid container, separating each layer with foil. Seal, label and return to the freezer.

To thaw and serve: place the biscuits (cookies) on a serving platter and thaw at room temperature for 1 to 2 hours. Sprinkle with icing (confectioners') sugar before serving.

MAKES 20

CHOCOLATE BROWNIES

METRIC/IMPERIAL

100 g/4 oz butter, softened
100 g/4 oz caster sugar
1 × 2.5 ml spoon/½ teaspoon vanilla essence
1 egg, beaten
150 g/5 oz flour
1 × 2.5 ml spoon/½ teaspoon baking powder
pinch of salt
100 g/4 oz plain chocolate, melted
100 g/4 oz walnuts, roughly chopped
a little milk, to mix

AMERICAN

½ cup butter, softened
½ cup sugar
½ teaspoon vanilla extract
1 egg, beaten
1¼ cups flour
½ teaspoon baking powder
pinch of salt
⅔ cup semi-sweet chocolate pieces, melted
1 cup roughly chopped walnuts
a little milk, to mix

Put the butter, sugar and vanilla essence (extract) in a bowl, beat together until light and fluffy, then beat in the egg a little at a time. Sift the flour, baking powder and salt together, then fold into the creamed mixture. Stir in the melted chocolate and the walnuts, and enough milk to give a soft dropping consistency.
Spoon the mixture into a greased 18 cm/7 inch square cake tin. Bake in a preheated moderate oven (180°C/350°F or Gas Mark 4) for 20 to 25 minutes until firm to the touch. Cut into 9 squares while still hot, then leave to cool in the tin.
To freeze: wrap in foil, then pack in a freezer bag. Seal, label and freeze.
To serve: remove wrappings and thaw the brownies at room temperature for 2 hours. Serve plain or coat with melted chocolate or chocolate icing if liked.
MAKES 9

HONEY BROWNIES

METRIC/IMPERIAL

200 g/7 oz self-raising flour
pinch of salt
150 g/5 oz butter
100 g/4 oz soft brown sugar
175 g/6 oz clear honey
1 × 15 ml spoon/1 tablespoon water
2 eggs
25–50 g/1–2 oz blanched almond halves

AMERICAN

1¾ cups self-rising flour
pinch of salt
⅝ cup butter
⅔ cup light brown sugar
½ cup clear honey
1 tablespoon water
2 eggs
¼–½ cup blanched almond halves

Grease a 28 × 18 cm/11 × 7 inch Swiss roll tin (jelly roll pan) and line with greased greaseproof paper or non-stick parchment.
Sift together the flour and salt. Put the butter, sugar, honey and water into a pan and heat gently until the butter has melted, stirring constantly. Leave to cool, then beat in the eggs one at a time. Add the flour and stir well to mix. Spoon the mixture into the prepared tin and press the almond halves on top. Bake in a preheated moderate oven (180°C/350°F or Gas Mark 4) for 30 to 35 minutes.
Leave to cool in the tin, then cut into about 12 squares.
To freeze: open (flash) freeze until firm, then pack in a rigid container, separating each layer with foil or freezer film. Seal, label and return to the freezer.
To thaw and serve: place on a serving platter and thaw at room temperature for 2 hours.
MAKES 12

FRENCH CHEW

METRIC/IMPERIAL

50 g/2 oz butter, softened
50 g/2 oz caster sugar
1 egg
1 egg yolk
1 × 15 ml spoon/1 tablespoon milk
75 g/3 oz self-raising flour
For the topping:
1 egg white
50 g/2 oz demerara sugar
50 g/2 oz desiccated coconut

AMERICAN

¼ cup butter, softened
¼ cup sugar
1 egg
1 egg yolk
1 tablespoon milk
¾ cup self-rising flour
For the topping:
1 egg white
⅓ cup raw brown sugar
⅔ cup shredded coconut

Grease an 18 cm/7 inch square cake tin and line the bottom with greased greaseproof paper or non-stick parchment.

Put the butter and sugar in a bowl and beat together until light and fluffy. Mix together the egg, egg yolk and milk and beat half into the creamed mixture. Beat in the remaining half with the flour. Spoon into the prepared tin and smooth the top.

To make the topping: beat the egg white until stiff, then fold in the sugar and coconut. Spread over the cake mixture and bake in a preheated moderate oven (180°C/350°F or Gas Mark 4) for 25 to 30 minutes.

Turn out onto a wire rack and remove the paper lining.

Leave to cool, then cut into 12 squares.

To freeze: pack in a rigid container, separating each layer with foil. Seal, label and freeze.

To thaw and serve: place the squares on a serving platter and thaw at room temperature for 2 hours.

MAKES 12

CHOCONUT BUNS

METRIC/IMPERIAL

225 g/½ lb flour
2 × 5 ml spoons/2 teaspoons baking powder
100 g/4 oz butter, softened
75 g/3 oz caster sugar
75 g/3 oz plain chocolate, chopped
25 g/1 oz walnuts, chopped
1 egg, beaten
2 × 15 ml spoons/2 tablespoons milk
a few drops of vanilla essence

AMERICAN

2 cups flour
2 teaspoons baking powder
½ cup butter, softened
⅜ cup sugar
½ cup semi-sweet chocolate pieces, chopped
¼ cup chopped walnuts
1 egg, beaten
2 tablespoons milk
a few drops of vanilla extract

Sift the flour and baking powder into a bowl, add the remaining ingredients and beat well to mix to a stiff dough.

Put 14 to 16 dessertspoons of the mixture on greased baking sheets, spacing them well apart. Bake near the top of a preheated moderately hot oven (200°C/400°F or Gas Mark 6) for 20 to 25 minutes until golden. Transfer to a wire rack and leave to cool.

To freeze: open (flash) freeze until firm, then pack in a rigid container, separating each layer with foil. Seal, label and return to the freezer.

To thaw and serve: place on a serving platter and thaw at room temperature for 2 to 3 hours.

MAKES 14 to 16

HONEY SQUARES

METRIC/IMPERIAL

100 g/4 oz flour
1 × 5 ml spoon/1 teaspoon ground ginger
1 × 5 ml spoon/1 teaspoon ground cinnamon
1 × 2.5 ml spoon/½ teaspoon bicarbonate of soda
0.5 × 2.5 ml spoon/¼ teaspoon salt
3 × 15 ml spoons/3 tablespoons vegetable oil
50 g/2 oz honey
50 g/2 oz black treacle
50 g/2 oz demerara sugar
1 egg, beaten
2 × 15 ml spoons/2 tablespoons milk
50 g/2 oz sultanas (optional)
25–50 g/1–2 oz chopped nuts (optional)

AMERICAN

1 cup flour
1 teaspoon ground ginger
1 teaspoon ground cinnamon
½ teaspoon baking soda
¼ teaspoon salt
3 tablespoons vegetable oil
3 tablespoons honey
3 tablespoons molasses
⅓ cup raw brown sugar
1 egg, beaten
2 tablespoons milk
6 tablespoons seedless white raisins (optional)
¼–½ cup chopped nuts (optional)

Grease an 18 cm/7 inch square cake tin and line the bottom with greased greaseproof paper or non-stick parchment.

Sift the dry ingredients into a bowl, add the remaining ingredients, except the nuts, and beat well to mix. Spoon into the prepared tin, smooth the top and sprinkle with chopped nuts if liked. Bake in a preheated moderate oven (180°C/350°F or Gas Mark 4) for about 30 minutes until firm to the touch. Turn out onto a wire rack and remove the paper lining. Leave to cool, then cut into 9 squares.

To freeze: open (flash) freeze until firm, then pack in a rigid container, separating each layer with foil. Seal, label and return to the freezer.

To thaw and serve: place on a serving platter and thaw at room temperature for 1 to 2 hours.

MAKES 9

FRUIT AND NUT SQUARES

METRIC/IMPERIAL

225 g/½ lb butter, softened
112 g/4 oz caster sugar
2 eggs, beaten
1 × 5 ml spoon/1 teaspoon vanilla essence
275 g/10 oz flour
1 × 5 ml spoon/1 teaspoon baking powder
pinch of salt
225 g/½ lb plain chocolate, melted
100 g/4 oz sultanas
100 g/4 oz walnuts, chopped
a little milk, to mix
whipped cream, to serve

AMERICAN

1 cup butter, softened
½ cup sugar
2 eggs, beaten
1 teaspoon vanilla extract
2½ cups flour
1 teaspoon baking powder
pinch of salt
1⅓ cups semi-sweet chocolate pieces, melted
¾ cup seedless white raisins
1 cup chopped walnuts
a little milk, to mix
whipped cream, to serve

Grease two 20 cm/8 inch square cake tins and line the bottoms with greased greaseproof paper or non-stick parchment.

Put the butter and sugar in a bowl, beat together until light and fluffy, then beat in the eggs a little at a time. Stir in the vanilla essence (extract). Sift together the flour, baking powder and salt and fold into the creamed mixture. Stir in the melted chocolate, sultanas (seedless white raisins) and walnuts and enough milk to give a soft dropping consistency.

Spoon the mixture into the prepared tins and smooth the tops. Bake in a preheated moderate oven (180°C/350°F or Gas Mark 4) for 20 to 25 minutes until golden brown and firm to the touch. Cut into squares, then leave to cool in the tins.

To freeze: wrap the tins in foil, then overwrap in a freezer bag. Seal, label and freeze.

To thaw and serve: remove wrappings and thaw at room temperature for 2 hours. Serve with whipped cream.

MAKES 32

COFFEE AND WALNUT SQUARES

METRIC/IMPERIAL

112 g/4 oz butter, softened
112 g/4 oz caster sugar
2 eggs, lightly beaten
1 × 15 ml spoon/1 tablespoon coffee essence
112 g/4 oz self-raising flour, sifted
For the topping:
50 g/2 oz walnuts, chopped
25 g/1 oz caster sugar
1 × 5 ml spoon/1 teaspoon ground cinnamon

AMERICAN

½ cup butter, softened
½ cup sugar
2 eggs, lightly beaten
1 tablespoon strong black coffee
1 cup self-rising flour, sifted
For the topping:
½ cup chopped walnuts
2 tablespoons sugar
1 teaspoon ground cinnamon

Put the butter and sugar in a bowl, beat together until light and fluffy, then beat in the eggs a little at a time and stir in the coffee. Fold in the flour until evenly blended. Divide the mixture equally between two greased 18 cm/7 inch square cake tins and smooth the tops.

To make the topping: scatter the chopped walnuts over the mixture. Mix the (caster) sugar with the cinnamon and sprinkle evenly over the walnuts. Bake in a preheated moderately hot oven (190°C/375°F or Gas Mark 5) for 10 to 15 minutes or until golden brown. Cut into 18 squares, then transfer to a wire rack and leave to cool.

To freeze: open (flash) freeze until firm, then pack in a rigid container, separating each layer with foil. Seal, label and return to the freezer.

To thaw and serve: thaw in the container at room temperature for 15 to 20 minutes.

MAKES 18

BLACKCURRANT AND ALMOND TARTLETS

METRIC/IMPERIAL

basic shortcrust pastry dough made with 150 g/5 oz flour
3 × 15 ml spoons/3 tablespoons blackcurrant jam
40 g/1½ oz soft tub margarine
50 g/2 oz caster sugar
1 egg, beaten
25 g/1 oz self-raising flour
50 g/2 oz ground almonds

AMERICAN
basic pie dough made with $1\frac{1}{4}$ cups flour
3 tablespoons blackcurrant jam
3 tablespoons soft margarine
$\frac{1}{4}$ cup sugar
1 egg, beaten
$\frac{1}{4}$ cup self-rising flour
$\frac{1}{2}$ cup ground almonds

Roll out the dough thinly on a floured surface and use to line 18 patty tins. Spoon a little jam into the bottom of each pastry case (tart shell). Put the margarine and sugar in a bowl, beat together until light and fluffy, then beat in the egg a little at a time. Stir in the flour and almonds until evenly blended, then divide the mixture equally between the pastry cases (tart shells). Bake in a preheated moderately hot oven (200°C/400°F or Gas Mark 6) for about 15 minutes until well risen and golden. Transfer to a wire rack and leave to cool.
To freeze: open (flash) freeze until firm, then pack in a rigid container, separating each layer with foil. Seal, label and return to the freezer.
To thaw and serve: place on a serving platter and thaw at room temperature for 2 hours.
MAKES 18

SWISS TARTLETS

METRIC/IMPERIAL
100 g/4 oz soft tub margarine
25 g/1 oz icing sugar, sifted
75 g/3 oz flour
25 g/1 oz cornflour
a few drops of vanilla essence
To decorate:
a few glacé cherries, sliced
a few strips of candied angelica, finely sliced

AMERICAN
$\frac{1}{2}$ cup soft margarine
$\frac{1}{4}$ cup sifted confectioners' sugar
$\frac{3}{4}$ cup flour
$\frac{1}{4}$ cup cornstarch
a few drops of vanilla extract
To decorate:
a few candied cherries, sliced
a few strips of candied angelica, finely sliced

Put the margarine and icing (confectioners') sugar in a bowl and beat together until smooth. Add the flour, cornflour (cornstarch) and vanilla essence (extract) and stir well to mix. Spoon the mixture into a piping (pastry) bag fitted with a 1 cm/$\frac{1}{2}$ inch star vegetable nozzle (tube) and pipe into 12 paper bun cases.
Decorate with slices of cherry and angelica, then bake in a preheated moderately hot oven (190°C/375°F or Gas Mark 5) for 10 to 15 minutes until well risen and golden. Transfer to a wire rack and leave to cool.
To freeze: open (flash) freeze until firm, then pack in a rigid container, separating each layer with foil. Seal, label and return to the freezer.
To thaw and serve: place on a serving platter and thaw at room temperature for 1 to 2 hours.
MAKES 12

CREAM HORNS

METRIC/IMPERIAL
225 g/$\frac{1}{2}$ lb frozen puff pastry, thawed at room temperature for 30 minutes
1 egg white, lightly beaten
25 g/1 oz sugar
For the filling (to finish):
1 × 15 ml spoon/1 tablespoon red jam
150 ml/$\frac{1}{4}$ pint double cream, lightly whipped

AMERICAN
$\frac{1}{2}$ lb frozen puff paste, thawed at room temperature for 30 minutes
1 egg white, lightly beaten
2 tablespoons sugar
For the filling (to finish):
1 tablespoon red jam
$\frac{2}{3}$ cup heavy cream, lightly whipped

Roll out the dough thinly on a floured surface, cut into long strips about 1 cm/$\frac{1}{2}$ inch wide, then wrap around metal cornet-shaped moulds, moistening the ends of the dough with water. Brush with egg white and sprinkle with the sugar.
Place the horns on baking sheets and bake in a preheated hot oven (220°C/425°F or Gas Mark 7) for 10 to 15 minutes or until the pastry is well risen and golden, turning the horns over after 7 minutes. Do not allow the sugar to become too brown. Transfer to a wire rack, leave to cool for 10 to 15 minutes, then remove the moulds.
To freeze: open (flash) freeze until firm, then pack carefully in a rigid container, separating each layer with foil. Seal, label and return to the freezer.
To thaw and serve: place the horns on a serving platter and thaw at room temperature for 1 to 2 hours. Fill with jam and whipped cream before serving.
MAKES ABOUT 24

COFFEE BUTTERFLY CAKES

METRIC/IMPERIAL

½ quantity of All-in-One Victoria Sandwich mixture (see page 276)
1 × 15 ml spoon/1 tablespoon coffee essence
20 g/¾ oz self-raising flour
For the butter cream icing:
25 g/1 oz butter
75 g/3 oz icing sugar, sifted
1.5 × 5 ml spoons/1½ teaspoons coffee essence
1.5 × 5 ml spoons/1½ teaspoons milk
14–16 walnut halves

AMERICAN

½ quantity of All-in-One Layer Cake batter (see page 276)
1 tablespoon strong black coffee
3 tablespoons self-rising flour
For the butter cream icing:
2 tablespoons butter
¾ cup sifted confectioners' sugar
1½ teaspoons strong black coffee
1½ teaspoons milk
14–16 walnut halves

Put the Victoria Sandwich (Layer Cake) mixture in a bowl and beat in the coffee and flour until evenly blended. Divide equally between 14 to 16 paper bun cases. Bake on the second shelf from the top of a preheated moderately hot oven (190°C/375°F or Gas Mark 5) for 15 to 20 minutes until well risen. Transfer to a wire rack and leave to cool.

To make the icing: put all the ingredients in a bowl and beat well to mix. Slice the tops off the cakes and cut the tops in half. Spread the icing on the bottom half of the cakes, then press in the halved tops to form butterfly 'wings'. Place a walnut half in the centre of each cake.

To freeze: open (flash) freeze until firm, then pack in a rigid container, separating each layer with foil. Seal, label and return to the freezer.

To thaw and serve: place on a serving platter and thaw at room temperature for 1 to 2 hours.

MAKES 14 to 16

ALPINE APPLE CAKES

METRIC/IMPERIAL

350 g/¾ lb cooking apples, peeled, cored and sliced
40 g/1½ oz sugar
basic shortcrust pastry dough made with 225 g/½ lb flour
50 g/2 oz icing sugar, sifted
2 × 5 ml spoons/2 teaspoons lemon juice

AMERICAN

¾ lb baking apples, peeled, cored and sliced
3 tablespoons sugar
basic pie dough made with 2 cups flour
½ cup sifted confectioners' sugar
2 teaspoons lemon juice

Put the apples in a pan with the sugar and a little water and cook gently until tender. Leave to cool. Roll out the dough on a floured surface and cut out 20 rounds using a 6 cm/2½ inch cutter. Place 10 rounds on a baking sheet and put 1 × 5 ml spoon/1 teaspoon of the apple mixture in the centre of each round. Moisten the edges of the dough, cover with the remaining 10 rounds and press firmly to seal. Trim and flute the edges. Bake in a preheated moderately hot oven (200°C/400°F or Gas Mark 6) for 20 minutes until golden brown, then transfer to a wire rack. Mix the icing (confectioners') sugar and the lemon juice together until smooth, then spread over the tops of the apple cakes when lukewarm. Leave to cool and set.

To freeze: open (flash) freeze until firm, then pack in a rigid container, separating each layer with foil. Seal, label and return to the freezer.

To thaw and serve: place on a serving platter and thaw at room temperature for 1 to 2 hours.

MAKES 10

DANISH PASTRIES

METRIC/IMPERIAL

For the dough:
15 g/½ oz fresh yeast, or 2 × 5 ml spoons/2 teaspoons dried yeast and 1 × 2.5 ml spoon/½ teaspoon sugar
5 × 15 ml spoons/5 tablespoons water
1 egg, beaten
15 g/½ oz caster sugar
225 g/½ lb flour
pinch of salt
175 g/6 oz butter, softened

AMERICAN

For the dough:

½ cake of compressed fresh yeast, or 1 package of active dry yeast and ½ teaspoon sugar
⅓ cup water
1 egg, beaten
1 tablespoon sugar
2 cups flour
pinch of salt
¾ cup butter, softened

Blend the fresh yeast with the cold water. (If using dried yeast, warm the water, dissolve 1 × 2.5 ml spoon/½ teaspoon sugar in it, then sprinkle over the yeast and stir well. Leave in a warm place for 10 to 15 minutes until frothy.) Then stir in the egg and sugar. Sift the flour and salt into a warm bowl, make a well in the centre and pour in the liquid. Mix to a soft dough.
Knead the dough lightly on a floured surface until smooth. Place in a lightly greased polythene (plastic) bag and leave to rest in a cool place for 10 minutes.
Beat the butter to a spreading consistency and shape into a rectangle about 1 cm/½ inch thick. Roll out the dough to a 25 cm/10 inch square, put the butter in the centre and fold over the dough, sides to middle, to enclose the butter, overlapping by 1 cm/½ inch.
Roll the dough and butter into a strip about 46 × 15 cm/18 × 6 inches. Fold evenly in three, then return the dough to the polythene (plastic) bag and rest again for 10 minutes each time. Divide the dough in two, using one half to make Windmills and the other half to make Fruit Snails.

WINDMILLS

METRIC/IMPERIAL

½ basic Danish pastry dough, rolled and folded 3 times as above
50 g/2 oz almond paste
beaten egg, to glaze
raspberry jam, to finish

AMERICAN

½ basic Danish pastry dough, rolled and folded 3 times as above
2 oz almond paste
beaten egg, to glaze
raspberry jam, to finish

Roll out the dough on a floured surface to a strip 46 × 15 cm/18 × 16 inches. Cut into 8 × 10 cm/4 inch squares and place on a baking sheet. Put a little almond paste in the centre of each square and brush the paste with a little beaten egg. Cut from the corners of each square to the centre, then fold one corner of each triangle to the centre and press the points firmly into the almond paste. Brush all over with beaten egg.
Cover the pastries with a greased polythene (plastic) sheet and leave in a fairly warm place for 10 to 15 minutes until puffy. Remove the sheet and bake in a preheated hot oven (220°C/425°F or Gas Mark 7) for 12 to 15 minutes until well risen and golden. Transfer to a wire rack and leave to cool, then put a little raspberry jam in the centre of each pastry.
To freeze: open (flash) freeze until firm, then pack in a rigid container, separating each layer with foil. Seal, label and return to the freezer.
To thaw and serve: place on a serving platter and thaw at room temperature for 2 hours.
MAKES 8

FRUIT SNAILS

METRIC/IMPERIAL

50 g/2 oz butter, softened
50 g/2 oz caster sugar
2 × 5 ml spoons/2 teaspoons ground cinnamon
½ basic Danish pastry dough, rolled and folded 3 times as above
25 g/1 oz sultanas
glacé icing made with 50 g/2 oz icing sugar

AMERICAN

¼ cup butter, softened
¼ cup sugar
2 teaspoons ground cinnamon
½ basic Danish pastry dough, rolled and folded 3 times as above
3 tablespoons seedless white raisins
glacé icing made with ½ cup confectioners' sugar

Put the butter, sugar and cinnamon in a bowl and beat together until well mixed and creamy. Roll out the dough on a floured surface to a strip 41 × 15 cm/16 × 6 inches. Spread with the creamed mixture and scatter over the sultanas (seedless white raisins). Roll up the dough from the shorter end, then cut into 8 slices and place cut side down on a baking sheet. Flatten the snails slightly, then leave to rise and bake as for Windmills. Coat with the icing when cool.
To freeze: open (flash) freeze until firm, then pack in a rigid container, separating each layer with foil. Seal, label and return to the freezer.
To thaw and serve: place on a serving platter and thaw at room temperature for 2 hours.
MAKES 8

PRAIRIE COOKIES

METRIC/IMPERIAL

225 g/½ lb self-raising flour
1 × 2.5 ml spoon/½ teaspoon grated nutmeg
100 g/4 oz butter
75 g/3 oz soft brown sugar
100 g/4 oz mixed dried fruit and candied peel
1 egg, beaten
caster sugar, for sprinkling

AMERICAN

2 cups self-rising flour
½ teaspoon grated nutmeg
½ cup butter
½ cup light brown sugar
⅔ cup mixed dried fruit and candied peel
1 egg, beaten
sugar, for sprinkling

Sift the flour and nutmeg into a bowl, add the butter in pieces and rub into the flour until the mixture resembles fine breadcrumbs. Add the brown sugar, dried fruit mixture and the egg and stir well to mix.

Place the mixture in 10 to 12 rough mounds on a greased baking sheet, then sprinkle with (caster) sugar. Bake on the second shelf from the top of a preheated moderately hot oven (200°C/400°F or Gas Mark 6) for 20 to 25 minutes until well risen and golden brown. Transfer to a wire rack and leave to cool.

To freeze: open (flash) freeze until firm, then pack in a rigid container, separating each layer with foil. Seal, label and return to the freezer.

To thaw and serve: place on a serving platter and thaw at room temperature for 2 hours.

MAKES 10 to 12

CARAMEL WALNUT SLICES

METRIC/IMPERIAL

112 g/4 oz butter, softened
112 g/4 oz soft brown sugar
2 eggs, beaten
112 g/4 oz self-raising flour
50 g/2 oz walnuts, chopped
1 medium cooking apple, peeled, cored and diced
approx 75 g/3 oz apricot jam, warmed and sieved

AMERICAN

½ cup butter, softened
⅔ cup light brown sugar
2 eggs, beaten
1 cup self-rising flour
½ cup chopped walnuts
1 medium baking apple, peeled, cored and diced
approx ¼ cup apricot jam, warmed and strained

Grease a 28 × 18 cm/11 × 7 inch Swiss roll tin (jelly roll pan) and line with greased greaseproof paper or non-stick parchment to come 1 cm/½ inch above the sides.

Put the butter and sugar in a bowl, beat together until light and fluffy, then beat in the eggs a little at a time. Fold in the flour, then stir in 25 g/1 oz/¼ cup walnuts and the diced apple.

Spoon the mixture into the prepared tin. Bake in a preheated moderate oven (180°C/350°F or Gas Mark 4) for 25 minutes or until well risen and golden. Turn out onto a wire rack and remove the paper lining. Brush the top of the cake with the warm apricot jam and scatter over the remaining walnuts. Leave to cool, then cut into 16 slices.

To freeze: open (flash) freeze until firm, then pack in a rigid container, separating each layer with foil. Seal, label and return to the freezer.

To thaw and serve: place on a serving platter and thaw at room temperature for 2 hours.

MAKES 16

ECCLES CAKES

METRIC/IMPERIAL

flaky or rough puff pastry dough made with 225 g/½ lb flour

For the filling:

25 g/1 oz butter
1 × 15 ml spoon/1 tablespoon soft brown sugar
100 g/4 oz currants
50 g/2 oz chopped candied peel
1 × 2.5 ml spoon/½ teaspoon ground mixed spice

To glaze:

a little milk
caster sugar, for sprinkling

AMERICAN

flaky or rough puff paste dough, made with 2 cups flour

For the filling:

2 tablespoons butter
1 tablespoon light brown sugar
⅔ cup currants
⅓ cup chopped candied peel
¼ teaspoon grated nutmeg
¼ teaspoon ground allspice and cloves, mixed

To glaze:

a little milk
sugar, for sprinkling

Roll out the dough thinly on a floured surface and cut out 16 rounds with an 9 cm/3½ inch cutter.

To make the filling: melt the butter in a pan, stir in the remaining ingredients and leave to

cool. Put a heaped 5 ml spoonful/teaspoonful of filling in the centre of each round of dough, moisten the edges with water, then gather the dough together over the filling. Press firmly together at the top to seal, turn the cakes over so that the joins are underneath, then roll gently to make flat round cakes.
Place on a baking sheet, then chill in the refrigerator for 15 minutes. Make 3 slits across the top of each cake, then brush with milk and sprinkle with (caster) sugar. Bake in a preheated hot oven (220°C/425°F or Gas Mark 7) for 20 to 25 minutes until well risen and golden. Transfer to a wire rack and leave to cool.
To freeze: open (flash) freeze until firm, then pack in a rigid container, separating each layer with foil. Seal, label and return to the freezer.
To thaw and serve: place on a serving platter and thaw at room temperature for 2 hours.
MAKES 16

ALMOND TARTLETS

METRIC/IMPERIAL
basic shortcrust pastry dough made with 100 g/4 oz flour
40 g/1½ oz butter
50 g/2 oz caster sugar
1 egg, beaten
50 g/2 oz ground almonds
3–4 × 15 ml spoons/3–4 tablespoons apricot jam

AMERICAN
basic pie dough made with 1 cup flour
3 tablespoons butter
¼ cup sugar
1 egg, beaten
½ cup ground almonds
3–4 tablespoons apricot jam

Roll out the dough on a floured surface and use to line 12 patty tins.
Put the butter and sugar in a bowl, beat together until light and fluffy, then beat in the egg a little at a time and fold in the ground almonds.
Spoon a little jam into the bottom of each pastry case (tart shell) and divide the almond mixture equally between them. Bake in a preheated moderately hot oven (200°C/400°F or Gas Mark 6) for 15 minutes until well risen and golden brown, then transfer to a wire rack and leave to cool.
To freeze: pack in a rigid container, separating each layer with foil. Seal, label and freeze.
To thaw and serve: place on a serving platter and thaw at room temperature for 2 hours.
MAKES 12

WALNUT BOATS

METRIC/IMPERIAL
rich shortcrust pastry dough made with 175 g/6 oz flour and 100 g/4 oz butter
For the filling:
50 g/2 oz walnuts, finely chopped
4 × 15 ml spoons/4 tablespoons crushed biscuit crumbs
50 g/2 oz icing sugar, sifted
finely grated rind and juice of ½ lemon
3 × 15 ml spoons/3 tablespoons milk
1 × 5 ml spoon/1 teaspoon rum
To decorate:
glacé icing made with 100 g/4 oz icing sugar
8 glacé cherries, halved

AMERICAN
rich pie dough made with 1½ cups flour and ½ cup butter
For the filling:
½ cup walnuts, finely chopped
4 tablespoons crushed Graham cracker crumbs
½ cup sifted confectioners' sugar
finely grated rind and juice of ½ lemon
3 tablespoons milk
1 teaspoon rum
To decorate:
glacé icing made with scant 1 cup confectioners' sugar
8 candied cherries, halved

Roll out the dough thinly on a floured surface and cut out 15 boat shapes, using boat-shaped moulds upside-down. Place the dough in the moulds, trim the edges and prick the bottom of the dough with a fork. (If boat-shaped moulds are not available, use patty tins.) Bake in a preheated moderately hot oven (190°C/375°F or Gas Mark 5) for 15 to 20 minutes until golden. Leave to cool slightly in the moulds, then transfer carefully to a wire rack and leave to cool completely.
To make the filling: put all the ingredients in a bowl and beat well to mix. Divide the mixture equally between the pastry boats and smooth over the tops. Pipe the glacé icing on top of the filling in a criss-cross pattern, then decorate each boat with half a cherry. Leave to set.
To freeze: open (flash) freeze until firm, then pack in a rigid container, separating each layer with foil. Seal, label and return to the freezer.
To thaw and serve: place on a serving platter and thaw at room temperature for 2 hours.
MAKES 15

ORANGE TOP KNOTS

METRIC/IMPERIAL

75 g/3 oz butter, softened
75 g/3 oz caster sugar
1 egg, beaten
1 × 5 ml spoon/1 teaspoon finely grated orange rind
150 g/5 oz self-raising flour
1 × 15 ml spoon/1 tablespoon orange juice
orange butter cream made with 100 g/4 oz icing sugar (see page 411)
icing sugar for sprinkling, to finish

AMERICAN

⅜ cup butter, softened
⅜ cup sugar
1 egg, beaten
1 teaspoon finely grated orange rind
1¼ cups self-rising flour
1 tablespoon orange juice
orange butter cream, made with scant 1 cup confectioners' sugar (see page 411)
confectioners' sugar for sprinkling, to finish

Put the butter and sugar in a bowl, beat together until light and fluffy, then beat in the egg a little at a time. Stir in the orange rind, then fold in the flour alternately with the orange juice.
Divide the mixture equally between 12 paper bun cases. Bake in a preheated moderately hot oven (200°C/400°F or Gas Mark 6) for 15 to 20 minutes until well risen and golden. Transfer to a wire rack and leave to cool. Cut a small circle out of the top of each cake, pipe a whirl of butter cream in the circle, then replace the top knot.
To freeze: open (flash) freeze until firm, then pack in a rigid container, separating each layer with foil. Seal, label and return to the freezer.
To thaw and serve: place on a serving platter and thaw at room temperature for 2 hours. Sprinkle with icing (confectioners') sugar before serving.
MAKES 12

CHERRY BUNS

METRIC/IMPERIAL

112 g/4 oz butter, softened
112 g/4 oz caster sugar
2 eggs, beaten
50 g/2 oz glacé cherries, finely chopped
150 g/5 oz self-raising flour
1 × 15 ml spoon/1 tablespoon milk
For the glacé icing:
225 g/½ lb icing sugar, sifted
2 × 15 ml spoons/2 tablespoons warm water
a few drops of pink food colouring
candied angelica 'leaves', to decorate (optional)

AMERICAN

½ cup butter, softened
½ cup sugar
2 eggs, beaten
¼ cup candied cherries, finely chopped
1¼ cups self-rising flour
1 tablespoon milk
For the glacé icing:
scant 2 cups sifted confectioners' sugar
2 tablespoons warm water
a few drops of pink food coloring
candied angelica 'leaves', to decorate (optional)

Put the butter and sugar in a bowl, beat together until light and fluffy, then beat in the eggs a little at a time. Stir in the cherries, then fold in the flour and milk until evenly blended.
Divide the mixture equally between 18 to 24 paper bun cases. Bake in a preheated moderately hot oven (190°C/375°F or Gas Mark 5) for 15 to 20 minutes until well risen and golden. Transfer to a wire rack and leave to cool.
To make the glacé icing: put the icing (confectioners') sugar in a bowl and gradually beat in the water and food colouring until smooth. Coat the top of each bun with a spoonful of icing and decorate with angelica 'leaves' if liked. Leave to set.
To freeze: open (flash) freeze until firm, then pack in a rigid container. Seal, label and return to the freezer.
To thaw and serve: place on a serving platter and thaw at room temperature for 2 hours.
MAKES 18 to 24

HONEY AND CHOCOLATE BUNS

Make as for Cherry Buns (see above), substituting 1 × 15 ml spoon/1 tablespoon honey and 25 g/1 oz chocolate dots (chips) for the glacé (candied) cherries.
Coat with honey glacé icing: put 2 × 15 ml spoons/2 tablespoons honey and 2 × 5 ml spoons/2 teaspoons lemon juice in a pan and heat gently until the honey has melted. Add 225 g/½ lb sifted icing sugar (scant 2 cups sifted confectioners' sugar) and beat until smooth. Coat the top of each bun with a spoonful of icing. Leave to set. Freeze, thaw and serve as for Cherry Buns.
MAKES 18 to 24

CHOCOLATE-DIPPED FLAPJACKS

METRIC/IMPERIAL
100 g/4 oz butter
50 g/2 oz soft brown sugar
100 g/4 oz golden syrup
175 g/6 oz rolled oats
50 g/2 oz glacé cherries, chopped
25 g/1 oz roasted hazelnuts, chopped
100 g/4 oz plain chocolate, melted

AMERICAN
½ cup butter
⅓ cup light brown sugar
⅓ cup light corn syrup
2⅓ cups rolled oats
¼ cup candied cherries, chopped
¼ cup chopped roasted hazelnuts
⅔ cup semi-sweet chocolate pieces, melted

Put all the ingredients, except the chocolate, in a bowl and beat for 2 to 3 minutes until well mixed. Spread the mixture in a greased 28 × 18 cm/11 × 7 inch Swiss roll tin (jelly roll pan) and bake in a preheated moderate oven (180°C/350°F or Gas Mark 4) for 25 to 30 minutes. Mark into 16 bars while still hot, then leave to cool in the tin. Dip the ends of the flapjacks in the chocolate, then leave to set.
To freeze: open (flash) freeze until firm, then pack in a rigid container, separating each layer with foil. Seal, label and return to the freezer.
To thaw and serve: place on a serving platter and thaw at room temperature for 1 to 2 hours.
MAKES 16

LEMON SHORTBREAD CIRCLE

METRIC/IMPERIAL
175 g/6 oz flour
finely grated rind of 1 lemon
50 g/2 oz caster sugar
100 g/4 oz butter
extra caster sugar, for sprinkling

AMERICAN
1½ cups flour
finely grated rind of 1 lemon
¼ cup sugar
½ cup butter
extra sugar, for sprinkling

Sift the flour into a bowl and stir in the lemon rind and sugar. Add the butter in one piece and rub in the flour until the mixture clings together. Transfer the dough to a floured surface, knead until smooth, then cut out a 20 cm/8 inch circle. Place on a baking sheet, trim and flute the edge and prick all over the dough with the prongs of a fork. Mark into 8 triangles with a knife, then bake in a preheated cool oven (150°C/300°F or Gas Mark 2) for 40 to 50 minutes until light golden and set. Leave to cool on the baking sheet for 15 minutes, then transfer to a wire rack. Sprinkle with (caster) sugar and leave to cool completely.
To freeze: pack in a rigid container, seal, label and freeze.
To thaw and serve: place on a serving platter and thaw at room temperature for 2 hours.
MAKES 8 PORTIONS

CHOCOLATE-COATED RINGS

METRIC/IMPERIAL
100 g/4 oz butter, softened
100 g/4 oz caster sugar
1 small egg, beaten
1–2 drops of vanilla essence
200 g/7 oz flour
25 g/1 oz cocoa powder
175 g/6 oz plain chocolate, melted

AMERICAN
½ cup butter, softened
½ cup sugar
1 small egg, beaten
1–2 drops of vanilla extract
1¾ cups flour
¼ cup unsweetened cocoa powder
1 cup semi-sweet chocolate pieces, melted

Put the butter and sugar in a bowl, beat together until light and fluffy, then beat in the egg and the vanilla essence (extract). Sift together the flour and cocoa, fold into the creamed mixture, then knead to a smooth dough. Chill in the refrigerator for 30 minutes.
Roll out the dough on a floured surface and cut out 24 × 6 cm/2½ inch rounds. Remove the centres with a smaller cutter, then place the rings on a lightly greased baking sheet.
Bake in a preheated moderately hot oven (190°C/375°F or Gas Mark 5) for 15 minutes, then transfer to a wire rack and leave to cool. Dip each ring into the melted chocolate until coated, place on a sheet of oiled greaseproof (waxed) paper and leave to set.
To freeze: pack in a rigid container, separating each layer with foil. Seal, label and freeze.
To thaw and serve: place on a serving platter and thaw at room temperature for 1 hour.
MAKES 24

EASTER BISCUITS (COOKIES)

METRIC/IMPERIAL
100 g/4 oz butter
65 g/2½ oz caster sugar
1 egg, separated
175 g/6 oz self-raising flour
40 g/1½ oz currants
15 g/½ oz finely chopped candied peel
1–2 × 15 ml spoons/1–2 tablespoons milk
caster sugar, for sprinkling

AMERICAN
½ cup butter
5 tablespoons sugar
1 egg, separated
1½ cups self-rising flour
4½ tablespoons currants
1½ tablespoons finely chopped candied peel
1–2 tablespoons milk
sugar, for sprinkling

Put the butter and sugar in a bowl, beat together until light and fluffy, then beat in the egg yolk. Fold in the flour with the currants and peel, then stir in enough milk to give a firm dough.
Knead the dough lightly on a floured surface, then roll out to 5 mm/¼ inch thickness. Cut out 15 to 20 × 6 cm/2½ inch rounds and place on greased baking sheets. Bake in a preheated moderately hot oven (200°C/400°F or Gas Mark 6) for 10 minutes. Brush with the egg white, lightly beaten, then sprinkle with (caster) sugar. Bake for a further 10 minutes until light golden. Transfer to a wire rack and leave to cool.
To freeze: open (flash) freeze until firm, then pack in a rigid container, separating each layer with foil. Seal, label and return to the freezer.
To thaw and serve: place on a serving platter and thaw at room temperature for 1 to 2 hours.
MAKES 15 to 20

SHORTBREAD WHEELS

METRIC/IMPERIAL
175 g/6 oz flour
50 g/2 oz caster sugar
100 g/4 oz butter
1 × 15 ml spoon/1 tablespoon cocoa powder
1 × 15 ml spoon/1 tablespoon drinking chocolate powder

AMERICAN
1½ cups flour
¼ cup sugar
½ cup butter
1 tablespoon unsweetened cocoa powder
1 tablespoon sweetened cocoa powder

Sift 100 g/4 oz/1 cup flour into a bowl and stir in the sugar. Add the butter in pieces and rub into the flour until the mixture resembles fine breadcrumbs. Divide into two equal halves.
Knead the remaining flour into one half of the dough and the cocoa and drinking chocolate into the other half. Roll out each piece to a 5 mm/¼ inch thickness, then cut out different-sized circles (6.5 cm/2½ inches, 3.5 cm/1½ inches and 1.5 cm/¾ inch in diameter).
Separate the circles and place on a baking sheet, making each biscuit (cookie) with three circles and interchanging the colours. Bake in a preheated moderate oven (180°C/350°F or Gas Mark 4) for 12 minutes. Transfer to a wire rack and leave to cool.
To freeze: open (flash) freeze until firm, then pack in a rigid container, separating each layer with foil. Seal, label and return to the freezer.
To thaw and serve: place the biscuits (cookies) on a serving platter and thaw at room temperature for 1 to 2 hours.
MAKES 14

CHOCOLATE WHIRLS

METRIC/IMPERIAL
225 g/½ lb self-raising flour
1 × 5 ml spoon/1 teaspoon baking powder
1 × 100 g/4 oz butter
2 × 15 ml spoons/2 tablespoons cocoa powder
6 × 15 ml spoons/6 tablespoons milk
2 × 15 ml spoons/2 tablespoons caster sugar
1 × 5 ml spoon/1 teaspoon ground ginger
1 × 15 ml spoon/1 tablespoon golden syrup
2 × 15 ml spoons/2 tablespoons lemon squash
extra caster sugar, for sprinkling

AMERICAN
2 cups self-rising flour
1 teaspoon baking powder
½ cup butter
2 tablespoons unsweetened cocoa powder
6 tablespoons milk
2 tablespoons sugar
1 teaspoon ground ginger
1 tablespoon corn syrup
2 tablespoons lemon squash
extra sugar, for sprinkling

Sift the flour and baking powder into a bowl, add the butter in pieces and rub into the flour until the mixture resembles fine breadcrumbs. Sift in the cocoa, make a well in the centre, then pour in the milk and mix to a soft dough.
Knead the dough lightly on a floured surface, then roll into a strip about 30 × 25 cm/12 × 10

inches. Scatter the sugar and ginger over the dough, moisten the edges with water and roll up from the longer side. Cut into 12 circles.
Put the syrup and squash in a greased 18 cm/7 inch square cake tin, then put the circles in the tin cut side down, allowing room for expansion. Bake in a preheated moderately hot oven (200°C/400°F or Gas Mark 6) for 20 minutes. Leave to cool slightly in the tin, then separate each whirl and place on a wire rack. Sprinkle with (caster) sugar and leave to cool completely.
To freeze: open (flash) freeze until firm, then pack in a rigid container, separating each layer with foil. Seal, label and return to the freezer.
To thaw and serve: place on a serving platter and thaw at room temperature for 1 to 2 hours.
MAKES 12

CHERRY SWIRLS

METRIC/IMPERIAL
50 g/2 oz flour
50 g/2 oz butter
50 g/2 oz caster sugar
50 g/2 oz ground almonds
a little beaten egg
1 × 15 ml spoon/1 tablespoon cocoa powder
1 × 15 ml spoon/1 tablespoon hot water
butter cream icing made with 150 g/5 oz icing sugar
approx 8 glacé cherries, halved

AMERICAN
½ cup flour
¼ cup butter
½ cup sugar
½ cup ground almonds
a little beaten egg
1 tablespoon unsweetened cocoa powder
1 tablespoon hot water
butter cream icing made with 1⅓ cups confectioners' sugar
approx 8 candied cherries, halved

Sift the flour into a bowl, add the butter in pieces and rub into the flour. Stir in the sugar and almonds and enough egg to bind the mixture. Roll out the dough thinly on a floured surface and cut out 15 to 16 rounds using a 6 cm/2½ inch fluted cutter. Place on a baking sheet and bake in a preheated moderate oven (180°C/350°F or Gas Mark 4) for 12 minutes. Transfer to a wire rack and leave to cool.
Mix the cocoa to a paste with the hot water, then beat into the butter cream icing until evenly blended. Pipe a swirl of icing on each biscuit (cookie) and decorate with half a cherry.
To freeze: open (flash) freeze until firm, then pack in a rigid container, separating each layer with foil. Seal, label and return to the freezer.
To thaw and serve: place on a serving platter and thaw at room temperature for 1 to 2 hours.
MAKES 15 to 16

LEMON CRUNCHIES

METRIC/IMPERIAL
225 g/½ lb flour
1 × 5 ml spoon/1 teaspoon baking powder
175 g/6 oz caster sugar
finely grated rind of ½ lemon
1 egg, beaten
1 × 5 ml spoon/1 teaspoon lemon juice

AMERICAN
2 cups flour
1 teaspoon baking powder
¾ cup sugar
finely grated rind of ½ lemon
1 egg, beaten
1 teaspoon lemon juice

Sift the flour and baking powder into a bowl. Add the butter in pieces and rub into the flour until the mixture resembles fine breadcrumbs. Stir in the sugar and lemon rind, then stir in the egg and lemon juice and mix to a fairly stiff dough.
Knead the dough lightly on a floured surface, then divide into two equal halves. Roll each piece into a 30 cm/12 inch 'sausage' shape.
To freeze: wrap each 'sausage' in foil, then pack in a freezer bag. Seal, label and freeze.
To thaw and serve: thaw in the foil wrappings in the refrigerator overnight. Cut each roll into 24 rounds and place on greased baking sheets, allowing room for spreading. Bake in a preheated moderately hot oven (190°C/375°F or Gas Mark 5) for 10 to 12 minutes until golden. Transfer to a wire rack and leave to cool.
MAKES 48

FORK BISCUITS (COOKIES)

METRIC/IMPERIAL

175 g/6 oz butter
25 g/1 oz icing sugar, sifted
100 g/4 oz flour
50 g/2 oz cornflour
25 g/1 oz drinking chocolate powder
1 × 2.5 ml spoon/½ teaspoon vanilla essence
extra icing sugar for sprinkling, to finish

AMERICAN

¾ cup butter
¼ cup sifted confectioners' sugar
1 cup flour
½ cup cornstarch
¼ cup sweetened cocoa powder
½ teaspoon vanilla extract
extra confectioners' sugar for sprinkling, to finish

Put the butter and icing (confectioners') sugar in a bowl and beat together until light. Sift in the dry ingredients, add the vanilla essence (extract) and beat well to mix.

Shape the dough into 20 small walnut-sized balls and place on greased baking sheets, spacing them well apart. Flatten each ball with the prongs of a wet fork into a rectangle about 6 × 3.5 cm/ 2½ × 1½ inches. Bake in a preheated moderately hot oven (190°C/375°F or Gas Mark 5) for 12 minutes. Transfer to a wire rack and cool.

To freeze: open (flash) freeze until firm, then pack in a rigid container, separating each layer with foil. Seal, label and return to the freezer.

To thaw and serve: place on a serving platter and thaw at room temperature for 1 to 2 hours. Sprinkle with icing (confectioners') sugar before serving.

MAKES 20

CHOCOLATE FRUIT FINGERS

METRIC/IMPERIAL

90 g/3½ oz butter
1 × 15 ml spoon/1 tablespoon golden syrup
225 g/½ lb muesli
25 g/1 oz seedless raisins, chopped
50 g/2 oz glacé cherries, finely chopped
100 g/4 oz plain chocolate, melted

AMERICAN

7 tablespoons butter
1 tablespoon light corn syrup
½ lb muesli
3 tablespoons seedless raisins, chopped
¼ cup candied cherries, finely chopped
⅔ cup semi-sweet chocolate pieces, melted

Put the butter and syrup in a pan and heat gently until melted. Remove from the heat and stir in the muesli, raisins and cherries. Press the mixture into a greased shallow 18 cm/7 inch square cake tin, spread the melted chocolate over the top and mark with the prongs of a fork. Chill in the refrigerator until set, then cut into 12 bars.

To freeze: open (flash) freeze until firm, then pack in a rigid container, separating each layer with foil. Seal, label and return to the freezer.

To thaw and serve: place on a serving platter and thaw at room temperature for 1 to 2 hours.

MAKES 12

MACAROONS

METRIC/IMPERIAL

100 g/4 oz sugar
100 g/4 oz ground almonds
2 egg whites
a few drops of almond essence
13–15 whole blanched almonds

AMERICAN

½ cup sugar
1 cup ground almonds
2 egg whites
a few drops of almond extract
13–15 whole blanched almonds

Put all the ingredients, except the whole almonds, in a bowl and beat for 5 minutes. Leave to stand for 5 minutes, then pipe or put 13 to 15 rounded teaspoonsful of the mixture onto baking sheets lined with non-stick parchment.

Place an almond on top of each macaroon and bake in a preheated moderate oven (160°C/ 325°F or Gas Mark 3) for 20 to 25 minutes until golden. Peel off the parchment carefully, transfer the macaroons to a wire rack and leave to cool.

To freeze: open (flash) freeze until firm, then pack in a rigid container, separating each layer with foil. Seal, label and return to the freezer.

To thaw and serve: place on a serving platter and thaw at room temperature for 1 to 2 hours.

MAKES 13 to 15

CHOCOLATE CRUNCH

METRIC/IMPERIAL

50 g/2 oz butter
3 × 15 ml spoons/3 tablespoons golden syrup
1 × 15 ml spoon/1 tablespoon cocoa powder
50 g/2 oz dried milk solids
25 g/1 oz rice crispies

AMERICAN

¼ cup butter
3 tablespoons light corn syrup
1 tablespoon unsweetened cocoa powder
⅔ cup dried milk solids
1 cup rice crispies

Grease an 18 cm/7 inch sandwich tin (layer cake pan) and line with greased greaseproof paper or non-stick parchment.
Put all the ingredients, except the rice crispies, in a pan and heat gently until melted, stirring constantly. Remove from the heat, stir in the rice crispies, then spoon into the prepared tin. Chill in the refrigerator until set, then cut into 8 slices.
To freeze: open (flash) freeze until firm, then pack in a rigid container, separating each layer with foil. Seal, label and return to the freezer.
To thaw and serve: place on a serving platter and thaw at room temperature for 1 to 2 hours.
MAKES 8

ALMOND CURLS

METRIC/IMPERIAL

65 g/2½ oz butter, softened
65 g/2½ oz caster sugar
40 g/1½ oz flour
50 g/2 oz slivered blanched almonds

AMERICAN

5 tablespoons butter, softened
5 tablespoons sugar
⅜ cup flour
½ cup slivered blanched almonds

Put the butter, sugar and flour in a bowl, beat for 2 to 3 minutes until well mixed, then fold in the almonds. Shape the mixture into about 24 small walnut-sized balls. Place on greased baking sheets, spacing them well apart.
Flatten each ball with the prongs of a wet fork, then bake on the second and third shelves from the top of a preheated moderately hot oven (200°C/400°F or Gas Mark 6) for 6 to 8 minutes until pale golden. Leave to stand on the baking sheets for a few seconds, then remove carefully onto a rolling pin. Transfer to a wire rack and leave until cool and set.
To freeze: open (flash) freeze until firm, then pack carefully in a rigid container, separating each layer with foil. Seal, label and return to the freezer.
To thaw and serve: place on a serving platter and thaw at room temperature for 1 to 2 hours.
MAKES 24

COCONUT COOKIES

METRIC/IMPERIAL

100 g/4 oz butter, softened
100 g/4 oz flour
25 g/1 oz custard powder
50 g/2 oz caster sugar
a few drops of vanilla essence
15 g/½ oz desiccated coconut
9–10 glacé cherries, halved

AMERICAN

½ cup butter, softened
1 cup flour
¼ cup custard powder
¼ cup sugar
a few drops of vanilla extract
2 tablespoons shredded coconut
9–10 candied cherries, halved

Put all the ingredients, except the coconut and cherries, in a bowl and beat for 2 to 3 minutes until well mixed. Press together to form a firm dough, then shape teaspoonfuls into 18 to 20 small balls. Roll in the coconut.
Place the balls 5 cm/2 inches apart on baking sheets and press half a cherry into each one. Bake in a preheated moderately hot oven (190°C/375°F or Gas Mark 5) for 20 to 25 minutes. Cool on the baking sheets for a few minutes, then transfer to a wire rack to cool completely.
To freeze: open (flash) freeze until firm, then pack in a rigid container, separating each layer with foil. Seal, label and return to the freezer.
To thaw and serve: place on a serving platter and thaw at room temperature for 1 to 2 hours.
MAKES 18 to 20

CORNFLAKE COOKIES

Make as for Coconut Cookies (see above), substituting 1 × 15 ml spoon/1 tablespoon cocoa powder (unsweetened cocoa) for the custard powder. Roll the mixture in crushed cornflakes instead of the coconut. Freeze, thaw and serve as for Coconut Cookies.
MAKES 18 to 20

CHOCOLATE CHIP COOKIES

Make as for Coconut Cookies (see above), adding 50 g/2 oz grated plain chocolate (⅓ cup semi-sweet chocolate pieces, grated) and the finely grated rind of 1 orange. Omit coconut. Freeze, thaw and serve as for Coconut Cookies.
MAKES 18 to 20

HONEY BISCUITS (COOKIES)

METRIC/IMPERIAL

225 g/½ lb honey
2 eggs, well beaten
50 g/2 oz butter, melted
175 g/6 oz flour
1 × 5 ml spoon/1 teaspoon baking powder
100 g/4 oz chopped nuts
1 × 5 ml spoon/1 teaspoon vanilla essence
225 g/½ lb stoned dates, chopped

AMERICAN

⅔ cup honey
2 eggs, well beaten
¼ cup butter, melted
1½ cups flour
1 teaspoon baking powder
1 cup chopped nuts
1 teaspoon vanilla extract
1¼ cups pitted dates, chopped

Put the honey, eggs and butter in a bowl and beat well to mix. Sift together the flour and baking powder and stir into the honey mixture, then stir in the remaining ingredients.
Spread the mixture in a lightly greased Swiss roll tin (jelly roll pan) and bake in a preheated moderate oven (180°C/350°F or Gas Mark 4) for 40 minutes. Mark into squares, then leave to set. Transfer to a wire rack to cool completely.
To freeze: open (flash) freeze until firm, then pack in a rigid container, separating each layer with foil. Seal, label and return to the freezer.
To thaw and serve: place on a serving platter and thaw at room temperature for 1 to 2 hours.
MAKES 24

DATE AND RAISIN CRUNCH

METRIC/IMPERIAL

5 × 15 ml spoons/5 tablespoons frozen concentrated orange juice, thawed
50 g/2 oz stoned dates, roughly chopped
25 g/1 oz seedless raisins
100 g/4 oz rolled oats
40 g/1½ oz caster sugar
40 g/1½ oz flour
75 g/3 oz butter, softened

AMERICAN

⅓ cup frozen concentrated orange juice, thawed
⅜ cup pitted dates, roughly chopped
3 tablespoons seedless raisins
1 cup rolled oats, firmly packed
3 tablespoons sugar
⅜ cup flour
⅜ cup butter, softened

Put the orange juice in a pan, make up to 150 ml/¼ pint/⅔ cup with water, add the dates and raisins and cook gently until thick.
Put the remaining ingredients in a bowl and rub together with the fingertips until evenly blended. Spread half the mixture in the bottom of a greased 450 g/1 lb loaf tin, spoon over the orange and fruit, then top with the rolled oat mixture. Bake in a preheated moderately hot oven (190°C/375°F or Gas Mark 5) for 40 minutes until golden brown. Leave to cool in the tin then cut into fingers (bars).
To freeze: open (flash) freeze until firm, then pack in a rigid container, separating each layer with foil. Seal, label and return to the freezer.
To thaw and serve: place on a serving platter and thaw at room temperature for 1 to 2 hours.
SERVES 6

SULTANA (WHITE RAISIN) AND CHERRY CRUNCH

Make as for Date and Raisin Crunch (see above), substituting 25 g/1 oz sultanas (3 tablespoons seedless white raisins) and 50 g/2 oz glacé cherries (¼ cup candied cherries), chopped, for the dates and raisins. Freeze, thaw and serve as for Date and Raisin Crunch.
SERVES 6

CARAMEL BARS

METRIC/IMPERIAL

For the base:
basic shortcrust pastry dough made with 225 g/½ lb flour
For the filling:
100 g/4 oz butter
50 g/2 oz caster sugar
2 × 15 ml spoons/2 tablespoons golden syrup
1 × 215 g/7½ oz can sweetened condensed milk
For the topping:
100 g/4 oz plain chocolate
15 g/½ oz butter

AMERICAN

For the base:
basic pie dough made with 2 cups flour
For the filling:
½ cup butter
¼ cup sugar
2 tablespoons light corn syrup
1 × 7½ oz can sweetened condensed milk
For the topping:
⅔ cup semi-sweet chocolate pieces
1 tablespoon butter

To make the base: roll out the dough on a floured surface and use to line the bottom of a 28 × 18 cm/11 × 7 inch Swiss roll tin (jelly roll pan). Prick the dough, then bake in a preheated moderately hot oven (200°C/400°F or Gas Mark 6) for 15 to 20 minutes until golden.
To make the filling: put all the ingredients in a pan and heat gently until dissolved, stirring constantly. Bring slowly to the boil, then simmer for 5 to 7 minutes until thick, stirring constantly with a wooden spoon. Remove from the heat and leave to cool slightly, then spread over the pastry and leave to cool completely.
To make the topping: put the chocolate and butter in a heatproof bowl, stand over a pan of simmering water and allow to melt. Spread over filling, leave to set, then cut into bars.
To freeze: open (flash) freeze until firm, then pack in a rigid container, separating each layer with foil. Seal, label and return to the freezer.
To thaw and serve: place on a serving platter and thaw at room temperature for 1 to 2 hours.
MAKES 20

SHORTBREAD

METRIC/IMPERIAL
225 g/½ lb butter
100 g/4 oz caster sugar
350 g/¾ lb flour, sifted
extra caster sugar, for sprinkling

AMERICAN
1 cup butter
½ cup sugar
3 cups flour, sifted
extra sugar, for sprinkling

Put the butter and sugar in a bowl, beat together until light and fluffy, then blend in the flour a spoonful at a time. Knead the mixture together, then divide into two halves and place each piece in a Swiss roll tin (jelly roll pan). Roll or press each piece out with the flat of the hand, prick well with a fork, then chill in the refrigerator. Bake in a preheated moderate oven (160°C/325°F or Gas Mark 3) for 35 minutes or until golden. Sprinkle with (caster) sugar, then mark each shortbread into 15 fingers (bars). Cool in the tins for a further 30 minutes, then transfer to a wire rack to cool completely.
To freeze: open (flash) freeze until firm, then pack in a rigid container, separating each layer with foil. Seal, label and return to the freezer.
To thaw and serve: place on a serving platter and thaw at room temperature for 1 to 2 hours.
MAKES 30

PEANUT CRISPS

METRIC/IMPERIAL
75 g/3 oz butter, softened
50 g/2 oz caster sugar
2 × 15 ml spoons/2 tablespoons salted peanuts, chopped
50 g/2 oz soft brown sugar
½ egg, beaten
100 g/4 oz self-raising flour
1 × 2.5 ml spoon/½ teaspoon ground mixed spice
extra caster sugar, for sprinkling

AMERICAN
⅜ cup butter, softened
¼ cup sugar
2 tablespoons salted peanuts, chopped
⅓ cup light brown sugar
½ egg, beaten
1 cup self-rising flour
¼ teaspoon nutmeg
¼ teaspoon ground allspice and cloves, mixed
extra sugar, for sprinkling

Put the butter and sugar in a bowl, beat together until light and fluffy, then beat in the peanuts, brown sugar and egg. Sift together the flour and spice(s), then fold into the mixture until evenly blended.
Shape the mixture into about 26 small walnut-sized balls and place on greased baking sheets, spacing them well apart. Flatten each ball with the prongs of a wet fork, then bake in a preheated moderately hot oven (190°C/375°F or Gas Mark 5) for 12 to 15 minutes. Sprinkle with (caster) sugar, transfer to a wire rack and leave to cool.
To freeze: open (flash) freeze until firm, then pack in a rigid container, separating each layer with foil. Seal, label and return to the freezer.
To thaw and serve: place on a serving platter and thaw at room temperature for 1 to 2 hours.
MAKES 26

GINGER PEANUT CRISPS

Make as for Peanut Crisps (see above), substituting 1 × 2.5 ml spoon/½ teaspoon ground ginger for the mixed spice (nutmeg, allspice and cloves). Do not sprinkle with (caster) sugar before freezing.
To freeze: as for Peanut Crisps.
To thaw and serve: thaw as for Peanut Crisps, then coat with ginger-flavoured glacé icing and decorate each biscuit (cookie) with a piece of crystallized (candied) ginger. Leave to set before serving.
MAKES 26

CHRISTMAS SQUARES

METRIC/IMPERIAL

175 g/6 oz butter, softened
75 g/3 oz caster sugar
finely grated rind of ½ lemon
100 g/4 oz ground almonds
175 g/6 oz flour
approx 100 g/4 oz redcurrant jelly, warmed
To decorate:
chocolate glacé icing made with 100 g/4 oz icing sugar
1–2 × 15 ml spoons/1–2 tablespoons chopped pistachio nuts or blanched almonds

AMERICAN

¾ cup butter, softened
⅜ cup sugar
finely grated rind of ½ lemon
1 cup ground almonds
1½ cups flour
approx ⅓ cup redcurrant jelly, warmed
To decorate:
chocolate glacé icing made with scant 1 cup confectioners' sugar
1–2 tablespoons chopped pistachio nuts or blanched almonds

Put the butter, sugar and lemon rind in a bowl and beat together until light and fluffy. Sift in the flour, then fold in with the ground almonds until evenly blended. Knead to a smooth dough, then chill in the refrigerator for 1 to 2 hours.
Roll out the dough thinly on a floured surface and cut out about 16 squares. Place on a baking sheet, allowing room for expansion. Bake in a preheated very hot oven (240°C/475°F or Gas Mark 9) for 5 minutes, then reduce the heat to moderate (180°C/350°F or Gas Mark 4) and bake for a further 15 minutes until golden. Transfer to a wire rack and leave to cool, then sandwich together in pairs with the warm redcurrant jelly. Spread a little glacé icing on each biscuit (cookie), then scatter over the chopped nuts and leave to set.
To freeze: open (flash) freeze until firm, then pack in a rigid container, separating each layer with foil. Seal, label and return to the freezer.
To thaw and serve: place on a serving platter and thaw at room temperature for 1 to 2 hours.
MAKES 16

VANILLA SHORTIES

METRIC/IMPERIAL

225 g/½ lb butter, softened
100 g/4 oz caster sugar
225 g/½ lb self-raising flour
1 × 5 ml spoon/1 teaspoon vanilla essence
a little icing sugar or glacé icing, to finish

AMERICAN

1 cup butter, softened
½ cup sugar
2 cups self-rising flour
1 teaspoon vanilla extract
a little confectioners' sugar or glacé icing, to finish

Put the butter and sugar in a bowl, beat together until light and fluffy, then fold in the flour and the vanilla. Mix to a smooth dough.
Turn the dough out onto a floured surface, knead lightly for 2 minutes, then chill until firm.
To freeze: shape the dough into a long roll about 5 cm/2 inches in diameter. Wrap in foil, then pack in a freezer bag. Seal, label and freeze.
To thaw and serve: thaw in the wrappings in the refrigerator for 30 minutes, then cut into thin slices and place on greased baking sheets. Bake in a preheated moderately hot oven (190°C/375°F or Gas Mark 5) for 10 minutes, then transfer to a wire rack and leave to cool. Sprinkle with icing (confectioners') sugar or coat with glacé icing before serving.
MAKES ABOUT 55

CHOCOLATE SHORTIES

Make as for Vanilla Shorties (see above), substituting 25 g/1 oz cocoa powder (¼ cup unsweetened cocoa) for the vanilla.
Freeze, thaw and serve as for Vanilla Shorties.
MAKES ABOUT 55

CHERRY SHORTIES

Make as for Vanilla Shorties (see above), adding 50 g/2 oz glacé cherries (¼ cup candied cherries), finely chopped.
Freeze, thaw and serve as for Vanilla Shorties.
MAKES ABOUT 55

NUT SHORTIES

Make as for Vanilla Shorties (see above), adding 50 g/2 oz/¼ cup chopped almonds or walnuts.
Freeze, thaw and serve as for Vanilla Shorties.
MAKES ABOUT 55

SWISS CHOCOLATE TARTS

METRIC/IMPERIAL

100 g/4 oz butter, softened
25 g/1 oz icing sugar, sifted
100 g/4 oz flour
2 × 15 ml spoons/2 tablespoons drinking chocolate powder
To finish:
2 × 15 ml spoons/2 tablespoons seedless raspberry jam
icing sugar, for sprinkling

AMERICAN

½ cup butter, softened
¼ cup sifted confectioners' sugar
1 cup flour
2 tablespoons sweetened cocoa powder
To finish:
2 tablespoons seedless raspberry jam
confectioners' sugar, for sprinkling

Put the butter and icing (confectioners') sugar in a bowl and beat together until light. Beat in half the flour and drinking chocolate (sweetened cocoa), then add the remainder and beat until smooth.

Pipe the mixture in whirls in 6 paper bun cases, beginning the whirls in the centre. Bake in a preheated moderately hot oven (190°C/375°F or Gas Mark 5) for 30 minutes.

To freeze: cool quickly. Open (flash) freeze until firm, then pack in a rigid container. Seal, label and return to the freezer.

To thaw and serve: place on a serving platter and thaw at room temperature for 1 to 2 hours. Put a little jam in the centre of each tart and sprinkle with icing (confectioners') sugar before serving.

MAKES 6

MARSHMALLOW COOKIES

METRIC/IMPERIAL

175 g/6 oz self-raising flour
2 × 15 ml spoons/2 tablespoons cocoa powder
100 g/4 oz caster sugar
100 g/4 oz butter
1 egg yolk
24 marshmallows

AMERICAN

1½ cups self-rising flour
2 tablespoons unsweetened cocoa powder
½ cup sugar
½ cup butter
1 egg yolk
24 marshamallows

Sift the flour and cocoa into a bowl, stir in the sugar, then rub in the butter until the mixture resembles fine breadcrumbs. Stir in the egg yolk and mix to a firm dough, adding a little water if necessary.

Roll out the dough thinly on a floured surface and cut out 48 rounds using a 5 cm/2 inch cutter. Cut out the centres of half the rounds using a 2.5 cm/1 inch cutter. Place the rounds and rings on greased baking sheets and bake in a preheated moderately hot oven (190°C/375°F or Gas Mark 5) for 10 to 15 minutes until set.

Remove the ring cookies, place a marshmallow on top of each round cookie, then return to the oven and bake for a further 3 minutes. Remove from the oven, press a ring over each marshmallow cookie, then leave to cool on a wire rack.

To freeze: open (flash) freeze until firm, then pack in a rigid container, separating each layer with foil. Seal, label and return to the freezer.

To thaw and serve: place on a serving platter and thaw at room temperature for 1 to 2 hours.

MAKES 24

CARNIVAL SQUARES

METRIC/IMPERIAL

100 g/4 oz plain chocolate, broken into pieces
50 g/2 oz butter
2 × 15 ml spoons/2 tablespoons golden syrup
15 marshmallows, quartered
75 g/3 oz rice crispies

AMERICAN

⅔ cup semi-sweet chocolate pieces
¼ cup butter
2 tablespoons light corn syrup
15 marshmallows, quartered
3 cups rice crispies

Put the chocolate, butter and syrup in a heatproof bowl over a pan of hot water and allow to melt, stirring once or twice. Leave to cool, then fold in the marshmallows and rice crispies. Spoon into a shallow 18 cm/7 inch square tin and smooth the top. Leave to set, then cut into 16 squares.

To freeze: open (flash) freeze until firm, then pack in a rigid container, separating each layer with foil. Seal, label and return to the freezer.

To thaw and serve: place on a serving platter and thaw at room temperature for 1 to 2 hours.

MAKES 16

SPICED FRUITY BISCUITS (COOKIES)

METRIC/IMPERIAL

112 g/4 oz butter, softened
112 g/4 oz caster sugar
1 small egg, beaten
1 × 15 ml spoon/1 tablespoon mincemeat
225 g/½ lb flour
1 × 2.5 ml spoon/½ teaspoon ground mixed spice

AMERICAN

½ cup butter, softened
½ cup sugar
1 small egg, beaten
1 tablespoon mincemeat
2 cups flour
¼ teaspoon grated nutmeg
¼ teaspoon ground allspice and cloves, mixed

Put the butter and sugar in a bowl, beat together until light and fluffy, then beat in the egg and the mincemeat a little at a time. Sift together the flour and spice(s), then fold into the creamed mixture and mix to a soft dough.

Roll out the dough thinly on a floured surface and cut out about 30 rounds with a 6 cm/2½ inch fluted cutter. Place on greased baking sheets and bake in a preheated moderate oven (180°C/350°F or Gas Mark 4) for 15 to 20 minutes until golden brown. Transfer to a wire rack and leave to cool.

To freeze: open (flash) freeze until firm, then pack in a rigid container, separating each layer with foil. Seal, label and return to the freezer.

To thaw and serve: place on a serving platter and thaw at room temperature for 1 to 2 hours.

MAKES 30

GINGER NUTS

METRIC/IMPERIAL

100 g/4 oz self-raising flour
1 × 5 ml spoon/1 teaspoon ground ginger
0.5 × 2.5 ml spoon/¼ teaspoon bicarbonate of soda
50 g/2 oz butter
50 g/2 oz golden syrup
50 g/2 oz caster sugar
2 × 5 ml spoons/2 teaspoons milk

AMERICAN

1 cup self-rising flour
1 teaspoon ground ginger
¼ teaspoon baking soda
¼ cup butter
3 tablespoons light corn syrup
¼ cup sugar
2 teaspoons milk

Sift the flour, ginger and bicarbonate of soda (baking soda) into a bowl. Put the butter, syrup and sugar in a pan and heat gently until melted, stirring occasionally. Leave to cool slightly, then pour into the dry ingredients with the milk. Beat well to mix.

Form the mixture into 18 to 20 small walnut-sized balls and place on greased baking sheets, spacing them well apart. Bake in a preheated moderate oven (160°C/325°F or Gas Mark 3) for 25 to 30 minutes, then transfer to a wire rack and leave to cool.

To freeze: open (flash) freeze until firm, then pack in a rigid container, separating each layer with foil. Seal, label and return to the freezer.

To thaw and serve: place on a serving platter and thaw at room temperature for 1 to 2 hours.

MAKES 18 to 20

MELTING MOMENTS

METRIC/IMPERIAL

175 g/6 oz butter, softened
100 g/4 oz caster sugar
1 egg, separated
1 × 5 ml spoon/1 teaspoon vanilla essence
225 g/½ lb flour
pinch of salt
25–50 g/1–2 oz cornflakes, crushed

AMERICAN

¾ cup butter, softened
½ cup sugar
1 egg, separated
1 teaspoon vanilla extract
2 cups flour
pinch of salt
1–2 cups cornflakes, crushed

Put the butter, sugar, egg yolk and vanilla essence (extract) in a bowl and beat together until light and fluffy. Sift together the flour and salt, then fold into the creamed mixture.

Beat the egg white lightly until frothy. Dip teaspoonfuls of the mixture into the egg white, then dip into the cornflakes until evenly coated. Place on greased baking sheets and flatten into disc shapes with the bottom of a glass. Bake in a preheated moderately hot oven (190°C/375°F or Gas Mark 5) until golden brown.

To freeze: cool quickly. Open (flash) freeze until firm, then pack in a rigid container, separating each layer with foil. Seal, label and return to the freezer.

To thaw and serve: place on a serving platter and thaw at room temperature for 1 to 2 hours.

MAKES ABOUT 40

GINGER SNAPS

METRIC/IMPERIAL

175 g/6 oz flour
1 × 5 ml spoon/1 teaspoon ground cinnamon
1.5 × 5 ml spoons/1½ teaspoons ground ginger
75 g/3 oz soft brown sugar
75 g/3 oz butter
1 × 15 ml spoon/1 tablespoon golden syrup
1 × 15 ml spoon/1 tablespoon black treacle
0.5 × 2.5 ml spoon/¼ teaspoon bicarbonate of soda
1 × 15 ml spoon/1 tablespoon milk
25 slivered blanched almonds, to decorate

AMERICAN

1½ cups flour
1 teaspoon ground cinnamon
1½ teaspoons ground ginger
½ cup light brown sugar
⅜ cup butter
1 tablespoon light corn syrup
1 tablespoon molasses
¼ teaspoon baking soda
1 tablespoon milk
25 slivered blanched almonds, to decorate

Sift the flour, cinnamon and ginger into a bowl and stir in the sugar. Put the butter, syrup and black tracle (molasses) in a pan and heat gently until melted, stirring occasionally. Leave to cool slightly, then pour into the dry ingredients and beat well to mix. Mix the bicarbonate of soda (baking soda) to a paste with the milk and stir into the mixture until evenly blended.
Shape the mixture into 25 rounds about the size of walnuts, then place on a greased baking sheet, spacing them well apart. Press a slivered almond on top of each, then bake in a preheated moderate oven (180°C/350°F or Gas Mark 4) for 20 to 25 minutes. Transfer to a wire rack to cool completely.
To freeze: open (flash) freeze until firm, then pack in a rigid container, separating each layer with foil. Seal, label and return to the freezer.
To thaw and serve: place on a serving platter and thaw at room temperature for 1 to 2 hours.
MAKES 25

ORANGE PEANUT COOKIES

METRIC/IMPERIAL

100 g/4 oz butter, softened
100 g/4 oz soft brown sugar
2 × 5 ml spoons/2 teaspoons undiluted orange squash
150 g/5 oz self-raising flour
0.5 × 2.5 ml spoon/¼ teaspoon ground cinnamon
100 g/4 oz salted peanuts, chopped

AMERICAN

½ cup butter softened
⅔ cup light brown sugar
2 teaspoons undiluted orange squash
1¼ cups self-rising flour
¼ teaspoon ground cinnamon
1 cup chopped salted peanuts

Put the butter and sugar in a bowl, beat together until light and fluffy, then beat in the orange squash. Sift together the flour and cinnamon, then fold into the creamed mixture with the peanuts to form a firm dough.
Form the mixture into 25 small walnut-sized balls and place on greased baking sheets, spacing them well apart. Flatten each ball with the prongs of a wet fork, then bake in a preheated moderate oven (180°C/350°F or Gas Mark 4) for 10 to 12 minutes. Transfer to a wire rack and leave to cool.
To freeze: open (flash) freeze until firm, then pack in a rigid container, separating each layer with foil. Seal, label and return to the freezer.
To thaw and serve: place on a serving platter and thaw at room temperature for 1 to 2 hours.
MAKES 25

FLAPJACK FINGERS

METRIC/IMPERIAL

75 g/3 oz butter, softened
75 g/3 oz demerara sugar
100 g/4 oz rolled oats

AMERICAN

⅜ cup butter
½ cup raw brown sugar
1 cup rolled oats, firmly packed

Put the butter in a bowl and beat until creamy. Mix the sugar and oats together and gradually work into the creamed butter until blended.
Press the mixture into a greased shallow 18 cm/7 inch square cake tin and smooth the top. Bake in a preheated hot oven (220°C/425°F or Gas Mark 7) for 15 minutes until golden brown. Leave to cool slightly in the tin, then mark into 12 fingers (bars) with a sharp knife and loosen the edges. When the mixture becomes firm, turn out onto a wire rack and break into fingers. Leave to cool completely.
To freeze: open (flash) freeze until firm, then pack in a rigid container, separating each layer with foil. Seal, label and return to the freezer.
To thaw and serve: place on a serving platter and thaw at room temperature for 1 to 2 hours.
MAKES 12

DOMINOES

METRIC/IMPERIAL

3 × 15 ml spoons/3 tablespoons golden syrup
40 g/1½ oz butter
25 g/1 oz cocoa powder
175 g/6 oz stoned dates, chopped
65 g/2½ oz rice crispies
a little glacé icing, to decorate

AMERICAN

3 tablespoons light corn syrup
3 tablespoons butter
¼ cup unsweetened cocoa powder
1 cup pitted dates, chopped
2½ cups rice crispies
a little glacé icing, to decorate

Put the syrup, butter and cocoa in a pan and heat gently until melted, stirring occasionally. Remove from the heat, then add the dates and rice crispies and stir well to mix.

Press the mixture into a greased 30 × 20 cm/12 × 8 inch Swiss roll tin (jelly roll pan) and leave in a cool place until set. Remove from the tin and cut into 16 bars. Decorate the tops of the bars with glacé icing, piping a pattern of spots to make the bars look like dominoes.

To freeze: open (flash) freeze until firm, then pack in a rigid container, separating each layer with foil. Seal, label and return to the freezer.

To thaw and serve: place on a serving platter and thaw at room temperature for 1 to 2 hours.

MAKES 16

CRACKLETTS

Prepare the mixture as for Dominoes (see above). Divide into 12 equal pieces, shape into balls, then push a lollipop (popsicle) stick into each. Freeze, thaw and serve as for Dominoes.

MAKES 12

PEPPERMINT BARS

METRIC/IMPERIAL

2 eggs
75 g/3 oz caster sugar
50 g/2 oz flour
20 marshmallows
1 × 15 ml spoon/1 tablespoon milk
a few drops of peppermint essence
2 egg whites
a few drops of green food colouring
To decorate:
a few marshmallows, halved
grated plain chocolate

AMERICAN

2 eggs
⅜ cup sugar
½ cup flour
20 marshmallows
1 tablespoon milk
a few drops of peppermint extract
2 egg whites
a few drops of green food coloring
To decorate:
a few marshmallows, halved
grated semi-sweet chocolate

Grease an 18 cm/7 inch square cake tin and line the bottom with greased greaseproof paper or non-stick parchment.

Put the eggs and 50 g/2 oz/¼ cup sugar in a heatproof bowl, stand over a pan of gently simmering water and beat until thick and creamy. Fold in the flour until evenly blended, then spoon the mixture into the prepared tin. Bake in a preheated moderately hot oven (200°C/400°F or Gas Mark 6) for 15 to 20 minutes, then turn out onto a wire rack, remove the paper lining and leave to cool.

Put the marshmallows and milk in a heatproof bowl, stand over a pan of gently simmering water and allow to melt. Stir in the peppermint essence (extract) and leave to cool.

Beat the egg whites until stiff, fold in the remaining sugar and beat again until stiff. Fold into the marshmallow mixture with the food colouring until evenly blended. Leave until just beginning to set.

Cut the cake in two, then sandwich together with some of the frosting and cover with the remainder. Decorate the top of the cake with marshmallow halves and grated chocolate, then leave to set.

To freeze: open (flash) freeze until firm, wrap in foil, then pack in a freezer bag. Seal, label and return to the freezer.

To thaw and serve: remove wrappings and thaw at room temperature for 2 to 3 hours. Cut into 6 bars before serving.

MAKES 6

TWILLS

METRIC/IMPERIAL

50 g/2 oz self-raising flour
50 g/2 oz demerara sugar
50 g/2 oz golden syrup
50 g/2 oz butter
50 g/2 oz blanched almonds, chopped

AMERICAN

½ cup self-rising flour
⅓ cup raw brown sugar
3 tablespoons light corn syrup
¼ cup butter
½ cup chopped blanched almonds

Put all the ingredients, except the almonds, in a heatproof bowl and stand over a pan of gently simmering water. Allow to melt, stirring occasionally, then remove from the heat and stir in the almonds.
Place 12 to 14 teaspoonsful of the mixture on greased baking sheets, spacing them well apart. Bake in a preheated moderate oven (160°C/325°F or Gas Mark 3) for 20 to 30 minutes until golden brown. Remove from the oven, leave until almost cool, then roll around a rolling pin. Leave on the rolling pin until crisp.
To freeze: open (flash) freeze until firm, then pack in a rigid container, separating each layer with foil. Seal, label and return to the freezer.
To thaw and serve: place on a serving platter and thaw at room temperature for 1 to 2 hours.
MAKES 12 to 14

FLORENTINES

METRIC/IMPERIAL

100 g/4 oz demerara sugar
100 g/4 oz butter
100 g/4 oz golden syrup
100 g/4 oz self-raising flour
40 g/1½ oz roasted hazelnuts, chopped
40 g/1½ oz blanched almonds, chopped
15 g/½ oz candied angelica, chopped
75 g/3 oz glacé cherries, chopped
plain chocolate, melted, for coating

AMERICAN

⅔ cup raw brown sugar
½ cup butter
⅓ cup light corn syrup
1 cup self-rising flour
⅓ cup chopped roasted hazelnuts
⅓ cup chopped blanched almonds
1½ tablespoons chopped candied angelica
⅜ cup candied cherries, chopped
semi-sweet chocolate, melted, for coating

Put the sugar, butter and syrup in a pan and heat gently until melted, stirring occasionally. Remove from the heat and stir in the remaining ingredients, except the chocolate.
Put about 36 teaspoonsful of the mixture onto greased baking sheets, spacing them well apart. Bake in a preheated moderate oven (160°C/325°F or Gas Mark 3) for 10 to 15 minutes, then transfer to a wire rack and leave to cool. Coat the back of the florentines with melted chocolate and leave to set.
To freeze: open (flash) freeze until firm, then pack in a rigid container, separating each layer with foil. Seal, label and return to the freezer.
To thaw and serve: place on a serving platter and thaw at room temperature for 1 to 2 hours.
MAKES 36

PEANUT BUTTER BISCUITS (COOKIES)

METRIC/IMPERIAL

75 g/3 oz butter, softened
50 g/2 oz peanut butter
100 g/4 oz soft brown sugar
150 g/5 oz flour

AMERICAN

⅜ cup butter, softened
3 tablespoons peanut butter
⅔ cup light brown sugar
1¼ cups flour

Put the butter, peanut butter and sugar in a bowl, beat together until light and fluffy, then fold in the flour until evenly blended. Knead lightly to give a fairly stiff dough, then divide into 4 equal pieces. Form each piece into a roll about 23 cm/9 inches long, then cut each roll into 6 or 7 rounds.
Place the rounds on greased baking sheets and mark with the prongs of a fork. Bake in a preheated moderate oven (180°C/350°F or Gas Mark 4) for 10 to 15 minutes until golden. Leave to cool on the baking sheets for a few minutes, then transfer to a wire rack and leave to cool completely.
To freeze: open (flash) freeze until firm, then pack in a rigid container, separating each layer with foil. Seal, label and return to the freezer.
To thaw and serve: place on a serving platter and thaw at room temperature for 1 to 2 hours.
MAKES 24 to 28

ORANGE CHEESE COOKIES

METRIC/IMPERIAL

100 g/4 oz butter, softened
100 g/4 oz caster sugar
1 egg yolk
50 g/2 oz cream cheese
175 g/6 oz flour
finely grated rind of 1 orange
1 × 15 ml spoon/1 tablespoon orange juice
caster sugar, for sprinkling

AMERICAN

½ cup butter, softened
½ cup sugar
1 egg yolk
¼ cup cream cheese
1½ cups flour
finely grated rind of 1 orange
1 tablespoon orange juice
sugar, for sprinkling

Put the butter and sugar in a bowl, beat together until light and fluffy, then beat in the egg yolk and cream cheese until evenly blended. Fold in the flour, then stir in the orange rind and juice. Place about 32 teaspoonfuls of the mixture on greased baking sheets, spacing them well apart. Sprinkle with (caster) sugar, then bake in a preheated moderate oven (180°C/350°F or Gas Mark 4) for 15 to 20 minutes until golden. Leave to cool on the baking sheets for a few minutes, then transfer to a wire rack to cool completely.
To freeze: open (flash) freeze until firm, then pack in a rigid container, separating each layer with foil. Seal, label and return to the freezer.
To thaw and serve: place on a serving platter and thaw at room temperature for 1 to 2 hours.
MAKES ABOUT 32

SUGARED SPICE COOKIES

METRIC/IMPERIAL

150 g/5 oz flour
1 × 5 ml spoon/1 teaspoon ground mixed spice
100 g/4 oz soft brown sugar
100 g/4 oz butter, softened
1 egg, separated
caster sugar, for sprinkling

AMERICAN

1¼ cups flour
½ teaspoon grated nutmeg
½ teaspoon ground allspice and cloves, mixed
⅔ cup light brown sugar
½ cup butter, softened
1 egg, separated
sugar, for sprinkling

Sift the flour and spice(s) into a bowl. Add the sugar, butter and egg yolk and work with the fingertips to give a fairly soft dough.
Knead the dough until smooth, then roll out thinly on a floured surface. Cut out about 28 rounds with a 6 cm/2½ inch fluted cutter, then place on greased baking sheets. Brush with lightly beaten egg white, then sprinkle with (caster) sugar. Bake in a preheated moderate oven (180°C/350°F or Gas Mark 4) for 15 to 20 minutes until golden, then transfer to a wire rack and leave to cool.
To freeze: open (flash) freeze until firm, then pack in a rigid container, separating each layer with foil. Seal label and return to the freezer.
To thaw and serve: place on a serving platter and thaw at room temperature for 1 to 2 hours.
MAKES ABOUT 28

GINGER DROP COOKIES

METRIC/IMPERIAL

100 g/4 oz butter, softened
50 g/2 oz caster sugar
50 g/2 oz stem or crystallized ginger, chopped
100 g/4 oz flour

AMERICAN

½ cup butter, softened
¼ cup sugar
¼ cup chopped preserved or candied ginger
1 cup flour

Put the butter and sugar in a bowl, beat together until light and fluffy, then stir in the ginger. Fold in the flour until evenly blended.
Place 12 to 15 teaspoonfuls of the mixture on greased baking sheets, spacing them well apart. Bake in a preheated moderately hot oven (190°C/375°F or Gas Mark 5) for 15 to 20 minutes until golden, then leave to cool on the baking sheets for a few minutes. Transfer to a wire rack and leave to cool completely.
To freeze: open (flash) freeze until firm, then pack in a rigid container, separating each layer with foil. Seal, label and return to the freezer.
To thaw and serve: place on a serving platter and thaw at room temperature for 1 to 2 hours.
MAKES 12 to 15

CHERRY DROP COOKIES

Make as for Ginger Drop Cookies (see opposite), substituting 50 g/2 oz/¼ cup glacé (candied) cherries, chopped, and 0.5 × 2.5 ml spoon/¼ teaspoon vanilla essence (extract) for the ginger.

Freeze, thaw and serve as for Ginger Drop Cookies.

MAKES 12 to 15

DATE AND WALNUT LOAF

METRIC/IMPERIAL

350 g/¾ lb self-raising flour
1 × 2.5 ml spoon/½ teaspoon salt
1 × 2.5 ml spoon/½ teaspoon ground mixed spice
75 g/3 oz caster sugar
75 g/3 oz stoned dates, chopped
75 g/3 oz walnuts, finely chopped
2 eggs, beaten
300 ml/½ pint milk
50 g/2 oz butter, melted

AMERICAN

3 cups self-rising flour
½ teaspoon salt
¼ teaspoon grated nutmeg
¼ teaspoon ground allspice and cloves, mixed
⅜ cup sugar
⅓ cup pitted dates, chopped
¾ cup finely chopped walnuts
2 eggs, beaten
1¼ cups milk
¼ cup butter, melted

Grease a 1 kg/2 lb loaf tin and line with greased greaseproof paper or non-stick parchment.

Sift the flour, salt and spice(s) into a bowl, then stir in the sugar, dates and walnuts and make a well in the centre. Mix the eggs and milk together, pour into the flour mixture with the butter and beat for 2 minutes until well mixed. Pour the mixture into the prepared tin and smooth the top. Bake in a preheated moderate oven (180°C/350°F or Gas Mark 4) for 1 hour or until a skewer inserted into the centre of the loaf comes out clean. Turn out onto a wire rack, remove the paper lining and leave to cool.

To freeze: wrap in foil, then pack in a freezer bag. Seal, label and freeze.

To thaw and serve: thaw in the wrappings at room temperature for 3 to 4 hours.

SERVES 8

WHOLEWHEAT FRUIT SLICE

METRIC/IMPERIAL

15 g/½ oz fresh yeast
1 × 2.5 ml spoon/½ teaspoon sugar
150 ml/¼ pint hand-hot milk and water, mixed
225 g/½ lb wholewheat flour
1 × 2.5 ml spoon/½ teaspoon salt
25 g/1 oz butter
For the filling:
100 g/4 oz stoned dates, chopped
50 g/2 oz sugar
25 g/1 oz walnuts, chopped
a little clear honey, to glaze

AMERICAN

½ cake of compressed fresh yeast
½ teaspoon sugar
⅔ cup hand-hot milk and water, mixed
2 cups wholewheat flour
½ teaspoon salt
2 tablespoons butter
For the filling:
½ cup pitted dates, chopped
¼ cup sugar
¼ cup chopped walnuts
a little clear honey, to glaze

Put the yeast, sugar, milk and water in a bowl, add 50 g/2 oz/½ cup flour and stir until evenly blended. Leave in a warm place for 10 to 15 minutes until frothy.

Put the remaining flour and the salt in a warm bowl and rub in half the butter. Add to the frothy yeast batter and mix well to give a soft dough. Cover and leave to rise in a warm place until doubled in bulk. Knead on a floured surface, then roll into a rectangle about 1 cm/½ inch thick.

Melt the remaining butter and brush over the dough. Mix together the dates, sugar and walnuts and spread over the dough, leaving a 1 cm/½ inch margin around the edge. Roll up like a Swiss (jelly) roll, moisten the edges with water and seal together. Place the roll on a greased baking sheet with the join underneath and make shallow diagonal cuts on the top. Leave to rise for 20 to 30 minutes, then bake in a preheated hot oven (220°C/425°F or Gas Mark 7) for 30 minutes or until golden brown. Transfer to a wire rack, brush with honey, then leave to cool.

To freeze: open (flash) freeze until firm, then pack in a freezer bag. Seal, label and return to the freezer.

To thaw and serve: remove wrappings and thaw at room temperature for 3 to 4 hours.

SERVES 6

APPLE AND WALNUT LOAF

METRIC/IMPERIAL

100 g/4 oz butter, softened
100 g/4 oz caster sugar
2 eggs, beaten
1 × 15 ml spoon/1 tablespoon honey or golden syrup
100 g/4 oz sultanas
50 g/2 oz walnuts, chopped
225 g/½ lb self-raising flour
0.5 × 2.5 ml spoon/¼ teaspoon salt
1 × 5 ml spoon/1 teaspoon ground mixed spice
1 medium cooking apple, peeled, cored and chopped

AMERICAN

½ cup butter, softened
½ cup sugar
2 eggs, beaten
1 tablespoon honey, or light corn syrup
⅔ cup seedless white raisins
½ cup chopped walnuts
2 cups self-rising flour
¼ teaspoon salt
½ teaspoon grated nutmeg
½ teaspoon ground allspice and cloves, mixed
1 medium baking apple, peeled, cored and chopped

Grease a 450 g/1 lb loaf tin and line with greased greaseproof paper or non-stick parchment.
Put all the ingredients in a bowl and beat for 2 minutes until well mixed. Spoon into the prepared tin, smooth the top and bake in a preheated moderate oven (180°C/350°F or Gas Mark 4) for 1 hour or until a skewer inserted into the centre comes out clean. Reduce the heat to 160°C/325°F or Gas Mark 3 and bake for a further 20 minutes. Turn onto a wire rack, remove the paper lining and leave to cool.
To freeze: wrap in foil, then pack in a freezer bag. Seal, label and freeze.
To thaw and serve: thaw in the wrappings at room temperature for 3 to 4 hours.
SERVES 6

WALNUT AND ORANGE TEA BREAD

METRIC/IMPERIAL

2 × 15 ml spoons/2 tablespoons golden syrup
75 g/3 oz soft brown sugar
75 g/3 oz butter
2 × 15 ml spoons/2 tablespoons undiluted orange squash
350 g/¾ lb self-raising flour
0.5 × 2.5 ml spoon/¼ teaspoon ground cinnamon
75 g/3 oz candied peel, chopped
75 g/3 oz walnuts, chopped
3 eggs, beaten

AMERICAN

2 tablespoons golden or light corn syrup
½ cup light brown sugar
⅜ cup butter
2 tablespoons undiluted orange squash
3 cups self-rising flour
¼ teaspoon ground cinnamon
½ cup chopped candied peel
¾ cup chopped walnuts
3 eggs, beaten

Grease two 450 g/1 lb loaf tins and line with non-stick parchment.
Put the syrup, sugar, butter and orange squash in a pan and heat gently until melted, stirring occasionally. Sift the flour and cinnamon into a bowl, stir in the peel and walnuts and make a well in the centre. Put the eggs in the centre of the flour, then gradually add the melted mixture, stirring constantly. Beat well until the mixture is smooth, then pour into the prepared tins. Bake in a preheated moderately hot oven (190°C/375°F or Gas Mark 5) for 40 to 45 minutes or until a skewer inserted into the centre of the cakes comes out clean. Transfer to a wire rack, remove the paper lining and leave to cool.
To freeze: wrap in foil, then pack in a freezer bag. Seal, label and freeze.
To thaw and serve: thaw in the wrappings at room temperature for 3 to 4 hours.
EACH LOAF SERVES 6

DATE AND RAISIN LOAF

METRIC/IMPERIAL

225 g/½ lb flour
pinch of salt
100 g/4 oz butter
100 g/4 oz stoned dates, chopped
50 g/2 oz walnuts, chopped
100 g/4 oz seedless raisins
100 g/4 oz demerara sugar
1 × 5 ml spoon/1 teaspoon baking powder
1 × 5 ml spoon/1 teaspoon bicarbonate of soda
150 ml/¼ pint milk

AMERICAN

2 cups flour
pinch of salt
½ cup butter
½ cup pitted dates, chopped
½ cup chopped walnuts
⅔ cup seedless raisins
⅔ cup raw brown sugar
1 teaspoon baking powder
1 teaspoon baking soda
⅔ cup milk

Grease a 1 kg/2 lb loaf tin and line the bottom with greased greaseproof paper or non-stick parchment.
Sift the flour and salt into a bowl, then rub in the butter until the mixture resembles fine breadcrumbs. Stir in the dates, walnuts, raisins and sugar and make a well in the centre. Mix the baking powder, soda and milk together, pour into the centre of the dry ingredients and stir well to mix.
Spoon the mixture into the prepared tin. Bake in a preheated moderate oven (180°C/350°F or Gas Mark 4) for 1 hour or until a skewer inserted into the centre of the loaf comes out clean. Turn out onto a wire rack, remove the paper lining and leave to cool.
To freeze: wrap in foil, then pack in a freezer bag. Seal, label and freeze.
To thaw and serve: thaw in wrappings at room temperature for 4 hours.
SERVES 8

CIDER MALT LOAF

METRIC/IMPERIAL
175 g/6 oz self-raising flour
1 × 15 ml spoon/1 tablespoon malted drinking powder
25 g/1 oz caster sugar
75 g/3 oz mixed dried fruit
2 × 15 ml spoons/2 tablespoons golden syrup
5 × 15 ml spoons/5 tablespoons sweet cider

AMERICAN
1½ cups self-rising flour
1 tablespoon malted drinking powder
2 tablespoons sugar
½ cup mixed dried fruit
2 tablespoons light corn syrup
⅓ cup sweet hard cider

Grease a 450 g/1 lb loaf tin and line the bottom with greased greaseproof paper or non-stick parchment.
Put all the ingredients in a bowl and beat for 2 to 3 minutes until well mixed. Spoon the mixture into the prepared tin. Bake in a preheated moderate oven (160°C/325°F or Gas Mark 3) for 1 hour or until a skewer inserted into the centre of the cake comes out clean. Leave to cool in the tin, then turn out and remove the paper lining.
To freeze: wrap in foil, then pack in a freezer bag. Seal, label and freeze.
To thaw and serve: thaw in the wrappings at room temperature for 3 to 4 hours.
SERVES 6

RAISIN, ALMOND AND GRAPEFRUIT LOAF

METRIC/IMPERIAL
450 g/1 lb seedless raisins, roughly chopped
5 × 15 ml spoons/5 tablespoons water
350 g/¾ lb self-raising flour
1 × 5 ml spoon/1 teaspoon baking powder
50 g/2 oz butter
50 g/2 oz caster sugar
100 g/4 oz blanched almonds, roughly chopped
3 × 15 ml spoons/3 tablespoons milk
5 × 15 ml spoons/5 tablespoons concentrated frozen grapefruit juice, thawed
2 eggs, beaten
finely grated rind and segments of 1 grapefruit
extra caster sugar for sprinkling, to finish

AMERICAN
2⅔ sups seedless raisins, roughly chopped
⅓ cup water
3 cups self-rising flour
1 teaspoon baking powder
¼ cup butter
¼ cup sugar
1 cup roughly chopped blanched almonds
3 tablespoons milk
⅓ cup concentrated frozen grapefruit juice, thawed
2 eggs, beaten
finely grated rind and segments of 1 grapefruit
extra sugar for sprinkling, to finish

Grease a 1 kg/2 lb loaf tin and line with greased greaseproof paper or non-stick parchment.
Put the raisins and water in a pan and cook gently until the raisins are plump and tender.
Meanwhile, sift the flour and baking powder into a bowl and rub in the butter. Stir in the sugar and nuts, then add the raisin mixture, the milk, grapefruit juice and eggs. Stir well to mix, then beat in the grapefruit rind and segments.
Spoon the mixture into the prepared tin. Bake in a preheated moderate oven (180°C/350°F or Gas Mark 4) for 1 hour or until a skewer inserted into the centre of the loaf comes out clean. Turn out onto a wire rack, remove the paper lining and leave to cool.
To freeze: wrap in foil, then pack in a freezer bag. Seal, label and freeze.
To thaw and serve: thaw in the wrappings at room temperature for 3 to 4 hours, then remove the wrappings and sprinkle with (caster) sugar before serving.
SERVES 8

GINGER AND CHERRY LOAF

METRIC/IMPERIAL

175 g/6 oz flour
1.5 × 5 ml spoons/1½ teaspoons baking powder
1.5–2 × 5 ml spoons/1½–2 teaspoons ground ginger
75 g/3 oz butter
25 g/1 oz crystallized ginger, finely chopped
50 g/2 oz glacé cherries, finely chopped
100 g/4 oz demerara sugar
7 × 15 ml spoons/7 tablespoons milk

AMERICAN

1½ cups flour
1½ teaspoons baking powder
1½–2 teaspoons ground ginger
⅜ cup butter
3 tablespoons finely chopped candied ginger
¼ cup candied cherries, finely chopped
⅔ cup raw brown sugar
7 tablespoons milk

Sift the flour, baking powder and ground ginger into a bowl, add the butter and rub into the flour until the mixture resembles fine breadcrumbs. Stir in the chopped ginger, cherries and 75 g/3 oz/½ cup sugar, then add the milk and mix to a fairly stiff dough. Spoon the mixture into a greased 450 g/1 lb loaf tin, smooth the top and scatter over the remaining sugar. Bake in a preheated moderate oven (180°C/350°F or Gas Mark 4) for 1 to 1¼ hours until a skewer inserted into the centre of the loaf comes out clean. Leave to cool in the tin for a few minutes, then turn out onto a wire rack and leave to cool completely.
To freeze: wrap in foil, then pack in a freezer bag. Seal, label and freeze.
To thaw and serve: thaw in the wrappings at room temperature for 3 to 4 hours.
SERVES 6 to 8

COCONUT LOAF CAKE

METRIC/IMPERIAL

100 g/4 oz butter, softened
100 g/4 oz caster sugar
2 eggs, beaten
175 g/6 oz self-raising flour
75 g/3 oz desiccated coconut
2 × 15 ml spoons/2 tablespoons milk

AMERICAN

½ cup butter, softened
½ cup sugar
2 eggs, beaten
1½ cups self-rising flour
1 cup shredded coconut
2 tablespoons milk

Put the butter and sugar in a bowl, beat together until light and fluffy, then beat in the eggs a little at a time. Fold in the flour, 50 g/2 oz/⅔ cup coconut and the milk and stir until blended.
Spoon the mixture into a greased 450 g/1 lb loaf tin, smooth the top and scatter over the remaining coconut. Bake in a preheated moderate oven (160°C/325°F or Gas Mark 3) for 1 to 1¼ hours until well risen and golden. Leave to cool in the tin for a few minutes, then turn out onto a wire rack and leave to cool.
To freeze: wrap in foil, then pack in a freezer bag. Seal, label and freeze.
To thaw and serve: thaw in the wrappings at room temperature for 3 to 4 hours.
SERVES 4 to 6

COTTAGE CHEESE AND WALNUT TEA BREAD

METRIC/IMPERIAL

225 g/½ lb cottage cheese, sieved
175 g/6 oz soft brown sugar
3 eggs, beaten
finely grated rind of 2 oranges
50 g/2 oz walnuts, chopped
225 g/½ lb self-raising flour
1 × 5 ml spoon/1 teaspoon baking powder

AMERICAN

1 cup strained cottage cheese
1 cup light brown sugar
3 eggs, beaten
finely grated rind of 2 oranges
½ cup chopped walnuts
2 cups self-rising flour
1 teaspoon baking powder

Grease a 1 kg/2 lb loaf tin and line with greased greaseproof paper or non-stick parchment.
Put the cottage cheese and sugar in a bowl and beat together until well mixed. Beat in the eggs a little at a time with the orange rind and the walnuts.
Sift together the flour and baking powder and fold into the mixture until evenly blended. Spoon the mixture into the prepared tin. Bake in a preheated moderate oven (180°C/350°F or Gas Mark 4) for 40 to 50 minutes until well risen and golden brown. Cool in the tin for 5 minutes, turn out onto a wire rack, then remove the paper lining. Leave to cool.
To freeze: wrap in foil, then pack in a freezer bag. Seal, label and freeze.
To thaw and serve: thaw in the wrappings at room temperature for 3 to 4 hours.
SERVES 6 to 8

HONEY AND BANANA TEA BREAD

METRIC/IMPERIAL

100 g/4 oz butter, softened
100 g/4 oz caster sugar
225 g/½ lb self-raising flour
1 × 2.5 ml spoon/½ teaspoon ground mixed spice
1 × 2.5 ml spoon/½ teaspoon salt
1 × 15 ml spoon/1 tablespoon honey
75 g/3 oz walnuts, chopped
100 g/4 oz sultanas
75 g/3 oz glacé cherries, halved
450 g/1 lb ripe bananas, peeled and mashed
2 eggs, beaten
juice of 1 small lemon

AMERICAN

½ cup butter, softened
½ cup sugar
2 cups self-rising flour
¼ teaspoon grated nutmeg
¼ teaspoon ground allspice and cloves, mixed
½ teaspoon salt
1 tablespoon honey
¾ cup chopped walnuts
⅔ cup seedless white raisins
⅜ cup candied cherries, halved
1 lb ripe bananas, peeled and mashed
2 eggs, beaten
juice of 1 small lemon

Grease a 1 kg/2 lb loaf tin and line with greased greaseproof paper or non-stick parchment.
Put the butter and sugar in a bowl and cream together until light and fluffy. Sift together the flour, spice(s) and salt, then fold into the creamed mixture until evenly blended. Stir in the remaining ingredients, mix well, then spoon the mixture into the prepared tin.
Bake in a preheated moderate oven (180°C/350°F or Gas Mark 4) for 1 hour, then reduce the heat to 160°C/325°F or Gas Mark 3 and bake for a further 30 minutes or until a skewer inserted into the centre comes out clean. Turn out onto a wire rack, remove the paper lining and leave to cool.
To freeze: wrap in foil, then pack in a freezer bag. Seal, label and freeze.
To thaw and serve: thaw in the wrappings at room temperature for 3 to 4 hours.
SERVES 8

AUTUMN LOAF

METRIC/IMPERIAL

300 g/11 oz self-raising flour
25 g/1 oz cocoa powder
1 × 5 ml spoon/1 teaspoon ground cinnamon
175 g/6 oz butter
225 g/½ lb soft brown sugar
100 g/4 oz stoned dates, chopped
100 g/4 oz glacé cherries, chopped
50 g/2 oz walnuts, chopped
1.5 × 5 ml spoons/1½ teaspoons bicarbonate of soda
3 × 15 ml spoons/3 tablespoons milk
300 ml/½ pint apple purée
3 × 15 ml spoons/3 tablespoons water

AMERICAN

2¾ cups self-rising flour
¼ cup unsweetened cocoa powder
1 teaspoon ground cinnamon
¾ cup butter
1⅓ cups light brown sugar
½ cup pitted dates, chopped
½ cup candied cherries, chopped
¼ cup chopped walnuts
1½ teaspoons baking soda
3 tablespoons milk
1¼ cups applesauce
3 tablespoons water

Grease a 1 kg/2 lb loaf tin and line with greased greaseproof paper or non-stick parchment.
Sift the flour, cocoa and cinnamon into a bowl, add the butter in pieces and rub into the flour until the mixture resembles fine breadcrumbs. Stir in 175 g/6 oz/1 cup sugar, the fruit and the nuts and make a well in the centre. Mix the bicarbonate of soda (baking soda) to a paste with the milk, then pour into the centre of the flour with the apple purée (applesauce). Stir well to mix, then spoon the mixture into the prepared tin.
Bake in a preheated moderately hot oven (190°C/375°F or Gas Mark 5) for 1 hour, then remove from the oven. Put the remaining sugar in a pan, add the water and boil for 3 minutes. Brush over the cake, then return to the oven and bake for a further 15 to 20 minutes until cracks appear in the top of the cake. Turn out onto a wire rack, remove the paper lining and leave to cool.
To freeze: wrap in foil, then pack in a freezer bag. Seal, label and freeze.
To thaw and serve: thaw in the wrappings at room temperature for 3 to 4 hours.
SERVES 8

BANANA NUT BREAD

METRIC/IMPERIAL

275 g/10 oz flour
1 × 5 ml spoon/1 teaspoon baking powder
0.5 × 2.5 ml spoon/¼ teaspoon bicarbonate of soda
1 × 2.5 ml spoon/½ teaspoon salt
50 g/2 oz soft tub margarine
100 g/4 oz caster sugar
3 ripe bananas, peeled and mashed
50 g/2 oz walnuts, chopped
finely grated rind of 1 orange
1 egg, beaten
6 × 15 ml spoons/6 tablespoons milk

AMERICAN

2½ cups flour
1 teaspoon baking powder
¼ teaspoon baking soda
½ teaspoon salt
¼ cup soft margarine
½ cup sugar
3 ripe bananas, peeled and mashed
½ cup chopped walnuts
finely grated rind of 1 orange
1 egg, beaten
6 tablespoons milk

Grease a 1 kg/2 lb loaf tin and line the bottom with greased greaseproof paper or non-stick parchment.
Sift the flour, baking powder, soda and salt into a bowl and make a well in the centre. Add the remaining ingredients and beat together for 2 to 3 minutes until well mixed.
Spoon the mixture into the prepared tin. Bake in a preheated moderate oven (180°C/350°F or Gas Mark 4) for 1¼ to 1½ hours until a skewer inserted into the centre of the bread comes out clean. Turn out onto a wire rack, remove the paper lining and leave to cool.
To freeze: wrap in foil, then pack in a freezer bag. Seal, label and freeze.
To thaw and serve: thaw in the wrappings at room temperature for 3 to 4 hours.
SERVES 8

CHOCOLATE MALT LOAF

METRIC/IMPERIAL

225 g/½ lb self-raising flour
pinch of salt
50 g/2 oz malted drinking chocolate powder
50 g/2 oz soft brown sugar
50 g/2 oz stoned dates, chopped
50 g/2 oz mixed dried fruit
2 × 15 ml spoons/2 tablespoons golden syrup, melted
approx 150 ml/¼ pint milk and water, mixed

AMERICAN

2 cups self-rising flour
pinch of salt
½ cup malted drinking chocolate powder
⅓ cup light brown sugar
¼ cup pitted dates, chopped
⅓ cup mixed dried fruit
2 tablespoons light corn syrup
approx ⅔ cup milk and water, mixed

Grease a 450 g/1 lb loaf tin and line the bottom with greaseproof paper or non-stick parchment. Sift the dry ingredients into a bowl, add the sugar, fruit and syrup and stir well to mix. Stir in enough milk and water to give a soft dropping consistency, then spoon the mixture into the prepared tin.
Bake in a preheated moderate oven (180°C/350°F or Gas Mark 4) for about 1 hour or until a skewer inserted into the centre of the loaf comes out clean. Leave to cool in the tin, then turn out and remove the paper lining.
To freeze: wrap in foil, then pack in a freezer bag. Seal, label and freeze.
To thaw and serve: thaw in the wrappings at room temperature for 3 to 4 hours.
SERVES 6

BANANA RAISIN LOAF

METRIC/IMPERIAL

75 g/3 oz butter
100 g/4 oz caster sugar
1 large egg, beaten
200 g/7 oz self-raising flour
0.5 × 2.5 ml spoon/¼ teaspoon salt
0.5 × 2.5 ml spoon/¼ teaspoon bicarbonate of soda
100 g/4 oz seedless raisins
2 large ripe bananas, peeled and mashed
50 g/2 oz walnuts, chopped (optional)

AMERICAN

⅜ cup butter
½ cup sugar
1 large egg, beaten
1¾ cups self-rising flour
¼ teaspoon salt
¼ teaspoon baking soda
⅔ cup seedless raisins
2 large ripe bananas, peeled and mashed
½ cup chopped walnuts (optional)

Grease a 450 g/1 lb loaf tin and line with greased greaseproof paper or non-stick parchment.
Put the butter and sugar in a bowl, beat together until light and fluffy, then beat in the egg a little at a time. Sift together the flour, salt and

bicarbonate of soda (baking soda) and fold into the creamed mixture until evenly blended. Stir in the raisins, bananas and walnuts (if using).
Spoon the mixture into the prepared tin. Bake in a preheated moderate oven (180°C/350°F or Gas Mark 4) for 50 minutes to 1 hour or until a skewer inserted into the centre of the loaf comes out clean. Transfer to a wire rack, remove the paper lining and leave to cool.
To freeze: wrap in foil, then pack in a freezer bag. Seal, label and freeze.
To thaw and serve: thaw in the wrappings at room temperature for 3 to 4 hours.
SERVES 6

FRUITY TEA BREAD

METRIC/IMPERIAL
225 g/½ lb self-raising flour
pinch of mixed spice
25 g/1 oz caster sugar
75 g/3 oz butter
100 g/4 oz sultanas
50 g/2 oz glacé cherries, chopped
1 × 15 ml spoon/1 tablespoon golden syrup
approx 7 × 15 ml spoons/7 tablespoons milk

AMERICAN
2 cups self-rising flour
pinch of ground cloves and nutmg, mixed
2 tablespoons sugar
⅜ cup butter
⅔ cup seedless white raisins
⅓ cup chopped candied peel
¼ cup candied cherries, chopped
1 tablespoon light corn syrup
approx 7 tablespoons milk

Grease a 450 g/1 lb loaf tin and line the bottom with greased greaseproof paper or non-stick parchment.
Sift the flour into a bowl, stir in the sugar, then rub in the butter until the mixture resembles fine breadcrumbs. Stir in the sultanas (seedless white raisins), peel and cherries, then add the syrup and enough milk to give a soft dough.
Spoon the mixture into the prepared tin. Bake in a preheated moderate oven (180°C/350°F or Gas Mark 4) for 1¼ to 1½ hours until a skewer inserted into the centre of the loaf comes out clean. Turn out onto a wire rack, remove the paper lining and leave to cool.
To freeze: wrap in foil, then pack in a freezer bag. Seal, label and freeze.
To thaw and serve: thaw in the wrappings at room temperature for 3 to 4 hours.
SERVES 6

WALNUT LOAF

Make as for Fruity Tea Bread, substituting 75 g/3 oz/¾ cup chopped walnuts for the peel and cherries.
Freeze, thaw and serve as for Fruit Loaf.
SERVES 6

CHERRY ORANGE LOAF

METRIC/IMPERIAL
120 ml/4 fl oz corn oil
2 eggs, beaten
2 × 15 ml spoons/2 tablespoons milk
150 g/5 oz caster sugar
275 g/10 oz self-raising flour
pinch of salt
225 g/½ lb glacé cherries, quartered
finely grated rind of ½ orange

AMERICAN
½ cup corn oil
2 eggs, beaten
2 tablespoons milk
⅝ cup sugar
2½ cups self-rising flour
pinch of salt
1 cup candied cherries, quartered
finely grated rind of ½ orange

Grease a deep 18 cm/7 inch cake tin and line the bottom with greased greaseproof paper or non-stick parchment.
Put the oil, eggs, milk and sugar in a bowl and beat together until well mixed. Sift the flour and salt into a separate bowl and stir in the cherries and orange rind. Beat the flour mixture gradually into the oil and egg mixture, then spoon into the prepared tin.
Bake in a preheated moderate oven (180°C/350°F or Gas Mark 4) for 1¼ hours or until a skewer inserted into the centre of the cake comes out clean. Turn out onto a wire rack, remove the paper lining and leave to cool.
To freeze: wrap in foil, then pack in a freezer bag. Seal, label and freeze.
To thaw and serve: thaw in the wrappings at room temperature for 3 to 4 hours.
SERVES 6

CHEESE AND CELERY LOAF

METRIC/IMPERIAL

450 g/1 lb self-raising flour
1 × 5 ml spoon/1 teaspoon salt
40 g/1½ oz butter
3 large celery stalks, finely chopped
175 g/6 oz Cheddar cheese, coarsely grated
1 garlic clove, peeled and finely chopped
1 egg
scant 300 ml/½ pint milk

AMERICAN

4 cups self-rising flour
1 teaspoon salt
3 tablespoons butter
3 large celery stalks, finely chopped
1½ cups coarsely grated Cheddar cheese
1 garlic clove, peeled and finely chopped
1 egg
scant 1¼ cups milk

Sift the flour and salt into a bowl, add the butter in pieces and rub into the flour until the mixture resembles fine breadcrumbs. Add the celery, cheese and garlic and stir well to mix.
Mix the egg and milk together, stir gradually into the flour mixture and mix to a soft dough.
Turn out onto a floured surface and knead lightly until smooth, then shape into a rectangle.
Place in a greased 1 kg/2 lb loaf tin and bake in a preheated hot oven (220°C/425°F or Gas Mark 7) for 55 minutes. Turn out onto a wire rack and leave to cool.
To freeze: pack in a freezer bag, seal, label and freeze.
To thaw and serve: thaw in the wrappings at room temperature for 3 to 4 hours.
CUTS INTO 12 to 16 SLICES

PLAIN SCONES (BISCUITS)

METRIC/IMPERIAL

225 g/½ lb self-raising flour
1 × 5 ml spoon/1 teaspoon baking powder
1 × 2.5 ml spoon/½ teaspoon salt
50 g/2 oz butter
approx 150 ml/¼ pint milk

AMERICAN

2 cups self-rising flour
1 teaspoon baking powder
½ teaspoon salt
¼ cup butter
approx ⅔ cup milk

Sift the flour, baking powder and salt into a bowl, then rub in the butter until the mixture resembles fine breadcrumbs. Make a well in the centre and stir in sufficient milk to give a soft dough.
Turn the dough out onto a floured surface, knead until smooth, then roll out to 2 cm/¾ inch thickness. Cut out 10 to 12 rounds with a 5 cm/2 inch cutter, place on a greased baking sheet and brush with a little milk. Bake in a preheated hot oven (230°C/450°F or Gas Mark 8) for about 12 minutes until golden brown. Transfer to a wire rack and leave to cool.
To freeze: pack in a single layer in a freezer bag, seal, label and freeze.
To thaw and serve: remove wrappings and place the frozen scones (biscuits) on a baking sheet. Reheat in a preheated moderately hot oven (200°C/400°F or Gas Mark 6) for 10 minutes.
MAKES 10 to 12

HERB SCONES (BISCUITS)

Make as for Plain Scones (see above), adding 1 × 15 ml spoon/1 tablespoon chopped fresh herbs or 1 × 5 ml spoon/1 teaspoon dried mixed herbs to the flour.
Freeze, thaw and serve as for Plain Scones.
MAKES 10 to 12

CINNAMON DROP SCONES

METRIC/IMPERIAL

150 g/5 oz flour
2 × 5 ml spoons/2 teaspoons baking powder
1 × 2.5 ml spoon/½ teaspoon ground cinnamon
pinch of salt
1 × 15 ml spoon/1 tablespoon caster sugar
1 egg, beaten
120 ml/4 fl oz milk
25 g/1 oz butter, melted
vegetable or corn oil, for frying

AMERICAN

1¼ cups flour
2 teaspoons baking powder
½ teaspoon ground cinnamon
pinch of salt
1 tablespoon sugar
1 egg, beaten
½ cup milk
2 tablespoons butter, melted
vegetable or corn oil, for frying

Sift the flour, baking powder, cinnamon and salt into a bowl, stir in the sugar and the beaten egg, then gradually add the milk and the melted butter. Beat well to mix to a smooth batter.

Heat a griddle or heavy-based frying pan (skillet) and grease lightly with oil. Pour 1×15 ml spoon/1 tablespoon of the mixture onto the griddle, cook for ½ minute until bubbles rise to the surface, then turn over and cook the other side until golden brown. Place on a clean tea (dish) towel to keep moist, then repeat with the remaining batter.
To freeze: interleave each drop scone with foil. Pack in a freezer bag, seal. label and freeze.
To thaw and serve: remove wrappings and thaw at room temperature for 1 hour.
MAKES 15

SAVOURY DROP SCONES

Make as for Cinnamon Drop Scones (see above), substituting 1 small onion, peeled and grated, 1×5 ml spoon/1 teaspoon mustard powder and 50 g/2 oz/½ cup grated Parmesan cheese for the cinnamon and sugar.
Freeze, thaw and serve as for Cinnamon Drop Scones.
MAKES 15

FRUIT SCONES (BISCUITS)

METRIC/IMPERIAL
225 g/½ lb flour
pinch of salt
2×5 ml spoons/2 teaspoons baking powder
1×5 ml spoon/1 teaspoon bicarbonate of soda
50 g/2 oz vegetable fat
50 g/2 oz caster sugar
50 g/2 oz seedless raisins
2×15 ml spoons/2 tablespoons currants
1 large egg, beaten
5×15 ml spoons/5 tablespoons milk

AMERICAN
2 cups flour
pinch of salt
2 teaspoons baking powder
1 teaspoon baking soda
¼ cup vegetable fat
¼ cup sugar
⅓ cup seedless raisins
2 tablespoons currants
1 large egg, beaten
⅓ cup milk

Sift the flour, salt, baking powder and soda into a bowl, rub in the fat, then stir in the sugar, raisins and currants. Mix together the egg and milk and stir into the fruit mixture to give a fairly stiff dough.
Turn the dough out onto a floured surface, knead lightly, then roll out to 1 cm/½ inch thickness. Cut out 10 to 12 circles with a 5 cm/2 inch cutter and place on a greased baking sheet. Bake in a preheated hot oven (230°C/450°F or Gas Mark 8) for 10 to 15 minutes until well risen and golden brown, then transfer to a wire rack and leave to cool.
To freeze: pack in a single layer in a freezer bag, seal, label and freeze.
To thaw and serve: remove wrappings and place the frozen scones (biscuits) on a baking sheet. Reheat in a preheated moderate oven (180°C/350°F or Gas Mark 4) for 15 minutes. Serve warm.
MAKES 10 to 12

HONEY SCONES (BISCUITS)

METRIC/IMPERIAL
225 g/½ lb self-raising flour
1×2.5 ml spoon/½ teaspoon ground mixed spice
2×5 ml spoons/2 teaspoons caster sugar
50 g/2 oz butter
2×15 ml spoons/2 tablespoons honey
6×15 ml spoons/6 tablespoons milk

AMERICAN
2 cups self-rising flour
¼ teaspoon grated nutmeg
¼ teaspoon ground allspice and cloves, mixed
2 teaspoons sugar
¼ cup butter
2 tablespoons honey
6 tablespoons milk

Sift the flour and spice(s) into a bowl, stir in the sugar, then rub in the butter until the mixture resembles fine breadcrumbs. Add half the honey and the milk and mix to a soft dough.
Turn the dough out onto a floured surface, knead until smooth, then roll out to 2 cm/¾ inch thickness. Cut out 10 to 12 rounds with a 5 cm/2 inch cutter. Place on a greased baking sheet and bake in a preheated hot oven (220°C/425°F or Gas Mark 7) for 12 to 15 minutes until golden brown. Transfer to a wire rack. Warm the remaining honey, brush over the scones (biscuits) and leave to cool.
To freeze: open (flash) freeze until firm, then pack in a rigid container, separating each layer with foil. Seal, label and return to the freezer.
To thaw and serve: reheat from frozen in a preheated moderately hot oven (200°C/400°F or Gas Mark 6) for 10 minutes. Or thaw at room temperature for 2 hours and serve cold.
MAKES 10 to 12

CHEESE SCONES (BISCUITS)

METRIC/IMPERIAL
225 g/½ lb self-raising flour
1 × 2.5 ml spoon/½ teaspoon salt
40 g/1½ oz butter
50 g/2 oz Cheddar cheese, grated
25 g/1 oz Parmesan cheese, grated
1 × 5 ml spoon/1 teaspoon mustard powder
approx 150 ml/¼ pint milk

AMERICAN
2 cups self-rising flour
½ teaspoon salt
3 tablespoons butter
½ cup grated Cheddar cheese
¼ cup grated Parmesan cheese
1 teaspoon mustard powder
approx ⅔ cup milk

Sift the flour and salt into a bowl, then rub in the butter. Mix the cheeses together and stir 50 g/2 oz/½ cup cheese into the flour mixture with the mustard. Stir in enough milk to give a soft dough.
Turn the dough out onto a floured surface, knead lightly, then roll out to 2 cm/¾ inch thickness. Cut out 10 to 12 rounds with a 5 cm/2 inch cutter and place on a greased baking sheet. Scatter over the remaining cheese, then bake in a preheated hot oven (230°C/450°F or Gas Mark 8) for 10 to 15 minutes until well risen and golden brown. Transfer to a wire rack and leave to cool.
To freeze: pack in a single layer in a freezer bag, seal, label and freeze.
To thaw and serve: remove wrappings and place the frozen scones (biscuits) on a baking sheet. Reheat in a preheated moderate oven (180°C/350°F or Gas Mark 4) for 15 minutes. Or thaw at room temperature for 2 hours and serve cold.
MAKES 10 to 12

WHOLEMEAL SCONES (WHOLEWHEAT BISCUITS)

METRIC/IMPERIAL
100 g/4 oz wholemeal flour
100 g/4 oz self-raising flour
1 × 2.5 ml spoon/½ teaspoon salt
2 × 5 ml spoons/2 teaspoons baking powder
50 g/2 oz butter
approx 150 ml/¼ pint milk

AMERICAN
1 cup wholewheat flour
1 cup self-rising flour
½ teaspoon salt
2 teaspoons baking powder
¼ cup butter
approx ⅔ cup milk

Put the wholemeal (wholewheat) flour into a bowl, then sift in the remaining flour, the salt and baking powder. Rub in the butter, then stir in enough milk to give a soft dough.
Turn the dough out onto a floured surface, knead lightly, then roll out to 2 cm/¾ inch thickness. Cut out 10 to 12 rounds with a 5 cm/2 inch cutter, place on a greased baking sheet and brush with milk. Bake in a preheated hot oven (230°C/450°F or Gas Mark 8) for 12 minutes until golden brown. Cool on a wire rack.
To freeze: pack in a single layer in a freezer bag, seal, label and freeze.
To thaw and serve: remove wrappings and place the frozen scones (biscuits) on a baking sheet. Reheat in a preheated moderately hot oven (200°C/400°F or Gas Mark 6) for 10 minutes.
MAKES 10 to 12

BACON SCONES (BISCUITS)

METRIC/IMPERIAL
75 g/3 oz streaky bacon rashers, rinds removed and chopped
225 g/½ lb flour
1 × 2.5 ml spoon/½ teaspoon salt
4 × 5 ml spoons/4 teaspoons baking powder
1 × 5 ml spoon/1 teaspoon mustard powder
40 g/1½ oz butter
approx 150 ml/¼ pint milk

AMERICAN
4–5 fatty bacon slices, chopped
2 cups flour
½ teaspoon salt
4 teaspoons baking powder
1 teaspoon mustard powder
3 tablespoons butter
approx ⅔ cup milk

Fry the bacon in its own fat until crisp and golden, then drain on paper towels.
Sift the dry ingredients into a bowl, rub in the butter, then stir in the bacon. Stir in enough milk to give a soft dough.
Turn the dough out onto a floured surface, knead lightly, then roll out to a circle 20 to 23 cm/ 8 to 9 inches in diameter. Cut into 8 equal triangles.
Place the triangles on a greased baking sheet and brush the tops with a little milk. Bake in a preheated hot oven (220°C/425°F or Gas Mark 7) for 10 to 15 minutes until well risen and golden brown. Transfer to a wire rack and leave to cool.
To freeze: pack in a single layer in a freezer bag, seal, label and freeze.
To thaw and serve: remove wrappings and place the frozen scones (biscuits) on a baking sheet. Reheat in a preheated moderate oven (180°C/ 350°F or Gas Mark 4) for 15 minutes.
MAKES 8

SCOTCH PANCAKES

METRIC/IMPERIAL
100 g/4 oz self-raising flour
25 g/1 oz caster sugar
1 egg, beaten
150 ml/$\frac{1}{4}$ pint milk
vegetable or corn oil, for frying

AMERICAN
1 cup self-rising flour
2 tablespoons sugar
1 egg, beaten
$\frac{2}{3}$ cup milk
vegetable or corn oil, for frying

Sift the flour into a bowl, then stir in the sugar and the egg. Stir in half the milk, beat until smooth, then beat in the remaining milk. Heat a griddle or heavy-based frying pan (skillet) and grease lightly with oil. Spoon the mixture into the pan in rounds, spacing them well apart. Cook for $\frac{1}{2}$ minute until bubbles rise on the surface, then turn over and cook the other side until golden brown. Place on a wire rack to cool while cooking the remaining mixture.
To freeze: stack in layers, interleaving each pancake with foil. Pack in a freezer bag, seal, label and freeze.
To thaw and serve: place the frozen pancakes on a baking sheet and reheat in a preheated moderately hot oven (200°C/400°F or Gas Mark 6) for 5 minutes or until heated through. Spread with butter while still warm and serve immediately.
MAKES ABOUT 18

CHEESE SCONE RING

METRIC/IMPERIAL
225 g/$\frac{1}{2}$ lb self-raising flour
pinch of salt
50 g/2 oz butter
150 ml/$\frac{1}{4}$ pint milk
100 g/4 oz cheese, grated
1 × 2.5–5 ml spoon/$\frac{1}{2}$–1 teaspoon dried mixed herbs

AMERICAN
2 cups self-rising flour
pinch of salt
$\frac{1}{4}$ cup butter
$\frac{2}{3}$ cup milk
1 cup grated cheese
$\frac{1}{2}$–1 teaspoon dried mixed herbs

Sift the flour and salt into a bowl, rub in the butter, then stir in the milk and mix to a firm dough. Turn out onto a floured surface and knead lightly, then roll out to an oblong about 33 × 23 cm/13 × 9 inches.
Scatter the cheese and herbs over the dough, then roll up like a Swiss (jelly) roll and cut into 8 equal pieces. Put the pieces cut side down in a circle on a greased baking sheet, arranging them so that they just touch each other. Bake at the top of a preheated hot oven (220°C/425°F or Gas Mark 7) for 15 to 20 minutes until golden. Leave to cool on the baking sheet.
To freeze: pack in a single layer in a freezer bag, seal, label and freeze.
To thaw and serve: thaw in the wrappings at room temperature for 3 hours, then reheat on a baking sheet in a preheated moderate oven (180°C/350°F or Gas Mark 4) for 15 minutes.
MAKES 8

BASIC WHITE BREAD

METRIC/IMPERIAL

2 × 15 ml spoons/2 tablespoons soft brown sugar
900 ml/1½ pints hand-hot water
15 g/½ oz dried yeast
1 × 15 ml spoon/1 tablespoon salt
1.5 kg/3 lb strong plain flour
25 g/1 oz butter
a little milk, to glaze

AMERICAN

2 tablespoons light brown sugar
3¾ cups hand-hot water
2 packages of active dry yeast
1 tablespoon salt
3 lb flour
2 tablespoons butter
a little milk, to glaze

Dissolve 1 × 5 ml spoon/1 teaspoon sugar in 300 ml/½ pint/1¼ cups water, sprinkle over the yeast and stir well. Leave in a warm place for 10 to 15 minutes until frothy. Add the salt and the remaining sugar to the remaining water.

Sift the flour into a warm bowl and rub in the butter. Pour in the water and the frothy yeast liquid, then work the flour and liquid together quickly with the fingertips to give a firm dough. (If it is too dry, add a little more water.)

Turn the dough out onto a floured surface and knead for 8 minutes until smooth and elastic, pulling the outside dough into the centre. Put into a lightly greased bowl, then cover with a clean dampened tea (dish) towel. Leave to rest in a warm place for 1 to 1½ hours or until doubled in bulk. Turn the dough out onto the floured surface, knock back (punch down) and knead again for 5 minutes, then divide in two and keep one half warm.

Knead one half of the dough into a smooth ball, shape into an oblong and put into a greased 1 kg/2 lb loaf tin. Divide the remaining dough in two, shape into two smaller oblongs and put into two greased 450 g/1 lb loaf tins. Brush the top of the loaves with milk, then leave to rise for 20 minutes or until the dough reaches the top of the tins.

Bake the loaves in a preheated hot oven (230°C/450°F or Gas Mark 8) for 20 minutes. Reduce the heat to moderately hot (200°C/400°F or Gas Mark 6) and bake for a further 20 minutes for the large loaf, 10 minutes for the smaller loaves, or until they are brown on the top and sound hollow when tapped on the bottom. Turn out onto a wire rack and leave to cool.

To freeze: pack in freezer bags, seal, label and freeze.

To thaw and serve: thaw in wrappings at room

temperature for 3 to 4 hours, or wrap in foil and reheat from frozen in a preheated moderately hot oven (200°C/400°F or Gas Mark 6) for 25 to 30 minutes until heated through.
MAKES ONE 1 kg/2 lb LOAF AND TWO 450 g/1 lb LOAVES

100 PER CENT WHOLEWHEAT BREAD

METRIC/IMPERIAL
1 × 15 ml spoon/1 tablespoon sugar
450 ml/¾ pint hand-hot water
1 × 15 ml spoon/1 tablespoon dried yeast
675 g/1½ lb wholewheat flour
1 × 5 ml spoon/1 teaspoon salt
15 g/½ oz butter

AMERICAN
1 tablespoon sugar
2 cups hand-hot water
1½ packages active dry yeast
6 cups wholewheat flour
1 teaspoon salt
1 tablespoon butter

Dissolve 1 × 5 ml spoon/1 teaspoon sugar in 150 ml/¼ pint/⅔ cup of the water, sprinkle over the dried yeast and stir well to mix. Leave in a warm place for 10 to 15 minutes until frothy.
Put the flour and salt in a warm bowl, rub in the butter, then stir in the sugar. Make a well in the centre, pour in the frothy yeast liquid and the remaining water. Stir well to mix.
Turn the dough out onto a floured surface and knead for about 5 minutes until smooth. Place in a lightly greased polythene (plastic) bag and leave in a warm place until doubled in bulk.
Turn the dough out onto the floured surface, then knock back (punch down) and knead again for 5 minutes. Divide in two, shape each piece into an oblong, then place in two greased 450 g/1 lb loaf tins. Leave in a warm place until the dough reaches the top of the tins.
Remove the bags and bake the loaves in a preheated hot oven (220°C/425°F or Gas Mark 7) for 20 minutes. Reduce the heat to moderately hot (200°C/400°F or Gas Mark 6) and bake for a further 10 to 15 minutes until the loaves are brown on top and sound hollow when tapped on the bottom. Turn out onto a wire rack and leave to cool.
To freeze: pack in a freezer bag, seal, label and freeze.
To thaw and serve: thaw in the wrappings at room temperature for 3 to 4 hours.
MAKES TWO 450 g/1 lb LOAVES

CIDER AND GINGER PLAIT

METRIC/IMPERIAL
150 ml/¼ pint cider
25 g/1 oz fresh yeast
450 g/1 lb flour
25 g/1 oz caster sugar
1 dessert apple, peeled, cored and grated
25 g/1 oz butter
1 egg, beaten
For the icing (to finish):
100 g/4 oz icing sugar, sifted
a little cider, to mix
25 g/1 oz crystallized ginger, chopped
25 g/1 oz walnuts, chopped

AMERICAN
⅔ cup hard cider
1 cake of compressed fresh yeast
4 cups flour
2 tablespoons sugar
1 dessert apple, peeled, cored and grated
2 tablespoons butter
1 egg, beaten
For the icing (to finish):

a little cider, to mix
3 tablespoons chopped candied ginger
¼ cup chopped walnuts

Put the cider in a pan, heat gently until lukewarm, then blend with the yeast. Put the flour, sugar and apple in a warm bowl, rub in the butter, then add the beaten egg and the cider mixture. Mix to a stiff dough, then turn out onto a floured surface and knead for about 5 minutes until smooth. Put the dough in a lightly greased polythene (plastic) bag and leave in a warm place until doubled in bulk. Turn out onto the floured surface and knead again for 5 minutes. Divide the dough into three equal pieces, shape each piece into a 38 cm/15 inch long roll, then plait (braid) the three rolls together. Shape the plait into a horseshoe, tucking under the ends, then place on a greased baking sheet. Leave in a warm place for about 20 minutes. Bake in a preheated hot oven (220°C/425°F or Gas Mark 7) for 15 to 20 minutes until golden brown. Transfer to a wire rack and leave to cool.
To freeze: pack in a freezer bag, seal, label and freeze.
To thaw and serve: thaw in the wrappings at room temperature for 3 to 4 hours.
To make the icing: put the icing (confectioners') sugar in a bowl, then add the cider a teaspoonful at a time to give a coating consistency. Drizzle over the loaf, then scatter over the ginger and walnuts. Leave to set before serving.
MAKES ONE 38 cm/15 inch PLAIT (BRAID)

RYE BREAD

METRIC/IMPERIAL

1 × 5 ml spoon/1 teaspoon sugar
300 ml/½ pint hand-hot water
25 g/1 oz dried yeast
350 g/¾ lb rye flour
350 g/¾ lb strong plain flour
1 × 5 ml spoon/1 teaspoon salt
1 × 2.5 ml spoon/½ teaspoon caraway seeds
150 ml/¼ pint milk
1 × 15 ml spoon/1 tablespoon black treacle
a little extra milk, to glaze

AMERICAN

1 teaspoon sugar
1¼ cups hand-hot water
4 packages of active dry yeast
3 cups rye flour
3 cups white flour
1 teaspoon salt
½ teaspoon caraway seeds
⅔ cup milk
1 tablespoon molasses
a little extra milk, to glaze

Dissolve the sugar in the water, sprinkle over the yeast and stir well. Leave in a warm place for 10 to 15 minutes until frothy.
Sift the flours and salt into a warm bowl, then add the caraway seeds and make a well in the centre. Put the milk and treacle (molasses) in a pan, heat gently until lukewarm, then pour into the flour mixture with the frothy yeast batter. Mix to a firm dough, then turn out onto a floured surface and knead for about 10 minutes. Place the dough in a lightly greased polythene (plastic) bag and leave in a warm place for about 1 hour until doubled in bulk. Knock back (punch down) the dough, then divide in two and shape into two long loaves.
Place the loaves on well-greased baking sheets and leave to rise in a warm place for about 40 minutes. Brush the loaves with a little milk. Bake in a preheated hot oven (220°C/425°F or Gas Mark 7) for 40 minutes or until the loaves are brown on top and sound hollow when tapped at the bottom. Turn out onto a wire rack and leave to cool.
To freeze: pack in a freezer bag, seal, label and freeze.
To thaw and serve: thaw in the wrappings at room temperature for 3 to 4 hours.
MAKES 2 LOAVES

NUTTY HONEY LOAF

METRIC/IMPERIAL

225 g/½ lb wholewheat flour
225 g/½ lb white flour
1 × 2.5 ml spoon/½ teaspoon salt
15 g/½ oz fresh yeast
5 × 15 ml spoons/5 tablespoons honey
50 g/2 oz butter
200 ml/⅓ pint milk
1 egg, beaten
75 g/3 oz walnuts, chopped
3 × 15 ml spoons/3 tablespoons milk, to glaze

AMERICAN

2 cups wholewheat flour
2 cups white flour
½ teaspoon salt
½ cake of compressed fresh yeast
⅓ cup honey
¼ cup butter
⅞ cup milk
1 egg, beaten
¾ cup chopped walnuts
3 tablespoons milk, to glaze

Put the wholewheat flour in a warm bowl, then sift in the white flour and salt.
Cream the yeast with 1 × 5 ml spoon/1 teaspoon honey, then put 2 × 15 ml spoons/2 tablespoons honey in a pan with the butter and milk and heat gently until the honey and butter have melted. Beat in the egg, then stir into the creamed yeast mixture.
Make a well in the centre of the flour, pour in the yeast batter and stir well to mix to a firm dough. Turn out onto a floured surface and knead until smooth. Put the dough in a lightly greased bowl, cover with a dampened tea (dish) towel and leave in a warm place until doubled in bulk.
Turn the dough out onto the floured surface and knead again. Work in the chopped nuts, shape the dough into a round and place in a greased 450 g/1 lb round tin. Leave in a warm place for 30 minutes until the dough reaches the top of the tin. Bake in a preheated moderately hot oven (200°C/400°F or Gas Mark 6) for 45 minutes until the loaf is brown and sounds hollow when tapped on the bottom. Return quickly to the oven if the loaf is not quite ready.
Put the remaining honey in a pan with the 3 × 15 ml spoons/3 tablespoons milk and heat gently until the honey has melted. Turn the loaf out of the tin and brush the top and sides with the honey glaze. Place on a hot baking sheet and return to the moderately hot oven for a further 2 minutes. Transfer to a wire rack and leave to cool.

To freeze: open (flash) freeze until firm, then pack in a freezer bag. Seal, label and return to the freezer.
To thaw and serve: remove wrappings and thaw at room temperature for 3 to 4 hours.
MAKES ONE 450 g/1 lb LOAF

PEANUT BREAD

METRIC/IMPERIAL
300 ml/½ pint milk
4 × 15 ml spoons/4 tablespoons smooth peanut butter
100 g/4 oz soft brown sugar
450 g/1 lb flour
1 × 15 ml spoon/1 tablespoon baking powder
100 g/4 oz butter
1 egg, beaten
100 g/4 oz salted peanuts, chopped
For the Topping:
25 g/1 oz salted peanuts
25 g/1 oz Gouda cheese, grated

AMERICAN
1¼ cups milk
¼ cup smooth peanut butter
⅔ cup light brown sugar
4 cups flour
1 tablespoon baking powder
½ cup butter
1 egg, beaten
1 cup salted peanuts, chopped
For the Topping:
¼ cup salted peanuts
¼ cup grated Gouda cheese

Put the milk, peanut butter and sugar in a pan and heat gently until the peanut butter has melted, stirring constantly. Leave to cool.
Sift the flour and baking powder into a bowl, add the butter in pieces and rub into the flour until the mixture resembles fine breadcrumbs. Make a well in the centre, add the egg, the cooled milk mixture and the chopped peanuts and stir well to mix.
Turn the mixture into a greased 1 kg/2 lb loaf tin and smooth the top. Scatter over the whole peanuts and the grated cheese. Bake in a preheated moderate oven (180°C/350°F or Gas Mark 4) for 1 to 1¼ hours until cooked through and golden brown. Turn out onto a wire rack and leave to cool.
To freeze: pack in a freezer bag, seal, label and freeze.
To thaw and serve: thaw in wrappings at room temperature for 3 to 4 hours.
MAKES ONE 1 kg/2 lb LOAF

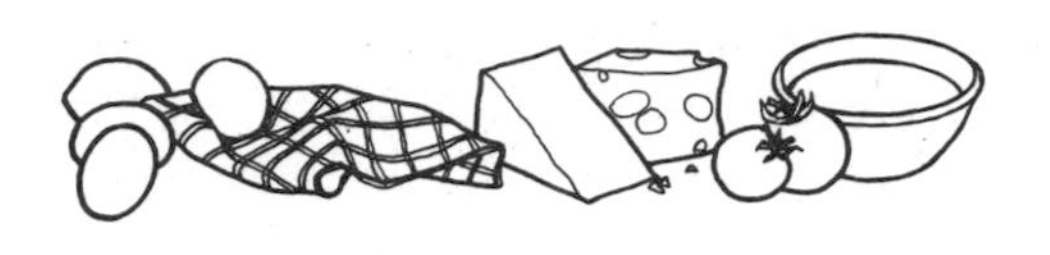

MALT LOAF

METRIC/IMPERIAL
15 g/½ oz fresh yeast
120 ml/4 fl oz hand-hot milk
1 × 15 ml spoon/1 tablespoon malt extract
225 g/½ lb wholewheat or strong plain flour
1 × 5 ml spoon/1 teaspoon salt
15 g/½ oz butter
50 g/2 oz currants
50 g/2 oz sultanas
25 g/1 oz candied peel, chopped
25 g/1 oz soft brown sugar

AMERICAN
½ cake of compressed fresh yeast
½ cup hand-hot milk
1 tablespoon malt extract
2 cups wholewheat or white flour
1 teaspoon salt
1 tablespoon butter
⅓ cup currants
⅓ cup seedless white raisins
3 tablespoons chopped candied peel
2 tablespoons light brown sugar

Dissolve the yeast in the milk and stir in the malt extract.
Sift the flour and salt into a bowl, rub in the butter, then add the dried fruit, peel and sugar. Make a well in the centre, pour in the yeast liquid and stir well to mix.
Turn the dough out onto a floured surface and knead until smooth and elastic. Place in a lightly greased polythene (plastic) bag and leave in a warm place until doubled in bulk.
Turn the dough out onto the floured surface, then knock back (punch down) and knead again for 2 minutes. Shape into an oblong and place in a greased 450 g/1 lb loaf tin. Leave in a warm place until the dough reaches the top of the tin.
Bake the loaf in a preheated hot oven (230°C/450°F or Gas Mark 8) for 10 minutes, then reduce the heat to moderately hot (190°C/375°F or Gas Mark 5) and bake for a further 25 minutes. Turn out onto a wire rack and leave to cool.
To freeze: pack in a freezer bag, seal, label and freeze.
To thaw and serve: thaw in the wrappings at room temperature for 3 to 4 hours.
MAKES ONE 450 g/1 lb LOAF

STOLLEN

METRIC/IMPERIAL

25 g/1 oz fresh yeast
2 × 15 ml spoons/2 tablespoons hand-hot water
6 × 15 ml spoons/6 tablespoons milk
75 g/3 oz caster sugar
pinch of salt
2 × 15 ml spoons/2 tablespoons rum
a few drops of almond essence
400 g/14 oz flour
1 egg, beaten
150 g/5 oz butter, softened
50 g/2 oz seedless raisins
25 g/2 oz currants
50 g/2 oz glacé cherries, chopped
25 g/1 oz candied angelica, chopped
65 g/2½ oz chopped candied peel
40 g/1½ oz slivered blanched almonds
icing sugar, for sprinkling, to finish

AMERICAN

1 cake of compressed fresh yeast
2 tablespoons hand-hot water
6 tablespoons milk
⅜ cup sugar
pinch of salt
2 tablespoons rum
a few drops of almond extract
3½ cups flour
1 egg, beaten
⅝ cup butter, softened
⅓ cup seedless raisins
⅓ cup currants
¼ cup candied cherries, chopped
3 tablespoons chopped candied angelica
½ cup chopped candied peel
⅓ cup slivered blanched almonds
confectioners' sugar for sprinkling, to finish

Dissolve the yeast in the water. Put the milk, 50 g/2 oz/¼ cup sugar and the salt in a pan and heat gently until the sugar has dissolved. Remove from the heat, then add the rum, almond essence (extract) and the yeast liquid.
Sift the flour into a warm bowl and make a well in the centre. Add the yeast mixture, the egg, 75 g/3 oz/⅜ cup butter cut in small pieces, the dried fruit, cherries, peel and nuts. Mix to a soft dough, then turn out onto a floured surface and knead for about 10 minutes until smooth.
Put the dough in a lightly greased bowl, cover with a clean, dampened tea (dish) towel and leave in a warm place until doubled in bulk. Turn out onto the floured surface and knead again for 5 minutes.
Roll out the dough thinly to an oblong 30 × 20 cm/12 × 8 inches. Melt the remaining butter, brush over the dough, then scatter over the remaining sugar. Fold the dough over from the long sides to form a split loaf shape, pressing the overlapping edges together and tapering the ends.
Place on a greased baking sheet, brush with melted butter and leave in a warm place until doubled in bulk. Bake in a preheated moderately hot oven (190°C/375°F or Gas Mark 5) for about 45 minutes, then transfer to a wire rack and leave to cool.
To freeze: pack in a freezer bag, seal, label and freeze.
To thaw and serve: thaw in the wrappings at room temperature for 3 to 4 hours, then sprinkle with icing (confectioners') sugar before serving.
MAKES ONE LARGE LOAF

HOT CROSS BUNS

METRIC/IMPERIAL

For the yeast batter:
100 g/4 oz flour
150 ml/¼ pint hand-hot milk
6 × 15 ml spoons/6 tablespoons hand-hot water
25 g/1 oz fresh yeast
1 × 5 ml spoon/1 teaspoon sugar
For the dough:
350 g/¾ lb flour
1 × 5 ml spoon/1 teaspoon salt
1 × 2.5 ml spoon/½ teaspoon ground mixed spice
1 × 2.5 ml spoon/½ teaspoon ground cinnamon
1 × 2.5 ml spoon/½ teaspoon grated nutmeg
50 g/2 oz butter
50 g/2 oz caster sugar
100 g/4 oz currants
25–50 g/1–2 oz chopped candied peel
1 egg, beaten
For the glaze, to finish:
50 g/2 oz sugar
4 × 15 ml spoons/4 tablespoons water

AMERICAN

For the yeast batter:
1 cup flour
⅔ cup hand-hot milk
6 tablespoons hand-hot water
1 cake of compressed fresh yeast
1 teaspoon sugar
For the dough:
3 cups flour
1 teaspoon salt
½ teaspoon ground allspice and cloves, mixed
½ teaspoon ground cinnamon
½ teaspoon grated nutmeg
¼ cup butter
¼ cup sugar
⅔ cup currants

3–6 tablespoons chopped candied peel
1 egg, beaten
For the glaze, to finish:
¼ cup sugar
¼ cup water

To make the yeast batter: sift the flour into a warm bowl and make a well in the centre. Blend together the milk, water, yeast and sugar, pour into the flour and stir well to mix. Leave in a warm place for about 10 minutes until frothy.
To make the dough: sift the dry ingredients into a bowl, rub in the butter, then stir in the sugar, currants and peel. Stir into the yeast batter with the egg and mix to a fairly soft dough.
Turn the dough out onto a floured surface and knead for 5 minutes until smooth. Place the dough in a lightly greased polythene (plastic) bag and leave in a warm place for 1 to 1½ hours until doubled in bulk.
Turn the dough out onto the floured surface, knock back (punch down) and knead again to a firm dough. Divide into 12 to 14 equal pieces and shape into buns. Place on a lightly floured baking sheet, spacing them well apart. Cover with the greased polythene (plastic) bag and leave to rise at room temperature for 30 minutes. Remove the polythene (plastic) bag, then mark a cross on the top of each bun with a very sharp knife. Bake in a preheated hot oven (220°C/425°F or Gas Mark 7) for 15 to 20 minutes until golden brown. Transfer to a wire rack and leave to cool.
To freeze: pack the buns in a single layer in freezer bags, seal, label and freeze.
To thaw and serve: remove wrappings and place the buns on a baking sheet. Reheat from frozen in a preheated moderately hot oven (200°C/400°F or Gas Mark 6) for 5 minutes or until heated through. Meanwhile, make the glaze: put the sugar and water in a pan, heat gently until the sugar has dissolved, then boil for 2 minutes. Brush over the buns and serve.
MAKES 12 to 14

STICKY CHERRY AND GINGER BUNS

Make as for Hot Cross Buns (see above), substituting 1 × 5 ml spoon/1 teaspoon ground ginger for the cinnamon and nutmeg and 50 g/2 oz chopped glacé cherries (¼ cup chopped candied cherries) for the chopped candied peel. Freeze, thaw and serve as for Hot Cross Buns, adding 1 × 15 ml spoon/1 tablespoon clear honey to the sugar and water for the glaze.
MAKES 12 to 14

FRUIT LOAF

METRIC/IMPERIAL
15 g/½ oz fresh yeast
1 × 5 ml spoon/1 teaspoon sugar
150 ml/¼ pint hand-hot milk and water, mixed
275 g/10 oz strong plain flour
1 × 5 ml spoon/1 teaspoon salt
40 g/1½ oz butter
25 g/1 oz caster sugar
25 g/1 oz sultanas
40 g/1½ oz currants
15 g/½ oz chopped candied peel
1 egg, beaten

AMERICAN
½ cake of compressed fresh yeast
1 teaspoon sugar
⅔ cup hand-hot milk and water, mixed
2½ cups flour
1 teaspoon salt
3 tablespoons butter
2 tablespoons sugar
3 tablespoons seedless white raisins
¼ cup currants
1½ tablespoons chopped candied peel
1 egg, beaten

Cream the yeast and sugar together in a warm bowl, add half the milk and water mixture and stir well to dissolve.
Sift the flour and salt into a warm bowl and rub in the butter. Add the sugar, dried fruit and peel, then make a well in the centre. Pour in the yeast liquid, the egg and the remaining milk and water. Mix to form a soft pliable dough. (If the mixture seems dry, add a little warm water.)
Turn the dough out onto a floured surface and knead for 5 to 10 minutes until smooth. Place in a lightly greased bowl, cover with a lightly greased polythene (plastic) bag and leave in a warm place until doubled in bulk.
Turn the dough out onto the floured surface, then knock back (punch down) and knead again for a few minutes. Shape into an oblong and place in a greased 1 kg/2 lb loaf tin. Leave in a warm place until the dough reaches the top of the tin.
Bake the loaf in a preheated moderately hot oven (190°C/375°F or Gas Mark 5) for 40 to 45 minutes. Cover the top of the loaf with foil if it becomes too brown during baking. Turn out onto a wire rack and leave to cool.
To freeze: pack in a freezer bag, seal, label and freeze.
To thaw and serve: thaw in the wrappings at room temperature for 3 to 4 hours.
MAKES ONE 450 g/1 lb LOAF

CONTINENTAL APRICOT SLICES

METRIC/IMPERIAL

25 g/1 oz fresh yeast
300 ml/½ pint hand-hot milk
4 × 15 ml spoons/4 tablespoons vegetable oil
450 g/1 lb strong plain flour
pinch of salt
2 × 5 ml spoons/2 teaspoons ground cinnamon
75 g/3 oz soft brown sugar
For the topping:
175 g/6 oz dried apricots, finely chopped, soaked overnight in cold water and drained
50 g/2 oz blanched almonds, chopped
75 g/3 oz currants
50 g/2 oz caster sugar
glacé icing made with 100 g/4 oz icing sugar, to finish

AMERICAN

1 cake of compressed fresh yeast
1¼ cups hand-hot milk
¼ cup vegetable oil
4 cups flour
pinch of salt
2 teaspoons ground cinnamon
½ cup light brown sugar
For the topping:
1 cup dried apricots, finely chopped, soaked overnight in cold water and drained
½ cup blanched almonds, chopped
½ cup currants
¼ cup sugar
glacé icing made with scant 1 cup confectioners' sugar, to finish

Dissolve the yeast in the milk, then stir in the oil. Sift the flour, salt and cinnamon into a warm bowl, then add the sugar and the yeast liquid and stir well to mix. Turn into a lightly greased bowl, cover with a clean, dampened tea (dish) towel and leave in a warm place for 30 minutes to rise.
Turn the dough out onto a floured surface and knead for 5 minutes. Divide in two, then roll into two squares to line the bottoms of two 23 cm/9 inch square cake tins. Put in the dough, then scatter over the apricots, almonds, currants and sugar. Bake in a preheated moderately hot oven (200°C/400°F or Gas Mark 6) for 20 minutes, then reduce the heat to moderate (180°C/350°F or Gas Mark 4) and bake for a further 20 minutes. Turn out onto a wire rack and leave to cool.
To freeze: open (flash) freeze until firm, wrap in foil, then pack in a freezer bag. Seal, label and return to the freezer.
To thaw and serve: remove wrappings and place on a baking sheet. Reheat from frozen in a preheated moderately hot oven (190°C/375°F or Gas Mark 5) for 45 minutes until heated through. Transfer to a wire rack and leave to cool, then drizzle over the icing. Leave to set.
MAKES 18 SLICES

CONTINENTAL FAMILY CAKE

METRIC/IMPERIAL

1 × 2.5 ml spoon/½ teaspoon sugar
5 × 15 ml spoons/5 tablespoons hand-hot milk
1 × 15 ml spoon/1 tablespoon dried yeast
For the dough:
275 g/10 oz strong plain flour
1 × 2.5 ml spoon/½ teaspoon salt
75 g/3 oz butter
175 g/6 oz currants
finely grated rind of 1 orange
50 g/2 oz caster sugar
2 eggs, beaten
For the topping:
25 g/1 oz butter
40 g/1½ oz flour
25 g/1 oz sugar
1 × 5 ml spoon/1 teaspoon ground cinnamon
3 × 15 ml spoons/3 tablespoons raspberry jam

AMERICAN

½ teaspoon sugar
⅓ cup hand-hot milk
1½ packages active dry yeast
For the dough:
2½ cups flour
½ teaspoon salt
⅜ cup butter
1 cup currants
finely grated rind of 1 orange
¼ cup sugar
2 eggs, beaten
For the topping:
2 tablespoons butter
⅜ cup flour
3 tablespoons sugar
1 teaspoon ground cinnamon
3 tablespoons raspberry jam

To make the yeast batter: dissolve the sugar in the milk, sprinkle over the dried (dry) yeast and stir well. Leave in a warm place for 10 to 15 minutes until frothy.
To make the dough: sift the flour and salt into a warm bowl, then rub in the butter. Add the currants, orange rind and (caster) sugar, then the frothy yeast batter and the eggs. Stir well to mix to a very soft dough, then turn into a greased 1 kg/2 lb loaf tin.

To make the topping: put the butter and flour in a bowl, rub together with the fingertips, then stir in the sugar and cinnamon. Spread the jam on top of the cake to within 2.5 cm/1 inch of the edges, then cover with the crumble mixture. Place inside a large lightly greased polythene (plastic) bag and leave at room temperature for 1 hour or until doubled in bulk. Remove the bag, then bake the cake in a preheated moderately hot oven (200°C/400°F or Gas Mark 6) for 35 to 45 minutes until golden brown. Leave to cool in the tin for 10 minutes, turn turn out onto a wire rack to cool completely.
To freeze: pack in a freezer bag, seal, label and freeze.
To thaw and serve: remove wrappings and thaw at room temperature for 3 to 4 hours.
SERVES 8

SCOFA BREAD

METRIC/IMPERIAL
1.5 kg/3 lb scofa flour
1 × 5 ml spoon/1 teaspoon salt
2 × 15 ml spoons/2 tablespoons brown sugar
50 g/2 oz lard
2 × 5 ml spoons/2 teaspoons baking powder
450 ml/¾ pint milk
450 ml/¾ pint water

AMERICAN
3 lb scofa flour
1 teaspoon salt
2 tablespoons brown sugar
¼ cup shortening
2 teaspoons baking powder
2 cups milk
2 cups water

Put the flour, salt and sugar in a bowl. Stir well to mix, then rub in the lard (shortening). Stir in the baking powder, then pour in the milk and water and mix to a fairly soft dough, adding a little more liquid if necessary.
Turn the dough out onto a floured surface, shape into a flattish round, then cut into six triangular shapes. Place on a floured baking sheet and bake in a preheated hot oven (220°C/425°F or Gas Mark 7) until the bread is light brown and crusty. Transfer to a wire rack and leave to cool.
To freeze: pack in a freezer bag, seal, label and freeze.
To thaw and serve: thaw in the wrappings at room temperature for 4 to 5 hours.
MAKES ONE LARGE LOAF

CHEESE BREAD

METRIC/IMPERIAL
15 g/½ oz fresh yeast
200 ml/⅓ pint hand-hot water
350 g/¾ lb strong plain flour
1 × 2.5 ml spoon/½ teaspoon salt
15 g/½ oz lard
100 g/4 oz cheese, grated
1 × 5 ml spoon/1 teaspoon caster sugar
25 g/1 oz onion, finely chopped
0.5 × 2.5 ml spoon/¼ teaspoon dried mixed herbs
beaten egg, to glaze

AMERICAN
½ cake of compressed fresh yeast
⅞ cup hand-hot water
3 cups flour
½ teaspoon salt
1 tablespoon shortening
1 cup grated cheese
1 teaspoon sugar
¼ cup finely chopped onion
¼ teaspoon dried mixed herbs
beaten egg, to glaze

Dissolve the yeast in the water. Sift the flour and salt into a warm bowl, rub in the lard (shortening), then add 75 g/3 oz/¾ cup cheese, the sugar, onion and herbs. Stir well to mix, make a well in the centre and pour in the yeast liquid. Mix to form a pliable dough.
Turn the dough out onto a floured surface and knead for 10 minutes until smooth. Put the dough in a lightly greased polythene (plastic) bag and leave in a warm place for about 50 minutes until doubled in bulk.
Divide the dough into three equal pieces. Shape each piece into a 30 cm/12 inch long roll, then join the pieces at one end with a little beaten egg. Place the dough on a floured baking sheet, plait (braid) the three rolls together loosely, then seal the ends with more egg. Leave in a warm place for about 40 minutes until doubled in bulk.
Brush the dough with the remaining egg and scatter over the remaining cheese. Bake in a preheated moderately hot oven (200°C/400°F or Gas Mark 6) for 20 to 25 minutes until the loaf is golden brown on top and sounds hollow when tapped on the bottom. Transfer to a wire rack and leave to cool.
To freeze: pack in a freezer bag, seal, label and freeze.
To thaw and serve: thaw in the wrappings at room temperature for 3 to 4 hours.
MAKES ONE 20 cm/8 inch PLAIT (BRAID)

GRANNY'S BROWN BREAD

METRIC/IMPERIAL

15 g/½ oz fresh yeast
300 ml/½ pint hand-hot water
1 × 15 ml spoon/1 tablespoon black treacle
225 g/½ lb wholewheat flour
225 g/½ lb strong plain flour
2 × 5 ml spoons/2 teaspoons salt
25 g/1 oz lard
1–2 × 15 ml spoons/1–2 tablespoons rolled oats

AMERICAN

½ cake of compressed fresh yeast
1¼ cups hand-hot water
1 tablespoon molasses
2 cups wholewheat flour
2 cups white flour
2 teaspoons salt
2 tablespoons shortening
1–2 tablespoons rolled oats

Dissolve the yeast in half the water and stir in the black treacle (molasses).

Put the wholewheat flour in a bowl, sift in the remaining flour and the salt, then rub in the lard (shortening). Make a well in the centre, pour in the yeast liquid and the remaining water and mix to a soft dough.

Turn the dough out onto a floured surface and knead for 10 minutes until smooth. Shape into 2 oblongs and place in two 450 g/1 lb loaf tins. Brush the tops with water and scatter over the rolled oats.

Place the loaves in a lightly greased polythene (plastic) bags and leave in a warm place until doubled in bulk. Remove the bags and bake in a preheated hot oven (230°C/450°F or Gas Mark 8) for 30 to 35 minutes. Turn out onto a wire rack and leave to cool.

To freeze: pack in freezer bags, seal, label and freeze.

To thaw and serve: thaw in the wrappings at room temperature for 3 to 4 hours.

MAKES TWO 450 g/1 lb LOAVES

FRUITY MALT LOAF

METRIC/IMPERIAL

75 g/3 oz malt extract
2 × 15 ml spoons/2 tablespoons black tracle
25 g/1 oz butter
1 × 2.5 ml spoon/½ teaspoon sugar
15 g/½ oz dried yeast
175 ml/6 fl oz hand-hot water
450 g/1 lb wholewheat flour
1 × 5 ml spoon/1 teaspoon salt
225 g/½ lb sultanas
clear honey, to glaze

AMERICAN

¼ cup malt extract
2 tablespoons molasses
2 tablespoons butter
½ teaspoon sugar
2 packages of active dry yeast
¾ cup hand-hot water
4 cups wholewheat flour
1 teaspoon salt
1⅓ cups seedless white raisins
clear honey, to glaze

Put the malt extract, molasses and butter in a pan, heat gently until melted, then leave to cool.

Dissolve the sugar in the water, sprinkle over the dried yeast and stir well to mix. Leave in a warm place for 10 to 15 minutes until frothy.

Put the flour and salt in a warm bowl, stir in the sultanas (seedless white raisins) and make a well in the centre. Pour in the frothy yeast liquid and the cooled malt mixture, then mix to a soft dough.

Turn the dough out onto a floured surface and knead for 10 minutes until smooth and elastic. Shape the dough into an oblong and place in a greased 1 kg/2 lb loaf tin. Leave in a warm place until doubled in bulk.

Bake the loaf in a preheated moderately hot oven (200°C/400°F or Gas Mark 6) for 40 to 45 minutes until the loaf is brown on top and sounds hollow when tapped on the bottom. Turn out onto a wire rack and leave to cool.

To freeze: pack in a freezer bag, seal, label and freeze.

To thaw and serve: thaw in the wrappings at room temperature for 3 to 4 hours.

MAKES ONE 1 kg/2 lb LOAF

MILK BREAD

METRIC/IMPERIAL

1 × 5 ml spoon/1 teaspoon caster sugar
15 g/$\frac{1}{2}$ oz fresh yeast
300 ml/$\frac{1}{2}$ pint hand-hot milk
450 g/1 lb strong plain flour
1 × 5 ml spoon/1 teaspoon salt
40 g/1$\frac{1}{2}$ oz butter

AMERICAN

1 teaspoon sugar
$\frac{1}{2}$ cake of compressed fresh yeast
1$\frac{1}{4}$ cups hand-hot milk
4 cups flour
1 teaspoon salt
3 tablespoons butter

Dissolve the sugar and yeast in half the milk. Sift the flour and salt into a bowl, rub in the butter, then make a well in the centre. Pour in the yeast liquid and the remaining milk and mix to a pliable dough.

Turn the dough out onto a floured surface and knead for 10 minutes until smooth. Put the dough in a lightly greased polythene (plastic) bag and leave in a warm place until doubled in bulk.

Shape the dough into an oblong and place in a greased 450 g/1 lb loaf tin. Or divide into 12 equal pieces, shape into rolls (buns) and place on a greased and floured baking sheet. Leave to rise at room temperature for 15 minutes.

Bake in a preheated moderately hot oven (200°C/400°F or Gas Mark 6) for 40 to 45 minutes for the loaf, 25 to 30 minutes for the rolls (buns). Transfer to a wire rack and leave to cool.

To freeze: wrap in foil, then pack in a freezer bag. Seal, label and freeze.

To thaw and serve: thaw in the wrappings at room temperature for 3 to 4 hours for the loaf, 1 to 2 hours for the rolls (buns). Or place the foil-wrapped bread or rolls (buns) on a baking sheet and bake from frozen in a preheated moderately hot oven (200°C/400°F or Gas Mark 6) for 30 minutes for the loaf, 15 minutes for the rolls (buns).

MAKES ONE 450 g/1 lb LOAF or 12 ROLLS (BUNS)

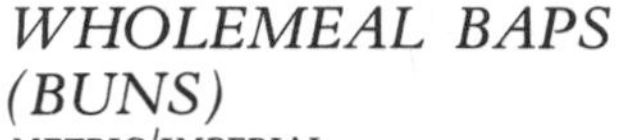

WHOLEMEAL BAPS (BUNS)

METRIC/IMPERIAL

1 × 15 ml spoon/1 tablespoon sugar
1 × 15 ml spoon/1 tablespoon dried yeast
450 ml/$\frac{3}{4}$ pint hand-hot water
675 g/1$\frac{1}{2}$ lb wholemeal flour
1 × 5 ml spoon/1 teaspoon salt
1 × 15 ml spoon/1 tablespoon vegetable oil

AMERICAN

1 tablespoon sugar
1$\frac{1}{2}$ packages active dry yeast
2 cups hand-hot water
6 cups wholewheat flour
1 teaspoon salt
1 tablespoon vegetable oil

Dissolve 1 × 5 ml spoon/1 teaspoon sugar in 150 ml/$\frac{1}{4}$ pint/$\frac{2}{3}$ cup water, sprinkle over the dried yeast and stir well to mix. Leave in a warm place for 10 to 15 minutes until frothy.

Put the flour and salt in a warm bowl, add the remaining sugar and stir well to mix. Make a well in the centre, pour in the frothy yeast liquid and the remaining water and the oil and stir well to mix.

Turn the dough out onto a floured surface and knead for about 5 minutes until smooth. Place in a lightly greased polythene (plastic) bag and leave in a warm place until doubled in bulk.

Turn the dough out onto the floured surface, then knock back (punch down) and knead for 5 minutes. Divide into 12 equal pieces and shape into baps (buns). Dust with flour, place on greased baking sheets and leave in a warm place until doubled in bulk.

Bake the baps (buns) in a preheated hot oven (220°C/425°F or Gas Mark 7) for 15 to 20 minutes. Cover with a tea (dish) towel and leave to cool.

To freeze: pack into a freezer bag, seal, label and freeze.

To thaw and serve: thaw in the wrappings at room temperature for 2 hours.

MAKES 12

BRIOCHE

METRIC/IMPERIAL
15 g/$\frac{1}{2}$ oz fresh yeast
1.5 × 15 ml spoons/1$\frac{1}{2}$ tablespoons hand-hot water
225 g/$\frac{1}{2}$ lb strong plain flour
0.5 × 2.5 ml spoon/$\frac{1}{4}$ teaspoon salt
1 × 15 ml spoon/1 tablespoon caster sugar
2 eggs, beaten
50 g/2 oz butter, melted
beaten egg, to glaze

AMERICAN
$\frac{1}{2}$ cake of compressed fresh yeast
1$\frac{1}{2}$ tablespoons hand-hot water
2 cups flour
$\frac{1}{4}$ teaspoon salt
1 tablespoon sugar
2 eggs, beaten
$\frac{1}{4}$ cup butter, melted
beaten egg, to glaze

Blend the yeast with the water. Sift the flour and salt into a warm bowl, stir in the sugar and make a well in the centre. Stir in the yeast mixture with the eggs and butter and mix to a soft dough. Turn the dough out onto a floured surface and knead for 5 minutes until smooth. Place the dough in a lightly greased polythene (plastic) bag and leave to rise at room temperature for 1 to 1$\frac{1}{2}$ hours until doubled in bulk.
Turn the dough out onto the floured surface, then knock back (punch down) and knead again. Shape three-quarters of the dough into a ball and place in the bottom of an oiled 1.2 litre/2 pint/5 cup fluted mould. Press a hole in the centre, shape the remaining dough into a small ball and place on top. Press down lightly.
Leave at room temperature for about 1 hour or until the dough reaches almost to the top of the mould. Brush the dough lightly with the beaten egg. Bake in a preheated hot oven (230°C/450°F or Gas Mark 8) for 15 to 20 minutes until the loaf is brown on top and sounds hollow when tapped on the bottom. Turn out onto a wire rack and leave to cool.
To freeze: pack in a freezer bag, seal, label and freeze.
To thaw and serve: thaw in the wrappings at room temperature for 3 to 4 hours.
SERVES 6 to 8

YORKSHIRE TEA CAKES

METRIC/IMPERIAL
25 g/1 oz caster sugar
300 ml/$\frac{1}{2}$ pint hand-hot milk
2 × 5 ml spoons/2 teaspoons dried yeast
450 g/1 lb flour
1 × 5 ml spoon/1 teaspoon salt
25 g/1 oz butter
50 g/2 oz currants
For the glaze:
2 × 15 ml spoons/2 tablespoons milk
4 × 5 ml spoons/4 teaspoons sugar

AMERICAN
2 tablespoons sugar
1$\frac{1}{4}$ cups hand-hot milk
1 package active dry yeast
4 cups flour
1 teaspoon salt
2 tablespoons butter
3 tablespoons currants
For the glaze:
2 tablespoons milk
4 teaspoons sugar

Dissolve 1 × 5 ml spoon/1 teaspoon sugar in 7 × 15 ml spoons/7 tablespoons milk, sprinkle over the dried yeast and stir well to mix. Leave in a warm place for 10 to 15 minutes until frothy. Sift the flour and salt into a warm bowl, stir in the remaining sugar, then rub in the butter. Make a well in the centre, then pour in the frothy yeast liquid with the remaining milk. Stir well to give a fairly soft dough.
Turn the dough out onto a floured surface and knead for 5 minutes. Place in a lightly greased bowl, cover with a lightly greased polythene (plastic) bag and leave in a warm place for about 1 hour until doubled in bulk.
Turn the dough out onto a floured surface, then knock back (punch down) and knead again, working in the currants until evenly mixed. Divide the dough into 6 equal pieces, form into balls and flatten with a rolling pin. Place on greased baking sheets and leave to rise in a warm place for 35 minutes. Bake the tea cakes in a preheated moderately hot oven (200°C/400°F or Gas Mark 6) for 20 to 25 minutes.
To make the glaze: put the milk and sugar in a pan and heat gently until the sugar has dissolved. Brush over the tea cakes while still hot, then transfer to a wire rack and leave to cool.
To freeze: open (flash) freeze until firm, then pack in a rigid container, separating each layer with foil. Seal, label and return to the freezer.
To thaw and serve: place on a serving platter and thaw at room temperature for 2 hours.
MAKES 6

HONEY AND CINNAMON DOUGHNUTS

METRIC/IMPERIAL

350 g/¾ lb self-raising flour
0.5 × 2.5 ml spoon/¼ teaspoon salt
1 × 2.5 ml spoon/½ teaspoon baking powder
1 × 2.5 ml spoon/½ teaspoon ground cinnamon
50 g/2 oz caster sugar
1 × 15 ml spoon/1 tablespoon honey
4 × 15 ml spoons/4 tablespoons vegetable oil
7 × 15 ml spoons/7 tablespoons milk
1 large egg, beaten
vegetable oil for deep-frying
extra caster sugar for sprinkling, to finish

AMERICAN

3 cups self-rising flour
¼ teaspoon salt
½ teaspoon baking powder
½ teaspoon ground cinnamon
¼ cup sugar
1 tablespoon honey
¼ cup vegetable oil
7 tablespoons milk
1 large egg, beaten
vegetable oil for deep-frying
extra sugar for sprinkling, to finish

Sift the dry ingredients into a bowl, stir in the sugar and make a well in the centre. Put the honey, oil, milk and egg in a separate bowl, beat well to mix, then pour into the flour mixture. Mix well to a soft dough, then turn out onto a floured surface and knead lightly until smooth.

Roll out the dough to 1 cm/½ inch thickness, then cut out rounds with a 6 cm/2½ inch plain cutter. Cut out the centres with a 2.5 cm/1 inch cutter, roll out again and cut into more rounds. Put a few of the rounds into hot oil and deep-fry for 2 to 3 minutes until golden. Drain on paper towels while frying the remainder.

To freeze: cool quickly, then pack in a freezer bag. Seal, label and freeze.

To thaw and serve: remove wrappings and place the doughnuts on a baking sheet. Reheat from frozen in a preheated moderately hot oven (200°C/400°F or Gas Mark 6) for 6 to 8 minutes until heated through. Sprinkle with (caster) sugar before serving.

MAKES 14 to 16

CROISSANTS

METRIC/IMPERIAL

450 g/1 lb strong plain flour
1 × 5 ml spoon/1 teaspoon salt
15 g/½ oz fresh yeast
1 × 5 ml spoon/1 teaspoon sugar
120 ml/4 fl oz hand-hot water
120 ml/4 fl oz hand-hot milk
100 g/4 oz butter
beaten egg and milk, to glaze

AMERICAN

4 cups flour
1 teaspoon salt
½ cake of compressed fresh yeast
1 teaspoon sugar
½ cup hand-hot water
½ cup hand-hot milk
½ cup butter
beaten egg and milk, to glaze

Sift the flour and salt into a warm bowl. Blend the yeast, sugar and liquid together, then stir into the flour and mix to a fairly stiff dough. Turn out onto a floured surface and knead lightly for 8 minutes, then place in a lightly greased polythene (plastic) bag and leave in a warm place until doubled in bulk.

Divide the butter into three. Roll out the dough to an oblong and dot one portion of the butter over two-thirds of the dough. Fold the dough into three and seal the edges together with the rolling pin. Repeat this process twice, using the remaining butter, then return the dough to the polythene (plastic) bag and leave to rest for 30 minutes.

Roll out the dough to 5 mm/¼ inch thickness and cut out ten 10 cm/4 inch squares. Divide each square into two triangles and roll up each triangle, starting at the longest edge and rolling towards the point. Bend into a crescent shape, then place on a greased and floured baking sheet and leave to rise for 10 minutes.

Brush the croissants with beaten egg and milk and bake in a preheated hot oven (220°C/425°F or Gas Mark 7) for 15 to 20 minutes until puffed and golden brown. Transfer to a wire rack and leave to cool.

To freeze: pack in a rigid container, seal, label and freeze.

To thaw and serve: place the frozen croissants on a baking sheet and reheat in a preheated moderate oven (180°C/350°F or Gas Mark 4) for 10 minutes or until heated through.

MAKES 20

WHOLEWHEAT AND OAT LOAF

METRIC/IMPERIAL

275 g/10 oz wholewheat flour
50 g/2 oz rolled oats
50 g/2 oz wheatgerm
50 g/2 oz soft brown sugar
1 × 5 ml spoon/1 teaspoon baking powder
1 × 2.5 ml spoon/½ teaspoon bicarbonate of soda
1 × 2.5 ml spoon/½ teaspoon salt
150 ml/¼ pint soured cream
25 g/1 oz butter, softened
2 eggs, beaten

AMERICAN

2½ cups wholewheat flour
½ cup rolled oats
⅓ cup wheatgerm
⅓ cup light brown sugar
1 teaspoon baking powder
½ teaspoon baking soda
½ teaspoon salt
⅔ cup sour cream
2 tablespoons butter, softened
2 eggs, beaten

Put the dry ingredients in a bowl and stir well to mix. Mix together the sour(ed) cream, butter and eggs, then add to the dry ingredients. Beat well to mix.
Turn the dough out onto a floured surface and knead until smooth. Shape into an oblong and place in a greased 450 g/1 lb loaf tin. Bake in a preheated moderately hot oven (200°C/400°F or Gas Mark 6) for 30 to 35 minutes until golden brown. Turn out onto a wire rack and leave to cool.
To freeze: pack in a freezer bag, seal, label and freeze.
To thaw and serve: thaw in the wrappings at room temperature for 3 to 4 hours.
MAKES ONE 450 g/1 lb LOAF

WHOLEWHEAT CARAWAY LOAF

Make as for Wholewheat and Oat Loaf (see above), adding 1 × 5 ml spoon/1 teaspoon caraway seeds to the dry ingredients.
Freeze, thaw and serve as for Wholewheat and Oat Loaf.
MAKES ONE 450 g/1 lb LOAF

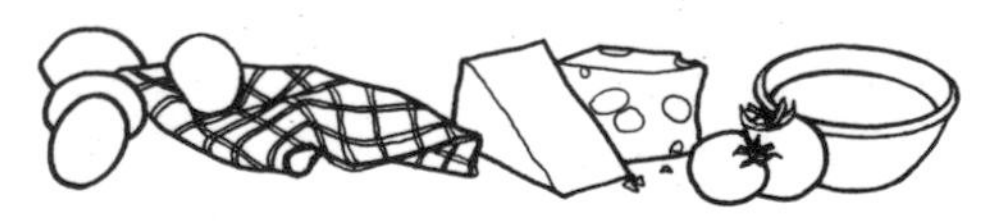

WHOLEWHEAT HERB LOAF

Make as for Wholewheat and Oat Loaf (see this page), adding 2 × 5 ml spoons/2 teaspoons dried mixed herbs to the dry ingredients.
Freeze, thaw and serve as for Wholewheat and Oat Loaf.
MAKES ONE 450 g/1 lb LOAF

KOLAC

METRIC/IMPERIAL

225 g/½ lb wholemeal flour
2 × 5 ml spoons/2 teaspoons baking powder
1 × 2.5 ml spoon/½ teaspoon salt
150 g/5 oz soft brown sugar
50 g/2 oz butter
1 egg, beaten
150 ml/¼ pint milk
2 dessert apples, peeled, cored and chopped
2 ripe bananas, peeled and chopped
225 g/½ lb cottage cheese, sieved

AMERICAN

2 cups wholewheat flour
2 teaspoons baking powder
½ teaspoon salt
scant 1 cup light brown sugar, firmly packed
¼ cup butter
1 egg, beaten
⅔ cup milk
2 dessert apples, peeled, cored and chopped
2 ripe bananas, peeled and chopped
1 cup strained cottage cheese

Put the flour, baking powder and salt into a bowl, stir in 100 g/4 oz/⅔ cup sugar, then rub in the butter. Add the egg and milk and mix to a soft dough.
Turn the dough out onto a floured surface and knead until smooth. Roll out to an oblong to fit a 28 × 18 cm/11 × 7 inch Swiss roll tin (jelly roll pan), place in the tin and press in the edges. Scatter over the apples and bananas, cover with the cottage cheese, then scatter over the remaining sugar. Bake in a preheated moderately hot oven (200°C/400°F or Gas Mark 6) for 30 to 35 minutes. Leave to cool in the tin for 10 minutes, then cut into 20 squares. Transfer to a wire rack and leave to cool completely.
To freeze: open (flash) freeze until firm, then pack in a rigid container, separating each layer with foil. Seal, label and return to the freezer.
To thaw and serve: place on a serving platter and thaw at room temperature for 1 to 2 hours.
MAKES 20 SQUARES

CHELSEA BUNS

METRIC/IMPERIAL

350 g/¾ lb strong plain flour
1 × 2.5 ml spoon/½ teaspoon salt
1 × 5 ml spoon/1 teaspoon mixed spice
40 g/1½ oz butter or margarine
15 g/½ oz fresh yeast
approx 150 ml/¼ pint lukewarm milk
1 egg, beaten
3 × 15 ml spoons/3 tablespoons caster sugar
50 g/2 oz butter
50 g/2 oz demerara sugar
50 g/2 oz currants or sultanas

AMERICAN

3 cups flour
½ teaspoon salt
½ teaspoon ground allspice
½ teaspoon ground cinnamon
3 tablespoons butter or margarine
1 cake of compressed fresh yeast
approx ⅔ cup lukewarm milk
1 egg, beaten
3 tablespoons sugar
¼ cup butter
⅓ cup raw brown sugar
⅓ cup currants or seedless white raisins

Sift the flour, salt and half the spice(s) into a warm mixing bowl. Work in the fat with the fingers. Dissolve the yeast in a little of the warm milk. Stir the egg and (caster) sugar into the flour, then make a well in the centre and gradually add the yeast and remaining milk, mixing with the hands until a soft dough is formed. If the dough is too dry, add a little more warm milk. Knead the dough on a lightly floured board until smooth. Return to the greased bowl, cover with a clean dampened tea (dish) towel and leave in a warm place until doubled in bulk.

Transfer the dough to a floured board and roll out 1 cm/½ inch thick into an oblong shape, approximately 30 × 23 cm/12 × 9 inches. Melt the butter in a small pan, then brush over the dough. Mix together the demerara (brown) sugar, fruit and remaining spice(s) and sprinkle over the butter. Roll up the dough from the long end like a Swiss (jelly) roll, dampening the edges and pressing down firmly to seal. Cut the roll into 10 to 12 slices, using a very sharp knife dipped in warm water and cutting with a sawing motion.

Grease a roasting pan, and lay the slices in it, cut sides up. Cover and leave in a warm place for 30 to 45 minutes or until well risen.

Bake in a preheated hot oven (220°C/425°F or Gas Mark 7) for 15 to 20 minutes or until browned on top. Remove from the oven, transfer to a wire rack and leave to cool.

To freeze: wrap in a single layer in foil, then overwrap in a freezer bag, seal, label and freeze.

To thaw and serve: remove overwrapping, put foil package on a baking sheet and reheat in a moderately hot oven (200°C/400°F or Gas Mark 6) for 10 to 15 minutes or until hot.

MAKES 10 to 12

BARA BRITH

METRIC/IMPERIAL

200 ml/8 fl oz hand-hot water
1 × 5 ml spoon/1 tablespoon dried yeast
450 g/1 lb flour
1 × 5 ml spoon/1 teaspoon salt
1 × 5 ml spoon/1 teaspoon ground mixed spice
75 g/3 oz butter
1 egg
50 g/2 oz demerara sugar
450 g/1 lb mixed dried fruit

AMERICAN

1 cup hand-hot water
1 teaspoon sugar
1½ packages active dry yeast
4 cups flour
1 teaspoon salt
1 teaspoon ground cloves and nutmeg, mixed
⅜ cup butter
⅓ cup raw brown sugar
2⅔ cups mixed dried fruit

Put the water and sugar into a small bowl and sprinkle over the yeast. Leave in a warm place for about 10 minutes or until frothy.

Sift the flour, salt and spice(s) into a bowl. Add the butter and cut it into small pieces, then rub it into the flour until the mixture resembles breadcrumbs. Stir in the yeast mixture and egg and mix well. Turn onto a floured board and knead thoroughly.

Place the dough in a lightly greased polythene (plastic) bag and leave to rise in a warm place until doubled in bulk. This will take about 1¼ hours. Turn onto a floured board and knead in the demerara (brown) sugar and dried fruit. Divide the dough in half and shape into loaves to fit into two 450 g/1 lb loaf tins. Leave to rise until the dough is 2.5 cm/1 inch above the rim. Bake in a preheated moderate oven (180°C/350°F or Gas Mark 4) for 50 minutes to 1 hour or until golden brown. Cool on a wire rack.

To freeze: pack in a freezer bag, seal, label and freeze.

To thaw and serve: thaw in the wrappings at room temperature for 4 hours.

MAKES TWO 450 g/1 lb LOAVES

CHOCOLATE FUDGE

METRIC/IMPERIAL

225 g/½ lb plain chocolate, broken into pieces
25 g/1 oz butter
1 egg
450 g/1 lb icing sugar, sifted
1 small can sweetened condensed milk
1 × 2.5 ml spoon/½ teaspoon vanilla essence
18 walnut halves, to decorate

AMERICAN

1⅓ cups semi-sweet chocolate pieces
2 tablespoons butter
1 egg
3½ cups sifted confectioners' sugar
1 small can sweetened condensed milk
½ teaspoon vanilla extract
18 walnut halves, to decorate

Put the chocolate in a heatproof bowl, stand over a pan of gently simmering water and allow to melt. Add the butter and egg and stir until evenly blended, then add the remaining ingredients and stir until the mixture begins to thicken.

Pour the mixture into a greased shallow 18 cm/7 inch square tin. Mark into 36 squares, then press a walnut half into half of the squares. Chill in the refrigerator until set, then cut into squares and remove from the tin.

To freeze: pack in a rigid container, separating each layer with foil. Seal, label and freeze.

To thaw and serve: remove from the container, and thaw at room temperature for about 1 hour.

MAKES 36 SQUARES

VANILLA FUDGE

METRIC/IMPERIAL

100 g/4 oz butter
4 × 15 ml spoons/4 tablespoons water
2 × 15 ml spoons/2 tablespoons golden syrup
575 g/1¼ lb caster sugar
1 small can sweetened condensed milk
1 × 5 ml spoon/1 teaspoon vanilla essence

AMERICAN

½ cup butter
¼ cup water
2 tablespoons light corn syrup
2½ cups sugar
1 small can sweetened condensed milk
1 teaspoon vanilla extract

Put the butter, water, syrup and sugar in a large heavy-based pan and heat gently until the sugar has dissolved. Add the condensed milk, bring to the boil, then boil for 10 to 15 minutes until the temperature reaches 115°C/240°F on a sugar thermometer or the mixture forms a soft ball when a little is dropped in a cup of cold water. Leave to cool, then add the vanilla essence (extract) and beat well until thick.

Turn the mixture into a greased 30 × 20 cm/12 × 8 inch tin. Leave until half set, then mark into 96 squares with a sharp knife. Leave until cold and firm, then remove from the tin.

To freeze: pack in a rigid container, separating each layer with foil. Seal, label and freeze.

To thaw and serve: remove from the container and thaw at room temperature for about 1 hour.

MAKES 96 SQUARES

CHERRY ALMOND FUDGE

Make as for Vanilla Fudge (see opposite), stirring 75 g/3 oz/¾ cup chopped blanched almonds and 75 g/3 oz/⅜ cup halved glacé (candied) cherries into the mixture before turning into the tin. Freeze, thaw and serve as for Vanilla Fudge.
MAKES 96 SQUARES

UNCOOKED CHOCOLATE FUDGE

METRIC/IMPERIAL
200 g/½ lb plain chocolate, broken into pieces
50 g/2 oz butter
1 × 5 ml spoon/1 teaspoon vanilla essence
450 g/1 lb icing sugar, sifted
3 × 15 ml spoons/3 tablespoons single cream

AMERICAN
1⅓ cups semi-sweet chocolate pieces
¼ cup butter
1 teaspoon vanilla extract
3½ cups sifted confectioners' sugar
3 tablespoons light cream

Put half the chocolate and the butter in a heatproof bowl, stand over a pan of gently simmering water and allow to melt, stirring once or twice. Remove from the heat and leave to cool slightly. Add the remaining ingredients, except the chocolate, and stir well to mix. Press the mixture into a greased 20 cm/8 inch square cake tin and smooth the top.
Leave in a cool place until firm, then cut into 50 to 60 squares. Melt the remaining chocolate and use to coat one side of the fudge. Leave to set.
To freeze: open (flash) freeze until firm, then pack in a rigid container, separating each layer with foil or greaseproof (waxed) paper. Seal, label and return to the freezer.
To thaw and serve: put the frozen fudge in sweet (candy) cases and thaw at room temperature for about 1 hour.
MAKES 50 to 60

MOCHA COCONUT SQUARES

METRIC/IMPERIAL
25 g/1 oz butter
225 g/½ lb plain chocolate, broken into pieces
2 × 5 ml spoons/2 teaspoons instant coffee powder
175 g/6 oz glacé cherries, halved
50 g/2 oz desiccated coconut, toasted
100 g/4 oz unsalted cashew nuts, roughly chopped

AMERICAN
2 tablespoons butter
1⅓ cups semi-sweet chocolate pieces
2 teaspoons instant coffee powder
¾ cup halved candied cherries
⅔ cup shredded coconut, toasted
1 cup roughly chopped unsalted cashew nuts

Put the butter and chocolate in a heatproof bowl, stand over a pan of gently simmering water and allow to melt, stirring once or twice. Remove from the heat, add the remaining ingredients and stir well to mix. Spoon into a greased 18 cm/7 inch square tin and smooth the top. Chill until set, then cut into 36 squares.
To freeze: pack in a rigid container, separating each layer with foil. Seal, label and freeze.
To thaw and serve: put the frozen squares in sweet (candy) cases and thaw at room temperature for about 1 hour.
MAKES 36

WALNUT FUDGE

METRIC/IMPERIAL
100 g/4 oz butter
150 ml/¼ pint evaporated milk
450 g/1 lb sugar
1 × 2.5 ml spoons/½ teaspoon vanilla essence
pinch of cream of tartar
25 g/1 oz walnuts, chopped

AMERICAN
½ cup butter
⅔ cup evaporated milk
2 cups sugar, firmly packed
½ teaspoon vanilla extract
pinch of cream of tartar
¼ cup chopped walnuts

Put all the ingredients in a heavy-based pan and heat gently until the sugar has dissolved. Boil rapidly for about 10 minutes until the temperature reaches 115°C/240°F on a sugar thermometer, or until the mixture forms a soft ball when a little is dropped in a cup of cold water. Remove from the heat and beat for 3 or 4 minutes until thick. Pour into a greased 18 cm/7 inch square cake tin, leave until half set, then cut into about 50 squares. Leave until completely cold, then remove from the tin.
To freeze: pack in a rigid container, separating each layer with foil. Seal, label and freeze.
To thaw and serve: put the frozen fudge in sweet (candy) cases and thaw at room temperature for about 1 hour.
MAKES ABOUT 50

RUM TRUFFLES

METRIC/IMPERIAL

100 g/4 oz plain chocolate, broken into pieces
3 × 15 ml spoons/3 tablespoons rum
100 g/4 oz stale cake crumbs
100 g/4 oz ground almonds
50 g/2 oz icing sugar, sifted
chocolate vermicelli, for coating

AMERICAN

⅔ cup semi-sweet chocolate pieces
3 tablespoons rum
2 cups stale cake crumbs
1 cup ground almonds
½ cup sifted confectioners' sugar
chocolate vermicelli, for coating

Put the chocolate and rum in a heatproof bowl, stand over a pan of gently simmering water and allow the chocolate to melt, stirring once or twice.
Meanwhile, put the cake crumbs and ground almonds in a bowl and mix together with the fingertips. Add the melted chocolate and the icing (confectioners') sugar and stir well to mix. Turn out onto a board sprinkled with icing (confectioners') sugar and knead lightly until smooth.
Shape the mixture into about 25 small balls. Put the chocolate vermicelli in a bowl, add the truffles one at a time and shake the bowl until evenly coated. Chill in the refrigerator.
To freeze: open (flash) freeze until solid, then pack in a rigid container, separating each layer with foil. Seal, label and return to the freezer.
To thaw and serve: put the frozen truffles in sweet (candy) cases and thaw at room temperature for about 1 hour.
MAKES ABOUT 25

COFFEE TRUFFLES

METRIC/IMPERIAL

175 g/6 oz plain chocolate, broken into pieces
1 egg yolk
25 g/1 oz butter
1 × 5 ml spoon/1 teaspoon single cream
2 × 5 ml spoons/2 teaspoons coffee essence
chocolate vermicelli, for coating

AMERICAN

1 cup semi-sweet chocolate pieces
1 egg yolk
2 tablespoons butter
1 teaspoon light cream
2 teaspoons strong black coffee
chocolate vermicelli, for coating

Put the chocolate in a heatproof bowl, stand over a pan of gently simmering water and allow to melt. Remove from the heat, beat in the egg yolk, butter, cream and coffee, then leave to set in a cool place for 30 to 45 minutes.
Shape the mixture into about 20 small balls. Put the chocolate vermicelli in a bowl, add the truffles one at a time and shake the bowl until evenly coated. Chill in the refrigerator until firm.
To freeze: open (flash) freeze until solid, then pack in a rigid container, separating each layer with foil. Seal, label and return to the freezer.
To thaw and serve: put the frozen truffles in sweet (candy) cases and thaw at room temperature for about 1 hour.
MAKES ABOUT 20

ORANGE TRUFFLES

Make as for Coffee Truffles (see above), substituting the finely grated rind of 1 orange for the coffee.
Freeze, thaw and serve as for Coffee Truffles.
MAKES ABOUT 20

BONFIRE TOFFEE

METRIC/IMPERIAL

100 g/4 oz butter
225 g/½ lb soft brown sugar
225 g/½ lb golden syrup

AMERICAN

½ cup butter
1⅓ cups light brown sugar
⅔ cup light corn syrup

Brush a large shallow tin with a little of the butter.
Put the remaining butter in a large pan and heat gently until melted. Add the sugar and syrup and heat gently until the sugar has dissolved, stirring occasionally.
Increase the heat and boil the mixture rapidly for about 10 minutes until the temperature reaches 155°C/310°F on a sugar thermometer. Remove from the heat and pour into the prepared tin.
Leave to cool for 10 to 15 minutes, then mark into squares and leave until completely cold. Remove the squares of toffee from the tin.
To freeze: pack into a rigid container, separating each layer with foil. Seal, label and freeze.
To thaw and serve: thaw at room temperature for about 2 hours.
MAKES ABOUT ½ kg/1 lb

CHOCOLATE NUT TRUFFLES

METRIC/IMPERIAL

25 g/1 oz butter
1 egg yolk
finely grated rind of 1 orange
25 g/1 oz walnuts, finely chopped
175 g/6 oz chocolate, melted
1 × 15 ml spoon/1 tablespoon brandy
chocolate vermicelli, for coating

AMERICAN

2 tablespoons butter
1 egg yolk
finely grated rind of 1 orange
¼ cup finely chopped walnuts
⅔ cup semi-sweet chocolate pieces, melted
1 tablespoon brandy
chocolate vermicelli, for coating

Put all the ingredients, except the vermicelli, in a bowl and beat together for 2 to 3 minutes until well mixed. Leave the mixture in a cool place until firm, then shape into about 20 balls. Put the chocolate vermicelli in a bowl, add the truffles one at a time and shake the bowl until evenly coated. Chill in the refrigerator until firm.

To freeze: open (flash) freeze until solid, then pack carefully in a rigid container, separating each layer with foil. Seal, label and return to the freezer.

To thaw and serve: put the frozen truffles in sweet (candy) cases and thaw at room temperature for about 1 hour.

MAKES ABOUT 20

COCONUT SHIES

METRIC/IMPERIAL

25 g/1 oz butter, softened
1 × 15 ml spoon/1 tablespoon lemon curd
1 × 15 ml spoon/1 tablespoon icing sugar, sifted
4 × 15 ml spoons/4 tablespoons desiccated coconut
For the coating:
25–50 g/1–2 oz desiccated coconut
a few drops of red food colouring
a few drops of yellow food colouring

AMERICAN

2 tablespoons butter, softened
1 tablespoon lemon cheese
1 tablespoon confectioners' sugar, sifted
¼ cup shredded coconut
For the coating:
⅓–⅔ cup shredded coconut
a few drops of red food coloring
a few drops of yellow food coloring

Put the butter and lemon curd (cheese) in a bowl, beat together until creamy, then beat in the icing (confectioners') sugar and the coconut. Turn the mixture out onto a board sprinkled with icing (confectioners') sugar, knead lightly until smooth, then shape into 14 to 16 small balls. Leave in a cool place until firm.

To make the coating: put a little coconut into two separate bowls and colour one with the red food colouring, the other with the yellow. Add the balls one at a time and shake the bowl until evenly coated.

To freeze: open (flash) freeze until firm, then pack in a rigid container, separating each layer with foil. Seal, label and return to the freezer.

To thaw and serve: put the frozen coconut shies in sweet (candy) cases and thaw at room temperature for about 1 hour.

MAKES 14 to 16

CANDY SLICES

METRIC/IMPERIAL

50 g/2 oz plain chocolate, broken into pieces
1 × 2.5 ml spoon/½ teaspoon vanilla essence
50 g/2 oz walnuts, chopped
1 egg
250 g/9 oz icing sugar, sifted
25 marshmallows, quartered
50 g/2 oz desiccated coconut

AMERICAN

⅓ cup semi-sweet chocolate pieces
½ teaspoons vanilla extract
½ cup chopped walnuts
1 egg
2 cups sifted confectioners' sugar
25 marshmallows, quartered
⅔ cup shredded coconut

Put the chocolate in a heatproof bowl, stand over a pan of gently simmering water and allow to melt. Stir in the vanilla essence (extract) and the walnuts.

Whisk the egg in a separate bowl, beat in the icing (confectioners') sugar, then stir into the chocolate mixture with the marshmallows.

Divide the mixture in two and form into long rolls. Roll in the coconut to cover completely, then wrap in foil and chill in the refrigerator until firm. Cut each roll into 20 slices.

To freeze: pack in a rigid container, separating each layer with foil. Seal, label and freeze.

To thaw and serve: put the frozen slices in sweet (candy) cases and thaw at room temperature for about 1 hour.

MAKES 40

TURKISH DELIGHT

METRIC/IMPERIAL

450 g/1 lb sugar
750 ml/1¼ pints water
0.5 × 2.5 ml spoon/¼ teaspoon cream of tartar
75 g/3 oz cornflour
200 g/7 oz icing sugar
50 g/2 oz clear honey
2 × 5 ml spoons/2 teaspoons rose water
a few drops of pink food colouring
15 g/½ oz cornflour
15 g/½ oz sugar

AMERICAN

2 cups sugar, firmly packed
3 cups water
¼ teaspoon cream of tartar
¾ cup cornstarch
1⅔ cups confectioners' sugar
3 tablespoons clear honey
2 teaspoons rose water
a few drops of pink food coloring
2 tablespoons cornstarch
1 tablespoon sugar

Put the sugar and 150 ml/¼ pint/⅔ cup water in a heavy-based pan and heat gently until the sugar has dissolved. Bring to the boil, then boil for 10 to 15 minutes until the temperature reaches 115°C/240°F on a sugar thermometer or until the mixture forms a soft ball when a little is dropped in a cup of cold water.

Remove from the heat, stir in the cream of tartar and set aside. Sift the cornflour (cornstarch) and icing (confectioners') sugar into a pan, add the remaining water and bring to the boil, stirring constantly. Boil for 2 minutes, then lower the heat and gradually pour in the sugar syrup, beating well with a wooden spoon. Return to the heat and bring to the boil. Lower the heat and simmer for 30 minutes, stirring. Add the honey and rose water and stir well to mix.

Pour half the mixture into a lightly greased shallow 18 cm/7 inch square tin. Add the food colouring quickly to the remaining mixture and pour over the mixture in the tin. Smooth the top and leave until cold.

Dip a sharp knife in icing (confectioners') sugar and cut the Turkish delight into 2.5 cm/1 inch bars. Mix the cornflour (cornstarch) and sugar together and spread this mixture over the bars. Leave for several hours, then cut into 2.5 cm/1 inch squares.

To freeze: pack in a rigid container, separating each layer with foil. Seal, label and freeze.

To thaw and serve: remove from the container and thaw at room temperature for about 2 hours.

MAKES 45 to 50

CHOCOLATE CHERRY DELIGHTS

METRIC/IMPERIAL

For the centres:
50 g/2 oz butter
2 × 15 ml spoons/2 tablespoons cocoa powder
50 g/2 oz icing sugar, sifted
25 g/1 oz ground almonds
1 × 15 ml spoon/1 tablespoon brandy
For the outer layer:
50 g/2 oz sugar
50 g/2 oz butter
2 × 15 ml spoons/2 tablespoons water
20 marshmallows
100 g/4 oz icing sugar, sifted
25 g/1 oz walnuts, chopped
25 g/1 oz glacé cherries, chopped

AMERICAN

For the centres:
¼ cup butter
2 tablespoons unsweetened cocoa powder
½ cup sifted confectioners' sugar
¼ cup ground almonds
1 tablespoon brandy
For the outer layer:
¼ cup sugar
¼ cup butter
2 tablespoons water
20 marshmallows
scant 1 cup sifted confectioners' sugar
¼ cup chopped walnuts
1½ tablespoons chopped candied cherries

To make the centres: melt the butter in a pan, add the cocoa and heat gently until dissolved, stirring occasionally. Remove from the heat and stir in the remaining ingredients. Chill in the refrigerator until firm, then roll into a 65 cm/26 inch sausage shape.

To make the outer layer: put the sugar, butter and water in a pan and heat gently until dissolved. Increase the heat and boil for 5 minutes, then remove from the heat and add the marshmallows. Stir until the marshmallows have melted, then stir in the icing (confectioners') sugar, walnuts and cherries.

Leave to cool, then roll into a strip 65 × 7.5 cm/26 × 3 inches. Place the mixture for the centres on top of the strip, then roll up and cut in half. Wrap each roll in foil, then chill in the refrigerator until firm.

To freeze: pack the foil-wrapped rolls in a freezer bag. Seal, label and freeze.

To thaw and serve: thaw the rolls at room temperature for 2 hours, then cut into 45 to 50 slices and put into sweet (candy) cases.

MAKES 45 to 50

FONDANT SWEETS (CANDIES)

METRIC/IMPERIAL

150 ml/$\frac{1}{4}$ pint water
450 g/1 lb sugar
0.5 × 2.5 ml spoon/$\frac{1}{4}$ teaspoon cream of tartar
pink, green, yellow and violet food colourings
vanilla, peppermint, lemon and almond essences

AMERICAN

$\frac{2}{3}$ cup water
2 cups sugar, firmly packed
$\frac{1}{4}$ teaspoon cream of tartar
pink, green, yellow and violet food colorings
vanilla, peppermint, lemon and almond extracts

Put the water and sugar in a large pan and heat gently until the sugar has dissolved. Bring to boiling point, then add the cream of tartar. Boil for about 10 minutes until the temperature reaches 115°C/240°F on a sugar thermometer, or until the mixture forms a soft ball when a little is dropped in a cup of cold water. Brush down the sides of the pan to prevent crystals forming during boiling.

Place a wetted baking sheet on a board, pour on the syrup and leave until a thin skin forms on the surface. Work the mixture quickly with a palette knife until cool, white and grainy in texture, then knead until smooth.

Divide the fondant into 4 equal parts and colour and flvour one part at a time. (Stand the remaining fondant in a heatproof bowl over a pan of hot water to keep it soft.) Roll out the fondant on a dry surface and cut out shapes with small cutters.

To freeze: pack in a rigid container, separating each layer with foil. Seal, label and freeze.

To thaw and serve: put the frozen fondants in sweet (candy) cases and thaw at room temperature for about 2 hours.

MAKES 450 g/1 lb

RUSSIAN CARAMEL

METRIC/IMPERIAL

100 g/4 oz butter
225 g/$\frac{1}{2}$ lb soft brown sugar
1 × 425 g/15 oz can sweetened condensed milk
2 × 15 ml spoons/2 tablespoons golden syrup

AMERICAN

$\frac{1}{2}$ cup butter
$1\frac{1}{3}$ cups light brown sugar
1 × 15 oz can sweetened condensed milk
2 tablespoons light corn syrup

Put all the ingredients in a large pan. Cook over a medium heat for 20 minutes or until the mixture thickens, browns and leaves the sides of the pan, stirring and scraping constantly. Pour immediately into a greased 18 cm/7 inch square tin, leave to set, then cut into 36 squares.

To freeze: pack in a rigid container, separating each layer with foil. Seal, label and freeze.

To thaw and serve: remove from the container and thaw at room temperature for about 2 hours.

MAKES 36

HONEY CRUNCHIES

METRIC/IMPERIAL

20 marshmallows, chopped
2 × 15 ml spoons/2 tablespoons honey
finely grated rind of 1 small lemon
finely grated rind of $\frac{1}{2}$ orange
65 g/$2\frac{1}{2}$ oz cornflakes or rice crispies, lightly crushed
25 g/2 oz seedless raisins

AMERICAN

20 marshmallows, chopped
2 tablespoons honey
finely grated rind of 1 small lemon
finely grated rind of $\frac{1}{2}$ orange
$2\frac{1}{2}$ cups cornflakes or rice crispies, lightly crushed
$\frac{1}{3}$ cup seedless raisins

Put the marshmallows and honey in a heatproof bowl, stand over a pan of gently simmering water and allow to melt, stirring constantly. Remove from the heat, add the remaining ingredients and stir well to mix.

Shape the mixture into 25 to 30 small balls with wet hands, place in sweet (candy) cases, then leave in a cool place until set.

To freeze: pack in a rigid container, separating each layer with foil. Seal, label and freeze.

To thaw and serve: place on a serving platter and thaw at room temperature for 1 to 2 hours.

MAKES 25 to 30

CHOCOLATE SWEETMEAT

METRIC/IMPERIAL
1 × 15 ml spoon/1 tablespoon golden syrup
100 g/4 oz butter
100 g/4 oz sugar
2 × 15 ml spoons/2 tablespoons cocoa powder
250 g/9 oz digestive biscuits, crushed
25 g/1 oz ground almonds
100 g/4 oz glacé cherries, chopped
75 g/3 oz plain chocolate, to finish

AMERICAN
1 tablespoon light corn syrup
½ cup butter
½ cup sugar
2 tablespoons unsweetened cocoa powder
3¾ cups Graham cracker crumbs
¼ cup ground almonds
½ cup candied cherries, chopped
½ cup semi-sweet chocolate pieces, to finish

Put the syrup, butter and sugar in a pan and heat gently until melted. Remove from the heat, add the remaining ingredients, except the chocolate, then stir well to mix. Leave to cool, then press the mixture into a shallow 20 cm/8 inch square cake tin.
To freeze: cover with foil, seal, label and freeze.
To thaw and serve: remove the foil and thaw at room temperature for 2 to 3 hours. Melt the chocolate and spread over the cake. Leave to set, then cut into 64 squares.
MAKES 64

CREAMY COCONUT DATES

METRIC/IMPERIAL
175 g/6 oz cream cheese
2 × 15 ml spoons/2 tablespoons double cream
450 g/1 lb stoned dates
1 egg white, lightly beaten
50 g/2 oz desiccated coconut

AMERICAN
¾ cup cream cheese
2 tablespoons heavy cream
2½ cups pitted dates
1 egg white, lightly beaten
⅔ cup shredded coconut

Put the cream cheese and cream in a bowl and beat until soft and smooth. Fill the dates with this mixture, coat in the egg white, then the coconut. Chill in the refrigerator for 1 hour.
To freeze: open (flash) freeze until firm, then pack in a rigid container, separating each layer with foil. Seal, label and return to the freezer.
To thaw and serve: put the frozen dates in sweet (candy) cases and thaw at room temperature for about 1 hour.
MAKES 30

PEPPERMINT CREAMS

METRIC/IMPERIAL
50 g/2 oz full fat cream cheese, softened
1 × 2.5 ml spoon/½ teaspoon peppermint essence
225 g/½ lb icing sugar, sifted
a few drops of green food colouring (optional)

AMERICAN
¼ cup cream cheese, softened
½ teaspoon peppermint extract
scant 2 cups sifted confectioners' sugar
a few drops of green food coloring (optional)

Put the cheese and pepper mint essence (extract) in a bowl, beat together until smooth, then gradually beat in the icing (confectioners') sugar. If using colouring, add to the mixture and knead until evenly blended.
Turn out onto a surface sprinkled with icing (confectioners') sugar, roll out to 5 mm/¼ inch thickness, then cut out about 30 rounds with a 2.5 cm/1 inch plain cutter. Place on greaseproof (waxed) paper and allow to dry overnight.
To freeze: pack in a rigid container, separating each layer with foil. Seal, label and freeze.
To thaw and serve: put the frozen creams in sweet (candy) cases and thaw at room temperature for about 1 hour.
MAKES ABOUT 30

ORANGE CREAMS

Make as for Peppermint Creams (see opposite), substituting 1 × 2.5 ml spoon/½ teaspoon orange essence (extract) and a few drops of orange food colouring for the peppermint essence (extract) and the green food colouring.
Freeze, thaw and serve as for Peppermint Creams.
MAKES ABOUT 30

COFFEE CREAMS

Make as for Peppermint Creams (see opposite), substituting 2 × 5 ml spoons/2 teaspoons coffee essence (strong black coffee) for the peppermint essence (extract) and the food colouring and adding an extra 25 g/1 oz /¼ cup sifted icing (confectioners') sugar.
Freeze, thaw and serve as for Peppermint Creams.
MAKES ABOUT 30

DATES STUFFED WITH ALMOND PASTE

METRIC/IMPERIAL
175 g/6 oz almond paste
450 g/1 lb stoned dates
50 g/2 oz caster sugar

AMERICAN
6 oz almond paste
2½ cups pitted dates
¼ cup sugar

Roll the almond paste into pellet shapes about twice the size of the date stones (seeds) and use to stuff the dates. Roll in (caster) sugar.
To freeze: pack in a rigid container, separating each layer with foil. Seal, label and freeze.
To thaw and serve: put the frozen dates in sweet (candy) cases and thaw at room temperature for about 1 hour.
MAKES 30

COCONUT ICE

METRIC/IMPERIAL
675 g/1½ lb sugar
300 ml/½ pint water
2 pinches of cream of tartar
225 g/½ lb desiccated coconut
1–2 drops of pink food colouring

AMERICAN
3 cups sugar, firmly packed
1¼ cups water
2 pinches of cream of tartar
2⅔ cups shredded coconut
1–2 drops of pink food coloring

Grease a 20 cm/8 inch square cake tin and line with greased greaseproof (waxed) paper. Put the sugar and water in a pan and heat gently until the sugar has dissolved. Add the cream of tartar, increase the heat and boil for 10 to 15 minutes until the temperature reaches 115°C/250°F on a sugar thermometer, or until the mixture forms a soft ball when a little is dropped in a cup of cold water.
Remove from the heat and stir in the coconut. Pour half the mixture into the prepared tin. Beat the food colouring quickly into the remaining mixture, pour into the tin and smooth the top. Leave until half set, then mark into about 36 squares. Leave until cold, then remove the squares from the tin.
To freeze: pack in a rigid container, separating each layer with foil. Seal, label and freeze.
To thaw and serve: thaw at room temperature for about 2 hours.
MAKES ABOUT 36

FISH AND CHIP BALLS

METRIC/IMPERIAL

225 g/½ lb smoked haddock fillets, poached, skinned and flaked
175 g/6 oz cream cheese, softened
2 × 5 ml spoons/2 teaspoons lemon juice
1 × 15 ml spoon/1 tablespoon freshly chopped parsley
freshly ground black pepper
50 g/2 oz potato crisps, crushed

AMERICAN

½ lb smoked haddock fillets, poached, skinned and flaked
¾ cup cream cheese, softened
2 teaspoons lemon juice
1 tablespoon freshly chopped parsley
freshly ground black pepper
1 cup crushed potato chips

Put all the ingredients, except the crisps (potato chips), in a bowl and beat well to mix. Roll into 30 walnut-sized balls with lightly floured hands, then roll in the crushed crisps (potato chips), pressing them well into the mixture.
To freeze: open (flash) freeze until firm, then pack in a rigid container, separating each layer with foil. Seal, label and return to the freezer.
To thaw and serve: arrange in a single layer and thaw at room temperature for about 2 hours.
MAKES 30

ALMOND BALLS

METRIC/IMPERIAL

100 g/4 oz cream cheese, softened
25 g/1 oz butter
1 × 15 ml spoon/1 tablespoon grated onion
1 × 15 ml spoon/1 tablespoon freshly chopped parsley
1 × 15 ml spoon/1 tablespoon snipped chives
1 × 15 ml spoon/1 tablespoon chutney
salt
freshly ground black pepper
50 g/2 oz almonds, finely chopped and toasted
0.5 × 2.5 ml spoon/¼ teaspoon paprika pepper

AMERICAN

½ cup cream cheese, softened
2 tablespoons butter
1 tablespoon grated onion
1 tablespoon freshly chopped parsley
1 tablespoon snipped chives
1 tablespoon chutney
salt
freshly ground black pepper
½ cup finely chopped almonds, toasted
¼ teaspoon paprika pepper

Put all the ingredients, except the almonds and paprika, in a bowl and beat well to mix. Form into 18 balls, then roll in the almonds and sprinkle with the paprika.
To freeze: open (flash) freeze until firm, then

pack in a rigid container, separating each layer with foil. Seal, label and return to the freezer.
To thaw and serve: arrange on a serving dish and thaw at room temperature for about 2 hours.
MAKES 18

SCONE (BISCUIT) VOL-AU-VENTS

METRIC/IMPERIAL
225 g/½ lb self-raising flour
1 × 5 ml spoon/1 teaspoon baking powder
pinch of salt
50 g/2 oz butter
120 ml/4 fl oz milk

AMERICAN
1 cup self-rising flour
1 teaspoon baking powder
pinch of salt
¼ cup butter
½ cup milk

Sift the flour, baking powder and salt into a bowl, add the butter in pieces and rub into the flour until the mixture resembles fine breadcrumbs. Stir in the milk and mix to a soft dough. Knead lightly on a floured surface until smooth, then roll out and cut into 6 rounds with a 7.5 cm/3 inch plain cutter. Mark out the centres with a 5 cm/2 inch plain cutter, without cutting right through the dough.
Place on a baking sheet and brush the top of the dough with milk. Bake in a preheated hot oven (220°C/425°F or Gas Mark 7) for 12 to 15 minutes or until golden. Cool slightly, scoop out the centres, then cool completely on a wire rack.
To freeze: open (flash) freeze until firm, then pack carefully in a rigid container, separating each layer with foil. Seal, label and return to the freezer.
To thaw and serve: place on a baking sheet and reheat from frozen in a preheated moderate oven (180°C/350°F or Gas Mark 4) for 25 minutes or until heated through. Fill with a savoury filling, replace the tops and serve immediately.
MAKES 6

HERB SCONE (BISCUIT) VOL-AU-VENTS

Make as for plain Scone (Biscuit) Vol-au-Vents (see above), adding 1 × 5 ml spoon/1 teaspoon dried mixed herbs to the flour when preparing the dough. Freeze, thaw and serve as for plain Scone (Biscuit) Vol-au-Vents.

BREAD CASES

METRIC/IMPERIAL
18 thin slices of bread, crusts removed
100 g/4 oz butter, melted

AMERICAN
18 thin slices of bread, crusts removed
½ cup butter, melted

Roll the bread carefully with a rolling pin until very thin. Trim into neat squares or cut into rounds with a 7.5 cm/3 inch plain cutter.
Brush both sides of the bread with the melted butter and place immediately into patty tins. Bake in a preheated moderate oven (180°C/350°F or Gas Mark 4) for 20 to 30 minutes or until golden brown and crisp.
To freeze: open (flash) freeze until firm, then pack in a rigid container, separating each layer with foil. Seal, label and return to the freezer.
To thaw and serve: arrange in a single layer on a serving dish and thaw at room temperature for 1 hour. Fill with a savoury filling of your choice.
MAKES 18

STUFFED DATES

METRIC/IMPERIAL
approx 28 dates, stoned
100 g/4 oz cream cheese, softened

AMERICAN
approx 28 dates, pitted
½ cup cream cheese, softened

Stuff the dates with the cream cheese, using a teaspoon or piping (pastry) bag.
To freeze: open (flash) freeze until firm, then pack in a rigid container, separating each layer with foil. Seal, label and return to the freezer.
To thaw and serve: arrange in a single layer on a serving dish and thaw at room temperature for about 2 hours.
MAKES ABOUT 28

CHEESE PASTRY BOATS

METRIC/IMPERIAL

100 g/4 oz flour
50 g/2 oz butter
50 g/2 oz cheese, finely grated
1 × 15 ml spoon/1 tablespoon grated Parmesan cheese
pinch each of salt, freshly ground black pepper, cayenne papper, paprika pepper and mustard powder
1 egg yolk
1–2 × 15 ml spoons/1–2 tablespoons water

AMERICAN

1 cup flour
¼ cup butter
½ cup finely grated cheese
1 tablespoon grated Parmesan cheese
pinch each of salt, freshly ground black pepper, cayenne pepper, paprika pepper and mustard powder
1 egg yolk
1–2 tablespoons water

Sift the flour into a bowl, add the butter in pieces and rub into the flour until the mixture resembles fine breadcrumbs. Stir in the cheeses and seasonings, then mix in the egg yolk and enough water to give a stiff dough.

Roll out the dough on a floured surface and use to line 18 barquettes (boat-shaped moulds). Bake in a preheated moderately hot oven (190°C/375°F or Gas Mark 5) for 10 to 15 minutes or until golden. Remove the moulds and cool the pastry quickly on a wire rack.

To freeze: open (flash) freeze until firm, then pack carefully in a rigid container, separating each layer with foil. Seal, label and return to the freezer.

To thaw and serve: arrange in a single layer on a serving dish and thaw at room temperature for 1 hour. Fill with a savoury filling of your choice.

MAKES 18

CHEESE STRAWS

METRIC/IMPERIAL

225 g/½ lb flour
1 × 2.5 ml spoons/½ teaspoon salt
freshly ground black pepper
50 g/2 oz butter
1 chicken stock cube, crumbled
100 g/4 oz Cheddar cheese, grated
50 g/2 oz Parmesan cheese, grated
2 egg yolks
1–2 × 15 ml spoons/1–2 tablespoons water

AMERICAN

2 cups flour
½ teaspoon salt
freshly ground black pepper
¼ cup butter
2 chicken bouillon cubes, crumbled
1 cup grated Cheddar cheese
½ cup grated Parmesan cheese
2 egg yolks
1–2 tablespoons water

Sift the flour, salt and a little pepper into a bowl. Add the butter in pieces and the stock (bouillon) cube(s) and rub into the flour until the mixture resembles fine breadcrumbs. Add the cheeses with the egg yolks and stir well, then stir in enough water to give a firm dough. Knead lightly until smooth.

Roll out the dough on a floured surface to a thin square or rectangle, then cut into straws about 5 mm/¼ inch wide and 6.5 cm/2½ inches long. Roll out the trimmings and cut out 6 to 8 circles about 7.5 cm/3 inches in diameter, then cut out the centres with a 5 cm/2 inch cutter to form rings.

Put the straws and rings on baking sheets and bake in a preheated moderately hot oven (200°C/400°F or Gas Mark 6) for 10 minutes or until golden brown. Cool quickly on a wire rack.

To freeze: open (flash) freeze until firm, then pack carefully in a rigid container, separating each layer with foil. Seal, label and return to the freezer.

To thaw and serve: place on a baking sheet and reheat from frozen in a preheated moderate oven (180°C/350°F or Gas Mark 4) for 10 minutes. Cool on a wire rack, then thread the straws through the rings.

MAKES ABOUT 80

CHEESE BLINTZES

METRIC/IMPERIAL

For the batter:

100 g/4 oz wholemeal flour
25 g/1 oz butter, melted and cooled
3 eggs, beaten
300 ml/½ pint milk
butter for frying

For the filling:

225 g/½ lb cottage cheese, sieved
2 × 15 ml spoons/2 tablespoons soured cream
0.5 × 2.5 ml spoon/¼ teaspoon paprika pepper
0.5 × 2.5 ml spoon/¼ teaspoon cayenne pepper
salt
freshly ground black pepper

To finish:

150 ml/¼ pint soured cream
1 onion, peeled and finely chopped

AMERICAN

For the batter:

1 cup wholewheat flour
2 tablespoons butter, melted and cooled
3 eggs, beaten
1¼ cups milk
butter for frying

For the filling:

1 cup cottage cheese, strained
2 tablespoons sour cream
¼ teaspoon paprika pepper
¼ teaspoon cayenne pepper
salt
freshly ground black pepper

To finish:

⅔ cup sour cream
1 onion, peeled and finely chopped

To make the batter: put the flour in a bowl and make a well in the centre. Add the butter, eggs and half the milk, beat until smooth, then beat in the remaining milk.

To make the filling: put all the ingredients in a bowl and beat well to mix.

Melt a knob of butter in a frying pan (skillet), pour in 2 to 3 × 15 ml spoons/2 to 3 tablespoons batter and fry over a high heat for 2 to 3 minutes on each side until golden brown. Make 12 blintzes in this way.

Divide the filling equally between the blintzes: place a spoonful in the centre of each, tuck in the sides and roll up. Put in a buttered ovenproof dish or foil container with the joins underneath.

To freeze: cover with foil, seal, label and freeze.

To thaw and serve: thaw at room temperature for 2 to 3 hours, then reheat in the covered dish or container in a preheated hot oven (220°C/425°F or Gas Mark 7) for 15 minutes or until heated through. Spread with the sour(ed) cream and sprinkle with the onion just before serving.

MAKES 12

DANISH BLUE CHEESE STRAWS

METRIC/IMPERIAL

100 g/4 oz flour
pinch of salt
0.5 × 2.5 ml spoon/¼ teaspoon paprika pepper
25 g/1 oz butter
25 g/1 oz lard
1–2 × 15 ml spoons/1–2 tablespoons water
50 g/2 oz Danish blue cheese, grated

AMERICAN

1 cup flour
pinch of salt
¼ teaspoon paprika pepper
2 tablespoons butter
2 tablespoons shortening
1–2 tablespoons water
½ cup grated Danish blue cheese

Sift the flour, salt and paprika into a bowl. Add the butter and lard (shortening) in pieces and rub into the flour until the mixture resembles fine breadcrumbs. Stir in enough water to give a stiff dough, then knead lightly until smooth.

Roll out the dough on a floured surface to a thin rectangle. Sprinkle the cheese over one half of the dough, then fold over the other half to enclose the cheese. Roll out again until the dough is thin enough to show the cheese inside. Cut into straws about 5 mm/¼ inch wide and 6 cm/2½ inches long.

Put the cheese straws on baking sheets and bake in a preheated moderately hot oven (200°C/400°F or Gas Mark 6) for 10 minutes or until golden brown. Cool quickly on a wire rack.

To freeze: open (flash) freeze until firm, then pack in a rigid container, separating each layer with foil. Seal, label and return to the freezer.

To thaw and serve: arrange in a single layer on a serving dish and thaw at room temperature for 1 to 2 hours.

MAKES ABOUT 50

SAUSAGE ROLLS

METRIC/IMPERIAL

450 g/1 lb pork sausagemeat
1 × 15 ml spoon/1 tablespoon freshly chopped mixed herbs
salt
freshly ground black pepper
basic puff pastry dough made with 350 g/¾ lb flour
a little milk, to glaze

AMERICAN

2 cups pork sausagemeat
1 tablespoon freshly chopped mixed herbs
salt
freshly ground black pepper
basic puff paste dough made with 3 cups flour
a little milk, to glaze

Put the sausagemeat, herbs and salt and pepper to taste in a bowl and beat well to mix. Divide into 4 portions and roll each one on a floured surface to make a long roll about 40 cm/16 inches long.

Roll out the dough on a floured surface and cut into 4 strips about 40 × 7.5 cm/16 × 3 inches. Place a roll of sausage on each piece of dough, brush the edges with water, then fold over the dough and seal well. Cut each roll into 8 equal portions, then make 2 to 3 cuts on the top of each portion.

To freeze: open (flash) freeze until firm, then pack in a rigid container, separating each layer with foil. Seal, label and return to the freezer.

To thaw and serve: place on a baking sheet, brush with milk and bake from frozen in a preheated hot oven (220°C/425°F or Gas Mark 7) for 25 minutes or until golden brown and heated through.

MAKES 32

CHEESE AND WALNUT SAVOURIES

METRIC/IMPERIAL

For the cheese pastry:
100 g/4 oz flour
pinch each of salt, freshly ground black pepper, cayenne papper, paprika pepper and mustard powder
50 g/2 oz soft tub margarine
65 g/2½ oz Cheddar cheese, finely grated
1 egg yolk
1 × 15 ml spoon/1 tablespoon water
For the filling:
1 egg white, beaten
15 g/½ oz walnuts, finely chopped
beaten egg or milk, to glaze

AMERICAN

For the cheese pastry:
1 cup flour
pinch each of salt, freshly ground black pepper, cayenne pepper, paprika pepper and mustard powder
¼ cup soft margarine
½ cup finely grated Cheddar cheese
1 egg yolk
1 tablespoon water
For the filling:
1 egg white, beaten
2 tablespoons finely chopped walnuts
beaten egg or milk, to glaze

To make the pastry: sift the flour and seasonings into a bowl, add the remaining pastry ingredients and mix with a wooden spoon to give a soft dough.

Roll out the dough on a floured surface to a thin oblong about 33 × 18 cm/13 × 7 inches. Cut in half lengthways, then brush one half with the beaten egg white. Sprinkle over the walnuts and place the remaining dough on top. Press lightly with a rolling pin, then brush all over the dough with beaten egg or milk. Cut into fingers (bars) about 2.5 cm/1 inch wide. Place on greased baking sheets and bake in a preheated moderately hot oven (190°C/375°F or Gas Mark 5) for 15 to 20 minutes until golden brown. Cool quickly on a wire rack.

To freeze: open (flash) freeze until firm, then pack carefully in a rigid container, separating each layer with foil. Seal, label and return to the freezer.

To thaw and serve: arrange in a single layer on a serving dish and thaw at room temperature for 1 to 2 hours.

MAKES 16

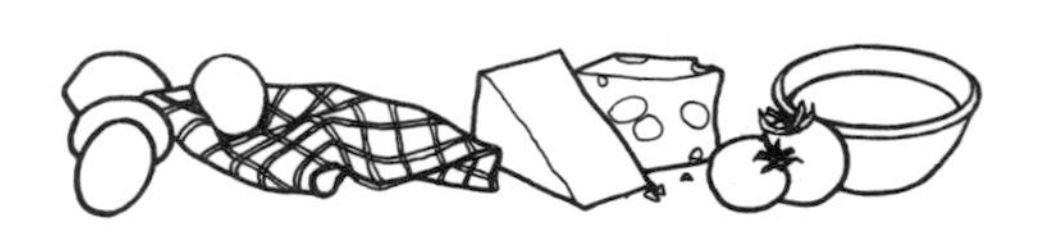

SAUSAGE TWISTS

METRIC/IMPERIAL

basic shortcrust pastry dough made with 350 g/¾ lb flour
16 chipolata sausages

AMERICAN

basic pie dough made with 3 cups flour
16 link sausages

Roll out the dough on a floured surface and cut into 16 strips about 25 × 1 cm/10 × ½ inch. Twist a strip of dough several times around each sausage, then place on a baking sheet. Bake in a preheated moderately hot oven (200°C/400°F or Gas Mark 6) for 25 minutes until golden brown. Cool quickly on a wire rack.
To freeze: open (flash) freeze until firm, then pack carefully in a rigid container, separating each layer with foil. Seal, label and return to the freezer.
To thaw and serve: thaw at room temperature for 1 hour, then reheat on a baking sheet in a preheated moderately hot oven for 10 to 15 minutes.
MAKES 16

SAVOURY HORNS

METRIC/IMPERIAL
basic puff pastry dough made with 225 g/8 oz flour
1 egg, beaten
poppy seeds
For the filling (to finish):
100 g/4 oz garlic sausage, finely chopped
1 tomato, peeled, seeded and chopped
2 × 15 ml spoons/2 tablespoons thick mayonnaise
6 stuffed olives
a few parsley sprigs, to garnish

AMERICAN
basic puff paste dough made with 3 cups flour
1 egg, beaten
poppy seeds
For the filling (to finish):
¼ lb garlic sausage, finely chopped
1 tomato, peeled, seeded and chopped
2 tablespoons thick mayonnaise
6 stuffed olives
a few parsley sprigs, to garnish

Roll out the dough on a floured surface to a strip about 65 × 10 cm/26 × 4 inches. Brush with the beaten egg and trim the edges with a sharp knife, then cut into 20 cm/8 inch ribbons. Wind each ribbon around a cream horn tin, egg side uppermost, then sprinkle with poppy seeds.
Put the horns on a dampened baking sheet with the joins underneath and bake in a preheated hot oven (220°C/425°F or Gas Mark 7) for 10 minutes. Cool on a wire rack, then carefully remove the cases from the tins.
To freeze: open (flash) freeze until firm, then pack carefully in a rigid container, separating each layer with foil. Seal, label and return to the freezer.
To thaw and serve: remove wrappings and thaw at room temperature for 30 minutes. Put the garlic sausage, tomato, mayonnaise and 4 chopped olives in a bowl and stir well to mix. Use to fill the horns, then garnish with the remaining olives and the parsley.
MAKES 15

CHEESE CRISPS

METRIC/IMPERIAL
150 g/5 oz flour
0.5 × 2.5 ml spoon/¼ teaspoon salt
0.5 × 2.5 ml spoon/¼ teaspoon mustard powder
pinch of cayenne pepper
100 g/4 oz butter
100 g/4 oz Cheddar cheese, finely grated
25 g/1 oz potato crisps, finely crushed
1 egg yolk
1–2 × 5 ml spoons/1–2 teaspoons water
salt, for sprinkling

AMERICAN
1¼ cups flour
¼ teaspoon salt
¼ teaspoon mustard powder
pinch of cayenne pepper
½ cup butter
1 cup finely grated Cheddar cheese
½ cup finely crushed potato chips
1 egg yolk
1–2 teaspoons water
salt, for sprinkling

Sift the flour and seasonings into a bowl, add the butter in pieces and rub into the flour until the mixture resembles fine breadcrumbs. Add the cheese and crisps (potato chips) and stir well to mix, then stir in the egg yolk and enough water to give a stiff dough. Knead lightly until smooth. Roll out the dough on a floured surface and cut out about 50 small rounds or squares about 2.5 cm/1 inch across. Place on greased baking sheets and bake in a preheated moderately hot oven (200°C/400°F or Gas Mark 6) for 12 to 14 minutes until golden brown. Sprinkle with salt, then cool quickly on a wire rack.
To freeze: open (flash) freeze until firm, then pack carefully in a rigid container, separating each layer with foil. Seal, label and return to the freezer.
To thaw and serve: arrange in a single layer on a serving dish and thaw at room temperature for 1 to 2 hours.
MAKES ABOUT 50

CHEESE CRISPIES

METRIC/IMPERIAL

For the cheese pastry:
100 g/4 oz flour
salt
pinch of cayenne pepper
75 g/3 oz Cheddar cheese, finely grated
1 egg yolk
1 × 5 ml spoon/1 teaspoon water
For the topping:
100 g/4 oz Cheddar cheese, finely grated
75 g/3 oz rolled oats
100 g/4 oz butter
freshly ground black pepper

AMERICAN

For the cheese pastry:
1 cup flour
salt
pinch of cayenne papper
¾ cup finely grated Cheddar cheese
1 egg yolk
1 teaspoon water
For the topping:
1 cup finely grated Cheddar cheese
scant 1 cup rolled oats
½ cup butter
freshly ground black pepper

To make the pastry: sift the flour and seasonings into a bowl. Add the butter in pieces and rub into the flour until the mixture resembles fine breadcrumbs. Stir in the cheese, egg yolk and water and mix to give a stiff dough. Knead lightly until smooth.
Roll out the dough on a floured surface and cut out 20 to 24 rounds with a 5 cm/2 inch plain cutter. Place on greased baking sheets.
To make the topping: put all the ingredients in a bowl and stir well to mix. Put a spoonful of topping on each round of dough and bake in a preheated moderately hot oven (200°C/400°F or Gas Mark 6) for 20 to 25 minutes until golden brown. Cool quickly on a wire rack.
To freeze: open (flash) freeze until firm, then pack carefully in a rigid container, separating each layer with foil. Seal, label and return to the freezer.
To thaw and serve: arrange in a single layer on a serving dish and thaw at room temperature for 1 to 2 hours.
MAKES 20 to 24

CHEESE AND HAM FINGERS

METRIC/IMPERIAL

basic flaky or rough puff pastry dough made with 225 g/½ lb flour
1 × 5 ml spoon/1 teaspoon prepared mustard
100 g/4 oz Cheddar cheese, grated
100 g/4 oz cooked ham or bacon, finely chopped
freshly ground black pepper
beaten egg or milk, to glaze

AMERICAN

basic flaky or rough puff paste dough made with 2 cups flour
1 teaspoon prepared mustard
1 cup grated Cheddar cheese
½ cup finely chopped cooked ham or bacon
freshly ground black pepper
beaten egg or milk, to glaze

Divide the dough in two and roll out each piece on a floured surface to a strip about 30 × 18 cm/12 × 7 inches. Put one strip on a dampened baking sheet, spread with the mustard and cover with the cheese and ham, leaving a 1 cm/½ inch margin all round. Sprinkle with black pepper to taste. Moisten the edges with water, place the second strip of dough on top and press firmly to seal.
To freeze: open (flash) freeze until firm, then wrap in foil. Seal, label and return to the freezer.
To thaw and serve: remove wrappings and place the dough on a baking sheet. Thaw at room temperature for 2 hours, then brush with beaten egg or milk and cut into thin fingers, separating them slightly. Bake in a preheated hot oven (220°C/425°F or Gas Mark 7) for 15 minutes, then reduce the heat to moderately hot (190°C/375°F or Gas Mark 5) and bake for a further 25 to 30 minutes until golden brown.
MAKES ABOUT 14

OVEN HOT DOGS

METRIC/IMPERIAL

2 × 15 ml spoons/2 tablespoons peanut butter
2 × 15 ml spoons/2 tablespoons prepared French mustard
16 thin slices of white bread, crusts removed
450 g/1 lb chipolata sausages
25 g/1 oz butter, melted

AMERICAN

2 tablespoons peanut butter
2 tablespoons prepared French mustard
16 thin slices of white bread, crusts removed
1 lb link sausages
2 tablespoons butter, melted

Put the peanut butter and mustard in a heatproof bowl, blend together, then warm over a pan of hot water. Spread the mixture on the slices of bread, then wrap around the sausages, pressing the rolls between the hands to make the bread stick together.

Arrange the sausages close together on a baking sheet with the joins underneath. Brush with the melted butter. Bake in a preheated moderately hot oven (200°C/400°F or Gas Mark 6) for 25 minutes or until golden brown. Cool quickly on a wire rack.

To freeze: open (flash) freeze until firm. Wrap individually in foil, then pack in a freezer bag. Seal, label and return to the freezer.

To thaw and freeze: thaw at room temperature for 2 hours. Reheat in the foil wrappings in a preheated moderately hot oven (200°C/400°F or Gas Mark 6) for 15 minutes, then remove the foil and reheat for a further 5 minutes or until crisp.

MAKES 16

CURRY HOT DOGS

METRIC/IMPERIAL

6 thin slices of white bread, crusts removed
75 g/3 oz butter
1 × 5 ml spoon/1 teaspoon curry paste or powder
6 frankfurters or skinless sausages, cooked

AMERICAN

6 thin slices of white bread, crusts removed
⅜ cup butter
1 teaspoon curry paste or powder
6 frankfurters or skinless sausages, cooked

Roll out the bread with a rolling pin until as thin as possible. Put 50 g/2 oz/¼ cup butter in a bowl with the curry paste or powder, beat well to mix, then spread on the bread. Wrap around the frankfurters or sausages, pressing the rolls between the hands to make the bread stick together. Melt the remaining butter and brush over the bread.

To freeze: open (flash) freeze until firm, then pack in a rigid container, separating each layer with foil. Seal, label and return to the freezer.

To thaw and serve: place on a baking sheet and bake in a preheated moderately hot oven (200°C/400°F or Gas Mark 6) for 30 to 35 minutes.

MAKES 6

SPINACH AND CHEESE PUFFS

METRIC/IMPERIAL

225 g/½ lb frozen chopped spinach, cooked and drained
50 g/2 oz butter
100 g/4 oz feta, Gruyère or Cheddar cheese, grated
0.5 × 2.5 ml spoon/¼ teaspoon grated nutmeg
1 small egg, lightly beaten
salt
freshly ground black pepper
225 g/½ lb uncooked fila or strudel pastry dough
vegetable oil for deep-frying

AMERICAN

½ lb frozen chopped spinach, cooked and drained
¼ cup butter
1 cup grated feta, Gruyère or Cheddar cheese
¼ teaspoon grated nutmeg
1 small egg, lightly beaten
salt
freshly ground black pepper
½ lb uncooked fila or strudel paste dough
vegetable oil for deep-frying

Put the spinach in a bowl, then add a small knob of the butter and the remaining ingredients except the dough and oil. Beat well to mix.

Melt the remaining butter. Spread out 1 sheet of dough and cover the remainder with a damp cloth. Brush the dough lightly with some of the melted butter and cut into long strips about 7.5 cm/3 inches wide. Put 1 × 5 ml spoon/1 teaspoon of the spinach and egg mixture 2.5 cm/1 inch from the top of the first strip. Fold the top of the dough over diagonally to form a small triangle so that the top edge lies over the side edge and the filling is completely covered. Fold this triangle down again so that the top edge of the strip is straight. Continue folding the triangle over on to itself until the whole strip has been used up. Repeat with the remaining strips and sheets of dough, brushing each sheet first with butter. Deep-fry in hot oil until golden brown, then drain on paper towels and cool quickly on a wire rack.

To freeze: open (flash) until firm, then pack in a rigid container, separating each layer with foil. Seal, label and return to the freezer.

To thaw and serve: reheat from frozen on a baking sheet in a preheated hot oven (220°C/425°F or Gas Mark 7) for 15 minutes or until heated through. Serve very hot.

MAKES 10

EGG AND BACON TARTLETS

METRIC/IMPERIAL

basic shortcrust pastry dough made with 225 g/½ lb flour
2 eggs, beaten
150 ml/¼ pint single cream or creamy milk
50 g/2 oz Cheddar cheese, grated
pinch of mustard powder
pinch of cayenne pepper
salt
freshly ground black pepper
100 g/4 oz streaky bacon rashers, rinds removed, grilled and chopped

AMERICAN

basic pie dough made with 2 cups flour
2 eggs, beaten
⅔ cup light cream or half-and-half
½ cup grated Cheddar cheese
pinch of mustard powder
pinch of cayenne pepper
salt
freshly ground black pepper
6 fatty bacon slices, broiled and chopped

Roll out the dough on a floured surface and use to line 18 to 20 deep patty tins. Bake blind in a preheated moderately hot oven (200°C/400°F or Gas Mark 6) for 15 minutes. Put the remaining ingredients, except the bacon, in a bowl and beat well to mix. Divide the bacon equally between the pastry cases (tart shells) and pour over the egg and cheese mixture. Bake in the moderately hot oven for 10 to 15 minutes.
To freeze: cool quickly. Open (flash) freeze until firm, remove the tins, then wrap the tartlets in foil. Pack in a freezer bag. Seal, label and return to the freezer.
To thaw and serve: remove wrappings and return the tartlets to the patty tins. Reheat in a preheated moderate oven (180°C/350°F or Gas Mark 4) for 15 to 20 minutes or until heated through.
MAKES 18 to 20

TOMATO AND ONION TARTLETS

METRIC/IMPERIAL

basic shortcrust pastry dough made with 225 g/½ lb flour
50 g/2 oz butter
2 onions, peeled and finely sliced
3 tomatoes, peeled and sliced
1 × 15 ml spoon/1 tablespoon tomato purée
pinch of dried basil or oregano
salt
freshly ground black pepper
2 × 15 ml spoons/2 tablespoons grated Parmesan cheese
To garnish:
9–10 black olives, halved and stoned
1 × 50 g/2 oz can anchovies, drained, soaked in milk and drained again

AMERICAN

basic pie dough made with 2 cups flour
¼ cup butter
2 onions, peeled and finely sliced
3 tomatoes, peeled and sliced
1 tablespoon tomato paste
pinch of dried basil or oregano
salt
freshly ground black pepper
2 tablespoons grated Parmesan cheese
To garnish:
9–10 black olives, halved and pitted
1 × 2 oz can anchovies, drained, soaked in milk and drained again

Roll out the dough on a floured surface and use to line 18 to 20 deep patty tins. Bake blind in a preheated moderately hot oven (200°C/400°F or Gas Mark 6) for 15 minutes.
Melt the butter in a pan, add the remaining ingredients, except the Parmesan cheese, and fry gently for 10 minutes. Remove from the heat and stir in the cheese, then divide equally between the pastry cases (tart shells). Garnish with halved olives and strips of anchovy. Bake in a preheated moderate oven (180°C/350°F or Gas Mark 4) for 25 minutes or until the filling is set.
To freeze: cool quickly. Open (flash) freeze until firm, remove the tins, then wrap the tartlets in foil. Pack in a freezer bag. Seal, label and return to the freezer.
To thaw and serve: remove wrappings and return the tartlets to the patty tins. Reheat in a preheated moderate oven for 15 to 20 minutes or until heated through.
MAKES 18 to 20

POTATO AND ONION TRIANGLES

METRIC/IMPERIAL

225 g/½ lb self-raising flour
pinch of salt
1 × 5 ml spoon/1 teaspoon mustard powder
100 g/4 oz butter
1 small onion, peeled and grated
1 large potato, peeled and grated
2 × 15 ml spoons/2 tablespoons freshly chopped parsley
50 g/2 oz Cheddar cheese, grated

1 egg, beaten
2 × 15 ml spoons/2 tablespoons milk

AMERICAN
2 cups self-rising flour
pinch of salt
1 teaspoon mustard powder
½ cup butter
1 small onion, peeled and grated
1 large potato, peeled and grated
2 tablespoons freshly chopped parsley
½ cup grated Cheddar cheese
1 egg, beaten

Sift the flour, salt and mustard into a bowl, then rub in the butter until the mixture resembles fine breadcrumbs. Add the onion, potato, parsley and cheese and mix to a fairly stiff dough with the egg and milk.
Turn the dough out onto a floured surface, knead lightly, then roll out to a circle 20 to 23 cm/8 to 9 inches in diameter. Cut into 8 equal triangles.
Grease a griddle or heavy-based frying pan (skillet) and heat until it is hot enough to turn a piece of the mixture golden brown in 30 seconds. Put in the potato and onion cakes and cook for 2 to 3 minutes on each side until golden brown.
To freeze: cool quickly. Open (flash) freeze until firm, then pack in a freezer bag. Seal, label and return to the freezer.
To thaw and serve: place the frozen cakes on a baking sheet and reheat in a preheated moderate oven (180°C/350°F or Gas Mark 4) for 30 minutes or until heated through.
MAKES 8

SANDWICH SPREADS

Put the ingredients for the chosen spread in a bowl and beat well to mix.
To freeze: pack into a rigid container, seal, label and freeze.
To thaw and use: thaw in the container at room temperature for 2 to 3 hours, then use as a filling for sandwiches and rolls (buns).
QUANTITY TO FILL 4 to 6 LARGE SANDWICHES

PILCHARD AND GHERKIN (DILL PICKLE) SPREAD

METRIC/IMPERIAL
50 g/2 oz butter, softened
1 small can pilchards, drained, boned and flaked
3 gherkins, finely chopped
freshly ground black pepper

AMERICAN
¼ cup butter, softened
1 small can pilchards, drained, boned and flaked
3 small sweet dill pickles, finely chopped
freshly ground black pepper

HONEY, RAISIN AND NUT SPREAD

METRIC/IMPERIAL
50 g/2 oz butter, softened
2 × 15 ml spoons/2 tablespoons honey
25 g/1 oz seedless raisins, chopped
25 g/1 oz almonds or walnuts, chopped

AMERICAN
¼ cup butter, softened
2 tablespoons honey
3 tablespoons seedless raisins, chopped
¼ cup chopped almonds or walnuts

CHEESE AND HERB SPREAD

METRIC/IMPERIAL
50 g/2 oz butter, softened
75 g/3 oz cheese, finely grated
1 × 15 ml spoon/1 tablespoon cream or creamy milk
1 × 5 ml spoon/1 teaspoon dried mixed herbs
salt
freshly ground black pepper

AMERICAN
¼ cup butter, softened
¾ cup finely grated cheese
1 tablespoon cream or half-and-half
1 teaspoon dried mixed herbs
salt
freshly ground black pepper

CHOCOLATE SPREAD

METRIC/IMPERIAL
50 g/2 oz butter, softened
50 g/2 oz plain chocolate, melted
1 × 15 ml spoon/1 tablespoon black treacle or golden syrup

AMERICAN
¼ cup butter, softened
⅓ cup semi-sweet chocolate pieces, melted
1 tablespoon molasses or light corn syrup

PEPPER ANCHOVY ROLLS

METRIC/IMPERIAL

75 g/3 oz cream cheese, softened
1 × 50 g/2 oz can anchovy fillets, drained and finely chopped
1 cap of canned pimento, finely chopped
2 × 15 ml spoons/2 tablespoons soured cream
freshly ground black pepper
16 slices of white bread, crusts removed
a little melted butter, to finish

AMERICAN

$\frac{1}{3}$ cup cream cheese, softened
1 × 2 oz can anchovy fillets, drained and finely chopped
1 cap of canned pimiento, finely chopped
2 tablespoons sour cream
freshly ground black pepper
16 slices of white bread, crusts removed
a little melted butter, to finish

Put all the ingredients, except the bread and butter, in a bowl and beat well to mix. Spread the mixture on the bread, roll up carefully, then cut each roll in half.
To freeze: pack the rolls in a rigid container, separating each layer with foil. Seal, label and freeze.
To thaw and serve: thaw in the container at room temperature for 2 hours, then brush with melted butter and put under a hot grill (broiler) until golden. Serve hot.
MAKES 32

ASPARAGUS ROLLS

METRIC/IMPERIAL

1 × 450 g/1 lb brown loaf, crusts removed
175 g/6 oz butter, softened
1 × 425 g/15 oz can green asparagus spears, drained

AMERICAN

1 × 1 lb brown loaf, crusts removed
$\frac{3}{4}$ cup butter, softened
1 × 15 oz can green asparagus spears, drained

Slice the bread thinly, then spread with the butter. Place an asparagus spear on each slice, then roll up carefully and cut each roll in half.
To freeze: pack the rolls in a rigid container with the joins underneath, separating each layer with foil. Seal, label and freeze.
To thaw and serve: thaw in the container at room temperature for 4 hours.
MAKES ABOUT 20

STUFFED SAUSAGE LOAF

METRIC/IMPERIAL

1 French loaf
75 g/3 oz unsalted butter, melted
1 green pepper, cored, seeded and chopped
2 celery stalks, chopped
50 g/2 oz button mushrooms, sliced
450 g/1 lb sausages, cooked and diced
175 g/6 oz Gouda cheese, grated
1 egg, beaten

AMERICAN

1 French loaf
$\frac{3}{8}$ cup sweet butter, melted
1 green pepper, cored, seeded and chopped
2 celery stalks, chopped
$\frac{1}{2}$ cup sliced button mushrooms
1 lb sausages, cooked and diced
$1\frac{1}{2}$ cups grated Gouda cheese
1 egg, beaten

Slice the loaf almost through lengthways, leaving a 'hinge'. Scoop out the soft bread from the centre of the loaf, then brush the inside of the shell with some of the melted butter. Put the scooped-out bread on a baking sheet, bake in the oven until crisp, then crumble into fine breadcrumbs.
Heat the remaining butter in a pan, add the green pepper, celery and mushrooms and fry gently until soft. Transfer to a bowl, add the breadcrumbs, sausages, cheese and egg and stir well to mix. Spoon the mixture into the hollowed-out loaf and close the lid.
To freeze: wrap in foil, then pack in a freezer bag. Seal, label and freeze.
To thaw and serve: thaw in the wrappings at room temperature for 2 hours, then place the foil-wrapped loaf on a baking sheet. Bake in a preheated moderately hot oven (190°C/375°F or Gas Mark 5) for 15 minutes, then fold back the foil to uncover the loaf. Increase the heat to hot (220°C/425°F or Gas Mark 7) and bake for a further 10 minutes until crisp.
SERVES 4 to 6

MUSTARD ROLLS (BUNS)

METRIC/IMPERIAL
50 g/2 oz butter, softened
2 × 5 ml spoons/2 teaspoons prepared mustard
1 × 5 ml spoon/1 teaspoon dried mixed herbs
4 bread rolls

AMERICAN
¼ cup butter, softened
2 teaspoons prepared mustard
1 teaspoon dried mixed herbs
4 bread buns

Put the butter, mustard and herbs in a bowl and beat together until evenly blended. Cut the rolls into diagonal slices without cutting right through the base, then spread the butter mixture between the slices and over the top of the rolls (buns).
To freeze: open (flash) freeze until firm, then wrap individually in foil and pack in a freezer bag. Seal, label and return to the freezer.
To thaw and serve: put the foil-wrapped rolls (buns) on a baking sheet and bake from frozen in a preheated moderate oven (180°C/350°F or Gas Mark 4) for 20 minutes. Fold back the foil to uncover the rolls (buns), increase the heat to hot (220°C/425°F or Gas Mark 7) and bake for a further 10 minutes until crisp.
SERVES 4

HAM AND CHEESE PINWHEELS

METRIC/IMPERIAL
1 × 450 g/1 lb brown sandwich loaf, crusts removed
75 g/3 oz butter, softened
225 g/½ lb cream cheese, softened
175 g/6 oz cooked ham, thinly sliced
freshly ground black pepper

AMERICAN
1 × 1 lb brown sandwich loaf, crusts removed
⅜ cup butter, softened
1 cup cream cheese, softened
6 oz cooked ham, thinly sliced
freshly ground black pepper

Slice the bread thinly, spread with the butter, then with the cheese. Arrange the ham on top of the cheese, sprinkle with pepper to taste, then roll up each slice carefully.
To freeze: pack the rolls in a rigid container with the joins underneath, separating each layer with foil. Seal, label and freeze.
To thaw and serve: thaw in the container at room temperature for 2 hours, then slice thinly into pinwheels. Place on a serving platter and leave to thaw completely.
MAKES ABOUT 60

SMOKED SALMON PINWHEELS

METRIC/IMPERIAL
75 g/3 oz butter, softened
2 × 5 ml spoons/2 teaspoons lemon juice
2 × 5 ml spoons/2 teaspoons freshly chopped parsley
1 × 450 g/1 lb white loaf, crusts removed and thinly sliced
175 g/6 oz smoked salmon, thinly sliced

AMERICAN
⅜ cup butter, softened
2 teaspoons lemon juice
2 teaspoons freshly chopped parsley
1 × 1 lb white loaf, crusts removed and thinly sliced
6 oz smoked salmon, thinly sliced

Put the butter, lemon juice and parsley in a bowl and beat together until evenly blended. Spread the mixture on the slices of bread, arrange the salmon on top, then roll up carefully.
To freeze: pack the rolls in a rigid container with the joins underneath, separating each layer with foil. Seal, label and freeze.
To thaw and serve: thaw in the container at room temperature for 2 hours, then slice thinly into pinwheels. Place on a serving platter and leave to thaw completely.
MAKES ABOUT 60

HUMMUS (CHICK PEA AND GARLIC DIP)

METRIC/IMPERIAL

225 g/½ lb dried chick peas, soaked in cold water overnight
2–3 garlic cloves, peeled and crushed
juice of ½–1 lemon, according to taste
3 × 15 ml spoons/3 tablespoons olive oil
2 × 15 ml spoons/2 tablespoons tahina paste
salt
freshly ground black pepper
To finish:
paprika pepper
3 × 15 ml spoons/3 tablespoons olive oil
1 × 15 ml spoon/1 tablespoon freshly chopped parsley

AMERICAN

1 cup dried chick peas, soaked in cold water overnight
2–3 garlic cloves, peeled and crushed
juice of ½–1 lemon, according to taste
3 tablespoons olive oil
2 tablespoons tahina paste
salt
freshly ground black pepper
To finish:
paprika pepper
3 tablespoons olive oil
1 tablespoon freshly chopped parsley

Drain the chick peas and rinse under cold running water. Cook in boiling water for 1 to 1½ hours or until tender. Drain and reserve the cooking liquid.
Put the chick peas and a little of the reserved cooking liquid in an electric blender and work to a smooth purée. Or work the chick peas to a smooth purée in a Mouli-légumes (food mill), then stir in a little of the reserved cooking liquid. Beat in the garlic, the juice of ½ lemon, the olive oil, tahina paste and salt and pepper to taste. Taste and add more lemon juice, if liked.
To freeze: pack in a rigid container, seal, label and freeze.
To thaw and serve: thaw at room temperature for 4 hours, then beat until smooth and spoon into a serving dish. Sprinkle liberally with paprika, pour over the olive oil and sprinkle with parsley. Serve chilled.
SERVES 4

LIVER SAUSAGE DIP

METRIC/IMPERIAL

225 g/½ lb liver sausage, softened
100 g/4 oz cream cheese, softened
75 g/3 oz butter, softened
1 × 15 ml spoon/1 tablespoon snipped chives
1 × 15 ml spoon/1 tablespoon sherry
1 × 5 ml spoon/1 teaspoon freshly chopped parsley
1 × 2.5 ml spoon/½ teaspoon salt
1 × 5 ml spoon/1 teaspoon freshly ground black pepper

AMERICAN

½ lb liver sausage, softened
½ cup cream cheese, softened
⅜ cup butter, softened
1 tablespoon snipped chives
1 tablespoon sherry
1 teaspoon freshly chopped parsley
½ teaspoon salt
1 teaspoon freshly ground black pepper

Put the liver sausage, cream cheese and butter in a bowl, beat together until smooth, then beat in the remaining ingredients.
To freeze: pack in a rigid container, seal, label and freeze.
To thaw and serve: thaw in the container at room temperature for 3 hours.

BLUE CHEESE AND GREEN PEPPER DIP

METRIC/IMPERIAL

100 g/4 oz Danish blue cheese, softened
2 × 15 ml spoons/2 tablespoons mayonnaise
150 ml/¼ pint soured cream
2 × 15 ml spoons/2 tablespoons finely chopped green pepper
freshly ground black pepper

AMERICAN

¼ lb Danish blue cheese, softened
2 tablespoons mayonnaise
⅔ cup sour cream
2 tablespoons finely chopped green pepper
freshly ground black pepper

Put all the ingredients in a bowl and beat well to mix.
To freeze: transfer to a rigid container, seal, label and freeze.
To thaw and serve: thaw at room temperature for 4 hours, then beat until smooth. Serve chilled with savoury biscuits (crackers).

BLUE CHEESE AND AVOCADO DIP

METRIC/IMPERIAL

100 g/4 oz Danish blue cheese, softened
150 ml/¼ pint soured cream
50 g/2 oz walnuts, chopped
1 avocado
1 × 15 ml spoon/1 tablespoon lemon juice
freshly ground black pepper

AMERICAN

¼ lb Danish blue cheese, softened
⅔ cup sour cream
½ cup chopped walnuts
1 avocado
1 tablespoon lemon juice
freshly ground black pepper

Put the cheese, sour(ed) cream and walnuts in a bowl and beat well to mix. Peel and halve the avocado and remove the stone (seed). Mash the flesh with the lemon juice, then add to the cheese mixture with pepper to taste. Beat well.
To freeze: transfer to a rigid container, seal, label and freeze.
To thaw and serve: thaw at room temperature for 4 hours, then beat until smooth. Chill before serving.

AVOCADO DIP

METRIC/IMPERIAL

2 avocados
75 g/3 oz cream cheese, softened
3 × 15 ml spoons/3 tablespoons lemon juice
1 × 5 ml spoon/1 teaspoon grated onion
1 × 2.5 ml spoon/½ teaspoon Worcestershire sauce
salt
freshly ground black pepper

AMERICAN

2 avocados
⅜ cup cream cheese, softened
3 tablespoons lemon juice
1 teaspoon grated onion
½ teaspoon Worcestershire sauce
salt
freshly ground black pepper

Peel and halve the avocados and remove the stones (seeds). Mash the flesh with a fork, add the remaining ingredients and beat well to mix.
To freeze: transfer to a rigid container, seal, label and freeze.
To thaw and serve: thaw at room temperature for 4 hours, then beat until smooth. Serve chilled with sticks of celery and carrot and sprigs of cauliflower.

PEPPER DIP

METRIC/IMPERIAL

225 g/½ lb cottage cheese
½ green pepper, cored, seeded and finely chopped
½ red pepper, cored, seeded and finely chopped
2 × 5 ml spoons/2 teaspoons tomato purée
50 g/2 oz butter, softened
4 × 15 ml spoons/4 tablespoons milk
salt
freshly ground black pepper

AMERICAN

1 cup cottage cheese
½ green pepper, cored, seeded and finely chopped
½ red pepper, cored, seeded and finely chopped
2 teaspoons tomato paste
¼ cup butter, softened
¼ cup milk
salt
freshly ground black pepper

Put all the ingredients in a bowl and beat well to mix.
To freeze: transfer to a rigid container, seal, label and freeze.
To thaw and serve: thaw at room temperature for 4 hours. then beat until smooth. Serve chilled.

MUSHROOM AND HAM DIP

METRIC/IMPERIAL

150 ml/¼ pint double cream, lightly whipped
150 ml/¼ pint natural yogurt
½ packet of dried mushroom soup mix
50 g/2 oz lean cooked ham, finely chopped
salt
freshly ground black pepper
paprika pepper, to finish

AMERICAN

⅔ cup heavy cream, lightly whipped
⅔ cup unflavored yogurt
½ package of dried mushroom soup mix
¼ cup finely chopped lean cooked ham
salt
freshly ground black pepper
paprika pepper, to finish

Put all the ingredients, except the paprika, in a bowl and stir well to mix.
To freeze: pour into a rigid container, seal, label and freeze.
To thaw and serve: thaw at room temperature for 4 hours, then beat until smooth. Transfer to a serving dish and sprinkle with paprika. Serve chilled.

CHOCOLATE SAUCE

METRIC/IMPERIAL

25 g/1 oz butter
25 g/1 oz cocoa powder
1 × 2.5 ml spoon/½ teaspoon vanilla essence
2 × 15 ml spoons/2 tablespoons water
25 g/1 oz sugar
2 × 15 ml spoons/2 tablespoons golden syrup

AMERICAN

2 tablespoons butter
¼ cup unsweetened cocoa powder
½ teaspoon vanilla extract
2 tablespoons water
2 tablespoons sugar
2 tablespoons light corn syrup

Put all the ingredients in a pan and heat gently until the cocoa and sugar have dissolved, stirring constantly. Bring to the boil, then simmer for 3 minutes.
To freeze: cool quickly, then pour into a rigid container. Seal, label and freeze.
To thaw and serve: thaw in the container for 1 hour, then reheat gently on top of the stove, stirring constantly. Serve with ice cream.
SERVES 4 to 6

RICH CHOCOLATE SAUCE

METRIC/IMPERIAL

100 g/4 oz plain chocolate broken into pieces
4 × 15 ml spoons/4 tablespoons evaporated milk
2 × 15 ml spoons/2 tablespoons golden syrup

AMERICAN

⅔ cup semi-sweet chocolate pieces
¼ cup evaporated milk
2 tablespoons light corn syrup

Put all the ingredients in a pan and heat gently until melted, stirring once or twice. Do not allow to boil.
To freeze: cool quickly, then pour into a rigid container. Seal, label and freeze.
To thaw and serve: thaw in the container at room temperature for 2 to 3 hours, then beat until smooth before serving.
SERVES 4

SYRUP SAUCE

METRIC/IMPERIAL

4 × 15 ml spoons/4 tablespoons golden syrup
150 ml/¼ pint hot water
1 × 5 ml spoon/1 teaspoon cornflour
2 × 15 ml spoons/2 tablespoons cold water
lemon juice, to taste

AMERICAN

¼ cup light corn syrup
⅔ cup hot water
1 teaspoon cornstarch
2 tablespoons cold water
lemon juice, to taste

Put the syrup and hot water in a pan and heat gently until the syrup has melted, stirring occasionally. Mix the cornflour (cornstarch) with the cold water, remove the pan from the heat and blend in the paste. Return to the heat and boil for 3 minutes. Add lemon juice to taste.
To freeze: cool quickly, then pour into a rigid container. Seal, label and freeze.
To thaw and serve: reheat from frozen on top of the stove, stirring occasionally. Stir in a little water if a thinner sauce is required.
SERVES 4

MARMALADE SAUCE

Make as for Syrup Sauce (see above), substituting 4 × 15 ml spoons/4 tablespoons/¼ cup marmalade for the syrup.
Freeze, thaw and serve as for Syrup Sauce.
SERVES 4

JAM SAUCE

Make as for Syrup Sauce (see above), substituting 4 × 15 ml spoons/4 tablespoons/¼ cup jam for the syrup.
Freeze, thaw and serve as for Syrup Sauce.
SERVES 4

CARAMEL (FUDGE) SAUCE

METRIC/IMPERIAL

25 g/1 oz butter
75 g/3 oz soft brown sugar
1 × 212 g/7½ oz can evaporated milk
1 × 15 ml spoon/1 tablespoon cornflour
pinch of salt
2 × 15 ml spoons/2 tablespoons water
25 g/1 oz walnuts, chopped, or blanched almonds chopped and toasted (optional)

AMERICAN

2 tablespoons butter
½ cup light brown sugar
1 × 7½ oz can evaporated milk
1 tablespoon cornstarch
pinch of salt
2 tablespoons water
¼ cup chopped walnuts, or blanched almonds, chopped and toasted (optional)

Melt the butter in a pan, add the sugar and stir until dissolved. Bring to the boil and simmer for 1 minute, then pour in the evaporated milk and bring slowly to the boil.
Mix the cornflour (cornstarch) and salt to a paste with the water, then pour slowly into the pan, stirring constantly. Simmer until thick and smooth, then remove from the heat and stir in the nuts, if using.
To freeze: cool quickly, then pour into a rigid container. Seal, label and freeze.
To thaw and serve: thaw in the container at room temperature for 2 hours, then reheat gently on top of the stove, beating constantly until smooth. Serve hot with ice cream.
MAKES 300 ml/½ pint/1¼ cups

BRANDY SAUCE

METRIC/IMPERIAL

25 g/1 oz cornflour
600 ml/1 pint milk
2 × 15 ml spoons/2 tablespoons caster sugar
2 × 15 ml spoons/2 tablespoons brandy
15 g/½ oz butter

AMERICAN

¼ cup cornstarch
2½ cups milk
2 tablespoons sugar
2 tablespoons brandy
1 tablespoon butter

Mix the cornflour (cornstarch) to a paste with 2 × 15 ml spoons/2 tablespoons milk. Heat the remaining milk until hot but not boiling, remove from the heat and stir into the paste. Return the mixture to the rinsed-out pan, bring to the boil and simmer for 2 minutes, stirring constantly. Remove from the heat and stir in the remaining ingredients.
To freeze: cool quickly, then pour into a rigid container. Seal, label and freeze.
To thaw and serve: reheat from frozen in the top of a double boiler, stirring constantly. Serve hot with Christmas pudding.
MAKES 600 ml/1 pint/2½ cups

CHERRY SAUCE

METRIC/IMPERIAL

100 g/4 oz fresh cherries, stoned
150 ml/¼ pint water
40 g/1½ oz caster sugar
juice of ½ lemon
2 × 5 ml spoons/2 teaspoons cornflour
1 × 15 ml spoon/1 tablespoon cherry brandy or kirsch (optional)

AMERICAN

¼ lb fresh cherries, pitted
⅔ cup water
3 tablespoons sugar
juice of ½ lemon
2 teaspoons cornstarch
1 tablespoon cherry brandy or kirsch (optional)

Put the cherries in a pan with the water, sugar and lemon juice. Cover and simmer for 15 minutes.

Mix the cornflour (cornstarch) to a paste with a little water, then stir in 2 × 15 ml spoons/2 tablespoons of the cherry liquid. Stir this mixture into the pan, then simmer for 2 minutes, stirring constantly. Remove from the heat and stir in the cherry brandy or kirsch, if using.

To freeze: cool quickly, then pour into a rigid container. Seal, label and freeze.

To thaw and serve: thaw in the container at room temperature for 2 to 3 hours.

SERVES 4

BUTTERSCOTCH SAUCE

METRIC/IMPERIAL

50 g/2 oz butter
175 g/6 oz soft brown sugar
4 × 15 ml spoons/4 tablespoons milk
1 × 15 ml spoon/1 tablespoon honey

AMERICAN

¼ cup butter
1 cup light brown sugar
¼ cup milk
1 tablespoon honey

Put all the ingredients in a pan and cook over gentle heat for 20 to 30 minutes until the sugar has dissolved and the sauce has become dark and thick.

To freeze: cool quickly, then pour into a rigid container. Seal, label and freeze.

To thaw and serve: thaw in the container at room temperature for 2 to 3 hours. Serve with ice cream.

SERVES 4

APRICOT SAUCE

METRIC/IMPERIAL

25 g/1 oz dried apricots, cooked in 300 ml/½ pint water and sugar to taste
1 × 15 ml spoon/1 tablespoon cornflour
1–2 × 15 ml spoons/1–2 tablespoons caster sugar
1–2 × 5 ml spoons/1–2 teaspoons lemon juice

AMERICAN

3 tablespoons roughly chopped dried apricots, cooked in 1¼ cups water and sugar to taste
1 tablespoon cornstarch
1–2 tablespoons sugar
1–2 teaspoons lemon juice

Drain the apricots and reserve 300 ml/½ pint/1¼ cups cooking liquid. Work the apricots to a smooth purée through a fine sieve (strainer). Put the cornflour (cornstarch) in a pan and gradually blend in the reserved cooking liquid and the sugar. Bring to the boil, then simmer for 3 minutes, stirring constantly. Stir in the apricot purée, taste for sweetness and add the lemon juice.

To freeze: cool quickly, then pour into rigid container. Seal, label and freeze.

To thaw and serve: thaw in the container at room temperature for 2 to 3 hours, then serve cold. Or reheat gently from frozen on top of the stove, stirring occasionally, and serve hot.

SERVES 4 to 6

BRANDY BUTTER

METRIC/IMPERIAL

100 g/4 oz unsalted butter, softened
2 × 5 ml spoons/2 teaspoons finely grated lemon or orange rind
100 g/4 oz caster sugar
2–3 × 15 ml spoons/2–3 tablespoons brandy

AMERICAN

½ cup sweet butter, softened
2 teaspoons finely grated lemon or orange rind
½ cup sugar
2–3 tablespoons brandy

Put the butter and grated rind in a bowl and beat together until creamy. Add the sugar and brandy together a little at a time, and beat until light and fluffy.

To freeze: pack in a rigid container, seal, label and freeze.

To thaw and serve: thaw in the container at room temperature for 2 to 3 hours. Serve with Christmas pudding.

SERVES 4

CUMBERLAND RUM BUTTER

METRIC/IMPERIAL

100 g/4 oz unsalted butter
1 × 5 ml spoon/1 teaspoon finely grated lemon rind
1 × 5 ml spoon/1 teaspoon lemon juice
100 g/4 oz soft brown sugar
2–3 × 15 ml spoons/2–3 tablespoons rum
pinch of grated nutmeg
pinch of ground cinnamon

AMERICAN

½ cup sweet butter
1 teaspoon finely grated lemon rind
1 teaspoon lemon juice
⅔ cup light brown sugar
2–3 tablespoons rum
pinch of grated nutmeg
pinch of ground cinnamon

Put the butter, lemon rind and juice in a bowl and beat together until creamy. Add the sugar and rum together a little at a time, and beat until light and fluffy. Beat in the nutmeg and cinnamon.
To freeze: pack in a rigid container, seal, label and freeze.
To thaw and serve: thaw in the container at room temperature for 2 to 3 hours.
SERVES 4

HONEY AND CINNAMON SAUCE

METRIC/IMPERIAL

1 × 15 ml spoon/1 tablespoon cornflour
0.5 × 2.5 ml spoon/¼ teaspoon ground cinnamon
0.5 × 2.5 ml spoon/¼ teaspoon salt
175 ml/6 fl oz water
4 × 15 ml spoons/4 tablespoons honey
1 × 5 ml spoon/1 teaspoon butter

AMERICAN

1 tablespoon cornstarch
¼ teaspoon ground cinnamon
¼ teaspoon salt
¾ cup water
¼ cup honey
1 teaspoon butter

Sift the cornflour (cornstarch), cinnamon and salt into a bowl and mix to a paste with a little of the water. Put the honey and the remaining water in a pan and heat gently until the honey has melted, stirring occasionally.
Stir the honey mixture into the paste, return to the rinsed-out pan and simmer until the sauce is thick and smooth, stirring constantly. Stir in the butter and beat constantly until melted.
To freeze: cool quickly, then pour into a rigid container. Seal, label and freeze.
To thaw and freeze: thaw in the container at room temperature for 2 hours, then reheat gently on top of the stove, stirring constantly.
SERVES 4 to 6

RASPBERRY SAUCE

METRIC/IMPERIAL

3 × 15 ml spoons/3 tablespoons redcurrant or raspberry jelly
175 g/6 oz fresh raspberries
2 × 15 ml spoons/2 tablespoons hot water
50 g/2 oz sugar
2 × 5 ml spoons/2 teaspoons arrowroot
1 × 15 ml spoon/1 tablespoon cold water
a squeeze of lemon juice, or to taste

AMERICAN

3 tablespoons redcurrant or raspberry jelly
6 oz fresh raspberries
2 tablespoons hot water
¼ cup sugar
2 teaspoons arrowroot flour
1 tablespoon cold water
a squeeze of lemon juice, or to taste

Put the jelly, raspberries, hot water and sugar in a pan and heat gently until the jelly and sugar have dissolved, stirring occasionally. Mix the arrowroot to a paste with the cold water and stir into the sauce. Bring to the boil and simmer for 2 minutes, then remove from the heat and rub through a fine sieve (strainer). Add lemon juice to taste.
To freeze: cool quickly, then pour into a rigid container. Seal, label and freeze.
To thaw and serve: thaw in the container at room temperature for 2 to 3 hours, then beat until smooth before serving. Serve with peaches and ice cream.
SERVES 4

APPLE SAUCE

METRIC/IMPERIAL
450 g/1 lb cooking apples, peeled, cored and sliced
120 ml/4 fl oz water
25 g/1 oz butter
To finish:
knob of butter
salt and freshly ground black pepper, or sugar, to taste

AMERICAN
1 lb baking apples, peeled, cored and sliced
½ cup water
2 tablespoons butter
To finish:
knob of butter
salt and freshly ground black pepper, or sugar, to taste

Put the apples, water and butter in a pan and bring to the boil. Cover and simmer for 15 minutes or until the apples are soft and fluffy. Cover and simmer for 15 minutes or 15 minutes or until the apples are soft and fluffy. Remove from the heat and beat with a wooden spoon until completely smooth.
To freeze: cool quickly, then pour into a rigid container. Seal, label and freeze.
To thaw and serve: melt the knob of butter in a pan, add the frozen apple sauce and heat through gently, stirring constantly. Add salt and pepper, or sugar, to taste. Apple sauce may also be served cold: thaw in the container at room temperature for 2 to 3 hours, then add salt and pepper, or sugar, to taste.

BLACKCURRANT SAUCE

METRIC/IMPERIAL
450 g/1 lb blackcurrants
4 × 15 ml spoons/4 tablespoons water
approx 100 g/4 oz caster sugar, or to taste

AMERICAN
1 lb blackcurrants
¼ cup water
approx ½ cup sugar, or to taste

Put the blackcurrants and water in a pan, cover and simmer until the fruit is soft. Sweeten to taste with (caster) sugar.
Work the fruit and juice to a smooth purée through a fine sieve (strainer), or work in an electric blender, then strain.
To freeze: cool quickly. Pour into a rigid container, then seal, label and freeze. Or freeze in an ice-cube tray until solid, then pack the cubes in a freezer bag. Seal, label and return to the freezer.
To thaw and serve: thaw in the container at room temperature for 2 to 3 hours. Use frozen cubes as required.
MAKES 300 ml/½ pint/1¼ cups

PIQUANT SAUCE

METRIC/IMPERIAL
20 g/¾ oz butter
20 g/¾ oz flour
300 ml/½ pint beef stock
1 × 15 ml spoon/1 tablespoon horseradish sauce
1 × 15 ml spoon/1 tablespoon prepared English mustard
salt
freshly ground black pepper

AMERICAN
1½ tablespoons butter
3 tablespoons flour
1¼ cups beef stock
1 tablespoon horseradish sauce
1 tablespoon prepared English mustard
salt
freshly ground black pepper

Melt the butter in a pan, stir in the flour and cook for 2 minutes, stirring constantly. Remove from the heat and gradually stir in the stock. Return to the heat and bring to the boil, stirring constantly. Simmer until thick, then stir in the remaining ingredients.
To freeze: cool quickly, then pour into a rigid container. Seal, label and freeze.
To thaw and serve: thaw at room temperature for 2 hours, then reheat in the top of a double boiler.
MAKES 300 ml/½ pint/1¼ cups

TOMATO CREAM SAUCE

METRIC/IMPERIAL

1 × 225 g/8 oz can tomatoes
1 × 5 ml spoon/1 teaspoon sugar
1 spring onion, trimmed and finely chopped
1 × 5 ml spoon/1 teaspoon Worcestershire sauce
salt
freshly ground black pepper
150 ml/¼ pint double cream

AMERICAN

1 × ½ lb can tomatoes
1 teaspoon sugar
1 scallion, trimmed and finely chopped
1 teaspoon Worcestershire sauce
salt
freshly ground black pepper
⅔ cup heavy cream

Put all the ingredients, except the cream, in an electric blender and work to a smooth purée. Stir in the cream.
To freeze: pour into a rigid container, seal, label and freeze.
To thaw and serve: thaw at room temperature for 4 hours, then beat until smooth before serving.
MAKES 300 ml/½ pint/1¼ cups

HORSERADISH CREAM

METRIC/IMPERIAL

1 × 5 ml spoon/1 teaspoon creamed horseradish
150 ml/¼ pint double cream, lightly whipped
juice of ½ lemon
paprika pepper, to finish

AMERICAN

1 teaspoon creamed horseradish
⅔ cup heavy cream, lightly whipped
juice of ½ lemon
paprika pepper, to finish

Fold the horseradish into the cream, then stir in the lemon juice.
To freeze: spoon into a rigid container, seal, label and freeze.
To thaw and serve: thaw in the refrigerator for 6 hours, then beat until smooth. Spoon into a serving dish and sprinkle with paprika.
MAKES 150 ml/¼ pint/⅔ cup

CRANBERRY RELISH

METRIC/IMPERIAL

225 g/½ lb fresh cranberries
1 cooking apple, cored and finely chopped
1 orange, peeled and minced, with the pips removed
1 lemon, peeled and minced, with the pips removed
225 g/½ lb sugar

AMERICAN

½ lb fresh cranberries
1 baking apple, cored and finely chopped
1 orange, peeled and ground, with the seeds removed
1 lemon, peeled and ground, with the seeds removed
1 cup sugar

Work the cranberries and apple to a smooth purée in an electric blender. Stir in the orange and lemon flesh and the sugar.
To freeze: pour into a rigid container, seal, label and freeze.
To thaw and serve: thaw at room temperature for 4 hours, then beat until smooth. Serve with turkey.

CRANBERRY SAUCE

METRIC/IMPERIAL

150 ml/¼ pint water
175 g/6 oz sugar
225 g/½ lb fresh cranberries

AMERICAN

⅔ cup water
¾ cup sugar
½ lb fresh cranberries

Put the water and sugar in a pan and heat gently until the sugar has dissolved. Add the cranberries and cook briskly for 2 to 3 minutes or until the skins pop open. Reduce the heat and simmer, uncovered, for 15 minutes or until the cranberries are soft.
For a smooth sauce, rub the hot sauce through a fine sieve (strainer).
To freeze: cool quickly, then pour into a rigid container. Seal, label and freeze.
To thaw and serve: thaw in the container at room temperature for 2 to 3 hours and serve cold. Or reheat from frozen on top of the stove, stirring occasionally, and serve hot. Serve with poultry, game and lamb.
SERVES 6

SIMPLE WHITE SAUCE

METRIC/IMPERIAL
50 g/2 oz cornflour
600 ml/1 pint milk
15 g/½ oz butter
salt
freshly ground black pepper

AMERICAN
½ cup cornstarch
2½ cups milk
1 tablespoon butter
salt
freshly ground black pepper

Mix the cornflour (cornstarch) to a paste with a little of the milk. Heat the rest of the milk, then stir into the paste. Pour into the rinsed-out pan and bring to the boil, stirring constantly. Simmer until thick, then remove from the heat and stir in the butter and salt and pepper.
To freeze: cool quickly, then pour into a rigid container. Seal, label and freeze.
To thaw and serve: reheat from frozen in the top of a double boiler, stirring constantly.
MAKES 600 ml/1 pint/2½ cups

WATERCRESS SAUCE

METRIC/IMPERIAL
1 bunch of watercress
150 ml/¼ pint chicken stock
1 × 5 ml spoon/1 teaspoon gelatine
150 ml/¼ pint double cream
salt
freshly ground black pepper

AMERICAN
1 bunch of watercress
⅔ cup chicken stock
1 teaspoon unflavored gelatin
⅔ cup heavy cream
salt
freshly ground black pepper

Put the watercress and stock in a pan and cook gently for a few minutes. Leave to cool slightly, then work to a smooth purée in an electric blender. Leave until cold.
Stir in the gelatine, then add the cream and salt and pepper to taste.
To freeze: pour into a rigid container, seal, label and freeze.
To thaw and serve: thaw at room temperature for 4 hours, then beat until smooth before serving.
MAKES 300 ml/½ pint/1¼ cups

BREAD SAUCE

METRIC/IMPERIAL
1 small onion, peeled and stuck with 4 cloves
6 peppercorns
1 blade of mace
½ bay leaf
300 ml/½ pint milk
25 g/1 oz butter
50 g/2 oz fresh white breadcrumbs
2 × 15 ml spoons/2 tablespoons single cream
salt
freshly ground black pepper

AMERICAN
1 small onion, peeled and stuck with 4 cloves
6 peppercorns
1 blade of mace
½ bay leaf
1¼ cups milk
2 tablespoons butter
1 cup fresh white breadcrumbs
2 tablespoons light cream
salt
freshly ground black pepper

Put the onion in a pan with the peppercorns, mace, bay leaf, milk and butter. Bring slowly to the boil. Cover and simmer for 15 minutes. Strain the milk into a bowl and stir in the remaining ingredients.
To freeze: cool quickly, then pour into a rigid container. Seal, label and freeze.
To thaw and serve: thaw at room temperature for 2 hours, then reheat gently on top of the stove, stirring occasionally.
MAKES 300 ml/½ pint/1¼ cups

SPICY CUMBERLAND SAUCE

METRIC/IMPERIAL
225 g/½ lb redcurrant jelly
finely grated rind and juice of 1 large orange
juice of ½ lemon
1.5 × 5 ml spoons/1½ teaspoons mustard powder
1 × 5 ml spoon/1 teaspoon Worcestershire sauce
pinch of ground ginger
pinch of cayenne pepper (optional)
4 × 15 ml spoons/4 tablespoons port

AMERICAN
¾ cup redcurrant jelly
finely grated rind and juice of 1 large orange
juice of ½ lemon
1½ teaspoons mustard powder
1 teaspoon Worcestershire sauce
pinch of ground ginger

pinch of cayenne pepper (optional)
¼ cup port

Put all the ingredients, except the port, in a pan and heat gently until the jelly has dissolved, stirring occasionally. Remove from the heat and stir in the port.
To freeze: cool quickly, then pour into a rigid container. Seal, label and freeze.
To thaw and serve: thaw at room temperature for 4 hours, then beat until smooth. Serve with lamb.
SERVES 4

SWEET AND SOUR SAUCE

METRIC/IMPERIAL
150 ml/¼ pint vinegar
150 ml/¼ pint water
4 × 15 ml spoons/4 tablespoons honey
1 × 5 ml spoon/1 teaspoon soy sauce
1 × 5 ml spoon/1 teaspoon ground ginger
1 × 225 g/8 oz can pineapple cubes or slices
1 × 15 ml spoon/1 tablespoon cornflour

AMERICAN
⅔ cup vinegar
⅔ cup water
¼ cup honey
1 teaspoon soy sauce
1 teaspoon ground ginger
1 × ½ lb can pineapple cubes or slices
1 tablespoon cornstarch

Put all the ingredients, except the cornflour (cornstarch), in a pan and bring slowly to the boil. Mix the cornflour (cornstarch) to a paste with a little cold water. Stir into the sauce, bring back to the boil and simmer until thick, stirring constantly.
To freeze: cool quickly, then pour into a rigid container. Seal, label and freeze.
To thaw and serve: thaw at room temperature for 2 hours, then reheat gently on top of the stove, stirring constantly.
SERVES 4

CHEESE SAUCE

METRIC/IMPERIAL
50 g/2 oz butter
50 g/2 oz flour
600 ml/1 pint milk
100 g/4 oz cheese, grated
salt
freshly ground black pepper

AMERICAN
¼ cup butter
½ cup flour
2½ cups milk
1 cup grated cheese
salt
freshly ground black pepper

Melt the butter in a pan, stir in the flour and cook for 2 minutes, stirring constantly. Remove from the heat and gradually stir in the milk. Return to the heat and bring to the boil, stirring constantly. Simmer until thick, then stir in the cheese and salt and pepper to taste.
To freeze: cool quickly, then pour into a rigid container. Seal, label and freeze.
To thaw and serve: reheat the sauce from frozen with 2 × 15 ml spoons/2 tablespoons milk on top of the stove, stirring constantly.
MAKES 600 ml/1 pint/2½ cups

TOMATO RELISH

METRIC/IMPERIAL
15 g/½ oz butter
1 small onion, peeled and finely chopped
150 ml/¼ pint stock or water
150 ml/¼ pint tomato ketchup
1 × 15 ml spoon/1 tablespoon capers
1 × 15 ml spoon/1 tablespoon chopped gherkins
salt
freshly ground black pepper

AMERICAN
1 tablespoon butter
1 small onion, peeled and finely chopped
⅔ cup stock or water
⅔ cup tomato ketchup
1 tablespoon capers
1 tablespoon chopped dill pickle
salt
freshly ground black pepper

Melt the butter in a pan, add the onion and fry gently until soft. Stir in the remaining ingredients, bring to the boil and simmer for 10 to 15 minutes or until thick, stirring constantly.
To freeze: cool quickly, then pour into a rigid container. Seal, label and freeze.
To thaw and serve: thaw at room temperature for 4 hours, then beat until smooth before serving.

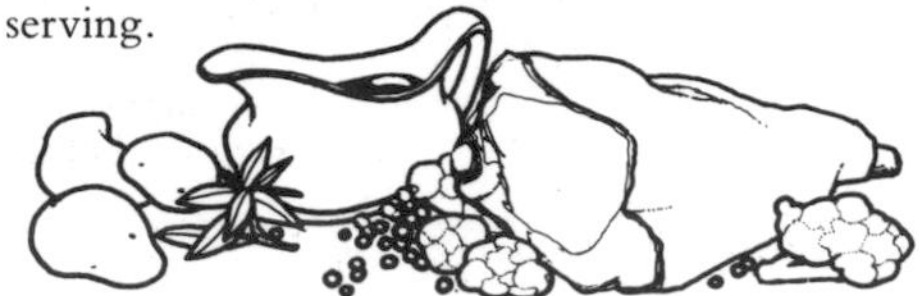

ALL-IN-ONE ESPAGNOLE SAUCE

METRIC/IMPERIAL
50 g/2 oz butter
50 g/2 oz flour
3 streaky bacon rashers, rinds removed and chopped
1 onion, peeled and chopped
1 carrot, peeled and sliced
100 g/4 oz mushrooms, sliced
600 ml/1 pint beef stock
2 × 15 ml spoons/2 tablespoons tomato purée
pinch of dried mixed herbs
salt
freshly ground black pepper

AMERICAN
¼ cup butter
½ cup flour
3 fatty bacon slices, chopped
1 onion, peeled and chopped
1 carrot, peeled and sliced
1 cup sliced mushrooms
2½ cups beef stock
2 tablespoons tomato paste
pinch of dried mixed herbs
salt
freshly ground black pepper

Put the butter, flour, bacon and vegetables in a pan and fry gently for 5 to 10 minutes, stirring occasionally. Stir in the remaining ingredients, bring to the boil and simmer for 1 hour. Strain, then taste and adjust the seasoning.
To freeze: cool quickly, then pour into a rigid container. Seal, label and freeze.
To thaw and serve: thaw at room temperature for 2 hours, then reheat gently on top of the stove, stirring occasionally.
MAKES 600 ml/1 pint/2½ cups

RICH BROWN SAUCE

METRIC/IMPERIAL
25 g/1 oz lard
2 streaky bacon rashers, rinds removed and chopped
1 onion, peeled and chopped
1 carrot, peeled and chopped
25 g/1 oz mushroom stalks, chopped
2 × 15 ml spoons/2 tablespoons flour
900 ml/1½ pints beef stock
2 × 15 ml spoons/2 tablespoons tomato purée
2 × 15 ml spoons/2 tablespoons Worcestershire sauce
salt
freshly ground black pepper

AMERICAN
2 tablespoons lard
2 fatty bacon slices, chopped
1 onion, peeled and chopped
1 carrot, peeled and chopped
¼ cup chopped mushroom stalks
2 tablespoons flour
3¾ cups beef stock
2 tablespoons tomato paste
2 tablespoons Worcestershire sauce
salt
freshly ground black pepper

Melt the lard in a pan, add the bacon and fry for 2 minutes. Add the vegetables and fry for a further 5 minutes. Stir in the flour and cook for 2 minutes, stirring constantly. Remove from the heat and gradually stir in the stock and the remaining ingredients. Return to the heat and bring to the boil, stirring constantly. Simmer for 1 hour, stirring occasionally, then rub the sauce through a sieve (strainer).
To freeze: cool quickly, then pour into a rigid container. Seal, label and freeze.
To thaw and serve: reheat from frozen on top of the stove, stirring occasionally.
MAKES 900 ml/1½ pints/3¾ cups

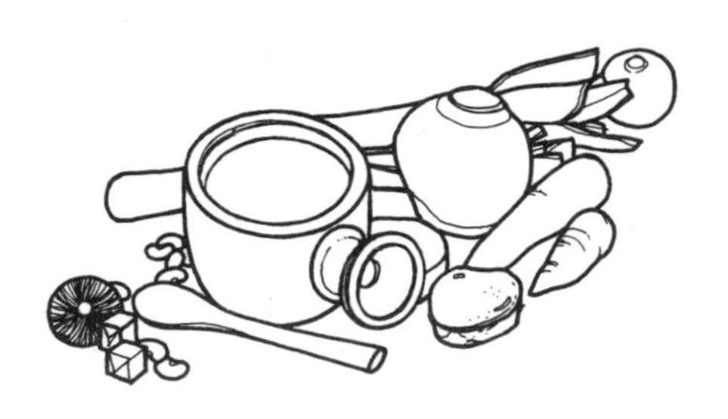

BARBECUE SAUCE

METRIC/IMPERIAL

1 × 15 ml spoon/1 tablespoon fruit sauce
2 × 15 ml spoons/2 tablespoons soy sauce
2 × 15 ml spoons/2 tablespoons clear honey
2 × 15 ml spoons/2 tablespoons tomato ketchup
1 × 15 ml spoon/1 tablespoon Worcestershire sauce
1 × 5 ml spoon/1 teaspoon prepared French mustard
freshly ground black pepper
2 × 15 ml spoons/2 tablespoons water

AMERICAN

1 tablespoon fruit sauce
2 tablespoons soy sauce
2 tablespoons clear honey
2 tablespoons tomato ketchup
1 tablespoon Worcestershire sauce
1 teaspoon prepared French mustard
freshly ground black pepper
2 tablespoons water

Put all the ingredients in a pan and stir over a gentle heat until the sauce is smooth. Boil briskly for 5 minutes or until thick.
To freeze: cool quickly, then pour into small pots or ice-cube trays. Freeze until firm, then remove the cubes of sauce and pack in a freezer bag. Seal, label and return to the freezer.
To thaw and serve: reheat gently from frozen on top of the stove, beating constantly until smooth. Serve with meat and poultry.

TOMATO SAUCE

METRIC/IMPERIAL

4 × 15 ml spoons/4 tablespoons corn oil
2 medium onions, peeled and chopped
2 garlic cloves, peeled and crushed
1 × 800 g/1 lb 12 oz can tomatoes
2 × 5 ml spoons/2 teaspoons sugar
salt
freshly ground black pepper
2 × 15 ml spoons/2 tablespoons tomato purée
2 bay leaves
300 ml/½ pint stock

AMERICAN

¼ cup corn oil
2 medium onions, peeled and chopped
2 garlic cloves, peeled and crushed
1 × 1 lb 12 oz can tomatoes
2 teaspoons sugar
salt
freshly ground black pepper
2 tablespoons tomato paste
2 bay leaves
1¼ cups stock

Heat the oil in a pan, add the onion and garlic and fry gently until soft. Add the remaining ingredients, cover and simmer for 30 minutes or until quite thick, stirring occasionally.
Remove the bay leaves, then work the sauce to a smooth purée in an electric blender or Mouli-légumes (food mill), or rub through a sieve (strainer). Return to the pan and simmer, uncovered, until thick. Taste and adjust seasoning.
To freeze: cool quickly, then pour into a rigid container. Seal, label and freeze.
To thaw and serve: reheat gently from frozen on top of the stove, stirring occasionally.
MAKES 900 ml/1½ pints/3¾ cups

BOLOGNESE SAUCE

METRIC/IMPERIAL

2 × 15 ml spoons/2 tablespoons corn oil
3 streaky bacon rashers, rinds removed and chopped
450 g/1 lb lean minced beef
1 medium onion, peeled and chopped
1 garlic clove, peeled and crushed
1 celery stalk, chopped
1 × 5 ml spoon/1 teaspoon dried oregano
1 × 2.5 ml spoon/½ teaspoon sugar
150 ml/¼ pint tomato purée
250 ml/8 fl oz beef stock
salt
freshly ground black pepper

AMERICAN

2 tablespoons corn oil
3 fatty bacon slices, chopped
1 lb lean ground beef
1 medium onion, peeled and chopped
1 garlic clove, peeled and crushed
1 celery stalk, chopped
1 teaspoon dried oregano
½ teaspoon sugar
⅔ cup tomato paste
1 cup beef stock
salt
freshly ground black pepper

Heat the oil in a pan, add the bacon and fry until golden brown. Add the beef, onion, garlic and celery and fry gently for 10 minutes until browned, stirring constantly.
Stir in the remaining ingredients and bring to the boil. Cover and simmer for 1 hour, then taste and adjust seasoning.
To freeze: cool quickly, then pour into a rigid container. Seal, label and freeze.
To thaw and serve: reheat gently from frozen on top of the stove, stirring occasionally.
SERVES 4 to 6

DIJON MUSTARD SAUCE

METRIC/IMPERIAL

20 g/$\frac{3}{4}$ oz butter
20 g/$\frac{3}{4}$ oz flour
300 ml/$\frac{1}{2}$ pint milk
1 × 15 ml spoon/1 tablespoon Dijon-style mustard
salt
freshly ground black pepper

AMERICAN

1$\frac{1}{2}$ tablespoons butter
3 tablespoons flour
1$\frac{1}{4}$ cups milk
1 tablespoon Dijon-style mustard
salt
freshly ground black pepper

Melt the butter in a pan, stir in the flour and cook for 2 minutes, stirring constantly. Remove from the heat and gradually stir in the milk. Return to the heat and bring to the boil, stirring constantly. Simmer until thick, then stir in the remaining ingredients.
To freeze: cool quickly, then pour into a rigid container. Seal, label and freeze.
To thaw and serve: thaw at room temperature for 2 hours, then reheat in a double boiler.
MAKES 300 ml/$\frac{1}{2}$ pint/1$\frac{1}{4}$ cups

APPLE AND ONION SAUCE

METRIC/IMPERIAL

15 g/$\frac{1}{2}$ oz butter
2 medium onions, peeled and chopped
450 g/1 lb cooking apples, peeled, cored and chopped
300 ml/$\frac{1}{2}$ pint chicken stock
2 × 15 ml spoons/2 tablespoons Worcestershire sauce
salt
freshly ground black pepper

AMERICAN

1 tablespoon butter
2 medium onions, peeled and chopped
1 lb baking apples, peeled, cored and chopped
1$\frac{1}{4}$ cups chicken stock
2 tablespoons Worcestershire sauce
salt
freshly ground black pepper

Melt the butter in a pan, add the onion and fry gently until soft. Add the remaining ingredients, bring to the boil, then simmer for 20 to 25 minutes until the apple is soft and pulpy.
To freeze: cool quickly, then pour into a rigid container. Seal, label and freeze.
To thaw and serve: reheat from frozen on top of the stove, stirring occasionally.

MINT SAUCE

METRIC/IMPERIAL

1 large bunch of mint
225 g/$\frac{1}{2}$ lb sugar
150 ml/$\frac{1}{4}$ pint water
vinegar, to finish

AMERICAN

1 large bunch of mint
1 cup sugar
$\frac{2}{3}$ cup water
vinegar, to finish

Wash and dry the mint leaves, then chop finely. Put the sugar and water in a pan and heat gently until the sugar has dissolved. Boil for 3 to 4 minutes. Leave to cool, then pour over the mint in a bowl and stir well to mix.
To freeze: pour the sauce into ice cube trays and open (flash) freeze until firm. Remove the cubes from the trays, then pack in a freezer bag. Seal, label and return to the freezer.
To thaw and serve: put the frozen cubes in a sauceboat, leave to thaw, then stir in a little vinegar to taste.

CURRY SAUCE

METRIC/IMPERIAL

100 g/4 oz lard
2 Spanish onions, peeled and chopped
2 medium cooking apples, peeled, cored and chopped
1 × 15 ml spoon/1 tablespoon curry powder
1 × 15 ml spoon/1 tablespoon ground coriander
1 × 5 ml spoon/1 teaspoon garam masala
50 g/2 oz cornflour
1 litre/1$\frac{3}{4}$ pints beef stock
2 × 5 ml spoons/2 teaspoons tomato purée
finely grated rind and juice of $\frac{1}{2}$ lemon
2 × 5 ml spoons/2 teaspoons brown sugar
2 × 15 ml spoons/2 tablespoons mango chutney
1 × 5 ml spoon/1 teaspoon salt

AMERICAN

$\frac{1}{2}$ cup lard
2 Bermuda onions, peeled and chopped
2 medium baking apples, peeled, cored and chopped
1 tablespoon curry powder
1 tablespoon ground coriander
1 teaspoon garam masala
$\frac{1}{2}$ cup cornstarch
4$\frac{1}{4}$ cups beef stock
2 teaspoons tomato paste
finely grated rind and juice of $\frac{1}{2}$ lemon
2 teaspoons brown sugar
2 tablespoons mango chutney
1 teaspoon salt

Melt the lard in a pan, add the onions and apples and fry gently for 5 minutes or until lightly coloured. Stir in the spices and cornflour (cornstarch) and cook for 2 to 3 minutes. Add the stock and bring to the boil, stirring constantly, then add the remaining ingredients. Cover and simmer for 30 minutes. Taste and adjust seasoning.
If a smooth sauce is liked, work to a smooth purée in an electric blender or Mouli-légumes (food mill), or rub through a sieve (strainer).
To freeze: cool quickly, then pour into a freezer bag placed inside a rigid container. Freeze until firm, then remove the bag from the container. Seal, label and return to the freezer.
To thaw and serve: reheat from frozen in the top of a double boiler. Beat until smooth before serving.
MAKES 1 litre/1¾ pints/4¼ cups

MUSHROOM SAUCE

METRIC/IMPERIAL
25 g/1 oz butter
2 onions, peeled and finely chopped
50 g/2 oz flat mushrooms, chopped
25 g/1 oz flour
600 ml/1 pint beef stock
½ × 15 ml spoons/2 tablespoons Worcestershire sauce
salt
freshly ground black pepper

AMERICAN
2 tablespoons butter
2 onions, peeled and finely chopped
½ cup chopped flat mushrooms
¼ cup flour
2½ cups beef stock
2 tablespoons Worcestershire sauce
salt
freshly ground black pepper

Melt the butter in a pan, add the onions and fry gently until soft. Add the mushrooms and fry for a further 2 minutes. Stir in the flour and cook for 2 minutes. Remove from the heat and gradually stir in the stock. Return to the heat and bring to the boil, stirring constantly. Simmer until thick, then add the Worcestershire sauce and salt and pepper to taste.
To freeze: cool quickly, then pour into a rigid container. Seal, label and freeze.
To thaw and serve: reheat gently from frozen on top of the stove, stirring occasionally.
MAKES 600 ml/1 pint/2½ cups

SAVOURY FILLINGS/SAUCES

METRIC/IMPERIAL
25 g/1 oz butter
25 g/1 oz flour
300 ml/½ pint milk
salt
freshly ground black pepper

AMERICAN
2 tablespoons butter
¼ cup flour
1¼ cups milk
salt
freshly ground black pepper

Melt the butter in a pan, stir in the flour and cook for 2 minutes, stirring constantly. Remove from the heat and gradually stir in the milk. Return to the heat and bring to the boil, stirring constantly. Simmer until thick, then add salt and pepper to taste.
Use with any of the following additions:

METRIC/IMPERIAL
1) *100 g/4 oz cooked chicken, finely chopped*
   50 g/2 oz cooked ham, finely chopped
2) *100 g/4 oz mushrooms, chopped and cooked in butter*
   2 back bacon rashers, rinds removed, chopped and fried until crisp
3) *100 g/4 oz peeled prawns*
   1 × 5 ml spoon/1 teaspoon lemon juice
   2 × 5 ml spoons/2 teaspoons chopped capers
4) *1 × 225 g/8 oz can sweetcorn, drained*

AMERICAN
1) *½ cup finely chopped cooked chicken*
   ¼ cup finely chopped cooked ham
2) *1 cup chopped mushrooms, cooked in butter*
   2 Canadian bacon slices, chopped and fried until crisp
3) *¾ cup shelled shrimp*
   1 teaspoon lemon juice
   2 teaspoons chopped capers
4) *1 × ½ lb can corn kernels, drained*

To freeze: cool quickly, then pour into a rigid container. Seal, label and freeze.
To thaw and serve: thaw at room temperature for 3 hours, then reheat gently on top of the stove, stirring constantly.

APPLE BUTTER (CHEESE)

METRIC/IMPERIAL

675 g/1½ lb cooking apples, quartered
600 ml/1 pint cider
0.5 × 2.5 ml spoon/¼ teaspoon ground cinnamon
3–4 whole cloves, or 0.5 × 2.5 ml spoon/ ¼ teaspoon ground cloves
350 g/¾ lb sugar for each 600 ml/1 pint apple purée

AMERICAN

1½ lb baking apples, quartered
2½ cups hard cider
¼ teaspoon ground cinnamon
3–4 whole cloves, or ¼ teaspoon ground cloves
1½ cups sugar for each 2½ cups applesauce

Put the apples and cider in a pan and simmer until the apples are soft and pulpy. Work to a purée through a sieve (strainer), then measure and calculate the amount of sugar needed.

Return the purée to the rinsed-out pan, add the cinnamon and cloves and the calculated amount of sugar. Stir over a gentle heat until the sugar has dissolved, then increase the heat and boil until thick and creamy, stirring occasionally.

Leave to cool slightly, then spoon into small dry containers or freezerproof jars.

To freeze: cool quickly, then seal, label and freeze.

To thaw and serve: thaw at room temperature for 3 hours, then store in the refrigerator once opened.

MAKES ABOUT 1 kg/2 lb

LEMON CURD (CHEESE)

METRIC/IMPERIAL

4 eggs, or 8 egg yolks
finely grated rind and juice of 4 lemons
225 g/½ lb butter
450 g/1 lb caster sugar

AMERICAN

4 eggs, or 8 egg yolks
finely grated rind and juice of 4 lemons
1 cup butter
2 cups sugar, firmly packed

Put the eggs or egg yolks in a heatproof bowl and beat thoroughly. Stir in the remaining ingredients, stand the bowl over a pan of gently simmering water and stir for 20 to 25 minutes until thick.
Strain into small dry containers or freezerproof jars, then leave to cool.
To freeze: seal, label and freeze.
To thaw and serve: thaw at room temperature for 3 hours, then store in the refrigerator once opened.
MAKES ABOUT 1 kg/2 lb

MINCEMEAT

METRIC/IMPERIAL

675 g/1½ lb seedless raisins, finely chopped or minced
225 g/½ lb cooking apples, peeled, cored and finely chopped or minced
100 g/4 oz candied peel, finely chopped or minced
350 g/¾ lb currants
225 g/½ lb sultanas
175 g/6 oz shredded suet
1 × 2.5 ml spoon/½ teaspoon ground mixed spice
finely grated rind and juice of 2 lemons
450 g/1 lb soft brown sugar
6 × 15 ml spoons/6 tablespoons dry cider

AMERICAN

4 cups seedless raisins, finely chopped or ground
½ lb baking apples, peeled, cored and finely chopped or ground
⅔ cup candied peel, finely chopped or ground
2 cups currants
1⅓ cups seedless white raisins
1 cup shredded suet, firmly packed
¼ teaspoon grated nutmeg
¼ teaspoon ground allspice and cloves, mixed
finely grated rind and juice of 2 lemons
2⅔ cups light brown sugar
6 tablespoons dry hard cider

Put all the ingredients in a bowl and stir well to mix. Cover the bowl, leave to stand overnight, then spoon into small rigid containers or freezer-proof jars.
To freeze: seal, label and freeze.
To thaw and serve: thaw at room temperature for 3 hours, then store in the refrigerator.
MAKES ABOUT 2.25 kg/5 lb

RASPBERRY FREEZER JAM

METRIC/IMPERIAL

1.25 kg/2½ lb raspberries, crushed
1.75 kg/4 lb caster sugar
4 × 15 ml spoons/4 tablespoons lemon juice
1 bottle of liquid fruit pectin

AMERICAN

2½ lb raspberries, crushed
8 cups sugar, firmly packed
¼ cup lemon juice
1 bottle of liquid fruit pectin

Put the crushed raspberries in a bowl, stir in the sugar and lemon juice and leave in a warm place for about 1 hour until the sugar has dissolved, stirring occasionally.
Add the liquid pectin, stir for 2 minutes, then spoon into small dry containers or freezerproof jars. Cover with foil and leave in a warm place for 24 hours.
To freeze: seal the containers or jars, label and freeze.
To thaw and serve: thaw at room temperature for 4 hours, then store in the refrigerator once opened.
MAKES ABOUT 2.75 kg/6 lb

STRAWBERRY FREEZER JAM

METRIC/IMPERIAL

575 g/1¼ lb strawberries, crushed
900 g/2 lb caster sugar
2 × 5 ml spoons/2 teaspoons lemon juice
½ bottle of liquid fruit pectin

AMERICAN

1¼ lb strawberries, crushed
4 cups sugar, firmly packed
2 teaspoons lemon juice
½ bottle of liquid fruit pectin

Put the crushed strawberries in a bowl, stir in the sugar and lemon juice and leave in a warm place for about 1 hour until the sugar has dissolved, stirring occasionally.
Add the liquid pectin, stir for 2 minutes, then spoon into small dry containers or freezerproof jars.
Cover with foil, then leave in a warm place for 48 hours.
To freeze: seal the containers or jars, then label and freeze.
To thaw and serve: thaw at room temperature for 4 hours, then store in the refrigerator once opened.
MAKES ABOUT 1.5 kg/3 lb

ANCHOVY BUTTER

METRIC/IMPERIAL
100 g/4 oz butter, softened
2 × 5 ml spoons/2 teaspoons anchovy essence
freshly ground black pepper

AMERICAN
½ cup butter
2 teaspoons anchovy extract
freshly ground black pepper

Put the butter in a bowl and beat until smooth. Add the anchovy essence (extract) and black pepper gradually and beat until evenly blended, then shape into a long roll.
To freeze: wrap in foil, then pack in a freezer bag. Seal, label and freeze.
To thaw and serve: remove wrappings and cut the frozen butter into slices using a knife dipped into hot water. Serve on canapés, or with poached fish.

MUSTARD BUTTER

METRIC/IMPERIAL
100 g/4 oz butter, softened
1 × 15 ml spoon/1 tablespoon prepared French mustard
salt
freshly ground black pepper

AMERICAN
½ cup butter, softened
1 tablespoon prepared French mustard
salt
freshly ground black pepper

Put the butter in a bowl and beat until smooth. Beat in the mustard gradually, add salt and pepper to taste, then shape into a long roll.
To freeze: wrap in foil, then pack in a freezer bag. Seal, label and freeze.
To thaw and serve: remove wrappings and cut the frozen butter into slices using a knife dipped in hot water. Serve with grilled (broiled) gammon and baked fish.

PARSLEY BUTTER

METRIC/IMPERIAL
100 g/4 oz butter, softened
2 × 15 ml spoons/2 tablespoons freshly chopped parsley
squeeze of lemon juice
salt
freshly ground black pepper

AMERICAN
½ cup butter, softened
2 tablespoons freshly chopped parsley
squeeze of lemon juice
salt
freshly ground black pepper

Put the butter in a bowl and beat until smooth. Add the remaining ingredients gradually and beat until evenly blended, then shape into a long roll.
To freeze: wrap in foil, then pack in a freezer bag. Seal, label and freeze.
To thaw and serve: remove wrappings and cut the frozen butter into slices using a knife dipped in hot water.
Serve with grilled (broiled) meats, fish and hot vegetables.

LEMON BUTTER

METRIC/IMPERIAL
100 g/4 oz butter, softened
2 × 5 ml spoons/2 teaspoons finely grated lemon rind
2 × 5 ml spoons/2 teaspoons lemon juice
2 × 5 ml spoons/2 teaspoons freshly chopped parsley
salt
freshly ground black pepper

AMERICAN
½ cup butter, softened
2 teaspoons finely grated lemon rind
2 teaspoons lemon juice
2 teaspoons freshly chopped parsley
salt
freshly ground black pepper

Put the butter in a bowl and beat until smooth. Add the remaining ingredients gradually and beat until evenly blended, then shape into a long roll.
To freeze: wrap in foil, then pack in a freezer bag. Seal, label and freeze.
To thaw and serve: remove wrappings and cut the frozen butter into slices, using a knife dipped in hot water.
Serve with chicken, fish and veal.

HERB BUTTER

METRIC/IMPERIAL

100 g/4 oz butter, softened
2 × 15 ml spoons/2 tablespoons finely chopped mixed fresh herbs
salt
freshly ground black pepper

AMERICAN

½ cup butter, softened
2 tablespoons finely chopped mixed fresh herbs
salt
freshly ground black pepper

Put the butter in a bowl and beat until smooth. Beat in the herbs gradually, add salt and pepper to taste, then shape into a long roll.
To freeze: wrap in foil, then pack in a freezer bag. Seal, label and freeze.
To thaw and serve: remove wrappings and cut the frozen butter into slices using a knife dipped in hot water. Serve with grilled (broiled) meats and hot vegetables.

TANGERINE STUFFING

METRIC/IMPERIAL

1 × 15 ml spoon/1 tablespoon vegetable oil
1 small onion, peeled and chopped
50 g/2 oz mushrooms, chopped
100 g/4 oz long-grain rice, boiled and drained
2 celery stalks, finely chopped
1 × 15 ml spoon/1 tablespoon freshly chopped parsley
1 tangerine
salt
freshly ground black pepper
1 egg, beaten

AMERICAN

1 tablespoon vegetable oil
1 small onion, peeled and chopped
½ cup chopped mushrooms
⅔ cup long-grain rice, boiled and drained
2 celery stalks, finely chopped
1 tablespoon freshly chopped parsley
1 tangerine
salt
freshly ground black pepper
1 egg, beaten

Heat the oil in a pan, add the onion and mushrooms and fry gently until soft. Transfer to a bowl and stir in the rice, celery and parsley.
Peel the tangerine and cut half the peel into very thin strips. Skin the segments, remove any pith and pips (seeds) and chop the flesh. Add the strips of peel and the chopped flesh to the stuffing with salt and pepper to taste. Bind with the egg.
To freeze: transfer to a rigid container, seal, label and freeze.
To thaw and use: thaw in the refrigerator overnight, or at room temperature for 4 hours, then use as for fresh stuffing.

CRANBERRY STUFFING

METRIC/IMPERIAL

100 g/4 oz fresh white breadcrumbs
175 g/6 oz prunes, soaked, stoned and chopped
1 large cooking apple, peeled, cored and chopped
40 g/1¼ oz blanched almonds, finely chopped
2 × 15 ml spoons/2 tablespoons cranberry sauce
finely grated rind and juice of ½ lemon
salt
freshly ground black pepper
1 × 15 ml spoon/1 tablespoon vegetable oil

AMERICAN

2 cups fresh white breadcrumbs
1 cup prunes, soaked, pitted and chopped
1 large baking apple, peeled, cored and chopped
⅓ cup blanched almonds, finely chopped
2 tablespoons cranberry sauce
finely grated rind and juice of ½ lemon
salt
freshly ground black pepper
1 tablespoon vegetable oil

Put all the ingredients in a bowl and stir well to mix.
To freeze: pack in a rigid container, seal, label and freeze.
To thaw and use: thaw in the refrigerator overnight, or at room temperature for 4 hours, then use as for fresh stuffing.

CELERY AND APPLE STUFFING

METRIC/IMPERIAL

50 g/2 oz butter
1 medium onion, peeled and finely chopped
4 celery stalks, finely diced
1 small cooking apple, peeled, cored and finely diced
175 g/6 oz fresh white breadcrumbs
finely grated rind of 1 small lemon
1 × 15 ml spoon/1 tablespoon lemon juice
2 × 5 ml spoons/2 teaspoons dried sage
salt
freshly ground black pepper
3 × 15 ml spoons/3 tablespoons concentrated giblet stock

AMERICAN

¼ cup butter
1 medium onion, peeled and finely chopped
4 celery stalks, finely diced
1 small baking apple, peeled, cored and finely diced
3 cups fresh white breadcrumbs
finely grated rind of 1 small lemon
1 tablespoon lemon juice
2 teaspoons dried sage
salt
freshly ground black pepper
3 tablespoons concentrated giblet stock

Melt the butter in a pan, add the onion and celery and fry gently until soft. Stir in the apple and fry for a further few minutes. Put in a bowl with the breadcrumbs, lemon rind and juice and the sage. Add salt and pepper to taste and stir well to mix. Bind with the stock.
To freeze: cool quickly, then transfer to a rigid container. Seal, label and freeze.
To thaw and use: thaw in the refrigerator overnight, then use as for fresh stuffing.

CHESTNUT AND SAUSAGEMEAT STUFFING

METRIC/IMPERIAL

1 × 440 g/15½ oz can whole chestnuts, drained and finely chopped
100 g/4 oz fresh white breadcrumbs
225 g/½ lb pork sausagemeat
50 g/2 oz butter
1 celery stalk, chopped
1 onion, peeled and chopped
salt
freshly ground black pepper
1 egg, beaten

AMERICAN

1 × 15½ oz can whole chestnuts, drained and finely chopped
2 cups fresh white breadcrumbs
1 cup pork sausagemeat
¼ cup butter
1 celery stalk, chopped
1 onion, peeled and chopped
salt
freshly ground black pepper
1 egg, beaten

Put the chestnuts in a bowl with the breadcrumbs and sausagemeat and stir well to mix. Melt the butter in a pan, add the celery and onion and fry gently until soft. Add to the bowl with salt and pepper to taste, then bind with the beaten egg.
To freeze: cool quickly, then transfer to a rigid container. Seal, label and freeze.
To thaw and use: thaw in the refrigerator over-overnight, then use as for fresh stuffing.

MUSHROOM AND BACON STUFFING

METRIC/IMPERIAL

175 g/6 oz fresh white breadcrumbs
1 × 15 ml spoon/1 tablespoon freshly chopped parsley
1 × 2.5 ml spoon/½ teaspoon dried thyme
1 garlic clove, peeled and crushed
50 g/2 oz butter
1 medium onion, peeled and chopped
6 streaky bacon rashers, rinds removed and chopped
100 g/4 oz mushrooms, chopped
salt
freshly ground black pepper
1 egg yolk
a little stock or water (optional)

AMERICAN

3 cups fresh white breadcrumbs
1 tablespoon freshly chopped parsley
¼ teaspoon dried thyme
1 garlic clove, peeled and crushed
¼ cup butter
1 medium onion, peeled and chopped
6 fatty bacon slices, chopped
1 cup chopped mushrooms
salt
freshly ground black pepper
1 egg yolk
a little stock or water (optional)

Put the breadcrumbs in a bowl with the parsley, thyme and garlic and stir well to mix. Melt the butter in a pan, add the onion and fry gently until soft. Stir in the bacon and fry for a further 3 to 4 minutes, then stir in the mushrooms and mix well. Add to the breadcrumbs with salt and pepper to taste, then bind with the egg yolk and moisten with stock or water, if necessary.
To freeze: cool quickly, then transfer to a rigid container. Seal, label and freeze.
To thaw and use: thaw in the refrigerator overnight, then use as for fresh stuffing.

APRICOT AND PEANUT STUFFING

METRIC/IMPERIAL

175 g/6 oz fresh white breadcrumbs
100 g/4 oz dried apricots, finely chopped
50 g/2 oz salted peanuts, finely chopped
1 × 15 ml spoon/1 tablespoon freshly chopped parsley
50 g/2 oz butter
1 large onion, peeled and chopped
finely grated rind and juice of 1 small orange
1 × 2.5 ml spoon/½ teaspoon curry powder
salt
freshly ground black pepper
1 small egg, beaten

AMERICAN

3 cups fresh white breadcrumbs
¾ cup dried apricots, finely chopped
½ cup finely chopped salted peanuts
1 tablespoon freshly chopped parsley
¼ cup butter
1 large onion, peeled and chopped
finely grated rind and juice of 1 small orange
½ teaspoon curry powder
salt
freshly ground black pepper
1 small egg, beaten

Put the breadcrumbs in a bowl with the apricots, peanuts and parsley. Melt the butter in a pan, add the onion and fry gently until soft. Remove from the pan with a slotted spoon and add to the breadcrumbs with the grated orange rind and mix well.
Stir the curry powder into the pan, fry gently for 1 minute, then stir in the orange juice. Bring to the boil, then add to the breadcrumbs with salt and pepper to taste. Bind with the beaten egg.
To freeze: cool quickly, then transfer to a rigid container. Seal, label and freeze.
To thaw and use: thaw in the refrigerator overnight, then use as for fresh stuffing.

FORCEMEAT STUFFING

METRIC/IMPERIAL

100 g/4 oz fresh white breadcrumbs
1 × 2.5 ml spoon/½ teaspoon dried mixed herbs or thyme
1 × 5 ml spoon/1 teaspoon freshly chopped parsley
finely grated rind of 1 lemon
50 g/2 oz butter, melted
salt
freshly ground black pepper
1 egg, beaten
a little milk

AMERICAN

2 cups fresh white breadcrumbs
½ teaspoon dried mixed herbs or thyme
1 teaspoon freshly chopped parsley
finely grated rind of 1 lemon
¼ cup butter, melted
salt
freshly ground black pepper
1 egg, beaten
a little milk

Put all the ingredients in a bowl and stir well to mix.
To freeze: pack in a rigid container, seal, label and freeze.
To thaw and use: thaw at room temperature for 4 hours, then use as for fresh stuffing.
Use for stuffing chicken, turkey and veal.

RICH FORCEMEAT STUFFING

Make as for Forcemeat Stuffing (see above), adding 75 g/3 oz/⅓ cup chopped cooked ham or bacon, a little grated nutmeg and ground mace. Freeze, thaw and use as for Forcemeat Stuffing.

APPLE AND RAISIN STUFFING

METRIC/IMPERIAL

1 large cooking apple, peeled, cored and chopped
100 g/4 oz seedless raisins
50 g/2 oz fresh white breadcrumbs
1 × 15 ml spoon/1 tablespoon sweet chutney
1 × 5 ml spoon/1 teaspoon Worcestershire sauce
salt
freshly ground black pepper
1 egg, beaten

AMERICAN

1 large baking apple, peeled, cored and chopped
¾ cup seedless raisins
1 cup fresh white breadcrumbs
1 tablespoon sweet chutney
1 teaspoon Worcestershire sauce
salt
freshly ground black pepper
1 egg, beaten

Put all the ingredients in a bowl and stir well to mix.
To freeze: pack in a rigid container, seal, label and freeze.
To thaw and use: thaw in the refrigerator overnight, or at room temperature for 4 hours, then use as for fresh stuffing.

CELERY, PARSLEY AND MINT STUFFING

METRIC/IMPERIAL

100 g/4 oz fresh white breadcrumbs
1 × 5 ml spoon/1 teaspoon dried sage
2 celery stalks, finely chopped
1 × 15 ml spoon/1 tablespoon freshly chopped parsley
1 × 5 ml spoon/1 teaspoon freshly chopped mint
finely grated rind of ½ lemon
50 g/2 oz butter, melted
salt
freshly ground black pepper
1 egg, beaten

AMERICAN

2 cups fresh white breadcrumbs
1 small onion, peeled and finely chopped
2 celery stalks, finely chopped
1 tablespoon freshly chopped parsley
1 teaspoon freshly chopped mint
finely grated rind of ½ lemon
¼ cup butter, melted
salt
freshly ground black pepper
1 egg, beaten

Put all the ingredients in a bowl and stir well to mix.
To freeze: pack in a rigid container, seal, label and freeze.
To thaw and use: thaw in the refrigerator overnight, or at room temperature for 4 hours, then use as for fresh stuffing.

PEANUT STUFFING BALLS

METRIC/IMPERIAL

175 g/6 oz fresh white breadcrumbs
15 g/½ oz fresh parsley, chopped
1 × 2.5 ml spoon/½ teaspoon freshly ground black pepper
100 g/4 oz salted peanuts, ground
50 g/2 oz butter
1 egg, beaten

AMERICAN

3 cups fresh white breadcrumbs
⅓ cup freshly chopped parsley
½ teaspoon freshly ground black pepper
1 cup salted peanuts, ground
¼ cup butter
1 egg, beaten

Put the breadcrumbs, parsley, pepper and peanuts in a bowl. Add the butter in pieces and work in with the fingertips. Bind with the beaten egg, then roll into 12 small balls about the size of walnuts.
To freeze: open (flash) freeze until firm, then pack in a rigid container, separating each layer with foil. Seal, label and freeze.
To thaw and serve: fry gently from frozen in hot shallow oil until crisp and heated through, turning occasionally. Or dot with butter and reheat from frozen in a preheated hot oven (220°C/425°F or Gas Mark 7) for 20 minutes or until heated through.
MAKES 12

HERB AND ORANGE STUFFING

METRIC/IMPERIAL

25 g/1 oz butter
2 onions, peeled and finely chopped
225 g/½ lb fresh white breadcrumbs
3 × 15 ml spoons/3 tablespoons finely chopped fresh herbs
finely grated rind and juice of 1 orange
salt
freshly ground black pepper
1 egg, beaten

AMERICAN

2 tablespoons butter
2 onions, peeled and finely chopped
4 cups fresh white breadcrumbs
3 tablespoons finely chopped fresh herbs
finely grated rind and juice of 1 orange
salt
freshly ground black pepper
1 egg, beaten

Melt the butter in a pan, add the onions and fry gently until soft. Add the remaining ingredients and stir well to mix.
To freeze: cool quickly, then transfer to a rigid container. Seal, label and freeze.
To thaw and use: thaw in the refrigerator overnight, then use as for fresh stuffing for lamb and poultry.

MUSHROOM STUFFING

METRIC/IMPERIAL

25 g/1 oz butter
50 g/2 oz mushrooms, chopped
1 small onion, peeled and chopped
75 g/3 oz fresh white breadcrumbs
1 × 2.5 ml spoon/½ teaspoon lemon juice
1 × 5 ml spoon/1 teaspoon freshly chopped parsley
salt
freshly ground black pepper
1 egg, beaten

AMERICAN

2 tablespoons butter
½ cup chopped mushrooms
1 small onion, peeled and chopped
1½ cups fresh white breadcrumbs
½ teaspoon lemon juice
1 teaspoon freshly chopped parsley
salt
freshly ground black pepper
1 egg, beaten

Melt the butter in a pan, add the mushrooms and onion and fry gently until soft. Add the remaining ingredients and stir well to mix.
To freeze: cool quickly, then transfer to a rigid container. Seal, label and freeze.
To thaw and use: thaw in the refrigerator overnight, or at room temperature for 4 hours, then use as for fresh stuffing.

SAGE AND ONION STUFFING

METRIC/IMPERIAL

40 g/1½ oz butter
2 medium onions, peeled and finely chopped
100 g/4 oz fresh white breadcrumbs
1 × 5 ml spoon/1 teaspoon dried sage
salt
freshly ground black pepper
1 egg, beaten

AMERICAN

3 tablespoons butter
2 medium onions, peeled and finely chopped
2 cups fresh white breadcrumbs
1 teaspoon dried sage
salt
freshly ground black pepper
1 egg, beaten

Melt the butter in a pan, add the onions and fry gently until soft. Add the remaining ingredients and stir well to mix.
To freeze: cool quickly, then transfer to a rigid container. Seal, label and freeze.
To thaw and use: thaw at room temperature for 4 hours, then use as for fresh stuffing. If liked, form into 8 balls, put in a greased ovenproof dish and bake in a preheated hot oven (220°C/425°F or Gas Mark 7) for 15 to 20 minutes.

RAISIN AND NUT STUFFING

METRIC/IMPERIAL

100 g/4 oz fresh brown breadcrumbs
50 g/2 oz seedless raisins
50 g/2 oz salted peanuts, chopped
1 × 15 ml spoon/1 tablespoon freshly chopped parsley
freshly ground black pepper
1 large egg, beaten

AMERICAN

2 cups fresh brown breadcrumbs
⅓ cup seedless raisins
½ cup chopped salted peanuts
1 tablespoon freshly chopped parsley
freshly ground black pepper
1 large egg, beaten

Put all the ingredients in a bowl and stir well.
To freeze: transfer to a rigid container, seal, label and freeze.
To thaw and use: thaw in the refrigerator overnight, or at room temperature for 4 hours, then use as for fresh stuffing.

LIVER STUFFING

METRIC/IMPERIAL

liver from the turkey, chopped
50 g/2 oz lamb's or calf's liver, chopped
100 g/4 oz fresh white breadcrumbs
25 g/1 oz shredded suet
1 streaky bacon rasher, rind removed and chopped
1 medium onion, peeled and finely chopped
1 garlic clove, peeled and crushed
1 × 2.5 ml spoon/½ teaspoon lemon juice (optional)
1 × 5 ml spoon/1 teaspoon freshly chopped parsley
1 × 2.5 ml spoon/½ teaspoon dried thyme
salt
freshly ground black pepper
1 egg, beaten

AMERICAN

liver from the turkey, chopped
¼ cup chopped lamb or veal liver
2 cups fresh white breadcrumbs
3 tablespoons shredded suet
1 fatty bacon slice, chopped
1 medium onion, peeled and finely chopped
1 garlic clove, peeled and crushed
½ teaspoon lemon juice (optional)
1 teaspoon freshly chopped parsley
½ teaspoon dried thyme
salt
freshly ground black pepper
1 egg, beaten

Put all the ingredients in a bowl and stir well to mix.
To freeze: transfer to a rigid container, seal, label and freeze.
To thaw and use: thaw in the refrigerator overnight, or at room temperature for 4 hours, then use as for fresh stuffing.

BACON AND HERB STUFFING

METRIC/IMPERIAL

100 g/4 oz bacon rashers, rinds removed and chopped
50 g/2 oz shredded suet
225 g/½ lb fresh white breadcrumbs
2 × 15 ml spoons/2 tablespoons freshly chopped parsley
1 × 15 ml spoon/1 tablespoon dried mixed herbs
finely grated rind of 1 lemon
salt
freshly ground black pepper
2 eggs, beaten
a little stock or water, to bind

AMERICAN

6 bacon slices, chopped
½ cup shredded suet
4 cups fresh white breadcrumbs
2 tablespoons freshly chopped parsley
1 tablespoon dried mixed herbs
finely grated rind of 1 lemon
salt
freshly ground black pepper
2 eggs, beaten
a little stock or water, to bind

Fry the bacon in its own fat until crisp. Remove from the pan with a slotted spoon, then mix with the remaining ingredients.
To freeze: pack in a rigid container, seal, label and freeze.
To thaw and use: thaw at room temperature for 4 hours, then use as for fresh stuffing.

CRÈME PATISSIÈRE (PASTRY CREAM)

METRIC/IMPERIAL

2 × 15 ml spoons/2 tablespoons cornflour
300 ml/½ pint milk
2 × 15 ml spoons/2 tablespoons caster sugar
2 egg yolks
4 × 15 ml spoons/4 tablespoons whipped cream
a few drops of vanilla essence

AMERICAN

2 tablespoons cornstarch
1¼ cups milk
2 tablespoons sugar
2 egg yolks
¼ cup whipped cream
a few drops of vanilla extract

Mix the cornflour (cornstarch) to a paste with a little of the milk. Put the remaining milk in a pan with the sugar, bring slowly to the boil, then stir into the paste. Return the mixture of the rinsed-out pan and simmer until thick, stirring constantly.
Remove from the heat and beat in the egg yolks, then return to the heat and simmer gently for a few minutes to cook the egg. Do not allow to boil. Leave to cool, then fold in

the whipped cream and vanilla essence (extract).
To freeze: pack in a rigid container, seal, label and freeze.
To thaw and use: thaw in the container at room temperature for 3 hours.
MAKES ABOUT 450 ml/¾ pint/2 cups

ALMOND PASTE

METRIC/IMPERIAL
250 g/9 oz ground almonds
125 g/4½ oz icing sugar, sifted
125 g/4½ oz caster sugar
1 × 5 ml spoon/1 teaspoon lemon juice
2 drops of almond essence
1 small egg, beaten

AMERICAN
2¼ cups ground almonds
1 cup sifted confectioners' sugar
½ cup sugar, firmly packed
1 teaspoon lemon juice
2 drops of almond extract
1 small egg, beaten

Put the ground almonds and sugars in a bowl and stir well to mix. Stir in the lemon juice and almond essence (extract), and enough beaten egg to give a pliable dough which is not sticky. Turn the dough out onto a board sprinkled with icing (confectioners') sugar and knead lightly with the fingertips until smooth.
To freeze: wrap in foil, then pack in a freezer bag. Seal, label and freeze.
To thaw and use: thaw in the wrappings at room temperature for 3 hours, then use as for fresh almond paste.
ENOUGH TO COVER THE TOP OF A 20 cm/8 inch ROUND or 18 cm/7 inch SQUARE CAKE

MOCK CREAM

METRIC/IMPERIAL
100 g/4 oz unsalted butter
1 × 15 ml spoon/1 tablespoon caster sugar
2 × 15 ml spoons/2 tablespoons hot water
2 × 15 ml spoons/2 tablespoons milk
1–2 drops of vanilla essence

AMERICAN
½ cup sweet butter
1 tablespoon sugar
2 tablespoons hot water
2 tablespoons milk
1–2 drops of vanilla extract

Put the butter and sugar in a bowl and beat together until light. Beat in half the water gradually, then half the milk, and continue beating until the mixture is very light and fluffy. Beat in the remaining water and milk, then the vanilla essence (extract) to taste.
To freeze: pack in a rigid container, seal, label and freeze.
To thaw and use: thaw in the container at room temperature for 2 to 3 hours.
ENOUGH CREAM TO FILL A 20 cm/8 inch CAKE

COFFEE MOCK CREAM

Make as for Mock Cream (see above), substituting 2 × 5 ml spoons/2 teaspoons coffee essence (strong black coffee) or instant coffee powder for the vanilla essence (extract).
Freeze, thaw and use as for Mock Cream.
ENOUGH CREAM TO FILL A 20 cm/8 inch CAKE

CHOCOLATE CREAM FILLING

METRIC/IMPERIAL
2 × 15 ml spoons/2 tablespoons custard powder
2 × 15 ml spoons/2 tablespoons cocoa powder
2 × 15 ml spoons/2 tablespoons sugar
300 ml/½ pint milk
3 × 15 ml spoons/3 tablespoons double cream, stiffly whipped

AMERICAN
2 tablespoons custard powder
2 tablespoons unsweetened cocoa powder
2 tablespoons sugar
1¼ cups milk
3 tablespoons heavy cream, stiffly whipped

Mix the custard, cocoa and sugar to a paste with a little of the milk. Put the remaining milk in a pan, bring to the boil, then stir into the paste. Return the mixture to the rinsed-out pan and simmer until thick, stirring constantly. Remove from the heat, cover with dampened greaseproof (waxed) paper and leave until cold. Fold in the whipped cream until evenly blended.
To freeze: pack in a rigid container, seal, label and freeze.
To thaw and use: thaw in the container at room temperature for 2 to 3 hours, then use as a filling for cakes and pastries.

PIPED CREAM STARS

Beat double (heavy) cream until just thick, fold in (caster) sugar and a few drops of vanilla essence (extract) to taste, then beat again. Place in a piping (pastry) bag fitted with a large star nozzle (fluted tube) and pipe stars or rosettes onto a foil-lined baking sheet.
To freeze: open (flash) freeze until firm, then pack in a rigid container, separating each layer with foil. Seal, label and return to the freezer.
To thaw and serve: arrange frozen cream on gâteaux or puddings with a warm palette knife. then allow to thaw for 30 minutes before serving.

CHOCOLATE FUDGE ICING

METRIC/IMPERIAL
150 g/5 oz icing sugar
25 g/1 oz cocoa powder
50 g/2 oz butter, thinly sliced
2 × 5 ml spoons/2 teaspoons honey
2 × 15 ml spoons/2 tablespoons milk
0.5 × 2.5 ml spoon/¼ teaspoon vanilla essence

AMERICAN
1¼ cups confectioners' sugar
¼ cup unsweetened cocoa powder
¼ cup butter, thinly sliced
2 teaspoons honey
2 tablespoons milk
¼ teaspoon vanilla extract

Sift the icing (confectioners') sugar and cocoa into a bowl. Put the remaining ingredients in a pan and heat gently until the butter has melted, stirring constantly. Pour immediately into the sugar mixture and beat with a wooden spoon until smooth. (If too thick, add a few drops of hot water.)
To freeze: pour into a rigid container, cool quickly, then seal, label and freeze.
To thaw and use: thaw in the container at room temperature for 2 hours, then beat well and use as for fresh icing.

FUDGE ICING

METRIC/IMPERIAL
225 g/½ lb icing sugar
75 g/3 oz butter
3 × 15 ml spoons/3 tablespoons milk

AMERICAN
scant 2 cups confectioners' sugar
⅜ cup butter
3 tablespoons milk

Sift the icing (confectioners') sugar into a bowl. Put the butter and milk in a pan and heat gently until the butter has melted, stirring constantly. Pour immediately into the sugar and beat with a wooden spoon until smooth.
To freeze: pour into a rigid container, cool quickly, then seal, label and freeze.
To thaw and use: thaw in the container at room temperature for 2 hours, then beat well.

CARAMEL FUDGE ICING

Make as for Fudge Icing (see above), substituting 1 × 15 ml spoon/1 tablespoon black treacle (molasses) for 1 × 15 ml spoon/1 tablespoon of the milk.
Freeze, thaw and use as for Fudge Icing.

RUM FUDGE ICING

Make as for Fudge Icing (see above), substituting 1 × 15 ml spoon/1 tablespoon rum for 1 × 15 ml spoon/1 tablespoon of the milk.
Freeze, thaw and use as for Fudge Icing.

GLACÉ ICING

METRIC/IMPERIAL
225 g/½ lb icing sugar
2 × 15 ml spoons/2 tablespoons warm water
a few drops of food colouring (optional)

AMERICAN
scant 2 cups sifted confectioners' sugar
2 tablespoons warm water
a few drops of food coloring (optional)

Sift the icing (confectioners') sugar into a heat-proof bowl, then stir in the water and the food coloring, if using. Stand the bowl in a pan half filled with hot water, then heat gently for 1 to 2 minutes until the sugar has dissolved, beating constantly.
Remove from the heat and continue beating until the icing is thick and coats the back of the spoon. If the icing is too thick, add a little more warm water; if too thin, add a little more sifted icing (confectioners') sugar.
To freeze: use immediately to cover small cakes or biscuits (cookies) etc. Leave until set, open (flash) freeze until firm, then pack in a rigid container, separating each layer with foil. Seal, label and return to the freezer.
To thaw and serve: place on a serving platter and thaw at room temperature for 2 to 3 hours.

ORANGE GLACÉ ICING

Make as for Glacé Icing (see opposite), substituting warm orange juice for the warm water.
Freeze, thaw and serve as for Glacé Icing.

COFFEE GLACÉ ICING

Make as for Glacé Icing (see opposite), substituting 1 × 15 ml spoon/1 tablespoon coffee essence (strong black coffee) for 1 × 15 ml spoon/1 tablespoon of the warm water.
Freeze, thaw and serve as for Glacé Icing.

COFFEE BUTTER CREAM

METRIC/IMPERIAL
100 g/4 oz butter, softened
225 g/½ lb icing sugar, sifted
1 × 15 ml spoons/1 tablespoon coffee essence
1 × 15 ml spoon/1 tablespoon hot water

AMERICAN
½ cup butter, softened
scant 2 cups sifted confectioners' sugar
1 tablespoon strong black coffee
1 tablespoon hot water

Beat the butter until light and fluffy; then beat in the icing (confectioners') sugar gradually with the coffee and water. Beat thoroughly until smooth.
To freeze: pack in a rigid container, seal, label and freeze.
To thaw and use: thaw in the container at room temperature for 3 hours.
ENOUGH TO FILL AND COAT THE TOP AND SIDES OF AN 18 cm/7 inch CAKE.

ORANGE BUTTER CREAM

Make as for Coffee Butter Cream (see above), substituting the finely grated rind and juice of 1 orange for the coffee.
Freeze, thaw and use as for Coffee Butter Cream.
ENOUGH TO FILL AND COAT THE TOP AND SIDES OF AN 18 cm/7 inch CAKE.

HONEY AND NUT BUTTER CREAM

METRIC/IMPERIAL
100 g/4 oz unsalted butter
225 g/½ lb icing sugar, sifted
2 × 5 ml spoons/2 teaspoons honey
1 × 15 ml spoon/1 tablespoon chopped nuts
2 × 5 ml spoons/2 teaspoons finely grated lemon rind

AMERICAN
½ cup sweet butter
scant 2 cups sifted confectioners' sugar
2 teaspoons honey
1 tablespoon chopped nuts
2 teaspoons finely grated lemon rind

Put the butter in a bowl and beat until soft. Beat in the icing (confectioners') sugar gradually until the mixture is light and fluffy, then stir in the honey, nuts and lemon rind.
To freeze: pack in a rigid container, seal, label and freeze.
To thaw and serve: thaw in the container at room temperature for 2 to 3 hours.
MAKES ENOUGH BUTTER CREAM TO FILL ONE 20 cm/8 inch CAKE

CREAM TOPPING

METRIC/IMPERIAL
1 egg
150 g/5 oz caster sugar
25 g/1 oz cornflour
juice of 1½ lemons
300 ml/½ pint double cream

AMERICAN
1 egg
⅔ cup sugar
¼ cup cornstarch
juice of 1½ lemons
1¼ cups heavy cream

Put the egg, sugar and cornflour (cornstarch) in a heatproof bowl and beat until light and fluffy. Beat in the lemon juice, then stand the bowl over a pan of simmering water and stir until the mixture becomes clear and begins to thicken. Remove from the heat and leave until cold, when it will become thick. Whip the cream lightly, then fold in the lemon mixture.
To freeze: pack in a rigid container, seal, label and freeze.
To thaw and use: thaw in the container at room temperature for 2 to 3 hours.
ENOUGH TO COVER A 20 cm/8 inch CAKE

INDEX

Illustrations by Mary Tomlin.

Jacket photograph by Paul Kemp.